ESSEX WILLS

THE ARCHDEACONRY COURTS 1577-1584

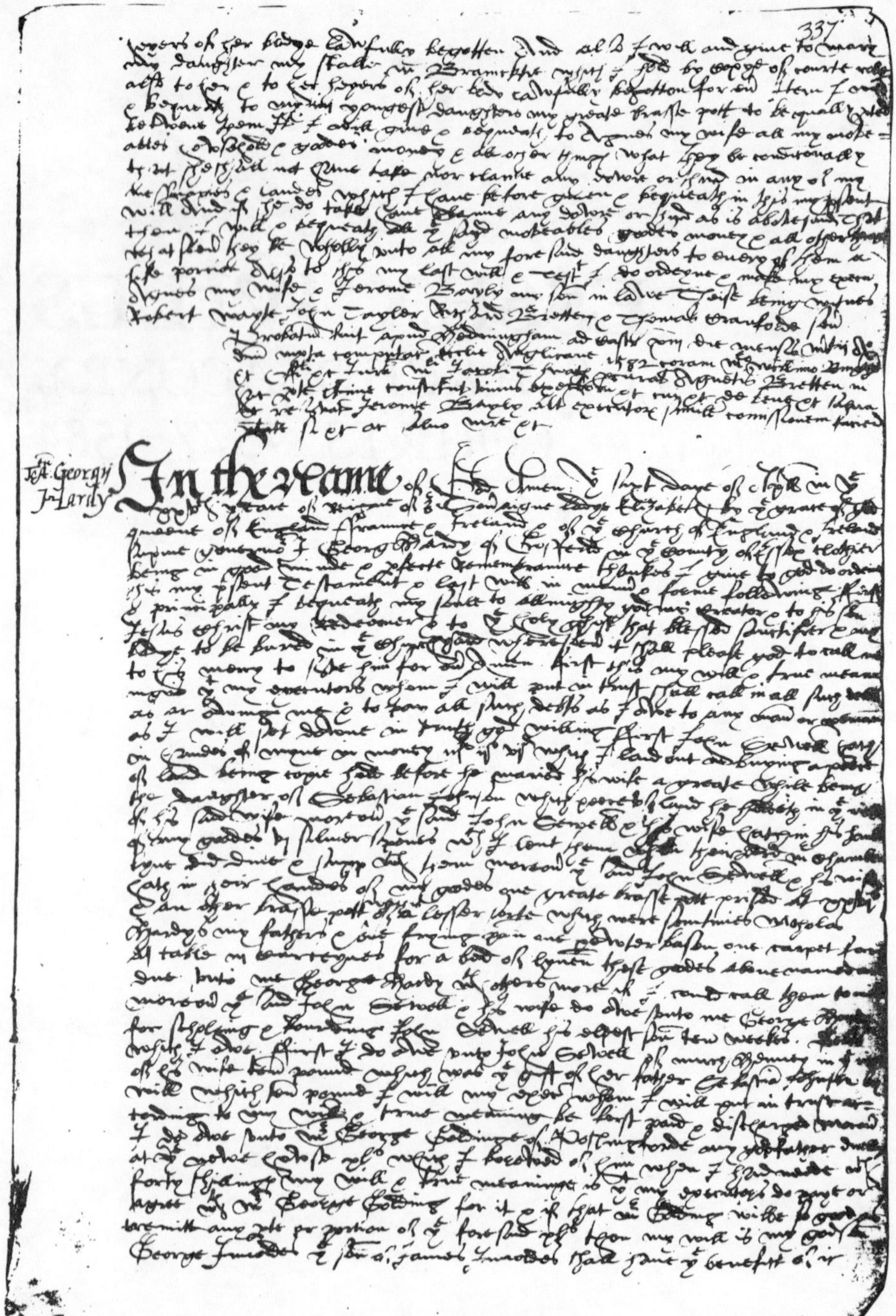

The registered copy of the Will of George Hardy of Gosfield, clothier, 1583 (no. 947), illustrating well the script of the period.

Essex Wills

The Archdeaconry Courts

1577-1584

abstracted and edited by

F.G. EMMISON

Essex Record Office

in collaboration with

The Friends of Historic Essex

1987

Published by the Essex Record Office,
County Hall,
Chelmsford, Essex
CM1 1LX

British Library Cataloguing in Publication Data

Essex Wills: the archdeaconry courts 1577-1584.
1. Wills—England—Essex—History—16th century.
2. Essex—Genealogy.
I. Emmison, F.G.
929'.34267 *CS435.E7*

ISSN 0-900360-69-0

Essex Record Office Publication No. 96

Printed by Essex County Supplies from copy prepared for Essex Record Office

CONTENTS

ACKNOWLEDGEMENTS

I am greatly indebted to The Friends of Historic Essex and especially to Mr Kenneth Neale, O.B.E., F.S.A., the Chairman, for undertaking financial responsibility for *Essex Wills* under the agreed arrangements for transfer of publication from the New England Historic Genealogical Society to the Essex County Council, as a result of which the volumes will now form part of the series of Essex Record Office Publications.

I am grateful to Mr J.T.A.Burton for his invaluable assistance in my editorial work and to Mr V.W.Gray, M.A., County Archivist of Essex, for generously lessening many of my problems.

The continued support and encouragement of Mr John B.Threlfall of Wisconsin, U.S.A., are immensely important.

F.G.E.

The cooperation is gratefully acknowledged of the New England Historic Genealogical Society in allowing the section on Editorial Method to be reproduced from Volume 3 of their *Essex Wills (England)* series.

The section on Probate Courts and their Jurisdictions is largely based upon *Fifty thousand ghosts return: Essex Wills 1400-1858*, an article by Dr Emmison which appeared in *Essex Review* no. 257, January 1956.

V.W.G.

FOREWORD

The ambitious scale of a project to publish detailed abstracts with indexes of every Elizabethan Will relating to the county of Essex speaks for itself. In no other English county has such a venture been tackled. Even given Dr Emmison's long and deepening study of this period in the county's history, carried through nearly forty years of publication, this is an undertaking of mammoth proportions. Anyone less committed and dedicated to the subject would long since have flagged in enthusiasm and energy.

It should surprise no-one that the realisation of so grand a scheme has involved a series of publishers, each carrying the programme nearer to its completion. It is, however, peculiarly fitting that the responsibility for carrying forward the series should now have been assumed by the Essex County Council as part of the long and distinguished publishing programme of the Essex Record Office first started by Derick Emmison himself in 1947. The Friends of Historic Essex, who have, over three decades, made so many important contributions to the furtherance of Essex historical studies, have demonstrated, through the establishment and work of their Essex Wills Sub-Committee, their determination to construct a firm financial base for the future of the series. This combination of clear enthusiasm and careful planning has been recognised as invaluable by the members of the County Council's Library, Museum and Records Committee, under the chairmanship of Mrs P.V.Wawn. They have seen, too, the continuing munificence of a number of benefactors, in particular Mr John Threlfall. They have above all understood the importance of the project to present and future social historians of the period and recognised that the publication of this series will ease the burden of responsibility which they bear for the preservation of many of the original Wills and Registers herein abstracted, which have hitherto inevitably been physically vulnerable to damage from over-use by researchers.

With the continuing support of the Friends, it is the earnest hope of the County Council that the series can now move forward speedily and confidently towards its completion, bringing into being a landmark in Essex historical studies and a tribute to one man's single-minded energy.

V.W.GRAY
County Archivist and General Editor,
Essex Record Office Publications

PREFACE

The compilation and publication of detailed and fully indexed abstracts of all the Elizabethan Wills in the Essex Record Office (approximately 12,000) is now assured as the result of arrangements made jointly by The Friends of Historic Essex and the Essex County Council. The Friends have decided to be financially liable for the printing and the Essex Record Office will act as publisher of the series. The abstracting and indexing are the responsibility of the Editor, who records his gratification with the arrangements for future publication.

The wish of the generous sponsor, Mr John B. Threlfall, that the volumes should contain an average of 1,000 Wills, in order to reduce the number of indexes to be consulted as well as the cost of production, is fully supported by the Editor, who draws attention to the large quantity of previously unpublished material which can thus be included in a single volume — about 10,000 personal name references and an immense amount of information on Essex local history and social history generally.

The task of editing Wills is not confined to the abstracts and the three indexes (persons, places and subjects). Reading 16th-century Wills gives rise to numerous and heterogeneous queries arising from both content and physical condition which involve a disproportionate amount of time and call for long experience with paleographical, topographical and archival problems. Even so, a few obstinate puzzles remain and, despite double checking, it is feared that some errors or inaccuracies may have passed unnoticed. Rare words are another matter on which the Editor is unwilling to hold up progress by disproportionate attention to this intriguing but time-consuming by-path.

It is important to draw special attention to the *principles adopted in making the abstracts* in order to reduce the cost of printing. These are set out in the section entitled *EDITORIAL METHOD* (after the Introduction), which users of this book are *strongly urged to read*, if only to avoid misunderstandings about what is included and what is not, and it would seem helpful to enlarge on them here.

The abstracts contain not only *every personal and place name* but also *retain in general the language of the Wills*. The Editor's omissions are mainly the 'legal' phraseology used in most Wills, especially the longer testaments drawn up by local attorneys, some of whom, doubtless to increase their fees, resorted to repeating many of the clauses to obviate misinterpretation. The length of some Wills was also doubled, if not trebled, by the insertion, in the event of the principal legatees dying without issue, of *remainders* to each of the younger sons in turn, then perhaps also to daughters, and occasionally to kinsmen and even to friends. Such a series of contingent remainders was of course a wise precaution in the case of a substantial estate, the span of life being much shorter than nowadays, and may have been dictated by affluent testators. The names of these 'remaindermen' are of course important, especially for family history. In abstracting it is, however, necessary only to give their names and relationship to the testator, without copying the repeated clauses.

The effect of leaving out legal and other tautology can be considerable and amount to as much as three-fourths of the longer Wills, but the Editor has to plough through the lot to ensure that no extra name or fact is overlooked! Brief Wills involve few omissions: little condensation, too, is practicable for those legacies of numerous articles of household and kitchen goods and of clothing, which furnish an intimate picture to the family historian and often include items of interest to the social historian. The Editor, however, makes one exception in the series. *The articles of bed-linen* (sheets, pillows, bolsters, blankets, coverings, etc.), *unless unusual, are excluded from the abstracts;* but beds, bedstead(le)s, featherbeds and flockbeds are always retained. Indeed, bed-linen items were so commonplace that many testators merely used the phrase 'with all the furniture appertaining to the bed'. In any case, retention of hundreds of lists of bed-linen, increasing the length of each volume by as much as twenty pages, would thus add little to our knowledge of this minor aspect of domestic life. We have Harrison's oft-quoted passage about the sleeping arrangements in his own time,[1] and in the present volume (Will no.747) it is interesting to find the first use of Harrison's delightful 'hap-harlot'.

This long explanation of editorial methods has also been given because some readers may raise the question, 'Is it still desirable [or even necessary] to obtain a facsimile reproduction [with or without a full transcript]?' The answer is a firm one: no extra factual information will normally be gained. If, however, some form of copy of an individual Will would be of special importance, the procedure for obtaining it is set out in the last paragraph of the 'Editorial Method'. But it should be remembered that, without some knowledge of palaeography, the enquirer may find it as difficult to read as the typical sample illustrated in the frontispiece.

Occasionally a date or other fact might have led the reader to query the Editor's accuracy. In order to obviate unnecessary enquiries to the Essex Record Office, he has resorted to the generous use of '[*sic*]', for example, where the date of a Will is nearly a decade (which is exceptional) before that of a probate, and he has often added '[not named]' where the christian name of a relation is not given by the testator.

The abstracts are prepared from photocopies or printouts from microfilms of the Wills registers, which are copies of the original documents, many being too fragile or faint for photocopying, but both registers and originals (where extant) are collated. Minor differences in spelling are not noted; the registered copies are found generally to be accurate.

Much care has been used in abstracting, but in books containing an average of nearly 10,000 personal name references, it is almost impossible to avoid errors.

Dealing now with the methods used in compiling the 'Index of Personal Names', it must be emphasized that the spelling of names in the 16th century (and much later) was erratic in the absence of standardized forms; often so inconsistent that a name may appear in two, three or four ways in the same document. Insofar as it was governed by any principles, the usage was largely phonetic; even so, some surnames occur with a wide variety of spellings. One of the pitfalls in consulting the index concerns the initial letter. If a name does not appear, it should be sought under other initials. Among such alternatives, the most usual are: Cowey/Kowye, Keame/Came, Cooke/Kooke, Jeffrey/Geffrey, Jermayne/German, Notte/Knott, Seton/Cytton, Varnam/Furname, Valentine/Folintine, Phillip/Fillippe. There are of course others, such as Ilford/Elforde. The chief problem relating to initials lies with names spelt (in a given volume) *only* with a form differing from what may be deemed normal. For example, Ginkinson; while it would be helpful to the reader to index this under Jenkinson, with a cross-reference from G, the Editor has followed, somewhat reluctantly in this respect, the principle set out in the standard work[2] and indexed it as in the original, i.e. Ginkinson, without cross-reference from J, obliging those interested in Jenkinson to search the index for possible alternatives. Other samples are Inglishe, no instance of English occurring in the volume; Sissell, which is a variant

---

[1] G.Edelen (ed.), *The Description of England, by William Harrison*, (Cornell Univ. Press, (1968), p. 201).

[2] R.F.Hunnisett, *Indexing for Editors* (Brit. Rec. Assoc., 1972). This concentrates mainly on problems affecting medieval records. For our period, I feel that it is unnecessary to add to the cost of printing by giving every variant at length, e.g. Boreham/Borham, Boram, Borram, which I have given as Bor(e)ham/Bor(r)am.

of the Barking name of Cecil; and Tawbutt, for Talbot. Similar results affect surnames derived from place-names which do not appear in their modern forms, e.g. the Essex 'parish' surnames Messing, Pitsea, Ulting, Weeley, Witham and Wix have to be found under Missing, Bytsey, Owltinge, Welye, Wittam and Wickes. The Editor of the New England Historic Genealogical Society has, however, urged, in the interests of American users (as well as British), the adoption in future, of the more normal form of surname, with cross-reference from the unusual. This has been agreed to; indeed, only an Editor with an intimate knowledge of local names would recognise some of the unusual variants.

In general, every effort is made to bring together variants. In some cases identity is established by their being found in use in the same or an adjoining parish or by their having already been equated in the published index to Essex Wills of the period[1]. Cuckoe/Cokkoke/Kacco; Onyon/Inion; Offyn/Oughan; and Thonder/Tonder are good examples; in the last case the draft abstract gave 'Tonder[Touder?]', but the completed index proved that the alternative could be deleted, and this brings us to the matter of palaeographical difficulties. The clerks employed in entering up the registers had their own problems in reading illiterate originals, but they in turn have not eased the Editor's work by their often small, cramped handwriting. In particular, there is the ubiquitous problem of minims (i, n, m, n, u and v, the first often carelessly placed or omitted, the last often written as u). Here again, consultation of other printed indexes has usually, but not always, helped in ensuring the correct form.

---

[1] Emmison (ed.), *Wills at Chelmsford, 1400-1620* (Brit. Rec. Soc., vol. 78, 1958)

INTRODUCTION

General

Wills are well known as invaluable for Family History, but it seems desirable to emphasize that they also yield an immense amount of material for Local and Social History, all the more so as when indexed by places and subjects as well as persons. Information on some subjects may be somewhat meagre in other sources[1] for our period (1558-1603). Admittedly, references to education, for instance, may occur only sporadically in Wills, but the series of *Essex Wills* when completed will, it is hoped, provide in the aggregate enough items to add considerably to our present knowledge, being drawn from the 10,000 or more Elizabethan Essex Wills in the Essex Record Office. Many more details will enable readers to visualize in general the circumstances in which Essex folk lived and the contents of their dwellings, livestock and tools, as well as other facets of domestic history: of special interest of course to readers with Essex ancestors. This new material may challenge local historians to identify the testators' farmhouses with those still surviving, many of which have been well restored in recent years.

The Family

The dominant note of most Wills is of course the Family, sometimes embracing quite distant relations. Family historians may even be provided with four (very occasionally, five) generations: parents, testator, children, and grandchildren.

One of the pleasant aspects of Elizabethan Wills, made in an age which the majority strove to get the bare necessities of life, is the kindly care shown by many a dying man for his wife, while at the same time feeling obliged to devise most of his lands, livestock and goods to his eldest son or brotherless daughters. Provision for the wife's material comfort may include, in addition to a cash annuity, the continued use of their bedchamber and unconditional access to the hall and kitchen. All the household goods may be left for her own use; if not, specified articles of furniture and kitchen equipment, resulting sometimes in valuable details. The heir or the executors may be instructed to ensure for her adequate 'meat, drink and apparel', corn, or quite commonly fuel for warmth and cooking, for life or a shorter period.

The short average lifespan resulted in the not unusual re-marriage of the widow which could invalidate all or some of her legacies, including of course houseroom. In the case of an affluent widow's remarriage, she or her second husband could be bound in £200 (717) or much larger sum 'for the performance' of the Will's provisions.

Children's marriage portions were occasionally dependent on the widow's or executors' approval (53, 491, 556, 717, 882); or the latter were empowered to withhold

---

[1] For a full calendar of the Essex Assize records, see J.S.Cockburn (ed.), *Essex Indictments: Eliz. I.* (H.M.S.O., 1978). For much information from Essex Quarter Sessions, archidiaconal and manorial records, see F.G.Emmison, *Elizabethan Life*, vols. I, II and III (Essex Record Office, 1970, 1973, 1976 respectively). Useful generally is *Local History Handlist: A select bibliography and guide to sources*, (comp. by A.T.Hall, 5th edn., Hist. Ass., 1980).

bequests because of disobedience.

Facing imminent death at a relatively early age, the Tudor testator may be leaving several young children or orphans. Their upbringing and maintenance therefore obliges him in some instances to make quite elaborate arrangements. Payment of their bequests years ahead at various ages from 14 to 24 or even later has to be entrusted to his widow, executors or supervisors, friends, or the eldest child, ensured perhaps by their having to enter into monetary bonds, and the legacy of cash or stock may be invested in various ways to increase for their ultimate benefit. The possibly premature death in turn of his heir apparent without issue may lead him to name as contingent legatees a succession of younger children, brothers, sisters, or kinsmen: all useful grist to the family historian.

Trades and Occupations

The index illustrates a useful cross-section of the male working population, except for menial servants and the poorest, though some labourers do appear among the testators. Whilst unspecified, certain occupations, e.g. mariners and a clothier (759), may be deduced; yeomen and husbandmen are certainly more numerous than those so termed, and others plied a craft as well as a little husbandry. Perhaps the most interesting record is that of a cutler in 1583 (995), referring to his stock of knives and weapons, and there is a second cutler in 1578 (845); these were among the few remaining craftsmen in the declining Thaxted industry which flourished there in medieval times. (Members of the Button family were to be the last surviving cutlers (1663) at Thaxted, apart from the Knappings (1626 and 1665); these may have been tradesmen, not manufacturers.[1]) The three north Essex blacksmiths in 1584 refer to some of their tools and to tally-accounting. The butterman (117) was probably a dealer, not a maker. 'Mr Charnocke', a virginal-maker, was presumably a Londoner, like the testator, though there are Romford links and a Hugh Charnocke of Hornchurch occurs in 1496.[2] The index reveals several other rare occupations.

Properties, Manors and Agriculture

Large estates devised are recorded mostly in the records of the Prerogative Court. But some of the gentry's Wills were proved in the Archidiaconal Courts, e.g. 69, 82, 94. Many manors also appear as leased to the testators by their non-resident lords, thus showing who actually lived in these manor-houses and farmed the demesnes, e.g. John Bridge with his large stock of cattle on the manor of Badnocks in Asheldham (350). Topographical facts abound. Names of farms especially provide a mass of information which supplements that in the standard work, some examples being earlier than those cited.[3] For field-names, Wills are particularly valuable where deeds and manorial records are not available.

Farming items include much about livestock and crops. Among the largest stocks found are those at West Tilbury (193), at Asheldham (350), and at Woodham Ferrers (116) where the numbers which the widow may choose suggest a still larger flock, as also at Hornchurch (94). All these probably pastured on the marshlands, though evidently not that apportioned among his sons by the gentleman-farmer of Runwell Hall (82). Agricultural implements were occasionally well listed (94). Among the less common crops saffron appears, as is well known, in the north-west corner of

---

1 F.G.Emmison (ed.), *Wills at Chelmsford, 1620-1720* (Brit. Rec. Soc., vol. 79, 1961).

2 Emmison, *Wills at Chelmsford, 1400-1619* (B.R.S., vol. 78, 1958).

3 P.H.Reaney, *The Place-Names of Essex* (English Place-Name Soc., vol. XII, 1935).

of the county, but 'scrull corn' is not readily explained, nor is the 2-acre 'salton' (at Grays Thurrock, 128), though presumably a salting.

It is somewhat rare to find any reference to husbandry methods (917). The late survival of two medieval measures for landholdings is of interest. Yardlands, half-yardlands and quarter-yardlands are known from other sources to have been common measurements in Great Waltham, Felsted, High Easter and Pleshey, all north and north-west of Chelmsford. The yardland represented the medieval virgate, probably the average size of a villein's holding and generally (though with local exceptions) reckoned at about 30 acres. In the current volume are a 'halfyardland' (348) and 'half a yard' (685); and in High Easter quarters were distinguished by names (865, 873). But another term is rarer: 'warland' (646) and 'wareland' (633), both at Saffron Walden. This defined in the *Oxford English Dictionary* as 'agricultural land held by a villein'. Among its quotations is '5 acres of wareland' (from the manor court rolls of Great Oakley, in north-east Essex), the 'ware' being etymologically connected with defence.

Houses

The few references to 'new' buildings or rooms are noted in the index. Local historians may perhaps be able to locate, if surviving, the surgeon's house at Castle Hedingham, with its 'great new chamber' and 'new parlour' (891). A Rochford man used a verb unrecorded by lexicographers in providing board to 'sollar' the house of the local glazier (216), meaning apparently to insert a sollar or attic under the roof, the noun (sollar or solar) being not uncommon. Among named rooms are the star chamber (216), the fish chamber (624), and the chapel chamber in another Castle Hedingham house (931). One of the most illuminating records is that of the innkeeper (122) of the 'Blue Boar' — undoubtedly on that side of Ingatestone High Street which lay in the parish of Fryerning. Here we have the names of seven rooms of a substantial hostelry, well equipped to serve travellers along the Great Essex Road from London to Colchester and Norwich. After bequests to his children by his first and second wives, the testator intended that the inn should descend only to those of his own surname. The building of a substantial house 30 foot long and 16 foot wide is of some interest (915). Separate kitchens, probably built as a fire precaution, are sometimes recorded; and we apparently find a separate bakehouse with its own bedchamber (824). The interest in old barns, recently aroused, has led the editor to index them, though only a small number of those still surviving are likely to be identified definitely; new barns are mentioned twice (447, 504).

Furniture

The present volume illustrates the gradual improvement in furniture. Except for the homes of the wealthy, most Elizabethan furniture was fairly rude and essentially utilitarian, judged by the standards of the next century. But the craft of the joiner, who used joints and might turn out superior or more ornamental pieces, was coming to the fore; although some testators distinguished 'joined' or 'joint' beds, chairs, chests and so on, while naturally those 'of carpenter's work' were rarely specified. Indeed, a choice article may occasionally be recognized in the testaments of grandfather, father and son. While some yeomen's and a few husbandmen's and craftmen's dwellings seem to have been adequately equipped, most homes remained sparsely furnished. However, a larger number boasted of beds with testers, 'ceilings' (screens or curtains), and occasional fine coverlets.

It was at the beginning of the period of the present volume (1577-84) that William Harrison, rector of Radwinter in north Essex (1558-93), had written his remarkable book *The Description of England* with its oft-quoted paragraph:-

> Our fathers, yea, and we ourselves have lien full oft upon straw pallets, on rough mats covered only with a sheet, under coverlets made of dagswain or *hapharlots*, and a good round log under their heads instead of a bolster or pillow. If it were so that our father or the goodman of the house had within seven years after his marriage purchased a mattress or flock-bed, and thereto a sack of chaff to rest his head upon, he thought himself to be as well lodged as the lord of the town [i.e. village], that peradventure lay seldom in a bed of down or whole feathers, so well were they contented and with such base kind of furniture. Pillows (said they) were thought meet only for women in childbed. As for the servants, if they had any sheet above them it was well, for seldom had they any under their bodies to keep them from the pricking straw that ran oft through the canvas of the pallet and rased their hardened hides.

His book was published in 1577 and a second edition in 1587. The worthy cleric felt it prudent to add after 'dagswain and hapharlots', both meaning coarse coverlets, '(I use their own terms)'. But although familiar to present-day scholars because of Harrison (and earlier use of both words is known to lexicographers), they were very rare. We now have a quotation, from Saffron Walden, a few miles from Radwinter (1579): 'To Agnes Rabbett my old covering called an hapharlott (747). In my reading of over 10,000 Essex Elizabethan Wills, this is the sole discovery of the word. As emphasized in the Preface and the Editorial Note, because of its commonplace nature, *bedlinen, (unless unusual) is excluded from the abstracts.*

Other articles of furniture sometimes showing superior workmanship are tables and chests. Most of the tables, however, were humble enough and often made of rough-hewn 'boards' or 'planks' resting on trestles: the top was the 'table' which could be lifted off when the pegs holding the two stretchers were removed; and the separate parts stacked against the wall, giving needed space in the room for other business. For example, 'my little table made of 2 boards (931) and 'my plank table and trestles belonging' (395).

Fixtures (to use the modern but not equivalent term), which were to remain with the house and not be removed, are indexed under that title; there is one unusually long list (624).

Readers are warned about equating the sums given in inventory valuations with total assets. Wide ranges are common. Yeomen's valuations lie between £36 and the unusually high sum of £702 (245), Husbandmen's £3 to £315, with a Yeoman of the Guard at £111, and an innkeeper(?) at £145. The 25 valuations are entered in the Subject Index under 'Wills — inventories (valuations)'. Plate is indexed under that word.

Education and Books

William Pawne, being childless, decided in 1578 (69) that his residuary estate should be used to build a school within his manor of Chivers in High Ongar, 'by the discretion of my executors', and the 'surplages' (surplus from 3 years' rent of his lands) used for its maintenance. But there is no proof of any action accordingly.[1] It may be that the residue proved insufficient. Pawne's three executors were local gentry: Elliott the lay rector[2], Wallinger of Chelmsford, lawyer and coroner[3], and Massie, apparently an East Ham gentleman[4].

There are a few bequests or directions for keeping sons at school until able to earn their living or 'shift' for themselves; more specifically, for two sons, one of whom is to be kept at school until able 'to write some plain, indifferent [tolerable] and legible hand' (800). A husbandman dealt with the schooling, boarding and books for

---

[1] *Charity Commissioners' Reports* (Essex Volume); *Victoria History of Essex* (1956), iv, 186.
[2] Morant, *History of Essex*, i, 133.
[3] *Calendar of Assize Records: Essex Indictments: Eliz. I* (1978).
[4] Morant, i, 133; Emmison, *Elizabethan Life: Disorder* (1970), 135.

the 'preferment and furtherance in living' of his younger son (873). Readers are again reminded, however, that 'education', as appearing in twelve Wills, had the contemporary meaning of bringing up or nourishing, even when tuition was also provided for (387); 'honest education' for a solitary girl may however mean tuition (318). While not referring to school, ten testators required children to be brought up 'in learning', some of whom are clearer: 'to learn English' (960); 'to be taught to read and write' (129, 204); 'to write, read and cast accounts and to place them with some honest men to learn some good art or science whereby to get their living another day' (223); or merely 'in learning or some other good trade or occupation' (807). Three were more concerned with religious education: to be brought up 'in the fear of God and especially in learning or otherwise in some godly exercise' (two boys and a girl, 469) and 'in learning, both of the Book [bible] and also in sewing and some other profitable exercise whereby she may be able in time to earn her living' (364). The general impression gained is that of a gradual increase of interest in education, albeit mainly vocational. There are the usual references to apprentices (16 in all).

University education claimed meagre attention. One man whose status is not given left his son £50 at 21 and £20 to keep 'at the school at Cambridge' [the University] for four years (185). A London merchant directed that, if all his children died before getting their legacies, the big sum of £160 was to be given to the universities of Cambridge and Oxford (188). A yeoman's youngest son was to have maintenance 'in the schools of learning' (387). Unfortunately there seems to be no evidence in the printed *alumni* lists that any of the three youths graduated. The munificent Thomas Brocke did not forget his erstwhile 'tutor in Oxford' (302). The index refers to three schoolmasters.

Charities and the Poor

Responsibility for the relief of the poor had been placed on every parish by the Acts of 1552, 1563 and 1572, gradually transforming charitable alms into a compulsory rate with the appointment of 'collectors' (220, 639, 764) and finally by the great Acts of 1598 and 1601 with that of 'overseers'. A few references to almshouses are found at Manningtree (503), while one was contemplated at West Bergholt (639). The proportion of men and women remembering or reminded of the poor by clerical draftsmen is fairly high, but such legacies were mostly trifling gifts of money; the occasional sums of 20s. in Tudor times were substantial. The '20s. in penny dole' at Harlow might suggest a misreading of '20d.' by the registrar's clerk, were it not for its being followed by another 20s. for bread, drink and cheese (668). Bread or corn might be supplemented by cheese or beer, usually at burial. More generous bequests include 'a sheep, bread, cheese, drink and other necessaries' as the executors 'think meet to make the poor cheer withal' (707), '1 quarter of wheat baked, with 1 lead of cheese' (400), and '10 dozen of bread and a barrel of beer' (654). By far the most charitably-minded testator was Thomas Brocke of Stock (302). By his general and specific gifts, the poor of Stock and Buttsbury received around £18, some neighbouring places nearly £10, and those at his burial also the astonishing sum of £10 and provision for 2 loads of fuel for every poor neighbour of his; yet little seems to be known of him.[1] A London clothworker left £5 to the poor children in Christ's Hospital (188). A legacy might be limited to the poor of the testator's hamlet (341). Winter hardship was occasionally relieved by bequests of wood, e.g. '200 of brush faggots' (233), and once (16) by 20s. every Christmas for 4 years in 'coals' (charcoal). A fuller rewarded four of his occupation (880). Very exceptional was the widow who gave a groat to four *women* accompanying her corpse (740). Funeral hospitality was not necessarily for the poor. 'My honest neighbours' got bread, wine and sugar (16); and a Romford innholder provided 40s. on a dinner

[1] F.W.Austin, *Rectors of Two Parishes and their Times* (1947), 83, 94.

'among my Tuesday's guests, the butchers of London', probably those attending the weekly market (136). Among non-religious gifts, four testators were to benefit roads and bridges and five contributed to the well-known charitable brief for repairing Colyton harbour in Devon.

Religion, Churches and the Clergy

By our period, Essex had become one of the chief centres of puritanism and other non-Catholic dissent. Clerical exponents were concentrating on biblical study, preaching, prayer, and 'godly exercises' (469). From such principles emerged the 'classis', a quasi-presbyterian group, of which the Dedham Classis three centuries later was to become known to historians because of the fortuitous survival and publication of its proceedings.[1] Drawn from ministers on the Essex-Suffolk borders, its leading member was Dr Edmund Chapman, the Dedham church lecturer. Some local testators showed gratitude for his spiritual guidance. The first was a Dedham shearman (728) who gave a legacy to him and small sums to neighbouring ministers; if his nephew and heir apparent died before 21, the shearman's implements were to be sold and half the money to go to 'such as fear God and love the Gospel'. His executor was Henry Sherman, a fellow parishioner and ancestor of the American general, William T. Sherman.

In addition to the occasional small grants for repairing the parish church (the normal income for which was the churchwardens' rate), specific church bequests were made only towards Heybridge (594) and Elmstead (726) church towers, Belchamp Walter bells (977), a new pulpit at Tollesbury (698), and a desk cloth at Earls Colne (689): ample confirmation of post-Reformation testators' preference for secular rather than ecclesiastical gifts. High Ongar church received a little land from William Pawne (69). An interesting item refers to the destruction of some stained glass in Fordham church, for the donor 'utterly disallows all manner of idolatry in glass windows as in all other places'.

The well-known emigration of the devout Flemings to Colchester and Halstead is represented by two 'Dutch' testaments (652, 951). Many testaments were drafted, written or witnessed by the clergy. Where not so described, most have been identified from the printed lists of Essex incumbents[2], which, however, do not record 'curates' (i.e. usually priests-in-charge, especially where the rector or vicar was non-resident). This may be useful to readers in eliminating clerics from testators' relatives, but other research on the clergy is not made by the editor.

Sickness, Burial and Probate

Apart from repaying charges for 'physic' (137) and the stock phrases in preambles, information about illness is limited to an occasional legacy by a bachelor or widow to the 'keeper' or 'host(ess)' who had been nursing or looking after him (239, 451, 290); in the last (nuncupative) Will the man confessed to being greatly indebted to his 'ostice', a widow in whose house he had lain sick 'of long time'. A mariner mentioned host and two keepers (563). Of the two surgeons, one may well have the usual meaning of barber-surgeon (710); the other 'chirurgeon' was perhaps qualified (981). We have no reference to any epidemic, except one slight hint (315).

The abstracts are indexed to requests for burial in chancel, in church, in 'church or

---

1 Emmison, *Elizabethan Life: Morals & the Church Courts* (1973), pp. 193–4.

2 R. Newcourt, *Repertorium...of the Diocese of London* [Essex clergy lists], vol. 2 (1710); there are numerous gaps, some filled by details from other sources (*Trans. Essex Archl. Soc.*, vols. 6,7, (1898, 1900)).

churchyard', or in the church porch. The five testators desiring interment in the chancel comprise a rector, an esquire, a gentlewoman, and two yeomen. Of the score of church burials, one (624) was to be in the chapel of South Weald church (whether north or south chapel is not stated). William Pawne of High Ongar provided for a tomb — in the chancel of the adjacent Norton Mandeville (69); but, as with his projected school, it is not known if his wishes were carried out or if the tomb was removed in later church alterations. No known church memorials figure in the present volume.

One testament proved in the Prerogative Court of Canterbury (John 'Medoes' in the records of that Court) occurs also in those of an Archdeacon's court (225).

Miscellaneous

The introductions to this series have explained terms for the receptacles and measures used for butter and cheese, especially the enormous size of the cheeses made from the milk of ewes pastured in the coastland marshes, e.g. 'half a wey of good cheese' (about 118 lb., 392). Unusual items of household provision are a bushel of salt (the first mention in fact of a large quantity of salt in our Wills), as much as 20 lb. of butter (both 94), and a roundlet of vinegar (563); a roundlet was not a fixed measure.

There is abundant material for visualising the clothes worn by the yeomen and husbandmen, and especially their wives and children. The coarse and scanty attire of the poor is less in evidence. The lengths and prices of cloth and '3½ yards of white sacking to make a doublet' (637) are noteworthy.

As usual there are good examples of armour and weapons for military and field use (especially 301, 753 and 995), a late reference to a long-bow (395), stone-bow (209), pellet-bow (908), shutting-bow, and prickshaft (717).

Of coastal craft, we find only one 'ship' - a one-eighth share of the 'John' of East Mersea (563). All other references are to small fishing craft - ketches, mongers, hoy, skey, and cocks - terms explained in previous volumes. Four testators (508, 563, 695, 785) thought of perils at sea, the second naming three local mariners absent on long voyages, John Slye at any rate surviving to make his own Will.

The remarkable number of cases in which a christian name is used for a second child (though rarely a daughter), an elder child not having died, has been demonstrated in our earlier volumes (in indexes, under 'Names, Christian'). The editor's interest in this phenomenon has led him to analyse figures elsewhere.[1]

In a period, long before the establishment of banks, the availability of, and security for, cash must have often posed a problem, except for the poorest. 'Ready money' (the testamentary term for cash) is common enough, but apparently inserted, with 'plate and jewels', as a matter of course for the richer testators by most draftsmen, and is therefore of little help. But occasionally a Will is more specific; for example, 'I have left in my chest 58s.3d. in good gold and money' (24) and the exceptional 'twelve score pounds of ready money' (376).

Rare Words

Note concerning 'howed'. In vols. 1-3 'howed' was defined as 'hamstrung', i.e. disabled by cutting the hamstring, hough or tendon of the hindleg of a quadraped, presumably to lame an animal from straying onto commons, etc. But frequent use

---

[1] F.G.Emmison, 'To my sons John the elder, Mark, John the younger, Peter...' (*Family History*, Inst. of Heraldic and Genealogical Studies, vol. 13, pp.447-50, 1986).

of 'black (or red) howed', or occasionally 'colour black howed', led the editor to query whether it meant 'hued'. However, 'howed cow', with no adjectival colour, confirms his earlier definition. 'Howed' is applied in Essex Elizabethan Wills to a cow, a bullock (female as well as male in Tudor times), a calf, and a heifer; and once (in a Will not yet published) to 'my red howed bull'. Since writing the above, 'lamed' has also been found (the first occurrence noted in 10,000 Essex Wills in this context): an ordinary bequest of 'a lamed cow' [D/ABW 40/83].

No satisfactory meanings for 'ronded' and 'oylie' have yet been found.

EDITORIAL METHOD

YEAR. Until 1752, the legal year began on Lady Day (25 March). All dates between 1 January and 24 March are therefore expressed thus, 1558/9, 1559 being the modern style.

PLACES. Unless otherwise stated, all places are in the county of Essex. Parishes, hamlets, etc., are given in their modern form. Field-names based on common words, e.g. Hyghe Feilde, are modernised, but not otherwise.

FORM OF ABSTRACTS.

a. *General.* The abstracts give *all* personal, place and field names; also all houses, lands, livestock, goods, money, etc., *except* the usual articles of bedlinen (sheets, pillows, pillowberes, blankets, coverlets, alternatively often referred to as 'my bed wholly furnished'); and all instructions, etc., of the testator. The language is retained as far as possible.

b. *Preambles and place of burial.* The vast majority of preambles are conventional and little more than affirmations of Christian faith, some slight variations being dictated by the clerical draftsmen. Preambles are therefore omitted, except where unusually long, when they are noted as '[Religious preamble.]'. Unless the place of burial is to be in a parish *other* than that of the testator, it is omitted.

c. *Legacies.* '...(to have and to hold) to him/her and his/her heirs and assigns (for ever)...' is generally to be assumed unless other directions are given. 'To be paid within one year/month after my decease...' or similar *short* term is omitted. 'To be paid at the age of 21' or 'to be paid at the age of 18 or at the day of her marriage, whichever is the sooner' is abstracted as 'at 21' or 'at 18 or marriage'. 'If X die, the one to be the other's heir' (a very common provision where there are two or more children) is omitted.

d. *Residuary legatee(s).* 'All the residue/rest of my goods (movable and unmovable) unbequeathed I give and bequeath to...' or similar phrase is abstracted as 'The residue/rest of my goods to...'.

e. *Successive remainders.* 'If my said son John do decease without heirs (male) of his body lawfully begotten, I bequeath my said house to my said son William and his heirs (male) and assigns (for ever)', when followed by similar clauses in respect of each younger child or other relation, is abstracted as 'If he die without heir (male), to remain (successively) to...'. Repeated descriptions of the property in such cases are omitted.

f. *Appointment of executors/executrices and overseers/supervisors.* The normal phrases referring to his/her duties, such as 'to see all things expressed in my Will', 'to pay my debts', 'to see me buried', etc. are omitted.

g. *Other omissions.* In addition to condensing long or repetitive clauses, various short 'legal' phrases, such as 'of good and lawful money of England' (after the sum), 'in the year of our Lord God', 'in the parish of', also an occasional clause cancelling all previous Wills, are omitted. Instructions to the widow to 'keep the said house(s) in good and sufficient reparations' or in the event of her remarriage to find sureties to be bound to pay legacies at a later date seem to be in some cases, as with other safeguards against contingencies, regularly inserted by the lawyer; if brief and in normal phraseology, they may be omitted, but any specific detail is included in the abstract.

h. *Probate clause* (always in Latin). This is often lengthy but normally yields merely date of probate/administration; unusual facts, e.g. widow's name if not in Will or renunciation of executorship, are given in the abstracts.

i. *Rare words.* Usually defined briefly in square brackets, but see special note concerning 'howed' and two other words on pp. xvii-xviii.

SPELLING. This is modernised, except for some very rare words, which may be briefly defined within square brackets or queried if doubtful. To obviate unnecessary examination of the Will in the Record Office, a doubtful year or word or apparent clerical error is followed by *sic* or *recte* according to the circumstances.

EDITORIAL RESEARCH. Where *surnames* are not clear or the reading difficult, other printed sources have been consulted, especially *Elizabethan Life*, volumes IV and V, ed. F.G.Emmison (1978, 1980) and *Wills at Chelmsford, 1400-1620*, ed. F.G. Emmison (1958) (British Record Society). Most names of *clergy* have been checked with the lists of incumbents in Newcourt's *Repertorium Ecclesiasticum Parochiale Londinense*, vol. 2 (1710), and the additional names in *Trans. Essex Archl. Soc.*, vols. 6,7 (1898, 1900), but further research to identify all names of clergy is not undertaken. Doubtful place-names are checked with Reaney's *Place-Names of Essex* (1935).

REFERENCES. The Essex Record Office references to the Wills, whether original or registered copies, have been omitted because of various complications. In case of enquiries, the references can be obtained from *Wills at Chelmsford, 1400-1620* or the numbers in this volume should be quoted if addressed to the County Archivist, Essex Record Office, County Hall, Chelmsford, CM1 1LX, enclosing (if from abroad) two international reply coupons.

F.G.EMMISON

THE PROBATE COURTS AND THEIR JURISDICTIONS

The *Essex Wills* series has, as its object, the abstracting of all the Elizabethan Wills from the three Archdeaconry Courts within the county and from that of the Commissary of the Bishop of London's Essex and Hertfordshire Jurisdiction. Readers should, however, be aware of the full complexity of probate jurisdictions within the county at the time.

The Prerogative Court of Canterbury (P.C.C.) granted probate of Wills of testators who had property worth over £5 in more than one diocese, except in certain cases, of which the diocese of London was one, where £10 was the amount. This latter therefore applied to persons who had property in Essex and in one or more other dioceses. Wills of persons dying at sea were also proved in this court. If there was doubt as to where, amid the numerous jurisdictions, small and large, a Will should be proved, it was cheaper in the long run to go straight to the Prerogative Court, rather than have the Will proved in a lower court and then find that it must proceed higher. There was also the question of prestige; the Prerogative Court was the highest and the most important. A large proportion of Essex Wills must therefore be sought for in the P.C.C. The original Wills and Registers are held in the Public Record Office. Printed indexes have been published by the British Record Society, for the period 1383 to 1700 (see *Bibliography* below).

The Consistory Court of the Bishop of London covered the whole diocese including Essex, with the exception of the courts of the Peculiars, noted below. The probate courts of the Vicar-General are included in it. This court had a concurrent jurisdiction with (i.e. alternative to) the Essex courts referred to below. The records are now in the Greater London Record Office.

The Commissary Court of the Bishop of London (London Division) was the court of the Bishop's Commissary, or deputy. It had jurisdiction over the City of London, many Middlesex and eight Essex parishes, all in the south-west of the county, viz. Chingford, Epping, Leyton, Loughton, Nazeing, Waltham Holy Cross, Walthamstow and Woodford. These Wills are now in the Corporation of London's Guildhall Library. Abstracts of the Wills of Essex testators for the Elizabethan period were published in 1983 as *Elizabethan Wills of South-West Essex* (see *Bibliography* below).

The Bishop's Commissary Court (Essex and Hertfordshire Division) had a corresponding jurisdiction within those two counties. It extended in theory to about a quarter (scattered) of the total number of Essex parishes and to six east Hertfordshire parishes (all listed in *Wills and their Whereabouts*; see below). In practice the court was used for probate of Wills in almost every Essex parish, not excepting the Peculiars. The records of this court, from 1483, are now in the Essex Record Office, Chelmsford (as listed in *Wills at Chelmsford*; see below) and are to be abstracted for the Elizabethan period in later volumes of this series.

There were three Archdeaconry Courts in Essex: the Archdeaconry of Essex, in the south; of Colchester, in two parts, in the north-west and north-east; and of Middlesex (Essex and Hertfordshire Jurisdiction), in the north and west of the county. The parishes contained in each are listed in *Wills and their Whereabouts*. The probate records of these three Archdeaconries are in the Essex Record Office. The earliest, those of the Archdeaconry of Essex, have survived from the year 1400, those of Colchester begin in 1500, and those of Middlesex (Essex and Hertfordshire Jurisdiction) in 1554. The Elizabethan Wills are abstracted in this present series.

The jurisdictions of the several courts of the Peculiars, i.e. those parishes exempt from the authority of the Archdeacons, are somewhat confusing but only in two cases do Wills survive from the Elizabethan period; in neither case are there any printed abstracts. The Peculiar of the Dean and Chapter of St. Paul's Cathedral included, in Essex, the parishes of Barling, Belchamp St. Paul's, Heybridge, Navestock, Tillingham and Wickham St. Paul's. The records begin about 1535 and are now in the Guildhall Library. A copy of an original index to the Wills is available on the shelves in the Manuscripts Department of the Library. An Essex Peculiar of the Dean and Chapter of Westminster was the parish of St. Mary, Maldon. The records of this jurisdiction, which also comprises parishes in London and elsewhere, are extant from 1504, and are in the City of Westminster Archives Department.

Wills from four other jurisdictions, the Peculiar of Bocking (covering, in Essex, Bocking, Borley, Little Coggeshal, Latchingdon, Southchurch, Stisted, Runsell in Danbury, and Milton in Prittlewell), the Peculiar of Good Easter, covering that parish alone, the Peculiar of Writtle and Roxwell, and the Peculiar of the Liberty of the Sokens (Kirby, Thorpe and Walton-le-Soken), survive only from the post-Elizabethan period. For details see *Wills and their Whereabouts*.

BIBLIOGRAPHY

Index of Wills proved in the Prerogative Court of Canterbury, vol. III, 1558-1583, ed. S.A.Smith and L.L.Duncan. Index Library, 1898. [Index of testators; also contains a county index.]

Index of Wills proved in the Prerogative Court of Canterbury, vol. IV, 1584-1604, ed. S.A.Smith and E.A.Fry. Index Library, 1901. [As vol. III above.]

Wills at Chelmsford (Essex and East Hertfordshire), vol. 1, 1400-1619, ed. F.G. Emmison. British Record Society, 1958. [Index of testators from the three Archdeaconry Courts, the Commissary Court (Essex and Hertfordshire) and the Peculiars of Writtle and Roxwell, and Good Easter.]

Elizabethan Life: Wills of Essex Gentry and Merchants proved in the Prerogative Court of Canterbury, ed. F.G.Emmison. Essex Record Office, 1978. [Abstracts of 339 selected P.C.C. Wills.]

Elizabethan Life: Wills of Essex Gentry and Yeomen, preserved in the Essex Record Office, ed. F.G.Emmison. Essex Record Office, 1980. [Abstracts of 277 selected Wills from the Archdeaconry Courts and the Commissary Court (Essex and Hertfordshire).]

Elizabethan Wills of South-West Essex, ed. F.G.Emmison. Kylin Press, 1983. [Abstracts of all Elizabethan Wills from the Essex parishes of the Commissary Court (London Division).]

Essex Wills (England), vol. 1, 1558-1565, ed. F.G.Emmison. National Genealogical Society, Washington, D.C., 1982. [Abstracts of all Wills proved in the three Archdeaconry Courts.]

Essex Wills (England), vol. 2, 1565-1571, ed. F.G.Emmison. New England Historic Genealogical Society, Boston, 1983. [As for vol. 1, above.]

Essex Wills (England), vol. 3, 1571-1577, ed. F.G.Emmison. New England Historic Genealogical Society, Boston, 1986. [As for vol. 1, above.]

Wills and their Whereabouts, A.J.Camp. Society of Genealogists, 4th edn., 1974. [County by county guide to probate jurisdictions and the survival and whereabouts of probate records. For Essex, lists the individual parishes over which the various courts had jurisdiction.]

Guide to the Essex Record Office, F.G.Emmison. Essex Record Office, 2nd edn. 1969. [Summary guide to archives in the Essex Record Office, including all probate material, giving dates covered and reference-numbers.]

1

ARCHDEACONRY OF ESSEX

This Archdeaconry covered central, south-west, south, south-east and east Essex. The abstracts were prepared from the Wills Registers, collated with the original Wills [Essex Record Office reference D/AEW]; occasional differences are noted in [ ]. Wills herein numbered 1-52, proved 1577-78, were abstracted from the Register [D/AER 13], nos. 53-441, proved 1578-83, from Register [D/AER 14], and nos. 442-467B, proved 1583-84, from Register [D/AER 15].

The Wills in the Register for 1577-1583 are not in order of date of probate, the order being as follows:-

folios			
1- 25	proved 1581-82	nos.	255-287
25- 45	proved 1581	nos.	288-308
46-103	proved 1580	nos.	180-254
104-202	proved 1578-79	nos.	53-179
203-end	proved 1582-83	nos.	309-441

In order to assist the reader, the editor has re-arranged these sections into chronological order. It appears that the Court scribe did not enter up this Register until several years after probate, and then he did not take up the annual bundles of original Wills in order of those years. He occasionally omitted to copy the probate clause giving the date; but he always added for quick reference the testator's name in the margin of the Register, sometimes giving a different or more 'literate' spelling, such differences being noted by the editor.

For unregistered Wills in the Archdeaconry of Essex see Appendix: nos. 998-1004.

HENRY HOLLAND of Rettendon yeoman, 19 Mar. 1576/7. (1)
I will that Anne my wife shall have the keeping and bringing up of Rd. my son and the custody of such goods as were in my possession to his use until full age, which were granted to me by letters of administration, 1 Dec. 1573. I will that she shall have only allowance for my expenses about my son until this day as in my book of accounts; henceforth she shall have nothing for keeping him but the use of the stock and shall find him all things necessary at her own costs. To my daughters Anne and Ellen each £10 at marriage or 20. To Rd. my best sword, dagger, bow and quiver of arrows. To six poor householders of Rettendon 12d. apiece, viz. father RAYSON, Joan TRYTTELS widow, Hugh COOLE, Edm. ELYE, Wm. GOODWYN, and widow NORRYCE. The residue of my goods to my wife towards the bringing up of my two daughters. I make her my executrix. I ordain for overseers my trusty friends Mr Th. CHURCHE, John LAKE and Th. BONNE, and for their pains 6s.8d. apiece. Witnesses: Rt. BUCKBERD rector of Rettendon, Th. RAWLINS, Wm. REEDE. Proved 6 Apr. 1577.

JOHN MARCHOLE of Fyfield husbandman, 10 Mar. 1576/7. **(2)**
To Eliz. my wife my house and land called Marchols for 8½ years after my death, in consideration to bring up my children; after, to Wm. my son, paying his mother [not named] 20s. a year for her third. If she die before, the profit of my house and land equally divided among my children. To Wm. 2 pewter platters. To my five children 2 pewter platters and 1 candlestick apiece. To them equally divided 1 cow and 3 of my sheep [*sic*]. To Wm. 1 featherbed and a pair of bedsteadles in the loft. To my daughters Agnes, Marion, Joan and Denis each 1 pair of trendle bedsteadles, 1 pair of sheets, 1 hutch, 1 brass kettle, and 10s. towards a bed. To Wm. my great hutch in the shop and 1 little hutch in the loft that my evidence [title-deed] is in, 1 cupboard in the hall, my little brass pot, and my broad brass pan. To my four daughters £5 each at 20, my brother-in-law John MOUNCK to receive it to their use until then. To Wm. 40s. to be paid at entrance on his house and land, except he be bound prentice to any man, then his master shall keep it for him so long as he is bound with him. If bound prentice, he shall be bound at the discretion of his uncle John MONCKE and his mother. The rest of my goods to my wife. I make her and John executors, and for his pains 2s. I make Nich. THOMAS and John HUBARD overseers. Witnesses: John GRAVE, Gilbert ASSHEWELL. Proved 27 Mar. 1577.

LAWRENCE FRANCIS of Fobbing husbandman, 17 — 1576 [1576/7?]. **(3)**
To Agnes my wife all my goods within the house as without, whom I ordain executrix. I pray goodman Ralph GLASKOKE of Basildon to be overseer, and for his pains 3s.4d. Witnesses: Wm. KNIGHTBRIDGE, John BECK, Roger BODY, Wm. SMYTHE. Proved 27 Mar. 1577.

MARGARET HAUCKIN of Great Waltham widow, 29 Apr. 1577. **(4)**
To the poor men's box 5s. at the day of my burial. To my daughters Clement, 'Marget' and Marian each £5 at marriage or 21, and my sons Th. the elder and Th. the younger each £5 at 21. To Marian my standing bed in my parlour with an over tester of silk and 1 standing cup with a cover of silver and gilt at 21. To 'Marget' a silver salt with a gilt cover at 21 or marriage. My 3 silver spoons shall be equally divided amongst 'Marget', Clement and Alice [*sic*] my three daughters. The rest of my goods to be equally divided amongst all my children, those already of full age within 1 year after my death, the others at 21. All the abovesaid to be delivered to my loving brother-in-law and most trusty friend John HAUCKIN, whom I make executor. Witnesses: Nich. YELDARD vicar of Great Waltham, Rt. HAUCKIN. Proved 22 May 1577.

WILLIAM INCKLEY of Wennington husbandman, 14 May 1577. (Nuncupative.) **(5)**
He gave his goods to Mgy. his wife, she therewith to pay his debts and bring up his children and to give to each, John and Henry INCKLEY, £3 6s.8d. of her own consent. He appointed her his executrix. Witnesses: Wm. AUDEN clerk, parson of Wennington, Charles NUTALL, Henry SYMNELL. Proved 25 May 1577.

JOHN EGELSTON of Stanford-le-Hope husbandman, 3 Apr. 1577. **(6)**
To the poor men's box 12d. To Joan my daughter my brown cow, £5, 3 good sheep, the greatest brass pot, 1 chest, 3 pewter platters, 3 saucers, and 2 pair of good sheets at 18 or marriage. To Agnes my well-beloved wife all my lands copy and freehold for her life; after her decease, to Joan and Mgy. my daughters. If both die having no heir, to remain to 'Barbery' EGELSTON my brother's daughter. The rest of my goods to my wife and Mgy. to be equally divided. I make my wife executrix and Eugeny GATTON gentleman and Wm. ROGER of 'Fookes here' [not identified] my overseers. Witnesses: Th. WAPULL, John FOLLY. Proved 23 May 1577.

WILLIAM SMYTHE of West Hanningfield yeoman, 5 June 1577. **(7)**
To the poor of West Hanningfield £3, Rochford 40s., and Eastwood 20s. To West Hanningfield church £3. To Eliz. my wife my half lease in Foulness [island] with my stock of cattle belonging. To her my two leases in West Hanningfield, viz. my house wherein I dwell and my lease of a farm called P[er]ages, with the stock belonging to the farms. To her my lands and tenements free and copy in Rochford and

Eastwood for her life; after her decease, to Jane GATES my sister, wife of Geo. GATES, for her life; after her decease, to Geo. GATES my sister's son; for want of issue, to Frs. GATES my sister's son. To him and Eliz. HAIES my sister's daughter £10 apiece, Wm. and Sebastian HAIES my sister's children 20s. apiece, Eliz. WEEKLEY £10, all at 21 or marriage, and the rest of my servants 6s.8d. apiece. To Rt. PARKER parson of West Hanningfield 1 spur ryal [coin worth about 15s.]. The rest of my goods to my wife, whom I make executrix. I appoint overseers John SKELTON and Rd. HUMFREY, to whom 40s. apiece for their pains. Witnesses: John NOBLE, John WELLS, John BATTELL, Th. WEEKLEY, Rt. PARKER clerk. Proved 13 June 1577 by Rd. HUMFREY proctor [in original only].

JANE BRYD [BRIDE *in original*] of East Tilbury widow, — 1577. (8)
To Wm. BRYDE [BIRDE in original] my son and Susan COUNCELL my grandchild my 6 kine going with John WORLEY to be equally divided, paying him 20s. for their going at Michaelmas next. To Wm. and Susan each 1 of my featherbeds and 1 of my flockbeds. To Joan TAYLOR 1 featherbed and my best petticoat and Cath. wife of the said John WARLEY my red furred petticoat and her child my goddaughter 6s. To Wm. and Susan each 1 dozen of pewter, 1 chest, and 1 brass pot. To 'Felice' WILKIN 1 woolbed, Joan WATER 1 flockbed, and Alice WIDOWES 1 featherbed, a pair of sheets, and ½ dozen of pewter. The residue of my goods to my executors. I make Edw. LAWRENCE and Geo. ABBOTT gentlemen executors. Witnesses: John FIELD, Matthew BRETT. Proved 12 June 1577 by Geo. ABBOTT, the other executor not coming.

JOHN EYRES [EYERS *in original*] of North Benfleet clerk [not the rector], 4 June, 18 Eliz. [1576]. (9)
To be buried where it shall please God. To Wm. DONCKEN, my host's son, 1 cow, 2 sheep and 26s.8d., my bible, 1 great chair, a mattress, a bolster, 1 covering, my war bill, and my 'skayne' [skein or skene, dagger or small sword], all at 17. To Mgy. DONCKEN 1 cow, 2 sheep, 20s., 1 featherbed, a covering, and a bolster, at 17 or marriage. To Charles KIRSPE 5 sheep, 3 hogs, 2 pitchforks, 1 saw, 2 bills, 2 axes, a mattock, 1 pair of 'gives' ['gyves' in original] [gyve, shackles?], and an iron wedge. To Th. HUTTON and Wm. HASELL my godsons and Eliz. OSBOURNE my goddaughter each 3s.4d. To the reparations of the chancel [of North Benfleet church] 2s.6d. To mother SOM[M]ER 2s.6d. To Mgy. DONCKEN my cloak that I bought of COPSHEIFT's widow. To John DRAPER my hose that LORKIN made. The residue of my goods to Mgy. SMITH, whom I ordain executrix. I request that Mr Wm. OSBORNE and John POOLE be my overseers and that Mr OSBORNE have the custody of my goods till the children come of age, and that my executrix be ruled by him. Witnesses: Edw. LEES, Rd. ARCHER clerk [instituted vicar of Little Wakering, 1578]. [No probate clause.]

ROBERT STELE of Woodham Mortimer carpenter, 2 June 1577. (10)
To the poor people of Woodham Mortimer at my burial 6s.8d. and of Great Braxted 10s. To Chris. STELE my eldest son at 22 my free messuage called Howse in Braxted, the free land belonging except that called Revells, with the ground called Scotches being copyhold lying on the south side of the highway thence to Tiptree Heath; on condition that he pay Isabel my wife 40s. yearly; if he die without heirs, to be equally divided between John and Th. STELE my sons at 22, paying my wife likewise. To Th. at 23 my copyhold lands called Revells and Scroppells with 3 roods in Mead in the occupation of John PORTER of Great Braxted yeoman. My sons John and Th. shall between them have the feeding of Loake Mead after the end of the lease of John PORTER; provided that they shall equally pay thereout such legacies of my predecessors to the church and poor people of Great Braxted. To my wife 9 kine which are now milked at home, 2 yearling bullocks, 1 wennel bull calf, 1 wennel cow calf, and 1 mare colour iron grey, such goods as were hers before I was married to her, and half my corn growing in Braxted and oats in Payne Field. To Mgy. IVAT 1 wennel cow calf and Mgt. GUBBON my maid 1 cow. The residue of my goods to Chris., John and Th. equally to be divided. I constitute John PORTER of [Great] Braxted yeoman and John WADE of Heybridge carpenter my executors, and 10s.

apiece for their pains. I appoint John BYNDER and Th. RAMSELL of Great Braxted yeoman my overseers, and for their pains 6s.8d. apiece. Witnesses: Edw. GIBBON of Tillingham, Hugh RICHMAN, Nich. JOHNSON clerk [the writer, uses his paraph]. Proved 14 June 1577.

NICHOLAS ELLES of Dengie, 16 June 1577. **(11)**
To the poor 5s. To the five children of the wife of Rt. HAIES of Dengie now living each 12d. To Grace BYCE and Joan TAYLOR my goddaughters and Edw. STEVEN my godson each 5s. To Eliz. RIVE, Agnes NEVELOCK and Abraham MAN each 12d. To John, Wm., Joan and Susan CLERKE, my wife's brothers and sisters, each 10s. To Priscilla BLAWERS, my wife's 1st husband's daughter, £5 at 21 or marriage; if she die before, to Wm. BLAWERS her brother. To Wm. BLAWER my wife's son £5 at 22; if he die before, £3 to his mother and 40s. to Th. COTTISFURTH, my faithful friend who shall have the custody of the £10 given to Priscilla and Wm. till the times appointed. The residue of my goods to Agnes my wife, whom I make my executrix. I will Th. COTTISFURTH to be supervisor, and towards his charges 5s. Witnesses: Roger NOWELL priest and writer of this [vicar of Heybridge], John FOWLE. [No probate clause.]

JOHN BRUAR of Great Wakering husbandman, 2 Nov. 1574. **(12)**
To Agnes my wife such goods as were her own before I married her. To her $1\frac{1}{2}$ quarters of wheat and $1\frac{1}{2}$ quarters of oats yearly for her life, 1 barrow hog, the poultry about the house except only the capons, and half the butter and cheese. To the poor people of Great Wakering 6s.8d. To John BRUAR my nephew at 21 and Joan and Mgt. my son's daughters each 10s. at 20 or marriage. To my brother Wm. BRUAR 2 bushels of wheat. To my servant Rt. HORSENAYLE 4s. The rest of my goods to my son Rd., whom I make executor. I make Rd. DANDY my overseer, and for his pains 6s.8d. Witnesses: Reynold KYROM, Wm. STOWE clerk [vicar of Great Wakering], John DEN, Giles TRYTTYLL [surname in original only]. Proved 11 July 1577.

THOMAS PASCALL of Great Baddow gentleman, 12 Feb. 1576/7. **(12A)**
To Mary my well-beloved wife my messuage and lands called Spenders in Nevendon and Basildon for her life, the remainder to my son John. To Edm. my son my messuage and lands called Lunsses in Nevendon, Basildon and Vange in the occupation of John BRODDOCKE; for default of issue, to Wm. my younger son. To my wife my mansion [i.e. dwelling] house and lands in Great Baddow and the profits of my farm lands called Apton Field for life, the remainder of my house and of my term unexpired to Wm. To him, by licence of the lord of the manor of Great Baddow, my customary lands there. To John my term of years in Waskettes [in Basildon], on condition that he pay each of my daughters Mary, Philippa, Mgt. and Eliz. £100 at marriage, also each of his brothers Edm. and Wm. during the residue of my term £10 a year; and my farm called Fryarn [in Basildon] and the stock and store thereon. To my wife my stock and store of cattle and corn on Spenders; she shall occupy during the term of years Rye Mead and have the profit of my cattle in Great Baddow, leaving it or the value to Wm. at her decease. To my wife and John my team or cart wain at Nevendon. To John my bay gelding. The residue of my goods, jewels, plate and household stuff to my wife, whom I make executrix. Witnesses: John LAYTHAM, Alex. PASCALL. Proved 25 June 1577.

WILLIAM RICHARDSON of Rochford tanner, 8 June 1577. **(13)**
To my six children, viz. John, Th., Mary, Dthy., Anna and Mgt., 40s. apiece at 23. To the poor people of Rochford 12d. The residue of my goods to Joan my wife to bring up my four daughters and pay my debts and legacies. I make her executrix. I constitute Geo. GATES and Rd. WYMAN overseers, and for their pains 20d. apiece. Witnesses: Wm. HILLS, Rd. WYMAN, Lawrence WILSON writer hereof. Proved 11 July 1577.

ELIZABETH REEDE [REDE *in margin*] of Rochford widow, 27 Apr. 1577. **(14)**
To the poor people 10s. at the day of my burial. To my son John HASTLER's three

children £6 to be equally divided at 21. To Susan his daughter 1 little brass pot, my daughter-in-law HASTLER my best double rail and best kercher. To Jane daughter of Th. HASTLER 6s.8d. at 21. To Roger REDE my son £13 11s.4d., my oldest featherbed, 1 hutch, a pillow wrought with black work, 2 long trowels, 1 tablecloth, 4 silver spoons, my least chair, least grindstone, 5 pewter platters, 5 pewter dishes, 2 saucers, a little brass pot, a kettle, a skillet, a skummer, another tablecloth, 5 canvas table napkins, and my carpet cushions. To my son[-in-law] Geo. GATES's two children £4 equally divided at 21. To Geo. son of Geo. GATES the biggest brass pot and Frs. son of Geo. the next biggest brass pot. To Roger my son 1 bedsheet. To Cath. BYSSHOPS and Avice HIDES each 12d. The residue of my goods to my executor, whom I ordain Geo. GATES. I make Wm. SMITHE overseer. Witnesses: Wm. TAYNTER, John WELLES, Wm. SMITHE. Proved 11 July 1577.

ANNE BRICE late wife of Thomas BRICE of Great Stambridge, 9 June 1577. (15)
To my eldest son Wm. BRICE 2 ewe sheep or else for the 2 sheep 8s. To my son Rd. BRICE my house in Foulness [island] with the lands belonging called Sutton Huckes; if he die without heirs, to remain to my daughter Rebecca. To Rd. 2 sheep at 21 or else 8s. To my daughters Emme and Susan my wearing apparel both linen and woollen equally divided. To Anne BRICE my daughter 1 cow and 40s., or if she like not the cow to have 40s., at marriage or 21. To Sarah and Rebecca my daughters 40s. at marriage or 21. The residue of my goods to Th. TERBUCKE of Paglesham towards the bringing up of my poor children, whom I make executor, desiring him as my trustee to be good to them. I appoint John CASLE of Great Stambridge my overseer, and to him 5s. Witnesses: Stephen BARWICK curate [rector of Hadleigh, instituted 1578], Rd. GRENEBANCKE. Proved 11 July 1577.

WILLIAM SHAWE of West Ham yeoman, 9 Mar. 1576/7. (16)
To be buried in Our Lady chancel in the north side of West Ham church as nigh to the place where my late wife [not named] lieth buried as conveniently my be. To Joan my wife for life the tenement with the orchard and garden as now enclosed with a pale in Upton in West Ham in the tenure of me and Th. MYLLER. Whereas he holdeth the tenement for 4¼ years to the Nativity of St. John the Baptist 1581, by reason whereof my wife cannot have the occupation until then, she shall have in lieu for 4¼ years the occupation of the house wherein I dwell with the orchard, garden, backsides and old houses, paying my overseers the yearly rent of a peppercorn if demanded; on condition that she be bound to them to deliver such goods and household stuff belonging to my children as be left in her custody at the end of the 4¼ years. To her for her life a yearly rent of £4 out of my lands in West Ham in recompense for her dower. To Susan wife of Nich. CRUE of London hosier, in compensation for legacies given her by Peter SMITHYMAN, a yearly rent of 40s. for 8 years out of ground called Little Stock in the tenure of James WOODLAND of West Ham in the same parish. To Susan for like consideration for 6 years after the 8 years an annuity of £4 out of the same ground. To my son Frs. SHAWE my lands and tenements free and copy in West Ham and East Ham and to his heirs male; for lack of such issue, successively to Th. son of my brother Rd. SHAWE and to my cousin John SHAWE and their heirs male. Provided that, in case my goods shall not be sufficient to pay my legacies, my overseers shall sell so much of my lands except my farm at Upton. To my wife my roan mare and 6 of my milch kine, 2 featherbeds and 2 bedsteads, being the best saving that which I lie on and the great bed in the hall. To her 6 pairs of sheets, 6 platters, 6 dishes, 6 saucers and 6 porringers, all of pewter, 2 pewter pots (i.e. a quart pot and a pint pot), 3 latten candlesticks, a latten chafing dish, 2 of the best brass pots saving the greatest, 2 kettles, 1 chafer, 3 tablecloths, 2 dozen napkins, 2 spits, and a pair of andirons. To my daughters Anne SHAWE 30s., 2 featherbeds, 3 tablecloths, 1 dozen napkins, 2 towels, 6 platters, 6 dishes, 6 saucers and 6 porringers, all of pewter, 2 pewter pots (a quart and a pint), 3 latten candlesticks, a latten chafing dish, 2 brass pots except the greatest, 1 kettle, 1 chafer, and 1 spit, and Eliz. £20, 1 featherbed, 6 napkins, 1 towel, 6 platters, [etc., as for Anne], each at marriage or 21. To my son Peter SHAWE £20 at 21. To Rt. SHAWE's wife a ring of gold of the value of 5s. I will that, if my wife at her costs shall keep and bring up Peter, Anne and Eliz. until

they are 16, she shall hold my field (10 acres) in my tenure at Upton abutting on my 2 acres in that of Peter UDALL for 16 years after my decease; if she refuse, my overseers shall have their bringing up and have the field. To my cousin John SHAWE barber my gown faced with budge, my leather jerkin of buck's leather lined with black bays, and 40s. To my maidservant Anne ARNOLD my wife's sister 40s. To Anne SHAWE my brother Rd.'s daughter a calf, my sister Dthy. SHAWE 40s., and Mgy. my maidservant 40s. and a featherbed. To SILVESTER my prentice 40s. at the end of his apprenticehood in recompense of his service, so that he honestly serve out the rest of his years with my brother Rd. To Rd.'s wife the ring which I wear. To John son of Henry SHAWE 40s. if he be living and come to ask for it. To Peter DAVY living in Gracious Street [in London] my black coat 1½ 'hundreth' of short faggots to be delivered there. I will that my overseers shall freely give Rt. WALKER of London innholder 2 months' grass in some of my pastures for a gelding or a mare yearly at such times as he shall send one during 4 years after my decease. To Mr John LEWES, proctor of the [Court of] Arches, and Rt. HODGESON gentleman each 3 months' grass yearly for 4 years for 1 gelding or 1 mare. To my cousin Rt. SHAWE in St. John's Street [in London] my gold ring with a red stone in it. To my brother Rd. the rest of my apparel. To my godchildren 2s. apiece. To the poor people in West Ham for 4 years yearly 20s. in coal about Christmas. To Th. REDFORD for making this my Will 20s. Towards the repairing of West Ham church 20s. I will that 20s. be spent in bread, wine and sugar among such of my honest neighbours as my overseers shall think fit. The residue of my goods, leases, money, rings, napery, bedding and household stuff to my son Frs., whom I make my executor. I ordain Anthony BRIDGES gentleman, Roger HODGESON, John LEWES, and my brother Rd. supervisors, desiring them to aid my executor, and to Anthony for his painstaking 20s. I will that Rd. shall have the keeping and bringing up of Frs. and of his goods and receive the rents of my lands till he is 21, and then to be accountable to him. To my cousins Th. and Thurston YATE each £15 at 24 in recompense of goods that came to my hands of their mother Anne SHAWE. Witnesses: Th. STAPLES, Wm. ROOKE, Th. HASTLER, Geo. DICKINS, John LYSTER. Administration committed, 10 May 1577, to Rd. SHAWE during the minority of Frs. SHAWE.

WILLIAM DAVY of Horndon-on-the-Hill, 30 Apr. 1577. (17)
To Sarah HALL my daughter's child a lamb, my wife to put it forth to the child's profit; if my wife die before the child come to age, she shall appoint it in lease with some honest man, paying for the keeping of it. If I see that Joan my daughter is not in case to profit by anything, I refer the distribution thereof to the discretion of my Joan my wife, to whom I give all my goods. To Davy CALLOWE my godson 12d. to buy him books. I make my wife executrix. Witnesses: Wm. BURNELL curate of Horndon, Rt. GOODWIN, John GOODWIN, John HOLLAND. Proved 23 July 1577.

AGNES ABELL of Stondon Massey widow, 19 May, 19 Eliz. [1577]. (18)
To the poor 2s. To Geoffrey ABELL my son 1 cow, 1 bed in the loft at the stair's head, £5, and 1 kettle. To Rd. ABELL my son 40s. To Th. my son 1 flockbed above in the chamber and a great brass pot. To Clemence my daughter my new brass pot, 1 cauldron, the little bed in the parlour, the painted cloths in the parlour, the little table in the hall, the painted cloth in the hall being the halling, and a posnet. The residue of my goods to Th., Rd. and Clemence part and part alike. Th. and Rd. to be executors and Wm. ABELL my son and Wm. TYMAN my son-in-law overseers, and to my son Wm. for his pains 10s. Witnesses: Andrew BROMAN, Geo. REYNOLD. Proved 23 July 1577.

RICHARD HAKESWELL of Padnoll Corner in Barking, 24 June [year not given]. (19)
To Francis HAWKESWELL [relationship not given] 2 kine, a mare colt of the year and the vantage, and my best apparel. To Andrew FRENCHE 1 ewe. To Agnes WARNER 1 cow. The residue of my goods to Eliz. my wife, whom I make executrix. I will that Th. HADDEN do see my Will performed. Witnesses: John PATCHE, Th. HADDEN, Th. SKINNER. [No probate clause.]

JOHN CUMBERS of High Ongar husbandman, 2 June [year not given]. (20)
To Wm. my son £6 13s.4d. and 1 colt at 21. To Mary and Parnell my daughters each £6 13s.4d. at 21. The residue of my goods to Cath. my wife to bring up my children; if my three children die before 21, to remain to my wife, paying my executors 13s.4d. apiece. I make Wm. STANE and Rd. BARRYAT my executors, and for their pains 6s.8d. apiece. Witnesses: Rd. POOLE, John LYKRIS, Th. BOWES, Harry YNGOWLLE. Proved 15 July 1577.

WILLIAM RAME of Broomfield, [date not given]. (Nuncupative.) (21)
He nominated John RAMME of Great Waltham and Lawrence SMYTHE *alias* SALMON of Broomfield his executors. To Lawrence SMITH and John SMITH sons to his wife each 53s.4d. at 21. To Agnes SMYTH daughter to the husband of Wm. RAMME's wife £6 at 21. The residue of his goods to Matthew RAMME at 21. Witnesses: Rd. CROWE, Wm. HAUCKSTED. Proved 17 Sept. 1577.

JOHN WELLS of Rochford linendraper, 27 Aug., 19 Eliz. [1577]. (22)
To Mgy. OWEN widow, my mother, £15. To my servants Th. SHEREWELL 3s.4d. and Mgt. EVANS 20d. To the poor of Rochford 3s.4d. at my burial at the discretion of Wm. TAYNETER my father-in-law. To John my son £10 and Mary my daughter £5, each at 21 or marriage. Mary my wife shall have their portions until then for their bringing up and education. To John my son my house and ground in Rochford called Yons after 21, my wife to have it until then. I make her my executrix. I make Th. BOOD and Wm. TAYNTER overseers, and to each for their pains 3s.4d. Witnesses: Wm. CORNEFORD, John EVE, John BERMAN, John BERMAN parson there. Proved 17 Sept. 1577.

THOMAS HUDSPECT of Purleigh husbandman, — 1577. (23)
To my sons John and Th. each £20 at 21; if both die before, to remain to the rest of my children equally divided, my sons at 21 and my daughter at 18 or marriage. The rest of my goods to my well-beloved in Christ, Rd. HAMOND of Little Baddow husbandman, whom I make executor, to see my younger children, viz. my sons James, Edw. and Wm. and my daughter Ellen, brought up honestly in the fear of God with sufficient meat, drink, cloth, lodging, washing, or other necessary to 15, then to provide for themselves. I appoint my brother John of High Easter husbandman overseer. Witnesses: Lawrence [misread by Registrar, Andrew in original] DOUNTON, Th. STANE, Rt. ROBINSON. Proved 19 Sept. 1577.

RICHARD ROSITER, [abode not given], 9 Sept. 1577. (24)
To be buried in Wanstead church. To Wm. ROSTER the lease which is called Talbot in the Forest of 'Roych' in the parish of 'Come' [Combe] (co. Somerset) in the hands of John CRID dwelling by Mr Henry LIGHT esquire. To Nich. ROSTER my eldest brother 20s., my sister, his wife, 2s.6d., my sisters each 2s.6d., my kinswomen dwelling in 'Come' each 12d., my brother Wm. ROSTER 20s., Mrs Jane LEYTE 2s.6d. in gold, Th. BARNUS 5s., his wife 2s.6d., my father Philip ROSTER 20s., my uncle Mr John MARRWOOD esquire and his wife each 10s., my uncle Barnard MARWOOD 10s., my aunts COURTNEY 10s. and THOMASON 2s.6d., my cousins dwelling at 'Haberton' [Harberton, co. Devon?] each 12d., and every one of my fellows dwelling in the house 12d. apiece; and John OSBORNE 2s. I owe Joan, servant in the house, 2s.6d. To Wm. TORNER 2s. and widow BAKER 8d. The rest to be given to the poor of this parish or elsewhere as my uncle Mr John MARWOOD shall think good. I have 6d. of Rt. TORNER's which I will to be paid. I make Mr John MARWOOD my executor and overseer. To my brother Wm. a bond lying in my chest new made. Debts — my brother Wm. ROSITER oweth me 40s., Wm. FIELD 55s.4d., Wm. TORNER 20s. I have left in my chest 58s.3d. in good gold and money. Witnesses: John WILLIAMS clerk [the clergy list for Wanstead is deficient at this period], Wm. ROSETOR, Th. BARNUS. Proved 8 Oct. 1577 [in original only].

HENRY LAKE of Little Ilford husbandman, 21 Oct., 19 Eliz. [1577]. (25)
To Alice my wife the use and occupying of my freehold tenement and land wherein I dwell for 9 years, on condition that she pay Mgy. my daughter £16 at marriage,

also keep and bring her up; if she decease before, the £16 to Th. my son at 21. Towards the reparation of Little Ilford church 6s.8d. The residue of my goods to my wife, whom I ordain executrix, on condition that she bring up and keep my sons Th. and Edm. I ordain Wm. RICHARDES clerk, parson of Little Ilford, and Wm. WALKER of East Ham my overseers. Witnesses: Wm. MALDEGILL, Ambrose BARKER, Wm. BROWN. Proved 9 Nov.1577 [in original only].

ROBERT TURNOR of Chipping Ongar, 25 Aug. 1577. (26)
To Alice ALLAT my daughter my mansion [i.e. dwelling] house in Chipping Ongar called Dyars, with the kitchen, barn, stable, and other buildings, and the garden and orchard, likewise the little hoppit or pightle adjoining to the end of the orchard called Wastells, renting to the lord [of the manor] 1d. a year. To my executors the residue of my houses and lands in Chipping Ongar to sell, the money to be employed to the performance of my Will. To Mary, Grace, Dthy., Alice and Joan, daughters of my daughter Alice, each £6 13s.4d. at 18. To Dthy. my best featherbed, best joined bedstead, the best half of all manner of tin and pewter, viz. platters, dishes, saucers, pottingers, salt cellars, 'flower' [for flour?] pots, pewter pots, basin and spoons, my best and greatest brass cauldron, 3 of my greatest and best brass pots, 3 of my best and greatest kettles and brass pans, 2 of the best brass posnets, 2 spits (a greater and a lesser of the best sort), a pair of the best cobirons, the best trivet, 2 of the best dripping pans, a pair of the best trammels, half of my tubs and barrels, a malt quern with a mustard quern, the best half of my chairs and of my joined stools, the long table in the parlour with the frame and best carpet, my best and greatest cupboard, a square little joined hutch with a cupboard in it, my best powdering trough, my best chafing dish, a great brass mortar with an iron pestle, 2 of my best and greatest candlesticks and 3 of the other sort, the best of all my linen, and £50. To Th. TURNOR my brother 40s.; if he die, to be divided among his children. To Dthy. 1 featherbed. To my godchildren 6s.8d. each. To the poor at Kelvedon [Hatch] 13s.4d., Chipping Ongar 13s.4d., and Great Parndon 13s.4d. to be disposed of by Rd. DEERY my tenant there dwelling. To him and his wife 6s.8d. To Mgt. BORNE my goddaughter a little salt cellar of silver and parcel gilt with the cover. To Wm. WILKINSON my brother[-in-law] 20s. To James MORRICE esquire my great silver goblet and the cover. The residue of my goods to be sold by my executors, and the money to be equally divided among my two daughters. I ordain Mr Wm. BOURNE and Mr Rd. ELLYOTT gentleman executors, and for their labour 40s. each. [Added] 26 Aug. 1577. To Th. son of my daughter Alice ALLET £6 13s.4d. at 18. Witnesses: James MORRICE, Rd. ELLIOTT, Wm. SAUNDERS. Proved 26 Nov. 1577; inventory exhibited at £31 4s.7d.

JOHN WOLMER of Pitsea miller, 23 Jan. 1577/8. (27)
To Jeremy ALLEN 1 brazen chafer and 10s. at 21 and Mabel ALLEN 5s. at marriage. To mother PAGE, widow FOBLYE and John HULKE each 2 pecks of wheat, all which shall be ground toll free. To Pitsea church 16d. to buy a spade. To my well-beloved in Christ Mr Th. READING 6s.8d. to make a sermon for me. The rest of my goods to my well-beloved wife Eliz., whom I ordain executrix, to have them for her life; after her decease, all that shall be left to her two sons Wm. and Th. BYRTON equally divided. I ordain my well-beloved in Christ Roger AUSTEN curate of Pitsea my overseer, and for his pains 10s. Witnesses: Henry HERLING, Eustace CLENCHE, John HEGEMAN. Administration committed, 29 Jan. 1577/8, to Wm. BYRTON and Th. BYRTON, Eliz. being dead before the execution of the Will [in original only].

JOHN DUBLE [DUBBELL *in original*] of Mucking husbandman, 26 Nov. 1577. (28)
To 'Hanan' [Hannah in original] my daughter 1 cow, 5 sheep, half a dozen of pewter, i.e. 3 platters and 3 dishes, a saucer, a porringer, a featherbed, a brass pot, a kettle, a posnet, a candlestick, a spit, and a chest; and to Eliz. POWMAN a pewter dish, a little chest, a saucer, a spit, a candlestick, a little posnet, and a pair of sheets; to both at 18 and not before. If both die before, to Alice my wife; if all three die before 'Haman' and Eliz. are 18, to remain to Miles HUNTER of East Tilbury and Rd. DUBBELL of West Tilbury. The rest of my goods to my wife, whom

I make executrix. I make Miles and Rd. overseers. Witnesses: James GOWER of Mucking, writer hereof, Proved 8 Jan. 1577/8.

THOMAS VALENTYNE of West Ham fisherman, 11 Jan. 1577/8. (29)
To Mary my wife my dwelling house for her life, she to pay the debt due yearly out of it; after her decease, to my son Wm. He shall pay Mary my daughter £5 and my son Edw. £10. I make my wife executrix and Wm. MUFFETT and Th. MUFFETT overseers. Witnesses: Th. POLLARD, John ARMESTRONG writer hereof. Proved 1 Feb. 1577/8.

WILLIAM MYLBORNE of Stanford Rivers husbandman, 1 Mar. 1577/8. (30)
To be buried in Stanford churchyard near where my father, my mother and my brother lie. I owe REYNOLDES of Brentwood 6s.8d. and Wm. STARKIE 5s. To my son Wm. 20s. and a chest joined; my son Robert 20s. and a greater chest; Joan my eldest daughter 20s. and a chest with a fair spring lock; and Mary my youngest daughter 20s. and a chest. The residue of my goods to Denis my spoused wife, whom I make executrix. I ordain John SARING and John MARCHALL overseers, and for their pains 20d. apiece. Witnesses: Rd. WILLIAMSON curate there, John SARING, John MARCHALL, Barthw. COMBERS. [No probate clause.]

ROGER GARNET of West Ham victualler, 28 Nov. 1577. (31)
To Agnes my wife all my goods, whom I make executrix. Witnesses: John ARMESTRONG, Edw. LOME, John NORTH, Andrew SKOTT, Geo. BAINEBREKE, Th. SHERIFF. Proved [blank].

RICHARD MORE of Stratford Langthorne in West Ham tailor, 13 Dec. 1577. (32)
All my goods to my wife Joan, whom I make executrix. Witnesses: Th. ADAMS, John CLEYTON of Langthorne. Proved 6 Apr. 1578 [in original only].

JOHN TABER of Dagenham husbandman, 19 May 1577. (33)
To Rt. my son a cow of the price of 33s.4d. and 20s. at 16, he to receive the cow and 20s. with the profit at 21, my wife to be bound to pay the legacies before she do marry. The rest of my goods to Elizabeth my well-beloved wife, whom I make executrix. I make Th. PEARSON overseer. Witnesses: Wm. BAYLY, James BENSON. [No probate clause.]

CONSTANCE PEACHE of East Horndon widow, 15 Dec. 1577. (34)
To Rt. my eldest son my freehold house in East Horndon and the rest of my goods, on condition that he pay Rd. and John his brethren and Constance his sister the legacies to them in their father's Will and give 40s. for the bringing up of his said sisters. I make Rt. executor and Allen BRUER and Wm. BUTTERWICKE overseers, and for their pains 20s. apiece. Witnesses: John DARBIE, Allen BRUER. [No probate clause.]

WILLIAM NEWSAM of Aveley, — Jan. 1576/7. (Nuncupative.) (35)
Persuaded by his friends to make his Will, he answered that Eliz. his wife should have his goods and dispose of them at her will. Witnesses: Mr [Wm.] TAYLER vicar of Aveley, [blank] HATTER. [No probate clause.]

JOHN BECKET of Rayleigh labourer, 26 Nov. 1577. (Nuncupative.) (36)
Two parts of his goods to Mgt. his wife and the third part to John his son. His wife his executrix. Witnesses: Rd. BLACKWELL minister of Christ and writer hereof, Geo. BADCOCKE. Proved 11 Dec. 1577 [in original only].

JOHN ELLET of Ramsden Crays, 3 Jan. 1577/8. (37)
To Denis my daughter 13s.4d. at 21 or marriage. To my brother Wm. my best hose and best doublet, he paying my wife 5s. The rest of my goods to Joan my wife, to bring up my children. I make her executrix. I ordain Wm. overseer. Witnesses: Th. ROBERTES clerk [rector of Ramsden Crays], Wm. ELLET, Th. FULLER. [No probate clause.]

CLEMENT LINCOLNE of Stapleford Abbots husbandman, 30 Sept. 1577. (38)
To the poor of the parish 6s.8d. To my brother Rt. 1 dun calf, on condition that he shall not demand of my wife that 15s. which I owe him before 1 year after my decease; if he so forbear, she shall keep the calf for a year. To her my land called Smithes Field in the said parish for her life; after her decease, to remain to the child that she goeth withal, but if a womanchild, after my wife's decease to Wm., on condition that after he enjoy the land he pay to the use of my said daughter £40 and to my brother Rt. £10; if she die before 20, the £40 to be divided, to my brother John £20 and my sisters Jane and Agnes each £10; if my wife die before the child is 20, my overseer shall be 'gardener' [guardian] to my child. To my overseer 10s. The rest of my goods to Eliz. my wife, whom I make executrix. I make Wm. LINCOLNE of Mountnessing my overseer. Witnesses: Rd. REYNOLDES, John REYNOLDES, John CONVERS, Wm. LODER, John WOOD, Rt. SAYDE. Proved 12 Nov. 1577.

WILLIAM PHILLIPES of Mucking tailor, 8 Dec. 1577. (39)
To my sister Martha BROWNE 1 cow, 6 yards of frize, and 20s.; to her husband my doublet, hose and felt hat; to my other sister [not named] my other cow; if she die before 18, Martha to have the cow. I will that my uncle CAR of Billericay shall have it at Michaelmas next to employ the profit thereof to my other sister. To my mother-in-law the rent of the 2 kine due at Michaelmas, which is 10s. To my aunt CAR 12d. and to her five children each 12d. To my dame CLERKE of Billericay 12d. and to her five children each 2s. To my aunt BOLLYBROOK 12d. and to her two children each 2s.6d. To the poor men's box of Mucking 2s.6d. To Simon HOPKIN 2 pressing irons and a pair of shoes. To Mr GOTE of Mucking clerk 5s. I ordain my uncle CAR my executor and my master Stephen CLERK my overseer. Witnesses: widow DUBLE and her brother, widow FROOD of Mucking, Stephen CLERCK, John RADLE. Proved 8 Jan. 1577/8.

PHILIP FRAUNCIS of Fobbing husbandman, 22 Jan. 1577/8. (40)
To my brother HARE a cow which goeth at 'Fayres' if my wife do not sell them; if she doth, he to have 1 of them at home. To his two daughters 'Tympathie' and Mary 2 sheep apiece. To Mary my daughter £20 at 20 or marriage, which is in Wm. TILFORD's hand, and my wife to have it in occupying to bring up the child withal; if the child die before, my wife to have it, paying my brother HARE £5; if he die, the two maids to have it. To my six godchildren 2s. To my brother HARE my best breeches and best short hose. To my father [not named] my best close hose and best jerkin. The rest of my goods to Joan my wife, whom I make executrix. I make Wm. TYLFORD and Edm. TEALE overseers, and for their pains 20s. Witnesses: John SPENDER, Nich. MARTEN, Wm. JEFFERY. Proved 27 Feb. 1577/8.

JOHN ARWAKER of Great Waltham yeoman, 21 Nov. 1577. (41)
To be buried in Great Waltham church or churchyard. To the poor people 6s.8d. To some learned man to make four sermons or exhortations to the people at my burial 5s. To Cath. my wife all my household stuff saving such things as shall hereafter be excepted. To John ARWAKER my eldest son a standing bed in the parlour, a great brass pot, a great spit, a great chest, a lead in the kitchen and a 'yauthing' [yotting, for brewing] vat, a great trough, 2 brewing tubs, a cart and cart harness, and a plough and plough harness, at 21. To James my son my house with the land belonging in Great Baddow, after my wife's decease; if he die before, to remain among my brother Th. ARWAKER's four sons equally, which be Edw., John, Wm. and Th. To James £40 at 21. To Eliz. and Cath. my daughters £20 each at marriage and Agnes my daughter £20 at 21. To 'Arkenwald' SMITH my brother-in-law and Cath. his wife my house and lands in Great Waltham, now in my occupation, for 5 years jointly. To Th.'s said four sons each a bullock of a year old and a good ewe sheep. To 'Arkenwall' and his wife my corn in the barn and on the ground, my horse, my brass, and the residue of my goods, whom I make my executors. I make Th. ARTORE and Wm. NORYS supervisors. Witnesses: Th. ARTORE, Wm. NORRIS. Proved 27 Feb. 1577/8 [in original only].

WILLIAM GYLL of Stifford yeoman, 3 Dec. 1577. (42)
To be buried in Stifford church or churchyard. To Rebecca my daughter, now wife of Rd. HAMMERS, the moiety of my house and ground in Aveley and of 2 acres belonging thereto; the other moiety to Frances, my wife's daughter, now wife of Ottwell BATTEN, on condition that Rebecca and Rd. pay Rd. WOLBAULL, my wife's son, £5 within 2 years after Michaelmas next, which I give to the said Richard WOLBAULL, on the like condition that Ottwell and his wife pay Rt. FISHE, my wife's son, other £5. To my kinswoman Mgt., daughter of James GILL my brother, £3 6s.8d. at marriage or 23. the residue of my goods to Jane my wife, whom I ordain executrix. I ordain Mr Rt. BADBY overseer. Witnesses: Rt. BADBY, Th. JOHNSON clerk, George HEARD. Proved 7 Jan. 1577/8.

DAVITH [DAVID *in margin*] ANVICKE of Grays Thurrock, servant with Thomas KIGHTLEY gentleman, 4 Oct. 1577. (43)
To Joan REDE servant with Rt. TRUMBLE my best hat, my chest, and 30s., Hum. LOWE my fellow [servant] and Wm. ROWLAND each 5s. in the hands of Alice MOORE, Zachary OBRIGHT my fellow my best doublet, Rd. WAKESTED my fellow my bow and 3 arrows, 2 shirts, and 1 pair of low shoes, Th. LYNCEY my fellow my working day hose and 3 shirts, Th. TOMSON my fellow my high shoes, Rt. LONGE my jerkin of sheep's russet, and Edw. RICHARDES my fellow my best gaskins and the 'moldes' [mules, slippers] to the same. To ten poor householders of Grays Thurrock 12d. each. To Lettice INGERSON of West Thurrock 12d. To John WALLES one of my fellows, 3s. More to Joan REDE 6s. which Rd. ENOTH of 'Ednaves End' doth owe me. To Th. HOLLAND of Chadwell my best blue coat. I ordain Rd. SHEPPARD of Grays Thurrock my executor, and for his pains my frize coat and 9 sheep, whereof 8 are in the custody of Rd. SHEPPARD and 1 black wether is with my own sheep. I appoint Mr Th. KIGHTLEY gentleman my overseer. Witnesses: Roger MOYS, Rd. WAKESTED, Th. KIGHTELEY. Proved 8 Jan. 1577/8 [in original only].

WILLIAM DUNCE of East Ham yeoman, 6 Feb. 1577/8. (44)
To my two sons Wm. and Th. my two leases of the lands [that] I hold of Sir John HUNGERFORD and Clement SISELEY esquire in East Ham and Little Ilford from Michaelmas next to the end of the leases. To my four daughters Joan, Denis, Anne and Cath. £40 at 20 or marriage. If my wife be now with child, if a son he shall have the like portion as my sons and if a daughter £40. To my brother John DUNCE and my sister Cath. JUSTICE each £6 13s.4d. To the poor people of East Ham 40s. To my manservants Chris. [blank] and Joan [blank] each 10s. The rest of my goods to Anne my loving wife. I ordain my well-beloved father-in-law Wm. GOUGHE and my brother-in-law Th. GOUGHE executors, and to each a gelding. I make my wife and my brother John DUNCE overseers. Witnesses: Wm. GOUGHE, John DUNCE, Geo. JUSTICE, Th. GOUGHE. Proved 3 May 1577 on the oath of Wm. JOHES notary public, proctor of Wm. GOUGHE and Th. GOUGHE. Proved 3 Mar. 1577/8 [in original only].

RICHARD ABELL of Stondon [Massey] bachelor, 15 Jan. 1577/8. (45)
I ordain executors my brothers Wm. and Th. BOTHE. To Wm. all my hay and 2 quarters of oats and Thomas the rest of my oats and the rest of my corn, viz. rye and barley, reserving to Geoffrey my brother half a quarter of rye only. To Geoffrey for the performance of his part in his mother's Will, i.e. 33s.4d., and a cow that I owe him. To Clemence and Agnes daughters of Wm. each a bullock of 2 years old and Ellen [their sister] the 3rd bullock of that age. To Mgt. daughter of Wm. my part of a yearling which is between Th. and me. To my sister Joan wife to John CHESTAND 1 cow. To my godson Rd. CHESTAN 1 wennel of a year old. To Clemence 1 brown 'howed' [for meaning see p. xvii] cow. To Th. my 7 sheep going on the ground at Stondon Hall, paying for them 22s. to Wm. TYMON my brother-in-law. To my keeper Joan HUTLEY 6s.8d. To my sister CHESTON 1 pair of sheets and Geoffrey 1 sheet. To Joan ASHELEY 3s.4d. To my brother Wm.'s wife [not named] 1 brass pan, 1 brewing tub and a kimnel. To the poor of Stondon 3s.4d. and of Blackmore 3s.4d. The rest of my goods to my executors. Witnesses: Wm. FERINGE parson there, Stephen WARNER of Stondon. Proved 4 Feb. 1577/8 [in original only].

NICHOLAS SUDBURY of Rayleigh, 22 Oct. 1577. (Nuncupative.) (46)
To Mgy. his wife the shop of linen as it was then standing and the lease of the house wherein she dwelleth so long as she keepeth herself a widow, otherwise to Eliz. his 2nd daughter. To his wife the commodities of all the milch kine and sheep until Michaelmas next, paying the rent of their pasture, except 2 kine, the milk whereof he gave to Wm. WEBB and John MARSHE a butcher until Michaelmas. To every of his daughters 100 marks, to be levied of his cattle and other movables appraised. He willed that his household stuff should be priced and equally divided between his wife and three daughters. To Agnes his eldest daughter the lease of the house wherein MARSHE dwelleth over and besides her 100 marks. To Joan his youngest daughter likewise his kine and sheep which one John BYRD, parson of Ashingdon, hath hired of him by writing between them, with their increase. If the youngest daughter should die before marriage, her portion to remain to the children of Th. SUDBURY his brother. To Th. all his wearing apparel, ½ seam wheat and ½ seam rye, 2 kine, his bridle and saddle. To Mr Edw. MOONE his black nag. To the poor of Rawreth half a bullock. To Mr APPLETON his best gelding in recompense of his pains, whom he made his executor, requiring him to have it called Sudbury because he might thereby remember him. To Th. REYNOLDES 1 of his best heifers. He willed him and his brother Th. SUDBURY to be the 'pricers' of his goods and cattle. [No witnesses.] Proved 11 Feb. 1580/1 by Mr Henry APELTON esquire.

JOHN HAMMOND of Fobbing yeoman, 14 Oct. 1577. (47)
To Joan my wife 13 kine, 40 sheep and 2 rams, also 6 lambs and 1 ram; after her decease, the 13 kine, 40 sheep and 2 rams to Rd. my son, and she shall maintain the stock. To Rd. my house with the lands belonging called Staplers in Stanford-le-Hope, my copyhold land with a tenement at the quay late John DEYOS [DOE's in original] in Fobbing. To Joan HAMMOND my daughter £20 and a featherbed at 24, to be delivered by John my eldest son out of his farm called Old Hall [in Corringham?], i.e. the rent thereof, for 3 years. To my wife, for her life, £6 yearly during the rest of the same years in the same lease not expired; after her decease, John shall pay Rd. yearly £3 out of Old Hall. To John my cart and 6 horses with all the things belonging, and he shall help his mother to carry the wood and other necessaries when need requireth. To Rd. my corn in the barn and the fields belonging to Staplers and to my wife the corn in the field in Fobbing. To Judith HAMMOND my brother's daughter £5. To Rd. 1 featherbed. The residue of my goods to my wife and John, whom I ordain executors. I ordain my brother Henry DOE the supervisor, and for his pains 6s.8d. Witnesses: Ralph WHITTING clerk, parson of Corringham, Henry DOE, John ARNOLD, John EELYOT [ELIOT in original], Wm. CROWDER writer hereof. Proved 15 Nov. 1577.

JANE STURME of Hornchurch widow, 11 Dec. 1566. (48)
To be buried in the chapelyard of St. Edward's in Romford. To Rt. my son my best bedstead, 1 tow tablecloth, 2 pewter platters the best, 2 pewter dishes, 2 saucers, 2 pothangers, 1 salt, 1 spit, 1 pair of cobirons, 1 great brass kettle, a kneading trough, a table, the hangings in my chamber, 1 great chest, 1 cupboard, 1 pair of racks, a frying pan, a gridiron, a chair, 6 pewter spoons, and 1 colt; also 1 form, 1 chafing dish, and 2 candlesticks. To my daughter Mary's two children 1 milch bullock towards their bringing up, to remain afterwards to them when they come to age; to them also 1 featherbed, 1 pewter platter, 2 pewter dishes, 2 saucers, and 2 kettles. To Wm. VOCHONE my daughter Jane's son, my mare, 1 coverlet, and 1 pewter dish. The rest of my goods to Mary, whom I make executrix. Witnesses: Henry SPITTLE [SPITTELL in original], John BROKYES. Proved 7 Jan. 1577/8 [in original only].

JOHN RUDLEY of Laindon husbandman, 14 Oct. 1577. (49)
To my son John a brass chafer, my daughter Mgt. RUDLEY my biggest brass kettle, and to both half the profit of the Church Field that GREGORY holdeth equally to be divided after Rt. COCKE be paid his legacy out of it, and he shall take up the rent for them until they are 20. To my son Thomas 1 chest, a featherbed that his

grandmother, mother RUDLEY, gave him, a brass pot, 2 candlesticks, 4 pewter dishes, a platter, a saucer, 1 salt, and a tablecloth. To Mgy. my wife and Th. the lease of my farm of Reames equally to be divided between them, also the stock on the ground, i.e. corn and cattle, equally. The rest of my goods to my wife. After her death, Th. shall have the lease of Remes. I make my wife and Th. executors and Rt. COCKE supervisor. Witnesses: John BROWNE curate of Laindon, Cuthbert SAULKILL. [Also entered later in Register: see no.531.]

HENRY PEACOCKE of Thundersley husbandman, 10 Mar. 1576/7. (50)
To the poor men's box 12d. To my three daughters Priscilla, Agnes and Amy £4 apiece, to be levied out of my land at Margaretting belonging to the lordship [i.e. manor] of Thristlinge [Fristling], my executrix to pay them at 15 to be employed to their benefit. The residue of my goods to Joan my wife, whom I make executrix. I make overseer Hum. DRYWOOD of South Benfleet. Witnesses: Th. JOLY clerk, Wm. FELIX, Henry CLERKE, Edw. ROBINSON. Proved 17 Mar. 1576/7 [in original only].

GEORGE JEFFERY of Barking husbandman, 1 Mar. 1577/8. (Nuncupative.) (51)
Made in the presence of John SNAGES the elder, yeoman, John JEFFERY yeoman and Davy OWEN husbandman. To John his son £10 to be delivered by his executor to Th. GOWER and Geo. GOWER for his use at 15, they to put it forth for his profit until he is 18. To Rt. his son £10 to be paid for his use to John CHAMPNYS and Rt. READE. To Joan and Mary his daughters each £5 at 18. To Joan a cupboard in the hall at 18. To Mary 2 table boards in the milkhouse 1½ feet broad apiece. If his wife die before the lease of [his] house be expired, it should remain amongst his four children until then. The rest of his goods to Eliz. his wife, conditionally that she should bring up Joan and Mary. He made her executrix. He made overseers John CHAMPNYS and Rt. READE, and for their pains 1 colt of a year old. Proved 17 Mar. 1577/8 [in original only].

JONAS WRIGHTE of Stanford-le-Hope, 4 Aug. 1577. (Nuncupative.) (52)
He desired his mother Ellen SANDALL, whom he made executrix, to bestow his goods as following. To his brother Matthew WRIGHTE his best doublet, a young colt, and his part of a quiver which he had; to Rd. SANDELL his father-in-law £4 of the £8 which he doth owe to him, also 4 sheep; to his brother 'Noye' WRIGHTE £6 13s.4d. to be put in the hands of 'Eugeny' GATTON gentleman to be kept to the use of the said 'Noeth'; to John R[ER?]N a lamb and his apparel with 2 old shirts; to his father-in-law's children 4d. apiece; to Alice PUTTYPOLE a pair of old shoes, with 2 pennyworth of hobnails; to Jonas STACYE his godson 6s.8d.; to Nich. son of [Jonas] STACYE 3s.4d. which he did owe him; to John BRUER 4d. which he doth owe him; and to Rd. PONDE 6s. with 2d. which he did owe him. The residue of his goods to his mother, to bestow on the poor and on Sarah WRIGHT his sister what she shall think good. Proved 17 Sept. 1577 [in original only].

GEOFFREY FINCHE of Greenstead[-juxta-Ongar], 7 Apr. 1578. (53)
To be buried in Greenstead churchyard beside my friends. To the parson for my tithes negligently forgotten 6s.8d. Towards the reparations of the church 20s. To Mgt. my wife the household stuff that she brought with her [at our marriage] and 3 kine presently after she doth go away; if she do remain here still, the kine to remain so long as she doth tarry here. To Grace FINCHE my daughter my joined bedstead in the parlour with a featherbed, and 2 of the best kine, 6 country ewes, and 2 store hogs to be kept on the farm called Greenstead Hall for 4 years; 2 small brass pots, 2 candlesticks, 2 pewter platters, 2 pewter dishes, 2 saucers, a salt cellar, 2 pair of sheets, a tablecloth, 2 table napkins, a towel, and a spit; Grace to have the commodity and profit of the cattle and household stuff after 4 years and not before. My will is that she be kept by my executor with sufficient meat, drink and raiment for 4 years. To Grace also ½ seam wheat and ½ seam malt. To Eliz. GREENE my daughter £10. To four of Th. GRENE's daughters, i.e. John, Agnes, Rd. and James GREENE, a cow bullock of a year old apiece. To Mgt. GREENE a cow of 4 years. To Mgt. FINCHE my daughter £10 at marriage, a featherbed, a brass pot, a kettle,

2 pewter platters, 2 pewter dishes, 2 saucers, a candlestick, a saltcellar, 2 good kine, 2 store hogs, 2 pair of sheets, a tablecloth, 2 table napkins, and a spit. To Joan ABELL my daughter 2 cow bullocks of 2 years old. To Wm. ABELL's three children, i.e. Clemence, Agnes and Ellen, a cow bullock of a year apiece. To Mgt. ABELL 2 cow bullocks of 2 years. To every one of my godchildren 12d. To John FINCHE my eldest son my tenement in Chadwell in the parish of Barking; if he die without issue, to remain to Andrew FINCHE, except that, if John overlive his wife, then to him and his heirs. To Andrew my son Harvies Grove in 'Byllchanger' [Birchanger] and my copyhold in Theydon Bois. To Grace my two tenements in North Weald Bassett for her life; after her decease to John; if she remain and be kept still with Andrew for 4 years, he shall have the profit for so long as she shall think good to be kept with him; if she marry contrary to my executor's and overseers' minds, they shall have authority to dispose [of] such lands and tenements as I have given her and to use them as they think good. To Andrew my tenement in Chipping Ongar. To Nich. WESTWOD a cow bullock of a year. To Nich. GLADWYN £3 6s.8d. and a quarter of wheat within ½ year after my years [lease] of my farm be expired. To John ROWGHE my servant a cow bullock of 2 years. To Geoffrey FINCHE my kinsman 2 cow bullocks of 2 years and a quarter of wheat. To Rebecca WOLLMAN 2 cow bullocks of 2 years. To John SALTMARSHE 3s.4d. To Nich. COWPER of London ½ seam of wheat. To Mgt. WATER a cow bullock of a year. To Annabel my sister 3s.4d. To John my son my Irish hobby and my silver drinking cup that my cousin COCKES gave me. I will that Andrew shall give to the poor of Chipping [Ongar] 3s.4d. To Th. GRENE of Chadwell my grey mare colt that John my son doth keep for me. To John £50. To Grace the joined table behind the parlour door and a silk cushion. To Mgt. a brass pan, a cushion and a fir table. To my cousin HILLS of London ½ seam of wheat. To 'Juda' NOKE 3s.4d. To Andrew my term of years in Greenstead Hall, with my goods and cattle, saving those given before in my Will. The rest of my goods to Andrew, whom I appoint executor. I make Robert FINCH of [Chipping] Ongar and John POOLE of Bobbingworh Hall my overseers, and for their pains 10s. apiece. Witnesses: Rd. VAUGHAN, Rt. FINCHE, John POOLE, Frs. STONE. Proved 18 July 1578.

AGNES SMYTH of Aveley widow, 15 Sept., 20 Eliz. [1578]. (Nuncupative.) (54)
Being demanded by goodwife DOONNE who should have her goods, whether PECOCKE her son or her daughter BEAMONDE, she answered 'No'; then being demanded again whether Kath. wife of Henry CRESWELL should have her goods, she answered 'No'; being further asked who should have the same, she answered 'This girl should have them', who stood then by her, being daughter to Henry CRESWELL. Witnesses: goodwife JOYCESON, the wife of Wm. DONNE, goodwife LANGLEY in the house of Henry CRESWELL. [No probate clause.]

NICHOLAS MARCAS, servant to Leonard HEATHER of Barking yeoman, 30 June 1578 (55)
To the poor men's box 6s.8d. To Rd. TYPTAPE, my cousin dwelling at the Tower in London, £5 at the end of his apprenticeship; Chris. his brother £5 at 21; and Joan their sister £5 at 18 or marriage. To the poor of the parish at my burial 20s. in bread. To my godson John FULLOR 5s. To the poor of Dagenham 10s. To Thomas COPINE's three children [not named] 10s.; 'Aycet' FURNER my fellow [servant] 5s.; Eliz. TURNER servant to Henry CLARKE 2s.; Henry, Ursula, John, Joan and Eliz., Henry CLARKE's children, 10s. among them; John son of Henry STRETTES 5s.; Agnes DAWLDON servant to Harry STRETTES 5s.; Susan STREETES 5s.; my fellow John [blank] 3s.4d.; and Joan HEATHER, my master's daughter, 10s. The rest of my goods to Henry STREETES and Rd. SMITHE my fellow, whom I make executors. I make overseers my trusty friends Masters Henry CLARKE and Leonard HEATHER, and for their pains 10s. Witnesses: Henry CLARKE, Leonard HEATHER, John GREENE, Th. HAYWARDE [parish] clerk. Proved 18 July 1578.

EMME STELLIMAN *alias* STELEWOMAN of Woodham Ferrers widow, 17 Apr. 1578. (Nuncupative.) (56)
She gave to [blank] HOCKLEY 10s., [blank] DANBURIE [DAUBURIE?] 10s., [blank]

NORTON 6s.8d., [blank] STOWE 6s.8d., Woodham Ferrers 20s. [the poor?], Wm. MABBES of Woodham Ferrers a black 'howed' [for meaning see p.xvii] cow calf, on condition that he pay 10s. to Th. STOCKELYE of Woodham, Eliz. CANNON of Leigh 40s. and a coat, her three children 6s.8d. apiece, Th. VICKEARS of Rettendon 10s., Agnes OWTINGE her maid 2 pair of sheets, 6 pewter dishes, a brass pot, ½ dozen napkins, and a tablecloth, Wm. CRESLIE of Woodham 3s.4d. and his wife 10s., a pair of flaxen sheets and a rail, and John, Henry and Rt. sons of John LORRAN 20s. to be equally divided among them at 20 or marriage. To Wm. STELLIMAN's daughter [not named] 20s., John OUTINGE 20s., Rd. OWTINGE 10s., Jane OWTINGE 40s., Jane her maid 3s.4d., and Henry NICHOLL 20s. She willed the rest of her household goods to be equally divided between her son John STELLIMAN and her two daughters, the wife of Rt. CAMPHER and the wife of John LORRAN. To Edw. STELEMAN *alias* STELLWOMAN and Rt., Henry and Rebecca, the children of Edw. STELLIMAN, each 5 nobles at 20 or marriage. To her son John STELLIMAN's children £7, 20s. apiece. To Rt. BATCHELLER's three children 10s. apiece likewise. To John son of Th. CAMPHER 20s. To John ROBINSON a coat. Witnesses: Mr Rt. PARSON parson [rector] of Cold Norton, Rt. CAMPEIRE, John LEWYN, Rt. BATCHELLER. Proved 13 Nov. 1578.

JOHN HARRIS *alias* BUTCHER of Little Baddow tanner, 22 Apr. 1578. (57)
To Thomas my son the elder and Thomas my youngest son each £20, whereof £3 6s.8d is due to each by the bequest of Th. LARKIN their grandfather at 21. To Anne HARRIS my daughter £10 whereof £3 6s.8d. is due to her likewise at 21 or marriage. To Ellen and Mgy. HARRIS £10 apiece likewise. To Martha, Priscilla and Mary my daughters £10 each at marriage or 21. To my two eldest daughters Anne and Ellen my 2 best featherbeds with the bedsteads. To Mary an annuity of £6 due to me out of West Land lease after the decease of Joan LARKYN my sister-in-law. To Mgy. 1 flockbed. To Joan LARKYN 1 bedstead and a featherbed. To Anne GREENE my sister-in-law the best coat that my wife had. To John MAPLE a black colt. To Mary my maid and Th. PASFEILD and Henry GYVER my two prentices 3s.4d. apiece. The rest of my goods to John HARRIS my eldest son at 24. Provided that my youngest children be sufficiently kept with my goods until they may be placed within a year after my decease. I ordain Th. LARKYN, parson of Little Waltham, and Rt. GOOSE of Writtle executors and John MAPLE of Woodham Ferrers supervisor. To the poor of Litle Baddow 2s. Witnesses: Wm. SEREDGE parson of East Hanningfield, Rd. AGNES. Proved 12 May 1578.

JOHN EXETER of Shenfield husbandman, 18 Oct. 1578. (Nuncupative.) (58)
He gave all his goods to Mgt. his wife. Witnesses: John EXETER the elder and his wife, Gregory NICHOLLES and Joan his wife. [No probate clause.]

WILLIAM ARCHER of the town of Barking baker, 18 May 1578. (59)
To my daughter Joan a bedstead over the hall called the green bed with a featherbed of the best except 1, the green curtains and hangings, a covering next the best, 2 pair of towen sheets, 1 pair of linsey woolsey blankets, 1 bearing sheet and 2 pillowberes of the same making, 1 'oylie' [for meaning see p.xviii] platter and 3 'oylie' pewter dishes, and 1 bell candlestick due to her at marriage. To Eliz. my daughter £3 to be paid her at marriage by Nich. ELLIOTT my brother-in-law. The rest of my goods to Agnes my wife, [my executrix]. I make John MARSHE and Andrew PAWSON overseers. Witnesses: Edw. CARTWRIGHT, Nich. ELLIOTT, Miles BOWDISHE writer. Proved 17 July 1578.

THOMAS PARKER of Brentwood, 18 Feb. 1577/8. (60)
I appoint £4 1d. [*sic*] to be paid to Henry WILDE of Dagenham before or on St. Bartholomew's day next, which I borrowed on a covenant. To my two children, i.e. Joan and Rachel PARKER, my house called 'Catternwhele' [Catherine] House part and part like, which Eliz. my wife shall have until they are of lawful age, to their honest education. The rest of my goods to my wife, whom I ordain executrix; but if she marry again whereby my goods may be alienated or wasted to the hurt of my children's education, then I appoint my next kindred to divide them equally, half and

the use or dwelling to my wife and the other half to the use and education of my children. Witnesses: Rd. BLACKWELL the writer, John HARRISON, John WAUDLEY [WANDLEY?], Hum. KITCHEN. Proved 17 Mar. 1578/9.

AGNES HALL of Shenfield, 14 Nov. 1578. (61)
To the poor of Stondon [Massey] 20s., Shenfield 20s., and Doddinghurst 13s.4d. To my brothers POKINS and BAYLIE that portion of £4 which my brother Geo. HALL oweth me, to be equally parted. To mother KECHE of Doddinghurst 10s.; Kath. HOTHERNWOOD 10s.; my brother BAYLIE's three children £5; my sister BAYLIE 13s.4d.; Agnes POSTLANDE 20s.; my uncle MANSFEILD's five children £7; my cousin Rebec[ca] MANSFEILD my best cassock, my black apron and my red petticoat; my cousin Mary MANSFEILD my silver hooks; Mary BAYLIE my silver pin; Alice BAYLIE my hutch at my brother POKINGE; Rt. MANSFEILD my hutc. at my uncle MANSFEILD; Anne BALLE half a dozen of pewter; my sister BAYLLIE's child that she goeth withal the other half dozen, if God send it to live, if not, to Anne BAYLIE and Mary; my aunt MANSFEILD a double kercher stitched round-about, a single rail, and a flaxen apron; my sister BAYLLE the rest of my linen; Kath. HOTHERNWOOD 2 neckerchers, 2 kerchers, and a frize cassock; my uncle ROWE 10s. and my hat; Mary BAYLIE my cassock. The rest of my goods to my executors, whom I nominate my uncle Geo. MANSFEILD and brother Th. BAYLIE. I nominate overseers Wm. PERRYMAN and John ELLIMENT, and for their pains 3s.4d. apiece. Witnesses: Wm. PERRYMAN, John ELLEMENT. [No probate clause.]

JOHN POWELL *alias* EVANS of Little 'Stilforde' [Ilford], 14 Mar. 1578/9. (62)
To Alice my wife all my goods, whom I make executrix. Witnesses: Wm. YOUNGE of East Ham minister [not the vicar], Th. MOMFETT, Rd. MOUMFORTE, Wm. WALKER. [No probate clause.]

THOMAS ATHAIES of Rettendon yeoman, 2 Nov. 1578. (63)
To Joan my wife my house and land called Chamberlaynes for 7 years, then to Th. HAYES my son; if he die without heirs, to remain successively to Wm. my son, to Sebastian my son, and to my daughters [not named]. To Th. my cupboard in the hall, a joined bedsteadle in the little chamber with a featherbed and a covering of needlework, 1 great chest, 1 brass pot that was my mother's, 4 pieces of pewter, 1 cushion of needlework, 1 candlestick, 1 silver spoon. my best doublet, and 40s. To Mgy. my daughter 1 silver spoon. To John WETHER my son-in-law my 'ronded' [for meaning see p. xviii] colt. To Anne WETHERS [*sic*] 1 dun bullock. To Joan my wife all the household [stuff] that she brought to me [at our marriage]. The rest of my household stuff shall be equally divided between Wm. and Sebastian HAYES and Bridget and Eliz. my daughters, and to each a silver spoon. To Bridget £5 at marriage or 21. To a godly preacher to make a sermon at my burial 5s. To Mgt. CROMER my wife's daughter, 1 silver spoon and 1 cushion. To Edw. HAYES my godson my sword. The rest of my movables to my wife, whom I make executrix. I make my brother Wm. ATHAYE overseer, and to him my best cloak for his pains. Witnesses: Wm. ATHAYE, Wm STYLLES, Henry HAYES. Proved 19 Dec. 1578.

THOMAS RATLE [RATTLE *in margin*] of Stanford-le-Hope yeoman, 5 Jan. 1578/9. (64)
To the poor 10s. To every one of my godchildren 12d. To my father [not named] 40s. at his next coming to Stanford, if he be alive; if deceased, to Wm. Ratle my brother. To Barbara my servant 12d. To Judith my wife such goods as came by her [at our marriage], i.e. 6 milch kine, 1 score of sheep being 3 years old, and her household stuff, the kine to be not above 6 years of age. To her 2 quarters of wheat, 3 sheets [skeats?] the cheese in my house, the firewood in my yard, the poultry, and 1 brown bay colt being 3 years old at Easter next. To Mgt. wife of John RAYNER of Stanford my right in a tenement called Hopillcockes for her life; after her decease, to Rd. SELAND her son; if he die without heirs, successively to Chris. SELANDE and to John RATLE my son. To John all my goods. I ordain him executor and John STELLIMAN and Rd. SANDELL my trusty friends overseers, and

for their pains 5s. apiece. Witnesses: John STELLYMAN, Rd. SANDELL, Rd. WOLLWARD, John GOODWYN, Th. SHEPPERD. Proved 4 Feb. 1578/9 by the oath of Walter HORSELL, proctor of John RATLE.

RICHARD WARNER of Woodham Mortimer husbandman, 16 Feb. 1578/9. (65)
To my servant Mgt. CLARKE that now doth dwell with me 6s.8d. To John PETER, my wife's son, my bay mare and 20s. The residue of my goods to Alice my wife, whom I make executrix. I make John PETER my son-in-law overseer. Witnesses: Rd. GUYE, John HAYWARDE, John WADE, Nich. JOHNSON parson of Woodham Mortimer. Proved 18 Mar. 1578/9.

ELIZABETH BOYLAND of Hutton widow, 14 Dec., 21 Eliz. [1578]. (66)
To be buried in Sutton [*recte* Hutton] churchyard. To the poor of Hutton 20s. To Rd. GLADINE's four children each 1 sheep. To Mary BOYLAND my youngest daughter the 2 best featherbeds; Anne GLADIN my daughter's child the greatest brass pot. I make Rd. GLADIN and Mary BOYLAND executors. The rest of my goods to them equally to be divided. Witnesses: Rt. PAYNE, John BAYLIE, John PAYNE. Proved 20 Jan. 1578/9.

ISABEL THORNEBROWGH, [abode not given], 23 June 1578. (67)
To be buried in Fobbing churchyard. To Phoebe my daughter my wearing linen and my chest. I will that the rest of my goods shall be sold to her use and that of Th. TOMSON, my first husband's son, and Roger THORNEBOROWGHE my son, and [the money] to be divided equally, excepting such things as Th. SMYTH shall think fittest not to be sold but kept to their use; he shall keep the goods and money till they are 21 or married, they to have their portions. I make him my overseer and 'doer of this my Will'. Witnesses: 'the parson of Fobbing' [Paul White?], Th. SMYTH. Proved 6 Oct. 1578.

AGNES OUTTINGE of Woodham Ferrers, 10 Jan. 1578/9. (68)
To Agnes OUTTINGE, my mother-in-law, my best cassock, a tablecloth, ½ dozen napkins, a posnet, a silver pin, and my best hutch; Rebecca my sister a cassock, a pair of sheets, a brass pot, my best silver hooks, best apron, best hat, and 1 hutch next the best; 'Dowse' [DOWSE?], my sister-in-law, my best russet petticoat, a pair of sheets, a kettle, a silver pin, my greatest hutch, and 1 apron next the best; Agnes SYMSON a petticoat, a double holland kercher, a cross cloth, a smock, and a strawen hat; to Anne MARSHALL a double lockram kercher, and a cross cloth; my cousin Rebecca CAMPER a silver pin; Mary BACHELER a pair of silver hooks; and Anne my sister and Harry my brother 3s. apiece. The residue of my goods to my mother-in-law, my sister Rebecca and my said sister-in-law, to be equally divided betwixt them. Rebecca's portion shall remain with Rt. CAMPER my cousin till she is 20. I ordain John OUTTINGE my father and Rt. CAMPER my cousin my executors. Witnesses: Roger NORTHERN curate, Mary WILSON *alias* READER, Mgy. CROFTE. Proved 19 Jan. 1578/9.

WILLIAM PAWNE of High Ongar esquire, 1 Apr. 1578. (69)
To be entombed on the right side of the chancel in Norton Mandeville church, to which work I give my executors 100 marks. To Mr Edw. ELLIOTT the advowson of Norton [Mandeville]. All debts between Th. BARKER and me I forgive. To Henry son of Th. BARKER and Wm. MASSIE my copyhold lands of the manor of Nash Hall [in High Ongar] and land called Kings Ridden holden of the manor of Pastle [Paslow] Hall [in High Ongar] and to their heirs, Henry to pay 100 marks for the charges of the tomb. To Th. WALLINGER of Chelmsford for the seat [site?] of Chevers Hall [in High Ongar] with the lands belonging in the tenure of Lawrence BINGHAM, paying all my debts except to Wm. MASSIE. To Lawrence son of Lawrence BINGHAM a tenement called Old Withers and the lands in that of Henry WITTHAM and John LYCORAS, on condition that he make to John LYCORAS a lease for 21 years after the end of the old lease for the yearly rent of £5 and shall set himself up a barn and shall suffer him to have the old barn to make a mill house. To the son and

heir of CHATTERTON allied to me the seat of Chevers Pawn with the lands and the profits of Chevers Hall, certain of the lands called Fullers in Blackmore, a mead called Howchins holden of the manor of Fingrett [in Blackmore], and a copyhold tenement and lands adjoining to the lands of Withers Pawn (18 acres) called Hauckes [Hanckes?] holden of the manor of Paslowe Hall. To Henry WITTOM my part of his house. To Th. SMYTHE my godson the 7 acres parcel of Fullers on condition that COX enjoy his bargain. To Michael HEIDON and Anthony FRAUNCIS a tenement and the lands wherein STAMMER dwelleth holden of the manor of Paslowe Hall, on condition that they pay £24 to Mr BELLANNE to discharge a statute. To High Ongar church Lord's Croft and the tenement therein, paying to the manor of Chivers 12d. and suit of court. I make executors Edw. ELLIOTT, Th. WALLINGER and Wm. MASSIE. The revenues of my lands shall be in stock for 3 years to the payment of Jeffrey GATTES and the residue to bring me to the ground and the furnishing of the same. To the ringers 2s. apiece. To PALMER my man 20s., BARTHOLOMEW 10s., and all Mr BARKER's servants 6s.8d. To Mr Edw. PINCHIN, Mr BARKER, Mr SMYTHE and Wm. BARKER 40s., and their wives, each a black gown, and Wm. BARKER 40s. To Wm. LYCORAS a piece of waste ground at Chivers corner with ½ acre of the wood there, paying 3s.4d., to enter after the end of Th. WYBERD's lease. To Ann BIRCHLEY [and] Mgt. MASSIE a black gown. To SHAWE 5s. The residue of Hauckes to the parish of Norton. To Sir Th. MILDMAYE £10 and a gown, whom I make my overseer. SAIER shall have his house with the wood of Chivers for such rents as he and Th. WYBERD pay for 21 years. The residue of my lands and goods I will to the building and maintaining of a school to be built within the manor of Chivers by the discretion of my executors. To PICKERING my buff hose. To my cousin Harry BARKER my green hose and doublet. The heirs of CHATTERTON shall suffer Rt PALMER to enjoy his house or else to have £26 13s.4d. WRIGHT and PEACOCKE shall enjoy their leases. I will the surplages [*sic*] of the 3 years to the school. Mr ELLIOTT shall have my bedstead with the furniture of my chamber and my counterfeit morning cloak, hose and doublet. Witnesses: John FARMERYE, Th. BARKER, Jeffery SMYTHE, John LYCKOREIS. Proved 19 Dec. 1578 by Wm. MASSIE, Edw. ELLIATT and Th. WALLINGER having renounced executorship.

RICHARD SEATON, [abode not given], 2 Nov., 20 Eliz. [1578]. **(70)**
To be buried in the churchyard of St. Peter in Maldon. To Susan my only daughter £20 at marriage or 20, and to be brought up by my wife; if Susan die before, the £20 to be divided equally among all my sister's [sisters'?] children. To John SEATON my brother £10. To my son-in-law Wm. KEELER's children, John, Th. and Chris., 20s. apiece, and to their three sisters, my daughters-in-law, 20s. apiece. Whereas I owe Anne HALLIWELL, my wife's sister, £9, I will to her 20s. over the £9. To John PERISHE 12 bushels of barley. To ELLIS my man my blue livery coat. To the poor of every parish in Maldon 10s. To John THURGOOD my sorrel bay mare. The residue of my goods to Joan my well-beloved wife, whom I make executrix. Witnesses: Wm. WYSEMAN, Th. EVE, Edm. TYLER, Augustine SHENE. [No probate clause.]

ELIZABETH HOWE of Shenfield, 16 Oct. 1576. **(71)**
I do desire my master Mr MANSFELD and goodwife PERRYMAN of Shenfield to sell all my goods to the only use of Th. BASENETT, my poor boy, which were sold to the value of £3 10s. by the rest of my neighbours. I appoint Geo. MANSFEILD and Wm. PERRYMAN overseers to the use of my boy. [Witnesses:] Geo. MANSFEILD, Wm. PERRYMAN. [No probate clause.]

STEPHEN WALKER of Collier Row [in Romford], 30 Mar. 1578. (Nuncupative.) **(72)**
He gave his son Rd. WALKER ½ dozen of pewter, viz. 3 platters, 3 dishes, a brass pot, a chafing dish, and a spit. The rest of his goods he gave to Eliz. his wife, whom he made executrix. Witnesses: John COMBERS of Colliers Row, [blank] SMYTHE. [No probate clause.]

WILLIAM KINGE servant with James MAYER of Leigh, 25 Sept. 1578. (Nuncupative.) (73)
He requested James MAYER and Th. SAVADGE to deliver to Rd. MASSON his brother-in-law 19s. which he had in his purse and likewise that £3 which was owing to him by his said brother-in-law should be equally distributed among the same brother-in-law's children and his sister BROOKE's [BROOKES'?] children. His apparel should be sold and the money likewise distributed. He appointed Rd. MASSON his executor. Witnesses: James MAYER, Th. SAVEDGE. [No probate clause.]

GILES PERMYTER of High Laver single man, 5 Oct. 1578 (74)
To the poor, viz. Reynold BREDGES 6s.8d., Reynold KINGE's wife 12d., Th. MORTON 2s.6d., widow BREDGES 2s.6d., old PAVELEY 12d. To Giles AYLETT my godson 8 sheep and 5s. that his father [not named] oweth me. To the children of Edw. PARMETER my brother each 6s.8d.; the children of my brother John 5s. betwixt them; my sister Ellen PARMETER and Agnes [surname not given] each £5 and half my boards; and the daughter of Andrew CLARKE 3s. The residue of my goods and cattle to Joan my well-beloved mother, whom I ordain my executrix. I make overseer Rt. KINGE, to whom I give 2s. Witnesses: Rt. KINGE, Peter REDE, Th. SHIPTON [see no. 76]. [No probate clause.]

THOMAS NICOULLES, [abode not given], 8 Oct. 1578. (75)
To be buried in Prittlewell churchyard. All my goods to Mgt. NICHOULLS my wife, whom I make executrix, also my house that I dwell in for her life, and after her decease to John WADE her son. Witnesses: John BRADOCKE, Edm. BARKER, Th. DOTTRELL. [No probate clause.]

PETER READE of High Laver husbandman, 12 Oct., 20 Eliz. [1578]. (76)
To the poor 10s. To Agnes my well-beloved wife my house and term of years in my dwelling house called Willmers; also my house in Matching called Huchins and the ground called Pekes belonging, for her life; after her decease, to my two daughters Dthy. and Mary, to each of whom £10 at marriage or 21. To them to be equally parted my lease of my house wherein Wm. TURTLE dwelleth. To Wm. PARMYTER my brother-in-law 4 bushels of wheat. The residue of my goods to my wife, to see my children honestly brought up, whom I make executrix. I desire Rt. KINGE of High Laver to be overseer, to whom for his pains 5s. Witnesses: Rt. KINGE, Reynold KINGE, Th. SHIPTON clerk [rector of High Laver]. [No probate clause.]

THOMAS BOONE of Bradwell-juxta-Mare husbandman, 12 Oct. 1578. (77)
To the poor 10s. Towards the repairing of Colyton Haven [co. Devon] 12d. To my sister Anne DERICKE widow 40s. To Bridget BINGLEY, my eldest daughter's daughter, £7 at 21 or marriage. To my daughter Anne PATTISON £5. To my kinswoman Thomasine BOONE £3 6s.8d. at marriage or 21. To my three servants Edw. PITMAN, Avice HUNTE and Joan [blank] 12d. each. The residue of my goods to Anne my wife, whom I ordain executrix. Witnesses: John COLEMAN curate, John BROOKE. [No probate clause.]

THOMAS CHAMPNEY of Dagenham yeoman, 1 Sept. 1578. (78)
To my six children, i.e. John CHAMPNEY, Alice PATTEN, Joan PATTEN, Joan CHAMPNEY, Mary CHAMPNEY and Jane CHAMPNEY, half of my goods to be equally divided at their ages of 20. To my son Harry CHAMPNEY 1 red cow bullock. The residue of my goods to Mgt. my well-beloved wife and the lease of the farm which I dwell in, towards bringing up my children. I ordain her executrix. I ordain overseers John SNAGGES and John PATCE. Witnesses: John SNAGGES and [John] PATCHE, John TANNER, John COMPORT. [No probate clause.]

THOMAS GOOSON of Rainham waterman, 3 May 1578. (79)
To my uncle Th. GOOSON of Barking my house in Barking, he paying my debts as followeth with other such charges as shall arise at the time of my sickness and my burial. I owe to Henry ILFORD 40s. by obligation dated 7 Feb. 1577/8, to Mr POWELES [POWELE's?] clerk 6s. on the score, to Henry ILFORD 6s.8d., to John

WALL 12d., and to Henry HODDE 6d. I ordain my uncle executor. Witnesses: Th. GOOSEN, Rd. PECOCKE, Th. PHILPOTTE, John CUTFORDE, Henry ILFORDE, John LAWRENCE clerk [vicar of Rainham]. [No probate clause.]

EDWARD SOMERSKALLE of Barking fisherman, — 1577. (80)
To the poor men's box 3s.4d. To Alice my wife my house which I dwell in in Barking, my 3 boats with all the craft belonging to them, and all other household goods, whom I ordain executrix. For my supervisors I make Rd. MASSON and Peter DEBITT of Barking, willing my wife to give them 3s.4d. apiece for their pains. Witnesses: John HORTON minister of Barking [the clergy list for Barking is deficient at this period]. [No probate clause.]

ROGER PARTRIDGE of Barking poulter[er], 12 June 1578. (81)
To the poor men's box 3s.4d. To Rt. CHASSIE of Barking my best frize coat. The rest of my goods to Eliz. my wife, whom I make executrix. I make overseers my friends Wm. NOAKE and Th. EDWARDES, and for their pains 2s.6d. Witnesses: Wm. NOAKE, Th. EDWARDES, Th. HAYWARD parish clerk of Barking. [No probate clause.]

JOHN CHURCHE of Runwell [Hall] gentleman, 26 Feb. 1577/8. (82)
To be buried in Runwell church and to the reparations 13s.4d. To the poor of Runwell 10s. To Mgt. my wife £40; 10 good kine and 30 good ewes well pastured and stovered on my farm of Runwell Hall during her widowhood, on condition that she pay my son Th. £3 6s.8d. yearly; and such goods as came to me by marriage; my houses and lands copy and free purchased of Wm. ROGERS in Runwell Street, for life, and she shall remain here in my house of Runwell Hall and have a chamber called Thomas CHURCHE's chamber and meat and drink at my executor's cost so long as she is unmarried; my young 'ronded' [for meaning see p.xviii] gelding, my dun mare and her colt which was hers before; and she shall have some convenient place appointed in my house to make the white meat that comes of her cattle. To Charles my son that portion of Runwell Hall called Southlands divided from the farm by the highway from Runwell Street to Rettendon during the lease, yielding Th. £8 a year; 16 kine and 80 ewes, a grey trotting gelding of 5 years old, the standing bedstead in Thomas CHURCHE's chamber, and my best featherbed but one; £10; a silver bowl; the said houses and lands at Runwwell Street; and if he depart his life without issue to remain to my son Edm.; a tablecloth, a dozen napkins, a towel, a basin and ewer, a wainscot table in the hall, a spit, and a pair of cobirons with 3 feet. To Edm. my lands in Takeley called the Great Park, sometime belonging to Colchester Hall [in Takeley], in the tenure of John SEALE, and if John's wife survive him she shall have 1 year without paying rent; copyhold land in Runwell called Princhettes purchased of one ONGE and his wife; if without issue, to Charles; part of Runwell Hall farm called East Field during the lease, yielding Th. £4; 12 kine and 70 ewes; a standing bedstead that I lie in, with my best featherbed save twain, a tablecloth, a dozen napkins, a towel, a basin and ewer, a wainscot table in the hall, a silver bowl, a bay bald colt of 3 years old, and a spit; and £10. To my son[-in-law] READE £10, and Edm., John and Mgt. READE, my daughter Martha's children, each £3 6s.8d. at 15. To Frs. GREENE 2 heifer calves of 1 year old to make him 2 kine, to be pastured on the ground and the profit to his use. To every of my menservants 5s. and maidservants 2s.6d. To my cousin Frs. CHURCHE 20s. and 20 ewe lambs of this year. To Charles FULLER 5s. The residue of my goods to Th., whom I make executor. I make Mr Geo. WHITT of Hutton esquire overseer, and for his pains £3 6s.8d. and a bay colt of 3 years which came of my black mare. Witnesses: Th. JOLIE parson of Thundersley, Howell GRIFFITH. Proved 10 June 1578.

THOMAS HOSEMAN of Romford yeoman, 8 Sept. 1578. (83)
To John WASTELL 20s., Joan PEATCHE 40s., and Agnes STODDARD 20s., being all my fellows [i.e. fellow servants] in Mr COOKE's house. To goodwife STEVENS 20s., Steven STEVENS her son 40s., Agnes STEVENS her daughter 20s., Alice her servant, and deaf Joan now her servant 10s. To Anthony HOWEMAN 40s., Giles SAUNDERS my godson 10s., goodwife HOLMES 20s., and Matthew her servant 10s., Lawrence

TAYLOR her other servant 10s. and my sword and dagger, BATCHILER's wife 10s., her daughter Frances 10s., Nicholas FREMAN 10s., mother HAMAN of the Almshouse 20s., mother STANDLEY 10s., and mother DUNCANE 10s. To the goodwife of the house in which it shall fortune me to die, £3 besides the charges. To John ELLIS dwelling with goodman Stephen STEVENS £5 at 21, in the meantime to be put forth by my executor for John's advantage; if he die before, to be given to ten poor folk such as my executor shall think most meet. To Rd. ATKYS minister of Romford 10s. To thirty of the poorest folk that is to be found in Romford and Collier Row within the Liberty of Havering £5. I give £5 to be bestowed on my burial and [a] dinner for those which accompany my body to the church. I ordain John HOLMES executor, and for his pains 26s.8d. I ordain my master Mr Stephen STEVENS overseer, and for his pains 26s.8d. Witnesses: Stephen STEVENS, John HOLMES, Rd. ATKYS. [No probate clause.]

ROBERT TURRELL of Little Wakering, 2 July 1578. (84)
I will by the licence of the lord [of the manor] that Joan my wife shall have my tenement and lands wherein I dwell for 14 years, keeping the 'housinge' of the farm in good reparations tenantable; after to remain to Th. my son; if he decease without heirs, successively to Rt. my son and to Joan my daughter. To my wife all my cattle and household stuff, she to bring up all my children at her cost, finding them meat, drink and apparel till they are 14. To my two younger children Rt. and Joan each 46s.8d. at 21 or marriage. To my brother Rd. TURRELL 1 of my kine and 2 of my sheep at the assignment of my father-in-law Th. BARNE in consideration of 4 marks which I owe to Rd. To my two sisters [not named] each 5s. The residue of my goods to my wife, whom I make executrix. I make Th. BARNE supervisor. Witnesses: John BOWDON, Lawrence FANNYNGE, Wm. HIDE. [No probate clause.]

ROBERT TROMBLE of Chadwell, 22 June 1578. (85)
To the poor people of the parish 20s. I will that there be preached at my burial a learned sermon for 5s. To Jane SMYTHE my servant 20s.; Th. TROMBLE my brother's son £22; and my master Rd. PITCHE's children 5s. apiece. I ordain Eliz. my wife executrix and my well-beloved friends Rd. PITCHE, John HOLLAND and John GRYFFIN overseers, and to each 5s. Witnesses: Rd. PITCHE the elder, John HOLLAND, John GRYFFIN, Th. SHEPPERD. [No probate clause.]

ROBERT TENDERINGE of Great Baddow husbandman, 25 June 1578. (86)
To John TEDDERINGE my son my house and lands called Coplyes in the occupation of Wm. SUCHE, on condition that he pay to Mgt. [*sic*] and also my two daughters each 40s. raised from the rent. To Rd., Wm. and Th., after the decease of Joan my wife, my land called Peyrseat Mead by even portions. To my wife my 2 acres of meadow in Great Baddow Common Mead for her life; after her decease, 1 acre to James and the other to Henry my sons. To James my lower acre in Bringey after my wife's decease. To Henry my youngest son my house called Rynde House. To my wife my 4 acres in Bringye and all my goods, whom I make executrix. I make my brother[-in-law] Th. BEAREMAN and John SPILLMAN overseers, and for their pains each 12d. Witnesses to this Will and the surrender [to the lord of the manor]: John PEASE instead of the bailiff, John SPILLMAN the elder, John COLLETT *alias* DEAVNYSSHE, John HILLES. [No probate clause.]

WILLIAM TURCKE of South Ockendon, 21 Sept. 1577. (87)
To my sons Rt. and Harry TURCKE each £30 and my daughters 'Matherye' and Agnes TURCKE each £20, all at 21. To Th. WATERWORTH my son-in-law £10 and the use of my daughters' portions. I will that Mr John LEGATT of Hornchurch Hall shall have the use of my sons' legacies and pay them at 21. To Th. WATERWORTH the rent of my land in Havering called Stratmans in the occupation of Mr Th. LEGATT for 5 years after my decease. To my son-in-law the rent and profit of my copyhold land in Cranham called Brockmans for 10 years towards the performance of my Will, whom I make executor. To Wm. my eldest son my lands in Havering called Stratmans. To Th. WATERWORTH my orchard in Hare Street in Havering [Romford]. To John TURCKE my son my land called Brockmans after the 10 years. I make John LEGATT

my overseer. I surrender my tenement in Cranham to Rt. DORE and Chris. WILSONE, customary tenants of the manor of Cranham, to the use of my Will. Witnesses: Rt. DORE, Chris. WILSON, Rt. WATTES, 'with my cousin' GILL'. [No probate clause.]

JOAN LERWYN [LARWYN *in margin*] of Rettendon, 4 Aug. 1578. (Nuncupative.) (88)
She bequeathed to the poor people 10s. She willed that 3 sermons be made by some learned man for 10s. She gave to her brother John LERWYN a cow and a napkin, to Joan his daughter £5, and to John, Rt. and Henry his sons £4 apiece, all to be paid to her brother for their use at 18 or marriage. She gave to her mother [not named] £20, Wm. GOODWYN 5s. and a pair of sheets, Wm. CHRISTOPHER 3s.4d., goodwife RUTTER a sheep and a kercher, Susan RUGGELLS, Ellen GOWERS and Mary TURRELL each a petticoat, Joyce 'wief' [WIES?] a neckercher and a lockram apron, Emme PEACHIE a black apron, Judith SELLEMAN a pair of silver hooks, Simon HOODE a little hutch, and Wm. GRYNNYNGES 8s. which he should have paid for the farm of a cow. The residue of her goods to Th. VICKARS her father-in-law, whom she ordained executor. Witnesses: Th. RADLEE, Henry RUTTER, Roger NORTHEN [curate of Woodham Ferrers]. [No probate clause.]

JOAN WAILE of Woodham Ferrers, 5 Apr. 1578. (Nuncupative.) (89)
In the presence of Mr Roger NORTHEN curate of Woodham Ferrers, Henry STELLIMAN the elder, Mary SAWNDERS, Amy ECKINGHAM, Alice LEWYS and divers others, she declared that she had sent for Mr NORTHERN and Henry STELLIMAN, her special friends and in whom she reposed her trust, that they should have the bringing up of her daughter Joan and have all her goods to that intent, and requested them very earnestly to be her executors. Mr NORTHEN requested her that she were better to put some of her own kindred in trust with the bringing up of her child as namely her sister and he were very loath to meddle with it. Henry STELLYMAN answered the like and refused to meddle therewith, but the testatrix was somewhat moved and answered that her sister should not meddle with her child or her goods, and her sister should have her frize cassock, 3 old petticoats, 1 old safeguard, and 1 woollen waistcoat, and no part else of her goods. Very earnestly she requested Mr NORTHEN to take upon him the bringing up of her child and her goods, and divers times before her death the testatrix as well before him and divers others her friends that came to visit her in her sickness she affirmed that she had committed the same at the discretion of Mr NORTHEN, whom she had made her executor, and that she was very glad that he had granted her to take it upon him, for there was none other that she could put so much trust as in him, and she did trust that he would bring up her child accordingly. Proved by Roger NORTHEN, 6 May 1578.

EDMUND DUKE of Barking labourer, 30 Aug. 1578. (90)
To Allen DUKE my brother my best coat and best breeches; John CIPGATE my blue coat and buckskin doublet; the said John CIPEGATE's wife Joan M[AR]WOODE's best cassock; John HORTON minister of Barking 1 of my best pewter platters; John GODDE sexton of Barking another pewter platter; James CAROWE my master a sow and 10 pigs; my master's wife, my dame, my wife's best neckercher; and each of his children a kerchief. To him 1 cow in the occupying of Wm. PATTERICKE of Collier Row [in Romford], with the profits past and to come, which he oweth me, being 23s.4d. I ordain the said James executor. Witnesses: John HORTON minister of Barking, John GODDE sexton, Kellam INYNRY [JUYNRY?]. On 9 Oct. 1578 James CAROWE appeared and renounced executorship of the Will and the judge committed administration, 'etc.'

KATHERINE PYGOTT [PIGOTT *in margin*] of Barking, 15 June 1578. (Nuncupative.) (91)
She bequeathed her money, apparel, and all other her goods to her cousin Henry LANGHSHOWE and Mgt. his wife to the behoof of their son Ralph. Witnesses: Witnesses: Agnes HOPKINS, Hum. PRYOR his servant of Barking, Eliz. DYGGISE. Proved 30 Sept. 1578; administration committed to Henry LANGSHAWE and Mgt. during Ralph's minority.

THOMAS MEADE, servant with Wm. EVEREAD of Fyfield, 28 June 1578. (92)
I ordain Chris. MEADE my brother executor and give him all that I have, so that my brother Edw. shall not have any part thereof. Witnesses: Giles SMITH curate of Fyfield, Wm. EVERED, Th. STOCKE, Abraham SMYTH writer hereof, John GULL. [No probate clause.]

WILLIAM FOOTT of Little Hazeleigh, 8 June 1578. (93)
To every of my children, i.e. Eliz. Mary, Susan, Mary [*sic*] and Grace, each £10 at 19 or marriage. To Th. LILLIE and Joan LILLIE each 10s., on condition that Wm. my son pay Peter my son £30 at 20. To Wm. my houses and lands free and copy [no details]. To John FOOTT my brother a weaning calf of a year old and the vantage at May Day next; to his two children [not named] each a lamb. To Wm. KINGE my daughter's son a bullock of 2 years old and the vantage, and John KINGE her son a dun cow of 4 years old. To my servants Edw. BOWER 3 lambs and John SOWMAN 12d. To Peter 2 oxen, not to be taken above 6 years of age, at 20. The residue of my goods to Mary my wife and Wm., whom I ordain executors. I make John TILER my son-in-law supervisor, and for his pains 3s.4d. Witnesses: Th. FARNISHE, Rt. BRYANT, Edm. TYLER, Th. SAMES. Proved 19 July 1578.

JOHN CARTMELL of Wisdens in [Romford in] the parish of Hornchurch gentleman, 7 Nov.1577. (94)
To Audrey my wife 6 silver spoons, a silver salt, and such bedsteads, bedding, linen, brass, pewter, cobirons, spits, andirons, dripping pans, trivets, pothangers, coffers, cupboards, presses, tables, stools, forms and household stuff as she brought at our marriage; a long cart, a little dung cart, a pair of wheels to the carts, a pair of iron harrows, a dung rake, a long saw and a short, a mattock, a shod shovel, a spade, a grinding stone and the iron to turn it, a plough with coulter and share, a plough bitch, a double hook, an axe, a hedding [*recte* hedging] bill, a long and short pitchfork, a chain for the plough foot with such augers and wimbles as she brought with her; a great wicker chair now at her house at Buttsbury, a little wainscot chest that she commonly lays her hats in, and a stool of an oaken plank; £20; my best black mare, 6 kine (she choosing one and my son Rd. another until her 6 be numbered), 10 sheep indifferently chosen among my flock, half my hogs, poultry, tubs, barrels, trays and cheese motes, my malt mill, the latten weights and scales, half as much linen as hath been spun in the house sithence our marriage (my servants' sheets only excepted); my ring with a red stone in it which I wear on my finger, a petticoat cloth of red (price 9s. the yard), my fox-furred cloak, and a brush. She and Rd. shall jointly keep house together at my executor's charge for a quarter of a year after my death, when she shall depart to Buttsbury. The division of the chattels given to her to be made at her departure, when Rd. shall give towards housekeeping a quarter of rye, a quarter of malt, a bushel of salt, a bushel of oaten meal, a lead of my best cheese and 20lb. of butter; and he shall carry her stuff, she finding him horse meat and man's meat. Whereas I stand bound to Mr WHIGHT and Mr JEFFERYE for payment of £20 due to Reynold BRUERTON at 21, Rd. shall discharge it. To Geo. my son £20 at 28 [*sic*] or before if my overseer think good; if he die before, £6 13s.4d. to Rd., £6 13s.4d. to the eldest daughter of my daughter KNAPE, and £6 13s.4d. divided among the children of my daughter ALLDRYTCHE, and a gimmal of gold with a death's head in it (price 6s.8d.). To every of my daughters and their husbands a gimmal of gold with a death's head (price 6s.8d.). To Frs. ALLDRYTCHE my son-in-law my grogram cassock, and to his son Frs. 2 silver spoons with knops in the ends. To the eldest daughter of my daughter KNAPE £10 at marriage; if she die before, to be divided among the rest of her children. To Th. HAYES my son-in-law a gimmal of gold with a death's head (price 6s.8d.), and to Clement his brother £3 6s.8d. To every one of my servants 12d. To the poor of Romford side 6s.8d. The rest of my goods to Rd., whom I make executor; provided that, if he die unmarried, I give all bequeathed to him to my other three children [not named] equally to be divided. I make Frs. overseer. Witnesses: John LEGATT, Wm. LAMBERT vicar of Corunte [co.?]. Proved 17 Mar. 1577/8.

JOHN CRIMBLE of Hawkwell yeoman, 4 July 1578. (95)
To the poor of Hawkwell 6s.8d. and of Rochford 6s.8d. To Jane my wife £100. To her £8 which Mr WEST doth owe me. I will that she shall pay Wm. YOUNGE her brother £13 6s.8d. which was delivered to my sister, his wife, to the behoof of his eldest daughter. To my wife 4 kine, 20 ewes, a ram, my sorrel gelding, a brown nag that she doth say is hers, 6 pairs of sheets, a dozen napkins, a diaper tablecloth, 6 diaper napkins, 2 plain napkins, my bedstead in the parlour, and her apparel. She shall remain in my house 1 month after my decease at my executor's charges if she will; if not, God speed her well. To her also 6 pewter platters, 6 dishes, 6 pottingers, 6 saucers, 2 brass pots, 2 brass kettles, a pewter basin, 2 pillows, 4 pillowberes, 4 towels (1 of diaper), a silver bottle, 3 silver spoons, and my silver bowl. To Rt. CRIMBLE £20, John CRIMBLE £3, my sister Eliz. £3, Martha CRIMBLE 40s., Mary CRIMBLE 40s., Mgt. BARNERD *alias* BASTLEYE 40s., Anne HAROLD 10s. I will that £9 be delivered to BASELEY of Hadleigh to the use of PRATT, he to have the bringing up of the girl; she must have a chest of linen which her father [not named] appointed her. The rest of my goods to my brother Wm., whom I make executor. I constitute overseers my friends Wm. BOURNE and Nich. WARDALL. Witnesses: Nich. WARDALL, Wm. ENGLAND, Th. COLLIN. Proved 6 Aug. 1578; Inventory exhibited at £330 9s.2d.

ANDREW GRENE of Chigwell, 28 Jan. 1577/8. (96)
To Susan GREENE my goddaughter 3s.4d. The rest of my goods to Th. my son, whom I make executor. I make overseers Adam HILL and Harry FULLER, and for their pains 3s.4d. apiece. Witnesses: Nich. HILL, John MILLS, Henry FULLER. Proved 31 May 1578.

THOMAS ANDEWE of Prittlewell, 16 May 1578. (97)
To my son Geo. ANDEWE my Latin bible and all my Latin books [no details]. To Wm. ANDEWE my son 3 pewter platters, 3 pewter dishes, 2 saucers, my cupboard in the buttery, and my counter table that my books be in, at 21 or marriage. To Harry ANDEWE my son all my English books, a great chafer, and a copper kettle, likewise. To Mgt. my daughter a [blank] of 'lattin' [latten or Latin?], likewise. The rest of my goods to Mgt. my wife, whom I make executrix. Witnesses: Joan VINSON, Henry WOOD, Th. FRANCIS, Rt. LARKYN. 26 May [1578], the executrix renounced executorship; administration committed, 'etc.'

WILLIAM GATTES of North Fambridge yeoman, 19 May 1578. (98)
To Magdalen my well-beloved wife for her life my house and land in Esher (co. Surrey); after her decease, to Geo. GATTES my kinsman; for lack of heirs, to Th. GATTES [relationship not stated]; according to a surrender which I have made. The rest of my goods to my wife, whom I constitute executrix. Witnesses: Edw. LEES, Wm. ELLIS, Th. ELLIS, Rd. BINGLEY. Proved 27 May 1578.

WILLIAM ALLEN of East Ham husbandman, 19 May 1578. (99)
To my mother [not named] 40s. half yearly till the money run out. To my brother Edm. ALLEN 1 brown cow that I bought last in Smithfield market [in London]; more I forgive 10s. due to me at Midsummer for keeping his cow. To my brother Th. ALLEN all my wearing apparel except my cloak; more I give him 5s. To Th. POLLMER's wife the lease of Moore Eves [Enes?] with the house belonging that she dwelleth in. To my godchildren 12d. apiece. To father SYMSON, FOLLENTYNE, Nich. MUFFETT, Rt. HEWARD, father FAUNCE, each 12d. To Rd. MOUMFORTHES in token of goodwill 5s. To my wife's daughter Sarah STAFFORT 2 beasts (1 coloured pied, the other a branded with sawn horns). I forgive the minister Wm. YOUNG [not the vicar] the debts between him and me. The residue of my goods to my well-beloved wife Mgy., whom I ordain executrix. I appoint my beloved neighbours Th. MONFETT the elder and Th. TINSELE smith of West Ham overseers, for whose pains 5s. Witnesses: Ralph HARRISON, Rd. MOUNTFORT, Edm. ALLEN, Wm. YOUNGE minister of the same parish. Proved 31 May 1578.

THOMAS LARKEN of Rayleigh, 8 May 1578. (100)
To Mgt. my wife all my goods for her life, whom I constitute executrix, if she abide single; if she chance to marry again, I will my goods to be divided equally into two parts, my wife to have one half, the other betwixt my four children, i.e. Th. my son and Agnes, Parnell and Mary my daughters. I constitute overseers Solomon TIE and Th. my son. Witnesses: Rd. BLACKWELL writer hereof, John CROBOURNE. Proved 26 May 1578.

SIMON NORRINGTON of Dunton, 3 May, 20 Eliz. [1578]. (101)
To Frances NORRINGTON my daughter 20 nobles and 1 of my best kine at 17. To the poor people in Dunton 2s.6d. The residue of my goods to Joan my wife, whom I ordain executrix. I appoint Henry NORRINGTON my father and John NORRINGTON my brother overseers. Witnesses: Henry NORRINGTON, John NORRINGTON, Th. MEREDITHE. Proved 30 May 1578.

ROBERT GRAYE of Fobbing, 14 Apr. 1578. (102)
[Religious preamble.] To Wm. and John my sons and Agnes my daughter each £4 at 20; my wife shall have the use of the £12 to bring up my children till then. I make her executrix. The residue of my goods to 'Urye' my wife. I ordain John TYLL-FORDE and Lawrence KENTE of Fobbing overseers, and to each 5s. for their pains. Witnesses: Wm. GRAYE, Henry THOMSON, Lawrence KEMPE [*sic*], Wm. SHER-BORNE, Wm. CROWDER writer hereof. Administration committed, 14 Nov. 1578, to John TYLLFORD, Lawrence KENT during 'etc.'

JOHN SILVESTER, [abode and date not given], husbandman. (103)
To be buried in Runwell churchyard. To Jane SYLVESTER and Sarah my daughters 6 ewe sheep and a cow or else £3 in money each at £16. To Samuel my son 10 ewe sheep and a cow or else £4 at 16. The rest of my goods to my wife [not named], whom I make executrix. I make my brother Th. SILVESTER and John LAKE over-seers. Witnesses: Chris. PEACOCKE minister, John WARNER, Th. SHORYE. Proved 28 June 1578.

WILLIAM BASEWICKE [BESWICKE *in margin*] of Steeple and Stansgate, 24 Mar. 1577/8. (104)
Forasmuch as my wife hath not the use of speech, I desire my cousin John BASE-WICKE of Stansgate in the parish of Steeple, whom I make my executor, to take my wife and child into his keeping and governance with such lands and goods as I now possess; and such as shall be left, if she chance to marry, to be divided, one half to Grace my wife and the other to Susan my daughter by equal portions, and John to have the keeping thereof until she marry and to pay himself for all charges. Whoso shall marry my wife shall have the keeping of the child during her mother's life or till she be able to go to service. If both die, John to have all my goods. I make him executor and Edw. SHUTE overseer. Witnesses: Chris: KNIGHT vicar of Steeple, John NICHOLL, Edw. SHUTE. Proved 27 May 1578.

LEVINGE DALE of Woodham Ferrers yeoman, 27 Apr. 1578. (105)
To be buried in Buttsbury churchyard. To the poor of Buttsbury 10s. and of Woodham Ferrers 10s. To Mgt. my wife all my goods. To her for her life a tenement and lands called Charvells and a tenement or house called Wymans with 3 crofts of free lands all in Stock; after her decease, to my brother Matthew DALE. To my wife for her life by surrender made to her in the presence of John LUTHER bailiff of the manor of Whites Tyrrells [in Buttsbury] and Chris. TAYLOR and Th. CLARCKE, customary tenants of the manor, a close being copy (2 acres) and 3 parcels of land and meadow called Mareland belonging to the manor of Blunts [in Great Burstead]; West Field (4 acres); and Lady Mead ($\frac{1}{2}$ acre of it being copy) surrendered to the bailiff of the manor of Blunts in the presence of John LUTHER and Chris. TAYLOR; all in Stock. To my brother Matthew £5. I make my wife executrix and overseers John LUTHER and Th. GOO[R?]HE, my brothers-in-law, to whom 5s. apiece. Witnesses: Edw. KENNETT, Chris. TAYLOR, Th. CLARKE. Proved 28 May 1578.

RICHARD BARBAR, [abode not given], 28 Apr. 1578. (106)
To be buried at the chapel of Romford near the gate on the south side of the chapel. To four bachelors which shall bear my body to church each 20s. [*sic*], Stephen SKELE, Wm. QUIKE, Stephen STEVENS the younger and Wm. SKELE. To six ringers for their pains 10s., John BAYLIE, John HARRODE, John CAVE, John WRIGHT, John DICKENSON, and Rt. THOROWGOOD. To Nich. SYMPSON gentleman 20 wethers, if they be found, which goeth upon the Common. To Mary SIMPSON his wife 10 ewes and 9 lambs. To Edw. CAROWE gentleman, John CAROE his brother, Julian SMITHE and Eliz. SPENCER each 20s., Mr [Rd.] ATKYS [minister of Romford] 5s., John NETTLETON 12d., Rd. CHARVELL my godson 10s., Geo. GOOSEBYE 6s.8d., Anthony HOLMAN and John HOLEMAN his brother each 20s. To Wm. HENCELY which he oweth me 15s. To the poor 10s. To STODDARD 3s.4d. To James CAROWE which he oweth me at 'Alholantyde' [1 Nov.] next 32s. To the poor £6 to be paid with 3 years quarterly. To Geoffrey CAROE the crop of my 2 fields now in my hands, paying my executors 15s. To Wm. QUYTE [*sic*] 10s., Emme NETTLETON 5s., John OSBORNE, widow BROKES, [blank] FOTE, John STRETE and John BROKES each 12d. To Rd.. LAWTOUN and Wm. WILLYTT each 3s.4d. The residue of my goods to Mr Geo. NODES, whom I make executor. I make Wm. OUTTRED overseer, and for his pains 20s. Witnesses: John BROKES, Geoffrey CAROWE, Wm. EVERED, Wm. HEDGE, Rd. LATOUN. Proved 31 May 1578.

EDWARD MADISON of Sandon yeoman, 20 May 1578. (107)
John OVERED of Sandon, whom I constitute executor, shall take into his hands all my goods, corn, cattle and movables and therewith pay my debts and discharge my funerals. The residue of my goods to Mgy. my wife. Witnesses: Patrick FERNE [rector of Sandon], John TAPPES, Simon BARBOR. 5 June 1578, John OVERED appeared before Mr Wm. BINGHAM, LL.D., Official of the Archdeacon of Essex, in the presence of Edm. HODYLOVE notary public, and exhibited the Will, and administration committed, the inventory to be exhibited before Michaelmas next.

THOMAS KNIGHT of Basildon yeoman, 20 May 1578. (108)
To the poor 13s.4d. To Joan my wife the lease of my farm that I do dwell on called Sommers [in Basildon] for the term of the lease, with the stock and store of corn and cattle except 1 bald gelding to my son Benjamin. To my wife all my household stuff except 1 featherbed to Benjamin. To her my house and lands called Juddes or Martins in Bradwell[-juxta-Mare] for her life; after her decease, to Benjamin. To him my moiety or lease in Wallettes [Wallasea Island] called Tillettes with the stock and store on it, on condition that he pay my wife £10 a year so long as the lease doth endure. To my son John £20. To my daughter DALE's four children [not named] 20s. apiece at 21. To my daughter ELLIS's daughter called Joan ELLIS 20s. at 21. I make Benjamin executor, and John SANDELL of Basildon overseer, and for his pains 20s. Witnesses: Henry DORE of Basildon, Rd.LOVE of [Ramsden] Crays, John BROWNE writer. Proved 7 June 1578.

THOMAS HERDE of North Ockendon husbandman, 10 May 1578. (109)
To the poor 5s. To my brother Rt. HERDE for the behoof of his son Rt. at 21 my house and lands in North Ockendon and 'Warley' free and copy. I will my brother to pay his son after 16 until 21 £3 16s.8d. a year and to give my two sisters Emlen WILSON and Eliz. HERDE out of my free lands £10 apiece, Eliz. at 21; if she die before, £5 to my mother [not named] and £5 to my other sister. The rest of my movables to my brother Rt., whom I make executor. I make my uncle Th. HERDE overseer. Witnesses: Nich. MASON, Th. ATKINS, Th. HALKINS minister [not the rector]. Proved 30 May 1578.

ALEXANDER CORNEWALL of Chigwell, one of the Queen's Majesty's Yeomen of the Guard, 15 Dec. 1577. (110)
To be buried in Chigwell church. I will that the lease of my house shall be appraised and [the money] divided between my wife and my three children [not named]; if she be with child, that child to have part with the others; all at 21 or marriage. She shall have the bringing up of my children with their portions. I make my cousin

Rd. CORNEWALL, citizen and skinner of London, executor. Witnesses: John STONERD of Chigwell esquire, Rt. SPACKMAN of Chigwell yeoman. 2 June 1578, Rd. CORNEWALL appeared before Mr FORTHE LL.D., surrogate of Mr Wm. BINGHAM LL.D., the Official, in the presence of Rt. LYNNE notary public, in the house of Mr Wm. BABHAM in Paternoster Row [in London], and exhibited the Will and renounced executorship. The same day administration granted to Mgt. CORNWALL *alias* FARMAR, widow of the deceased. Inventory exhibited at £111 16s.4d. by oath of Wm. FARMAR of Islington [co. Middlesex] gentleman.

JOHN BRAND of Barking fisherman, 9 May 1578. (111)
To the poor men's box 5s. To my two sons Rt. and John each £4 at 21; if both die before, to the next of my kin. If Mgy. my wife be with child, to the same 40s. To John BRAND my father my best doublet and best cap. I forgive my sister Anne BARRETT the 5s. she doth owe me. The rest of my goods to my wife, whom I make executrix. I make overseers my loving father Rd. MASON and Fabian PYTCHER, and for their pains 20d. apiece. Witneses: John HORTON, curate [of Barking], Rd. MASON tailor, Fabian PITCHER fisherman, Th. HAYWARD [parish] clerk. Proved 31 May 1578. Inventory exhibited at £20 11s.2d.

ELIZABETH ROCHE of Chadwell widow, 4 May 1578. (112)
To the poor men's box 20d. To father HAWSE, Rt. BAYLIE, widow HUNSDEN, goodwife POWLMER, widow MATCHINGHAM and WESTE's widow, each 12d. at my burial. To my brother James SAMOND 1 cow called Great and 20s. and at harvest time next a seam of bread corn, ½ wheat, ½ rye, also 2 ewes; to his wife my best garment. To Wm. CLARKE 1 ewe; Susan HAWLE 1 ewe and a pair of good flaxen sheets; Th. CROWE 1 ewe; Emlen SMITH 2 ewes. To Emlen SMYTH 10s. and a ring of silver and gilt which was her mother's. To Eliz. CLARKE, Wm. son of Lawrence CLARKE, Edw. FELSTED, Hum. FELSTED, and Phoebe FELSTED, each 5s.; to Phoebe also the younger of my 2 bullocks. To my goddaughter Eliz. ENSER and my godson Barthw. CROXSTOLLE each 20d. To Mgt. BONNAMES 5s. and the eldest of my 2 bullocks, committed to the keeping of Harry PITCHEY until she is of lawful years. To 'Grissell' SAMOND, Th. TROWAR, Isaac TROWAR and James TROWAR, 3s.4d. apiece. To my daughter Dthy. CLARKE my best bed. To my son-in-law John TROWAR my best mare. I will that my mother HAWSE shall have my grey cassock and widow HUNSDEN a petticoat. I will that Emlen SMYTH and her stock be committed to the keeping of Harry PITCHEY or Rt. BEETE. Whatsoever of these men following be indebted to me, I freely forgive, viz. John LAWRENCE, Rt. BAYLEY, Wm. WETHERHEDDE, John WOOD, and father COLE the butcher. The debt of Rd. TOMPSON and SMYTHE the butcher I give to Susan HAWLE my servant. I will that £4 given by the Will of my husband [not named: see *Essex Wills*, Volume 3 (no.26)] for Wm. ROCHE of Chadwell] to Edw. FELSTEDE's children be committed to the keeping of Lawrence CLARKE my son-in-law to their use, for that he hath of theirs £10 already. The rest of my goods to Mgt. TROWAR and Dthy. CLARKE my daughters to be equally divided. I ordain Lawrence CLARKE and John TROWAR executors, they to provide a godly and learned sermon at my burial to the edification of those present. I appoint my well-beloved friend and neighbour Rt. BEET overseer, and for his pains 3s.4d. Witnesses: Frs. WHITE parson of Chadwell, Th. CRO, James SAMOND, Rd. PITCHEY, Harry PITCHEY, Rt. BEET, Lawrence CLARKE, John TROWARE. Proved 10 May 1578.

THOMAS PAYNE of South Weald husbandman, 28 Mar. 1578. (113)
To the poor of South Weald 13s.4d., and of Doddinghurst 6s.8d. To my sister Ellen wife of George BAYLIE of Doddinghurst the lands with a tenement in South Weald and Doddinghurst during the years of the lease from my brother John. To Ellen 2 kine and 2 'hoskers' [heifers] in the hands of Th. RUSBROCKE. To Mary BAYLIE my goddaughter 3s.4d.; the rest of my brother BAYLIE's children each 20s. To my brother Reynold PAYNE 2 kine (1 with Wm. NOT of Navestock, the other with widow KINGE), a colt which now halteth of 5 years, 20s., and another cow in the occupying of James BRETTON of Laindon. To my brother Wm. PAYNE 20s.; Mgt. PAYNE my goddaughter 20s.; the rest of his children each 6s.8d. To the children of John my

brother each 6s.8d.; Dthy. LEWIS my sister's child 53s.4d. to bring her up; Mgt., Dthy's sister, 10s.; Rd. CRAMPE £3 6s.8d., a colt, 6 sheep, and 20s. he oweth me; Wm. CRAMPE £3 6s.8d. at 24; my brother Rt. PAYNE's six children [not named] £6 13s.4d. among them. To eight poor men to carry me to church 8s. To Th. PILES of South Weald 3s.4d. I make Rt. PAYNE and Geo. BAYLIE executors. The residue of my goods to them equally. Witnesses: Th. REDRITCHE [vicar of Childerditch], Wm. TINGE. Proved 10 May 1578.

AGNES KIRKBYE of Burnham widow, 13 Apr. 1578. (114)
To Grace FREAKE my daughter £5, a pair of flaxen sheets, a pair of linsey woolsey blankets, and ½ dozen table napkins. To Jane my youngest daughter £13 6s. 8d., a bedsteadle with the ceiling and painted cloths which I had of John FREAKE, a featherbed, a trundle bedsteadle, a flockbed, a long chest, a cupboard with a press, 8 pieces of pewter, my biggest and least brass pots, my greatest kettle except 1, my biggest spit, 2 tablecloths, 7 table napkins, a couple of kerchiefs, 2 rails, a little hutch, a little framed table, 2 joined stools, and 2 milch kine, all at 18. Towards the repairing of Colyton Haven 4s. [co. Devon]. To Geo. POWGGLEE an old plain bedsteadle with a bed. To Th. EVERINGE a covering already in his hands. To Nich. KYRBYE a new broadcloth coat that was his brother's, a small water barrel, and 2 boards or planks. The rest of my goods to John PEEKE my son-in-aw, whom I make executor. I make Wm. AYLETT overseer. Witnesses: Wm. AYLETT, Nich. BAWNE, John PEEKE senior, Wm. ARTHURES. Proved 19 May 1578.

HENRY HUNTER of West Ham badger, 29 Mar. 1578. (115)
To Joan RAYNOLDES my eldest daughter 2 kine, a pair of open-seamed sheets, a brass pot, my lesser kettle, a chest, my wife's 2nd cassock, her stammel [red] petticoat, my table in the parlour, Jane [*sic*] to receive them at marriage. To Elizabeth my 2nd daughter 2 kine, a cupboard in the hall, my greatest kettle, and a chest. To Susan RAYNOLDES my 3rd daughter 3 kine, a brass pot, my worst kettle, and a chest. To my son Wm. 4 kine, a brass pot, a joined chest, another chest, my table in the hall, and my best featherbed. My pewter and linen to be equally divided amongst my children Joan, Eliz., Susan and Wm. at the discretion of Rt. GOLDSTONE my brother-in-law. To Anne DALTON my gelding, mare and colt, and my wife's hat and worsted apron. All my other goods to Rt. GOLDSTONE, whom I make executor, he to be good to my children. Witnesses: John ARMESTRONGE clerk [not the vicar], Geo. WHITTWAYE, John MARWOOD. Proved 9 May 1578.

HARRY STELEWOMAN *alias* STILLIMAN of Woodham Ferrers, 20 Apr. 1578. (116)
To the poor people of Woodham Ferrers 20s., of Stow [Maries] 10s., and of [Cold] Norton 10s. To some godly preacher to make 2 sermons, 1 at my burial, the other within a month after in Woodham, 10s. for his pains. To my well-beloved wife Emme STELEWOMAN my 2 tenements and lands belonging in Woodham Ferrers called Cookes and Doores and in Danbury called Hill House for her life; after her decease, to my son and heir John STELEWOMAN *alias* STILLIMAN. To Rt. CAMPER my son-in-law and my daughter Rebecca his wife £50 between them. To my wife all my household stuff, 30 milch kine, 160 sheep called ewes of the best at her choice, and 2 geldings at her choice. To John's children £20 among them part and part at 21 or marriage. To the children of Edw. STELEWOMAN *alias* STILLIMAN by his 1st wife, my wife's daughter, i.e. Edw., Rt., Harry and Rebecca, £20 likewise. To my daughter Judy LERWYN £5 and her children £5 among them. To the children of my cousin Rt. STILLIMAN of Stow £5 part and part like at 20 or marriage. To John OWTINGE 10s. and Wm. MABBES 10s. To my servants dwelling with me 3s.4d. apiece. The residue of my goods to my wife and John, whom I make executors. Witnesses: Wm. ROGER, Th. VYCKERS, Wm. SHETHER the writer, Rt. BACHELLER, Th. POPEEL. Proved 13 May 1578 by Emma STELLIMAN the widow, the other executor having died.

JOAN AWSTEN of West Ham, 1 May 1578. (117)
To my son John MARVILL all my goods. To Th. MICHAELL 2 milch kine with certain household implements for the behoof of Wm. AWSTEN. I make my well-beloved

in Christ Gregory WARLOWE tanner executor and John LITLE of West Ham butterman overseer. Witnesses: John DORRINGTON minister and curate of West Ham, John FOORDE, Th. WILKINSON, Edw. LUMBE. Proved 6 May 1578.

JOAN BEELLS, [abode not given], 11 Mar., 20 Eliz. [1577/8]. (118)
To be buried in Fobbing churchyard. To John SAWANSON 1 collander, 1 pewter dish, 1 platter, 1 candlestick, 1 kettle (the biggest save 1), 1 new sheet, and 13s. To Mich. KENT the bed that I lie on, 1 pewter platter, 1 lockram sheet, and to his son Mich. 1 sheep. To my son's son Wm. JAMES 1 sheep. To my sons Edw. JAMES and Th. JAMES each 20s. To Wm. BELL my husband's godson 12d. The rest to my son John JAMES, whom I make executor. Witnesses: Harry THOMSONE, Wm. WADE, Agnes DAVID, Philip WHITE parson of Fobbing. Proved 9 Apr. 1578.

JOHN HINDE of Great Ilford in the parish of Barking husbandman, 24 Sept. 1577. (119)
To Wm. HINDE my son my new buck's leather doublet and my best cloak or 20 marks in money. To Thomasine LEY my wife's sister 10s. To Isabel ROCKAR my maidservant 6s.8d. To the poor of [Great] Ilford 6s.8d. To every one of my godchildren 12d. To Mary HARTE 40s. The rest of my goods to Eliz. my wife, whom I make executrix, to perform my Will by the help and advice of Roger HIERON and Rt. COMYN, whom I make overseers, and for their pains 6s.8d. Witnesses: Geo. STODDERD, Matthew COOPER, John THACKWELL. Proved 27 May 1578.

WILLIAM PEASE, [of Hornchurch or Walthamstow], 9 Apr. 1578. (Nuncupative.) (120)
To Mgt. his wife all such goods as were hers before he married with her. He gave her £13 6s.8d., conditionally that she pay the legacies given by Frs. THOROWEGOOD, her 1st husband to her two children by him, for which legacies he entered into bonds to Nich. TRIPLOWE of Hornchurch smith and Wm. TURCKE of Puttloos [now Putwells] in Brentwood husbandman. To the poor of Hornchurch side 20s. and of Walthamstow 10s., and to Isabel his maid 10s. To Rt. and Joan PEASE his children the rest of his goods, cattle, horses, colts, kine, bullocks, sheep, and 'household', and his house in London inhabited by one SKYNNER a chandler, with all sollars, cellars, shops, backsides or gardens belonging, to be divided between them in equal portions, to Joan at 18 and Rt. at 20. He made Geo. PEASE, his brother's son, his executor; his overseers John POOLE of Hornchurch husbandman and [blank] COLLIER [collier, i.e. charcoal burner?] of Abridge [in Lambourne], his brother-in-law. Witnesses: John POOLE, Wm. STEVEN, Nich. TRIPLOE. Proved 18 Apr. 1578.

EDWARD LOWE of Vange, 10 Mar. 1577/8. (121)
To Mgy. my wife all my lands and tenements in Fobbing and Corringham free and copy for her life; after her decease, to the poor people of Fobbing for ever, save only that there shall be paid out of the lands to Wm. LOWE my son for his life £3 a year; if he die without heirs, they shall remain to the poor of Fobbing. The churchwardens of Fobbing, after my wife's death, shall have their letting and pay themselves 3s.4d. a year for their painstaking. The residue of my goods to my wife, whom I make executrix. A true copy of this my Will shall remain in the register book of Fobbing so that the churchwardens may always see from time to time what they may do. Wm. shall have my house and lands to dwell in during his life lying in Corringham called Tregoes for 26s.8d. a year as part of his £3. Witnesses: John LAKE, Th. BREDGE[S], Henry POTTER. Proved 13 Apr. 1578.

WILLIAM LEAFPHINGWELL of Fryerning, 10 Apr. 1579. (122)
Towards the reparations of Fryerning church 3s.4d. To the poor men's box 3s.4d. To Parnell my wife my tenement or inn called the 'Blue Boar' in Fryerning with the stables, barns, orchards and gardens belonging, for her life; my kitchen being parcel of my customary tenement called Stockens adjoining my house which I dwell in, for her life; and 22 featherbeds with the bedsteadles as they stand in 7 chambers, i.e. the New Chamber 4, Hadley Chamber 4, Newdome Chamber 2, Barfolde Chamber 2, Little Hadley Chamber 4, the High Chamber 4, and the Parlour 2, all which beds she

shall have the occupying of during her life. To my son Henry LEAFPHINGWELL a featherbed. To my sons Geo. and Peter, after my wife's decease, my tenement called the 'Blue Boar' with the stables [etc.]; for lack of heirs, to remain to the rest of my children, part and part alike; also my kitchen and tenement called Glasiers with a little freehold garden plat adjoining; if she die without heirs, successively to my daughter Anne and to Elizabeth DAWNY my wife's daughter. To Anne LEAFPHINGWELL a tenement called Turners with the barns, stables and gardens; if she decease without heirs, to the rest of my children. To Mgt. and Anne each a featherbed and a silver spoon at marriage. To Henry and Peter each a silver spoon at marriage. To my wife's four children, i.e. Edw., Alice, Thomasine and Eliz. DAWNYE, each a featherbed at marriage and 50s. apiece to be paid within 6 years after my wife's decease by Geo. and Peter. To Mgt. and Anne each 2 pewter platters, 2 pewter dishes and 2 saucers at marriage. I will that my cupboard in the parlour and my great chest in my bedchamber shall not be removed out of the 'Blue Boar' but remain there to Geo. and Peter, and they shall not sell the 'Blue Boar' unless to some of my own children or kinsmen called by my name, and whosoever of them that is so disposed to buy it shall have it £20 better cheap than any other man. If Geo. and Peter decease before my wife without heirs and no sale made, to remain to be divided amongst the rest of my children part and part alike. To Wm. PONDE my godson a featherbed. He who shall happen to marry with my wife shall be bound to my overseers in £100 to keep the 'Blue Boar' in good reparations and to leave the bedding in as good value as they shall be appraised by honest men. The rest of my goods, cattle and corn to my wife for her life; after her decease, to Geo. and Peter. I ordain Peter my executor with her, and my brother John LEAFPHINGWELL and John WALFFORD, my wife's brother, overseers, and for their pains 6s.8d. apiece. Wm. PAGE my servant shall have his dwelling during his life in the cottage that MUNDES dwelleth in for a groat a year after the decease of Mrs ROYDON, paying it yearly to Anne LEAFPHINGWELL, to whom I have given the house. Witnesses: Rt. CLARKE, Edw. HILLS, Edm. WORNE, Roger WAIGHT. Proved 8 Sept. 1579 by Parnell the widow, power reserved to the other executor when he shall come. Inventory exhibited at £145 12s.4d.

CHRISTIAN LUCAS widow of John LUCAS the elder of Brentwood, 27 Jan. 1578/9. (123)

To Wm. WELLES brewer and Roger HOLTE shoemaker, both of Brentwood, £11, on condition that they or either of them keep James and Michael INGRAM, my daughter's children, until they are 14 and find them meat, drink, linen, woollen, hose, shoes and all other things needful, Wm. and Roger shall have to their own use the rent of the house wherein John POLSTEAD gentleman dwelleth and be accountable to James and Michael after they are 21 for the rent. To Joan INGRAM my daughter 40s. to be paid to her or such person as my executors shall think good towards her keeping or relief for a year after my decease. To my executors £9 6s.8d., on condition that they or one of them shall keep and bring up John INGRAM, brother to James and Mich. to 20, finding him meat, [etc.]. To Ralph ASKEWE my tenant 10s. which he oweth me and to Eliz. his wife a black cassock, a red petticoat and a kercher. The residue of my goods to Wm. and Roger, whom I make executors. I make John WOODDELL the elder and John COCKE baker, both of Brentwood, oversers, and for their pains each 5s. Witnesses: Henry WALLER, Ralph ASKEWE, Rd. BROOKE the writer. Proved 24 May 1579.

RICHARD NELSON of Ramsden Crays, 27 Jan. 1578/9. (124)

To Joan my daughter 20s., 1 kettle and 1 pewter platter. To my son[-in-law] Wm. SPACYE my best hose, best coat, 1 new shirt, 1 pair of new high shoes, and 1 bullock of 2 years old. To my son[-in-law] Th. REWS 20s., my best doublet, 1 shirt, a black coat, and 1 pewter platter; to his daughter 1 sheep. To my daughter Sarah EXETER 20s. with 1 new chest, 1 red little chest, 1 brass posnet, 2 pewter porringers, 6 pewter spoons, and 1 pewter platter at marriage or 21. To my daughter Mary 2 lambs of a year old, my best cupboard, 1 cauldron, 1 kettle, 1 pewter platter, 1 new pewter pot, and 1 pillow at 21 or marriage. To Th. ROBARTES clerk [rector of Ramsden Crays?] for preaching a sermon at my burial 3s.4d. The rest of my goods to Eliz. my wife, whom I make executrix. Witnesses: Wm. KEYCKIRRKE, John WALTER, Rt. ADAMS, Th. ROBARTES the writer. Proved 24 Mar. 1578/9.

RICHARD BUSHOPE of Barking single man, 18 Aug. 1578. (125)
To the poor of Barking 40s. To Mgy. daughter of John BUSHOPE my brother 40s. The rest of my goods to Edw. BUSHOPE my brother, whom I make my executor. Witnesses: John HORTON minister of Barking, Rd. WALLETT of London. Proved 31 Mar. 1579.

ROBERT BACHELER of Stow Maries, 14 Feb. 1578/9. (126)
To the poor 20s. To the reparations of Stow Maries church 6s.8d. To a godly learned preacher for his painstaking in making 2 sermons 10s. To Alice my wife 40 of my best beasts, all my sheep, horse, colts, mares and geldings, my carts and ploughs and all my corn except 60 quarters of oats to my executors towards paying my debts and legacies. To my wife all my household stuff, the butter and cheese in the house, and my hogs. She shall have the occupying and profit of my farm called Maris [now Morris Farm, in Stow Maries] except the Marsh and ground belonging (by estimation 50 acres) during the lease which I have of the manor, on condition that she shall pay yearly £44 rent. She shall bring up my children at her costs with meat, drink, cloth and learning until they are 21 and be bound with sureties to my executors to do no act prejudicial to my lease. To Mary my daughter £40 at 20 or marriage. To Frs. BACHELER my brother 40s. The residue of my goods and my lease of the manor with the profits to my executors, they to take so much as above; then the residue of my goods to my two sons John and Henry equally divided. I make John STELLYMAN and John LORAINE executors, and for their pains each 10s. I make Wm. SOAME supervisor, who shall request my executors to make a yearly account of the profits of my farm. Witnesses: Henry SALISBURYE clerk [rector of Creeksea], Edw. STELLIMAN, James BRI[D]GES. Proved 3 Mar. 1578/9.

WILLIAM DALE of Bradwell-juxta-Mare husbandman, 10 Jan. 1578/9. (127)
To Joan DALE my daughter 1 featherbed with the posted bedstead with the white ceiling, 3 pewter platters, 3 pewter dishes, and a kettle of $1\frac{1}{2}$ gallons at marriage or 24. To John MEDCALF of Bradwell my black fustian doublet and black frize jerkin. To Wm. ELLIS of Fambridge [*sic*], my brother-in-law, 3s.4d., whom I ordain overseer. The residue of my goods to Alice my wife, whom I ordain executrix. Witnesses: John COLMAN, John NEVELOCKE, John MEDCALF, Th. SMITH. Proved 2 Mar. 1578/9.

JOHN CARTER of Grays Thurrock husbandman, 5 Feb. 1578/9. (128)
To Joan my wife and John my son all my goods jointly for the time of the longer liver of the twain. To my wife my tenement in Little Thurrock with the land belonging called Howchins for her life and the wood there growing to be 'dispent' jointly between her and my son at my tenement at Grays [Thurrock] so oft as needful occasion arise. To John my two tenements in Grays which I bought of John COMENS of Ilford, a marsh of 5 acres called Gossoppes Mead in Little Thurrock, 1 'salton' [salting?] in Grays (2 acres), and a parcel of arable (1 acre) in Grays. I ordain my wife and my son executors and my brother Rd. RAISTELL overseer. Witnesses: Rd. RAISTELL, John ALLANN, Wm. CROWDER writer hereof. The rent of my land at Orsett shall also be deducted to the payment of my debts. Proved 3 Mar. 1578/9.

RALPH WHITLOCKE of Rainham yeoman, 11 Jan. 1578/9. (129)
To Wm. my son £40 at 21 and Kath. my daughter £20 at marriage or 18. My executrix shall bring up my children well and honestly, the boy as soon as may be to be taught to read and write well. To my brother's son [not named] a cow called Broad Horn and his daughter a cow called Little Cherres. The rest of my goods to Agnes my wife, whom I make executrix. I make overseers Rt HOLDEN, Wm. RADLE and John LAWRENCE vicar of Rainham. Witnesses: Wm. WHITLOCKE, Rt. HOLDEN, Wm. RADLEY, John LAWRENCE. Proved 4 Mar. 1578/9.

ALICE MAKYN of South Weald widow, 25 Sept. 1577. **(130)**
To the poor 3s.4d. The residue of my goods to Th. COWPER, he to be executor. I make John WRIGHT of Wealdside [in South Weald] overseer, and for his pains 3s.4d. Witnesses. Th. MARIEGE, Wm. REIGNOLD, Geo. REIGNOLD. Proved 2 Mar. 1578/9.

ROBERT HARVIE, [abode not given], 4 Feb. 1578/9. **(131)**
To Joan my wife all my goods, whom I make executrix. Witnesses: John BRANSONNE, Geo. WYATT, Th. BRIDGIS, Th. STUDLY. Proved 9 Feb. 1578/9.

JOHN BILLERICA *alias* MILLER of Great Waltham husbandman, being grown in age, 26 Dec. 1579 [*recte* 1578?] **(132)**
To the poor people of Great Waltham 20s. to be distributed by my executor with the advice of Joan my well-beloved wife. To her £6 13s.4d. to be yearly paid by Rd. my son for her life, on condition that she demand no dower in my lands; the occupation of the low parlour and the little buttery in the house wherein I dwell; and necessary firebote to burn in the parlour, to be yearly felled and laid ready by Rd.; 1 quarter of wheat and 1 quarter of malt yearly paid likewise; and the best cow at her choice. Rd. shall keep on his lands in Rowhey [now Rolphy, in Great Waltham] 1 milch cow with winter meat and pasture for her use. To her my best featherbed, the joined bedstead in the parlour, 1 round table, 1 joined stool, 2 chests in the parlour, 1 other chest, the hangings in the parlour, all my linen and napery, 6 pewter platters, 6 pewter dishes, 6 saucers, 1 iron pot, 1 great kettle, 1 little kettle, 1 brass pot, 1 brazen mortar, 2 posnets, 1 spit, 1 pair of andirons, 1 dripping pan, 2 little beer barrels, and 1 cowl. To Joan my daughter, now wife of John DAVENISHE, 40s. To Eliz. my daughter £13 6s.8d. at 21, and 1 featherbed (the 2nd in goodness). To Mgt. DAVENISHE, the daughter of Joan my daughter, £3 6s.8d. at 21. To Joan BILLERICA *alias* MILLER, daughter of Rd., £3 6s.8d. at 21. To Mary DAWTON my niece 40s. to be paid to my loving friend Rd. EVERARDE of Waltham Bury [in Great Waltham] to her use at 21. To every of my godchildren 12d. The residue of my goods to Rd., whom I ordain executor. My wife shall have the third part of the fruit on my lands in Rowghleighe End [now Rolphy Green] for her life. To Rd. PONDE my neighbour, to be overseer, 5s. Witnesses: Rd. EVERARDE of Waltham Bury, Rd. PONDE, Henry DAVENISHE of Springfield. [No probate clause.]

JOHN MOUNDES of South Benfleet, 28 Jan. 1578/9. **(133)**
To Alice my wife all my goods. To her my house to dwell in for her life; after her decease, to Wm. MOUNDES my brother. I will that my wife be my executrix. Witnesses: Wm. LEACHE, Avice HUNT, Henry COLMAN minister [curate of South Benfleet, *Transactions of Essex Archaeological Society*, New Series, vi (1898), 136] and writer hereof. Proved 9 Feb. 1578/9.

PHILIP BURTEN of Great Waltham, 8 Oct. 1577. **(134)**
To six of the poorest householders 2s. To Mary my well-beloved wife all my goods in consideration of her pains and true intent done to me lovingly and kindly. I ordain her my executrix. Witnesses: Th. GOODYFFE, Rd. PONDE. Proved 8 Feb. 1578/9.

ANTHONY MILES of West Ham carpenter, 14 Nov. 1566 [*sic*]. **(135)**
To Eliz. MILES my daughter 2 kine (1 white, 1 brown) and Grace MYLES my daughter 2 kine (1 black with a white back, 1 brended), each at marriage. I make Mgt. my wife executrix. To John MYLES my brother my best coat. To my wife all my goods. I make overseers Rd. FOX and Miles LEEDES, and to each 3s.4d. for their pains. Witnesses: Stephen DICKSONE, Rd. FOXE, John CLARKE, Miles LEEDES. If my overseers see that my wife's goods go to waste, they shall take as much of her goods as the 4 kine shall be appraised at by them. Proved 1 Feb. 1578/9; administration committed to Mgt., the testator's widow.

JOHN BRIGHT of Romford innholder and yeoman, 27 Aug. 1578. **(136)**
To the five daughters of my brother Geo. BRIGHT of Westminster, i.e. Eliz., Mgt., Jane, Mary and Anne, each 20s. at marriage. To Eliz. BRIGHT, daughter of my brother Thomas, 20s. at marriage. To my servants Lucy LAMBE and Eliz. STICHE

each 20s. To Eliz. BRIGHT, my servant and daughter of John BRIGHT my ostler, 20s. when her covenants are ended. I bequeath among my poor neighbours of Romford £5, half at my executors' discretion on Ash Wednesday after my death and the other half twelve months following. To the discharging of my burial £3. I bequeath other 40s. on a dinner among my Tuesday's guests, the butchers of London; Mr Wm. HEARD and Th. PHILPOTT shall be overseers of this dinner. To John my godson, son of my brother Stephen BRIGHT of Barking, £5, Th. son of my brother Rd. 20 nobles, and John son of my brother Th. £10, each at 24; if all three die before, all three portions to Andrew eldest son of my brother Rd. The residue of my goods to Eliz. my wife and Justinian BALDWYN my son-in-law, whom I make executors; provided that, if she marry, she shall pay £20 to my brother Stephen. Mr Frs. RAME of Hornchurch gentleman, goodman John SKEALE of Hornchurch yeoman, and goodman Rt. DICKENSON of Romford shall be supervisors, and for their labour 6s.8d. apiece. To my wife and Justinian all my lands and tenements in Havering. Witnesses: Frs. RAME, Th. STONE, Rt. DYKINSON, John SKEALE. Proved 13 July 1579.

MANUEL CHAMBERLYN of Magdalen Laver, — 1579. (137)
To the poor people 12d. To my father Rt. CHAMBERLYN 40s. To him my tenement and land in Great Hormead [co. Hertford] for his life; after his decease, to my brother Wm. CHAMBERLYN. To Mgt. DENNES ½ quarter of barley, Susan BUTLER 3s.4d., and John RAMSYE 4s., all of Magdalen Laver. To my brother Wm. 40s. To Agnes COMFORT 3s.4d. To Harry DOWSETT my fellow [servant] my knit hose, leather doublet and cloth hose; Geoffrey HILL my hutch; the said John RAMSY my old russet hose; Alice DOWSETT of Weald [North Weald Bassett] my gold ring; my dame DOWSETT of Weald my woollen yarn which she did spin for me, she considering her maid that did help spin it 2s. To my master Mr THURGOOD with whom I dwell 40s. towards the physic bestowed on me and other charges and for bringing me honestly to the earth. To Harry DOWSETT my best hat and best hatband; mother HARRISON of Weald 12d.; Geoffrey aforesaid my doublet with leather sleeves. All my other old raiment to the poor people of Magdalen Laver at Mr THURGOOD's discretion, saving my boots which I give to George BEAVESSE of Weald and my canvas doublet to Reynold BREDGES. The residue of my goods to the poor of Laver. I make executor Mr THURGOOD, and for his pains 12d. I make overseer Mr Rd. DOWSETT, and for his pains 2s. If my goods will not extend to these legacies, every person's portion shall be so much abated as shall seem good to my executor and overseer. Witnesses: Th. HUSKYN clerk [rector of Magdalen Laver], Th. KINGE the elder, Wm. KINGE. Proved 21 Dec. 1579 by Rt. THURGOOD executor.

GEORGE HUBBLETHORNE *alias* SKEATH of Shenfield carpenter, 16 Nov. 1579. (Nuncupative.) (138)
To Rt. my son the lease of my dwelling house with the lands belonging which I have of John EXETER in Shenfield, to enter at Michaelmas 1581 during the term of the lease; also now 6 young sheep, a featherbed, 2 plain bedsteads, 3 table napkins, a little brass pot, a chafing dish, a form, a table, 2 chests, a great cobiron, 2 platters, 2 dishes, 2 saucers, and a pewter pot. The rest of my goods to Joan my wife, whom I make executrix with Rt. my son. I make John SALMON overseer. Witnesses: John EXETER, Th. EVE of Shenfield. Proved 12 Jan. 1579/80.

HELEN ROWLES of Leigh widow, 3 Dec. 1579. (139)
To Rachel and Eliz. daughters of John ROULE my son deceased all the stuff in the loft and chamber where I lie, viz. 2 beds being featherbeds and 1 flockbed with the bedsteads, and 3 chests and all things in them, to be equally divided; if both decease before 16, to my son's two children, i.e. Wm. and John sons of Wm. ROULE my son. To Wm. my son's son a brass pot and a pewter platter. To John ROULE a brass pot and a spice mortar. The residue of my goods to Wm. my son, whom I make executor. Witnesses: John BOWDON, Agnes SALMON, Clere CLARKE, Mgy. DAVY, Mgy. SALLOWE. Proved 11 Jan. 1579/80.

GEORGE STEVEN, [abode not given], 27 Sept., 21 Eliz. [1579]. (140)
To be buried in Hornchurch churchyard. To Anne my wife and Geo. my son my house and lands called Baldwens and term of years of King's land in my occupying, for her life; after her decease, to Geo. To my wife and Geo. my tenements called Lingcones and Norysses in Hornchurch 'town' and 3 crofts of land called Veltes, late Rt. FABATTE of Hornchurch, for 3 years after my decease; then my tenement called Lingcones late John COBE's deceased and Veltes to John my son and Norysses to Wm. To Wm. £5. To my sons Geoffrey and Th. each £20 at 22. To Mgt. my daughter 1 featherbed which I bought last. To Joan my daughter £20 and my best bedstead and featherbed after my wife's decease. To John my best chest in the parlour after his mother's decease. I will that Anne my wife and Geo. my son shall pay John PAYNE of Hadlye [now Hardley] Green the elder £31 16s., due to him by writing made by Rt. FABOTT to Geo. STEVEN at All Saints' Day after my decease. To Wm. my 2nd chest in the parlour after his mother's decease. To Geo. my son my cupboard, table and form in the parlour, my 2 best sheets [*recte* spits], and a pair of racks belonging to the same spits. The residue of my goods to my wife and Geo., whom I make executors. Witnesses: Rd. HAWRWAIE, Rd. COMVERS, Harry PORLAND, John CORTES, Th. BALDWYN, Rt. MAWLE, Th. CRAB. Proved 30 Oct. 1579 by Anne WHITE one of the executors, Geo. STEVEN being dead.

ROBERT FAWBOT of Hornchurch, 5 Apr. 1579. (141)
To John and Geo. FAWBOT my younger son my 2 crofts called Stone Field and Stone Mead (5 acres) which abutteth on Howe Lane on the north, the river on the west, the land late Wm. LEGAT on the south, the residue now Rt. FAWBOT on the east; if both die before lawful age, to Rt. my eldest son. To Geo. STEVENS of Hadley Green [see no.140], my well-beloved in Christ, my 3 crofts called Ivettes at the Green at Howe Lane end, abutting on the land late John LUCING's mortgaged to John PAYNE conditionally that Geo. STEVENS pay him £41. To Rt. my tenement called Cotters with the residue of my land belonging after the decease of Isabel my wife (12 acres), on condition that when he comes of age he make a good assurance to Geo. STEVENS of Ivettes. To Rt. my house called Leases with the said condition at 21. Geo. STEVENS shall be guardian to Rt. and receive the profits of Leases until he is 21. Geo. STEVENS shall pay Mr John LEGAT of Hornchurch Hall 43s.4d. out of the rent of Leases and shall let to farm [i.e. lease] Leases to my wife until Rt. come to age. To my wife all my goods and ready money, to see my children brought up. I make her my executrix. I ordain Geo. STEVENS and Th. COCKE overseers. Witnesses: John COCKE of Brentwood, John CLARKE of Upminster, Th. THOMKYNS, Mich. MEANE. Proved 30 May 1579.

THOMAS LYTMAN of South Weald yeoman, — 1579. (142)
To Joan my wife my house and lands free and copy until Th. my son is 18; then he to have my land in Bades lordship [in South Weald] except 1 barn and a stable. To my daughters Alice and Susan each £20 at 18. The residue of my goods to my wife. To the child that my wife goeth withal, if a son, £20 and a copy croft called Evens Croft at 21, and if a daughter £15 at marriage. To Alice my cupboard in the parlour, Susan my bedsteadle in the parlour, and Th. my table in the hall and meal trough in my boulting house. To my wife my barn and stable next the hallhouse for her life. I make Henry CRAMPE, John FINCHE and Rd. REVE overseers, and for their pains 3s.4d. apiece. Proved 24 Nov. 1579.

ROBERT STELLOMAN of Stow Maries husbandman, 15 Oct. 1579. (143)
To be buried in Stow Maries church or churchyard at my executrix's discretion. To the poor 3s.4d. To some godly preacher of God's Word for his pains in making an exhortation to the people after my decease 5s. To Edw. STELLOMAN my son £10 at 21. To Susan and Anne my daughters each £20 at 20 or marriage. To Joan my wife my land called Skynners (3 acres), a parcel in North Field (7 acres), and a croft called Barn Field (1 acre) towards the bringing up of Edw. till he is 21. To her all my goods. I make her my executrix. I will Edw. GIBSON my father-in-law and Edw. STELLOMAN my brother to be overseers, and for their pains each 3s.4d. Witnesses: Henry SALISBURYE clerk [rector of Creeksea], Rt. BACHELER, John LORAINE. Proved 23 Nov. 1579. Inventory exhibited at £135 18s.

WILLIAM PITTMAN, [abode not given], 28 Sept. 1579. (144)
To be buried in Fobbing churchyard. To Eliz. PITMAN my daughter, besides her grandmother's bequest, a cupboard, 20s., a cow, 4 sheep, 4 pewter platters, 4 pewter dishes not of the best nor of the worst, 1 brass pot, 2 great chests (1 of spruce, 1 of oak), and 1 table and form at PEWSEE's house, at marriage or 20. To Benet PITMAN my daughter my house that I now lie sick in, with the land, at marriage or 18; for want of issue, successively to Joan PITMAN and Eliz.; in the meantime the commodities of the house to the bringing up of Joan my youngest daughter. To John PITMAN my brother my best doublet and hose and bow and arrows. To John FENILL half a lead of cheese. To JOHNSONNE and John SMITH each 20 lb. of cheese. To goodman BURNITT my best shirt, goodman DANITT [DAVITT?] my best coat, and widow COPER 1 featherbed. I forgive mother ALLICE 11d. that she oweth me. All my movables shall be sold by my overseers with the consent of the parson, and distribution to be made to Benet and Joan by even portions. If all my daughters die before the times appointed, all to my brethren by even portions. Clement JAGSONNE shall have Benet and her portion towards her bringing up, and my brother Lawrence PITMAN shall have Joan with her portion with the profit of Benet's house towards the bringing up of Joan for 8 years. I make John HAMAN and John ARNOLL overseers, and for their pains 6s.8d. between them. I make Lawrence and Clement executors. Witnesses: Philip WHITE, John HAMON, Rd. HAMON, Clement JAGSONE, Lawrence PITMAN. Proved 29 Oct. 1579.

THOMAS SPENCER of Woodham Mortimer husbandman, 9 Apr. 1579. (145)
To Joan my wife my customary tenement and 3 crofts of land belonging (6 acres) called Brodheddes in Woodham Mortimer, holden of the manor of Woodham Mortimer, for her life; after her decease, to 'Moyses' SPENCER my son. To my wife my free croft called Katherine Croft (2 acres) in Woodham Mortimer for her life, on condition that she not only redeem it from Mr John BROOKE of Great Baddow by paying him £10 when due but also pay Agnes and Tabitha SPENCER my daughters each £5 at 21. After her death, Katherine Croft to Moses. The residue of my goods to my wife, whom I make executrix, desiring her to see my children virtuously brought up in the fear of God and the knowledge of their duty towards the world. I nominate Rd. BRAINEWOOD of Langford, my wife's father-in-law, overseer, and for his pains 2s.6d. Witnesses: Gilbert WOODWARD, John HARRYSON, John PAYSE, Nich. JOHNSON clerk [rector of Woodham Mortimer]. Proved 23 Nov. 1579.

THOMAS MUNES of Springfield, 6 Sept., 21 Eliz. [1579]. (146)
To the poor people 10s. To the repairing of Springfield church 3s.4d. To Anna my wife my lease of the manor of 'Duckes' [now Dukes, in Springfield] for the term of 18 years, to see my children virtuously brought up; after, she shall deliver the lease to Th. my son; for the better performing hereof, if she marry again, she and her husband shall be bound jointly with sufficient sureties in £200 to Wm. MUNE my brother, Th. CLARKE of Buttsbury and Gabriel BEE of Billericay, my trusty friends, to deliver the lease to Th. To him my tenement in the town of Chelmsford which Wm. HERICH dwelleth in; 20 marks at 21; and my long table, form and painted cloths in the hall when he entereth on the lease. To John MUNE my son £30 at 21 and Kath. and Joan my daughters each 20 marks at 20 or marriage. To my five servants [not named] each 20d. The rest of my goods to my wife, to see my Will fulfilled. I ordain Wm. my brother and Gabriel BEE overseers, and for their pains each 10s. Witnesses: Geo. WOOD, Lawrence ROCHELL, John BREWER. Proved 29 Oct. 1579.

HENRY DOE [DOWE *in margin*] of Fobbing yeoman, 7 Apr. 1579. (147)
To the poor 5s. To Rabage my wife £20 in the hands of Wm. PONDE of Langdon Hills yeoman; 3 heifers of 3 years old, 1 gelding, 1 mare and a colt which were her own in her widowhood, all the household stuff and other furniture belonging to husbandry which remaineth and was her own in her last widowhood; and 20 ewes. She shall have her abode for herself and her two children [not named] in my house called Hofild [now Hovels, in Fobbing] until Michaelmas after my decease, with com-

petent meat and drink, also pasture for her great cattle above rehearsed only. To Roger DOE my son 1 tenement in Fobbing called Walcockes and £20 at 21. To Geo. DOE my youngest son 1 tenement and 4 acres of land in Vange called Filpottes at 21 and £20 at 21. To Mary my daughter, wife of Lawrence KENT, and Joan my daughter, wife of Wm. JEFFERY, each £10 at Christmas after my decease. To Sarah and Clare my daughters each £10 at 21. To Mgy. daughter of Th. KENT and Joan DOONE my servant each 1 ewe or mother sheep of the best. The residue of my goods, my children brought up in the fear of God, to Rd. my eldest son, whom I make executor. I nominate Geo. MUNES of Fobbing and John SANDELL of Basildon overseers, and for their pains 10s. apiece. I will that Rd. shall stand bound to them in £200 for the performance of my Will. Witnesses: John TYLLFORDE, Wm. NORTHEN writer hereof. Proved 10 Apr. 1579.

RICHARD LACKE of East Ham yeoman, 22 Mar., 21 Eliz. [1578/9]. (148)
To Agnes CHAMBER [*recte* CHANLER], my daughter's child, a plain bedstead, an old table, 3 pewter platters, and a red horned cow which her mother gave her. To my daughter Joan's child a pair of towen sheets and to Joan 10s. I will that Alice POWELL widow pay Wm. PATTE my overseer £20 which I should have for ground called Stonynge Donne (5 acres) already delivered by surrender to me by the court roll, also pay Wm. PATTE £5, and Wm. PATTE shall pay the same £5 to my wife. Alice POELL [*recte* POWELL] shall pay the other £15 to Wm. PATTE and 2 quarters of rye for the rent of the said field on which the corn now grows, and my wife shall have the rye. Wm. PATTE shall pay Agnes CHAUNLER the other £15 at 22 or marriage. To the poor of East Ham 10s. The residue of my goods to Christian my well-beloved wife, whom I make executrix. I constitute my well-beloved neighbour Wm. PATTE overseer, and for his pains 5s. Witnesses: Th. MUFFETT, Wm. YOUNGE minister [not the vicar] of East Ham. Proved 7 Oct. 1579.

FRANCIS WOOD of Rayleigh, 9 July 1579. (149)
To Judith my wife all my household stuff (except 2 chests by my bedside), my mare, my brinded cow, and a sow with 4 pigs. To my brother[-in-law] John BARNES all my wearing apparel, saving 1 sheep's coloured coat which I give to John CURRUDERS. To my sister, John BARNE's wife, a crown of gold of 5s. To my two daughters Alice and Mgt. WOOD my house that I dwell in to be equally divided, the said 2 chests, and 4 kine or £4 in money at their choice according to a bond which I have for the kine from John BONER the younger. Whereas Nich. CURRUDERS oweth me 24s., if he will pay 17s. with quietness I forgive him the rest. The rest of my goods to my wife, whom I ordain executrix; she shall dwell in my house till Michaelmas come twelvemonth rent free. I appoint overseers Mr BADOKE and John WARDLY, and for their pains 3s.4d. apiece. Witnesses: Rd. BLACKWELL minister [the clergy list for Rayleigh is deficient at this period] and writer hereof, Geo. HAPKYN. Proved 5 Oct. 1579.

JOHN BROOKE of Bradwell-juxta-Mare yeoman, 20 July 1579. (150)
To be buried in Bradwell church. To the poor of Bradwell £5. To the repairing of Bradwell church 40s. and of Colyton Haven [co, Devon] 2s.6d. To Mary BOND my servant 30s. at marriage and Barnabas BOND my godson 10s. at 21. To John BROOKE my son all my household stuff, as well the cupboard, tables, forms, wainscot, painted cloths, etc. in the hall, also the cupboard, tables, stools and wainscot in the upper parlour. To Rt. my son my best bedstead with the bed, and 2 tables, chest and painted cloths in the great chamber. To Joan BOVER my daughter my bed with the table, stools, bench, chest, wainscot and painted cloths in the lower parlour. All which legacies to my children to remain in my wife's custody for her life. To John my land in Asheldham called Noke and my land in Southminster called Leteland, at Michaelmas 1583. To Rt. my land in Barling and Wakering free and copy in the jurisdiction of the [manor] court of Canewdon, my tenements and customary lands in Lawling and Latchingdon, and my tenement and land called Merywethers in Bradwell, all at Michaelmas 1584. If John shall not suffer Rt. peaceably to have these lands, Rt. shall have my free lands and also my tenement and lands called New Hall and Cookes in Bradwell after the decease of Mary my wife. If she do fell, lop or carry

away any wood or timber from any of the lands bequeathed to John and Rt. before they enter on them, except for reparations about the houses and grounds when need shall require, the owner of the tenement where such default shall be made may enter presently on his lands. The residue of my goods to Mary my wife, whom I ordain executrix. Witnesses: John DEBANKE, John COLEMAN, Rt. WADE. Proved 5 Oct.1579.

RICHARD HULKE of Rayleigh, 30 June 1579. (151)
To my sister Agnes wife of Ezechiel WILLSHEERE 40s. a year during the time of the moiety of my lease called Goldsmithes in Langdon Hills. To my brother John HULKE £5 at 21, Mary daughter of Geo. HULKE £5 at 20, and John her brother £5 at 21. To Sarah daughter of Henry HULKE £6 at 20; if she decease before, to her brother Wm. HULKE. To him a featherbed and a brass pot. To my brother Henry the moiety of my lease of Goldsmithes in his occupation, on condition that he pay all the legacies. I make him executor. Witnesses: Rd. HULKE, Rd. BLACKWELL minister, writer hereof, John HARRISON. Proved 9 Sept. 1579.

JOHN GLOVER of Brentwood blacksmith, 17 Mar. 1577/8. (152)
To be buried in South Weald churchyard. To Joan my wife all my goods. If she be with child, the goods to her child and mine after her decease; if she and the child die, the goods to the children of Joan BOLTON and of 'Dynnes' FULLER, my two daughters, to be equally divided. I make my wife executrix and overseer Th. DANWOOD *alias* BEEN, and for his pains 12d. Witnesses: Th. DANWOOD *alias* BEEN, Rd. SPRINGFEILD, John FULLER, Leonard OXCLYFF. Proved 8 Sept. 1579.

JOHN HAYES of Corringham, 6 May 1579. (153)
To the poor of Corringham 40s. To Th. HAYES my son my leases of Mardens with the store [of cattle] thereon. To Phobe my daughter £100 at 20. To Rd. DREAMER £5. To Susan my daughter-in-law 40s. and every one of her children 20s. To Rd. HEATH my cousin £5 at 21. To Th. the bed in the little loft next the window and the 'leassayer' [lesser?] bed in my chamber, 4 brass pots, 3 kettles, 2 dozen of pewter, 6 pair of sheets, and 2 walnuttree chests. To Susan the standing bed in the maid's [maids'?] chamber. To Th. the cupboard in the hall. To Rt. WRIGHT £5. To every one of my servants 5s. To my sister BAGSHAT 40s. and every one of her children 6s.8d. To John son of John ARNOLD 3 lambs. To goodman ROGER of the Hall [Corringham Hall?] my ring with the seal, John ARNOLD 1 of the rings on my finger and his wife the other ring on the same finger, 2 kerchiefs and 2 neckerchers. To Th. £100 within 10 years after my decease and the stock that I have at Brumfordes [now Bromfords, in Nevendon] when the lease is expired. To Mr AYLEFF a ring worth £3 and his wife a ring worth 40s. for a remembrance. The residue of my goods to John my son. I ordain him and Rt. WRIGHTE my son-in-law executors. Witnesses: Th. REDDRICHE [vicar of Childerditch], John ROGER. Proved 8 Sept. 1579 by John HAYES, Rt. WRIGHTE renouncing executorship.

THOMAS NEWELL of Dunton, 11 Aug., 21 Eliz. [1579]. (154)
To goodwife FRYDAY of Stock 3s.4d. and 1 cloth brown cassock; the two daughters of Wm. SANSOME of Laindon 16d.; Eliz. FYFEILDE of Dunton 12d.; Rt. TAYLOR of Dunton my best blue coat, 1 lockram sheet, and 1 quiver; father FRYDAYE of Stock 1 pair of russet hose; Th. HARDINGE of Dunton 1 lamb; John JOYCE of Dunton my pair of white hose; and James MALBROOKE of Dunton my leather doublet and best pair of russet hose. The residue of my goods with my house in Stock to Mary my daughter at 16; if she decease before, my goods and house shall be equally divided between Wm., Joan and Mary NEWELL, my brother and sisters portion and portion like. I ordain James MALBROOKE executor and Rd. MARSHALL of Preston Oak in South Hanningfield supervisor, and for his pains 3s.4d. Witnesses: Th. MEREDITHE, Rt. TAYLOR. Proved 8 Sept. 1579.

JOHN HARROWER of Hornchurch husbandman, 27 July 1578. (155)
To Th. my son my house with such land as lieth on the same side of the way that the house standeth on and 2 acres of marsh (10 acres in all), at 26 and not before. If he die without heirs male or go about to alienate the title, the house and land

shall come to John my other son. To John my youngest son 2 crofts called Trotters Crofts, Long Pot Field, 2 other crofts called Davies Crofts, Goar Field, and an elm spring adjoining, at 25 and not before. If he die without heirs or go about [as above], the lands shall come to Mary and Joan HARROWER my daughters. To them each £3 6s.8d. at 21 or marriage. To Mgt. my wife, whom I make executrix, until Th. and John fulfil the years, my said houses and lands, conditionally that she pay my legacies and keep my two daughters while she hath my land. I make overseers Mr Wm. LAMBERT vicar of Hornchurch, and Henry HUMFRYE husbandman of the said parish. Witnesses: Henry HUMFREY, Mr Wm. LAMBERT, Geoffrey WAIGHT, Wm. AWGUR. Proved 7 Sept. 1579.

JOHN STONARDE of Purleigh, 11 Jan. 1578/9. **(156)**
To Henry GOLY my brother[-in-law] and Joan GOLY my sister my house and land equally to be divided at Stock. To them 8 sheep likewise. To widow FLYMINGE's boy 1 lamb. To Mgy. GOSSE 1 lamb. I ordain my uncle POLENE of Horley [*recte* Purleigh] executor, and for his pains 1 ram lamb. I give certain wool which I have in my master's house amongst them that take pains with me in this my sickness at the time of my death. Witnesses: John COBERE [*recte* COKERE], Wm. SONE. Proved 22 July 1579.

THOMAS HOCKAM of Brentwood butcher, 22 Mar. 1578/9. **(157)**
To Eliz. my wife my messuage and the buildings belonging and a garden on the backside in Brentwood in the tenure of Rd. COWPER fletcher, for her life; after her decease, to John my son, on condition that he pay my son Matthew £8 after my wife's decease; if John default in payment, to Matthew, paying John £10 at the messuage within a year after such default. To Eliz. daughter of Michael LONDON of Brentwood and Anne LONDON her sister each 20s. at 18; to Sarah LONDON her sister 1 cow or 33s.4d. at 18. To Rt. HOCKAM my son's son 1 cow or 33s.4d. at 18. To Susan POMFRETT my servant 20s. at 20. The rest of my goods to my wife, whom I make executrix. I make overseers Wm. COCKE mercer, and Roger HOLTE shoemaker, both of Brentwood, and for their pains 3s.4d. apiece. Witnesses: Wm. COCKE, Rd. BROOKE. Proved 21 July 1579.

WILLIAM PERYMAN [PERRYMAN *in margin*] of Shenfield husbandman, 1 May 1576. **(158)**
To the poor 3s.4d. To my sons Wm. and Th. each £3 at 24. To my three daughters Martha, Mary and Alice PERRYMAN £3 apiece at £20. To my two youngest sons Stephen and Abraham £3 apiece at 21. To my two eldest sons all my apparel equally divided. The rest of my goods to Agnes my wife, whom I make executrix. I desire my neighbours John CRAMPE and Geo. MANFEILD to be overseers, and for their pains 3s.4d. apiece. Witnesses: Edw. WALKER, curate of Shenfield, John CRAMPE, Geo. MANFEILD, Th. HOWE, Wm. FULLER, John NOTT. Proved 21 July 1579.

WILLIAM ROSSE, [abode not given], 10 July 1579. **(159)**
To be buried in Great Burstead churchyard. To Wm. my son my house that I dwell in and the orchard belonging at 21. To Mgt. my daughter my house that one EDGATT holdeth with the backside and orchard at 18. To my son Wm. my mead called Marsh lying beneath the Mill at 21. I will that my wife [not named] shall have these tenements with the mead to the bringing up of my children. To Wm. a bed and a great chest in the shop. My movables to be equally divided between my wife and two children. To her my cow and my bullock. I ordain her my executrix and Th. FULLER overseer. Witnesses: Timothy OCKLE vicar [of Great Burstead], Th. FULLER, Edgate THRINGE, John TREWE. Proved 21 July 1579.

GEORGE WEBBE of the city of London, 17 Dec. 1578. **(160)**
To my wife and children all my goods according to the custom of London, and whatsoever shall remain of my part, my debts and funerals discharged, to be equally divided among my children. I make my wife Kath. executrix, to see my children

brought up in the fear of God. She shall have my house and land at Stondon [Massey] for her life; after her decease, to my children, Th., Susan the elder, Kath., Mary, Eliz. and Susan the younger, equally between them. Witnesses: Geo. YOUNGE, Wm. YOUNGE, Geo. KYRBIE, Otwell MAYTRENGHAM, Eliz. FARRANDE, Eliz. WHITEHEADE. Proved 21 July 1579.

ROBERT DORE the elder of Cranham, 18 Aug. 1578. (161)
I will have 5 pair of sheets that are at the tile kiln brought to my house called Terkes, 2 tablecloths, a little brass pot, 1 bucking tub, 2 old tubs, 1 good handsome kettle, 3 cushions, half my other wife's wearing linen, 1 long towel and 2 pillowberes also brought, which I will that Eliz. my now wife shall have, also all the goods in my house that I dwell in called Terkes. Witnesses: Th. BRAYNE curate [of Cranham]. [No probate clause.]

ALICE MAWLE of Blackmore widow, 29 Oct. 1575 [*sic*]. (162)
To be buried in the church of St. Lawrence, Blackmore, at my pew where my father and mother [not named] were buried. To Kath. MAWLE my goddaughter my greatest brass cauldron and a pewter platter; to Jane her sister my harness girdle, my brass pan with the broad chines, a brass kettle called a tinker's kettle, a brass posnet, and a pewter platter. To Mgt. GRENE my new cauldron that I am wont to brew with, my black chest in the sollar next the press, 3 pair of the newest flaxen sheets, my best flaxen tablecloth, 4 table napkins, 2 of my best pewter platters standing on my cupboard, a pewter basin, a pewter cornered saucer, 2 of my best pewter platters in my chest, the best bell candlestick, the little candlestick, my best featherbed, the bedsteadle, tester, headcloth, 2 pillows with tassels at the corners, and my saltcellar next the best. To Geo. MAWLLE my cupboard, a brass pot that was his grandfather's [not named], my new chest, and 2 pewter porringers. To Wm. MAWLLE my great 'landed' cow. To Wm. TURKE a brass pot that I bought myself and a pewter platter. To John TURKE my godson 2 sheep. To Alice daughter of Rt. MAWLLE the younger a pair of flaxen sheets. To Geoffrey GRENE a cow in the hands of Rt. MAWLLE. To Th. GIE my godson a pair of flaxen sheets. To Eliz. WALKER my goddaughter a bullock of a year old. To Alice wife of Wm. STANE a mattress and my bail cauldron. To Joan wife of Rd. TURNER my bailed kettle and a pair of sheets. To Alice WALKER a pair of sheets and a posnet of pan brass. The residue of my goods to Alice ROBIONTE and Agnes MAWLLE my daughters, whom I ordain executrices, and Henry FINCHE clerk, vicar of Blackmore overseer, and for his pains 2s.6d. Witnesses: Chris. DALE, John son of Henry FINCHE. Proved 21 July 1579. Inventory exhibited at £45 15s.8d.

JOHN LEGAT of Theydon Garnon yeoman, 28 Mar. 1579. (163)
To the poor men's box 5s. To John my son my house and land, which Gerrard DOWSETT holdeth, at 21. To Anne my wife my land called Lowges, which I bought of my brother Henry LEGATT, for her life; after her decease, to Rd. my son. My wife shall procure Henry to make such further assurance for Lowges as shall be advised by her learned counsel. To John my son £5, my shop gear and my old brown horse, conditionally that he confirm a lease of Wardes land which I have demised by indenture to Chris. my son. To my daughters Anne, Susan and Hester each £10 at 21. My cousin Wm. STACE shall have the letting of Wardes and be accountable to Chris. at 21. The residue of my goods to my wife, whom I ordain executrix, trusting that she will see my children virtuously brought up. I ordain my cousin Wm. STACYE overseer, and for his pains 6s.8d. Witnesses: Rd. COPLANDE, Wm. GORE, Silvester ASHBYE. Proved 20 July 1579.

PETER SUCHE [*recte* SACHE?] of Widford pedder [pedlar], 17 May 1579. (164)
To Henry PALMER parson there 3s.4d. To John BUSSHE, John HEDE and Peter MIDDLETON each 3s.4d. To John SUCHE my son my best blue coat, best gascons [kind of breeches], and all my horse and all that belongeth to them, he to see his mother [not named] kept. To Barnard TYLER my old frize coat, John BUSSHE my black fustian doublet and my canvas gascons, Amy HERDE widow 5s., Eliz. HAWARDE my servant 10s., and Walter HAYDON my godson 12d. The rest of my goods

to Agnes my wife and John, whom I make executors. To the poor of Widford 6s.8d. I make John WAYLETT supervisor, and for his pains 2s. Witnesses: John WAYLETT, John ELYETT, Henry PALMER writer hereof. Proved 2 June 1579.

ROBERT KIMBERLEY of Hornchurch husbandman, 29 May 1579. (165)
To be buried in the chapelyard of St. Edward at Romford in the south side of the yard between the chapel and the wall next the street. To Frs. my son and Kath. my daughter each 1 cow and 1 bullock of a year old and 20s. at 14. If my wife be with child, 5 marks to the child. To my sister Isabel the great brown cow in the Park and 1 bulchin in Rofes Field at Nearles [Nelmes, in Hornchurch?], 1 flitch of bacon, 4 bushels of wheat, 24s. in the hands of Geo. LARDER at Upminster, 8s. in those of Mr [Wm.] WASHER [rector] at Upminster, paying him 2s., and 14 trusses of hay in those of Andrew BARRYTT at Upminster. The rest of my goods to Eliz. my wife, whom I make executrix. I make John SPITTELL overseer, and for his pains 10s. Witnesses: Lewis GOFE, Edw. DOWNCER, John BROKES. Proved 22 June 1579.

NICHOLAS TABOR of Fryerning innholder, 20 Aug. 1578. (166)
To ten of the poorest householders 3s.4d. To Rd. my son £30 16s.8d. and 1 featherbed with all things belonging to be worth in value 40s. at least. To Edw. my son £20 at 22; he shall be put into the custody of Mr Edw. ELIOT of Newland Hall [in Roxwell], his godfather, in whom I repose my trust for bringing him up. To George my son £20, to be in the custody of Th. OFFEN, my brother-in-law of Boreham, to his use. To Eliz. and Mgt. my daughters each £10 at 21 or marriage. To Anne GILDER my daughter 1 cow or 40s. at her election and Joan GILDER my goddaughter 1 black 'howed' [for meaning see p.xvii] heifer of 1 year and the vantage. The residue of my goods to my wife, whom I ordain executrix. I ordain my well-beloved friends Th. DOWNES of Sandon and Th. OFFEN of Boreham my overseers. Witnesses: Anthony BRASIER [rector of Ingatestone], Chris. DALE. Proved 25 June 1579.

RICHARD SMYTHLYE of Burnham, 28 May 1579. (167)
To Martin SAFFOLDE the younger 10s. To Eliz. BUTTLERS 12d. The rest of my goods to Anne my wife, whom I make executrix. Witnesses: John NEWTON, Martin SAFFOLD, Rt. HEWES. 'This will must be made as a will nuncupative.' Proved 3 June 1579.

ALICE THOMSON of East Tilbury widow, 6 Dec. 1578. (168)
To Rt. my son my cupboard, a table and a form, a tablecloth, a bedsteadle, a featherbed, a cauldron, a brass pot, 3 candlesticks, 2 platters, a pewter dish, and a latten chafing dish. To ANDREWES' children, Wm., Th. and John, each 1 of the youngest sheep. To Dinah MARSHALL a sheep. To ANDREW and Rt. my son the rest of my sheep and my cow equally to be divided. The residue of my goods to Matthew ANDREWE my son-in-law, whom I make executor. Witnesses: John FYNCHE vicar, Isaac HATCHE. Proved —1579.

AGNES READE of Burnham widow, 27 Apr. 1579 (169)
To Avice PAGE, my daughter's daughter, my long table and 2 pewter dishes, to be delivered to her father [not named] until she be married. To Agnes PAGE, sister to Avice, 2 pair of sheets and 2 pewter dishes, to be kept to her use likewise. To my daughter Avice my brewing lead or brass and my malt quern. To John READE, my son's son, an iron pot, 3 pieces of pewter, and a white and black coverlet. I forgive Emmanuel PAGE all that he oweth me. The rest of my goods to my daughter Joan, whom I make excutrix. I make goodman OGHAM overseer. Witnesses: John PEEKE senior, John PEEKE junior, Wm. ARTHUR. Proved 3 June 1579.

JOHN BARKER of Great Waltham, 8 Apr. 1579. (170)
To the poor people 6s.8d. To the reparations of Waltham church 6s.8d. To Joan SPENSER my servant £4, 3 milch beasts, 6 sheep, 2 hogs, the best bed in the parlour, 4 pewter platters, 4 pewter saucers, 2 latten candlesticks, a latten mortar, 2 hutches, a saltcellar next the best, a little kettle, a brass pot, and a frying pan, on condition that she remainand dwell with me and Joan my wife for our lives or so long

as we have no other person dwelling with us; otherwise she shall have no legacy. To James son of James BREDGE of Stebbing 13s.4d., and Wm., Henry and Mgt. BREDGE his brothers and sister, each 13s.4d. To Joan SPENSER my servant, on condition aforesaid, half of such corn and grain in the house and on the ground with half the hay left growing on the tenement and lands in my tenure, after our deceases. The residue of my goods to my wife, whom I ordain executrix. I desire my well-beloved friend Rt. WOODHAME to be supervisor, and for his pains 3s.4d. Witnesses: James BREDGE the elder, Rd. EVE, Rt. GRENEFEILD, Ralph SMITHE. Proved 7 May 1579.

JOHN BROWNE of Ingatestone white tawer, 25 Feb. 1578/9. (171)
To Anne my wife one house with the lands called Gardeners and another tenement called Parnells in Little Waltham, for her life. After her decease, Gardeners to Chris. my son, he to pay 'Edie' my daughter 20s. for 10 years, i.e. £10, and Parnells to Joan my daughter for 10 years to let, and after 10 years to be divided between my two daughters [other not named] equally. To Chris. 1 of my beasts and a silver spoon. To my two daughters each a cow at 21. The rest of my goods to my wife, on condition that, if she marry, she give each of my three children £6 13s.4d. and be my executrix. I will that Reynold SMYTHE be overseer, and for his pains 3s.4d. Witnesses: Anthony BRASIER [rector of Ingatestone], Chris. DALE. Proved 7 May 1579

JOHN BECKE of Stapleford Tawney joiner, 24 Jan. 1578/9. (172)
To Th. my son my black mare and 2 young heifers of 2 years, to be in the keeping of his mother [not named], she to have the profit until he is 21, if she keep herself a widow; if she marry, to deliver his portion to my overseer, he to have the putting forth of his stock; if Th. die before, to be divided equally betwixt my two daughters. To my eldest daughter Mgt. 5 nobles and my youngest daughter Julian 4 nobles, each at marriage. I will that my wife keep Th. until he be able to be put forth to service and to get his own living. The residue of my goods to my wife, also my cattle and lease of my house. I make her my executrix. I ordain Wm. NICHOLSON of Stapleford Tawney overseer, desiring him to take pains if so be my wife fail in anything. Witnesses: Wm. CAVELL, Rt. LEVET. Proved 4 May 1579.

AGNES PRESICKE of Stanford[-le-Hope] widow, 21 Mar. 1578/9. (173)
To John PRESICKE my son 1 round table, 1 mattress, 1 coverlet, 2 pair of sheets, a tablecloth, 1 pillow, 1 pillowbere, 1 blanket, and 1 candlestick. To Mary PRESICKE my daughter 1 table, a form, 1 mattress, 1 coverlet, 2 pair of sheets, 1 tablecloth, 1 pillowbere, 6 trenchers, 1 candlestick, 1 chest, and 1 blanket. To Isabel wife of Oliver EDENS my woollen apparel, 1 pair of sheets, and 1 pillowbere. To John 1 chest. I will that all my brass and pewter and certain painted cloths be equally divided between John and Mary. I make John executor. Witnesses: Nich. MASON clerk [the clergy list for this parish is deficient at this period], John SLAWTERFORDE. Proved 5 May 1579.

THOMAS ELKYN of Abbess Roothing husbandman, 21 Sept. 1576. (174)
To Joan born of the body of Joan ESTWICKE 1 cow and 1 old tub price 12d., after my wife's decease. The rest of my goods to Agnes my wife, whom I institute my executrix. Witnesses: Weston EWESE, John WRIGHT, Gilbert PEOBE [PARBE?], John INGLANDE. Proved 17 June 1576 [*sic*].

HENRY NUTTALL of Aveley yeoman, 5 Mar. 1578/9. (175)
To Eliz. my daughter £16 at marriage or 21, 5 silver spoons of the price of 5 nobles, and my lesser goblet or 45s. To my boy Henry NUTTALL £6 13s.4d., and my bedstead and bed in the lower parlour. To the poor of Aveley 20s. I make my well-beloved wife Agnes executrix, to whom I give the residue of my goods. If Eliz. die before 21, as God forbid, or be married, the £16 to remain to the use of the poor of Aveley and the residue of the things to my wife. She shall deliver Henry and the things to my trusty cousin Roger NUTTALL, whom I heartily pray to receive him and his bequest and to bring him up; he shall be bound to my wife and my cousin Charles NUTTALL to pay them to Henry at 21; if he die before age, Roger shall be allowed

for every year that he keep him 20s. and the residue to remain to my daughter. I make Charles overseer, and for his pains 10s. to buy him a ring to wear for my remembrance. Witnesses: Wm. TAYLOR vicar of Aveley, Wilfred LUTIE. To my wife my title of reversion and remainder in the messuage called Corts [now Courts] and the lands belonging in Aveley; if the daughter of Charles and my daughter Eliz. die without heirs, after my wife's death, to Charles [*sic*]. This codicil added in the presence of Wm. TAYLOR, Wilfred LUTIE, John BAYLIE, Rd. KITCHEN. Proved 10 Apr. 1579.

CHRISTOPHER OWTRAM of Barking yeoman, 3 Jan. 1578/9. (176)
To be buried in Barking church or churchyard. To Gillian my wife and Godfrey my son all my goods, to be equally divided. She shall have the education and bringing up of Godfrey and the occupying of his stock until he is 21. I make executors Mr Godfrey FANSHAWE and my wife. I humbly desire Mr Th. POUNSETT gentleman and Andrew FULLER, high constable, my father-in-law, to be overseers. Witnesses: John HORTON, minister of Barking, Mr Godfrey FANSHAWE, Andrew FULLER, John LATHETHAM. 25 Apr. 1579, Geoffrey FANSHAWE appeared and exhibited the Will before Mr Wm. BINGHAM, LL.D., and administration committed 31 Oct. next.

JOHN COWPER of North Weald Bassett, 2 Dec. 1577. (177)
To the poor men's box 4d. To Rd. my son 1 cow, 1 bullock, 1 joined bed, 1 joined chest, 2 hutches, 1 brass pot, 1 little kettle, 2 pewter platters, 1 pewter dish. 1 saucer, 1 salt, the painted cloths that hang from the door to the window about his bed, 1 great bolster, 1 plank to make a table, 2 forms, 11 boards 13 foot apiece, 2 slabs 13 foot apiece; also 40s. at marriage. To Agnes COWPER my daughter 1 cow, 3 hutches, 1 joined bed, 1 great kettle, 1 little kettle, 2 pewter platters, 1 pewter dish, 1 saucer, 1 salt, 1 cupboard, 1 round table, and my best candlestick. The rest of my goods to John, whom I make executor. Witnesses: Ralph FEILDE curate, Lawrence SEARLE. Proved 10 Apr. 1579.

ROBERT BUNDOKE of Ramsden Bellhouse yeoman, 15 Jan. 1578/9. (178)
To the poor people of Ramsden Bellhouse 5s. and of Downham 5s. I will that Mr [Th.] REDREDGE [vicar of Childerditch] make 2 sermons, 1 to be preached at Ramsden, the other at Downham, my executrix to content him for his pains. To my son John and my daughters Eliz., Dthy. and Anne, each 3 kine. To Rt. BUNDOKE my servant 3 kine. To my daughter 'Madyon' wife of Th. WYTTHAM and Rt. and Th. his sons each 1 cow. Th. WYTTHAM my son-in-law shall have 10 acres this year to sow oats on a ground called Downes and the oats in covenant between us to stand void, he to help sow the rest of the corn. To Hum. and Alice HODE each 1 sheep. To my said five children and Rt. my servant 41 sheep equally to be divided. All the kine and sheep to be delivered at the end of my lease of Castlinges. The rest of my goods to my wife, whom I make executrix. Witnesses: John COX clerk [not rector of either parish], Rd. FREMAN, Th. WYTTHAM. Proved 10 Apr. 1579.

JOHN PAPRELL of Prittlewell, 7 Dec. 1578. (179)
To Eliz. my wife my house called Gates *alias* Welbeloved in Prittlewell in the tenure of widow ANDEWE, on condition that she pay my debts; if she will not, my overseers shall sell the house and pay my debts with the money as it will extend and take out of my goods so much as will pay the residue of my debts. To John my son at 21 and Frances and Judith my daughters at 18 each £10. The residue of my goods, my children being brought up by my wife, to her, whom I make executrix. I ordain Mr Nich. MARSHALL and John VINCENT to be overseers, and for their pains each 10s. Witnesses: John HARRYSON, Wm. HODSON, John VINCENT, Th. DUE. Proved 8 Apr. 1579 by Edmund BARKER clerk, vicar of Prittlewell, proctor of Eliz. Inventory exhibited at £61 13s.4d.

NICHOLAS WHITE of Brentwood, 2 Dec. 1580. (180)
To Rose my wife all my goods. I make her my executrix. Witnesses: Th. DANWOODE. Benjamin COLTHERSTE, Rd. DARBIE, Leonard OXCLIFFE. Proved 21 Dec. 1580.

JOAN NEVELL of Rettendon, 24 May 1580. (181)
To Joan ERDLYE 1 covering, 1 brass pot, 1 pillow, 1 pillowbere, and 1 pewter dish. The rest of my goods to be equally divided between my two daughters, i.e. Joan TURELL and Mary TURELL, whom I make executrices. I make Hum. HAIES and Wm. HAIES overseers. [No witnesses.] Proved 25 June 1580.

CYPRIAN JAMES of Hadleigh, 15 Dec. 1580. (182)
To Agnes HARRISON my aunt's daughter of Southchurch 20s. and Mgt. her sister 20s. To John PECHIE my cousin £3, which my father-in-law Th. ANDREWES of Beeleigh Abbey at Maldon oweth me, being gven to me by the Will of my father John JAMES. To Matthew BUNGE of Hadleigh for his pains about me my russet cassock; Mary CHANLER my hat; Mary BARWICKE my silver hooks; goodman FRESE's wife my red petticoat that I bought of her; Eliz. TUNBRIDGE 3 yards of red cloth; goodwife KETTER a lockram kercher. All other things to my master BARWICKE in consideration of such charges as he hath been and shall be in seeing my Will performed. I constitute John PECHIE executor. Witnesses: Joan KETTER, Joan BUNGE, Stephen BARWICKE. Proved 18 Mar. 1580/1.

RICHARD DEANE of Lambourne yeoman, 30 June 1580. (Nuncupative.) (183)
He gave his son Rd. and his daughter Dthy. DEANE each £20; if both die, the £40 to his friends. To Th. GOLDINGE £5 being a legacy from John GOLDINGE his father. To Rt. DEANE his brother £6, whereof £3 3s.4d. being a debt. He willed that whosoever should marry with Dorothy his wife be bound with sufficient surety in £100 to pay his debts and legacies. Witnesses: John REYNOULDE clerk, curate of Lambourne, Lawrence PERSON, Th. CURTESSE. Administration committed, 11 Nov. 1580, to Dthy. the widow.

MARGERY BAILIE of South Ockendon, 10 Jan. 1580/1. (184)
To the poor 2s. To Mgt. BAILIE, my son Rd.'s daughter, 1 half angel, 1 brass pot, 2 platters, 2 pewter dishes, 1 salt, 1 saucer, a pair of flaxen sheets, a flaxen tablecloth, and my least cupboard at 20. To my son John's two daughters, i.e. Martha and Joan, each 10s. in gold. To Agnes my maid my best gown. To my cousins RAMSES my new frize gown and a hat and IVES my brown cloth gown. To Wm. MAYE my man 26s.8d., Rd. WIGGLESWOODE my boy 20s., widow MELLES my old frize gown, goodwife REVELL my 2nd red petticoat, widow HUMFRYE 1 towen sheet, Eliz. my maid 2s., and my cousin IVES my great hat, a cap, a neckercher, and a kerchief. The residue of my goods to John, whom I make executor. Witnesses: John REVELL, Wm. MAYE. To my godchildren 12d. apiece. Proved 15 Mar. [1580/1].

THOMAS SALMON of Doddinghurst, 26 July, 23 Eliz. [1581]. (185)
To be buried in Doddinghurst church or churchyard. To 'Roberge' my wife 100 marks, i.e. 20 nobles within 10 weeks after my decease and the rest within 1 year, on condition that she shall not have or claim above the value of £4 a year of my lands for her life in recompense of her thirds and because my lands be most of them copyhold by reason whereof I cannot charge them with the rent of £4. To Agnes my daughter £40 at marriage or 20. To Th. my son £50 at 21, also £20 to keep him at the school [i.e. university] at Cambridge; my executor shall keep him [t]here at the school these 4 years and pay for his board for the 4 years. To John [struck through] HUYN my son-in-law £20. To Wm. REVE my brother-in-law £8 6s.8d. at 21. To my servants each 2s. To the poor at Doddinghurst 20s. at my burial. To Doddinghurst church 10s. I ordain Wm. my son executor and Henry CRAMPE, Walter GUYE and Wm. REVE overseers, and to each for their pains 20s. Witnesses: Rd. GLASCOCKE, Th. SALMON, Th. MARDEN, Rd. BEAMONT. Proved — Dec. 1580.

WILLIAM RALENES of West Ham reed layer, 30 Jan. 1580/1. (186)
To Agnes RALENES my daughter and Joan CRAIGES my daughter-in-law each 1 standing bedstead and 1 featherbed, 1 brass pot, 2 pewter platters, a brass kettle containing 3 gallons, and 1 latten candlestick. The rest of my movables to Mgt. RALLENES my wife, whom I make executrix. I ordain overseer my trusty friend

Martin BRUESTER, and for his pains 12d. Witnesses: Martin BRUESTER, Miles LEEDES, Rt. HASSELL. Proved 4 Mar. 1580/1.

JOHN KENNETT of Burnham, 13 Dec. 1580. (187)

To Anne my wife my house and lands at Woodham Ferrers called Dawberies and Reynouldes for 14 years; then or after her decease, to John my son. To him £10 at 21. To Anne and Rebecca my two daughters £20 apiece at 21 or marriage. To John PASFEILDE my servant 1 wennel calf. The rest of my goods to my wife, whom I make executrix. I make Mr Wm. KINGE overseer, and for his pains 20s. Witnesses: Hum. KYNWELMARSHE, Benjamin HARRIS, Wm. KINGE. Proved 10 Mar. 1580/1. Inventory exhibited at £58 3s.4d.

EDWARD BRISLEY [BRYSLEY *in margin*], citizen and clothworker of London, 19 Nov., 23 Eliz. [1580]. (188)

I will that my substance shall be divided into three equal parts according to the laudable custom of the city of London, whereof one to my well-beloved wife Grace, one to my children Henry, Jane and Anne BRISLEY equally amongst them, and one to pay my debts and legacies. Henry shall have so much money as shall make up his part to £100 and that according to the custom it be paid at 24. If the portions to Jane and Anne shall not amount to £60 apiece, to be made up to £60 and likewise paid at 21. If all die before their portions become due, I give £160, parcel thereof, to the two Universities of Oxford and Cambridge equally between them and £60 residue to my wife. To Henry my gold ring with the seal and to Henry, Jane and Anne each a mourning garment of the price of 10s. a yard. To my cousin Eliz. GIBSON 40s. To my father-in-law Mr Frs. MICHAELL £5 and my mother [not named], his wife, 20s., to my uncle Henry ISHAM mercer £3 and my aunt, his wife, 20s., to Th. GRAY the elder of London grocer £3 and his wife 20s., and to my sister HARTLEY 20s., to make each a ring for remembrance. To the poor children harboured in Christ's Hospital in London £5. To my wife's brothers John CARLETON 20s. and Frs. MYCHELL my best black cloak with sleeves. To Rt. GIBSON 10s. to buy him a coat cloth. To the poor inhabitants in Epping and 'Garnesey' [Theydon Garnon] £6. To four poor men that shall carry my body to the church 12d. apiece. The rest of my goods to my wife, whom I ordain executrix, and Henry ISHAM and Th. GRAY overseers. Witnesses: Jonas FRINGE scrivener, Rt. GOTHER, James JUYS [INYS?], Wm. GIBBENS. Proved before Rt. KINGE, S.T.P., Commissary of John Bishop of London in the parts of Essex, 8 Mar. 1580/1, by Rt. LYNNE notary public, proctor of Grace.

WILLIAM WOLRYE *alias* HALL of Chignall St. James, 16 Dec. 1580. (Nuncupative.) (189)

To Jane his wife all his goods, if she keep herself unmarried; if she should marry, to pay out of them for the use of his seven children [not named] to John BOWSIE, John WOLRYE *alias* HALLE and Th. WOLRIE *alias* HALLE £20 at 21 and in the meantime to be improved to some increase for their best preferment equally. He named Joan [*sic*] his wife executrix and [the three men] overseers. Witnesses: [the same three]. Proved 18 Jan. 1580/1 by Joan his widow.

THOMAS PECHIE of Doddinghurst husbandman, 27 Jan. 1578/9. (190)

To Parnell my wife a featherbed (the best saving 1), the painted cloths about it, a new kettle, the little posnet, the middle spit, 2 pewter dishes, 2 pewter platters, 1 brazen candlestick (the best saving 1), 1 salt, 1 saucer, all her apparel, half the poultry, a pair of pothangings, a spinning wheel, and £4, and 20 marks towards the bringing up of my two youngest daughters Thomasine and Ellen PECHIE (5 marks yearly for 4 years). To Ellen a joined bedstead, the better brazen pot, the greater of the 2 hutches in the parlour against the west window, a greater platter, a pottinger, a saucer, a flaxen wheel, the half part of a mortar and pestle, a candlestick, and 40s., at 16. To Thomasine a cupboard, the great cauldron, a great platter, a saucer, a pottinger, a brazen candlestick, a hutch in the parlour against the west window, the half part of a mortar and pestle, and 40s. at 16. I will that my wife have the keeping of the said household stuff till they be 16. To Eliz. and Mary PECHIE my daughters 40s. each. To my brother's children [not named] of Dagenham 26s.8d. equally divided at 16. To Geoffrey my son a pewter platter, a hutch in the loft, a trundle bedstead, and a candlestick. To Henry my son a chafer, Th. my son a posnet, and Geo. my son a frying pan. To my daughter's child Th. MOUNT 6s.8d. To the poor people of Doddinghurst 3s.4d. I ordain Wm. and John my sons executors; they shall have all my goods unbequeathed to pay my debts and legacies. I make Geo. BAILIE of Doddinghurst and Th. TOMPKIN of Upminster overseers, and for their pains each 2s. Witnesses: Th. WESTE clerk [not the rector], Th. TOMKIN. Proved 16 Feb. 1580/1.

JOHN COLMAN of Bradwell-juxta-Mare, 3 Nov. 1580. (191)
To be buried in Bradwell church. To Wm. COLMAN of Thorrington all my goods, on condition that he bring up my son John in the fear of God and see that he have meat, drink, cloth and necessaries until he be able to get his living. I ordain Wm. executor, to see John be put to prentice. Witnesses: John COLMAN, John DEBANCKE. Proved 15 Feb. 1580/1.

ANDREW THURE [THAYER/THEIRE *in original Will*] of Little Wakering, 4 Feb., 23 Eliz. [1580/1]. (192)
To the poor inhabitants 3s.4d. apiece at the discretion of my master and our vicar Mr ARCHER. To the four that carry my corpse to church 12d. apiece. The residue of my goods to Joan SAMON and Anne CRAFORDE, daughters of my master and dame. I make them my executrices. I desire my master and Mr ARCHER to be overseers, to see the overplus of my goods equally divided between my executrices at 18 or marriage. Witnesses: John WHAILES, Rd. ARCHER vicar of Little Wakering, Th. GATWARDE, Joan WORMES. Proved 15 Feb. 1580/1.

EDWARD CAMBER of West Tilbury yeoman, 30 Nov. 1580. (193)
To the poor people of West Tilbury 20s. To Mgy. my wife the lease of my farm wherein I dwell, with 12 kine and 60 ewes to be chosen by her and the use and profit of 8 other kine and 40 ewes until Michaelmas next, to be pastured on my farm called Palewicke in West Tilbury without paying anything therefor; also 4 horses, geldings or mares to be likewise chosen from the rest, and all husbandry implements and my corn on the ground and in the barn, with all my household stuff; and £40. To Th. CAMBER my brother £20 and my lands in West Tilbury which I purchased of John CAMBER my brother. To my cousin Rt. BRETTON the younger and my sister GASLINGE £10 each, to Isaac and Isabel her children £5 apiece at 20; Th. FIPPE £10; Avice now the wife of Th. HAMMONDE 40s.; and Alice FIPPE 40s. at 20. To my cousins John GRAYE of South Benfleet and every one of his children severally 40s. and ENGLEFEILD's three children, i.e. John, Wm. and Th. £5 apiece at 20. To Th. CHARVELL my wife's brother £5. To Joan RYVERS and Gabriel PRESSON my servants each 10s. To my sister TOMPSON of London 40s. and both her children, 'Auburoughe' and Judith, 40s. apiece at 20. The residue of my goods, jewels and implements to John my eldest brother to perform my Will, whom I make executor. I ordain Rd. GASLINGE gentleman overseer, and for his pains 40s. Witnesses: James SPRINGE of East Tilbury, John LUCKYN writer hereof. Proved 12 Feb. 1580/1.

THOMAS TAPSTER of Great Wakering marshman, 10 Dec. 1580. (Nuncupative.) (194)
To Joan his wife all his goods, she therewith to bring up his children [not named]. She should have for her life his cottage called Nobles in Great Wakering. He willed her to be executrix. Witnesses: Rd. HODDGE of Little Wakering, John DEANE of Great Wakering, the wife of the said HODGE. Proved 15 Feb. 1580/1.

WILLIAM BLACKMOORE of Buttsbury yeoman, 15 Dec. 1573. (195)
[Religious preamble.] To the poor people of Buttsbury 40s., i.e. 20s. within 14 days before Easter ensuing my decease and 20s. 12 month following. To John ALDREY the younger, Kath. and Mary ALDREY each 20s. To my men and women servants which dwell with me each 6s.8d. To Rd., Wm., Walter and Wm. the younger my son an obligation wherein Rt. STAMMER of Rawreth yeoman is bound to me in £200 about 10 years yet to come [for payment of] £100, to be equally divided at marriage

or 21. To each of my children 2 kine at 21. All to remain in the possession of Kath. my wife until then. The residue of my goods to her to bring up my children to the age of 12. I ordain my cousin Wm. BLACKMOORE of Southminster and John AWDRYE citizen and painter stainer of London executors and Rt. STAMMER and John COOPER citizen and painter stainer of London overseers, and for their pains 20s. apiece. Witnesses: Henry PICKERINGE servant to Rd. DUNKIN scrivener of London, Th. ANDREWE, Frs. OSLANDE, Wm. BLACKMOORE, Rt. GOMERSALL. Proved 20 Jan. 1580/1 by Edw. WILLETT, proctor of John AWDREY. 6 Feb. 1580/1 appeared Wm. BLACKMOORE of Asheldham [*sic*] and renounced executorship. 16 Feb. 1580/1 in the chapel of Brentwood before Wm. BINGHAM appeared John AWDREY and alleged that no goods of the deceased had come to him, and he exhibited the Will and renounced executorship, which at his petition was granted.

NICHOLAS SUDBERYE of Rayleigh, 12 Oct. 1577. (Nuncupative.) (196)
[Entered before,see no.46, no differences.]

THOMAS ADDAMS the elder of West Ham yeoman, 27 Nov. 1580. (197)
To 12 of the poorest people of Stratford Street [in West Ham] 12d. To Maud my wife my freehold lands in Stratford for her life; after her decease, to Th. my eldest son; provided that Th. the younger [son] have his way with horse, cart and carriages through the freehold of Th. my eldest son to his copy[hold], paying him 12s. a year. I will that Th. the eldest have his dwelling in the tenement he now dwelleth in, paying his mother [not named] for her life 6s. a quarter. To my wife my copyhold land that I hold of the manor of West Ham Burnells for her life. To Elizabeth ADDAMES my daughter after my wife's death a little tenement in Stratford next the gate where I dwell. To Th. my youngest son the rest of my copyhold after my wife's death. The rest of my goods to her. I make her my executrix and my trusty friends Th. SPIGHTE and Th. HOUNTE, John HEADLE and Rd. STAYNES overseers. Witnesses: Th. SPIGHTE, John HEDLE, Th. HOUNTE, Miles LEDES. Proved 21 Jan. 1580/1. Inventory exhibited at £36 8s.6d.

RICHARD GRENEBANCKE of Great Stambridge husbandman, 22 Nov. 1580. (198)
[Long religious preamble.] Towards the reparations of Great Stambridge church 10s. To the poor 10s. To Eliz. and Mary GRENEBANCKE my daughters £30 to be equally divided at 21; if both die before, to Eliz. my wife, and because the £30 is in the hands of Rd. PEASE of Ulting I will that he shall pay it to her to their use and she be bound to my overseers for payment at their ages; if she refuse, some other honest and substantial man that will be bound shall have the use, helping her towards their finding and good bringing up during their minority. To Eliz. and Mary each at 21 a brass pot, 1 chest, 2 platters and 2 pewter dishes, and to Eliz. my silver spoon. The residue of my goods to my wife, whom I make executrix. I constitute Rd. RULE, John CASLIN and Th. WRAIGHTE of Great Stambridge overseers, and for their pains 2s.6d. each. Witnesses: Wm. BOADE, Rd. WATERMAN. Proved 18 Jan. 1580/1.

WILLIAM ELEMENTE of Shenfield, 28 May 1579. (199)
To the poor of Shenfield 20s. To Joan daughter of John ELEMENT a little brass pot. To Mary daughter of Th. WIATT the great brass pot. The residue of my goods to John my son and Th. WYATE my son-in-law to be equally divided, they to be executors. I make Geoffrey CLEMENT [probably CLEMENT rather than an error for ELEMENT (Wills of Geoffrey and other CLEMENTS of Doddinghurst, the next parish)], overseer, and for his pains 2s.6d. Witnesses: Geo. BULLIN, Geo. REYNOULDE. Proved [date not given].

JOHN GLASCOCKE of Danbury, 6 Dec. (200)
To Wm. my godson my son Wm.'s son, John GOULDINGE my daughter Agnes' son, John PARKER my daughter Eliz.'s son, and Joan SPIKERNELL my daughter Mgt.'s daughter, each 1 young sheep. To Anthony GLASCOCKE my servant and kinsman 1 young cow and 2 ewe lambs and Mgt. WARDOLL my servant 1 cow bullock of a year and 1 ewe lamb. The residue of my goods to Joan my wife, whom I make executrix. I make Wm. my son overseer, and for his pains 4 bushels of barley. Witnesses: Mich. FOX, John PEASE the writer. Proved 18 Jan. 1580/1.

RICHARD CAMBER of Burnham, 8 July 1580. (201)
To the poor 3s.4d. at my burial to be paid to the collectors of the parish. To Agnes my wife my house wherein I dwell called Billettes. The rest of my goods to my wife, whom I make executrix. I make Wm. ARTHURE clerk [not the vicar] overseer. Witnesses: Rd. MANN, Wm. LYSTE. Proved 18 Jan. 1580/1.

RICHARD THUNDER of Dagenham, 7 Nov. 1580. (202)
To the poor folks of Dagenham 10s. To Geo. PORTER 30s. I forgive my brother John THUNDER 20s. what he doth owe me and give him 20s. more. To my wife's two sons John and Th. GRENE and her two daughters Mary and Joan GRENE 40s. apiece at 21. To eight poor men which shall carry me to the grave 6s. apiece and their dinner. If my wife be with child, my house and lands towards its bringing up to lawful age; if not with child or it fail before lawful age, my house and lands to my wife for 12 years, paying yearly to my sister Mary THUNDER 40s. if then living with my wife, and after the 12 years to my sister; if she default without heirs, to my brother John, on condition that he pay Geo. PORTER 40s. after his [John's] entrance on the lands. The rest of my goods to Eliz. my wife, whom I make executrix. I ordain Th. COOPER and Rd. HAROWER overseers, and 4s. apiece for their pains. Witnesses: David JEFFERAY clerk [the clergy list for this parish is deficient at this period], John SPARROWE, Th. FIDOLE, Lewis GOSSE. Proved 20 Jan. 1580/1.

THOMAS GRAY of Burnham, 5 Dec. 1580. (203)
To Winifred my wife my half part [share] of my hoy called 'Repentance' and my cock called the 'Wenne', with all things belonging to them. To her my household stuff, saving that, if she be with child, she shall give the child £5 at 18. I make her my executrix. Witnesses: Rd. FOXE, Wm. LEPER, Rd. WISEMAN, John KNYFE. Proved 18 Jan. 1580/1.

JOHN QUICKE of Hornchurch yeoman, 13 Dec. 1580. (204)
To Hornchurch church 3s.4d. To the poor people 30s. To Mgt. CLARKE of Hornchurch widow and John and Rd. CLARKE her sons 20s. apiece; the children of Th. GIBBES of Stapleford Abbots 30s. to be equally divided; John COPPEROUS the elder of Loughton 20s., his children 30s. among them, Wm. COPPEROUS of Woodford 10s., and Henry MOUNDAIE of Edmonton [co. Middlesex] 20s. To Henry MOUNDAIE my servant 1 cow, 2 sheep and 5s., Alice HOMES of Limehouse [co. Middlesex] widow 20s.; Joan USSHARE of Stifford 10s.; Rt. CLARKE my servant my doe's leather doublet, a sheep, and a leather jerkin; Agnes daughter of James BUSSHE a sheep; and Joan STANLOWE of Dagenham 20s. To my godchildren 12d. apiece. To Geoffrey WRIGHT, Ralph WRIGHT and widow BAWDEN each a bushel of rye, and their children 12d. apiece. To Th. QUICKE my son all my lands and tenements [no details]. My will is that James TURCKE of Stapleford Tawney be guardian and governor of Th. until he is 21, bringing him up in learning to write and read and to some other good exercise and making him a true account at 21, and for his pains 26s.8d. To my son 1 joined cupboard in the parlour, 1 folding table, 1 great spit, and my greatest brass pot. The rest of my goods to Mary and Susan my daughters to be equally divided betwixt them; if Susan die before 18, to Mary. My will is that a sermon be made at my burial and that Mr LEAFEILDE, if he can be gotten, do make it and have 5s. To Th. a great ship chest and 2 other chests. I ordain Mary and Susan QUICKE executrices. I add to them to be overseers James TURCKE, John SKELE and Rd. HARROWARE, and for their pains 13s.4d. apiece. Witnesses: Hum. PEACOCKE, Rd. HARROWARE, Geoffrey WRIGHT, John HODGESON writer hereof. Proved 20 Jan. 1580/1 by Mary QUICKE; power reserved to the other executrix when she shall come; administration committed to James TURKE during the minority of Susan. Inventory exhibited at £120 8s.4d.

MARTIN TREDSALL of Bradwell-juxta-Mare mariner, 2 Feb. 1579/80. (205)
To the poor 10s. To Joan my wife my house and term of years in my tenement called Starlinges by North and Tomsons Croft; 4 of my beasts and 8 sheep; and half of my household stuff. To Mgt. my daughter £8 at 18; if she die before, to my children's children; also to her a joined chest in the parlour. To Bridget [my daughter

omitted?] £6 13s.4d. To John my son 2 angels. The residue of my goods to Timothy my son, whom I ordain executor. Witnesses: John COLMAN, Rt. WADE. Proved 2 Apr. 1580.

THOMAS CHAPMAN of Danbury, 13 Nov. 1580. (206)
To John my son £10, my bed in the parlour and my little brass pot at 23 or marriage. To Joan my daughter my joined bedstead in the loft and the bed, my best brass pot, and £10 at 21 or marriage. The residue of my goods to Joan my wife, whom I make executrix. I make John ALLEN overseer, and for his pains 5s. Witnesses: Edw. PAYNE, Wm. BOVAR. Proved 19 Dec. 1580.

EDWARD COTTRELL of Rochford yeoman, 20 March 1579/80. (207)
To be buried in Rochford church. To my mother Joan COTTRELL of Sutton Coldfield (co. Warwick) widow £8. To my brother Th. COTTRELL £3, his son Nich. 20s., and my brother Hum. £10 which Wm. BACON of Great Leighs oweth me, not molesting him before his day of payment, All Saints next. To Wm. BACON 13s.4d. which he oweth me, he to pay the poor of Little Leighs 8s. To my brother Raphael COTTRELL £4. To David CLONNER all reckonings betwixt us. To Mistress ALLINGTON 1 cow in the custody of Wm. BACON. To John WALPOLE, clerk of my Lord's [Rt. 2nd LORD RICH] kitchen, 1 bullock in the same custody. To Mistress Frances RICHE, my Lord's daughter, my silver spoon in my purse. To Wm. BLYTHE, Philip PURKAS, John NASHE, Rt. BOROWE, Th. CLOUGHE, Th. LORDE, John MODYE, Rt. PARE, Susan MARSHE, Jane Mistress RICHE's maid, and Mgy. each 2s. [probably LORD RICH's servants]. To the yeoman [superior servant] for taking pains with me in my sickness 6s.8d. To my godchildren Edw. LORDE and Alice ENOWES 6s.8d. each. To Mr [probably Wm.] BOURNE, my Lord's steward, my 2 great dripping pans. The residue of my goods to my brother Rd. COTTRELL, whom I ordain executor. I will that John WALPOLE be overseer. Witnesses: John SANDFORD, Frs. COOKE, John WALPOOLE. Proved 21 May 1580.

NICHOLAS HOLMAN of Noak Hill in [Romford in the parish of] Hornchurch, tanner, 4 Oct. 1580. (208)
To be buried in the chapelyard of St. Edward at Romford. To my well-beloved wife Agnes 4 kine, a cauldron, 1 featherbed, 2 woolbeds, 1 bearing sheet, 2 bedsteads, 2 kettles, 1 brass pot, $\frac{1}{2}$ dozen pewter platters, 1 latten candlestick, 1 dripping pan, 1 gridiron, a frying pan, 1 pewter pottinger, 3 chests (2 with lids, 1 without), a little table, 2 hand towels, 2 tablecloths, 1 long towel, 1 long other fine towel, 2 table napkins, and 3 pillowberes. To four of my sons, i.e. John, Rd., Th. and Anthony, and their heirs male or female, Barn Croft and the houses there standing at Noak Hill, to be equally divided at 21; my wife shall have them towards the bringing up of my children till they are 21; if all die before, to the next of their kindred, male or female. To each £5 at 21. To John, Rd. and Th. each a cow; to Anthony a grisled colt; all at 14. To Stephen my son all my stock of the trade of a tanner, on condition that he pay therefor 20 marks to my wife towards bringing up my said four other children. To my wife and Stephen the lease of my house wherein I dwell for the term not yet expired equally between them. To Anne HOLMAN my daughter £6. To three of my daughter BARNES' children, i.e. Th., Agnes and Eliz., 20s. apiece at 21, Agnes to have their parts to her use. To my wife my grisled mare. To my children each 1 pewter platter and 1 pewter dish, 1 pair of sheets, 1 kettle, and a chest, Rd. to have the yellow chest. The residue of my goods to Stephen, whom I make executor, Th. my brother and my wife to see my Will executed. Witnesses: John COMPORTE, Th. HOLMAN. Proved 26 Nov. 1580.

JOHN HAYES of Rettendon yeoman, 8 May 1580. (209)
To my sisters Eliz. HAYES and Hester HAYES my messuage called Goodwynes in Rettendon, with the lands, meadows, woods, feedings and pasture free and copy belonging, in the tenure of RAWLINS, to be sold to their behoof, except a croft (1 acre), one head abutting on the east on Goodwynes, one head abutting on a tenement called Hoddes on the west and south, the other head abutting on Rettendon Common on the north, which I give to Anne wife of Wm. DURRANT. I appoint Th.

HASTLER and Wm. FULLER executors to sell the premises, the money equally between them at marriage; if both die before, all to my brother Th. HAYES. To Rd. RAYSON's children 10s. amongst them. To ten poor householders in Rettendon 4d. apiece. To my godsons Edw. HAYES 20s. in gold and my saddle and John LOLLY 10s. To a preacher for 3 sermons 20s., the 1st at the day of my burial. To John FAWKENER, Rd. HUMFRYE, Rt. HUMFRYE, Wm. HUMFRYE, Th. WOORTHAM, Rd. KITRIDGE, John ANDERKYN, Alice HILS, Mgt. HARRIS and Edw. DURRIVALL, all servants to Mr CANNON, 10s. apiece. To John FAWKENER my gun and John ANDERTON [*sic*] my stone bow. To goodman MEADE and his wife 40s. apiece, Ellen BUCKBERD my goddaughter 13s.4d., Th. HAIES' wife 6s.8d., Rd. WALLIS a 20s. piece in gold, Edw. HASTLER 10s., John ELY my plain fustian doublet and my buff leather hose, goodman MEADE my cloak, and widow RAWLINS the 40s. due to me in her hands and 3 old trees. The residue of my goods to my executors. Witnesses: John BIRD, John LOLLYE. Proved 11 Aug. 1580.

JOHN BRIDGEMAN of Bradwell-juxta-Mare husbandman, 15 May 1580. (210)
To the poor 13s.4d. To John and Henry my sons at 21 each £13 6s.8d. and Eliz. my daughter at 21 or marriage £10. The residue of my goods to Thomasine my wife, whom I ordain executrix. Witnesses: John COLMAN, Rt. WADE. Proved 10 June 1580.

WILLIAM SOAN of Hornchurch husbandman, 20 July 1579. (211)
To Wm. my son Horse Croft (½ acre) in Havering Marsh in the Hassock and his heirs male, paying 1d. quitrent at my house in 'Hakeford' [now Hacton, in Upminster] called Warders, which I will to my executors and overseers to let on Wm.'s behalf and paid to him at 21. If he die without heirs male, the money to be divided equally to my two daughters, but the land to come to Samuel my eldest son and his heirs male; for default of such issue, to my two daughters for life and after to the next of kin. My meadow called Leye Brook and 2 parcels of ground called Want Fields shall be let until Samuel is 24 to the payment of my debts and the overplus to my two daughters. To Cecily my wife for her life my house in 'Hackfield' with the buildings, backsides, gardens, orchards and 3 or 4 closes behind it called the Orchard and Home Field (5 acres), with 3 other parcels called Man Field, More and Downe, conditionally that she maintain and repair all housing, pale, hedges, ditches and other enclosures; after her decease, to be let to pay my debts. I make my wife executrix. To her the rest of my goods, except the bench boards, all shelves, planks, an old counter table, my greatest brass pot sometime my father's, my quern, my furnace [oven], a salting and kneading trough with the covers, 1 bedstead, curtains, tester and painted cloths hanging in the hall which were my father's, 1 pair of pot-hangers, pothooks, and my still with the cover, all which are reserved and I give to Samuel, not to be removed but the use of them to my wife for her life, conditionally that she leave them in good state. I make overseers John SKEALE of Wyebridge [in Hornchurch], John BAYLIE my brother-in-law, and Wm. AUGUR, and for their pains 20d. apiece. Witness: Wm. LAMBERT vicar of Hornchurch. Proved 18 May 1580.

JOHN HILL of Lambourne husbandman, 9 May 1580. (212)
[Religious preamble.] To Frs. SYCER of Chigwell my green coat and his son John, my godson, 2s.6d.; Th. son of Wm. GILMAN of Lambourne and Kath. CLARKE my servant each a bullock of 1 year; and Eliz. now wife of Andrew JENNYNGES of Dagenham 2 bullocks or young kine of 1 year and £4, but if she die before she receives them, to Adam son of Rd. HILL of Chigwell. The residue of my goods to Mgy. my wife. I make her my executrix and my brother Adam HILL overseer, and for his pains 3s.4d. Witnesses: John RAYNOLDES clerk, curate of Lambourne, Th. SPYCER, Roger PICKMAN, Henry PITCHE, Th. BURLES. Proved 11 June 1580. Inventory exhibited at £42 4s. 10d.

THOMAS LUKIN of Great Baddow yeoman, 5 Apr. 1578. (213)
To be buried in Great Baddow church or churchyard. To my sisters Joan BARNARDE, 'Dennys' BARDEN, Mgt. OFFYN, Kath. STANES and Mary RENOLDE each £20. To my cousins Edm. KINGE, John KINGE and Priscilla PORTRICE each £10. To Frances

HIGGONS, Alice DINGLEY, Mgt. BACON and Mary BUNTTINGE each 10s. To my aunt KINGE of Baddow 30s. To Katherin KINGE my cousin £5. Whereas my brother BARNARDE hath been at divers great charges with me as well for my keeping as for money lent and other reckonings between me, him and my cousin John LUKINGE, I will that he be allowed all his charges and be discharged of bonds undertaken on my behalf. To the poor people of Great Baddow, Roxwell, Chelmsford and Writtle, each [parish] 40s. To John and Grace, my sister Eleanor CLARKE's children, each £5 at 21. To Wm. BARNARDE, my sister's son, £10 at 21. To Jonas CARSEY £10 at 21. To Ellis GARROLDE, my cousin KINGE's servant, 3s.4d., my cousin Abraham KINGE 10s., and his wife 10s. To John PEACHIE and Agnes PEACHIE each 10s. I ordain my brother Henry LUKIN executor, to whom I leave all my lands and tenements [no details]. Witnesses: John LUKYN, John PEASE, Rt. STURGEON, John BETT, Ambrose HALSOE, Th. DAVIE. Not proved, because the executor renounced executorship and administration.

WILLIAM COLYN of [South] Weald, 20 March, 'one thowsande fyve hundred fiftie and five'. (214)

To Joan my wife all my household stuff, goods and cattle on my farm in which I dwell in Weald. To my sister BROWNE's five children [not named] each 20s. after the death of my mother Agnes. To Rt. BRIGHTE's four children each 20s. To my brother John's eldest son [not named] 20s. To 20 poor households in this parish 20s. To every godchild 4d. To my wife £3 after my mother's death. To Mgt. WALLER, my wife's daughter, 20s. To Christian LAKES and Wm. BELL each 6s.8d. To Edw. COLYN my brother my messuage with the lands called Goodales, another messuage with 3 crofts, and Little Croft in Beauchamp Roothing, conditionally that he discharge my legacies and debts; if he do not pay them, my lands in Beauchamp Roothing to John PAYNE of Crowes [now Crow Green, in South Weald] with the like condition. All other my goods to Edw. COLYN and John PAINE, whom I make executors; overseer I make Roger POWLE; and to each 6s.8d. I owe Wm. WALLER £12, which is a stock of Hum. WALLER, to be paid. I owe Edw. £14, my sister IVES £3, and John POWLE 7s.3d. Witnesses: Henry COTON, Chris. MOORE curate, Wm. WALLER, John MAYNE. Proved 11 June 1580.

LEONARD BRAKETT of Dagenham husbandman, 11 May 1580. (215)

To my daughter Joan 6 sheep, 2 red kine, 2 silver spoons, and 1 brass pot which was her granddame's [not named] at 18. I owe Th. BRAKETT my brother 4 calf skins. The residue of my goods to Joan my wife, whom I make executrix. I appoint my friend Rd. BROWNE overseer, and for his pains 20d. Witnesses: Rd. BROWNE, Rd. HUMFRYE. Proved 11 June 1580. Inventory exhibited at £30 6s.8d.

RICHARD NOBLE of Rochford yeoman, 26 Feb. 1579/80. (216)

To Joan my wife my tenement in Rochford with the garden, which WYMAN the glazier now dwelleth in, for her life; after her decease, to Martha and Mgy. my daughters to be divided equally as they shall think good. To my wife the little table in the parlour, the form and the chest at my bedside with the featherbed, all my linen (4 pair of the best sheets excepted), all such goods as she brought me [at our marriage], and £4. She shall have my house that I dwell in and the occupying of my household stuff for a $\frac{1}{4}$ year after my decease (my brewing kettle and tubs excepted, which my daughter Mary shall have to sell to pay my debts). To Susan my daughter my featherbed in the star chamber with the bedsteadle. To Mgy. the bed in the chamber at the stairs head with the bedsteadle. To Eliz. my daughter a wool bed. To my daughter LORDE the featherbed in the great bedstead over the buttery with the bedsteadle. To Mary the joined bedsteadle in the chamber over the hall, the featherbed, and the table and the form in the star chamber. To Mary, Susan, Mgy. and Martha each a table. To Eliz. my copyhold that Rd. DAMARKIN now possesseth with a little parcel of ground on the south end of the house, with a several 'buttle' [separate abuttal] and band as the bank goeth. To my daughter LORDE a long copper kettle. All my brass and pewter shall be divided among my four daughters equally, viz. Mary, Mgy., Susan and Martha. To my wife all my firewood and a sow. To Mary the house that I dwell in, with the croft and garden, on condition that she shall pay her sisters £5 apiece. The residue of my goods to Mary, whom I ordain executrix, and supervisor I make Nich. BRADWER [*recte* BRODWATER] of Eastwood, and for his pains 10s. To my wife my russet gown and so much board as shall serve to sollar the house that WYMAN the glazier dwelleth in. To Temperance LORDE my daughter the trundle bedstead in the long chamber, and her children 3s.4d. each. To the poor of Rochford 2s.6d. Witnesses: Wm. WOODE, John KNIFE, John MEEKE, John BERIMAN parson there. Proved 23 May 1580.

DOROTHY BOYLAND of Woodham Walter widow, 2 May 1580. (Nuncupative.) (217)
Being on the point of death. I give to the little child Th. ALBERTE, my eldest son's son, £6, whereof £4 is in the hands of John OFFYN the elder and 40s. in those of John FLETCHER of Woodham Walter. To Th. a bed, a brass pot, a kettle, my best cow, a bushel of corn in the house, and 6s.8d. I will that John EASTWOODE shall have his bringing up to 21, setting him to school and teaching him his occupation of a tailor and also the said goods and the £6 to his own use, and he shall enter into bond for the payment. To John ALBERT my youngest son a cupboard next the best, a brass pot, my best great kettle, a cow, a bullock, a hog, a sheep, a lamb, 1 silver spoon, and a bed. To Rose my daughter a sheep, a tub, and a cow. To Joan SUERSBYE 1 of my coats and my wheel and my cards. To Amy BOYLAND a coat and Ellen BOYLAND a brass posnet. The residue of my goods to John my eldest son, whom I ordain executor. I constitute Th. BOYLAND my overseer, and for his pains 3s.4d. Witnesses: John ESTWOOD tailor, Th. BOYLAND of Woodham Walter husbandman. [No probate clause.]

MARGERY DARBY of Romford widow, 29 Apr. 1580. (218)
To Nich. COMPORT my godson 1 down bed and Th. his brother 1 featherbed. To John RICHARDSON my kinsman a pair of coarse sheets. The residue of my goods to Agnes COMPORT my daughter. I ordain John COMPORT my daughter's husband executrix. Witness: John RICHARDSON. Proved 18 May 1580.

THOMAS RAWLINS the elder of Stock brickmaker, 9 Apr. 1580. (219)
To Eliz. my wife 2 beasts, 2 bullocks and a mare, only for the education and bringing up of my two sons Rt. and John RAWLINS. To Rt. and John at 21 a brass pot and a kettle each. The rest of my goods to my wife, on condition that she shall bring up my other three children [not named]. I make her my executrix and overseer John TABER my neighbour. Witnesses: Edward KENNETT, clerk and curate of Stock, John TABER, John CROSELEY, Amy TABER, Ellen PINCHINE. Proved 19 May 1580.

JOHN BRETT of Ramsden Bellhouse yeoman, 22 March 1579/80. (220)
To Eliz. my wife and John my son the tenement wherein I dwell by the licence of the lord [of the manor], with all the goods, equally to be divided betwixt them. To John the lease of my farm called Castelinges [now Castledon]. To Wm. my son 3 kine, 22 sheep, and 1 mare (12 of the sheep and 1 cow being at farm to Rt. ELLIS of White Notley, 10 sheep at farm with John STRANGE of Terling, 1 cow with Rt. PAYNE of Braintree, and the other with John MARKES of Terling Street). To Rt. my son £13 6s.8d. to be paid to him by 'Chrispian' NORRIS of Terling at 22. To Alice my daughter £40 to be paid likewise at 22. To poor households in Ramsden Bellhouse 3s.4d. to be paid by the collectors. To my four children my household stuff equally divided. To 'Chrispian' NORRIS money owing to me, with the corn on the ground and in the barn at my house and that which is betwixt us to pay my children before bequeathed, trusting that he will be good to them. To Rt. a dowry of 20s. a year for the life of Wm. BRETT's wife. To Rt. a little tenement called Marchantes in Terling after my wife's decease. I make her and John executors and 'Chrispian' overseer. Witnesses: Rt. BOOTHE clerk [rector of Ramsden Bellhouse], Rd. FREEMAN, John PEVERELL, Rt. HAWKIN, Rd. BRETT. Proved 19 May 1580.

NICHOLAS PERRYN of South Fambridge mariner, 28 Nov. 1580. (221)
To my daughters Mary and Eliz. at 18 and my son John at 21 each £6 13s.4d. To John and Rt. DOWEMAN each 20s. To John DOWMAN my best jerkin and best breeches and Benjamin DOWMAN the rest of my apparel. To Helen my wife my

customary tenement called Bacons in Burnham for her life; after her decease, to John; for want of issue, to Mary and Eliz. To my uncle John PERRYN of Rayleigh 6s.8d. To Prudence my servant a black sheep. To four persons that shall carry my body to the church 2s. The residue of my goods to my wife, whom I constitute executrix, to see my children well brought up in the fear of God. I appoint Nathaniel CAWSTON of Canewdon supervisor, and for his pains 40s. Witnesses: Rt. DOWMAN, Nathaniel CAWSTON writer hereof. Proved 19 Dec. 1580.

RICHARD PARIS of Dagenham labourer, —, 10 Eliz. [1580]. **(222)**
To Mary my wife the lease and term of years of my house wherein I dwell, which I had of my master, Geo. SCOTT of Chigwell esquire; after her decease, the residue of the years if she live so long to my two sons John and Wm. equally divided. To John 5 of my best ewes, put out to his best benefit, and 40s. at 21. To Wm. 40s. at 21. To Wm. PARIS my brother 2 ewes and all my wearing apparel, i.e. coats, hosen, doublets, shoes, boots, and 1 shirt. To my old master, Mr Geo. SCOTT of Chigwell, and Mr Wm. and Mr Rt. SCOTT his sons, each half a crown of gold for a token and remembrance of me. If my wife marry, he with whom she intendeth to marry shall be bound with surety in £10 to my overseers to perform my Will. The residue of my goods to my wife, whom I make executrix, and I hope she will be good and loving mother to my two sons and see them brought up in the fear of God and be a careful mother for them to the uttermost of her power. I make overseer Wm. SCOTT of Chigwell and Rt. SCOTT of Hornchurch gentlemen. Witnesses: Wm. SCOTT, Rt. SCOTT, John HOTHERSOLLE *alias* GILBERD, Lewis GOFFE, Rd. SMITH. Proved 18 May 1580.

RICHARD SANDELL the elder of Stanford-le-Hope yeoman, 26 Mar. 1580. **(223)**
To the poor 3s.4d. To the reparations of Stanford church 2s. To Ellen my wife all my goods. I will her to bring up my children Rd. and Th. to school to learn to write, read and cast accounts and to place them with some honest men to learn some good art or science whereby to get their living another day. My wife shall take up my debts to instruct them withal, pay my debts, and give meat, drink, lodging and raiment to Rd. and Th. until they can write, read and cast accounts, as shall be best for her conscience. To her all my lands and tenements freehold and copyhold for 11 years after my decease, on condition that she pay Th., Rd. and Joan SANDELL my children £50, i.e. £20 each to Joan at 21 or marriage, Rd. £10 at 21, and Th. £20 at 21, 40s. to be received for his use by my cousin John SANDELL. I ordain my wife executrix. My intent is to choose for my overseers my brother Rt. TAYLOR and Henry EGLESTON to see my Will performed without fraud or guile. Witnesses: Rd. JOHNSON minister [the clergy list for Stanford-le-Hope is deficient at this period], Henry EGLESTON, Wm. ROGER, John RATTELL. [No probate clause.]

MARGARET BARBOR of Stock widow, 27 Mar. 1580. **(224)**
To Rt. BARBOR my eldest son a mattress, a bolster and a covering, and a gallon brass posnet. To Th. BARBAR my 2nd son 20s. with a great hutch. To my daughters Joan and Dthy. BARBOR the residue of my household stuff between them part and part like. To Dthy. a cow which I have at Romball TAVENER's with the profits at 20, to be delivered by Rd. BATTISSONE my neighbour, whom I make executor, he to have the placing of my children. I make Rt. BARBOR my eldest son overseer. Witnesses: Edw. KENNET clerk, curate of Stock, Lettice HARVIE, widow CHOPINGE. Proved 18 Apr. 1580.

JOHN MEDOWES of Wickford husbandman, 9 Feb. 1579/80. (Nuncupative.) **(225)**
To the reparations of Wickford church 5s. To the poor 10s. To goodman SMITHE 10s. I forgive my cousin SMITH £10 which he oweth me. The rest of my goods shall be divided into three parts, to Joan my wife and Ellen and Judith my daughters. Witnesses: John TAYLOR parson [of Wickford], Wm. CLARKE, Wm. SMITH. Proved in the Prerogative Court of Canterbury, administration committed to the widow.

RALPH GYBBINS [GIBBINS *in margin*] of Barking labourer, 29 Mar. 1580. (226)
To Rd. LYNLEY of the town of Barking all my goods, he to have the bringing up of my daughter Mgt. GIBBINS in the fear of God until lawful age, at which time he to have the bestowing of her at his discretion. To him 46s. which my brother-in-law David INGRAM oweth me; for default of payment Rd. shall recover it by law. I make him executor. Witnesses: John WILKENSON, Wm. GIBSON, Morrice ap HEWE. Proved 20 Apr. 1580.

JOHN SEABROWE of Little Wakering mariner, 18 Nov. 1580. (227)
To the poor people, my neighbours, in Little Wakering 20s. To John NOBLE one half of my ketch or vessel called 'John' with half the tackling and apparel, on condition that he pay within 3 years after my decease £10 to John GATES and Joan my wife. To Edw. SEBROWE my brother £6 13s.4d. if he shall demand the same. My executors yearly during the years which I have yet to come in the tenement and lands I hold of my bargain from widow CHALLIS shall pay Edw. for the better relief of him, his poor wife and children, 1 seam of such corn and grain as shall be sown on the same grounds, if demanded by him or his wife. To Edw. his son £3 6s.8d. at 21; if he die before, to Priscilla SEABROWE his sister at 21 or marriage. My wife for her life shall have the use of the half part of the ketch called the 'Jonas' now to her belonging, with the profit that can be made, she bearing half of the reparations. To John GATES, in satisfaction of his part and half of a skey called the 'Swallow', one half part of my skey or dredging cock called the 'James' with half her tackling and apparel. The other half of the 'James' to my wife, together with my skey or dredging cock called the 'Prudence' to be kept with all reparations. To her and John GATES my half lease which I took with John COCKE of the Bailiffs, Burgesses and Commonalty of Maldon of certain fishing ground in the Liberty of the Town and Borough of Maldon, with the years yet to come; if she die before they be expired, the half to Wm. GATES. To him one half part of the 'Jonas', after her death. To her all my oysters which are now on all my laynes, to be taken up and carried by her before Easter Day next to her own use. All other my goods to her and John GATES, and £10 to be paid to Rachel GATES at marriage or 21. I make John and my wife executors and my very loving friend Wm. COLLEN supervisor, and for his pains 10s. Witnesses: Wm. COLLEN, Th. GATES, John PRESTON. Proved 19 Dec. 1580.

ROGER GROMWELL of Rochford shoemaker, 23 Nov. 1580. (228)
To Th. POWELL my son-in-law my house that I dwell in, to occupy it freely until his son Roger is 21, then to Roger. To him my best bed, a fir chest, the best cupboard, 9 pewter dishes, a holland cupboard cloth, the table and 1 pair of trestles, 1 form, and all the stained cloths in the house; also my stock of leather and shoes. To the poorest people of Rochford 3s.4d. To Roger my greatest brass kettle. All other my goods to Roger's son [not named]. To Th. POWELL my greatest wire kettle and my debts and money. I ordain him executor. Witnesses: Th. SKOTT, Edm. KILBY, Th. SELLAN. Proved 19 Dec. 1580.

WILLIAM GARDENER of Hornchurch husbandman, 13 Nov. 1580. (229)
To my son Wm. my white mare. The rest of my goods to Eliz. my wife, whom I ordain executrix. Witnesses: Th. HAYES, John BAKER, Th. NOKES, Rd. EVENT. Proved 26 Nov. 1580. Inventory exhibited at £3 16s.2d.

MARGARET PAINTER of Great Ilford in the parish of Barking widow, 17 Nov., 23 Eliz. [1580]. (230)
To goodwife TUTTELL's maid 1 neckercher. To my goddaughter Susan WOOD a fine sheet. The residue of my goods to Hugh EDWARDES, whom I make my executor. Witnesses: Mistress FANSHAWE, Mgt. TAVERNER, Barnard WHITHEADE, NICHOLAS's wife, mother FOSTER, Eliz. WOOD, goodwife STODDERD. Proved 17 Dec. 1580.

JOHN DRAPER of Rettendon husbandman, 6 Nov. 1580. (231)
To John CAMPER the 40s. which he oweth me, 10 of my best sheep, and my best suit of apparel. To my sister Anne CAMPER all my implements of household and to

Joan and Anne CAMPER, my sister's daughters, each £5 at 20 or marriage. To my cousin Th. HOLDER 20s. at 21. To Joan PAVETT and Joan TYBBELL each 10s. at 20 or marriage. To my uncle Wm. PAVETT 10s. and my aunts HOLDER and COOK each 3s.4d. To the poor of Rettendon 5s. To some honest preacher to make a sermon in Rettendon church 3s.4d. The rest of my goods to Th. BONE my father-in-law, whom I make executor. Witnesses: Rt. BUCKBERD parson of Rettendon, 'Radoffe' GOULER. Proved 24 Nov. 1580.

JOHN LANGFORD of South Ockendon, [no date]. (Nuncupative.) **(232)**
Divers times within this 12 months and lastly a little before his death before sundry witnesses, as namely MORGANE's wife, [blank] BEAMONT, FOSTER's wife, Mr SAMPSON and Mr BADBYE, he confessed that, at what time soever it pleased God to call him and his wife [not named], Henry PATRICKE his cousin and his two children should have all such goods as they left, for (quoth he) he is all the comfort and help that I have, being always ready to help me at my need. [No probate clause; see no.242.]

FABIAN PITCHARE of Barking fisherman, 26 May 1580. **(233)**
To the poor of Barking town 200 of brush faggot where most need is. To Eliz. PITCHARE my daughter £10 at 21 and the child that my wife is withal £4 at 21. The rest of my goods to my wife Eliz. whom I make executrix. I ordain supervisors John TIRRIE and Peter DEBBETT of Barking fisherman, and for their pains 20d. apiece. Witnesses: John HORTONE minister, John TIRRIE, Peter DEBBETT. Proved 4 Oct. 1580.

NICHOLAS CANLER of Brentwood, 13 Nov. 1580. **(234)**
I make Alice my wife executrix. To her all my goods, on condition that she do bring up my son John CANDELER orderly as a child ought to be brought up. To her also my house at Yarmouth [co. Norfolk] which I mortgaged to Nich. LEME; she shall redeem and pay him £46. Witnesses: Geo. BORRS, John CLARKE, Rd. HALSHED. Proved 25 Nov. 1580.

RICHARD ALLCOCKE of Brentwood cobbler, 19 Nov. 1580. (Nuncupative.) **(235)**
To his five children, i.e. Philip, Rd., Th. ALLCOCKE, Kath. LOCKSMITH and Eliz. [blank], all his goods to be equally divided. He gave his copyhold house wherein he dwelt to Rd., according to the custom of the manor, on condition that he pay Philip and Th. each 40s. He nominated John COCKE of Brentwood baker executor. Witnesses: Rd. MASSHLEN, John WHITE, Mich. LONDON. Proved 25 Nov. 1580.

JOHN PASFEILD of Woodham Mortimer yeoman, 10 Sept. 1580. **(236)**
Whereas one Rd. BERDEN of Black Notley is bound to Th. BARNARD of Felsted and Nathaniel BARNARD of Broxted, all yeomen, for payment of £20 yearly at Michaelmas (£100 in all) to my own use, I ordain that the £100 be paid by them to Magdalen my wife; she shall out of the £100 pay my debts and the residue to my children as followeth. To John and Lewis my sons each £10, my daughters 'Dennys' PASFEILD and Barbara now wife of John WADE the younger each £3 6s.8d., and Rd. my son 40s. To him all my apparel, my best gown excepted. To Th. 40s. and Mary my daughter 20s. I ordain that, if it shall please Almighty God to continue my sickness whereby part of the £100 be diminished, my wife may abate my children's legacies. The residue of my goods, ready money, plate, jewels and other things to my wife, whom I ordain executrix. I constitute Th. BARNARD and Nathaniel BARNARD overseers, and to each for their pains 10s. Witnesses: Gilbert WOODWARD, John HARRISON, Nich. JOHNSON clerk [rector of Woodham Mortimer]. Proved 4 Nov. 1580.

JOAN BAWDEN of Upminster widow, — 1580. **(237)**
To the poor men's box 20d. To the maintenance of the church 12d. The residue of my goods, the debts and legacies of my husband Wm. BAWDEN being paid, to Thamer my daughter and John my youngest son equally divided at 21. I ordain John executor and overseers and guardians Th. HERDE of Upminster, Rt. HEARD of [North?] Ockendon, Rt. HUDSON of Upminster and John SKELE of Hornchurch, giving them

power to sell any part of my goods, and what remaineth to Thamer and John. Witnesses: Rd. BAWDEN, Rd. [blank], Wm. WASSHER parson of Upminster. Proved 27 Nov. 1580; administration committed during minority of John BAWDWIN to the overseers.

RICHARD WENTWORTH of Little Stambridge gentleman. (Nuncupative.) (238)
About 2 or 3 days before his death on 24 Nov. 1580 he gave to Mgt. his well-beloved wife for her better maintenance and towards the better education and bringing up of his children [not named] all his goods, and he constituted her his executrix. Proved 26 Nov. 1580 by the oath of Rd. WINDOR, notary public, proctor of the widow.

THOMAS HAMERTON of Rochford, 26 Oct. 1580. (239)
To WYMAN's wife my keeper my old featherbed and John WYMAN her husband 1 of my coats. My joined form be appraised and sold and Th. SELANDE's wife to have a good pennyworth in it. To Eliz. my wife all the goods in her custody, which I freely gave her when we parted, she not to meddle with any other of my goods. The residue of my goods, my keepers contented and pleased, to Eliz. PERYMAN, my daughter-in-law dwelling in St. Katherine's Without, in London, whom I make executrix. I ordain goodman BARTELETT of Eastwood and Mr ROWLAND parson of Sutton overseers. Witnesses: John BARTLETT of Eastwood, WYMAN's wife, widow MOYSE, Rt ROWLAND parson of 'Sutton Magna'. Proved 18 Nov. 1580.

WILLIAM BAYLIE of Rainham, 18 May 1579. (240)
To the poor of South Ockendon 20s. and of Rainham 13s.4d. To my cousin John BAYLIE's children, i.e. Matthew, Joan and Wm. my godson, £10 apiece at 18 or marriage, Wm. not to have his before 20. To my cousin James IVE 40s. To my cousin John RAMSE's daughters Agnes 40s. and Eliz. my goddaughter £3, each at 18 or marriage. To Rt. BALDEN my master's man 40s. To my cousin Joan RAMSE a bed which her mother gave me, a brass pot, and 10s. which she oweth me. To my cousin John BAYLIE's son Wm., my godson, a silver spoon that was my father's [not named], John HABRAHAM 13s.4d., Rd. FRITHE and Wm. FRITHE 6s.8d. each, and Kath. HOWE [and] Eliz. DIXSON 5s. apiece. I will that the £34 that my master Mr IVE doth owe me he shall have 4 years' day of payment for it after my death. To Wm. SHARPE and young UPNE's wife 5s. apiece. I forgive Th. LARKEN 20s. of the £3 he oweth me on condition that he pay my executor 20s. at Bartholomewtide next and 20s. at Michaelmas next after. The rest of my goods to my cousin John BAYLIE, whom I make executor. I ordain John GOLDINGE overseer, and for his pains 3s.4d. Witnesses: Rt. HOLDEN, John IVE. Proved 4 Oct. 1580.

JOAN AWBOROWE of Mundon widow, 24 Apr. 1578. (241)
To Th. STEVEN and Joan STEVEN my daughter all my goods, in consideration whereof Th. shall pay Rd. GILBARD at 21 £30; if he die before, the £30 equally divided between John NICHOLAS and Clement NICHOLAS, son and daughter of Joan STEVEN. I ordain Th. STEVENE executor. Witnesses: Th. THRUSTON the elder, Wm. BAKEN of Mundon. Proved 7 Oct. 1580. Inventory exhibited at £8 14s.6d.

JOHN LANGFORD of South Ockendon, 28 Sept. 1580. (Nuncupative.) (242)
He gave his goods to Dthy. WYTHAM his servant, saying these words to her or the like, viz. 'Dthy., Look that you look well to your dame and tend her well in her sickness, for if God call her I know I shall not live long after, wherefore look when God doth call us all the goods that we have shall be yours, my debts paying paid.' Witnesses: Mr Th. LEWYS [curate of South Ockendon], Rd. SHIPLEY, widow GODSTOCKE, Nich. DOLARD. Administration committed, [no date], in the absence of an executor, to the said Dthy. [See no. 232.]

AGNES NEWMAN of Romford widow, 27 July 1578. (243)
To Mgy. my daughter my cow, 3 ewes, my best featherbed, my woolbed, the tester and the bedstead, the chest that was my son Th.'s, my best cassock, a blue worsted kirtle, a pewter platter, a porringer, my brass pot, a quart pewter pot, a kettle, 2 pewter dishes, my best broad pan, and 3 pair of sheets. To Stephen my son 2 ewes,

the woolbed that Frs. my son lieth on, the bedstead, a pewter platter, a pewter dish, a porringer, a pair of towen sheets, a pair of twilly sheets, a short tablecloth, an old [blank], and a candlestick. To Th. my son my little brass pot. To Eliz. BAWDEN my frize cassock, my russet petticoat the best, a new kercher, and a new neckercher. To Peter MOYSE's wife my old russet cassock, a new kercher, and a new neckercher. To Mgy. more a little kneading trough, a broad tub, and a long tablecloth. The rest of my goods to Frs., [whom] I make executor. I make overseers Stephen my son and Wm. SMYTH, and to each 3s.4d. Witnesses: Philip REIGNOLDES, Rd. COOKE, John NETTLETON. Proved 3 Sept. 1580. Inventory exhibited at £11 9s.

THOMAS LAMBE of Romford, 23 July 1580. (244)
I ordain that all my goods be divided into three parts, one to pay my debts if they will reach so far, the 2nd to my wife [not named], whom I make executrix, and the 3rd to my two children Th. and John at 21. Witnesses: Nich. COTTON, John GREENE, John HOLMES, Rd. ATKYS minister [of Romford]. Proved 27 July 1580 by [blank] the widow.

JAMES SYMONDE of Billericay yeoman, 27 May 1580. (245)
To Anne my wife my house wherein I dwell, with the barns, stables, and the vessels and other implements concerning the working and tanning of leather, and the orchards, gardens, and the lands, meadows, pastures and feedings in Great Burstead, Mountnessing and Buttsbury, during the term of 16 years; if she die before, all to Wm. SYMONDE my son; for want of issue, to James my son. To my wife my customary garden called Gutters garden for 16 years likewise; after to Wm. To my wife my two leases, one whereof is holden of John SIDNAM esquire, the other of Geo. DRIWOOD gentleman, for term of years to come; also the half of my household stuff, corn and cattle; the other half to Wm. at 23; which shall be indifferently and equally parted by Wm. SYMONDE my brother, Th. WHITEBREADE of Margaretting and Wm. HALES, and my son's part to remain with my wife until he is 23. To the poorest people of Great Burstead £3 6s.8d., half at my burial, the other half within 3 months after given by Mr [Timothy] OCKELAYE [vicar of Great Burstead], James HARRYS and Wm. HALES. Towards the repairing of Great Burstead church 5s. and of the chapel [Billericay chapel] 10s. To my servants John ASHLIE £3 at 24, 'Persie' FINCHE [female] 20s. at 21, Henry HAUKER my son 20s., and the residue of my servants dwelling with me each 3s. To Th. SYMOND 20s., Henry KINGE 6s.8d., and GOOSBYE my tenant 20d. To Colyton Haven [co. Devon] 12d. The rest of my goods as my stock of leather, hides, bark, skins, debts and ready money shall be sold, tanned, taken up or otherwise ordered in sale by Wm. SYMOND my brother and Th. WHITEBREAD. Out of the stock, to Wm. my son another £100 at 23, my wife to occupy it until then. The residue of the stock and of my goods to James at 21. If both James and Wm. die before 21, to my sisters BROWNE's and ASHLEY's children equally to be divided at 21. I ordain my wife and Wm. my son executors and Wm. HALES and Wm. BIRKETT overseers. Witnesses: Timothy OCKELYE, John NORRYS, Wm. HALLES. Proved 12 July by Anne, power reserved to Wm. the son when he shall come. Inventory exhibited at £700 8s.

ROBERT BENTON of Magdalen Laver, 20 Feb. 1579/80. (246)
To the poor people 6s.8d. To Rd. and Th. my sons my tenement called Quintons in Magdalen Laver, with the lands belonging in Magdalen Laver, High Laver and Harlow, equally between them at 24; if both die before, to remain equally to my daughters, viz. Helen, Mary, Alice, Kath., Eliz., and Joan. Geo. BENTON of Harlow, my brother's son, John BENTON of Latton, son of Th., and Th. WAYLET of Harlow, son of Geo. WAYLETT, shall have the manuring [i.e. working] and occupying of the tenement and lands until Rd. and Th. are 24, paying £5 a year towards their bringing up and on condition that, if at any time there be no more ground ploughed than was ploughed within a year before my decease except it be Stony Field, then [the three men] shall pay the yearly rent of £15. When Rd. is 24 he shall have the occupying of the tenement and land until Th. is 24, paying yearly to my executors to the use of the rest of my children £3. To my six daughters £20 apiece at 21 or marriage. I will that my great hutch, my cupboard in the hall, the table and frame, 6 joined

stools and the quern in the kitchen chamber shall always remain to my tenement. Geo. BENTON, John BENTON and Th WAILETT, who shall be executors, shall have the ordering and bringing up of my children to 18 and place them with their stocks as they shall see most meet. If my goods and rent will not extend to answer my daughters' portions, they shall be abated. The rest of my goods to my six daughters equally. To my executors for their pains 10s. apiece. I make overseers my brother John READE and John JABEN and Th. JENEN of Magdalen Laver, and for their pains 3s.4d. apiece. Witnesses: Th. HOSKYN clerk [rector], Th. JENEN, John READ. [No probate clause.]

JOAN DASON [DAWSON *in margin*] of Margaretting widow, 2 Apr. 1580. (247)
To Bridget PACHIE 1 cow; Joan LENSAY an old featherbed, a cauldron, 4 pewter platters, a pillow, a pair of sheets, 2 pewter dishes, a candlestick, a salt, and a lesser kettle; Th. LENSAY a brass pot, a platter and a pewter dish; John LENSAY 1 lamb; Wm. LENSAY 1 lamb; Joan RAYLINGE 1 cow that was bought of BARKER; my daughter COLLINGES a pair of sheets and 3s.4d.; Grace YOUNGE a featherbed, a platter, a pewter dish, a pillow, a bolster, a sheep and a lamb; 'Doll' YOUNGE a sheep, 1 platter and a pewter dish; Joan YOUNGE a red cow; and Jane YOUNGE a mattress and a cupboard. The rest of my goods to my daughter YOUNGE, now widow. I ordain her my executrix. I appoint my brother BONYNGE overseer. Witnesses: David WYNGAT, Th. GILL, Adam GORE. [No probate clause.]

LAWRENCE RICKERD [RICKARD *in margin*] of Billericay, 9 Mar. 1579/80. (248)
To Agnes my wife 2 kine. To Susan RICKERD, my brother's daughter, 53s.4d. which is due to her by the Will of her father [not named]. Of the residue of my goods, half to my wife, half equally between my two brothers Edw. and Rd. I appoint my wife and Rd. executors; if they refuse to prove my Will, Wm. BURKETT and Wm. COLLINS of Billericay shall be executors. I desire my well-beloved friend Wm. HOLDEN to be supervisor. Witnesses: Th. FREEMAN, Th. ROBARTES. [No probate clause.]

RICHARD HORSENAILE of Little Wakering husbandman, 7 Jan. 1579/80. (249)
To Agnes my wife my tenement and lands in which I dwell in [blank] for her life; after her decease, to Susan my daughter, wife of John FOSTER. All other my goods to my wife, whom I make executrix. Witnesses: Wm. CREK, Th. SHEPPERD. [No probate clause.]

EDWARD WEBB of Horndon[-on-the-Hill], 5 Apr. 1580. (Nuncupative.) (250)
To Sarah MOORE daughter of John MOORE 4 bullocks. The residue of his goods to John. He nominated him executor. Witnesses: Wm. JOHNSON, [blank] SHORDEN. Proved 12 July 1580.

ALICE DOWSETT of Ingrave widow, 15 Dec. 1579. (251)
To Th. KELLE my son 1 mattress, 1 bolster, 2 pillows, a covering, 2 pairs of sheets, 1 blanket, a brass pot, and 1 frying pan. To my eldest daughter Olive BROWNE a pair of sheets. To Rd. KELLE, my son's son, 1 chest. To Eliz. HEARD my daughter 2 pair of sheets, 2 holland kerchers, 1 of lockram, a holland rail, my new smock, my best gown, and 1 russet petticoat. To 'Kenborowe' HEARD my daughter's daughter 1 bedstead. The residue of my goods to 'Kenborowe'. I nominate him and Wm. WITTAM of Ingrave executors and Nich. NEVELL my overseer, and for his pains 12d. Witnesses: John DOWSETT, Nich. NEVELL. Proved 28 July 1580.

WILLIAM AT HAYE of Rettendon yeoman, 5 May 1580. (252)
To my son Henry AT HAYES [*sic*] 15 acres of land called Millers, so that he shall let Cecily his mother have the land for her life, paying him 40s. a year; after her decease, the land to him. He shall have no part of my household [stuff]. The residue of my goods shall be divided at Michaelmas next, if God shall call me, between my wife and my children, Edw. the elder, Th., Hugh, Edw. the younger, Anne SEMSONE, Jane AT HAYE, and Cecily, my wife one half and the other to be parted equally; after her decease, her part to be equally parted among my children. My

wife shall see my children virtuously brought up; they that are under age to have their portions at 21. If Henry die without heirs, the land to descend from one to the other of my children, the longest survivor of them. All the glass shall remain in the windows of my house without any removing. I make my wife and my eldest son Henry executors. To Henry, Th., Edw. the younger, Jane and Cecily each a silver spoon. Witnesses: John BIRDE the writer, Wm. AT HAYE, Th. ARXDEN. Proved 10 June 1580.

WILLIAM SMYTHE *alias* REIGNOLDES of Maldon butcher, 22 Feb. 1579/80. (253)
To be buried in All Saints' church in Maldon as nigh to my father's grave as may be convenient. To Eliz. my wife my messuage, lands and gardens which I purchased of Reynold SMYTHE late of [Saffron] Walden butcher, being my father, and Kath. his wife. Also to my wife all my goods, in consideration that she, for the messuage and the goods, shall pay my debts and creditors so far as the value shall extend, trusting that she will be good mother to my two daughters Alice and Mary and see them godly and virtuously brought up either with herself or preferred by her good means to some other honest service. I make her my executrix. Witnesses: John LUFKIN, Henry KEME, Ralph SMYTHE. Proved 23 June 1580.

HUMPHREY BENTON, [abode not given], 18 Apr. 1580. (254)
To be buried in Upminster churchyard. To Constance my daughter 2 bedsteads, 2 chests, the hangings in the chamber beneath, a square table in the hall, a cupboard, a brass cauldron, a brass pot, a brass kettle, 4 pewter platters, 4 pewter dishes, 2 latten candlesticks; and 3 beasts called Chill, Petchey and the black bullock. To John GLADWINE's children, John and Andrew, 4 sheep, Alice daughter to John YOUNGE 1 sheep, Joan BAYLIE 1 sheep. To John GLADDEN [*sic*] 1 quarter of wheat. To my wife's six children, Rd., Wm., Mgy., Mgt., Mgt. [*sic*] and Eliz. COLE, 2 sheep apiece. To Eliz. COLE a branded bullock. To John GRAYGOSE, in consideration of legacies I received to his wife in his youth, 2 geldings and a young wether sheep, my wife to have the use of them till the first fallow be ended. To the same John £5 in consideration of rent which I received of his. The rest of my goods to my well-beloved wife Alice, whom I make executrix. I make Charles NUTTALL and John WILLETT overseers, desiring them to be aiders to my wife. Witnesses: Th. HEARD of Upminster, Geo. HEATH, Th. TOMKINS, Charles NUTTOME [*sic*], Th. SALTON schoolmaster of Upminster.

GEORGE BREWER of Dagenham yeoman, 27 Mar. 1581. (255)
To Joan my wife her dwelling in this my house until Michaelmas next, with the use of the buildings belonging, Long Croft, Groves Brook, the field adjoining the house now stubble, and the croft that the wheat is in with the crop now on it, 6 kine, 10 ewes, 1 black mare with a woman's saddle, 4 hogs, my hens and geese, and the household stuff that she had when I married her, paying therefor at Michaelmas to Mr Alderman HARVIE £3. To Agnes WREIGHT of South End in Hornchurch, my cousin, 1 cow of 3 years. To Joan BREWER my sister 1 cow of 3 years and my 2nd featherbed, on condition that she seal to my brother John BREWER a general acquittance for her legacy by the Will of our father [not named]. To Joan daughter of John 1 grey mare with her colt and to John his son 1 cow of 3 years. To John my brother my load cart, half my cart harness, plough chains, great table in CHAMPNEY's house, and all other household [stuff] that I have there, my 2nd brass pot, 2 little candlesticks, and 2 pottingers. To Agnes TURNER of Romford 4 sheep. To the poor of Dagenham 10s., of Hornchurch 5s., and of Romford 5s. To Geo. FEILD my godson 1 sheep, Joan STEVEN my maidservant 2 sheep, and Geo. CHARLES of Barking 3 sheep. The rest of my goods to Mgt. BREWER my daughter, whom I constitute executrix. I ordain Jeffery HUMFREY of Dagenham and Wm. AWGUR of Hornchurch yeomen supervisors, and for their pains 6s.8d. Written by me John BERYMAN, vicar of Dagenham. Witnesses: Geo. BREWER, Ambrose FEILD, Wm. STRATTON. Proved 12 Apr. 1581.

WILLIAM HARRIS of Childerditch husbandman, — Mar. 1580/1. (256)
To my three children, Geo., Wm. and Joan HARRIS, half of my stock of cattle and corn equally amongst them. The other half, with my household stuff, to Emme my wife and Th. my son. If my three children will be ruled by her, she to keep them or else to deliver their whole stock with them. The rest of my goods to my wife, whom I make executrix. Witnesses: Th. VEER, John HARRIS, Wm. HARRIS. Proved 13 Apr. 1581.

HENRY ALMON of Burnham mariner, 6 Feb. 1580/1. (257)
To my son John ALMON my cottage called Waskettes, he to pay yearly to Ellen my wife 10s. as long as she doth keep herself a widow. To her my boat or cock [dinghy] called the 'Helen' and to John my boat or cock called the 'Brouninge', with all that belong to them as nets. I will that John shall pay my daughter Eliz. £3. To my wife and Eliz. my household stuff equally divided by two or three honest men. My wife and John shall take the 'ware' off from the lambs to Lady Day next and then the lambs to remain to John, whom I make executor. I ordain my loving and trusty friend Th. OWGHAN overseer. All my other goods to John. Witnesses: Th. OWGHAN, Wm. LECE, Nich. FILBYE, Isaac STEVEN. Proved 14 Apr. 1581.

ALICE CLEMENT of Doddinghurst widow, 12 June, 22 Eliz. [1580]. (258)
To the poor 20s. To my godchildren each 4d. I will that Wm. CLEMENTE my son shall pay out of my copy lands at Epping to my three daughters Joan, Alice and Eliz. and to Alice TURNER, my daughter's daughter, £3 6s.8d. each. To Wm. CLEMENT my son 1 cow. To Geoffrey CLEMENTE my son 1 featherbed, the cupboard in the hall, and the table in the hall. To Henry CLEMENT my son a featherbed, the brass pot, and the broad lidded hutch. To Joan my daughter a kneading trough and a table. To Alice my daughter's daughter 1 'howed' [for meaning see p. xvii] cow, 1 little chest, a brass pan, the best pewter platter, and the best basin. To Geoffrey [the house omitted?] Flanckers after my decease and shall pay out of it £6 13s.4d. to my children's children. I ordain Geoffrey and Henry executors, he to discharge the legacies as I stand charged with by the Will of Wm. CLEMENT the elder of Doddinghurst deceased [*Essex Wills*, vol.1, no.22]. The rest of my goods to my seven children part and part like. My overseer I make Geo. MANFELD, and for his pains 3s.4d. Witnesses: John CLEMENT, Geo. MANFELD, Geo. BULLEN. Proved 13 Apr. 1581.

THOMAS BOXWORTH of Stock husbandman, 8 Feb. 1580/1. (259)
To Eliz. my wife my house for her life; after her decease, to Th. BOXWORTH my middle son, so that he pay Ralph BOXWORTH my youngest son £3. To Th. BOXWORTH the younger, after my wife's decease, my cupboard in the parlour, my featherbed, and my brass pot. To Ralph my cupboard in the hall, my great kettle, a table, my bed that I lie on, and a mortar, after my wife's decease. The rest of my goods to her; after her decease, to Th. my middle son and Ralph to be equally shifted. I ordain her my executrix and Edw. HAUKINE overseer, and for his pains 5s. Witnesses: Th. BOXWORTH, Edw. HAUKINE, Alexander GARRETT. Proved 14 Dec. 1581.

JOHN BRADDOCKE of Little Stambridge husbandman, 31 Mar. 1581. (260)
To Alice my wife 5 good ewe sheep, and the profit of my cow till Michaelmas next; and all my household stuff. To Th. BRADDOCKE my brother 5 ewe sheep and all of my own sheep and of them I hire of Philip GOLDINGE and he also to have my cow at Michaelmas, so as Th. is to satisfy himself with this my gift for all that I owe him. My wife shall pay 5s. which is my debt to Hugh TYE's widow. I ordain Th. executor. [No witnesses.] Proved 12 May 1581.

GEORGE GOODMAN of Rochford yeoman, 16 Mar. 1580/1. (261)
To Joan my wife all my goods and cattle (except as hereafter excepted). To Agnes and Mary GOODMAN my daughters £20 apiece at 18 or marriage, to be paid by my wife, she to put in bond to Th. COLLINS of Ash End [in Rochford] gentleman; if both die before without issue, the £40 to be paid to the four children [not named] of Wm.

GOODMAN, my brother, of Great Shelford (co. Cambridge) husbandman. To my wife my copyhold land in Eastwood called Hill Field and Pery Grove for her life; the remainder to Mary; if she die without heirs, to Agnes my elder daughter. To Joan, Giles and Mgt. HATCHE, my wife's children, such money as was bequeathed to them by the Will of Henry HATCHE of Hawkwell, her husband. To the poor of Rochford 2s.6d. To Mgt. EVANS my kinswoman 20s. at marriage. The rest of my goods to my wife, whom I make executrix. Witnesses: John BERIMAN rector there and the writer, Rd. KINGE. Proved 15 Apr. 1581.

WILLIAM STOOKES of Fyfield, 25 Apr. 1581. **(262)**
To Agnes my wife, whom I make executrix, my house in which I dwell, with the buildings and lands belonging in Fyfield for 16 years after my decease. She shall have sufficient firebote to dispend on the premises and not elsewhere and maintain the spring. At the end of the term, to give over all the premises to my son John; if he die before, leaving no issue, to my daughter Joan, she to give each of her two sisters Agnes and Mary £20. If all my children die without issue, to Th. STOOKES my brother for life; after his decease, to my son-in-law Th. PETCHIE. To my three daughters £3 6s.8d. apiece at marriage or 20, also 33s.4d. apiece to be paid by John after his entrance on his lands. The rest of my goods to my wife. I ordain Th. PETCHIE overseer, and for his pains 13s.4d. Witnesses: John MONKE, Rt. EATTUE [EATTNE?], Abraham SMYTHE the writer. Proved 8 June 1581.

THOMASINE GLASCOCKE of Fyfield widow, 23 Apr. 1581. **(263)**
To be buried in Fyfield church at the discretion of well-disposed people. To Fyfield church where I shall lie 6s.8d. I ordain Th. PHERE and Wm. PHERE my brothers executors. To 'Mault' MOTE my maid 1 joined bed in the 'gu[est's?] chamber next to the great chest, the featherbed, the cupboard in the parlour, ½ dozen of pewter of the greater sort, ½ dozen porringers, ½ dozen saucers, the best brass pot, the lesser cauldron of the twain, 1 of the great spits, 1 posnet, 1 cow, 1 sheep, 2 lambs, my best gown, best kirtle, best red petticoat, 2 of my best kerchiefs, and my best neckercher. To Thomasine TODGELL my goddaughter 1 bed in the chamber over the parlour with the head abutting towards the garden next the street, the cupboard in the same chamber, 4 pewter dishes, 4 porringers, 4 saucers, 1 kettle, 1 posnet, 1 cow, 1 sheep, 1 lamb, my broad cloth gown with the plain sleeves, 1 red petticoat welted about beneath, 2 kerchiefs and 2 neckerchers. To Agnes EVERARD my goddaughter 1 bullock of the 1st calf, 1 sheep and 1 lamb. To Thomasine RAYNOULD my goddaughter 1 cow, 1 sheep and 1 lamb. To Thomasine VERE of Childerditch Hall my goddaughter the bed in the chamber over the parlour next the chamber door, the hutch at the bed's feet, 1 brass pot, 1 kettle, 1 posnet, and 3 pewter platters. To Wm. STOOKES, my brother-in-law, the great ship chest in the great chamber; Joan STOOKES his daughter the great cauldron; and Mary STOOKES his daughter 1 kettle, 1 posnet, and 2 small pewter platters. To Rd. BUSHE my servant 1 flockbed. To Joan STOOKES 1 pair of sheets. To Stephen HAMON my godson 1 cow, and the rest of my son HAMON's children 12d. apiece. To mother ROBARD of Willingale my old russet gown and my frizado petticoat. To my cousin Rt. STAMMER 40s. To my brother John WEARE [*recte* VEARE] 40s. and and 3 bushels of wheat and his wife my best russet gown. To Phoebe VEARE, my brother Th. VEARE's daughter, the chest with the spring lock. To Magdalen LACKE and Joan LAKE my goddaughters 10s. apiece; the rest of my son LAKE's children 12d. apiece. To Thomasine GLASKOCKE 10s.; the rest of my son GLASKOCKE's children 12d. apiece. To my servants John KENE and Wm. YONGE each 4s. To every poor householder in Fyfield ½ bushel of wheat. To 'Dynis' MITUE [MITNE?] my goddaughter 4s. To Joan TODGELL my goddaughter, dwelling at 'Eenfeildes' [now Envilles, in Little Laver or Fyfield], 5s. To Thomasine STOKES my goddaughter, Wm. STOOKES' daughter, 5s. The rest of my goods shall be equally divided between my brothers Th. and Wm. I ordain Edw. HAMMON of Willingale Doe and Wm. EVERED of Fyfield overseers, and for their pains 6s.8d. apiece. Witnesses: John MONCKE, Rt. STAMER, John MITTUE [MITTNE?], Abraham SMITHE the writer. Proved 5 May 1581 by Th. VEARE and Wm. VEARE so named.

CHARLES NUTTAW of Wennington yeoman, 13 Nov. 1581. (264)
To be buried in Wennington church. All my goods shall be equally divided, the 1st part to Mgt. my well-beloved wife, the 2nd amongst my children Charles, James, John and Mary NUTTAW at 21, Mary's at 18, and the 3rd to pay my debts. To the poor people of Aveley 10s., Wennington 10s., and Rainham 10s. To every servant dwelling with me at my decease 12d. I ordain my wife executrix and my trusty friends Wm. ARDEN parson of Wennington, James SHAWCROFT, John PAYNE and John IVE of Wennington overseers, and to each for a token of remembrance 3s.4d. trusting that they will accept my goodwill more than the value. If my wife be at any time minded to sell my lease which I have of my son-in-law John PAYNE and Eliz. his wife, my daughter, she shall do so only to them. Witnesses: Wm. ARDEN, Wilfred LEWTIE. Proved 17 Jan. 1581/2.

BARTHOLOMEW STEVENS of Hornchurch, 7 Feb. 1581/2. (265)
To my brothers Th. £8, John £7, Wm. £3, and Anthony STEVENS at 21 £3; if he die before, to my sister Agnes at 21; if Anthony and Agnes die before 21, to my brother Frs.'s children and Th.'s children equally divided. To my aunt LYNEYS 30s., my cousin ARNOBE's wife and Joan HINED's each 20s., Jane WARRENER 20s., and my uncle WILKOCKE's five children 30s. equally divided. To Rt. PRIER's wife 6s.8d. I will 33s.4d. to be bestowed at my burial and 20s. to 40 poor folks at the Feast of All Saints by my uncles Wm. STEVENS and Rt. WILKOCKE as they think good. To my brothers Frs. a bedsteadle and 1 pewter dish and Th. a mattress, a bolster, 2 pair of sheets, 1 platter, 1 saucer, 1 towel, 2 table napkins, and the greatest chest at his uncle STEVENS. To my cousin Martha STEVENS a cauldron with 2 ears, Rt. HANAN a platter and 2 porringers, Agnes SANDER a pewter dish, Agnes HINDS a platter and a saucer, Joan HINDS a covering and the best chest at my uncle WILKOCKES, Jane WARNER the other chest, my brother Anthony my best hose and best doublet, a spit and a candlestick, my sister Agnes a tablecloth, John FORRIST a canvas doublet and a pair of russet hose, Th. HINDES a leather doublet and a pair of hose, and my brother Th. my best frize coat. I make him executor and my uncle WILKOCKE overseer, and for his pains 10s. Witnesses: Th. BAULDON, Wm. GOLDRINGE. Proved 9 Mar. 1581/2.

THOMAS PARKER of Barking yeoman, 12 Oct. 1581. (266)
To be buried in Barking church or churchyard. To Mgt. my wife 1 milch cow and 6 sheep or 20. for the sheep, 1 quarter of rye, a staple bedstead with a featherbed standing in the loft at the south end of the house, a table and a form, 2 chests (1 greater, 1 smaller) in the chamber where my wife lieth, a cupboard in the hall, half of my brass in the house (except 1 great brass pot which I give to my executrix over and above her part); all my pewter (except to my executrix 1 pewter basin), 1 spit, 2 pair of sheets, and half the kimnels and other stuff in the milkhouse. To my executrix my lease and term of years of Mr FYNNYS, citizen and haberdasher of London, of a cottage and 14 acres of ground by lease, 9 Nov. 1576, so that she permit Rt. PARKER my brother jointly to occupy the cottage for 4 years, paying her the moiety of the profits. I ordain Joan my daughter executrix and my loving brother Rt., Rd. BETT and Th. NORDEN aiding her, and for their pains 10s. apiece. Witness: John PIERSON writer. Not proved or administered [because] no goods.

THOMAS KIRTON of Ramsden Bellhouse, 18 Feb. 1581/2. (267)
To my brother Wm. KIRTON 40s. To Jeremy ALLEN 40s. To my father-in-law Wm. COALE, whom I make overseer, 10s. To Phoebe MAY 5s. The rest of my goods to Agnes my wife, whom I make executrix. Witnesses: Bennet STRETT, Th. SAXTON, James BUTTER. Proved 8 March 1581/2.

ROBERT JOHNSON of Stapleford Abbots husbandman, 17 Jan. 1581/2. (268)
To my son Wm. £8 at 21; if he die before, to my daughters equally divided. To my daughters Christian 40s. and Eliz. 33s.4d., and my other daughters [not named] each 10s., all at marriage. The rest of my goods to Joan my wife, whom I make executrix. Witnesses: Rd. REIGNOULDES clerk, parson of Stapleford Abbots. Proved 9 Mar. 1581/2.

ROBERT SAYER of Hadleigh at the Castle, 1 Oct. 1581. **(269)**
To Mgt. my wife my lease of my house and ground and all my cattle and goods for her life, with liberty to let or sell the lease if need constrain her. Such goods as it shall please God to suffer her to leave behind her shall be equally distributed among my children, and John SAYER and Henry my sons to see to it. I constitute my wife executrix and appoint Stephen BARWICKE parson [of Hadleigh] and John KITTER overseers. Witnesses: John SARE, Anthony FELIX. Proved 27 Feb. 1581/2.

JOHN BURMAN [BURNEHAM *in margin***] of Brentwood painter, 9 Feb. 1581/2.** **(270)**
To Kath. BURMAN my wife all my goods. I make her my executrix and Geo. BUR[R]E overseer, and for his pains 8d. Witnesses: Geo. BUR[R]E, Roger HALTE, Rd. BIRLINGE, Leonard OXCLIFFE. Proved 23 Feb. 1581/2.

WILLIAM TYHAM of Horndon-on-the-Hill, 15 June 1581. **(271)**
To be buried in Orsett churchyard. To the poor men's boxes of Horndon 20d. and Orsett 20d. To my wife's children, Rd. TYPTAP, Chris. TYPTAP each £3 and Kath. TYPTAP £4, the best bed, 6 pewter platters and 6 of the best pewter dishes; all at marriage or 21. To John MOCKE 2 sheep, Eliz. MERIALL 1 sheep, my godchildren 8d., 'Enilen' SPARROWE 2 theaves, and Agnes YNYSA 12d. The rest of my goods to Agnes my wife, whom I ordain executrix. I make Th. TAYLOR and John SLATERFORD overseers, and for their pains each 3s.4d. Witnesses: Edm. BICKNOLL vicar there, Th. TAYLOR. Proved 21 Feb. 1581/2. Inventory exhibited at £50 10s.8d.

KATHERINE BOXOR of Stanford-le-Hope, — 1580. **(272)**
To John BOXOR my son my best featherbed, a cauldron in the lead, a lathe, and a churn. To Th. my son a featherbed, a flockbed, a tablecloth, a ceiling, a brass pot, ½ dozen of pewter, a chafing dish, the least latten basin, a candlestick, a table in the milkhouse, a board, 2 pillows, a cupboard, a couple of bowls, a chair, a great joined stool, and a chest. To Mgt. my daughter a featherbed, a flockbed, a ceiling, the best tablecloth, a couple of long towels, 6 napkins, a table, a form, a cupboard, 2 chests, 2 chairs, the painted cloths about the hall, ½ dozen of pewter, a great basin, a cauldron, a brass pot, a kettle, a spit, a pair of andirons, a dripping pan, a pair of pothooks, the great bowl, 2 latten candlesticks, a saltcellar, and the best chafing dish. To John 2 of the best platters and a chest. I make him executor. Witness: Rd. JOHNSON. Proved 13 Feb. 1581/2.

ROBERT CLARKE of Shenfield husbandman, 11 Jan. 1581/2. **(273)**
To my sons John £12, Th. £3, Wm. and Rt. each 40s., all at 22, and my daughters Avelin 20s. and Mgt. 26s.8d., both at 18. The rest of my goods to Kath. my wife, whom I make executrix. I appoint Wm. BOXER and Rt. HEHE overseers. Witnesses: Rt. PARKER, Wm. WHARTON, Wm. HAMOND. Proved 13 Feb. 1581/2. Inventory exhibited at £24 12d.

GREGORY BROOKE of Burnham, 29 Nov. 1581. **(274)**
To Barbara my wife my cow and my 9 lambs, all my household stuff, and £10. If she now be with child, £8 of the £10 shall remain to be paid at his or her marriage or 21. To John THURROCKE a pair of breeches, a jerkin and a doublet; Edw. KINGE a pair of the best breeches and a frize jerkin; and BUTTELL a pair of breeches. To the poor of Burnham 20s. To father FOXE 5s. I ordain Benjamin HARRIS executor, and for his pains 40s. The residue of my goods to him. I appoint for making my funeral sermon 3s.4d. Witnesses: John FISHER, Benjamin HARRIS, Wm. BETHAM curate. Proved 23 Feb. 1581/2.

EDWARD WHITE of Brentwood single man, 6 Dec. 1581. (Nuncupative.) **(275)**
To my brother[-in-law] Wm. LYAT of Barking all my goods. I will him to be good to my sister Barbara COOKE's children, to give them as he shall think good as my hope is he will do. I make him executor. Witnesses: Rt. CORALL, John HORNE. Proved 18 Dec. 1581.

MARGARET BULMAN, [abode not given], 26 Nov. 1581. (276)
To be buried in Great Wakering churchyard. To the poor there 2s. All other my goods to Rachel FRENCHE my daughter, whom I make executrix. Witnesses: John MEBORNE, Rt. TENDERINGE, John PEICKE, John DEANE. Proved 17 Dec. 1581.

ANTHONY SMYTHE of Great Wakering bricklayer, 29 Sept., 22 Eliz. [1580]. (277)
I make my daughter Joan SMYTHE executrix. To her and Jane SMYTHE my lease of 'Aldomes' [in Great Wakering?] with 1 milch cow, 14 sheep, 2 fat hogs, and the barley in my barn and kitchen. To Joan my eldest daughter half of my household stuff. I command her to see Jane her sister brought up at Joan's charges until she is able to go to service. The other half to Jane at 21 or marriage. To Marion my wife her dwelling in the west end of ALDOME's house for 4 years, she to make her fire in the hall with my daughter and to occupy it when need shall require without let or blame. To my wife a garden plat to set beans or such like at the west end of the house. To her 1 milch cow to be pastured and stovered at the charge of the executrix for 4 years in Aldomes Mead; 3 lambs to be brought up in Aldomes, every year 2 lambs till they be a year old till 3 years be expired; a hog, 3 small sheats, half my household stuff, the wheat that grew in the orchard, ½ seam of barley, and 3 hens to go in Aldomes. To her for 4 years every year 2 lops of wood to be burnt in Aldomes or else she must not have them and ½ seam of wheat or if barley groweth on the ground ½ seam of barley. I appoint Rd. SMYTHE of Little Wakering and John HENBONE of 'Burstead' overseers, and for their pains 2s.6d. apiece. Witnesses: John MARSHALL, John DANE, Rt. TENDERINGE. Proved 12 Feb. 1581/2.

HUGH BRIDGE of Mundon yeoman, 20 Dec. 1581. (278)
To John my son my house and land called Bramble Hall, Scottes and Garlands Marsh in Mundon. To my son Hugh £40 within 7 years after my decease and to my daughter Joan wife of Rt. FAUNCE £20 within 3 years, both to be paid by John out of my land. I will that he shall keep Joan my wife if she keep herself unmarried, if she shall think good to continue with him or else to be at his keeping, paying her yearly £6 13s.4d. To my wife my best featherbed with a joined bedsteadle, 3 of my best platters, 2 of my 2nd and 1 of my worst, my worst chafing dish, 1 of my best and 1 of my worst candlesticks, my 2nd brass pot, 2nd brass kettle, 1 little posnet, 1 table with a pair of trestles and form to it, my best hutch, best chair , a frying pan, and a chafer. To Hugh my 3rd featherbed, 3rd brass pot, 3rd brass kettle, 3 pewter platters, 3 pewter dishes, 1 andiron, 1 spit, 1 short table, 1 hutch, and 1 candlestick. My executor shall pay £4 to Stephen OSTINE and Emme COOTES, which I owe them. To John SOANE 20s. The rest of my goods to my son John, whom I make executor. Witnesses: Abraham GARINGTON, Lawrence CLAITOR, Daniel GARINGTON, Th. WISEMAN. Proved 12 Feb. 1581/2.

THOMAS BODE [BODIE *in margin*] of Rochford yeoman, 18 June, 23 Eliz. [1581], (279)
[Long religious preamble.] To be buried in Rochford church. To the poor people of the town 20s. To every one of my household servants 10s. To my sister HILLES of Hawkwell 10s. To the poor people of Great Stambridge 5s., of Canewdon 5s., and of Paglesham 5s. To Alice MELLER of Paglesham my sister my house and lands called Pakes in Paglesham free and copy, which John MELLER her husband holdeth, 2 other crofts which I hold, also another copyhold tenement in Eastwood in the occupation of Wm. KEIS. To Alice's children each 40s. and to her 40s. To Thomasine my wife my tenement and lands called Moones in Great Stambridge. To her my tenements and lands called Birds, conditionally that she claim no thirds in my other lands in Boreham and the lands I purchased of John LARGDE in the tenure of John PORTER of Boreham, for her life; after her decease, one half to Geo. CRIMBLE, my wife's son, and the other to Edw. and Wm. BODE, my brothers. To my wife another tenement in Terling, with all the lands and tenements which I purchased of John ROCHESTER of terling, in lieu of her general third of my other lands, for her life; after her decease, to Edw. and Wm. She, in consideration aforesaid, shall have the lands and tenements which I have of Edw. my brother in Rayleigh, for her life; after her decease, to Edw. and Wm. To Th. son of Rt. STEPHEN my brother of Brentwood

deceased 40s. and to his two other children each 10s. To the children of my cousin Rt. STEPHANE of Leigh deceased each 20s. at 18 or marriage. To my brother STEPHEN of Maldon, my brother Th. COLLINS and Mary his wife, my sister, and their son, each 2 angels for a remembrance. To my wife my tenement and lands which I purchased of RINGE in the tenure of [blank] HADLEIGHE in Althorne for her life; after her decease, to Alice MELLER. To Wm. CORNEFORD of Rochford, for his life, my house in Rochford which I purchased of John CRIMBLE; after his decease, to Mary CORNEFORD his daughter, begotten of Clement CORNFORD deceased; for default of heirs, to Wm. son of Wm. HILLES, saving the orchard, to my wife for her life. As to my lands and tenements called Whites in Great Stambridge, to Edw. and Wm. according to the Will of John BODE their father. To my wife 2 crofts in Great Stambridge (4 acres) in the occupation of KILLINOUSE. To Judith BODE my sister £5, my cousin Edw. JENYNS 2 angels to make him a ring, my cousin Th. JENYNS 10s. for a remembrance, Wm. RICHARDSON 40s., my brother Edw.'s wife and my brother Wm.'s wife each 4½ angels to make them a ring, and every of Wm.'s children 2 angels. To Wm. RICHARDSON my orchard in Prittlewell. The residue of my goods to my wife, whom I make executrix. I make Edw. and Wm. overseers, and to them £4 between them. Memorandum that this was copied the very same night in which he departed and with the very same witnesses, viz. John ADAMS, Geo. GATES, Lawrence FANINGE. Proved 23 Aug. 1581 by his wife; thereupon, 19 Dec. 1581, proved by definitive sentence at the instance of Alice SAMMON *alias* MILLER, sister of the deceased.

EDMUND CHAMBERLANE of Burnham, 10 Dec. 1581. (280)
To my eldest son John 3 cottages, whereof twain are under one roof, with 3 several garden plats in Bocking called Bockinges at the end of 8 years. To my two younger sons John and Th. 5 marks apiece at 24. To Phyllis my daughter the new featherbed, and a cow at 18. To Mary my wife a featherbed and a cow. If any of my children die before, their legacy to remain to the child wherewith my wife now goeth; if not with child, to the rest of my children. The rest of my household stuff to be divided into three parts, 1 to my wife, the other 2 equally divided amongst my four children. The rest of my goods to Henry EVE, whom I make executor, to bring up Phyllis, he shall have the use of my cottages to the end of the 8 years, paying my eldest son John for the last 4 years so much money yearly as surmounts above 5 nobles. I make Rd. FOX overseer, and for his pains 40d. Witnesses: John PEEK senior, John PEEKE junior. Proved 23 Feb. 1581/2.

HENRY SELAKE [SELACKE *in margin*] of Dagenham, 28 Nov. 1581. (Nuncupative.) (281)
He very earnestly and very often wishing that Th. REED were there with him at his Will-making, saying, I do give him my part of my house and land in Tiverton (co. Devon) at the end of Hauwtes Lane in the occupation of Rt. BERRIE over against the Cross, willing him to make the best thereof, and the rest of my goods, which is very small, all which is not able to recompense his great gentleness and goodwill towards me in always helping me in my necessity. I make him executor. Declared in the house of widow MOILES in Dagenham, then present with him, [also] Eliz. SPICER. Proved [date not given].

WILLIAM CURLEWE of Rawreth, 30 Nov. 1581. (282)
To Rawreth church to help to repair it 5s. To the poor people 5s. To the children of my brother Th. CURLEWE each 13s.4d. at 21. To the children of John CURLEWE each a lamb. I forgive Th. the debts he oweth me. To my godchildren each 12d. To John CURLEWE a red young bullock. The rest of my goods to Agnes my wife, whom I make executrix. I constitute Rd. MASON parson of Rawreth overseer, and for his pains 6s.8d. Witnesses. Wm. GEFFERAY, Wm LAYE. Proved by Rd. MASON, proctor of Agnes. Inventory exhibited at £49 16s.8d.

JANE LEGATE [LEGATTE *in margin*] of Hornchurch widow, — 1581. (Nuncupative.) (283)
Being demanded by Mr John LEGATE whether she would that her husband's Will

should be performed, she answered , Yea. Being demanded what should be done with the overplus, if any, she answered, I give £10 thereof to Walter LEGAT my son and £10 to my cousin John. Being demanded what she would do with the residue, if yet more remained, she answered, it shall be equally divided amongst all my children. At another time, she said, I give to Jane SONNE and Dthy. BUSSHE each 1 cow and 3 sheep, to my two men servants Th. JACKMAN and John BETT 10s. apiece, mother HIGGINS widow 20s., HARWELL and his wife 20s., John HANDLIE 20s., BROWNE's wife 20s., Henry PATRICKE 10s., JOHNSON's wife 10s., and all my godchildren 2s. apiece. Witnesses: Mr John LEGATTE, goodman Rt. WATTES, goodman Henry PATRICKE, Th. LEGATT of Sutton [now Suttons, in Hornchurch], Wm. LEGATTE. Administration committed 10 Jan. 1581/2, to Th. LEGATTE and Wm. LEGATTE the sons.

KATHERINE DAVIES servant to Mistress BLACKWELL of Barking, 7 Oct. 1581. (284)
To Henry BLACKNY my son [blank], Rd. STANTON 8s., Judith JEFFERAY my fellow [servant] my black cassock, JARETTE's wife my russet gown and a flaxen apron, and Constance DOWNER my best gown, conditionally that she pay Wm. WARDE, Mr BLACKWELL's servant, 20s. To the poor men's box 6s.8d. The rest of my goods to Jarett TRICE my fellow, whom I make executor. To my mistress a pair of flaxen sheets. Witnesses: Th. BREWER, Th. HAYWARDE parish clerk of Barking. Proved 20 Dec. 1581.

WILLIAM LOCKE of Little Warley yeoman, 17 Aug. 1581. (285)
To my sons John LUCKE, Th. LUCKE, Wm. LUCKE, and Rd. LUCKE, each £15 at 21. To Rt. LUCKE my son 40s., 1 ship chest bound with iron, 1 great chair, 2 pair of sheets, 2 candlesticks, my best brass pot, 2 platters, and my best covering. To John 1 brass pot, 2 pair of sheets, 2 platters and 1 candlestick. To Th. 1 brass pot, 2 pair of sheets, 1 candlestick, 1 posnet and 1 little hutch. To Wm. 1 great cauldron new unbound, 2 pair of sheets, 1 candlestick, 2 platters, and 1 litte hutch. To Rd. 2 pair of sheets and 2 platters. To every of my servants 5s. To my godchildren 12d. apiece. The residue of my goods to Ellen my wife. I ordain Henry BICKNER of Ulting, my trusty friend, executor, and for his pains 3s.4d. Witnesses: Wm. BROWNE, John MONDES, John FRITTON. Proved 21 Nov. 1581.

JOHN PACE of Barking fisherman, 28 Oct. 1581. (286)
To be buried in Barking church or churchyard. To my three daughters Mgt., Joan and Eliz. £13 6s.8d. divided equally at 21 or marriage, my executrix to have the use of their stocks until then. To my brother Geoffrey PACE my best breeches. To my wife's brother John MEDDOWES my best shirt. To the poor people of Barking 5s. on the day of my burial. The residue of my goods to my well-beloved wife Eliz., whom I make executrix, towards her better maintenance and the better and virtuous bringing up of my said children. Overseers I make my loving friends John TERRYE and Th. NORTHEN fishermen, and for their pains 2s. apiece. Witnesses: John TOMPSON, John PEARSON writer, Proved 18 Nov. 1581.

WILLIAM LAKE of Upminster, 13 Oct., 23 Eliz. [1581]. (287)
To my wife 10 sheep, 5 kine, 1 mare and a colt, and my swine. The rest of my sheep to be equally divided among my young children [not named]. The rest of my goods to Joan LACKE my loving wife, whom I make executrix. I have according to the custom of the manor surrendered my house and land into the hands of the tenants to the use of Rd. my eldest son, on condition that he pay every one of my other children 20s. at their full age. I make Rd. LAKE my brother and Wm. PRIOR overseers. Witnesses: Rd. LACKE, Hum. FRYTHE, John CLARKE, Geo. WISEMAN the writer. Proved 22 Nov. 1581.

ANNE BROWNE of Rayleigh widow, 30 Aug. 1581. (288)
To be decently buried in Rayleigh church or chancel. To the poor folks of Rayleigh 10s. at my burial. To widow MAWBROOKES my frize cassock next the best. To Eliz. KNIGHTE of Leigh 6s.8d. To four poor men to bear me to the church 16d. To Edw. HARTE the younger £8, 1 featherbed, 1 frying pan, and a dripping pan, to be delivered to Edw. HARTE his father, he to put in bonds to repay when his son

is 20; if he die before, to be equally divided amongst the other children of Edw. the father. To Edw. the son, after the decease of my son John BROWNE, my best chafing dish. To Judith now wife of Edw. HARTE the elder all my wearing linen except the parcels hereafter given, my gold ring next the best, my worst diaper tablecloth, ½ dozen of my best table napkins, a bearing sheet, my best black apron, my least welling kettle, 2 pewter platters, 2 pewter dishes, 2 saucers of the best sort, 1 of my best latten candlesticks, a spit, an andiron, a dripping pan, a heckle [comb for flax or hemp] and a frame, my new frize cassock, and the rest of my apparel. To Anne daughter of Edw. HARTE £10, my silver girdle, the least trundle bedstead, the featherbed, the flockbed, 2 pewter platters, 2 pewter dishes, 2 saucers, a saltcellar, 2 candlesticks, and a chafer at 18 or marriage. To Edw. HARTE the elder the forepart of a worsted kirtle to make him a doublet. To my sister, Mr Wm. STODALL's wife, and my cousin Edw. BODE's wife, each 10s. to make a ring with a death's head for a remembrance. To my sister HAIES my worsted kirtle. To my son John BROWNE my free lands and tenements in Wickford in the tenure of [blank] CHAPPLE, £60; and cloth of a gown to make him a cloak on condition that he shall wear it for me; 4 kerchiefs and worsted to make him a doublet. To Joan MAPLE my maid a holland kerchief, a silk girdle, a crosscloth, a lockram neckerchief, an apron, a frize cassock, canvas for 2 smocks, a hat, and 20s. To WRAIGHTE's widow frize to make her a cassock. The residue of my household stuff to my son John. To Mr BADCOCKE 10s. I make my brother John BARTLETT of Eastwood overseer, and for his pains 20s. To my cousin Edw. BOODE 40s., whom I constitute executor. Witnesses: John BOODE, Wm. HARTE, Hum. HARTE, Henry BADCOCKE. Proved 24 Nov. 1581.

JOHN HARRISON of Woodham Mortimer, 24 Oct. 1581. (289)
To the poor 10s. at the day of my burial. To a preacher at my burial 3s.4d. To Ellen my wife the house wherein I dwell with the land belonging for her life; after her decease, to Th. my son. To her all my goods within my house, 5 of my best kine at her choice, 16 sheep, half my hogs, 1 seam of barley, 2 seams of oats, sufficient winter store [*recte* stover?] for all her cattle for the year to come, my bald mare with her colt, and my own poultry; and £10 at All Saints' Day 1583. To Edw. my son my 2 acres in Press Mead in Woodham Walter which I bought of Mr John STONARDE esquire. To Joan WADE, my sister's daughter, 1 cow bullock and 6 ewe lambs. To Agnes my daughter, now wife of Hum. OFFIN of Great Baddow, £3. The residue of my goods to Th., whom I make executor. I nominate John WADE of Woodham Mortimer overseer, and for his pains 2s.6d. Witnesses: Gilbert WOODWARDE, John STOCKER, Edw. AYER, Nich. JOHNSON clerk [rector of Woodham Mortimer]. Proved 21 Nov. 1581.

WILLIAM KINGE of Great Wakering, 23 Nov. 1580. (Nuncupative.) (290)
Being demanded what recompense he would give to his 'ostice' [hostess], [blank] MASON widow, in whose house he had lain sick of long time, to whom he was indebted for all his charges, he, confessing that he was greatly indebted to her and was not able to make her a recompense with all that he had, but, quoth he, widow NEALE hath of mine in keeping, 25s. in money, a gold ring and 1 old angel which he, my godfather LARGE had in keeping, all which I give to my 'ostis', and if there remain anything, she being paid, I will the poor of Great Wakering shall have it. Witnesses: Rd. DANDIE, John PIKE, Philip DUDE, Th. SMYTHE, Wm. HILLES. Administration committed, 12 Oct. 1581 to Charles PATENSON and Mary PATENSON *alias* MASON his sister, creditors.

ALICE BROWNE of Mundon widow, 2 May 1581. (291)
To my brother Edw. FELIX 20s., 1 flockbed, my best hutch, my best canvas tablecloth, my least brass pot, my biggest kettle save 1, and 2 of my best platters. To my brother John FELIX 20s., my 2nd hutch, 1 spit, 1 iron dripping pan, 2 of my 2nd platters, 1 long table, my 2nd tablecloth, 1 pillow, 1 sheet, 1 ceiling to hang over a bed, and 1 old stained cloth. To Edw.'s four children [not named] 20s. to be equally divided. To Sarah daughter of John FELIX 20s. To Susan daughter of Rt. WOODWARDE 40s. at 20, to remain in the hands of Rt. SOALE of Mundon until then, on

condition that he pay Amy WOODWARDE, mother of Susan, 2s. yearly for 20 years or the 20s. to be put into some other honest man's hands that will do the same. To Susan 1 cupboard, 2 platters, 1 dozen white trenchers, ½ dozen wooden spoons, and 1 flockbed. To widow SWIFTE of Maldon 2 lockram kerchiefs and 1 lockram apron. To Amy WOODWARDE 1 pair of malt querns, 1 brewing tub, 1 little broad keeler, my biggest brass pot, my 3rd kettle, the rest of my pewter, 1 spice mortar with a pestle, 1 dozen trenchers, 2 hutches; and the rest of my linen between Amy and Susan. To Edw. my best stained cloth, 1 joined stool, and my biggest chair. To Amy 1 joined stool, 1 chair and 1 form, and a frying pan. To Daniel GARINGTON the younger son of Daniel of Mundon my biggest kettle and 1 round table with a hutch in it. The rest of my goods to Wm. EROLL and Daniel GARINGTON, whom I make executors. Witnesses: Henry PRIOR, Amy WOODWARDE. Proved 12 May 1581.

ELIZABETH KEBELL widow, [abode not given], 22 Oct. 1581. (292)
To the poor people of the ward of Plaistow in West Ham 40s. To Roger son of Jasper KEBELL and his two sisters Agnes and Joan KEBELL 40s. apiece at 21 or marriage. To their father Jasper 20s. To James ALLEN of Plaistow 10s. The rest of my goods to Hugh GRIFFIN, whom I make executor. I make overseers Wm. MERITON the younger, Th. POLLARDE and John PRAIGHTE [*recte* PRAGELL?] the younger, and for their pains 6s.8d. apiece. Witnesses: John PRAGELL, Wm. MERITON, Th. POLLARDE. Proved 31 Oct. 1581.

WALTER ANDROES [ANDREWES *in margin*] of Brentwood saddler, 10 Aug. 1581. (293)
To Eliz. ANDROWESmy wife my two tenements in Brentwood for her life; after her decease, my greatest tenement in Brentwood in which widow BAYWARDE dwelleth to John my son, on condition that he shall not sell it, and my little tenement to Wm. my son that John FORDE dwelleth in. To Joan ANDROWES my daughter £6 13s.[4d.] at marriage. The rest of my goods to my wife, whom I ordain executrix. I make John WYELLS of Brentwood overseer, and for his pains 12d. Witnesses: John CHAMBER, John WYELL, Leonard OXCLIFFE. Proved 4 Oct. 1581. Inventory exhibited at £7.

RICHARD TAILOR of Rayleigh, 21 Dec., 15 Eliz., [1572]. (294)
To my wife's son, Anthony NEWMAS [*recte* NEWMAN?], 20s. in moneyworth in house stuff. To Edw. TAILOR my son 10s. To the poor 12d. The rest of my goods to Eliz. my wife, whom I make executrix. I owe Edw. 10s. Witnesses: Giles COMFORDE, John LOANE of the 'Chequer' the elder, Henry COLMAN minister, Nich. BRODEWATER. Proved 13 Sept. 1581.

WILLIAM TRIPLOWE of Cranham, 29 July 1581. (295)
To Agnes daughter of Th. SHAWE £40 to be paid by my executrix to John LEGATT of Hornchurch and Wm. SPARROWE of Bulphan, they to put it forth to her use and pay it again with the profits when she is 18 or at marriage. To 'Rabrige' SHAWE £20 at marriage, if she be obedient and guided and ruled by her mother, or else nothing. The rest of my goods to my wife, whom I make executrix. I make John LEGATT and Wm. SPARROWE overseers, to whom I give 10 groats apiece. Witnesses: Th. HAWKINS minister [not the rector], Th. WRIGELSWOOD of North Ockendon, Rt. WHELPESON. Proved 15 Sept. 1581.

HENRY EGELSTON [EGGLESTON *in margin*] of Stanford-le-Hope yeoman, 5 July 1581. (296)
To the poor people 3s.4d. and so forth yearly for 20 years at the Feast of the Nativity of our Lord. To my daughters Barbara and Susanna each £20 at 18 or marriage. To the child with which my wife now goeth £20, if a daughter at marriage and if a son at 21. To Barbara the press in the parlour, my wife to have the use of it for her life. To Susan the table and form in the hall. To Mgy. my wife my free and copyhold tenements and lands in Stanford and West Tilbury for her life; after her decease, to the child if a son, and if a daughter to my daughters. The residue of my goods to my wife, whom I make executrix. I make John STELWOMAN supervisor, and 3s.4d. for his pains. Witnesses: James GOWRE the writer, vicar of

Mucking, Wm. BURNELL clerk [the clergy list for Stanford-le-Hope is deficient at this period], John STOCKES, Rt. BEAMOND of London draper. Proved 21 July 1581. Inventory exhibited at £63 7s.

JOAN VYNCENTE [VINCENT *in margin*] of Great Stambridge widow, 16 Aug. 1581. (297)

[Religious preamble.] To my eldest son Jehu STOUTE my house called Marshalls *alias* Marchantes with 4 crofts of land called Cotsalls tenements in Great Stambridge in the tenure of [blank] HOUSE. To my youngest son John STOWTE my 2 crofts called Mottes in Great Stambridge in the tenure of one KETTLE of Canewdon. I will that Jehu pay John for 8 years 40s. towards his better bringing up. To Alice STOWTE my daughter my customary house wherein I dwell called Trittles Hall *alias* Thinskilxton and a pightle or croft of land belonging and the orchards and gardens in the lordship of Great Stambridge, also my oyster layne and fishing place which I hold in fee simple by copy of court roll of the manor of Great Stambridge. My goods shall be appraised and sold or otherwise equally divided between my said three children. To Rd. COALE of Stambridge aforesaid 5s., whom I desire to be overseer. I will Jehu to be executor. Witnesses: John DANYELL minister [not the rector] of Great Stambridge, James STEVEN, John RACHELL, Wm. FANNER. Proved 13 Sept. 1581.

WILLIAM MINTON [MYNTON *in margin*], [abode not given], 17 Feb. 1580/1. (298)

To be buried in Great Waltham churchyard. To Anne my wife for her life my house in Great Waltham; after her decease, to John my son, on condition that he pay Rd. my son 40s. To Rd. 2 looms with the furniture belonging except 2 sleys (1 of 30, the other of 24), which I give to John. To John and Rd. my scales and weights to be equally divided. They shall occupy the looms and sleys together until Michaelmas next. To Rd. 2 boards lying over the entry and 1 mattress at marriage. To John the great brass pot after my wife's decease. To Agnes my daughter 1 kettle with 2 rings and 6s.8d. To Joan my daughter 6s.8d. The residue of my goods to my wife, whom I make executrix. I make Rt. WOODHAM overseer, and for his pains 12d. Witnesses: Edm. MARYN, Wm. DREAKES, Rt HAYEARDE, Th. BRIDGE. [No probate clause.]

ANNE ROGER of Stanford-le-Hope widow, 26 Apr. 1581. (299)

To Rt. ROGER my son the best featherbed, a cupboard and the greatest brass pot. The residue of my goods to John, Th. and Rt. my sons to be equally divided at 21. John STILLIMAN my father shall have the lands with the house called Littles in as ample sort as Wm. ROGER my late husband did give it to me to the bringing up of my said three sons. To the poor 2s. To my father half the oats growing on Littles. If all three sons die without enjoying the goods, the same to my father and John WHITE now dwelling with him. To the wife of Chris. SNOMON my frize cassock and a red petticoat and widow STACE a russet petticoat. The rest of my goods to my father to bring up my children. I make him executor and Henry EGLESTON and John RATTLE of Stanford overseers, and for their pains 3s.4d. apiece. Witnesses: Wm. BURNELL [see no.296] clerk, Henry EGLESTON, John RATTLE. Proved 27 June 1581.

EDWARD GOODINGE of Moreton husbandman, — 1581. (300)

To my brother John GOODINGE a cow, a bullock, 2 sheep, a sow, 4 pigs, 2 lambs, and my crop of corn, and my time that I have there to be a comforter to his father and mother. To Kath. my wife a joined bed, a joined table, a hutch without a lid, 3 sheep, 4 pigs, and half a quarter of bullimong corn [mixed grain]. I make my brother John executor. Witnesses: Th. KINGE of Moreton, John SETTEN of the same, writer. Proved 21 July 1581.

WILLIAM GLASCOCKE of Fyfield yeoman, 6 Apr. 1579. (301)

I ordain Wm. my son executor. To the poor of High Easter, Fyfield and East Ham, each parish 10s., of Shelley 2s., and of Moreton 3s. To my servants 3s.4d. apiece. To Wm. my best brass pot, my best cupboard in the hall, ½ dozen of my greatest silver spoons, my scales with the iron beams, 4 of my greatest leaden weights, 2 coats of plate, the best bow with the best sheaf of arrows, the best 2 gorgets, the best sword and dagger, and 2 steel caps; the goods that he hath of mine in his custody; the debts that he oweth me; my cauldron that hangeth, the iron bar and a pair of pothooks, all hanging in the kitchen chimney, but he shall not remove them so long as my wife dwell in the house, neither will any person hereafter take out the iron hooks but they to remain still with the house. To Wm. my timber squared and unsquared, my 'scrull' that I 'scrull' corn with and my hangers that I ride withal. To Wm. my house with the lands in Fyfield, and my wife's gift. To him my house and lands in Dagenham, to him and his heirs male after my wife's decease; if he die without heirs male, to my daughter Mgt., provided that he shall give her for her life £5 a year. To her £20, Wm. LAIKE her son £20, and the rest of her children £10 apiece yearly. To her also ½ dozen of silver spoons of the lesser sort and a little joined hutch in the middle chamber. To Th. GLASCOCKE my brother 40s. and my best coat, best doublet, best hose and shoes, best russet jerkin, best hat, and 2 of my best shirts, if he be alive. To John FERE the rest of my apparel and 3s.4d. I will that Thomasine my wife shall have my house in Fyfield and the lands so long as she keepeth herself a widow, she to have for her firebote every year 13 of the best lops and 1 old husband [a pollarded tree (used in Kent; Halliwell, *Dict. of Archaic Words*)] to make her logs, so that she shall fell no timber or 'spoores' [for speres?, saplings (Fisher, *Medieval Farming Glossary*)], what wood soever they be, and shall keep the house in good reparations, paying the lord's rent, i.e. 4d. a year; if she marry, to take the profit until Michaelmas next and then quietly depart and take her jointure in Dagenham; if Wm. chance to fell any timber for his own use, my wife to have the lops and offal towards her firebote. The rest of my goods to Thomasine my wife. I make Wm. my son executor. My body to be buried either in Fyfield or in High Easter church, to which church 3s.4d. If my son refuse to prove my Will, Th. LAIKE my son-in-law shall prove it and take the use of one of my houses. I ordain John GLASCOCKE of Roxwell and John WRIGHT of Kelvedon [Hatch] gentlemen and Th. LAIKE of Waltham Holy Cross yeoman supervisors, and for their pains 6s.8d. apiece. Witnesses: Wm. STOOKES, John MOUNCKE, Abraham SMYTHE the writer. Proved 20 July 1581.

THOMAS BROCKE of Stock, 19 June, 23 Eliz. [1581]. (302)

To Rt. son of Wm. BROCKE my brother £20; my sister Joan CARPENDER £20; the children of Agnes MEACHAM my sister departed £20 among them part and part like; Th. son £20 and Agnes and 'Edgeth' [for Edith?] daughters of Wm. each 10 marks. To Mgt. wife of John BUSSIE [*recte* BUSSHE?] and Joan wife of Th. BANNESTER each £6 13s.4d. To the children of Th. HUNTE of 'Marshe Baldea' [in?] deceased £10 to be equally divided. To the poor people of the town where I was born [not stated] 40s. To John DENNYS and Wm. BROWNE of Stock 20s. apiece; widow GRENE and widow HARVIE, father WHISKARDE and widow HOLMAN, all of Stock, 10s. apiece. To widow KINGE £3 6s.8d. goodman WHOLIE 10s., Rd. COOPER 20s., PETYGREWE, REVELL, Hugh MILES, Saunder [Alex.] GARRET, mother STARLINGE, Nich. BUSSHE, BARTON the sawyer, widow CHIPPINGE, Mich. WEALDE, PARNELL, PAYNE the butcher, and John BUSSHE, all of Stock, 10s. apiece. To the poor of Buttsbury £3 to be distributed by my cousin Rd. BROCKE as he shall see occasion of need. All which legacies to these poor people of Stock and Buttsbury shall be distributed before the day of my burial. To my godchildren in Stock and Buttsbury 10s. apiece. To Edw. FINCHE dwelling over against the 'Spread Eagle' in Fryerning £3. To the poor of Ingatestone and Fryerning 40s., of Mountnessing 20s., and of Margaretting 20s. To BYNDER of the Park, John AMATT surgeon, Henry NUTTINGE, PARKER, and RICHARDSON, and 'CHAREFOWLE' [for CHARVELL] potter, all of Stock, each 10s. To the children of my brother John BROCKE £10. To BRAYE of Stock 10s. I will that at my burial my executor shall distribute, over and above that which already is recited, to the poor people which shall be at my burial £10 ['ten poundes']. To the poor of Chelmsford 20s., of Moulsham [in Chelmsford] 20s., and of Brentwood 20s., and to the hospital of Moulsham 10s. To Mr WOODWARDE[1] that was my tutor

[1] John Woodward, Sir William Petre's chaplain and former rector of Ingatestone (F.G.Emmison, *Tudor Secretary: Sir William Petre at Court and Home* (1961), 278-9).

in Oxford [University], to be delivered to my Lady PETER [widow of Sir Wm. Petre of Ingatestone Hall] to his use £5. Towards the reparations of Stock church 20s. To HOPTON the smith, HITTES the sawyer and mother HEMINGES, all of Buttsbury, 5s. apiece. To my brothers Wm. and Rd. BROCKE £60 between them equally to be divided. To my fellows in household, as well menservants as maidservants, to be distributed by my executor, 40s. To BATESON of Stock 5s., HAWLE 10s. and Edw. HAWKEN 10s. To my loving friends Roland TANSEY £5 and Th. FITCHE £3, whom I make overseers. I will that, at the next winter at the felling of my woods, my executor shall assign to each of my poor neighbours in Stock a place where each shall for their firing have the felling and making of 2 loads of wood apiece. To Rd. son of Wm. BROCKE my brother my messuage in Buttsbury wherein John READER the elder liveth. The rest of my goods to Rd., whom I make executor. Witnesses: 'Row.' TANSEY, Rd. BATESON, John AMATT. Proved 28 June 1581.

JOAN BROWNE of Stock widow, [date not given]. (303)
To my brother-in-law John PETCHIE 26s.8d. which he oweth me, on condition that he shall pay the charges of my burial and bestow on my neighbours and friends that doth help to bring me to the church in bread and drink 3s. To PETYFEW's [*sic*] wife, FRIDAIE's wife and HOPTON's wife each 4d. To my daughter Dthy. TOMPSON £3 now in the hands of Rd. WILSON of Buttsbury mercer and due to be paid at Michaelmas next. The rest of my goods to Dthy. Geo. YOUNGE of Buttsbury shall have the custody of Dthy. and the governance of her portions until she is 20; if she die before, to the five children of my brother POOL 5s. apiece, to my sister PETCHIE 20s., to five of Rd. WILSON's children 12d. apiece, to my cousin Toby FRISTER's eldest son Wm. 6s.8d., and to three of Geo. YOUNGE's children 5s. apiece. I make my well-beloved in Christ Geo. YOUNGE of Buttsbury executor. I ordain overseers John PETCHIE and Rd. WILSON, and for their pains each 6d. To PETYGREW's wife 5s. after Dthy.'s death. All my goods shall be sold by the discretion of Geo. YOUNGE and Rd. WILSON. Witnesses: John PETCHIE, Geo. YOUNGE, Rd. WILSON. 12 May 1581, Geo. YOUNGE appeared and renounced executorship; administration committed to him during the minority of Dthy.

CHRISTOPHER TAILOR of Stock potter, 21 Mar. 1580/1. (304)
To Dthy. my wife and my sons John and Chris. all my lands and tenements freehold and copyhold for term of their lives and to the heirs of Christopher; if he die without heirs, to be equally divided amongst my daughter's children. To my wife and John all my household stuff equally divided, saving to Chris. my long table with the frame, the 2 forms and the settle in the house wherein I dwell. To my daughters Agnes and Joan each £20, the £20 to Joan to be paid equally between my wife and my sons to her husband to discharge my bond for him to Mr BERRY of Eastwood. To my daughter Mary £20 for which I stand bound to her husband, for it to be paid. Whereas there is due to Wm. STERLINGE at the end of his years 4 marks, I make it up to £5. To Th. STERLINGE 10s. My uncle [not named] shall have his chamber and his bed for his life as he hath had it heretofore. To the poor at my burial 20s. The rest of my goods to my wife and John my eldest son equally divided, whom I ordain executors. I ordain Abraham DRAINE and Chris. TAILOR overseers, and for their pains 5s. Witnesses: Th. BELLINGHAM, John ROBIENTE, Frs. MOTTE, Alex. GARRETT. 12 May 1581, the executors appeared and renounced executorship; the judge committed letters testimonial to collect to Th. SHERIFFE the apparitor, 'etc.'

WILLIAM JENNINGES of Romford glover, 27 Apr., 21 Eliz. [1579]. (305)
To Romford chapel 5s. To the poor 5s. To my daughters Jane, Joan and 'Grisell' JENNINGES each 20 marks at 18 or marriage. To my son Stephen JENNINGES £10 at £18. To him a cottage which I have in mortgage of Frs. NEWMAN at Noak Hill [in Romford], if he do not repay £12 specified in the mortgage or bill of sale; but if he pay, to pay the £12 to Stephen at 18. To John BENNAT my best doublet and buff venetians and my best coat. The residue of my goods to my well-beloved wife Mgy., whom I ordain excutrix. I make overseers John GRENE and Rt. DICKENSON, and for their pains 6s.8d. Witnesses: John BENNATE, Edw. CLEISTE [*recte* CLEIFTE], John COMPORTE. Proved 3 June 1581.

ALICE LAUNSIE of Rettendon widow, 18 Oct. 1580. (306)
To Samuel SEYMER, John LAUNSIE, Nathaniel LAUNSIE, Rt. WOODE the younger and John HAIES each a sheep. To Sarah THORNTON and Wm. PERCE's children each 2s. To my goddaughters, i.e. Ellen MILLER, Judith LAUNSIE and Sarah WOODE, each 5s. To a preacher to make 3 sermons 10s. To John FRANCIS and John my son each a shirt of flaxen cloth, Judith LAUNSIE a smock of flaxen cloth, Agnes EGEOTT my daughter my best chair and best table, my sister Christian my worsted kirtle, best petticoat and best hat, and Anthony FOOTE's wife a red petticoat. To John LAUNSIE my service book. To John my son and my three daughters each a pair of sheets of the best. To widow GOODWYN, John PASFEILDE and Frances THORNTON each 1 sheet. To my three daughters my wearing linen. To Sarah EDGIOTT my black apron and Rebecca EDGIOTT 1 table napkin, Dthy. my son's wife my double cupboard cloth, Dthy. my son's daughter 1 holland apron and 1 frame to make tape, Agnes 1 little brazen mortar with the pestle, Judith 1 diaper napkin, and widow GOODWYNE my frize cassock and 1 petticoat with a linen upperbody. To John HAISE and Emma HAIES each 5s. The residue of my goods to my three daughters equally divided. I make John my son and Wm. EGIOTT my son-in-law executors, and for their pains each 2s., and my son-in-law Rt. WOODE overseer, and for his pains 2s. To the poor of Rettendon 10s. Witnesses: Th. HOPKINS, Eliz. WILLINGALE. To Mgt. PERCE my old kettle and 5s., mother PASFEILDE my black coat and my hat, Dthy. my son's wife the turned form, Emme HAIES 1 pair of sheets or else all the yarn and flax, also 2 tick pillows marked with blue, Martha SUDBURYE a flaxen kerchief and a workday apron, Th. PASFEILDE's wife 1 towen sheet, my son my flannel waistcoat, Emme HAIES a coverlet, and John HAIES to have of Emme HAIES 10s. The apples to be given to poor folk. Witnesses to this latter part: mother PASFEILD, mother JACKSON. 12 May 1582, the executors appeared and renounced executorship and all right and interest in deceased's goods, and the judge decreed letters testimonial, 'etc.' and ordered them to exhibit the inventory.

THOMAS BOWTH (or BOOTHE) of Stratford Langthorne in West Ham, 25 Mar. 1580. (307)
To my son Vincent BOWTH a standing wainscot bedstead, a truckle bed, and a red cow. To my daughter Alice a wainscot cupboard in the hall, a joined bedstead in the parlour with the featherbed, and a cow. The rest of my goods to Joan my wife, whom I ordain executrix, appointing my very friends and neighbours Wm. MAPLES and Hugh BENNETT overseers. Witnesses: Th. FORRESTE clerk [not the vicar], Wm. MAPLES, Hugh BENNETT, Rd. MOMPORTE. Proved 5 May 1581.

WILLIAM BROWNE of Rayleigh, — 1581. (308)
To Mary MEDCALF 1 joined bedstead, a flockbed, and 40s. at 21. To certain of the poorest in Rayleigh 3s.4d. To Mary my wife, whom I make executrix, my house that I dwell in and all my goods. I appoint my cousin Edw. BODE of Canewdon overseer, and for his pains 10s. Witnesses: Charles WORLINGTON, John SMYTHE. Proved by definitive sentence for Mary BROWNE, 20 Feb. 1581/2, by the oath of Geoffrey CLARKE, her proctor.

JOHN COOPER of Corringham, 21 Oct. 1582. (309)
To Mgt. RAMSE 2s. to buy her such things as she needs; to her five children [not named] 12d. apiece likewise; to Th. RAMSIE a pair of my best russet drawers and a pair of new shoes. To Rd. ARNOULD my best shirt; to Wm. BLOWER a frize coat, a doublet and a pair of russet breeches; to John BOONE a russet jerkin. To my three godchildren 5s. apiece. To my wife [not named] 40s. that John ANDREWE's wife of Barking doth owe me. To mother CURRAN 12d. To Stephen DRAPER my best knit hosen and my mattock. I will that at my burial a bushel of good wheat shall be bestowed in white bread and a godly sermon preached and he to have for his pains 6s.8d. To the poor all my apparel linen and woollen. To my maid a russet petticoat cloth that is a-spinning to be made for her and a hat that I bought last. The residue of my goods to my wife, whom I make executrix. Overseers I desire to be Rt. DRAPER and John and Rd. ARNOULD. Witnesses: Rt. DRAPER, John ARNOULD. Proved 15 Nov. 1582.

THOMAS LEYCETER of Grays Thurrock, 10 Mar. 1581/2. (310)
To Mgy. my wife and my two sons Th. and John half my lands, cattle and goods; the other half to be divided between my two sons. I make my wife executrix. Witnesses: Roger HOLDEN, Th. KIGHLEY, John FILLOPPE. Proved 3 Apr. 1582.

WILLIAM HAIES of Cranham, 26 Feb. 1581/2. (311)
To Beatrice my daughter 40s. at marriage. The residue of my goods, cattle, corn and household stuff to Mary my wife, whom I make executrix. I make overseers Wm. MUSCHAMP esquire and my cousin Hum. HAIES. To my wife for her life, towards the bringing up of my children, my lands and tenements in Carshalton, Beddington and Wallington (co. Surrey); after her decease, to Hum. my son, conditionally that he pay to his two sisters Anne HAIES and Eliz. HAIES, my daughters, 20 marks apiece when he is 21 and in possession of the lands. If he refuse to pay, the lands to Anne and Eliz. equally apportioned; for default of their heirs, successively to Wm. HAIES my godson, son of my brother John, and to the children of my brother Edw. HAIES. Witnesses: Wm. MUSCHAM esquire, Mary his wife, Wm. MANSWORTHE servant with Wm. HAIES, Wm. HAIES. Proved 3 Apr. 1582.

MARY widow of Rd. PARIS of Dagenham, 2 July, 24 Eliz. [1582]. (312)
To be buried as near to my late husband as conveniently may be. To my son John PARIS £10, besides 40s. given him by his father's Will [no.222], the £12 to be paid to my very friends Wm. SCOTT of Barking and his brother Rt. SCOTT of Hornchurch gentlemen, both to be bound to my executor and my brother Andrew MAN of Hertford [co. Hertford] tanner for payment to John at 21. To him my best featherbed, a towel, a tablecloth, and 2 of my least brass pots. To Wm. my son £10 besides 40s. [as above], at 21. To him my 2 best brass pots, 3 silver pins, a pair of silver hooks, a silver ring, and a silver whistle. If both my sons die before 21, their parts to be equally divided among the children of my brother-in-law Wm. PARIS and of my youngest sister Agnes MAN. To Agnes my old servant 4s., the little bed whereon she lieth, my old cassock, and my worst petticoat. To my godchildren 12d. apiece. To my mother [not named] my best cassock but 1, best red petticoat and best smock. To Agnes my youngest sister my best cassock and Joan COCKES my eldest sister my best russet petticoat. To old mother SUDBERE my frize cassock and an old russet petticoat. To my landlord Mr SCOTT a silver ring, Mistress Anne SCOTT a little silver jewel, and Eliz. SCOTT a silver jewel. The residue of my goods and the lease of my house to my brother-in-law Wm. PARIS of Dagenham labourer, whom I make executor, towards the bringing up and finding to school my young son Wm., hoping that he will be a good and friendly uncle to both my children and be careful as I know his brother was always for him while he lived. I make Wm. SCOTT, Rt. SCOTT and Andrew MAN overseers; to my said brother for a token of remembrance a little silver goblet and to Mr Wm. SCOTT and Rt. SCOTT each half a crown in gold. Witnesses: Wm. SCOTT, Rt. SCOTT, Geoffrey UMFRIE. Proved 13 Sept. 1582.

PETER BROOKE of Barking fisherman, 20 Nov. 1582. (Nuncupative.) (313)
Being demanded of Eliz. his wife how he would dispose his goods, he answered, I give all freely unto you and to bring up my daughter 'Timothie' as you would bring up your own. Witnesses: Rose HOLLIS, goodwife BURCHEALL, goodwife HOWE, John ATKINSON. Proved 25 Feb. 1581/2.

ANTHONY ERINGTON of Horndon-on-the-Hill gentleman, 14 Sept. 1582. (Nuncupative.) (314)
To 'Rubie' his son a debt of £21 which one Mr LISTLEY 'ought' [oweth] Anthony and a sword or 5 marks which Mr LISTLEY 'ought', and a gold ring worth £3 6s.8d., all at 18; if he die before, to the child wherewith his wife went withal. The rest of his goods to Mgy. his wife. [No executor or witnesses.] Proved 15 Nov. 1582; administration committed to the widow.

THOMAS HAWARD, parish clerk of Barking, 29 Oct. 1582. (315)
To the poor men's box 3s.4d. To my brother Wm. HAYWARD all my woollen apparel, coats, doublets, hosen, hats and shoes, but not my gowns. The rest of my

goods to Kath. my wife, whom I make executrix. If she die of this sickness that God hath laid upon us, I make Wm. executor. I make overseer my brother. [No witnesses.] Proved 10 Jan. 1582/3 by Kath. Inventory exhibited at £11 12d.

GEORGE FASBIE of Barking fisherman, 19 Jan. 1582/3. (316)
To be buried in Barking churchyard near to the place of my other wife deceased. To my loving wife Joan all my goods as well quick as dead, provided that she keep my two children John and Edw. FASEBIE with meat, drink, learning, lodging and apparel during their minority, i.e. to 21. I ordain her my executrix and overseer my trusty friend John PIERSON of Barking writer, desiring him to aid her. Witnesses: Stephen BIRD, Rd. MASSON. Proved 21 Jan. 1582/3.

JOHN IVE of Wennington husbandman, 6 Mar. 1581/2. (317)
To Susan IVE my daughter £4 and to Joan IVE my daughter £4 at 20. The residue of my goods to Mgt. my wife, whom I make executrix. Witnesses: Mr [Wm.] ARDEN, parson of Wennington, James SHAWCROFTE. I make John IVE supervisor, and for his pains 3s.4d. Proved 4 Apr. 1582.

JOHN BARKER of Rayleigh, 22 May 1582. (318)
I will that my uncle Simon DALE shall have my daughter Mary BARKER to bring [up] in honest education, he to have all my goods to her education, except 2 kettles, a posnet and a pewter platter which I give to Mary at 18. To my brother Rd. BARKER my black fustian doublet. To Hum. BARKER my godson 2s. to buy him 2 shirts. I ordain Simon DALE executor. Witnesses: Rd. BLACKWELL minister, John HARRISON, John BONNER. Proved 31 May 1582.

WILLIAM DRAKE of Great Waltham yeoman, 10 Feb. 1582/3. (319)
To Eliz. my well-beloved wife my house and land called Drakes, free and copy, for her life, on consideration that she bring up my children in fear and nurture of our Lord God; after her decease, to Wm. DRAKE my eldest son. To my two daughters [not named] £6 13s.4d. apiece at 20. To Th. DRAKE my brother 40s. To the child that my wife is withal, if a manchild £10 at 21 but if a womanchild but £6 13s.4d. at 21. The residue of my goods to my wife, whom I make executrix. Witnesses: Edm. MARION, Rt. WOODHAM, Rt. HAWARD, Joan GOODEF, Rd. POND writer hereof. Proved 21 Mar. 1582/3.

JOHN RADLEY of Ramsden Bellhouse, 15 Mar. 1581/2. (320)
To my daughters Kath. and Mgt. each £4 13s.4d. and Joyce £6 13s.4d. The rest of my goods, cattle, lands and leases to John my son, whom I make executor. I make Nich. TABOR overseer, and for his pains 6s.8d. Witnesses: Rt. BOOTHE clerk [rector of Ramsden Bellhouse], Rt. WATESON, Th. WHELER. Proved 23 Apr. 1582.

ROBERT BRUER [BRUARE *in margin*] of Hornchurch husbandman, 4 July 1582. (321)
To the poor of Hornchurch 15s. at the day of my burial. To my sister MILBORNE's children £6 13s.4d. to be equally divided at 20, to be delivered to Th. MILBORNE their father, so that he put in sufficient assurance to my overseers. To my brother Geo. BRUARE 1 of the kine that I bought sithence I was married and 30s., to be paid by Rd. HARROWER of 'Southend' [South End in Hornchurch] for a mare sold to him. To Geo.'s sons Rd. 40s. and Wm. 6s.8d. at 20 and his daughters Mgy. and Agnes each 10s. at 18. To the children of my brother Wm. BRUARE £3 equally between them at 20. To Lewis JOHNSON my godchild 40s. and Jane and John his children each 20s. at 20. To Lewis JOHNSON my godchild 2 sheep. To John EDLIN, Rd. EDLIN the younger, and Joan daughter to Joan BREWER my wife each 20s. To John BRUER my younger brother 40s. and a chest which was my father's [not named]. To Th. FABUTT my sister's son 4 sheep. To the said John BRUER my best doublet and black coat, Geo. BREWER my mare colt, John BRUER the younger the best colt, and Lewis JOHNSON the black horse colt. To John son of Th. MILBORNE the bald horse colt. The rest of my goods to my wife, whom I make executrix. I make the overseers Henry HUMFRAYE and John BRUARE my eldest brother, and for their pains 5s. between them. Witnesses: Rt. BREWER, Wm. LAMBERT, Rd. HARWARE, John HAWOOD. Proved 28 July 1582.

THOMAS CHRISTOVER [CHRISTOFER in margin] of Chigwell tanner, 7 Aug. 1582. (Nuncupative.) **(322)**
He gave his goods to Kath. his wife and nominated John LEWIS of Chigwell, his master, executor. Witnesses: Th. FOULKES vicar of Chigwell, Eliz. wife of 'Dionisse' HARVIE. Proved -- 1582.

JOHN WRIGHTE of West Tilbury, 24 May 1582. **(323)**
To the poor of West Tilbury 20s. To the repairing of Tilbury church 6s.8d. To Roger ROGARES and Th. SIMONDES each 20s. To Mgy. my wife and Mgt. my daughter all my goods to be parted equally, my daughter at 18. To my wife my copyhold land in Mucking called Danymaires *alias* Garnettes for her life; after her decease, to Mgt. To her after her mother's decease my freehold in Chadwell. I make overseers John EDGIAT and John BRUARE. Witnesses: Rd. CAWOOD [not the rector], John RIPTEN, John EDGIOT, Roger WEST, John BRUERE. Proved -- 1582.

MARY daughter of John CUCOCKE of Rivenhall deceased, 6 Nov. 1582. **(324)**
To be buried in Purleigh churchyard. To my mother Lettice wife of Rt. STRAIGHT for her life my lands in Rivenhall; after her decease, to my sister Winifred wife of John MYNOT, to whom I bequeath my black gown which my father made me, on condition that she agree that my mother enjoy my lands for her life. To my mother my best gown, my hat, my black apron, my 2 best neckerchiefs, 1 of my best crosscloths, and my frize gown. To my sister Alice STRAIGHT my red petticoat, a lockram kercher, a crosscloth, and a pair of grogram sheets. To my sister Lettice a pair of linsey woolsey sleeves, a crosscloth, a kerchief, and a waist [girdle or waistcoat]. My cow to be sold and the money parted equally between my brethren Edw., John, Th. and Rt. the sons of Rt. STRAIGHTE. To Edw. 1 of my hutches, the other to Alice. To Wm. MASON of Ulting my 4 lambs, paying my father-in-law STRAIGHT for the keeping of them. To my three godchildren each 12d. To Mgt. WITHERS my waistcoat. The rest of my goods to be divided between my two sister Susan and Rebecca. I make executor my father Rt. STRAIGHT. Witnesses: Rd. ALISON minister [not the rector], John ARGENT, Rt. HUMFRIE. Proved 23 Nov. 1582.

RICHARD WEALD of Great Stambridge, 17 Mar. 1581/2. **(325)**
To Rt. my son being 8, 50s., to be paid by Eliz. my wife to Wm. RODOCKE of 'Stambridge', to whom I will the keeping and bringing up to lawful age. To Agnes my daughter, being 10, 1 dun cow and 1 red bullock of a year old which are judged to be worth 40s.; I will that Henry HOWSE of Great Wakering have the keeping and bringing her up to lawful age and the keeping of her cow and bullock and at 20 to give her instead 40s. To her 3 sheep worth 10s., Henry HOWSE likewise to pay her 50s. To my two children 2 flitches of bacon judged to be worth 8s. Whereas John BOUN of Rayleigh oweth me 30s., to my wife 10s. and my children 20s. The residue of my goods to my wife, whom I make executrix. Witnesses: Peter WALKER, Edw. KEMPE, Wm. RODOCKE, John FRANCES. [No probate clause.]

RICHARD BURLEY of Ramsden Bellhouse, 8 June 1582. **(326)**
To John DANIELL my right and interest in a ground called Wick Hatch in Wickham [Bishops?], he paying Kath. my wife £5 so soon as he shall enjoy the ground. To him my best hose. The rest of my goods to my wife, whom I make executrix. Witnesses: Rt. BOOTHE clerk [rector], Anne MARSHE, Alice HILLES. [No probate clause.]

THOMAS KEME [KEMPE *in margin*] of Great Waltham, 8 Aug. 1582. **(327)**
To Kath. BONE 3s.4d. The residue of my goods to Florence my well-beloved wife, whom I make executrix. Witnesses: Rd. POND, John POND. Proved 11 Dec. 1582.

THOMAS BREWER of Barking husbandman, 28 Sept. 1580. **(328)**
To the poor men's box 3s.4d. To Jane DUNNE my servant, if it happen [that] my wife put her away after my death for her misbehaviour towards her, 20s. To Eliz. PARKER my daughter-in-law 1 brown milch bullock. The rest of my goods to Mary my wife, whom I make executrix. I make overseers my loving and trusty friends John JEFFREY my brother-in-law and Henry CLARKE my neighbours, and for their

pains each 3s.4d. Witnesses: John JEFFREY, Henry CLARKE yeoman, Th. HAYWARDE, [parish] clerk of Barking. Proved 6 May 1583.

THOMAS TURNISHE of Purleigh, 29 Nov. 1579. (329)
To Mary TURNISHE my daughter all my goods, on condition that she shall bring up my two children Wm. and Rt. TURNISHE with meat, drink and apparel until each be 15. She shall release and give to Rt. my son the £3 6s.8d. given her by copy of court rolls out of the yearly rent of my three parts of the house in Purleigh called Nether House at marriage or 21; if she refuse, the value of the 5 marks be taken out of my goods by the inventory by the estimation of Th. KINGE and James BRETT of Purleigh to Rt.'s use. If Rt. die before marriage or 21, the £3 6s.8d. to Mary, whom I make executrix. Witnesses: Rt. PEARSON clerk, parson of Cold Norton, Th. KINGE, James BRETT, Wm. BATES of Purleigh. Proved 12 Dec. 1582.

JOHN GREENE of Romford yeoman, [date not given]. (330)
To Jane my wife my lands and tenements in Romford and Havering for her life; after her decease, the tenement, backside and garden in the tenure of John PYBORNE, a field next the windmill and another field called Lee Field to John the elder my son and my tenement wherein Geo. COLLIN dwelleth with the orchard and garden to Wm. my son. To Geoffrey my son, after my wife's decease, the house wherein Wm. BETT doth dwell, with the garden and the little field adjoining the highway and John BASTWICKE's ground. To Th. and John the younger my son, after my wife's decease, my other close adjoining ground in the tenure of Geo. NODES gentleman and land of John BASTWICKE. To Eliz. my daughter, after my wife's decease, my 2 shops called the Shambles. To my children, John my eldest son 100 marks at marriage, Wm., Geoffrey, Th., John my youngest and Eliz. each £10 at 24, and Geo. £20 at 30. To the churchwardens of Romford towards the reparations of Romford chapel 20s. To the poor people in the town of Romford 20s. The residue of my goods to my wife. To Mr FEILD, preacher of Romford, for making my funeral sermon 10s. To Th. CHARVELL weaver, Denis wife of James BROOKE, Alice wife of James SHAWCROFTE, and Joan my mother, each 10s. I make my well-beloved wife executrix, and Rt. DYCKENSON overseer. Witnesses: Fr[ancis] RAME gentleman, Wm. FEILD, John HARNAR. [No probate clause.]

MARGARET WILLOUGHBYE of Barking widow, 9 Apr. 1583. (331)
To be buried in Barking churchyard near the grave of my late husband John WILLOUGHBYE. To the poor people of the town of Barking 3s.4d. To my cousin Winifred NIGHTINGGALE spinster my wainscot press, my long table with the frame and a long form in the hall of my dwelling house, 1 pewter basin, 2 pewter candlesticks, a pewter salt, and 3 stone pots standing on the head of the same press. I forgive Abraham SOWCHE of Erith [co. Kent] fisherman 6s.8d. and [blank] YOUNGE of Erith 2s.6d. which they oweth me. To John WATSON my apprentice 1 pair of russet hose which were my husband's. To Wm. NIGHTINGGALE's wife my best red petticoat, best neckerchief and kerchief, and russet petticoat laid on with lace. To widow EASTON my old red petticoat, Joan BEARE my old russet petticoat, and Joan HEWES widow a kerchief and a neckercher. To John WATSON and Th. FLYNTE, my two apprentices, now sick, 10s. between them towards their comfortable relief. To Wm. NIGHTINGGALE my red and yellow bed quilt. The rest of my goods to be sold, the legacies to be paid accordingly. I make my trusty and well-beloved in Christ Wm. NIGHTINGALE executor and Miles BOWDISHE of Barking the writer, supervisor, and for his pains 10s. [No witnesses.] Proved 23 Apr. 1583.

JOHN DOUSETT of High Laver, 6 June 1581. (332)
To mother GOODDINGE, WILLIAMSON and MORETON of this parish and John PAVELEE each 4d. To Frs. my son £3 6s.8d. out of my tenement and lands wherein I dwell called Wenneswick. To him, Rt. and Andrew my sons and Joan my daughter £40 out of my tenement by the yearly sum or rent of £4 by even portions. To Th. my son my said tenement and land, Strawberry Croft and 2 parcels of land called Malkins Croft and Malkins garden, all in High Laver, to him and his heirs male; if he decease without heirs male, successively to my sons Frs., Rt. and Andrew. To Th.

my cupboard, the table and the form in the hall, the shelves and boards and a salting trough placed in the 2 nether chambers at the entry of the house, my best spit, my brandiron in the hall, 1 pair of pot hangings and the bar or iron fixed in the chimney in the hall, my yotting [for brewing] vat and the malt quern in the yotting house, a lead or pan hanged in the kitchen, my cheese press, my best shoed cart, a dung coop with a pair of shoed wheels to the same, my plough with chains, share and coulter, and 1 bed. To Geo., John and Harry my sons and Agnes my daughter 30s. apiece. To Andrew and Joan each a cow, a bed and bedstead. I will that Th. shall suffer Mary my wife to have and use her third and dower of the premises and show her duty and courtesy during her life. The residue of my goods as corn on the ground and in the barn, horse, beasts and household stuff to my wife, whom I make executrix. I make supervisors John COLLIN of Otes in High Laver and Edw. TAGELL of Matching, and for their pains 3s.4d. apiece. Witnesses: John COLLIN, Edw. TAGELL, Th. HOSKINS clerk [rector of Magdalen Laver]. Proved 17 Mar. 1582/3 by Geoffrey CLERKE notary public, proctor of the widow.

JOHN SILVESTER of Margaretting, — Mar. 1582/3. (333)
To my wife Joan 1 cow, a featherbed, a flockbed, a cupboard, a table, and all the pewter and brass that I had with her [at marriage]. To my son Rd. my house and land in Margaretting and Ingatestone. He shall keep my daughter Helen as long as she shall live with meat, drink and cloth and the chamber that she hath now, and he shall be bound to perform the same in £20. To my daughter Mgy. SILVESTER 40s. at marriage or 4 years after my decease. To Mary SILVESTER my daughter 20s. To Th. WAST my daughter's son 1 sheep at 20. The rest of my goods to Rd., to be my executor. I ordain overseer David WINGATE, and for his pains 5s. Witnesses: David WINGATE, Rt. HATCHMAN, Rt. CHESSONN, Rt. TABER, Edw. HACHMAN. Proved 19 Mar. 1582/3.

HENRY PITSEY of Chadwell yeoman, 27 Mar. 1583. (334)
To be buried in Chadwell church. To Hester DEMAN £4 at 18; if she die before, 20s. each to John BEARDMAN and widow BEARDMAN. To my brother[-in-law] Rt. DEMAN 20s. and to his son Rt. a great brass kettle. To Wm. WOOD of Chadwell 6s.8d. To Th., John WOOD's son, 3s.4d. To my godson Henry STURTE a weaning lamb or else 3s.4d., which[ever] he 'had latherest' [lieferest, would] have. To each of John MARLER's children 12d. To Edw. GOOSE my godson 12d. and each of the rest of my cousin GOOSE's children 8d. To my two maidservants and Rt. SICKETT my man 20d. apiece. To Agnes SYMONDES 12d. To John PYTSEY £16 at £4 a year. To my brother Rt. DEMAN my Kentish black bullock and Agnes, John WOOD's daughter, 12d. The rest of my goods to Agnes my wife and my cousin Geo. HULKE to be equally parted, whom I constitute executors. I appoint Miles HUNTER and Wm. WOOD overseers, and to each for their pains 4s. Witnesses: Miles HUNTER, Wm. WOOD, Wm. SAUNDERS, John HOLLAND. Proved 6 May 1583 by the widow, Geo. HULKE renouncing executorship.

JOHN EDWARDES *alias* HOSIER of Rochford the elder, 1 Mar., 26 Eliz. [1583/4]. (335)
To Mgt. my wife my black jet cow, 4 lambs, my round table with the hutch to it, my best chest, a woman's chair, a table press in the parlour, and 5 bushels of wheat; she shall have her dwelling in my house until Michaelmas after my decease. To John my son 1 flockbed and my dungcart, on condition that he suffer my son Wm. to have quiet possession of his part of the house and land until the same time, paying John for the occupying thereof 26s.8d. To the poor of Rochford 4s. To my wife the goods she brought to me [at our marriage], also the lesser of my 2 bigger kettles and 1 skillet. The rest of my goods to Wm., whom I make executor. I appoint overseers Wm. BRIDGE and John COLLIN, and for their pains 6s.8d. apiece. Witnesses: John COLLIN, Wm. BRIDGE, [Mark of 'John HOSYER'.]. Proved 20 Mar. 1583/4.

WILLIAM KNIGHBRIDGE of Great Stambridge, 22 Jan., 26 Eliz. [1583/4]. (336)
To Joan my daughter 1 joined bedstead in the parlour, 1 featherbed in the sollar, a brass pot, the best holland rail, 2 holland kerchiefs, 1 platter, and 2 pewter dishes.

To Andrew my son my best featherbed, 1 brass pot, my greatest kettle, 1 little kettle, 1 posnet, 1 platter, 2 pewter dishes, 1 canvas tablecloth of the longest, 1 middle cloth called a drinking cloth, and 1 covering. To John KNEIGHBRIDGE my son's son my best coverlet. To Ambrose my son[-in-law?] 40s. due to be paid to him, his prenticeship being expired; if he die before, the 40s. to be equally divided between Joan my daughter and John KNIGHBRIDGE my son's son. To Ambrose RAVEN, my son-in-law, 1 flockbed now at his uncle's at Purleigh and 5s. which his uncle hath. To my daughter-in-law Thomasine the rest of my kerchers and rails. My mare to be sold and the money equally divided between Th. KNIGHBRIDGE and Andrew KNIGHBRIDGE my sons. the rest of my goods to Th. my eldest son, whom I make executor. I appoint Andrew overseer. Witnesses: Peter WALKER, Th. WAFERD, Chris. MARCER. Proved 11 Feb. 1583/4.

JOHN LURWEN of Stow Maries, 27 Dec. 1583. (337)
I will that some learned man shall make 2 sermons, 1 at my burial or some convenient time, the other at the appointment of my executrix, and for his pains 10s. To widow WESTWOOD, Wm. WHYTE, widow AYERS and Wm. FELLIXE of [Cold] Norton each 5s. To my cousin GOODEN of Rettendon widow 40s. To John LURWEN my son my house and lands called Buckhach and Redenes in Rettendon (40 acres) at 21, on condition that he shall not make any claim to a messuage called Holders; for the time of his nonage the profits of the house and lands to Judith my wife. To her my other tenements and lands in Rettendon called Doores, Chandellers and Holders. To Rd. my son at 21 and Emme and Joan my daughters at 20 or marriage each £40. To my servants 3s.4d. apiece. The residue of my goods to my wife towards the bringing up of my children. I ordain her executrix, and Th. VICKERS of Rettendon and John STELEWOMAN of Woodham Ferrers overseers, and for their pains each 10s. Witnesses: Edw. STELEWOMAN, James BRYGE, John LANCYE. Proved 11 Feb. 1583/4.

ROBERT BECKE of South Shoebury mariner, 3 Dec. 1583. (338)
To Eliz. my wife my land in Barling until John my son is 21, then to him; if he die before, successively to Mary my daughter at 21 and to my wife for her life, the remainder to Wm. son of Henry HASELL of South Shoebury. To John and Mary each £20. To my sister Parnell LASHAM £5. To the church 10s. and to the poor of South Shoebury [blank]. The residue of my goods to my wife, to whom I bequeath the education of my children and the occupying of their stock. I make overseers Matthew COLTHURSTE and John FRENDE. Witnesses: Matthew COLTHURST, Th. FERRYS, Susan COLTHURSTE, Mgy. COLSTON [*recte* GOLSTON]. 20 Mar. 1583/4, appeared Eliz. the widow and renounced executorship; administration committed to her.

WILLIAM ALAMER of Great Leighs husbandman, 20 Jan. 1583/4. (339)
To Wm. ALAMER my son 20s. at 20. To Bridget and Susan ALAMER my daughters each 40s. at 21. The residue of my goods to 'Dennys' my wife, whom I ordain executrix. Witnesses: Chris. SHREVE, Rd. EVE, John FOSTER, John BARNARDE. Proved 12 Feb. 1583/4.

THOMAS RICHE of Springfield, 5 Apr. 1583. (340)
To Rose my wife all my goods, whom I make executrix. Witnesses: Charles DABB notary public, John RYSON. Proved 14 Jan. 1583/4.

WILLIAM BARRET of Collier Row [in Romford], — Jan. 1583/4. (341)
To Joan DUNCAN and mother HOLMAN, both of the Almshouse, 12d., Geo. GLASTON 12d., and Nich. FREEMAN 6s. To the poor of Collier Row 16s. 8d. To Mgy. HOCKLEY my goddaughter 20s. My executrix shall bestow at my funerals 20s. To Th. SKYNNER my sister's son 10s. To Rt. LONDON 10s. To Rt. SKYNNER 10s. The residue of my goods to Ursula my wife, whom I make executrix. I ordain overseers Wm. STEVENS and Rd. HUTT, and for their pains 3s.4d. apiece. Witnesses: Wm. OWTRED, Wm. STEVENS, Rd. HUTT, John COMPORTE the writer. To Rd. HUTT's children 12d. apiece. Proved 14 Feb. 1583/4.

KATHERINE MADYSON of Danbury widow, 9 Feb. 1580/1. **(342)**
[Long religious preamble.] To Geo. MARADGE son of Ralph MARAGE of Danbury husbandman 1 cow, 1 sheep, a lamb, the cupboard in the parlour with a drawer in it, 1 chest, a platter, 2 pewter dishes, 1 porringer, 1 'salfer' [saucer] of the best, 1 salt, a spit, a brass pot, 1 little kettle, a posnet, a chafing dish, the standing bedstead and the featherbed. To Ralph MARAGE of Danbury which married with Mgt. daughter of Ralph CASSE my son all my goods. I make Ralph executor and Wm. GLASCOCKE of Danbury overseer, and for his pains 3s.4d. Witnesses: Rd. REYNOLDES, John ESTWOOD, Wm. BENETT. Proved 14 Jan. 1583/4.

ANNE GUDGE of Chigwell single woman, 24 Oct. 1583. (Nuncupative.) **(343)**
To Nich. son of Rt. GUDGE 1 ewe and a lamb at 10 and 40s. at 18. To Nich. CAMPE her brother[-in-law?] the rest of her goods, whom she made executor. Witnesses: John ANDROWES the elder, John CAMPE, Henry FOWLER, Isabel CAMPE. Administration committed 30 Jan. 1583/4.

EDWARD PULLYVER of East Ham, 14 Jan. 1583/4. **(344)**
I ordain Jane PULLIVER my wife and Cecily my daughter executrices and John SOUTHWELL of London clothworker and Rt. SLEPE of Walthamstow yeoman overseers. To Cecily half of my goods. To her and if my wife should chance to be with child then to them both £5 a year during my years; if she be not, then the £5 to Cecily. To the poor of East Ham 5s. To my brother Th. 20s. 20 Feb. 1583/4, appeared Chris. ROBINSON notary public, the widow renouncing executorship; administration committed to her, power reserved to Cecily being a minor when she shall come. [No witnesses.]

JOHN ELLIS of Burnham husbandman, 28 Apr. 1583. **(345)**
To Wm. ELLYS my son 4 kine, 10 sheep, my best bed which I lie on, 5 pewter platters, 1 pewter dish in my chest, my best brass pot, my table and form with the frame in the hall, my best chest, and my best chafer. To Millicent my wife 3 of my kine, 7 ewes, 1 ram, and 1 [blank] of the best, if they live. The rest of my goods to her. To my dame [*recte* master?] Jasper ANDERKIN 1 hog. My master Jasper ANDERKIN shall have my son's portion in his hands till he is 22; if he die before, his stock to be sold and 26s.8d. given to the poor of Burnham. The residue of my goods to my master, whom I make executor. Witnesses: John PEIKE the elder, Th. RICHMAN, Jasper ANDERKIN. [No probate clause.]

JOAN FELYX [FELIX *in margin*] widow, [abode not given], 28 Apr. 1583. **(346)**
To be buried in Purleigh churchyard. To my two daughters, Mary wife of Wm. BLACKMORE and Dthy. wife of Wm. WOOD of South Benfleet, each 20s. To Philip ROCHESTER my russet coat which I wear every day and my wafer iron. The rest of my goods to my son Chris. FELIX, paying my brother John TURNIDGE of Writtle the 5s. which I owe him. I make Chris. executor. Witnesses: Rd. ALLISON, James BRETT, Wm. ROBJOHN. [No probate clause.]

RICHARD FOSTER of South Ockendon wheelwright, 27 Nov. 1583. **(347)**
To Peter my eldest son my dwelling house, kitchen and stable with the orchard on the south side of the house. To Walter my son the house that Mr Th. LEWES minister dwelleth in with the workhouse unto the church pale. To James my youngest son the house that old Joan dwelleth in with the loft over it and the barn adjoining towards the south. For the division of the yard on the east side of the house, stable, barn and workhouse, I put it to the good discretion of my overseers to determine it for the best use of each of my sons to be laid to each house. To Eliz. FOSTER my daughter my tenement with the yard adjoining the said house and the yearly rent thereof in her nonage towards her bringing up at the discretion of Th. SHERWELL and his wife [not named]. To Peter and James all my tools, boards, timber and logs equally between them. To Walter £5, 1 cloak, 1 joined table in the parlour with a form, and 1 featherbed with the bedsteadle in the little parlour. To Agnes my wife 3 of my best kine, 1 standing joined bedsteadle with the featherbed, and £5. To Anne my youngest daughter 50s. towards her bringing up. To my wife

and Eliz. all my pewter equally, with 1 brass pot and a kettle to each. To Eliz. 1 cow, 1 joined table being the best in the chamber above the parlour, the featherbed, 1 little chest in the parlour with all that is in it, and 40s. To my wife 2 pair of sheets, 2 tablecloths not the best nor the worst, a coverlet in the hutch above, a little kettle, a posnet, a table, a piece of new cloth, 1 old gown, the cupboard and a great chest in the parlour. If she be with child, a fit portion according to the discretion of my overseers. The residue of my goods to Peter and James, whom I constitute executors. I make Mr Hum. BAGESHAE, Geo. HEARD, Th. SHEERWELL and Geo. BAYLIE overseers, and for their pains 5s. apiece. Witnesses: Th. LEWES curate, Amos LEWES. Proved 17 Dec. 1583.

THOMAS BARNARDE of Great Waltham the elder, 23 Nov. 1583. (348)
To the curate 12d. for my tithes forgotten. To Agnes my wife my house called Bowyers and my lands for her life, and at Michaelmas the profits, i.e. the corn, grass and hay; after her decease, to Th. my son the house and the half yardland. To my four daughters, i.e. Mgy., Mgt., Joan and Prudence, my field called Five Acres; Th. shall pay them £5 apiece. To Mary my daughter £6 13s.4d., and in each of the successive years to my other four daughters £5 apiece. To Clemence COWLAND my daughter 2 beasts, on condition that, if she trouble my wife or children, my gift is void. To Anne DUNCKEN my daughter 6s.8d. and her son John 6s.8d. To Th. his chamber that he hired of me. If my wife do not marry I give her all my goods; if she marry, to my four daughters equally divided. Witnesses: John OWTTINGE, John TONNAR of Palmers [now Palmers Farm, in Great Waltham], Rd. BARNARDE the tanner the elder, Rd. BARNARDE the younger, Chris HOWLDE. I make my wife executrix and Rd. BARNARDE overseer. [No probate clause.]

JOHN HUMFREY of Little Thurrock, — 1583. (349)
To be buried in East Tilbury churchyard. To my sons John and James and my daughters Agnes and Eliz. each 4-s. at 21. To each a pewter dish. To my two daughters each a candlestick at 21. The rest of my goods to Joan my wife, she to be executrix. Witnesses: Wm. HUMFREY, Bennett WELCHE. Proved 15 Jan. '1585' [*recte* 1583/4?].

JOHN BRIDGE of Asheldham yeoman, 24 Jan. 1582/3. (350)
To be buried in Asheldham church. To the poor householders 6s.8d. at the day of my burial. To 'Jellian' my wife all my household stuff excepting things belonging to the dairy and husbandry. To Abraham my son my stock of cattle being 40 kine and 15 score ewes. My wife shall have the use of the half stock of cattle being 20 kine and 7 score ewes and 10 with their young feeding on the farm of Bodnicke [now Badnocks, in Asheldham] during the term of years, if she do not marry again, paying the rent according to her part. If she marry, Abraham shall have the whole stock of cattle, disbursing yearly £10 to his mother. If she do not marry, it shall be at her choice whether she take £10 every year with her dwelling in the house of Bodnycke or else the occupying of the half stock and then to pay half my legacies, and to give an answer within 6 months after my decease. To Benjamin my son £20. To Wm. my son £3 a year till he is 21, and 10 ewes and a gelding pasturing and feeding and £40 at 21. To Miles BRIDGE the younger 3 'gemmels' of gold price 20s. at 18 and 1 'portingue' [Portuguese gold coin worth about £4] at 21. To Isaac STEVENS my son-in-law 1 gelding price 20s. To Rd. WAKMAN my son-in-law 3s.4d. a year for 4 years. To Miles, whom I make overseer, 1 gold ring for his pains worth 40s. The rest of my goods to Abraham, whom I make executor. Witnesses: John BROOKE, Th. SKARLETT, Henry BREDGE. Proved 14 Jan. 1583/4.

ELIZABETH WILLFORD of West Ham widow, 12 Oct. 1583. (351)
To Edw. WILLFORD my son-in-law, £20 according to my husband's Will [*Essex Wills*, vol.2, no.264], being in the hands of Th. HUNTE carpenter by an obligation. To the poor of West Ham 3s.4d. To Ellen LEE my sister a petticoat, a bolster, and 6s.8d. To my godson Miles COOKE 6s.8d. To Chris. FOSTER's wife 3s.4d. I appoint James PRYCE, one of the Ordinary Yeomen of the Queen's Majesty's Chamber, and Th. HUNTE of West Ham overseers, and to them 12s. apiece. The residue of my goods and ready money to Joan COLE, whom I ordain executrix. Proved 2 Nov. 1583.

ALAN GOGNEY of Barking bricklayer, 31 Dec. 1583. **(352)**
To Olive my wife all my goods, whom I make executrix. Witnesses: Wm. TAYLOR, Wm. SQUIRE, Mgy. BLAKESLEY. Proved 4 Feb. 1583/4.

WILLIAM ROBINSON of Rayleigh shoemaker, 13 Feb. 1582/3. **(353)**
To be buried in Great Burstead churchyard. I will that my goods be divided into three equal parts, to Mgt. my wife and Th. my son and Eliz. my daughter, and Harry BOODE of Rayleigh gentleman shall have the keeping of her part for a year and then to her. I make Th. and Eliz. my executors and Nich. BRODEWATER my landlord overseer. Witnesses: John SPARKE, Th. SPICER, Th. HULL. Proved 14 Jan. 1583/4.

JOHN SMITHE of Tillingham husbandman, 26 Nov. 1583. **(354)**
I ordain Rt. SMITHE and Rd. ROBINSON executors. I will that my messuage with the yards and gardens in Rayleigh, if it shall please them to sell, now in the tenure of Wm. JOHNSON and John FOWLER, and that the money be distributed to my two daughters Agnes and Frances equally, but Frances to have £5 more than Agnes. Agnes shall be in the government of Rd. ROBINSON and Frances in that of Rt. SMITHE, he to have the £5 more only to bring up and instruct her in learning, both of the Book [the Bible?] and in sewing and some other profitable exercise whereby she may be able in time to earn her own living. The residue that remaineth of my house being sold equally to be divided between my said daughters at 21, also my goods which are known to be mine. To each of my daughters 1 brass pot, which pots are in the custody of John WITH in Rayleigh, and each 1 kettle, 1 in like custody and the other in that of one old Jane. I have in the custody of John FOWLER 5 chests, some great, some less, 1 spit, 2 pair of cobirons, 1 pair of trammels in the hall and another in the loft in the custody of JOHNSON; I have 1 flockbed and 1 framed table with a form; I have in the said house 2 bedsteadles, plain ones, and whatsoever are in the chests that are known to be mine; and whatever else known to be mine I will my executors to divide them equally to my children. If Wm. SOMMER have received any rent for me according to my request, he to deliver it to my executors. Witnesses: Nathaniel DOBSON clerk [instituted rector of Creeksea, 19 Apr. 1585], Ralph FRANKE, Th. SEAGAR, John STANE, Edw. KENE, Clement MAN. Proved 14 Feb. 1583/4.

THOMAS FOWLE of Burnham husbandman, 3 Jan. 1583/4. **(355)**
To the poor people of Burnham 20s. at the day of my burial, some godly preacher to make godly exhortation, to whom 6s.8d. To Eliz. my wife my house and lands in which I dwell called Romans [now Romans Farm, in Burnham] for 16 years after my decease. She shall at the court holden for the manor of Burnham next after my decease surrender her third or dowry out of my house at the town's end called Rood House to my son Peter FOWLE; after the 16 years, Romans to my two younger sons Jasper and Th. to be indifferently divided, paying the third part to their mother during her life. To Peter my half [share of a] boat called the 'Dorothy' with all that belongeth to it and £5 at the court day after my decease. To my daughters Eliz. and Grace FOWLE each £4 and to Mary and Susan each £20 at 20 or marriage. The residue of my goods to my wife, whom I ordain executrix. I ordain Th. OWGHAM overseer. Witnesses: John PYKE the elder, Edw. BECKE, Alex. HARVYE, Th. OWGHAM. Proved 28 Jan. 1583/4; administration committed to Eliz. the widow in the person of Mr Rd. WYNDOR notary public, her proctor.

WILLIAM LANE of Childerditch tailor, 26 Dec. 1583. **(356)**
To 'Ede' LANE my daughter dwelling in Chew Stoke (co. Somerset) 40s. The rest of my goods to Ann PUTLEY, whom I nominate executrix. I nominate John BRAMSON overseer, and for his pains 2s.6d. Witnesses: Nich. NEVILL, Geo. RAYNEBARDE, John BRAMSTON. Proved 4 Jan. 1583/4; administration committed to executrix in the person of Rt. STAINE her proctor.

JAMES GEALE [JEALE *in margin*] of Ramsden Bellhouse yeoman, 5 June 1582. **(357)**
To Simon GEALE my brother my lands and tenements in Ramsden called Brachetes, holden of the manor of Barringtons, wherein Wm. ALLEN and [blank] SPARROWE

inhabiteth; and my household stuff in my chamber where I lie, saving 1 bed there, also my timber and board in my chamber within the hallhouse. To my godchildren 12d. apiece. The residue of my goods to Th. GEALE my brother, whom I ordain executor. I ordain my very friend Th. BURGES of Runwell gentleman overseer. Witnesses: Wm. ALLEN, Th. ALLEN. Proved 15 Sept. 1582.

EDWARD STEWARDE of Stanford-le-Hope husbandman, 24 June 1583. (358)
To the poor 12d. To my son Edw.'s two children [not named] each 3s.4d. To my daughter Amy ROWELL's children each 3s.4d. The residue of my goods to Joan my wife, whom I make executrix. She shall keep John my son according to her ability with meat, drink and clothing. I ordain overseers Mr Th. GYTTINGE of London, John GOODWINNE of Horndon[-on-the-Hill] brewer and Edw. my son, and for their pains each 20d. Witnesses: Th. HOUGHTON clerk [not the rector], Th. STAMER. Proved 28 Nov. 1583.

JOHN THOROWGHGOOD of Fyfield husbandman, 10 June 1583. (359)
To Th. ANDREWES, mother BURDE and mother GULL, parishioners, 4d. apiece on my funeral day. To Lambert THOROWGOOD my son and heir all my movables amounting to £6 6d., which were appraised by John CHAMPNEIS of Elsenham, John SILVESTER of Fyfield and Wm KEY the writer; on condition that Lambert shall pay out of my land or movables £5 6s.8d. to the children of Th. LONGE my son-in-law and Dthy. now his wife, i.e. to Eliz. LONGE the elder, sometime my servant, 40s. in the 2nd, 3rd and 4th years after my decease at 13s.4d. a year, and 13s.4d. each to John, Rt., Helen, Eliz. the younger and Ralph LONGE in the 5th to the 9th years. I make Lambert executor. I ordain Gilbert ASHEWELL supervisor, and for his pains 20s. Witnesses: John CHAMPNEIS, John SILVESTER, Wm. KEYE. Proved 28 Nov. 1583.

WILLIAM BROWN of Great Ilford in the parish of Barking, 11 June 1583. (360)
Anne my wife shall occupy my messuage wherein I dwell in Great Ilford and 6 acres of land called Barnes Riddens with the barns, stables and orchards and the profits for her widowhood only; if she marry, she shall no longer occupy the same, which shall remain to Oliver son of Ralph BURNWOOD; if he die without heirs, to Wm. BURNWOOD his brother. My tenement with 3 acres at Ilford Bridge called Stoneowldes shall remain to such uses as are expressed in a surrender of the same. To Ralph BURNWOOD £10. To the four children of Mr Barker, i.e. John 40s., and Mary, Rachel and Eliz. BARKER at lawful age or marriage each 40s.; to Edw. their brother £5. To Rd. HANGER [HAUGER?] which was sometime my prentice 40s. To my wife's three children, i.e. Edw., John and Mgt. FRANCKE, each £5. To the poor of Barking parish 40s. and of West Ham 40s. To John THACKWELL a pair of smith bellows, an anvil, a bickern [anvil], and a vice. To John DUNCE 10s. To John RICKARDES, Mr POWELL's man, 10s. To my godchildren, viz. Wm. BURNWOOD, Wm. BUCKLEY, Rd. DEANE, Henry ALLEN, Wm. COMING, John BARKER, Anne TYRRETT and one MYSKYNE, each 5s. I will that the lease I have at Stratford Langthorne [in West Ham] which I bought of Th. HUNTE be sold towards payment of my legacies. Towards the reparations of Barking church 3s.4d. The rest of my goods to my wife, whom I make executrix. I require Wm. WALGRAVE gentleman and Th. SPYKE yeoman to be supervisors, and to each 20s. for their travail. John shall have the legacy when he cometh out of his prenticeship or at marriage. Witnesses: Wm. SQUIRE, John THACKWELL, John FRANCKE. Proved 23 Nov. 1583.

ROBERT ALBERDE of Little Leighs tiler, 5 Aug. 1583. (361)
To Joan my well-beloved wife my tenement in Little Leighs for her life, the re mainder to Mary ALBERDE my daughter. If my wife (now great with child) be delivered of a manchild, the remainder to him, he to pay Mary £6 13s.4d. at her marriage, if he be in possession. The residue of my goods to my wife, whom I make executrix. Witnesses: Bartw. BROCKE, Th. BRIDGE. Proved 27 Nov. 1583.

JOAN SPANSBYE of Rochford widow, 25 Apr. 1582. (362)
To the children of John PLAT, Mgt. WRIGHT and the wife of one POWLTRYE where I now lie 2s.8d. To POWLTRYE's wife my frize cassock, PLAT's wife my 2nd russet

petticoat, and Mgt. WRIGHTE my best russet petticoat. The rest of my goods to Agnes and Mgt. SPANSBY my daughters, whom I make executrices, to be divided equally. Witnesses: John BERYMAN parson of Rochford, writer hereof, John EVE. Proved 28 Apr. 1583.

CHRISTOPHER KINGE of Great Leighs labourer, 31 Oct. 1583. (363)
To my son Wm. 2 pewter dishes, a table, 2 chests, a brass pot, and a bolster. My wife [not named] shall deliver to him the featherbed that was given to him by his grandmother [not named] and a bedstead. The rest of my goods to my wife and my two children, i.e. Lettice and John, to be equally divided. My wife shall have the bringing up of them and their goods until they are of age and are able to go to service and get their own livings. I make my wife executrix. Witnesses: Mr FITCHE, Geo. BOOTH clerk. Proved 27 Nov. 1583.

GEOFFREY CLEMENTE of Doddinghurst husbandman, — 1583. (364)
To my son Th. the cupboard, table and form in the hall, the trammels as they hang, and a salting trough. To John, Geoffrey and Geo. my sons and Anna my daughter each a hutch. To my daughter Rabage the cupboard in the parlour. All to be received from my wife Eliz., their mother, at her discretion. To Geoffrey, Geo., Anna and Rabage each a cow at my wife's decease. The rest of my goods to my wife, whom I make executrix. My brothers John CLEMENTES and Henry I make supervisors, to whom in remembrance 20d. apiece. Witnesses: Rd. FOSTER of Doddinghurst, Luke PONDE, Geo. PECHE. Proved 28 Nov. 1583.

ROBERT BROOKES of Hare Street in Hornchurch yeoman, 9 Jan., 25 Eliz. [1582/3]. (365)
To be buried in Romford chapelyard. To Joan my wife for her life a messuage with the outhouses, gardens and yards in Pottenhurst in the Liberty of Havering-atte-Bower in the occupation of one CARLILE, also 2 messuages in Romford called Windoes Garden in the occupations of Rd. CHARVELL carpenter and John INGERSON labourer; after her death, the messuage at Pottenhurst to remain to Mgt. now wife of Weston FIFEILDE, Weston and Mgt. to pay Edw. BROKES now my servant £5 after my wife's decease. To Joan wife of John UPHAVERING, my daughter, my 2 messuages in Romford called Windoes Garden after my wife's decease, John or Joan to pay Joan daughter of Weston £8 after my wife's decease. To Philip son of Rd. BROKES 40s. To Parnell BROKES 20s. To Rd. son of John DOWNEHAM 1 cow or 33s.4d. The rest of my goods to my wife, whom I make executrix. I ordain overseer John DOWNEHAM, and for his pains 10s. Witnesses: Edw. RAMME, John DOWNEHAM, John HOLLMAN. [Mark of 'Robert BROKES'.] Proved 29 Nov. 1583.

THOMAS BOVER of Bradwell[-juxta-Mare], 22 Nov. 1583. (366)
To Joan my wife £10 and all the goods remaining in her house called Whittes in High Easter, the bed in the little chamber, a milch cow or the price of 33s.4d., 1 horse of price 26s.8d., and 2 ewe sheep or the price of 40s. for them; if she like not the cattle, she may choose the money. To her £8 a year for 6 years, on condition that she bring up my two youngest children Geo. and Mary BOVER at school to learn to write and read, also to find them sufficient meat, drink and clothes for 6 years. She shall have to her own use the little chamber, also her board, i.e. meat and drink, at my executors' costs for a year after my decease, if they may have the house wherein I dwell. To my sons Rt. and Geo. each £50 at 21 and my daughter Mary £30 at 20. To my brother BOVER 40s. To Joan my daughter, now wife of Timothy RAVEN, £10 after her husband's decease. To Mgt. SURRICHE 40s., Roger BOVER 20s., 'Percilla' KINGE £3 at 20, and Timothy RAVEN the younger 10s. The rest of my goods to Th. my son. I make John and Th. my sons executors, and 10s. each for their pains. Th. shall not intermeddle with my legacies or goods until he is 21; till then John shall have the executing of my Will. I nominate Wm. SMITHE of Great Ilford supervisor, and for his pains 20s. Witnesses: Wm. SMITHE, Alice FORDE, ALSEFORDE, Th. BOVER, John NEWLOCK, Th. KINGE. Proved 9 Dec. 1583 by John; power reserved to the other executor when he is 21. [Added in margin (in Latin)] Void because there is another Will [see no.467A].

WILLIAM THORNETON of Rettendon yeoman, 7 Nov. 1583. (367)
To Josias my son my houses and lands in Hockley called Seppes, Boynardes and Garners and my lands in Rochford. To Rt. my son my houses and lands in Paglesham called Winton Hall and Huntes and my lands in 'Stambridge' called Cookes Croft. To 'Mathew' my daughter £20 within 3 years after my decease. To the poor of Rettendon 5s. To my servants Agnes SWYLLE 3s.4d. and Phoebe SWYLL 5s. To my daughter's children 50s. Such interest as I have in my farm at Vange to Wm. my son. The residue of my goods to be divided between Josias, Wm. and Rt. I make Josias and Wm. executors and Rt. GRIGES the elder overseer. Witnesses: Th. HASTLER, Rt. GREGES, Wm. WARDALL, Wm. THORNETON. Proved 27 Nov. 1583.

HENRY NORRINGTON of Dunton yeoman, 10 June, 25 Eliz. [1583]. (368)
To my son £8, 1 great cauldron with 2 iron ears, and ½ dozen of pewter. To Simon his son 8s. and his daughters Alice 6s.8d. and Dthy. 10s. To Frances daughter of Simon 10s. To John DAYNS' wife and John JOYCE, both of Dunton, each 2s.6d. To Barthw. MAYE my son-in-law 40s. The rest of my goods to Amy my wife. To her and Nich. MAYE my son-in-law the lease of my house and my cattle with the corn growing on my ground during the term of the lease, the 2 latter years only excepted which I will to John. I make my wife executrix. Witnesses: Rt. WYTHERS, Rd. SAWELL. Proved 28 Nov. 1583.

HUGH PIGOTT of Danbury tanner, 12 Sept. 1583. (369)
To Joan my wife for her life my freehold lands and sheds, paying the lord's rent; after her decease, the head tenement which I dwell in with the garden to Mary PIGOTT my daughter; for default of issue, successively to the next child of my son John and to the next heirs of my daughter Agnes SHERIFFE. Wm. SHERYFFE my son-in-law shall pay my wife for her life 20s. for his yearly rent. After my wife's decease, the new builded tenement with the yard to Agnes for her life; after her death, to Hugh SHERIFFE her son; for default of issue, successively to Daniel his son, to the heirs of Agnes, to the next child of John and to the heirs of the name of PIGOTT. John shall pay my wife for her life 26s.8d. After her decease, to John 1 shed and his dwelling house and the yard for his life; for want of issue, to Mary. To my wife and Mary my goods equally divided. I appoint my wife executrix and Edw. SOAME of Danbury overseer, and for his pains 5s. Witnesses: Jasper LYON, Wm. RAYNER, Rt BROOKE. Proved 6 Nov. 1583.

WILLIAM CLERKE of Dagenham yeoman, 30 June 1583. (370)
To the reparations of Dagenham church 3s.4d. To Wm. son of John CLERKE my brother deceased my freehold lands in Dagenham, as well marsh as upland grounds, on condition that he shall not demand any legacy remaining in my hands. To Joan LAWRENCE my sister's daughter 20s., to my godchildren 6d. To Alice my well-beloved wife my household stuff. My executors shall bestow at my burial £5. The rest of my goods to my wife and to John HUMFREE of Dagenham, whom I ordain executors. I ordain Henry CLERKE of Ripple Side in Barking yeoman overseer, and for his pains 5s. Witnesses: John BERYMAN vicar of Dagenham, and writer hereof, John SPARROWE. Proved 4 Nov. 1583.

THOMAS GYLLIAN the elder of Rawreth tanner, 28 Sept. 1583. (371)
To the poor people 3s.4d. Towards the repairing of Rawreth church 5s. To Agnes my wife my farmhouse called Trendy [now Tryndehayes] in Rawreth with the lands belonging for 3 years after the date of my Will; thereafter I will that my wife and Henry GILLIAN my son occupy my farm jointly for the years yet to come in my lease; if she marry before, she be amoved from the farmhouse and appurtenances and Th. and Henry my sons to occupy jointly the same. To Bridget GILLIAN my daughter £20 at 21 or marriage. To Th. £10 within 8 years; if he die before, to be equally divided to his children at 21. In consideration of the debts I owe, to my wife my stock and store of cattle of every sort, my corn, the stock of leather and other implements in my tanhouse, with my household goods, for 3 years after my death; thereafter, the surplusage to be equally divided between my wife and Henry. The residue of my goods to my wife, whom I make executrix. I constitute Rd. HAYES

the elder of Rawreth overseer, and for his pains 6s.8d. Witnesses: Rd. MASON writer hereof, Geo. HAYES, Rt. UNDERWOOD. Proved 6 Nov. 1583.

THOMAS WEST, [abode not given], 18 Oct. 1583. (372)
To be buried in Rayleigh churchyard. To Agnes my daughter 1 standing bed with a new featherbed, ½ dozen mean pewter, a brazen candlestick, a chafing dish, a brass pot, a posnet, and a little chest; after my wife's death, 1 cupboard at her choice. The rest of my goods to Joan my wife, whom I appoint executrix. Witnesses: Rd. BLACKWELL clerk [not the rector], Arthur NEWMAN. Proved 6 Nov. 1583.

MARGARET MASON widow, [of Corringham], 27 Aug. —. (373)
To Agnes and Sarah my daughters all my wearing apparel . To Agnes my best bed. To John KENTE my son 4 sheep and Agnes and Sarah each 2 sheep. To Agnes 22s. that Lawrence PERRYE oweth me and Sarah 20s. which [blank] oweth me. The residue of my goods to John, whom I make executor. Witnesses: John ROGER, Rt. LACKE, John ARNOLDE. Proved 4 Nov. 1583.

JOHN BONNER of Rayleigh, 23 Oct. 1583. (374)
To Anne my wife for her life my house that I dwell in; after her decease, to John my eldest son; if he die without issue, to be sold and equally divided betwixt my three children, Th., Edw. and Susan BONNER, to whom John after my wife's decease shall give each 13s.4d. To John HALL my daughter's child 10s. I make my wife executrix. Witnesses: Rd. BLACKWELL clerk and writer, [blank] WEBBE, Arthur NEWMAN. Proved 6 Nov. 1583

WILLIAM SAUNDERS of Chadwell husbandman, 17 July 1583. (Nuncupative.) (375)
Being demanded by Mr Rd. CAWOOD, curate of West Tilbury, if his mind was that Alice his wife should have half his goods and John his son and Magdalen SAUNDERS his daughter the other half and that John should have more by 5 marks than Magdalen, he answered, 'Yea', and that his wife should have the keeping of them until they come to full age. He appointed John BREWER overseer. Witnesses: Rd. CAWOOD, John ROBINSON, John BREWER. Administration, 3 Oct. 1583, committed to the widow.

GEORGE BLACKLOCKE, [of Corringham], 4 Sept. 1583. (376)
I set my brother Rd. BLACKLOKE as executor. To joan my wife my house at 'Barfould' [West Bergholt] and my ground for her life, to dwell in or let, paying out of it 40s. a year to my sister's son Geo. HAYWARDE; after her decease, to Rd. To my brother HAYWARDE a mare and a colt. To my sister for Geo. a colt. To my wife 2 nags, my sister's son a steer, my sister and her daughter Eliz. each a cow, a hog and 5 lambs. I have twelve score pounds of ready money, whereof 3 score is in the house, my wife hath it, whereof I give £100 to my brother; £40 to my brother HAYWARDE and his wife, £10 to my sister'son, and to her daughter Eliz. 20 nobles, and the rest to my wife. Witnesses: John WARRYNER, Wm. RAYNE. Proved before Mr Wm. RUSTE [vicar of Felsted], surrogate of Mr Edw. STANHOPE, LL.D., Official in the Visitation of the Bishop of London. [Date of probate not given.]

MARGARET BLACHE of Great Waltham widow, 16 May 1581. (377)
To be buried in Waltham church. to Th. BLACHE my son 4 spur ryals [gold coin worth 15s.] and 1 [blank] and to his wife 1 angel and 1 side saddle. To Chris. BLACHE my son's son 1 joined bedstead with the trundle bed, 1 featherbed, 2 flockbeds, 1 tablecloth wrought with blue, 1 diaper towel, a joined press with a great hutch, a joined form, a great kettle, a little kettle, a skillet, a little spit, a pair of andirons, a great grate in the hall, a dripping pan, a basting ladle, a wafer iron, 11 pieces of pewter, a brazen candlestick, a brazen mortar and a pestle, a tray, a fire shovel, a salt, ½ dozen table napkins, an elm bowl, a brewing tub, a chair, a great gridiron, and a spur ryal. To John BLACHE 1 joined bed in the parlour and the hangings, the trundle bed, a lockram towel, ½ dozen table napkins, a tablecloth, a round tablecloth, the cupboard in the parlour, a chair, a bowl, a brass pot, a great kettle, a little kettle, a posnet, a frying pan, ½ dozen of pewter, a candlestick a

saltcellar, a spur ryal, and 1 spit. To Kath. BLACHE 1 joined bed with the trundle bed, 1 featherbed, 1 flockbed, 1 'melled' [milled, thickened] tablecloth, 1 flaxen towel, ½ dozen table napkins, 1 holland sheet, 2 kettles, a posnet, ½ dozen of pewter, a candlestick, a salt, a bowl, a hutch of pear tree, a spur ryal, 1 press in the parlour, and a leaf table with a cupboard in it and the cloth thereto. To Eustace BLACHE 20s., a tablecloth, 6 napkins, a pair of sheets, 1 pair of pillowbere, and 1 great brass pot. To Wm. BLACHE a spur ryal, a pair of sheets, 6 table napkins, and a pair of pillowberes. To the poor women of the South End [of Great Waltham] 10s. To Joan BLACHE my son's daughter 1 angel, a pair of sheets, 1 lockram curtain, 1 new hutch, and 6 table napkins. The pewter is to be equally divided between the three children, Chris., Joan and Kath. To Eliz. BLACHE my son's daughter the little hutch, 1 angel, 1 sheet with a black seam, and 6 table napkins. To Mary daughter of Mr EVERERD 1 cushion of strawberry work. To my sister MEADE 1 angel. To Jane HAYES a pair of sheets; if she die, as God forbid, Cecily to be her heir. To Emme HAYES a pair of sheets, John HAYES her brother to be her heir. To Eliz. daughter of John HAYES a pair of sheets, Agnes her sister to be her heir. All those goods to be delivered at the age of 20 or marriage. The residue of my goods to be equally divided amongst the children of my son Th. I make him executor. Witnesses: Th. SAWEN, Chris. PARKER. Proved 4 Oct. 1583.

WILLIAM NORRIS of Fyfield husbandman, 13 Aug. 1583. [See no. 1001.] (378)
To Mgy. my wife, whom I make executrix, all my goods. I make overseer Mr MAN our minister [the clergy list for Fyfield is deficient at this period], and for his pains 2s. Witnesses: Mr MAN minister, Wm. KEY the writer. Proved 3 Oct. 1583.

JOAN KINGE of Dunton widow, 29 Aug., 25 Eliz. [1583]. (379)
To Edw. WITTAM 3 of my best kine, 5 ewe sheep, my cupboard in the hall, my best bed being a featherbed, an almain rivet with a bill thereto belonging [armour], a bedstead, ½ dozen of pewter, viz. 3 great platters, 3 middling dishes, 3 pottingers, and a pair of cheese weights. To Mgt. SHEPPERD my daughter £5. To the poor of Dunton 3s.4d. To PAYN's wife of Billericay 12d., COOPER's wife and HARDINGE's wife of Laindon, and HARDINGE's wife's daughter, 4d. apiece. To Joan STOKES of Childerditch 4d. To John and Grace my daughter's maids 12d. apiece. To John son of John INGALL a lamb. To four carriers to convey my body to the earth 8d. apiece. To my son's three menservants 5s. To Anthony SAUNDER of Margaretting 2s., Th. PEPPER my godson, HARRISE my tenant, and POULTER my tenant of Margaretting, each 12d. The rest of my goods to Edw. WITTAM my son and John GYLL my son-in-law equally, whom I make executors. Witnesses: Rt. WITHERS, Th. WITTAM, Edw. WITTAM, Benjamin WITTAM. Proved 3 Oct. 1583 by Edw.; power reserved to the other executor when he shall come.

ROSE BAGGETT of Rettendon widow, 4 Jan. 1581/2. (380)
To be buried in Rettendon churchyard nigh the place where my late husband Nich. was buried. To my daughter Mary now wife of Wm. BYSSHOPE 1 cow, 2 ewe sheep, 1 mattress and a bolster for a bed, 1 pewter basin, a latten candlestick, 2 joined stools, 2 cushions, and 1 pair of sheets. To Barbary daughter of my son-in-law Wm. BISSHOP 1 bullock of a year, 1 little cupboard with a table joining, and 1 holland kercher, at 14. To Wm. son of Edw. WHITE 1 chest which was my sister LINCON's. To Mary 2 bushels of wheat. The residue of my goods to my daughter Susan BAGGETT, whom I ordain executrix. Witnesses: Anthony PAGE, Rd. HUMFREY. Proved 4 Oct. 1583.

THOMAS HARDYE [see footnote to no.385] of Fyfield millwright, 18 July 1583. (381)
[Religious preamble.] To Mary my wife my part of such profits as shall arise from the millhouse and from a windmill, both in Little Laver, until Mary and Joan HARDYE my daughters are 14, when they shall be equally divided into three parts and Mary and Joan shall have their parts. To my wife the yearly rent of 50s. until Mary and Joan are 14, when each to have one-third part, from a tenement and a windmill in 'Asledham' [see no.385]. To my wife such right and title as I have in Mill Lane in Fyfield, she paying to the right honourable Lord Robert RICHE 2s. yearly during the term that I have. To Mary my daughter my cupboard in my parlour at

16. To Joan my best featherbed complete worth 8s. or 8s. [in money] at 16. To John HARDYE my brother my best cloak. To John BARNARDE my brother-in-law 10s. To the poor inhabitants of Fyfield 10s. I make Mr MAN [see no.378] and John POOLE of Stondon [Massey] my father-in-law overseers, and for their pains 3s.4d. apiece. I make my wife executrix, to whom the residue of my goods. To my brother Edw. HARDYE and my sisters Anne, Alice, Eliz. and Joan HARDYE each 6s.8d. at Michaelmas 1585. Witnesses: Mr MAN, Wm. KEY the writer hereof, Geo. BUTCHER. Proved 3 Oct. 1583.

THOMAS CHILDE of Great Waltham yeoman, 27 July 1583. (382)
To the poorest people of [blank] of North End [in Great Waltham] 3s.4d. To widow CHAMPNES and HOWDE's wife each 1 bushel of malt and WADE's wife 1 bushel of wheat. To John my eldest son my house called Old Childes with the lands belonging; and a croft by Pamar's barn on the north side to Black Chapel [in Great Waltham] by the highwayside and on Broom Field leading to Little Sawens, on condition that he pay PAMMARS 6s.8d. yearly as a rentcharge into that tenement called Pamers. To Stephen my son my tenement called Pamers with the barn and other buildings and 2 crofts abutting on the hall and kitchen (2½ acres); another croft before the great barn door (1 acre); and a croft called Linwood (8 acres) abutting on the land of John ELES at wall and on the ground sometime Old Park and on the highway. To Stephen my bed that I lie on, 1 brass pot the 3rd in goodness, 1 kettle with a piece in the bottom, 1 table the best saving 1, a pair of great trestles, the best form in the carthouse, 2 pewter platters, 2 pewter dishes, and a backchair. To Th. my son £20 to be paid to John GOODAY my brother-in-law to keep to his use till he is 22, a featherbed, a brass pot broken-rimmed the 4th in goodness, 2 pewter platters, and 2 pewter dishes. To Joan my daughter 20 marks within 1 year after my decease or at marriage, 1 featherbed and a chafer. To Dthy. my daughter 20 marks, 3 pewter platters, and 3 dishes. To Rose my daughter 20 marks at 20, 3 pewter platters, and 3 pewter dishes. The residue of my goods to John my son, whom I make executor with my loving brother Wm., and for his pains 1 mare colt. I make my brother-in-law John GOODAYE of Braintree overseer. To my wife my white ambling mare. Witnesses: John CHILDE the elder, Wm. COULLANDE, Rd. PONDE writer. Proved 4 Oct. 1583 by Wm.; power reserved to the other executor when he shall come.

JOAN SHOCKE of Burnham widow, 7 Oct. 1583. (383)
To Mary BOWLES my best featherbed; Isaac BOWLES' children 1 dozen of pewter, i.e. 6 platters, 4 dishes, 3 saucers and 1 salt, equally between them; Joan BOWLES 1 featherbed, a round table, and a hutch; Justina SAFFOLDE 1 flockbed; Th. BALLARDE 1 hutch, a brazen strainer, a brass pot, a trammel, and a tub with a board on it; Isaac son of Isaac BOWLES 1 frying pan; and Wm. BOWLES 1 little table and a kettle. The rest of my goods to Isaac BOWLES and Th. BALLARDE, whom I make executors. Witnesses: Alex. BOREHAM the writer, John OFFIN. Proved 6 Nov. 1583.

JOHN MALL the younger of Hornchurch husbandman, 31 May 1583. (384)
To the poor people of Hornchurch 6s.8d. at the discretion of my brother Wm. MALL. The rest of my goods to Cecily my wife, whom I make executrix. Witnesses: Rt. WATTES, Rd. KELLWEY. Proved 17 July 1583.

PETER HARDINGE[1] of Hornchurch miller, 18 June 1583. (385)
To John HARDINGE my son my part of the house and mill at Little Laver, the rent whereof shall be paid to Agnes my wife to the bringing up of him till he is 14. To Anne HARDINGE my daughter the rent of my part of the house and mill in 'Ashindon' for 27½ years, provided that my wife shall have the rent until the child is 14. If John 'let' his life before he is 21, my part of the house and mill to Edw. HARDY [*sic*] my brother. The rest of my goods to my wife, whom I make executrix. Witnesses: Wm. LAMBERT, Rt. WATTES. Proved 17 July 1583.

[1] Entries for HARDING and HARDY in *Wills at Chelmsford, 1400-1620* (ed. F.G.Emmison) show that they are alternative surnames. As to 'Asheldam' (381) and 'Ashingdon' (385), Harding testators occur in both parishes in the same volume; a windmill at Ashingdon is recorded in 1678 (K.G.Farries, *Essex Windmills*, vol.3 (1984), p.19).

JOHN GLASCOCKE the elder of Downham, 8 Oct. 1583. (386)
To Susan my wife my tenement called Sudburies with my copyhold lands belonging, for her life. If she be with child and have a manchild, the same to have them; if not a son, to descend to Rd. FREEMAN, on condition that he pay for them £70 after my wife's decease, i.e. £20 to the girl and the residue to Th. HOLYWELL my brother[-in-law], but if she be not with child, he to have £70. My free land I commit to the use and custody of Rd. FREEMAN and Wm. CROXTON during the nonage of John BAILYE, and at his full age, if he pay £10, to enjoy the lands in consideration of £20 given him by the Will of Rd. BAILYE his father. If he be not able to pay the £10, FREEMAN and CROXTON to enjoy the premises, paying the £20 to BAILIFFE. To Th. son of Geo. GREGORYE 40s. at 21 or at such time as my wife do bind him to any science and in the meantime she to keep him as her own. To the poor of Downham 10s. To Downham church 10s. I make FREEMAN and CROXTON executors, and to them 6s.8d. apiece. I make my brother Th. HALLYWELL [*sic*] and Edw. RUTTER overseers, and to each 3s.4d. Witnesses: Andrew RUTTER, Rt. BUCKLEY, Henry CHAPMAN. Proved 28 Nov. 1583.

NICHOLAS POOLE of Fyfield yeoman, 21 May 1583. (387)
To John my eldest son my messuage and lands in Willingale Spain called Aldredge *alias* Alderstande. To Hum. my son my other tenement in Willingale Spain called Home Croft. To Geoffrey my son my tenement and garden in Chipping Ongar in the occupation of John CRABBE. To Simon my youngest son my little tenement and orchard plat in Fyfield called Trevettes, also my indenture of lease of the croft in Fyfield called Mynsons Croft from his age of 21 to the end of my years. To Agnes my wife my best bedsteadle, the best featherbed, 8 of my best pewter platters, 4 of my best candlesticks, best cupboard, 4 of my best coffers or chests, my round or small table in my chamber, 8 pair of sheets, 5 of my best tablecloths, and all her wearing linen, money and jewels, my milch cow with cut horns, also £20. To Nich. my son £20. To Simon £40 at 21 and £40 1 year after. To Geoffrey son of Nich. 6s.8d. To Thomasine STOOKES 3s.4d. and Agnes REED 20d. my servants. The rest of my goods to John, Hum. and Geoffrey equally betwixt them, to pay my legacies and to suffer my wife and their mother to have her abode in the house together with them, keeping her with meat, drink and apparel, being their guide while she keep herself unmarried if she will, also to educate and bring up Simon with meat, drink and apparel and in the schools of learning until he is 21; also to finish the ditches of the orchard as already begun and fence it 6 foot long of assize and hang a great gate in the gate room. I will that John pay Hum. and Geoffrey £15 betwixt them equally. I ordain John, Hum. and Geoffrey executors, they to bestow 40s. at least about my burial, and Th. my brother and John HUBBARDE smith supervisors, and for their pains 3s.4d. apiece. Witnesses: Th. POOLE, John HUBBARD, Wm. NEALE. Proved 16 July 1583, before Edw. STANHOP, LL.D., Official of the Bishop of London in the Visitation.

THOMAS URSLER of West Ham blacksmith, 8 June 1583. (388)
To the poor of the parish 20s. To my three children, i.e. my eldest Rt., my 2nd Henry, and Mgt. each £6 13s.4d., at 16 or marriage. I make my wife [not named] executrix and my friends Rd. STAINES and Henry ETHERIDGE of West Ham overseers, and for their pains 5s. apiece. To Rt. my shop with the implements. To my three children the lease of my house after my wife's decease. [No witnesses.] Proved 22 July 1583 before Edw. STANHOP, LL.D., Official, by John DANBYE, proctor of the executrix.

THOMAS BALDINE of West Ham, 2 Nov. 1581. (389)
To Rd. MOYLE my brother-in-law and my overseer my best cloak, to my sister a tablecloth, and to Wm. PEELE [*recte* MOYLE] overseer my dagger and 3s.4d. The residue of my goods to my three daughters [not named] at the discretion of my overseers. [No witnesses.] Administration committed, 18 Nov. 1583, to Rd. MOYLE and Wm. MOYLE supervisors.

JOHN JOHNSON of Great Wakering, 4 Apr. 1582. (390)
To Joan my wife 6 kine, 1 horse, 1 mare and a colt, 3 featherbeds, and 4 flockbeds. To my son John 2 featherbeds, 3 pieces of pewter, a mortar with a pestle, 3 latten candlesticks, a pewter salt being at Prittlewell, 9 pieces of pewter in my house at Wakering, and 1 bearing sheet, 1 brass pot the best, and 5 kettles at Prittlewell, also £4 at 21; if he die, to 'Urye' KENTE and Mary BELL equally, saving the £4 to remain to my wife. To 'Urye' and Agnes KENTE 2 brass pots at Prittlewell, 3 pieces of pewter at Prittlewell which were my mother's [not named], and each 20s. at 21 or marriage. To John 1 cupboard at Prittlewell. The rest of my goods to my wife, whom I constitute executrix. I make Wm. CROXTON of Milton [in Prittlewell] and Hugh DANIELL of Prittlewell overseers. If my wife marry, to put in bond to my overseers for bringing up John and for discharging of the bonds which goodman RICHMOND hath. Witnesses: Th. DANIELL, Rt. CHAPMAN. Proved [date not given].

THOMAS GORE of Romford, 15 Apr. 1583. (Nuncupative.) (391)
All my goods to Grace my wife, saving 1 gold ring or 26s.8d. to Kath. my daughter at 18 or marriage and 1 cow or 33s.4d. Witnesses: Rd. ATKIS of Romford minister, Wm. CREAMER, Th. KEMPE. Administration committed, 17 July 1583, to Grace GOORE *alias* CROFTE during the minority of Kath.

JOHN WALKER of Chadwell yeoman, 4 Oct. 1582. (392)
To be buried in Chadwell chancel. To the poor people of Chadwell 4 dozen of bread and ½ lead of cheese at my burial. To Thurston my son 20 marks when his apprenticeship doth come out or at 24 if he serve out his apprenticeship. To Rd. my son 20 marks at 20. If either or both die before, the whole to remain to John my son; if he die before, to the next of my kin. To Joan ELLYTT and Sybil MOCKE my sisters each 5s. To Mgt. WRIGHTSONNE my wife's sister ½ wey of good cheese. I appoint John HOLLAND parson of Chadwell to preach a funeral sermon, and for his pains 6s.8d. The residue of my goods to Elizabeth my wife and John equally divided, whom I make executors. I appoint John FRIER and Rt. HURTE both of Milton [in Prittlewell] and John BASTARD of Little Thurrock overseers, and for their pains 5s. apiece. Witnesses: John [blank], John HOLLAND, John FRYER, Rt. HURTE. Proved 15 Nov. 158[3] by the widow, the other renouncing executorship.

WILLIAM TAMMAS of Rochford, 18 May, 23 Eliz. [1581]. (393)
To Rt. HASELLWOOD 1 scythe and a cradle as it hangeth, also a flail. All other movables to Joan TAMMAS my wife, whom I make executrix. After her decease, my goods equally divided betwixt my three children Wm., Joan and John TAMMAS. Mich. LORKIN of Eastwood to be supervisor. Witnesses: Henry PAYNELL, Mich. LORKIN, Rt. HASELLWOOD. [No probate clause.]

RICHARD WYMANNE of Rochford tawer, 1 Apr. 1583. (394)
Ellen my wife shall have my house that I dwell in for my term of years and my house and ground belonging in Purleigh for her life; after her death, to Agnes, Mary, Susan, Thomasine and Anne my daughters. If Helen my wife be with child with a son, to my son after her death; if he die without heirs, to my daughters. To them 20s. apiece at 21. I ordain my wife executrix and Wm. RICHARDSON and Nich. HORSENAILE overseers. Witnesses: Ezechiel RAYNER, John COLLIN, Th. POWELL, Rd. BURGEIS, James KELE. Proved 16 May 1583.

JOHN WYLLOUGHBYE [WILLOUGHBY *in margin*] of Barking fisherman, 25 Mar. 1583 (395)

To the poor men's box 4d. To Frs. NEVILL my sister's son my long bow, my sheaf of arrows, and 4 shafts. To Kath. WILLOUGHBYE my brother's daughter my best pewter platter. To my brother Wm. WILLOUGHBYE my plank table and trestles. The residue of my goods to my loving wife Mgt., whom I make executrix. I make my trusty and well-beloved in Christ Miles BOWDISHE of Barking clerk supervisor, and for his pains 20d. Witnesses: Wm. WILLOUGHBYE, Wm. NIGHTINGGALE, Miles BOWDISSHE. Proved 13 Apr. 1583.

HENRY PAGE of Stock husbandman, 20 Apr. 1583. (396)
To John my son £3 at 21 and my four daughters Joan, Jane, Anne and Mary PAGE 40s. apiece at 20 or marriage. To John 1 cow priced at 33s.4d. at 21 and my daughters each a sheep priced at 5s. apiece at marriage or 20. To Rd. son of Hum. WORTHAM of Corringham 5s. at 24. To the poor of Stock 2s. The rest of my goods, cattle and money to Agnes my wife, whom I ordain executrix. I appoint John PAGE my brother of Southminster overseer, and for his pains 5s. Witnesses: Alex. GARRETT writer hereof, Rd. DAYE. Proved 15 May 1583.

ROBERT TRETELL of Rettendon labourer, 11 Feb., 25 Eliz. [1582/3]. (397)
To Alice my wife all my goods towards the honest bringing up of my children [not named]. I ordain her my executrix. Witnesses: Th. HASTLER, Wm. HAYES. Proved 10 Apr. 1583.

JOHN GIFOR [GYFOR *in margin*] of Rochford, 25 Mar., 25 Eliz. [1583]. (398)
To Agnes CREAKE, Joan CREKE, Mary CREKE and Susan CREKE, my sister's daughters, the over[-plus] of my goods, my debts and other charges deducted. I make Henry PAYNELL and Wm. CORNEFORD of Rochford executors. To Wm. GYFORD and Henry GYFORD, my brother's sons, my wearing apparel. Witnesses: Th. WHITTOP, Rt. WIXE, John PIGGOTT. [No probate clause.]

GEORGE SMITH of Barking husbandman, 18 May 1583. (399)
To Frs. my son £3 6s.8d. at 21. To Kath. my daughter £5 at 21 or marriage. My wife Jane shall have their bringing up with the use and safe keeping of their gifts so long as she keep herself a widow. If she marry before their age and her husband being thought of as a good and honest man, putting in security for payment thereof as shall be thought best to my overseers, they to be answerable to my children. The residue of my goods to my loving wife, whom I make executrix. I make my trusty and well-beloved in Christ John and Frs. SMITHE, my two brethren, overseers. Witnesses: John REED, Wm. SAWYER, Miles BOWDISHE writer hereof. Proved 24 May 1583.

AGNES widow of Rt. RAMME of Great Waltham, 8 Jan. 1581/2. (400)
To the poor people 20s.; I will that 1 quarter of wheat be bought, baked and given, with 1 lead of cheese, to them on the day of my burial. To Th. my son 1 bedstead in the house where Th. NEWTON dwelleth, my best great chest, and 1 pair of sheets. To Agnes SHETTELLWORTHE my daughter 1 featherbed which I lie on. To Jane my daughter, wife of John SERICHE, a double rail, a kerchief, and 1 pair of sheets. To Jane [*sic*] my daughter, wife of Rd. PONDE, a pair of sheets and 1 holland rail. To Eliz. my daughter, wife of John MARSHE, a pair of sheets, a double rail, a kerchief, and a chest. To Th. RAMME my godson 3s.4d. To Agnes PONDE my goddaughter 3s.4d., 1 chest and a pair of trammels. To Joan [*sic*] SERICHE my goddaughter 3s.4d., a 'fosser' [forcer, coffer], a pair of sheets and a blanket. To Alice RAMME my cousin the mattress which I lie on, a white and black covering, a pair of sheets, and a pair of trammels. To Jane BRAYNWOOD my cousin a kettle of 3 gallons. The residue of my goods to my said five children equally divided. I make Th. and Rd. PONDE my son-in-law executors and my loving brother Th. CHILDE overseer. Witnesses: John HAUKIN, Walter HAARE, Th. FEILDE. Proved — 1582 by Rd. PONDE.

JOAN GREENE of South Ockendon widow, 5 Mar., 24 Eliz. [1581/2]. (401)
To John BRETTON my elder son such money as he hath in his hands. To Joan his daughter and my goddaughter £5 at 21 or marriage, a brass pot, and a chafing dish. Whereas Rt. GREENE my son doth owe me 46s.8d., the poor of Orsett to have 20s. and 20s. to the poor of South and North Ockendon. The rest of my goods to John BRETTEN my younger son, whom I make executor. Witnesses: John BAILYE, Rd. BROCKES, Th. COTTON. Proved 28 Apr. 1582.

WILLIAM SPARROWE of Hornchurch husbandman, 29 March 1582. (402)
To my two children Wm. and Joan each 40s. at 18 or marriage. The rest of my goods to Agnes my wife to bring up my children. I make her my executrix and

Geoffrey HUMFREY of Dagenham, my brother-in-law, overseer. Witnesses: Wm. LOVE, John HODSONNE. [No probate clause.]

WILLIAM IPSEE, [abode not given], 20 Oct. 1582. **(403)**
To be buried in Purleigh churchyard. To my three children John, Eliz. and Mgy. and the infant whereof my wife is now with child, each £5 at 20. To John 6 sheep, a crossbow, a buckler, and a dagger. To John, Mgy. and Eliz. each a chest and a gold ring, and to Mgy. and Eliz. each a table and a form. The rest of my goods to my wife [not named], whom I make executrix. I appoint Th. KINGE and James BEST supervisors. Witnesses: Rd. ALISON minister [not the rector], Th. KINGE, James BRETT, Hugh COLE. [No probate clause.]

LAWRENCE FANYNGE [FANINGE *in margin*] of Great Stambridge, 27 Jan. 1582/3. **(404)**
To Joan my wife all my goods. I make her my executrix. Witnesses: John LAUGAR, Th. WRIGHTE, Geo. KINGE, Th. HASELL, Rt REAXE. Proved 22 Feb. 1582/3.

GEORGE STONARDE of Horndon-on-the-Hill glover, 6 Aug. 1582. **(405)**
To Henry my son £60 at 21; if he die before, to my wife £40 and £20 to my brothers and sisters equally divided. To my brother Wm. £3 and his son Wm. dwelling with me 40s. at 28 [*sic*] and his daughter Mary STONARDE 40s. To the poor people of Horndon 10s. The rest of my goods to Joan my wife, whom I make executrix. I make John STONARDE and Rt. HARVEY overseers, and for their pains 10s. Witnesses: Th. TAYLOR, Rt.HARVYE, Anthony HORNE. Proved [date not given].

RICHARD JOYCE, [abode not given], 31 Mar. 1583. **(406)**
'Certain things given by Rd. JOYCE'. To my father 22s. which he oweth me and I forgive him. To my mother the profits of 5 sheep, my sister Joan 10 sheep, and my other three sisters 10 sheep or else 66s.8d. equally between them. To my four sisters the 5s. which my uncle [not named] gave me by his Will. [No witnesses or probate clause.]

JOHN NEVILL of Mountnessing blacksmith, 9 Apr. 1582. **(407)**
To Eliz. my wife my house and land in Mountnessing. To John WOODLEY my kinsman my frize jerkin and a pair of russet hose. To my brother Wm. NEVILL my best white canvas doublet. The rest of my goods to my wife, whom I make executrix. I make my neighbour Rt. WHISKARDE overseer, and for his pains 2s. Witnesses: Edw. COLTHERST, Edw. LORKIN, Geo. WYSKERD. Proved 29 May 1582.

JOHN STRAUNGE of Purleigh husbandman, 4 Dec.1581. **(408)**
[Religious preamble.] To the poor 20s. at the day of my burial. To John my eldest son £60 at marriage or within a year after my decease, 1 gelding and the keeping of 1 gelding, 1 seam of wheat at marriage, my best featherbed, 1 dozen table napkins, 2 tablecloths, a great brass pot, 2 kettles, 1 chafer, 1 great brass pan, 3 of the best silver spoons, 1½ dozen of pewter, 2 candlesticks, and 1 good chest. To Paul my youngest son £50 at 23 or marriage; if he die before, to my wife £20, John my eldest son £20, and John [my] middle son £20. To Paul 1 horse and the pasturing of 1 horse during the lease of Eastwrightes, 4 pair of sheets, 2 tablecloths, 2 pillows, 3 of the best silver spoons, 1 great brass pot, 1 chafer, 1 candlestick, 1½ dozen pewter, and 2 kettles. To Ursula WEBBE £10 which I have received of Wm. FANINGE to her use. To Mr BARNARDISTONE of Maldon 1 horse pasture at Wrightes till Michaelmas next. To him and his wife each 1 half crown of gold. I forgive my brother Roger STRAUNGE of Prittlewell 20s. which he oweth me. To my sister NEWMAN of Thorrington 40s. To Abraham LYNSEY 5s. To Mgt. FREAKE and Ursula WEBB each 1 half crown of gold. To Arthur HARRYS esquire my silver ear pickers. To Mr Edm. WALGRAVE, Mr Rd. WALGRAVE and my brother[-in-law] John LEVETT each 1 angel of gold to make a ring. To my brother Wm. LEVETT and Th. KYNGE each 1 crown of gold to make a ring. To Augustine my man 1 half crown of gold and Mary and Mgy. my maids each 2s. To mother GARDENER 12d. To Eliz. my loving wife and John my middle son my lease of East and West Wrightes and the

rest of my goods, whom I make executors. I make John LEVETT the elder of Southminster and Th. KINGE my neighbour overseers. Witnesses: John FREAKE, Th. KINGE, John SAFFOLDE. Proved 2 Apr. 1582.

RICHARD CASTLE of Woodham Walter, 1 Apr. 1583. (409)
To Alice my wife my standing bed in the chamber; Eilz. my younger daughter a flockbed; Joan my daughter a covering of the bed in the sollar, a great chest and a brass pot; Th. my son the table in the sollar; Joan a basin and a chafing dish; Mgt. my daughter-in-law a trundle bed; Eliz. a cauldron and 2 pewter dishes; Th. a cob-iron and 4 wedges if they can be found, a 'perser', 2 wimbles, a wrybit, and a mattock, my best doublet and jerkin and gaskins; Eliz. the long table in the hall and 2 forms; and Joan the cupboard in the buttery. The rest of my goods to my wife. I make her executrix. Witnesses: John CHILDE, John FLETCHER, John ROBERTES, Lewis MORRICE. Proved 11 Apr. 1583.

JANE daughter of Thomas EMRIS of Loughton yeoman, 27 Apr. 1582. (410)
To my sister Anne the house and land which my father [not named] bequeathed to us, and 40s. To my aunt Joan TURNOR widow 20s. and my cousin Eliz. STEVENS my best neckercher and 20s.; Nich. her son 20s.; Kath. FULLER, my master's daughter, 5s.; my cousin Th. STEVENS 15s. on condition that he pay Th. BOLTER 8d. To Th. STEVENS 2 lasmbs and Nich. his son and Ellen TURNOR each 1 ewe sheep. To Anne TURNOR my best hat, best petticoat, 5 kerchers, a crosscloth, 2 white aprons, 3 kerchers, and 1 pair of white sleeves. To my sister my blue apron and a safeguard; Anne TURNOR my 2 waistcoats (the white and other red), also 2 smocks and 1 pair of shoes, the best I have I give to my sister. I ordain Th. STEVENS executor and Mr Rt. FULLER overseer. Witnesses: Edw. [blank], John HARE, Rd. ATKYS minister [of Romford]. Proved 1 May 1582.

ELEANOR FORBYE of Rayleigh widow, 16 Feb. 1581/2. (411)
To John HYAM my son the biggest kettle in my house, 2 pewter platters, and a joined frame; to his wife 1 russet cassock. To Mary MAKINS my daughter my best russet cassock, a russet petticoat, 2 kerchiefs, and 2 pewter platters. To my son Th. FORBYE 1 featherbed in the loft, my best cupboard in the hall, 1 round table in the hall, 1 joined stool, best chair, and white hutch in the chamber, 2 pewter platters, and 1 pair of sheets. To Alice BAKER my daughter 1 featherbed, 1 cupboard and best great chest in the chamber, a table and form, my great chair and the hangings in the hall, 1 pair of sheets, and 2 pewter platters; this portion shall remain to her son Hum. BAKER. My son Edw. HYAME shall pay my daughter Mary MAKINE 20s. and 20s. more to John HYAME my son. The rest of my goods to be equally divided between Edw. and Th. and Alice. I make Th. and Alice executors and Edw. overseer. Witnesses: Rd. BLACKWELL minister and writer hereof, Wm. HARTE, Edw. HARTE. Proved 2 Apr. 1582 by Th.; power reserved to Alice when she shall come.

GREGORY KENE of Canewdon husbandman, 30 May 1582. (412)
To the poor people of Tillingham 6s.8d. and of Canewdon 6s.8d. To Joan my wife half the profits of the ground that I sold to my father [blank] for 4 years and my 4 kine, on condition that she shall not claim the third of my land at Tillingham. To John my son the residue of my lease with the stock of 9 kine, 45 sheep and 1 horse. To Henry my son my house and land at Tillingham; for default of heirs, successively to John, to Anne and to Alice my daughters. To Henry the bed that I lie on. To John the 2nd bed and the cupboard in the parlour. To Anne KENE my daughter a bed and 2 of the best candlesticks that were mine and a little joined table. To Henry and John each £10, Anne £20 and Alice £5, each at 21 or marriage. To 'Mathewe' [blank] 40s. at marriage if she live so long. To Anne the best covering. To Henry 2 kine. To my wife the rest of my 'household'. I will that my lease remain equally among my wife and children. To Henry LOCKE my godson my mare colt. The rest of my goods to my wife and John, whom I ordain executors. I appoint John LOCKE overseer, to have my children the better ruled, and for his pains 20s. Witnesses: Gregory KETTELL, John HULL. Proved 25 June 1582 by James THWAITES, proctor of the executors.

THOMAS SKYNNER of Collier Row [in Romford] husbandman, 1 June, 24 Eliz. [1582]. (413)
[This Will is repeated on folio 8 of next Register [D/AER 15] in identical language.]

THOMAS WYATE of Upminster husbandman, 13 July 1582. (414)
To Anne WYATE my daughter my table and form in the hall at lawful age. To my sons John and Th. each £3 6s.8d. at 21. To Anne £3 6s.8d. at 16. If all die before, to my sister HEATHE's children. My wife shall keep and bring up my children with meat, drink and raiment at her own costs and pay their legacies. To Anne WHITE my servant 1 lamb. The residue of my goods to Joan my well-beloved wife, whom I ordain executrix. I ordain Th. TOMKINS and Th. GRYFFIN overseers. Witnesses: John HEATHE, Th. PEACHEY, Th. BOYLAND writer hereof. Proved 28 July 1582.

JOHN STEVEN of Canewdon husbandman, 26 Feb. 1582/3. (415)
To nine poor widows of this parish and John MORRYCE's wife and Moses TEDYMER 11s. equally divided. To Ambrose PORTER 12d. To widow SAVERY ½ bushel wheat. Whereas my sister Jane did deliver me in her lifetime £16 to be equally divided between her three children John, Wm. and Anne JARMAN, my executor shall pay them, and they discharge him against John WYSE of St. Lawrence in Dengie Hundred. To John STEVEN the younger of St. Lawrence 6s.8d. The rest of my goods to Henry HURRELL my son-in-law, whom I make executor. I constitute Gregory KETTELL and Nathaniel CAWSTON overseers. Witnesses: Th. HARRISON, Rd. LAYE. Proved 11 Apr. 1583.

RICHARD HAWLE of Barking labourer, [date not given]. (416)
My worldly goods to be divided between my wife one half and the other to my children [not named]. I make Grace my wife executrix. Witness: John ROBINSON. [No probate clause.]

JOHN BURLE of Dagenham labourer, 3 Apr. 1582. (417)
To Agnes BURLE and John BURLE my daughter and son, John FULLER my wife's son, and Mary BURLE my daughter 1 ewe apiece. The rest of my goods to Eliz. my wife, whom I make executrix. Witnesses: John BERYMAN vicar of Dagenham and writer hereof, Th. LOOFTIS weaver. Proved 23 Apr. 1582.

WILLIAM WITH *alias* KENTE of Basildon yeoman, 30 Nov. 1582. (418)
To Kath. my wife my leases and terms of years in my two farms called Butlers and Olivandes to their expiration. To Wm. my son £100 at 21, 1 bed in the bedchamber next the door, 6 pewter platters, my best brass pot, 1 press cupboard in the little parlour, and a table. To John my son £100 at 21, one bed in the chamber over the hall, 6 pewter platters, 1 brass pot, 1 cupboard, and a table. To Eleanor my daughter 100 marks at 21, 1 bed in the great parlour next the door, 6 pewter platters, 1 brass pot, 1 cupboard at my brother WRIGHTE's, and a table. If all die before 21, my executrix shall pay Th. WYTH *alias* KENTE of Vange, Th. WITH *alias* KENTE of Southminster, Wm. WITHE *alias* KENTE of West Hanningfield, Lawrence WITH *alias* KENT of Horndon-on-the-Hill and John WITHE *alias* KENT, brother of Lawrence, each £10. To my kinswoman Rachel ADDAMS of Vange 2 ewe sheep; Rt. LESSON, Th. MOSIER, John PYGRUME and Th. CHURCHE my servants each 1 ewe sheep; Wm. WITHE *alias* KENT of West Hanningfield a cow; and Rose HALL, Sarah DOVE, Denise ELLETT and Agnes BOYETT my servants each 1 ewe sheep. To Rd. RICHBELL 10s. To Rd. EYVETT 10s. To John son of my brother Th. WRIGHTE 1 gelded brown colt. The residue of my goods, my children brought up without any allowance to be paid for their board or learning, to my wife, whom I make executrix, on condition that she shall enter into a bond of £500 to John WRIGHTE of Brook Street [in South Weald] and John ROOE of North Benfleet; if she marry, he that shall marry with her to enter into like bonds. Witnesses: John BROWNE curate, John WRIGHTE. Proved 21 Feb. 1582/3.

AGNES WENDEN late of Gosfield widow, 30 Aug. 1582. (419)
To Anne HAWKINS daughter of Gilbert HAWKINS, my son, £10 by 40s. a year. To

my daughters Agnes CLAYTON, HUNTMAN and Alice HILLS each 50s. To 'Jeph' [Geoffrey?], John and Ralph CLAYTON each 10s. To Anne my pewter locked in my hutch at Gosfield with 1 brass pot there. To Henry son of John HAUCKINS my son and heir my copyhold lands wherever they lie holden of Mr John WENTWORTH of Gosfield esquire. I appoint John my son executor. I have in the possession of John HUNTMAN 2 kine or else £3 at my choice; he oweth me £3 for rent due. John WENDEN of Great Tey oweth me 10s. for rent due. Witnesses: Th. WISEMAN, 'Jeph' CLAYTON, Oliver ROBERTES clerk [the clergy list for Gosfield is deficient at this period]. Proved 18 Jan. 1582/3.

JOHN ESEGORE of West Ham husbandman, — Oct. 1580. **(420)**
To my mother Alice RIGBYE now wife of Gilbert RIGBYE £10, parcel of £18 which my late master John RIGBYE of Waltham Holy Cross gentleman hath of mine in his keeping. To her a milch cow. To Susan GRACE my sister's daughter the other £8 at 21; my master shall put it to her most advantage till then, when my executrix shall give her a good milch cow. To Gilbert 40s. To my mother and my sister Mary CRECE wife of Th. CRECE my cottage wherein I dwell with the yard which I hold in fee of the lord of the manor of West Ham; provided that my mother shall have it for her life. The rest of my goods to my mother, whom I make executrix. I heartily desire my master to have the oversight of my Will, and for his pains 3s.4d. Witnesses to Will of John EDGOORSE [*sic*]: Henry REGBE, Henry ETREGE, Th. USSLYE, Wm. RANDE, Wm. MILLER. 'By me John OSGOR'. Proved 21 Jan. 1582/3.

ABRAHAM NEVELL of Barking fisherman, 7 Dec. 1582. **(421)**
To be buried in Barking churchyard near my first wife [not named]. To my daughter Magdalen my best cupboard with a press in the hall at marriage, she to pay her sister Sarah NEVELL 10s. The residue of my goods to my loving wife Eliz., whom I make executrix. I make overseers John PIERSON scrivener and Titus BACON, and for their pains 20d. apiece. Witnesses: John PIERSON, Titus BACON, Th. NEWTON curate of Barking [the writer?]. Proved 15 Dec. 1582.

JOHN SILVESTER of Hornchurch husbandman, 6 Dec. 1582. **(422)**
To Eliz. my daughter 1 brass posnet, 3 ewes, and 1 horse colt of a year. The rest of my goods to Joan my wife, whom I make executrix. I make overseers Th. WILLOTT and Wm. STEVEN, to whom 12d. apiece. Witnesses: John SKELE, Hugh SILVESTER, Rd. SILVESTER. Proved 16 Jan. 1582/3.

ROBERT BENETT of Romford husbandman, 22 Dec. 1582. **(423)**
To my six children Kath., Edw., Wm., Nich., Rt. and Frs. each 13s. 4d. at 21. To my three youngest sons Nich., Rt. and Frs. each a lamb or 2s.8d. to buy a lamb at 8, which lambs to be delivered into the hands of some friend to be kept for them with the profits at 21. The rest of my goods to Eliz. my wife, whom I make executrix. I ordain overseers my brother John BENNETT and Mich. CARTER. Witnesses: John BENNETT and Mgy. his wife, Rd. ATKIS minister [of Romford]. Proved 16 Jan. 1582/3.

ROBERT ROBINSON of Brentwood saddler, 11 July 1582. **(424)**
To my daughter-in-law 'Mathewe' GATSON £5 at marriage or 21. The rest of my goods to Agnes my wife, whom I make executrix. I make overseer Wm. PEASE of Brentwood, and for his pains 3s.4d. Witnesses: Th. CASELIN, Wm. PEASE, Leonard OXCLIFFE. Proved —.

THOMAS BRETTON of West Tilbury, 3 Sept. 1582. **(425)**
To the poor 3s.4d. To my brother Rt. my best doublet, provided that he give my sister MASON 6s.8d. To her my 2nd doublet. To my mother [not named] my lease that I have of Th. CAMBER. All my other goods to Mgy. my wife, whom I make executrix, with my part of land and houses given by my cousin [not named] for her life; if she be with child, to the child after her decease; these being overseers Rt. BRETTON and Rt. EYRE. Witnesses: Rd. CAWOOD minister [not the rector]. [No probate clause.]

ROBERT MANNINGE, [abode not given], 22 Oct. 1582. **(426)**
To be buried in Purleigh churchyard. To my mother [not named] a sheet, a halfsheet and a russet petticoat. To John PRATT my servant my shop board, a hutch, a pressing iron, a pair of shears, and 12d. The rest of my goods to my wife [not named], whom I make executrix. Witnesses: Rd. ALISON minister [not the rector], John ARGENT, James BRETT, Wm. COLLIN. [No probate clause.]

WILLIAM GYBBES [GIBBES *in margin*] of Stapleford Abbots yeoman, 15 Apr. 1577. **(427)**
To Mgt. my wife £10, the best featherbed, 1 chest which she brought [at our marriage], 1 of the best kettles, 4 pieces of pewter; also 1 cow at what time she shall refuse any longer to dwell with my son. Whereas unto my son Wm. at his I did freely give him so much in goods and cattle as amounteth to £30, if he die without issue, the £30 in goods or money shall remain over to my nephew Wm. son of my youngest brother Wm. GIBBES; for want of him, to my daughter's children equally. To my daughter CORDYE 16s., and to each of her children 3s.4d. To the poor 5s. The rest of my goods to Wm., whom I ordain executor. Witnesses: Rt. JOHNSON, John FINCHE, Rd. REIGNOLDES rector of Stapleford Abbots. Proved 16 Oct. 1582.

JOHN WHITE of Brentwood yeoman, 30 Sept. 1582. **(428)**
To Anne my wife my great bed in the one bedchamber, the plate cupboard in the buttery, and 1 pair of sheets. To Mgt. RUTTER my daughter 1 featherbed, 1 bedsteadle, and 1 brass pot. To Thomasine WHITE my daughter 1 pair of sheets and 1 posnet. The rest of my goods to my three sons, saving my debts which I give to Rd. my son, whom I make executor, and the goods to be equally divided between Rd., John and Wm. I make overseers John WHITE and Th. DANWOOD, and for their pains 12d. apiece. Witnesses: John [blank], Wm. REIGNOLDE, Th. DANWOOD, Leonard OXCLYFFE. Proved 16 Oct. 1582.

RICHARD GYBBES [GIBBES *in margin*] [abode not given] carpenter, 21 Sept. 1582. **(429)**
To be buried in East Horndon churchyard. To Joan GYBBES my daughter 1 cow, 2 lambs, 1 joined bedstead in the loft over the parlour, 1 featherbed, my 2nd cauldron of brass, 3 latten candlesticks, 1 latten mortar, 1 latten chafing dish, 2 joined stools, and 3 pillowberes. To Agnes GIBBES my daughter 1 cow, 2 lambs, 1 joined bedstead in the parlour, 1 featherbed, my best cauldron, 1 brass pot, 1 dozen of pewter, 3 latten candlesticks, 1 brass mortar, 1 latten chafing dish, 2 joined stools, 3 pillowberes, and 6 table napkins. To Rt. GRACE, John QUINTIN, Th. MAGOT, John BROWNE, John WALDROPE, and Reynold PARDYE each 12d., John QUINTIN 1 pair of hose, Reynold PARDYE 1 pair of high shoes, and Rt. GRACE my leather doublet. My daughters to have their parts at 20 or marriage. To Th. MAGETT 1 canvas doublet. To my godchildren each 6d. To Agnes my joined press in the parlour. If Mgy. my wife refuse to keep and bring up Eliz. SEDCOLE as I have promised, she shall pay Clement JAXON of 'Thorndon' [East or West Horndon] £6 and deliver her to him. The rest of my goods to my wife, whom I nominate executrix, and Nich. NEVILL overseer, and for his pains 5s. Witnesses: John HOWSSE, Nich. NEVILL, Alice QUINTIN. Proved 15 Nov. 1582.

WILLIAM WITTAM of Dunton, very sick, 19 Aug. 1582. **(430)**
Towards the reparation of Dunton church 10s. To the poor 6s.8d. To my sons Wm., Th. and Andrew WYTTAM each £30 at 20 and to 'Thomson' [Thomasine], Eliz. and Anne WITTAM each £20 at 20 or marriage. To my brother young John's children Edw. and John £5 apiece at 21. To Rebecca WITTAM, my brother young John's daughter, 5s. at 15, and to my brother young John 5s. To my sister SAKINS' children 20s. between them. If all my sons die before age, to my daughters £20 apiece and the residue to Kath. my wife; if all my daughters die before age, to my sons £10 apiece and the residue to my wife. To my servant Rt. GYVER 1 sheep and every one of my servants 12d. apiece. The residue of my goods to my wife, whom I make executrix. I make Henry FOSTER of High Laver and my brother Th. WITTAM supervisors, and for their pains 10s. apiece. Witnesses: Henry FOSTER, Th. WITTAM, Rd. PRENTYCE. [No probate clause.]

WILLIAM AYDES of Rettendon, 25 Nov. 1582. **(431)**
To my wife [not named] all such movables saving that I give to my son Wm. AUDES [*recte* AYDES] 20s. out of the said goods at 20, and my wife to ask and receive of my debtors such debts as any man or woman do owe. After her decease my son shall have all my goods and the 20s. to Barbara BENCONE [*recte* BENTONE], my daughter-in-law. I ordain my wife executrix and overseers Th. VIKERS and Rd. PASFEILD. Witnesses: Roger GEBENS, Andrew HODE, John HAMANE. [No probate clause.]

ROBERT PACWOODE of Stanford-le-Hope husbandman, 13 Dec. 1582. **(432)**
To my daughter's son Wm. TERY 1 cow and 3 sheep and 30s. at 21 and her daughter Joan TERY 1 cow and 3 sheep at 18. The rest of my goods to Thomasine my well-beloved wife. I make her my executrix and John STELYMAN overseer. Witnesses: 'Ewgeny' GATTON, John STELYMAN. Proved 17 Jan. 1582/3.

RICHARD WELLES of Fyfield wheelwright, 23 Nov. 1582. **(433)**
To Jane my wife in consideration that she shall honestly keep and bring up all my children to their full age my house and land in Fyfield called Finches for her life; after her decease Th. my eldest son shall have part of the croft adjoining my house, from the great ash at the garden end right over to Hayrones ground, the nether part to be his. To him the mead in Hayrones ground, on condition that, [if] he do not molest or trouble any of his brothers or sisters for my wife's right in Finches, he shall have the house, barn, yard and a press; if he refuse, John my son and my two daughters Joan and Olive shall have them. To John the other part of my croft adjoining Finches and the croft beyond the river on the left hand of the highway from my house. To Joan and Olive Walnut Croft abutting on the right side of the highway for their lives after my wife's decease. To my wife my lands and tenements in Bobbingworth so long as she keep herself a widow; if she marry or die, to my son Walter and the child that she now goeth withal and the longer liver of them. To John the cupboard in the hall after her decease. The rest of my goods to my wife, whom I make executrix. I choose my brother Edm. of Navestock to be overseer, and for his pains 10s. Witnesses: Wm. RAMSYE, John DICKINSON, Edm. WELLES, Rt. CRANNYSE. Proved 21 Feb. 1582/3.

NICHOLAS GROSSER of London innholder, 19 Oct. 1582. **(434)**
To the poor of the parish of St. Katherine Creechurch in London 20s. To Th. SPENCER of the same parish, joiner, 20s. To Alice GROCER my maid 20s. and 1 silver spoon. The rest of my goods to Rd. COTMAN and Joan his wife, which Rd. COTEMAN I make executor. I make Wm. BATEMAN bricklayer, Henry LEY girdler and Frs. BRADSHAWE salter overseers, and for their pains 2s.6d. apiece. Witnesses: Th. IDELL bricklayer, Frs. BRADSHAW the writer hereof, Wm. BATEMAN. [No probate clause.]

WILLIAM BRETTON of Boreham yeoman, -- 1582. **(435)**
To the reparations of Boreham church 20s. to be paid to the churchwardens. To the poor of Boreham at my burial 20s. To the reparations of Widford church 20s. and the poor of the same 20s. To John MASON of West Thurrock and to Cecily wife of Th. TENDRINGE for their lives to be equally divided my freehold lands in Widford or Writtle; after their decease, to Rt. MASON and Charles HAYES (except 2 crofts or closes in Writtle and Moulsham [in Chelmsford] in the tenure of Th. BUSSHE and widow BROWNE, which I give to Priscilla daughter of Th. TENDRINGE). To Charles HAYES my lands in Boreham called Ardeleys purchased of Frs. EGLESFEILD gentleman. To Th. and Cecily my lands in Boreham called Newhightes with Hobbes Croft and 1 acre in Wrosney Mead thereto belonging, and to their heirs. To my kinswoman Phoebe wife of John TENDRINGE my two tenements in BOREHAM wherein one Edw. STANE dwelleth and the other in Moulsham, for her life; after her decease, to Mary her daughter the tenement in Boreham and to Phoebe her daughter the tenement in Moulsham. To the two sisters of John MASON out of the money that he doth owe me each £5, and the other £30 I give to him. To widow SYNKE 6s.8d. yearly for her life. To every of my servants 10s. To every of my godchildren 5s. and to

Wm. SEREDGE 20s. To Charles HAIS a silver salt. To Mgy. STURDYE a cow price 30s. To Roger IZAD and Alice his wife together 10s. and a silver spoon. The residue of my goods to my kinswoman Cecily TENDRING and Charles HAIES her son. I ordain executors John MASON and Charles HAYES and nominate Roger BRAMPSTON gentleman and Th. TENDRINGE of Brent Hall [in Boreham] overseers, and for their pains an old ryal of 20s. Witnesses: Th. SORRELL, Edw. STANES, John TENDRINGE, Gilbert ARNNOUD. Proved 16 Oct. 1582.

JOHN JOYCE of Rettendon, 22 Mar. 1582/3. (436)
To Hugh COLE 20s. To the poor 20s. To Anne my wife, on condition that she do not take away any of my goods without my executors' consent so much in value as in an inventory of Wm. CURLEWE deceased amounting to £50, such sum, debts and legacies as have been satisfied for his debt being deducted by my executors. To my wife £10. To Anne my daughter £30, my best posted bedsteadle, best featherbed, best bearing sheet, and best casting sheet. To her and Henry my son each 1 dozen of my best pewter. To her my best cauldron, best kettle, best brass pot, and 2 of my best candlesticks. To Harry my son £30, my next best featherbed and bedsteadle, 1 cauldron, 1 kettle, 1 brass pot, 4 pair of sheets of the next best, 2 candlesticks next the best. To Wm. my son, Judith and Joan my daughters and John my son each £30, daughters at 18 and sons at 20. To my two maidservants and Rd. my man 5s. apiece. The residue of my household stuff shall be sold and the money equally divided amongst my four youngest children, i.e. Wm., Judith, Joan and John. To my wife the tenement and lands in her occupation when I did marry with her at Michaelmas next and not to receive any legacy before except the £10 and her 'household'. To her ½ seam of wheat and ½ wey of cheese and her being in a chamber until Michaelmas if she keep her so long unmarried and 'uncontract'. I ordain John BARON and Henry BARON executors, and my brothers-in-law and Th. ARKSDEN supervisors. Witnesses: Th. ARKSDEN, Th. BOONE, Henry ATHAYES. 11 Apr. 1583 appeared John BARON, to whom the judge committed letters to collect the deceased's goods at the Feast of [All] Saints next; 1 May 1583 appeared John BARON and exhibited the Will, to whom administration committed, power reserved to Henry BARON when he shall come.

PETER WILSON of Barking fisherman, 11 May 1582. (437)
To the poor men's box 12d. I make Agnes my wife executrix, she to pay debts and legacies due to the children of Rt. SAVAGE at their full age. I make overseers my trusty friends Peter DEBETT fisherman and Rd. MASON tailor, and for their pains each 3s.4d. Witnesses: Stephen BURDE, Wm. GYLLETT, Rd. MASON, Peter DEBETT, Th. HAYWARD clerk of Barking. Proved 28 May 1582.

EDWARD SWETING of Margaretting husbandman, 15 Oct. 1582. (438)
To my brother John SWETING 1 red crimple-horned cow, my colt, 1 seam of wheat, and £5. To John SWETING the younger, son of John my brother, 20s. To Agnes GREENE my sister 1 little black cow and 20s. and her daughter Anne HINTLEY 5s. To my brother Rt. SWETINGE £3 and a ½ quarter of wheat. To my sister PERRYMAN 30s. To my brothers Th. and Wm. SWETINGE each 40s. To the poor of Margaretting 6s.8d. at my burial and of Ingatestone, Fryerning, Stock and Buttsbury each parish 3s.4d. To Mr [David] WINGATE, vicar of Margaretting, 5s. and his daughter Hester 12d. To Rd. WEALD, Edm. PEPPER and Daniel JERVIS each 12d. To Wm. BURRE 1 bushel of wheat. To John son of Th. SWETINGE, Wm. son of Wm. SWETINGE, Benet JOHNSON and Anne JOHNSON each 20s. To Mgt. JONESON 40s. in the hands of Henry BORNE. To Th. son of Th. SWETINGE and Mary JOHNSON each 10s. To Joan JOHNSON my sister's daughter £12 in the hands of Th. WHITEBREADE of Margaretting at 20; if she die before, equally divided among the rest of her sisters. To the same Joan JOHNSON my wheat growing in Smethers Croft, to be sold by Th. WHITEBRED to her profit; also 1 covering, 1 blanket, 2 pair of towen sheets, 1 tablecloth, 3 new platters, 2 pewter dishes, 2 saucers, 1 great salt, 6 pewter spoons, 1 latten mortar, 1 latten chafing dish, my great brass pot, my biggest posnet, 1 gridiron, 2 shredding knives, 1 bedstead with the ceiling and headcloth, 1 great chest

in the parlour and all that is in it, 1 great spit, 1 dripping pan, 1 andiron, all my feathers in a tub in the loft, my best kettle, 6 new trenchers, the cupboard in the hall, and all my wool. The rest of my goods to my brothers Wm. and Th. equally. I name Wm. executor, to whom I give Bridge Mead on condition that he fulfil my Will; if he refuse, to Th. on the same condition. I appoint Th. WHITEBREADE overseer, and 5s. for his pains. Witnesses: Henry BORNE, Th. WEALD, Th. GLYE. Proved 12 Dec. 1582.

JOHN WRIGHTE of Hornchurch husbandman, 20 Dec. 1582. (439)
To my sons John and Wm. each 1 chest. To Augis [written above Agnes struck through] my wife for 3 years each year 1 lop of wood towards her provision of fire, to be taken on my lands in the tenure of my sister THORNEDON and Henry HUMFREY. My will is that, my brother Wm. WRIGHTE's Will be performed concerning my lands, the profit of which he gave for certain years yet unexpired, after which my wife shall have the profits for 10 years of the lands in the South End of Hornchurch in consideration that she bring up my two sons decently and seemly at the discretion of Henry HUMFREY, Th. GYLL, Wm. AUGER, Rd. HARROWER and John HODSONNE and keep the house and land in good reparations, making no waste and reserving all woods and underwoods, and pay yearly 50s. to Rd. HARROWER of South End of Hornchurch yeoman, the first 5 years' rent to Wm. my youngest son and the other 5 years' rent to Th. GYLL of Dagenham yeoman, Wm., Rd. and Th. to enter into bonds to Geo. WRIGHTE my brother for payment to Wm. at 21. If Wm. die before, they are to pay John my son £10, my wife £5, my sister THORNEDON's two children 20s. apiece, and the residue equally to my brothers. My wife shall take sufficient timber for the reparation of the houses and 3 lops yearly for her fire. She shall enter into a bond of £30 to Henry HUMFREY of Hornchurch to perform my Will; if she refuse, Geo. my brother shall have the profits of my lands in like order, and to enter into bond; if Geo. die, my brother John WRIGHTE to deal as aforesaid in my lands. To John my son all my said land, to enter at the end of the 10 years. The rest of my goods to 'Augis' my wife. I make executors my wife and Geo. and overseers Henry HUMFREY and Wm. AUGER. Witnesses: Henry HUMFREY, Th. GILL, Wm. AWGER, Rd. HARROWARE, John HODSON. Proved 23 Mar. [1582/3].

ROSE BUTLER of Bradwell-next-the-Sea widow, 15 Sept. 1581. (440)
To Gregory BUTLER the elder my cow. To Joan FRAUNCES, my sister's daughter, my best featherbed, a joined chest, a kerchief, a crosscloth, a smock, and an apron. To Mgt. daughter of Rd. MANFEILDE a little plain chest, a new holland kerchief, a new lockram neckerchief, and a kerchief. To Rose MANFEILD my best rail. To Joan wife of Rt. LOVEDAYE a spice mortar. To Olive wife of John ELLETT my best coat, best hat, best waistcoat, a kerchief, a rail, an apron, a smock, and a pair of foresleeves. To THURGOOD's wife a russet petticoat and a new lockram neckerchief. The residue of my raiment to Dorothy daughter of Th. BUTLER, late of Bradwell, deceased. To Gregory BUTLER the younger my russet yarn and Dthy. BUTLER my best blanket. To John ELLETT the younger 6d. and to John, Abraham and Jerome, children of John CHAMPNES 2d. apiece. The residue of my goods to be sold by my executor, half the money thereof to Gregory BUTLER and the other divided at the discretion of Mr [John] DEBANCKE parson of Bradwell and my executor to Dthy., Rt., Gregory the younger, Rd. MANSFEILD's children, and John NEWLOCKE's children. If Gregory the elder be not satisfied with my gifts but shall trouble my executor he shall be void of my gifts. I make John NEWLOCKE of Bradwell husbandman executor, and for his pains a little brass pot. Witness: John ROBERTES. [No probate clause.]

JOHN EXETOR the elder of Shenfield yeoman, 23 Jan. 1581/2. (441)
To the poor people of Shenfield 20s. and of Brentwood 20s. To the necessary reparations of Shenfield church 20s. To my sister Mgt. £5 and to her children £4 apiece. To Joan EXETOR £4. To my godson John MILBORNE 6s.8d. and his brother Th. 3s.4d. To Eliz. wife of Geo. KELHAM 6s.8d. To John BARNARDE my godson 6s.8d. and his sister Joan 6s.8d. To Rt. MYLBORNE 40s. To Mgt. wife of Walter PAMPLIN 40s. To Alice my wife for her life my customary lands and tenements

wherein Wm. FULLER dwelleth in Shenfield Street; after her decease, to my godson John EXETOR. To my wife my freehold lands in Shenfield called Marsh Land. She shall have my house with the Chantrey land belonging (10 acres) nigh Sawiers Lane in the tenure of Rt. HUBLETHORNE for 1 year after my decease, then to my brother John EXETOR for his life; after his decease, to Henry his son. To John my brother a featherbed. To Th. MILBORNE dwelling in Brentwood 40s. for aiding my wife in the execution of my Will, whom I make executrix. Witnesses: Chris. MYLLES, Lawrence MATHEW, Geo. KYLHAM, Rt. MYLBORNE. Debts owing to John EXCETOR the elder, which he confessed to be due to him — Th. STODDARD of Abridge [in Lambourne] 40s. by specialty [i.e. bond]; Th. CODWELL oweth £31 by specialty; Wm. COOKOWE oweth £16 6s.8d.; Geo. EVERSALL oweth £8 12s.; John WOOLSTONE oweth 57s.; Th. PETCHEE of Maldon oweth £10; Wm. BATT of Chadwell [in Dagenham] oweth 13s.4d. Proved 8 Mar. 1581/2; sentence read, 27 July 1582.

[End of Register D/AER 14.]

[The corners of the first two leaves of the Register D/AER 15 beginning in 1583 have been eaten away by a rodent; the missing parts have been taken from the original Wills, but there is no original for John Draper (no.442).]

JOHN DRAPER of Woodham Walter, — M— 1582. **(442)**
To --- one tenement called D--- --- in Curlye [now Curling Tye] Green in Woodham Walter --- SQUIRE --- son of Arthur DRAPER --- in Little Baddow to Arthur DRAPER ---. To Rose DRAPER my daughter --- 1 harness girdle --- linen divided equally between Rose and --- my daughter-in-law, Arthur's wife, --- John BURNETT *alias* GILBERDE ---. To Arthur BASTWICKE 1 bullock of a year. --- To Harry BASTWICKE 10s. at 21. To --- 10s. at 21 in the hands of ---. To John BURNETT *alias* GILBERDE 1 cow, 2 sheep, a cupboard, a table, 1 pewter dish, 2 platters of the best, 4[?] pigs, 1 sheat hog, and the best brass pot of the 2 little ones; if God call me away in my sickness, John shall have the profits of my cattle and ground until Michaelmas next, saving the wool and lamb that is excepted; also 1 spit that was his father's, 1 flockbed, 1 good coverlet, half my corn in Little Baddow, and a croft of oats in Woodham Walter. To Anne RAIGNOLDE 1 white-back bullock, the best of the 3 at Little Baddow. To Isaac SAFFOLDE 1 bullock. To Joan DRAPER, my son's wife, 1 stone yelt [young sow]. To Arthur DRAPER's sons 2 calves. The residue of my goods to Harry and Arthur my sons, whom I make executors. I make John BURNETT *alias* GILBERDE overseer, to be recompensed for his pains. Witnesses: Edw. HAMONDE, John ---. Proved ---.

RICHARD HEATH of Barking fisherman, 11 May 1582. **(443)**
To the poor men's box 12d. To my son Th. £5 to be paid by 'Dennys' my wife, at 21, also £3 by my brother Wm. HEATH. I forgive my brother all other debts that he oweth me. If my son die before 16, the £3 to be paid by my brother to my wife, and then she to deliver to him such bonds as I have of him in my keeping. To my son my fir chest and the little cupboard in the chamber and 1 great chest in Rt. PERPOYNTE's house, a pair of flaxen sheets, 2 pewter dishes, and a candlestick. The rest of my goods to my wife, whom I make executrix. I make my loving friends Mr Th. MOORE of Dagenham gentleman and my father-in-law Th. NICHOLSON overseers, and for their pains 3s.4d. apiece. Witnesses: Th. MYLLOR, Wm. JONESON, fishermen, Th. HAYWARDE parish clerk of Barking. [No probate clause.]

THOMAS KINGE of East Ham yeoman, 23 July 1580. **(444)**
To the poor folk of East Ham 10s. whom Emme my wife shall think best. To Nich. SNARE [SUARE?] 40s. which is some part of his debt he oweth me, to Thomas SWAYETES 30s., and to Wm. SNARE [SUARE?] 20s. which are some parts likewise. To the son of John WASSE 1 black bullock with calf. To Kath. daughter of Edm. FOLLINTINE £3. To Alice daughter of John BROWNE deceased of East Ham 50s. over and above the legacy of her father's goods, as by an obligation in the hands of Mr DOWNCE, to be paid to her at 18 or marriage. The residue of my goods to my

wife, whom I make executrix. I ordain my well-beloved and trusty friend John WASSE overseer, and for his pains 10s. To my godchildren 12d. apiece. To Christian daughter of Rd. REYNOLDES 2s. at marriage. To Alice BROWNE 1 pair of good flaxen sheets. To four men to bear me to church 12d. apiece. To Wm. WOODLANDE my best cloak. To WOODLAND of Barking my wife's kinsman [blank] and my best sheep's russet coat. Witnesses: Edm. HARTLEY, T[homas] HAIWRD [*sic*]. Proved 8 Mar. 1582/3.

THOMAS FLETCHER of Barking tanner, 13 Mar. 1582/3. (445)
To be buried in Barking churchyard near my late wife Jane. All my bark, tan vats, hides, leather and all other utensils belonging to the trade of a tanner shall be indifferently valued by the joint advice of Agnes now my wife, Rt. COMMYNS, Th. FISHER and Wm. PREBLE and sold forthwith, Th. FISHER to have the refusal before any other so that he put in sufficient bond with surety for answering such money as shall arise to the use of my wife and my four children, Th., Matthew, Jane and Joan FLETCHER, one half to my wife and the other to them. I will that he keep so much of the other half as shall accrue to Th. and Matthew at 21 to their own uses. Wm. WRIGHTE of Matching shall have the custody and education of Jane and my dear friend John POOLE of Little Waltham that of Joan and of their legacies until they are 21 or married. To my wife 2 featherbeds with the bedsteads, 1 in the loft over the hall next the window and the other in the parlour behind the street door, 12 pair of sheets, and 1 flockbed. The rest of my household stuff, brass, pewter, bedding and other household implements shall be equally divided, half to my wife and half sold by my overseers, with the advice of Wm. PREBLE, and the money employed to my children's benefit equally. To my son John, if he be living, 40s. To Dthy. MEADOWES my wife's daughter 20s. The rest of my goods to my beloved wife, whom I make executrix. I make my dear friends Rt. COMMYNS and Th. FISHER overseers, desiring them to aid her. Witnesses: Th. FLETCHER, Th. NEWTON minister [curate of Barking], Wm. PREBLE, Th. FISHER, Griffin GOOSE. Proved 23 Mar. 1582/3.

RICHARD SWALLOWE of Hare Street in [Romford in] the Liberty of Havering-atte-Bower husbandman, 18 Nov., 23 Eliz. [1580]. (446)
To be buried on the south side of St. Edward's [chapel] in Romford. To four of the poor folks 16d. To my sister Mgy. 1 bed in the west end of the house, 1 pewter dish, 1 pewter platter, and a saucer. To my sons-in-law John BURTON my greatest colt and Rd. BURTON 1 of my best sheep. To Mary BURTON my daughter-in-law my youngest colt. The residue of my goods to Joan my wife, whom I make executrix. I make my brother-in-law John MAISTER of 'Gubbins' [now Gobions, in Romford] overseer, and for his pains 12d. Witnesses: Avery FRITH, Wm. MAULE of the Almshouse, Wm. MAWLE of 'Gubbendes', John PAYNE of Dagenham. Proved 16 Jan. 1582/3.

CHRISTOPHER STEVENS of Stanford-le-Hope yeoman, 16 Nov. 1582. (447)
To Joan my daughter all my goods to pay my debts and legacies withal. To Wm. CLEMENTES my daughter Helen's youngest son now living 2 good sheep. To my son-in-law all my apparel which I wear, 1 mattress and 1 coverlet. To John my son all my lands [no details], except 1 yard and 1 barn with sufficient timber to make the same, a house to dwell in to be assigned by my overseer; for want of issue, to Joan for her life; after her decease, to her heirs; for lack of issue, to Wm. CLEMENTES and his heirs male; if the lands descend to him, being under 21, my very friend Mr 'Eugeny' GATTON gentleman shall keep him and the receipt of the lands until then to bring him up. If all my legatees decease without heirs, my lands shall be sold by the churchwardens, or for want of churchwardens by the constables, and for their pains 6s.8d., to Mr GATTON, he giving as much as any other will give. To Edw. DENTON £6 13s.4d. and to the issue male and female of my daughter Ellen the rest of the money. To the sister [not named] of Edw. DENTON 40s. To my cousin Joan BANCKE's two sons £5 each. To Mr GATTON 2 0f the best trees, 1 in Finches, the other in the other ground. The residue of my goods to Joan. I make her my executrix. The residue of the money coming of the sale to the use of Ellen. If

John or his heirs doth come and enjoy my lands, he or they shall pay Joan £13 6s.8d. Witnesses: Th. SOMERFEILD, 'Eugenye' GATTON, Proved 17 Jan. 1582/3.

THOMAS SORRELL of Great Waltham yeoman, 1 June 1582. (448)
To Wm. SORRELL my brother my messuage that I dwell in, with the lands in my occupation, free and copy, until John my son is 21. Wm. shall pay out of the lands to Anne my wife £10 yearly during John's minority in recompense of her third or dower of all my lands, or she to take her third at her choice; the residue of the profits to be employed to the bringing up of all my children; Wm. shall have my tenement called Rowland Tailours until John is 21 towards their bringing up. If the tenement called Fullers with the lands belonging shall happen to fall during John's minority, Wm. shall have it likewise. To John all my messuages and lands in use, remainder or reversion; for default of issue, to Wm. on condition that he pay my daughters Mary and Alice 100 marks apiece. To my wife, John, Mary and Alice all my household stuff, goods, corn, cattle and other implements equally divided. If my wife be with child, that child shall have as good a part. I ordain Wm. executor. Witnesses: Th. EVERARDE, Rt. HAYWARDE, Edm. MARRIAN. Proved 21 Mar. 1582/3 by definitive sentence for the validity of the Will as appears by the sentence remaining in the Registrar's custody.

ELLEN GAUNTE of Rochford, 16 Nov. 1580. (449)
To Mgt. ABBLOTT, my daughter's child, my house and the orchard and all the household stuff within. I make her my executrix. Witnesses: John BERYMAN, Wm. RICHARDSON. Proved 28 Apr. 1582.

ROBERT JOHNSON of Stapleford Abbots husbandman, 17 Jan. 1581/2. (450)
To my son Wm. £8 at 21. If he die before, to my daughters to be equally divided at such time as shall seem good to their mother or any other friend whom she shall put in trust. To my daughters Christian 40s., Eliz. 33s.4d., and to 'either' of my other daughters 10s., all at marriage. The rest of my goods to Jane my wife, whom I make executrix. I make Mr Clement STONARDE overseer. Witness: Rd. REYGNOLDS clerk, parson of Stapleford Abbots. Proved 9 Mar. 1581/2.

'MARSCELIN' OWTRED of London, 8 Oct. 1582. (451)
[Very long religious preamble.] I will that my annuity of £10 a year for 14 years yet to come which my cousin Wm. OWTRED is bound to pay me quarterly 50s. be sold to him that will give most for the same; if Mr Frs. RAMME will give £80, he shall have for the said term. To the poor people in the town of Romford 40s. To Mr [John] PYTTES, minister [rector] of All Hallows-in-the-Wall, London, 20s. To my cousin John OWTRED and his sisters Anne and Eliz. each £4. To goodwife BALLE in Grub Street [in London] 20s.; Mr Rd. ATKIS, minister of Romford, 40s.; Mr CHARNOCKE virginal maker 20s. To Beatrix STRAUNGE my keeper 40s.; Mr St. CLERE minister 20s. To Mgy. HOLMAN my aunt's daughter, 40s. To Mr Frs. RAME, Mr PHACKE, Mr ADKYS, and my brother Rd. BOWERS, each 4 yards of cloth to make him a gown; to my hostess HALL 3 yards to make her a gown; to Randall Hall and Rt. DICKENSON each 1½ yards to make him a coat; all of the value of 16s. a yard, and the same shall be worn by them at the time of my burial. To my aunt HOLMAN 3 yards to make her a gown of the price of 6s.8d. a yard, and £4. Whereas I ought to pay her an annuity of 13s.4d. by year out of a tenement in Romford in the tenure of Rd. CHARVEL, my desire is that my executors compound with her husband Anthony HOLMAN for £8, whereof he receive but £4 and the other £4 be paid by my executors to her; if he will not compound, they shall retain the £8 towards paying the annuity. I make my loving friends Mr Rd. ADKIS and Rt. DICKENSON executors. I nominate my friend Mr Frs. RAMME overseer, desiring him to assist them. Witnesses: John GREENE, Randall HALL. Proved 9 Mar. 1582/3 by Mr ADKIS, the other executor renouncing executorship.

THOMAS CRAWLEY of Grays Thurrock, 20 Feb. 1577/8. (452)
To Alice my well-beloved wife all my goods. I make her my executrix. Witnesses: John WILLIAMS clerk [vicar of Grays Thurrock], goodwife DOWNY. Proved 24 Apr. 1582.

WILLIAM CHAUNDLER [CHAUNDELER *in margin*] of South Ockendon, 13 Apr. 1582. (453)
To Christian my wife my lease of Hamptons with the lands belonging in South Ockendon. To John and Geo. the sons of 'Poule' CHAUNDELER my eldest sons 40s. apiece when my wife thinkest best. To Th. son of Peter CHAUNDELER my son 40s. and Wm. son of John COTSALL 40s., both at my wife's discretion. To Joan my daughter, wife of John COTSALL, £5. The residue of my goods to my wife, whom I make executrix. Witnesses: Th. LEWES curate, Th. LONGE, Amos LEWES. Proved 29 May 1582.

'PHRYSWITHE' [Frisewide] FOSTER, servant to John BEST of Stock, 6 May 1582. (454)
To John BUNTING 20s. To my sister TWED my best gown, best neckercher and a crosscloth, and my table standing in my master's hall. To Eliz. and 'Dennys' daughters of Hum. PALMER, the rest of my linen equally between them. To them and John and Th. children of Th. CHARVEL 2s. each. To Arthur PERRIN's wife a spit, an andiron, a kettle, a pewter dish, a little table, a bedsteadle, a pair of trammels, a pair of pothooks, a pillow and a bolster. To Wm. STONARDE's wife a skillet, a saltcellar, a little kettle, a saucer, and a pillow. The rest of my household stuff to Hum. PALMER of Stock, whom I make executor. If my goods will not reach so far, John BUNTINGE shall have but 13s.4d. To Edm. FRYDAYE's wife [blank]. Witnesses: Rt. BONINGE, Th. LENSEYE, Alex. GARRATT writer of this. [Mark of 'Phriswith' FOSTER.] She confesseth that her master oweth her 30s. There is in the hands of Hum. PALMER 7s.6d. Proved 29 May 1582.

MARGARET PYTMAN [PITMAN *in margin*], [abode not given], 17 June 1582. (455)
To be buried in Corringham churchyard. To Joan daughter of Wm. PITMAN [PETTMAN in original] over and above her father's portion given her by Will 1 pair of sheets and 1 pewter dish. My father Th. SKANBEE shall have her and her portion as specified in her father's Will to bring her up in the fear of the Lord. To John PITMAN, my husband's son, over and above the portion that the law doth give him, 1 good sheep for love and goodwill to both. To my brother BLOWER 2 load of wood and his eldest daughter a new white russet cassock, 1 kerchief and neckerchief. To Susan BLOWER 1 white waistcoat, a safeguard, 1 old petticoat, 1 kerchief and 1 neckerchief. To Joan BLOWER a kerchief and a neckercher. To their mother Ursula FOSTER 2 pair of sheets, 2 table napkins, and a bearing sheet. To my brother and sister [blank] 2 pair of sheets, 2 pillowberes, and I forgive him 20s. that he oweth me. To Susan WARLEY 1 russet cassock, 1 russet petticoat, 1 kerchief, and a neckerchief. To [blank] his daughter 1 neckerchief, 1 kerchief, and 1 lockram apron. To my servant 'Al.' HOWSONE 1 new petticoat, 1 old cassock and 1 canvas apron. To James SKANDLE my husband's best doublet and best hose. To mother COPER ½ load of wood and my old russet gown, to my brother John PYTMAN [PITMAN in original] my husband's best black coat, and to Chris. his son my husband's russet breeches. The rest of my goods to my father Th. SKANDLE and he should pay my debts and legacies, whom I make executor. Witnesses: Philip WHITE, John SEYMER, John HAMON, Wm. BRODE [BRAD in original]. [No probate clause.]

RICHARD TYLER of Rochford yeoman, 22 Feb., 24 Eliz. [1581/2]. (456)
To Lucy my wife for her life my freehold and copyhold lands and tenements in Rochford; after her decease, my freehold tenement, yards and gardens on the south side of the Back Lane in Rochford to Edw. and Frs. my sons; if both die without issue, to Th. my eldest [son]. My wife paying my debts shall have all my goods. I ordain her my executrix. Witnesses: Th. SCOTT, Rd. EVE, Rt. MOUNTAIGUE, Jeremy MORTON. Proved 31 May 1582.

ALICE ROWE [ROO *in margin*] of Horndon[-on-the-Hill] widow, 22 Mar. 1581/2. (457)
To 'Tacye' my daughter a featherbed, the best bedstead, 1 bearing sheet, all my wearing apparel woollen and linen, 3 sheep, half the pewter, 1 brass pot next the best, the biggest kettle and the least kettle, 2 chests of the best, 4 joined stools, 1 pair of cobirons, 3 cushions, the best chafing dish, 2 candlesticks, a square table

and trestles to it, 1 tablecloth, a chair, 3 milk vessels, 1 goose and 1 gander, 1 frying pan, and 1 linen wheel. The rest of my goods to John my son, whom I make executor. My daughter's portion shall be delivered to John STONARDE of Horndon, whom I make overseer, until she is 20 or married. Witnesses: John STONARDE, Geo. STONARDE. Proved 28 Apr. 1582.

JOHN KIRBYE of Corringham smith, 15 May 1582. (458)
To Joan my daughter £4. To Mary my daughter £4, 1 cow and 2 sheep. To the poor 10s. To Mgy. my wife for her life the house at Fobbing that Rd. DAVYES doth dwell in; after her death, to Joan. To Mary the kitchen that Daniel dwelleth in, he to have it for 2 years after my death,paying the rent, if he will dwell in that kitchen. The rest of my goods to my wife, whom I make executrix. Witness: Rt. DRAPER parson of Corringham, the writer hereof. [No probate clause.]

THOMAS SKYNNER of Collier Row [in Romford] husbandman, 1 June, 24 Eliz. [1582]. (459)
To the poor men's box of St. Edward's in Romford 3s.4d. To Mgt. my daughter my field that I bought. My will is that my executors pay £20 concerning my land and they to have the profit of it for the full term of 21 years, reserving all woods on the same to her use. To Olive my daughter my lease that I have in reversion, paying my daughter Joan £3 after her entry. To Barbara my wife my bedsteadle that I lie on in the old chamber, the featherbed, all the woollen wearing clothes in the house, a piece of russet, a piece of red [cloth], also £5. To Susan my daughter £5 at Michaelmas, also £5 more at 21, to be paid by Olive £3 and by Mgt. 40s.; if Susan die before, my wife to have £5 and the other £5 to my three daughters. My wife shall have the profit of my cattle between this and Michaelmas after my decease, reserving the corn, hay and fallow. To John HARROWLDE my best doublet and best hose, with a flaxen shirt. To my wife the cow she brought with her [at our marriage] and the linen, brass and pewter likewise. The rest of my goods to my three daughters. To Rd. JONES my best coat. If Olive, Mgt. and Joan die wihout heirs, to Mgt. COLLINS their parts and my field that I bought her. I make my brother[-in-law] John COLLINS and Nich. HEARD my executors and 'Marselyn' HEARD my overseer. If Nich. who now lieth very sick die, my brother 'Marselyne' shall be executor and Anthony HEARD overseer. Witnesses: John COXE, John HARROLDE, Proved 27 June 1582 by John COLLINS, power reserved to Nich. HEARD when he shall come. [This Will is a duplicate entry of no.413.]

WILLIAM TURKE of Romford, 24 July, 24 Eliz. [1582]. (460)
To Romford church 5s. To the poor of Romford 3s.4d. To my kinsfolk that are nearest to me of my blood all my apparel, to be divided amongst them equally. To Stephen TURKE that dwelt with QUICKE 10s. To Jane QUICKE, one of his daughters, 10s. To my cousin TURKE of Hornchurch 10s. To Geo. OWTRED, Eliz. OWTRED and John COMPORTE's wife each 20s. To my two keepers 3s.4d. apiece. To my master OWTRED £3, part of that money he oweth me. To WILLETT my fellow my great chest which I bought of him. To Mgt. my maid my other chest. The residue of my goods to my executor, Wm. OWTRED my good master. [No witness.] [No probate clause.]

JOHN FAUNCE of Purleigh, 31 May 1582. (461)
To the poor men's box in Purleigh 3s.4d. To Alice CORSYE a lamb, Alice REINOLDE, a sheep, and John WEBBE a lamb, all at Michaelmas 1584. I will that my goods be truly appraised, half of the value to my three sons John, Rt. and Jonas part and part like at Michaelmas 1584. If John decease before, his part be equally divided amongst his children at 21. The residue of my goods to Mgt. my wife, whom I make executrix. I make John GAYWOOD overseer. Witnesses: Daniel GARRINGTON, Henry HURRELL, Th. TWISTE. [No probate clause.]

AGNES RUSSELLS of Rochford, 11 Mar. 1582/3. (462)
To goodwife ZELAND [*recte* IRELAND] of Rochford my red petticoat of stammel [red] colour. The residue of my goods to goodwives CLARKE, FORDE and DAMERKIN,

whom I make executrices. Witnesses: Jeremy NORTON, John MEEKE, John CORSAR. [No probate clause.]

WILLIAM MARRYAN of Canewdon weaver, 2 July 1582. (463)
To my daughter Anne my house in Prittlewell that I last dwelt in at 21; for want of issue, successively to Wm. my son at 21 and to Judith my wife. To Anne and my daughter Eliz. each 2 silver spoons, a great platter, 2 little platters, 2 porringers, and a saucer. To Eliz. my freehold tenement called [blank] at 21; for want of issue, successively to Anne and to Wm. at 21. To Wm. my 3 looms in my house at Prittlewell, a great silver whistle, 2 silver spoons, a great platter, 2 little platters, 2 porringers, and a saucer, at 21. To my wife all my lands and tenements copy and free until my children are 21. The rest of my goods to my wife, whom I make executrix, she to bring up my children well and in the fear of God. I constitute overseers my brother[-in-law] Edw. KINGE of Rochford and Hugh DAVYE of Prittlewell, and for their pains each 3s.4d. Witnesses: Nathaniel CAWSTON, John DUBBIN, Rt. VINCENTE. Proved 26 July 1582.

JOHN CHARVELL of South Shoebury husbandman, 28 Jan. 1581/2. (464)
To the poor 5s. To John my son my house and shop in Prittlewell, on condition that he give at the barn in the farm grounds called Hamstalls [now Hamstel] in Prittlewell to Frances my wife 10 seams or quarters of wheat of his best that this year shall be growing there and also pay Stephen BARTLET, my daughter's son, at 21 £5; if he die before, the £5 to Alice MARSHALL his mother, my daughter. To John all debts owing to me, he to discharge my debts to Mr EDMONDES of Prittlewell. To John my gelding which I usually did ride on and 2 of my smallest colts, viz. a grey mare and a bay horse; also my term of years yet to come in the lease of Hamstalls. To Eliz. my daughter £10 if my wife shall or may enjoy 4 of the years yet to come in my farm called Dawes in South Shoebury and other £10 within 8 years after the expiration of the 4 years. To my wife all other my goods, whom I ordain executrix. Witnesses: John MARSHALL the elder, Th. MYNNETT, John PRESTON. To John his son 4 quarters of wheat out of his farm called Dawes. Proved 28 Apr. 1582.

JOHN SMITHE of Rayleigh [cooper?], 31 Mar. 1582. (465)
To my three children, i.e. 'Saunder' [Alexander] SMITHE 20s. at 21 and all my working tools when he shall have discretion to use them and Alice and Jane SMITHE 20s. each at 21. To my brother Th. SMITHE 1 doublet, a pair of upper stocks and nether stocks, and 5s. To certain of the poorest in Rayleigh 2s. on the day of my funeral. To Wm. SOMMER 1 round table. To Roger FOSTER my arrows. To Saunder my great charger, greatest basin, porringers, and great table, at 21. To Alice and Jane half a dozen of pewter platters apiece at 21. To my said three children 1 pewter salt apiece. To Saunder my ship chest, next greatest chest to Alice, and best chest next that to Jane, all at 21. To Th. KNIGHTESBRIDGE 100 hoops which he shall work and make out himself. To Mgy. my wife my house in Rayleigh for her life; after her decease, to Saunder; if he fail without issue, to Alice and Jane. I ordain my wife executrix. The rest of my goods to her. I appoint my brother Th. and Wm. SOMMER overseers. Witnesses: Rd. BLACKWELL minister, the writer, John HARYSON, Edw. IRELAND. Proved 28 May 1582.

WILLIAM KINGE of Dunton Wallet yeoman, 25 Jan. 1582/3. (466)
To Joan my wife all my goods in the house wherein I dwell, £10, 5 of my best kine, 10 of my best ewe sheep, and my best horse. To my father Th. KINGE £20 and my land (8 acres) purchased of my sister Mary KINGE by deed dated 25 Feb., 23 Eliz. [1580/1], provided that he pay her £30. To Mgt. WITHAM my daughter-in-law £10 at marriage. To Mary daughter to my sister Ellen DOUSETT £20, which my father shall keep until she is 18. To Bridget LYNDSELL daughter to my sister Joan LYNSELL £20 at 18. To my goddaughter 'Denise' LINSELL £20 at 20. To Mary daughter to my sister Agnes NEALE £20 at 20. To Mr WITHERS [Geo., rector of Danbury?], for his pains and for a funeral sermon 20s. To the poor parishioners of Dunton 20s., of Little Burstead 20s., of Great Burstead 20s., of Margaretting 20s., of Stock 10s., and of Magdalen Laver 20s. To Stephen INGALL 10s., Rd. STACE 5s., John WOOD-

WARDE 10s., John son to John INGALL 40s., and Joan my servantmaid 5s. The rest of my goods and the lease of my house wherein I dwell to Mary WITTAM, whom I make executrix, if she will abide and remain with my father or at his appointment until it shall please God the said Mary to marry. I make my father, Peter MORGAN and Th. MORGAN overseers, to whom 6s.8d. [each?]. Witnesses: Th. KINGE, Rd. MORGAN, Rt. WYTHER[S?]. Proved 21 Feb. 1582/3.

THOMAS ANDROW of Collier Row [in Romford], [date not given]. (467)
To the poor folk of Collier Row 3s.4d. To Geoffrey my son £10 to be paid to my overseers by my executrix, they to put the money to the most profit for him and to pay him at 16. To him my best joined bed with the ceiling of the same, with 1 woolbed and a featherbed, a pair of linsey-woolsey blankets of the best, my great brass pot with 2 long legs; my wife to have the bedstead with the great brass pot for life. Alice my wife shall bring up Geoffrey and set him to school until he be able to earn his living and put him prentice to some honest man. If Geoffrey die before 21, my overseers shall have 6s.8d. apiece out of the £10, and the residue of the £10 with the profits to my brother[-in-law] John LOCKSMITHE's children and Avery ANDROWE's children. The residue of my goods to my wife. I make her my executrix and Wm. OWTRED and John LOCKESMITHE overseers. Witnesses: Wm. OWTRED, John LOCKESMITHE, Giles OSBORNE, Geo. TURKE. Proved 28 May 1582.

THOMAS BOVER of Bradwell-next-the-Sea yeoman, 29 Nov. 1583. [see no.366.] (467A)
To the poor of the parish 5s. To my sons Th. £60 at 20, Rt. £40 at 24, Geo. £30 at 21, and to Mary my daughter £30 at marriage or 21. John my son shall have the use freely of the money given to Rt., Geo. and Mary for 6 years after my decease now remaining in his hands. My executrix to keep at school and learning my two youngest children, finding them meat, drink and apparel during their minority. The residue of my goods to Joan my wife, whom I make executrix. I make John MALDON of Bradwell supervisor, and for his pains 10s. Witnesses: John DEBANKE, John BOVER, John ROBERTES. Proved 20 Mar. 1583/4.

STEPHEN SUTTELL, [abode not given], 27 Feb. 1581/2. (467B)
To be buried in Corringham churchyard. To Agnes my wife my house and lands free and copy in Fobbing and Corringham, paying 5s. yearly apiece to Eliz. SUTTELL and Mary ST(E)ANTE my daughters during my wife's life. To Eliz. and Mary the same lands in Fobbing after my wife's decease divided by even portions. To John son of Th. SUTTELL of Writtle my house and lands in Corringham after her decease. To goodman FOLLYE of Rochford 6s.8d. The rest of my goods to my wife, whom I make executrix. Witnesses: Philip WHITE parson of Fobbing, the writer hereof, Hum. WORTHAM and his wife [not named]. Proved — 1590 [in original only].

2

ARCHDEACONRY OF COLCHESTER

This Archdeaconry covered north-east and north-west Essex. (For Wills relating to north and west Essex, see Section 3.) No original Wills of this Archdeaconry being extant before the year 1586, the abstracts were prepared solely from the Wills Register [Essex Record Office reference D/ACR 7] and are numbered 468-819.

AUGUSTINE BERYFFE of St. Leonard at the New Hythe, Colchester, clothier, 26 Aug., 19 Eliz. [1577]. (468)
To Susan BERIFFE my daughter my tenement in St Mary Magdalen in Colchester, and the heirs of her body; in default of such issue, it shall be sold and the price thereof coming to be given to the rest of my children part and part like. To Kath. my wife the stable room, shop and fishhouse adjoining to the north side of my new dwelling house in St. Leonard; on condition that she do not claim any third or dowry in the tenement. To my other children, i.e. Rd., Wm., 'Awsten', John, Mgt., Eliz., Kath. and Priscilla BERIFFE, 40s. apiece. To the poor of St. Leonard 5s. The rest of my goods to my wife, whom I ordain executrix. Witnesses: Rt. ILES, Wm. BERIFFE, Rd. BERIFFE, Alice FES, Alice OSBORNE, Rd LAMBART, John WOOD, Ralph KING. Proved 14 May 1577.

STEPHEN BULL of [Saffron] Walden tailor, 25 Apr. 1577. (469)
To my maidservants Agnes MAYE and Barbara BURDALL and my servant John WOOLLWARD each a quarter of malt at marriage. To my son Rd. £60 at 24 and my daughters Mary and Eliz. BULL each 40 marks at 21 or marriage. My will is that Mary my wife shall bring up Rd., Mary and Eliz. at her own costs decently and orderly in the fear of God and especially in learning or otherwise in some godly excercise until they shall be able to help themselves; in consideration whereof I give her all my goods, she to stand bound to my supervisor to pay their legacies. I make her my executrix. I will that at the next [Church] court holden for the town of Walden, she shall prove my Will. I ordain my well-beloved friend in Christ Wm. WOODDALL of Walden gentleman my supervisor, and to him 1 doublet of black satin. Witnesses: Wm. WOODDALL notary public, John CLERKE, Geo. DEVELL. Proved 4 Sept. 1577.

THOMAS PARIS of Heydon husbandman, 14 June 1569. (470)
To Mgt. my wife my house and lands for her life, on condition that she bring up my children and see them well bestowed until marriage; then to my son Wm. PARIS. To Mgt. my eldest daughter 1 acre of my best land or else 5 marks which Wm. shall pay her if he will have it; and to Mercy, Joan, 'Royce', and Agnes, my 2nd, 3rd, 4th and 5th daughters, each 1 acre or else 5 marks likewise, to be paid to them at marriage or 25; they shall choose their acres according to their ages. To my wife all my goods, to distribute them among my children equally. I make her my executrix. Witnesses: Wm. SHEPPARD parson of Heydon, John KINGE, Nich. MADELL, John SE[VERIN?]. Proved 12 Nov. 1577.

JOHN RANKE of Goldhanger, 5 June 1577. (471)
To my daughter Agnes, using herself as becometh to her mother, a bullock. The rest of my goods to Agnes my wife. [No executor appointed.] Witnesses: Hugh ANDREAS curate, 'Barnaby' DICKMAN constable, Lawrence VALENCBYE. [No probate clause.]

THOMAS HALE, [abode not given], — 1577. (472)
To Mgt. my daughter a featherbed with a postbed at marriage, and my lands free and copy; if she die before, to Mary my wife. To Joan BATES my servant 10s. at marriage. The rest of my goods to my wife, making her executrix. I make overseer my brother Frs., and for his pains 3s.4d. God save the Queen. Witnesses: Rt. SURTANE, Henry STEVEN, Giles BRETT, Th. BOWEN. [No probate clause.]

MARGARET widow of William BROWNE, [abode not given], 7 June 1577. (473)
To Anne my daughter a cupboard, a brass pot, a posnet, a kettle, 3 sheets, a tablecloth, the best flockbed and featherbed, a bedsteadle, 20s., 3 pewter dishes, a saucer, a salt, a candlestick, 2 aprons, 3 kerchiefs, a bearing sheet, and a smock. To John my son 1 flockbed, a 'cloke' [probably cloak], 3 kerchiefs, 1 ryal, 5s., the greatest kettle, a frying pan, and a casting sheet. To Joan my daughter 1 flockbed, 3 kerchiefs, 1 rail, 1 kettle, a posnet, a table, a trough, a dripping pan, 3 sheets, a tablecloth, 2 aprons, a casting sheet, 5s., and a smock. The rest of my goods to James my son, whom I make executor. I make my faithful overseers Giles BREATT and Henry STEVEN. Mr VINTON, Th. BOWEN, John FLOWREDAYE, Ralph BIDGETT: the legacies shall be delivered into the hands of these my honest neighbours. If any of my children die before 21 or marriage, the goods to be divided among the rest. Witnesses: Giles BREATT, Henry STEVEN, John MATHER the vicar [vicar of Tolleshunt Major]. [No probate clause.]

AGNES BAKER of Great Bromley, 15 Dec., 20 Eliz. [1577]. (474)
To Eliz. BAKER my daughter a dry bullock, a yearling calf, my best flockbed, my biggest kettle, my least brass pot, 2 pieces of pewter, 2 saucers, a cheese 'lare', my great hutch, 4 yards of black russet to make her a loose gown, a press, a boarded chair, my long table and form, a pair of trestles a pair of querns, my red petticoat, a pair of fire tongs, a spit, my best spinning wheel, a pair of cards, and half the hay in the barn. To Mary BAKER my daughter 1 cow, a flockbed, my best brass pot, my little kettle, 2 pewter dishes, 2 saucers, a latten chafing dish, a back chair, my table in the hall and a form, my little hutch, and a salting trough with a cover. To Mgy. BAKER my daughter 1 cow, a flockbed, 2 pieces of pewter, 2 saucers, a little candlestick, a skillet, a kneading trough with the cover, a press, my biggest hutch, my little coffer, a high-back chair, my little table and a form, my middle kettle, and my cupboard. All these legacies at 20. If it can be spared, a flockbed and bedstead to my son Mark at 21. The rest of my goods shall be divided among my two youngest daughters. I appoint John LYCCORIS of Great Bromley executor, and for his pains 5s. Witnesses: John BALL, John SEAMAN. Proved 17 Mar. 1577/8.

PRISCILLA LISTER of Peldon maid, [date not given]. (475)
To my brothers[-in-law] David GEORGE and John GEORGE each 20s. at 21. To Alice LISTER my sister 13s.4d. and my linen and woollen. To John a brass pot, my pewter, a bed, and 7s. To each of my brethren a coffer. To my fellow servants

12d. apiece. All other my goods to Alice, whom I make executrix. I make Mr TEY of Peldon supervisor. Witnesses: Wm. TEY parson of Peldon, Th. PEVERELL, widow WILKINSON. Proved 27 Mar. 1578.

KATHERINE WEST of Manningtree widow, 22 Aug. 1554 [*sic, recte* 1574]. (476)
To be buried in Mistley churchyard. To John GILBERT *alias* HAYELL and Barbara his wife my house in Manningtree with an orchard and to the longer liver; after their deceases, to Alice daughter of Gilbert; if she decease without heirs, to Kath. her sister. I will that John pay Agnes SEVERALL my daughter 20s. To her a great chest. To her children and to the children of John LEYS each a pewter dish. To Marion LANDEN a brass pot. To Alice HAYLES *alias* GILBERT abovesaid a kettle pan and a spruce coffer. To Agnes LANDEY [*sic*] a little kettle. I ordain John GILBERT *alias* HAYLE and his wife executors, to whom I give the residue of my goods. Witnesses: Cuthbert DAWSON, Rt. WENT, Geo. DOWETT, Geo. WOOD, John SMYTHE the elder. To Agnes my daughter half the fruit of the garden of my house as is now planted for her life and a stained cloth hanging in the hall. Witnesses: John CLERK parson of Lawford, Rt. KECHE, Rt. WENT, John KIRKER. Proved 13 Mar. 1577/8.

PARNELL REINOLD [REINOLDES *in margin*] of Wivenhoe, -- July 1577. (Nuncupative.) (477)
She did give to Mgt. REYNOLD her mother-in-law 30s. Witnesses: Edw. BURGES clerk [rector of Wivenhoe], [blank] clerk, [blank] SAM[M]ON. Proved 2 Sept. [blank].

ROBERT THORNE of Great Chishall yeoman, 17 Dec., 20 Eliz. [1577]. (478)
To Reynold my son my lands and tenements for his life; after his decease, to Geo. son of Reynold; for default of issue, successively to Henry another son and to Anthony my eldest son, according to certain uses expressed in a deed of feoffment by me made to Th. FREVELL of Heydon gentleman and John COSEN of Heydon husbandman, dated 16 Dec. [1577], when I was lawfully seized in fee simple by a grant to me by Reynold. To Anthony 1 pair of my best towen sheets and a brass pan already appointed to him by me. The residue of my goods to my well-beloved son Reynold, whom I constitute my executor. Witnesses: John STEAD, Th. SURDELL, Rt. BARTHED. Proved 18 Feb. 1577/8.

RICHARD WENLOCK of Langham, 30 Jan. 1577/8. (479)
To the poor people of Langham 40s., at 13s.4d. a year. To Alice my wife, in consideration of her third of my house and lands, £8 every year for her life, to be paid by Rd. my son. To her £10, all my household stuff, i.e. in my parlour, on the parlour chamber, and on the sollar over the parlour chamber, and in the maid's [maids'?] chamber, with my brass and pewter. I will that she have her dwelling in my parlour chamber, the sollar and the maiden's [maidens'?] chamber, the use of the 'backhouse' [backhouse or bakehouse] and the garden, sufficient firewood to serve her necessity and the third part of the fruit, as pears, apples, plums [and] nuts, also a cow and a gelding pastured as long as she keep herself a widow; if she marry, to take her £8 a year, her household stuff and money, and so depart. To Rd. my houses and lands, meadows and woods in Langham and Boxted, conditionally that he pay John the elder and John the younger, my two sons, each £10, also to each £20 to be paid out of my goods. To Jane my daughter £10, conditionally that she and her husband that now is, according to her other husband CHAUNDLER's Will, give to Joan CHAUNDLER his daughter 10 sheep to be delivered by my executors and put forth to her profit. To Susan my daughter £20. To Christian WARNER and Jane BALL my daughters each £6 13s.4d. To Timothy my brother, Kath. my sister, and my brother[-in-law] FENKLE each 20s. The rest of my goods to Rd., conditionally that he discharge the parish of Langham for the keeping of Daniel son of Eliz. VERES [NERES?]. I ordain Rd. my son and Th. my son-in-law executors. Witnesses: Th. DEBNAM, Allen HINES, Th. BRIDGES. Proved 21 Feb. 1577/8.

WILLIAM LINGWOOD of Peldon, 31 Jan. 1577/8. **(480)**
To Agnes my wife all my goods, to bring up my children; if she marry, I will that she take order as Mr GYLL and Mr TEY of Peldon shall think meet according to the ability of my wife at that time. Witnesses: Wm. TEY [rector] of Peldon, Th. PEVERELL. Proved 21 Feb. 1577/8.

AUDREY BRAY of Ardleigh widow, 2 Feb. 1577/8. **(481)**
I bequeath my house and the yard and the rest of my goods to be sold by my friends John BRAGGE and Rd. KENT to the behoof of the parish, on condition that my children may be the better and more honestly and godly brought up, as I hope and trust in God they shall be. I therefore desire my said friends to be executors. Witnesses: Lawrence LYDE [vicar of Ardleigh], Wm. HECKFORDE, Henry WHELLER. Proved 21 Feb. 1577/8.

MATTHEW HARVY of St. Botolph, Colchester, husbandman, 2 Feb. 1577/8. (Nuncupative.) **(482)**
He willed that Samuel HARVYE his brother should have his 2 mares and his gelding with his plough and cart irons for £7 5s., whereof he willed £5 to be paid for his debts and the rest with the residue of his goods to Anne his wife, whom he made executrix. Witnesses: Geo. MANNERS, Rd. PASFEILD, Adam HOLLAND. Proved 21 Feb. 1577/8.

WILLIAM RUNHAM of Great Chesterford, 25 Jan. 1577/8. **(483)**
To Mgt. my wife my house wherein I dwell and all my other lands, for her life; if she marry, only until John and Th. my sons are 21, committing no strip or waste in the woods but yearly during their minority to have 2 reasonable cartloads of wood and not above. If both my sons die before 21, she shall have the lands and tenements for life although married; after her decease, my house with 3 acres of arable land which was given by Jane RUNHAM my mother deceased and 1 acre of wood at Burton [in Great Chesterford] to remain to the use of John and all other lands to Th., on condition that they pay to the child wherewith my wife now goeth £3 13s.4d. after they have entered upon them. If all my children die before 21, to remain to Samuel, Th. and Philip, sons of John RUNHAM my brother the younger, to be equally divided among them. To John my son 1 rood of saffron ground. I have surrendered my said lands into the hands of the lords of the manors of Great Chesterford and Strethall by Th. TAYLOR, tenant of both manors, in the presence of Th. SWALLOW and John my brother, likewise tenants of the same manors. The residue of my goods to John my brother, to be supervisor, and for his pains 12d. Witnesses: Th. PAYNE clerk, vicar there, Th. SWALLOW, Th. TAYLOR, John SAWYER, Th. ROWLAND, John RUNHAM the younger, Roger AMYE. Proved 18 Feb. 1577/8.

ALICE BEWTELL of Debden, 10 Dec. 1577. **(484)**
To Edw. BEWTELL my son 40s. and his daughter [not named] 6s.8d. To my sons Frs. and Geo. each 53s.4d., a mattress and a hutch. To my daughter Blanche 5s.4d. To Anne BEWTELL my daughter £4 13s.4d. at marriage, my 2nd bed, and all my linen, saving 6 pair of sheets to be divided among my executors. To Blanche and Anne one half of my pewter and brass. The rest of my goods to Th., Wm. and Barnaby BEWTELL my sons, which three witnesses requested and desired HODSEN with others. Proved 14 Jan. 1577/8.

THOMAS BRANDE of Little Bardfield husbandman, 16 July 1570 and 12 Eliz. **(485)**
To 'old' John BRAND my son 1 cow and 1 seam of wheat to be delivered by Joan my wife so soon as she may spare any of them. To Th. my son 1 horse and 1 bullock. To Wm. my son 1 horse called Baell. To Edw. my son 1 horse named Jack and 1 cow. To Oliver my son 1 horse called Cony and 2 yearlings. To 'young' John my son 1 cow and 40s. which my wife shall pay him. To John THORNE my son-in-law 1 cow and 1 bullock. To my sons each 1 seam of wheat and 1 seam of malt at marriage. To Esdras BRANDE $\frac{1}{2}$ seam of wheat and a wennel. To the children, i.e. Edw., Mary, John and Paul, of old John, and the children, i.e. Edw. and Alice, of Edw. my son, each a sheep. To Eliz. GOORE my servant 2 bushels of wheat at

marriage. To my wife the lease and term of years of my farm and the occupying of all my other goods for her life, except she can spare any of these my gifts to my children and hers. I will that Oliver shall be a guide with her. All my other goods to my wife, whom I ordain executrix; William to be always a guide to her. I institute my trusty and well-beloved friend John WINTERFLOOD the elder to be supervisor, and for his painstaking 3s.4d. Witnesses: John WINTERFLOOD senior, Rt MAYHEW. Proved 14 Jan. 1577/8.

GILES COOTE of Radwinter, 2 Jan. 1577/8. (486)
To the poor men's box 5s. To my uncle Rd. COOTE's children 20s. to be equally divided. I ordain Alice COOTE my sister my executrix. The remainder of my goods, also my lease of Bery Field to her. Witnesses: Wm. SAMSON, Lancelot ELLIS, John SMYTHE, Th. WAKEFEILD, Th. MUMFORDE. Proved 14 Jan. 1577/8.

WILLIAM SELL of Littlebury, [date not given]. (487)
[Religious preamble.] To Mgt. and Mary my daughters and Wm. and Michael my sons each 26s.8d., all at 21. The rest of my goods to my wife [not named], whom I make executrix. Witnesses: John SELL, John HELYE. Proved 14 Jan. 1577/8.

WILLIAM LAW of Newland in Arkesden, 4 Oct. 1577. (488)
To Andrew my son my messuage in Arkesden and my lands, meadows, woods and pastures free and copy in Arkesden and Elmdon; if he die without issue, to my own heirs. I will that Anne my wife shall have for her life my house, with sufficient meat, drink, fire and candle at Andrew's costs; if she shall not like of her using by him, he shall pay her £6 13s.4d. a year. [I give my wife omitted?] one half of the sheets, pillows and pillowberes, 1 mattress, 1 pair of blankets, 1 great chest, 1 little chest, 1 covering, and 1 bolster. To my sons Philip £6, Rt. the elder my 2nd son 50s.[53s.?]4d., and Rt. the younger £4. To Grace [my daughter omitted?] 1 cow bullock of a year. The rest of my goods to Andrew to the performance of my Will. I make him executor. Witnesses: John BROMBRIGE [*recte* BROWNRIGE] clerk [vicar of Arkesden], Geo. LAWE the elder, 'Mathie' GYPPES, Rt. LAWE, John SILVESTER, Rt. BAYNETT. Proved 14 Jan. 1577/8.

RICHARD COOLE of Little Bentley yeoman, 18 Dec. 1577. (489)
To the poor folk 10s. To every one of my wife's children [not named] a sheep. To my brothers all my apparel to be equally divided. To my sister Eliz. COOLE a cow bullock of a year and the vantage. To my son Wm. 4 good beasts, my best featherbed with the best bedsteadle, and my best brass pot, at 21. To Mgt. my wife my houses and lands in Little Bentley called Warrins and Wyates for her life; after her decease, to William. The rest of my goods to my wife, bringing up my son. I make her my executrix; if she do marry, to my brothers Simon and John COOLE for fulfilling this Will, whom I ordain supervisors. Witnesses: Edw. HYLLES, Rd. KINGE, Stephen ESTWOOD. Proved 17 Jan. 1577/8.

MARGERY LITTLEBURY [of Peldon], [date not given]. (Nuncupative.) (490)
She said to me, Wm. TEY parson of Peldon, that her mind was that Eliz. WILKINSON, goddaughter to her sister Anne, should have 20s. of the money that her father-in-law TASILER had in his hands, also that John WILKINSON should have the rest of the other 20s. that should be left. She willed that her linen and woollen and suchlike things should be distributed between the widow WILKINSON, Anne, Susan, Eliz. and John WILKINSON. She desired me to see it executed. Witnesses: widow WILKINSON, LINGWOOD's wife, MILLER's wife, Anne WILKINSON, John MYLLER, Proved 13 Dec. 1577.

WILLIAM GARDINER of Langham husbandman, 14 Dec. 1577. (491)
To Anne and Joan my daughters £10 apiece at marriage or 21; provided that, if they do contract matrimony with any, not making their mother and brethren privy to the same and will not be ruled by them, then they shall lose the benefit of my gift. To Edw. BARKER 2 bullocks (1 to be brought up this year and the other next year), he to have them kept up on my farm until he may sell them to his advantage, then buy

other with the money, and to have the running of 2 in this sort free, so long as he shall think good to dwell here at Langham Park Lodge. I will that James COCKE and Geo. COCKE shall have the running of the cattle they now have here until May Day next and thence the running of only 3 apiece until Michaelmas following. To Joan SEWELL and her husband the seam of barley that he hath already in his hands. To Beatrice FORDE a calf to be weaned next year and to run in the ground free until it be a cow, then to let it out to her advantage, conditionally that she learn the Ten Commandments and other principles of Christianity and behave herself honestly and obediently to her master and dame. To Mgy. my wife one half of my goods for her life; after her decease, her half shall be equally divided, one half between my two daughters Anne and Joan and the other to Edw. my son. The rest of my goods to Edw. He and my wife shall have the occupying of my farm houses jointly; after her decease he shall have the whole farm; if he die before he be married, his whole portion shall go to my [*recte* his] sisters Anne and Joan; if all my children die, my wife shall have all my goods and the lease of my farm to give and to sell. If she and Edw. in occupying my farm and dwelling together shall not well agree, they shall equally divide my goods and shall depart either from the other within the gates as may be most to their quiet. I ordain them executors. Witnesses: John REIGNOLDE, Th. FARROUR, James COCKE. Proved 17 Jan. 1577/8.

RICHARD COLE [COOLE *in margin*] of Boxted, 14 Nov. 1577. **(492)**
To the poor men's box 3s.4d. To Alice my wife my houses and lands in Boxted for her life; after her decease, to Rd. my son. To Rt. my son £10 at 23; within 1 year after my decease he shall be preferred to some honest master by the discretion of Rd. HAWKINS and Th. DEBNAM, my faithful friends, and his master have the occupying of the £10 during his apprenticeship, putting in bonds for payment with some profit to Rt's use as my friends shall think good; if Rt. die before 23, the £10 to remain to Rd. and Jane my daughter part and part like. To Jane £6 13s.4d. at 24; if she die before, to my wife. The rest of my goods to my wife, whom I ordain executrix. Witnesses: Th. DEBNAM, Rd. HAWKINS, Rd. MORSE, Wm. HOWE. Proved 13 Dec. 1577.

JOHN PARKER of Messing, 30 Oct. 1577. **(493)**
To Mgt. my wife all such household stuff as is in my chamber where I lie (except the bed standing under the stairs), my oak cupboard in the hall, my greatest kettle and another next it, the best skillet posnet, the best brass pot, 2 pewter platters, and 6 pieces which she brought [at our marriage], my brass mortar, my black cow, and my butter and cheese such as I have. To Th. my son my bed under the stairs, 1 sheet, 2 blankets, a bolster, a pillow and a coverlet, with the steadle and hangings. To Anne my daughter the bed on the sollar. To Mgt. my daughter 40s., which was delivered to her master when he received her, she to have it when her master is bound to deliver it to me. To Nicholas my son my other cupboard, he to pay Th. and Anne 5s. apiece. To the child that my wife is withal 20s., to be paid to my wife. The rest of my goods to my executor to pay my debts, and for his pains 6s.8d., the overplus to be divided equally between my wife and my children. I ordain my well-beloved brother[-in-law] Wm. BORLEY executor. Witnesses: my wife, L[OO?]NES' wife, Wm. BORLEY, John LUFKIN. Proved 13 Dec. 1577.

WILLIAM LAMBARD of Stanway, 25 July 1577. **(494)**
To Rendall THEDOM 6 sheep with the increase at 21, and my cupboard; if he die before, to his brother Th. THEDOM. To my brother[-in-law] Rd. VARLAND, paying to Mr [Th.] UPCHER, the parson of 'the Heathe' [St. Leonard, Colchester] 6s.8d. and to John CLERKE of 'the Heathe' 16d. which he lent me, first 2 selfgrow jerkins, a sky-coloured jerkin, 1 'sacking' [sackcloth] doublet, and a pair of sky-coloured hose. To Andrew CROMER a twybill and a cutting saw. The residue of my goods to Eliz. my wife, whom I make executrix. Witnesses: John THEDOM, Th. POLEFOOTE, Rt. PORRIDGE. Proved 20 Dec. 1577.

JOHN LOCKE of Great Bentley, 26 Oct. 1577. **(495)**
To Joan LAWDAME, mother TANNER, mother ROOTES, Anne TABOR, Joan JACOB

and Joyce GOLDATOR each 3s.4d. To Joan my wife my houses and lands free and copy for her life; after her departure, to John my son; if he die without heirs, my freeholds to John HALE, my sister's son. To John my son £10 at 21, the best featherbed, 1 dozen of the best pewter, the best brass pot, 2 of the best beasts, 10 of the best ewes, 2 good kettles, 2 good hutches, 2 cushions, 1 chair, 1 trammel, a pair of pothooks, a trivet, a spit, a table and a form, all at 21. To John HALE 40s. at 21. I will that my wife do keep my son to school 2 years after my departure. To every one of my godchildren 12d. To my servants Anne PARKE and John PARKE each 12d. To Eliz. NASHE 1 ewe sheep of 2 years. To Rd. LOCKE, my brother Rd.'s son, and to Wm. LOCKE, my brother Wm.'s son, each 20s. The rest of my goods to my wife, whom I make executrix. I make John HARRIS my supervisor, and for his pains 3s.4d. Witnesses: Wm. THORNE vicar, Rt. HUBBERT, John CARNSDALE. Proved 20 Nov. 1577.

NICHOLAS INGERAME of Great Birch, 7 June 1577. (496)
To Mgt. my wife for her life a half part of my tenement called Hommans in Great Birch; after her decease, to John INGRAM my son; if he die before her, the half part to Th. my son. To Wm. my son my best flockbed. To Th. 20s., paying 10s. to my wife which he oweth me and my daughter 9s.8d. To Eliz. my daughter 1 featherbed. The rest of my goods to be equally divided among my wife, John and Eliz., my wife to have the custody of these two parts until their marriages. I make her my executrix. I will John WAKINGE supervisor, and for his labour 2s.8d. Witnesses: John SMYTHE, Rd. BROCKE, Th. SYMOND clerk [rector of Great Birch]. Proved 20 Nov. 1577.

JOHN CHALLIS of Little Walden in the parish of 'Great' [Saffron] Walden, 1 July 1577. (497)
To Mgy. my wife all my lands and tenements for her life; after her decease, to John CORNELL and Mgt. his wife for 1 year; after, my tenement called the Hailewiny to Alice PURKES my daughter. To John CHALLIS my son and Emme his wife a close of pasture called Famelyes (4 acres); for want of their heirs, to Alice; on condition that which of them do enjoy the close shall pay Mgt. my daughter £3 6s.8d. To Barthw. my son my tenement called Peter Fryers with an acre of land called Fryers Hill, parcel of a tenement called Dalmers. To Mgt. my daughter a form, a table with 2 joined stools, a cupboard, 6 pieces of the best pewter, 3 saucers, the best kettle, the best brass pot, a hutch, and a cow. To John and Barthw. each a cow after my wife's decease. The rest of my goods to my wife, whom I ordain executrix. Witnesses: John WOLLARD, John FREMAN, Wm. FREMAN. Proved 5 Nov. 1577.

RICHARD LORKIN of Weeley, 25 July 1577. (498)
To Joan my wife my 2 cottages called Crabtrees ($1\frac{1}{2}$ acres) in Weeley for her life; after her decease, to be sold and the money divided to my four daughters, i.e. Joan, Mary, Mgt. and Susanna LORKIN. To Joan 1 great kettle and 1 spit; Mary a kettle and a spit. To Wm. GARDINER, Rt. GARDINER, John ARNOLDE and Rd. ARNOLDE each a lamb. The rest of my goods to my wife. I ordain my executors Th. HAYMER and Rd. HEWETT of Weeley. I have surrendered into the hands of the lord [of the manor] my cottages [to] John COLMAN, Th. HAYMER and Rd. HEWETT tenants. Proved 20 Nov. 1577.

DOROTHY WOOD of Fingringhoe widow, 10 Aug. 1577. (499)
To my son John WOOD 1 cow and my cauldron. To my son Isaac WOOD 1 bullock of a year and the vantage, my best brass pot, and my best candlestick at 21. To Eliz. WOOD my daughter 1 cow, 1 flock[bed], a transom, a little spit, and my best latten chafing dish. To my daughter Lucy WOOD a cow, my best flockbed, and a salt at 21. The residue of my goods to Anthony, to see his brother Isaac honestly kept and brought up. I ordain Anthony executor. Witnesses: Henry CONSTABLE, John STONE. Proved 25 Oct. 1577.

JOHN SMYTHE of Dovercourt labouring man, 19 Sept. 1577. (500)
To Elizabeth my wife a piece of free land called Bremed lands (2 acres) on the west

side of Dovercourt for her life; and my house called Smyth with the lands belonging in Dovercourt for her life; to hold after the decease of Mgt. SMYTHE my mother. I make my wife executrix, to whom I bequeath all my goods. I will her to bring up my children [not named]. Witnesses: John COTTINGAME the writer, John HAYLE the younger. Proved 20 Nov. 1577.

THOMAS KEYES of Tolleshunt Major, 31 May 1577. **(501)**
To Anne my eldest daughter £20 at 21, also the posted bed, the table with the 2 forms, 1 hutch which was her mother's, all in the parlour, the greatest iron spit and greatest brass pot, a brass chafer being her grandfather's [not named] gift, a brass posnet, a brazen mortar with the pestle, a kettle to hold 10 gallons, a firepan, a pair of tongs, a pewter pot, a white wrought bended neckerchief, a white pair of sleeves, a pair of purled ruffs, a double yard rail with 1 stitch, a fine kerchief with an eyelet hole of blue silk, a cornered kerchief of holland with an eyelet hole of white, a fine crosscloth with an eyelet hole of red silk, another white one with a rent behind, a pair of silk sleeves, a black apron with the silver twitches, a holland pillowbere with a white seam, a lockram table-cloth the best, 3 diaper table napkins, my wife's best gown, a bearing sheet, the best 'kull' [caul, netted cap], a fine flannel swaddle bend, a round kirtle of mockado, her mother's best hat and satin purse, a velvet pin pillow, a fine holland rail, and the Katherine wheel. To Eliz. my daughter £20 at 21, the best flock coverlet, the best plank of elm and the frame, the 2nd iron spit, a fine iron fork, a cobiron, the 2nd brass pot, a latten chafer given in her grandfather's Will, a kettle of 7 lb., a hutch nearest the parlour door, the greatest pewter pot given in his Will, a white purled neckerchief, a pair of white sleeves edged with white bonelace, the best pair of wrought ruffs, a fine white holland kerchief with a black mark at the end and a white eyelet hole in the middest, a new holland double rail with a round hem, a yard kerchief with a black mark in the end and a white eyelet hole, a cornered kerchief with a black mark and eyelet hole, a crosscloth with a black mark, an iron 'moule' [spade] in the one side by the marks, 2 crosscloths marked with a red silk, an ell of new holland to make her a pillowbere, a cupboardcloth of diaper, 4 diaper napkins, a worsted kirtle with a chamlet upper-body and a tablecloth. If both die before 21, it is my will that John DEAMMON my brother shall have the £40 at such time as they should have it. To John DAIMMON £5 at 29 [*sic*] and all my wearing raiment except the cloak and the gown. To my servants Th. DYER and Jane PUR each a lamb. To my wife's goddaughter Susan BUSHE a holland rail and 1 crosscloth double stitched. To my sister BUSHE 1 fine holland kerchief and the best greatest crosscloth. To Jane and Kath. my maids a holland yard kerchief betwixt them and each a side holland crosscloth; to Jane my wife's black petticoat and Kath. a pair of knives. To my brother John DAMMYN a white yard kerchief with a blue eyelet hole. To my wife's nurse a lockram apron with a flat hem, the best of the twain. To widow BROWNE a yard kerchief of lockram. To the seven children of my brother old John, i.e. Anne, Mgt., Wm., Th., Samuel, Mary and Phyllis, each a lamb. The rest of my goods to Edw. SPARLINGE, whom I ordain executor. I ordain Geo. KINGE of Lawling in Latchingdon a faithful overseer. Witnesses: Th. BOWEN, Giles BREATT, John MATHER the vicar. Proved 8 July 1577.

JOAN PEPPES of Debden widow, 10 Feb., 19 Eliz. [1576/7]. **(502)**
I will that Philip BYRD my son shall sell my lands in the tenure of Simon BARKER of Wimbish and so much of my other lands and tenements to pay my legacies. To Wm., Edw. and Chris., the sons of my son, each £20 (to Chris. at 21 or 24 as my executor shall think meet), and to the residue of my son's children [each] £3 6s.8d. at marriage or 21, viz. Philip, Geo., Mary, Mgt., Th., Anne and Alice. The residue of my lands to Philip my son, whom I make executor. Witnesses: Rd. HODSON, Edw. BYRDE. Administration committed, 10 Oct. 1577, to the executor.

'EM' DASON of Manningtree widow, 24 June 1574. **(503)**
To be buried in Mistley church or churchyard. To the reparations of the 'almeshousen' of Manningtree 6s.8d. and of the church 3s.4d. To my godchildren 12d. apiece. To Edw. and Hugh ROBINSON 10s. apiece. To Eliz. ROBINSON my best garment. To 'Jude' HULL 1 bed, a bedstead, 2 candlesticks, 6 pieces of pewter, and

a chest. To my kinswoman Alice CHRISTEMAS 5 silver spoons. To my four sons [not all named] all my goods and lands and tenements to be parted among them equally. I set this my house in which I dwell to be valued at £60 with the brewing vessel and baking vessel, with a long table and cupboard in the hall, and my sons to buy out another's part, which of them be disposed to sell. I ordain Wm. DASON and Th. DASON my two eldest sons my executors. To Phoebe, my eldest son's daughter, 1 bedstead with a featherbed, 1 chest of linen, and 2 silver spoons in it. 'By me Th. DAWSON the writer.' Proved 14 Oct. 1577.

JOHN LYNE of Wix, 10 Sept. 1577. (504)
To Agnes my wife for her life the house wherein I dwell with the ground belonging; after her decease, to my daughter Joan. To my wife all the household stuff that she brought with her [at our marriage] and the half of my household stuff not given to my son and the other half to be equally divided between my son and my daughter, after my wife's decease, to whom I give the use for her life. To her all my corn and cattle. The rest of my movables, saving to my son John 1 cow and 4 sheep after probate and the cupboard and the querns after my wife's decease, to him. To my daughter the table in the hall. To John my house and land called Braysers free and copyhold at 24 and not before. My brother shall have the occupying of it to bring up John CROSSE and to pay him at 21 £4 and my wife 30s. towards the setting up of a new barn. To my wife 1 piece of fallow called Great Borrowes and half the two pightles called Braysers to sow them in convenient time and to receive her croft quietly, paying my executor 1 seam of clean wheat. To the poor of this parish 2s. I appoint my brother Rd. LYNE executor. Witnesses: John BATLE the elder, Rt. WILLIAMS parson of Tendring. Proved 24 Oct. 1577.

ELIAS BECKQUITH of Cressing bachelor, 16 June 1577. (505)
To the poor inhabitants of Cressing 6s.8d. and of Rivenhall 6s.8d. To my sister Agnes, late the wife of Wm. HALLES and now widow, 20s. To my sister Christian, late the wife of Henry HALLES and now widow, 20s. To my brothers Henry and Rt. BECKQUITH each 20s. and John BECKQUITH 13s.4d. To Wm. ELLIS my best doublet, John KINGE my coat cloth, John SPILLMAN 3 platters, and Rd. BECKQUITH, my brother's son, a kettle. The residue of my goods to my brother Robert, whom I ordain my executor. Witnesses: Th. BARATT, John KINGE, John SPILLMAN. Proved 24 Sept. 1577.

HUGH WALDEN of Great Totham, 26 June 1577. (506)
To Joan my wife my houses and lands in Tolleshunt Major free and copy for 6 years towards the payment of my legacies, on condition that she shall claim no third; after, to John my son. To my wife my house and lands in Little Totham called Hawkins for her life; after her decease, to Abraham my son; for lack of issue, to Th. my son; if he die before 24, the profit to the performance of my legacies. To John my son 2 kine at Straytes and the hire for the same now due and my 2 young heifers. To Abraham a cow bullock at 21. To Wm. and Th. my sons each £20 at 21. To Eliz. my daughter £18 at 21 or marriage and 1 red bullock of 3 years, going in the Heath. To Anne my daughter £20 at 21 or marriage. To Wm. HARWARD my servant 5s. To 'Annyner' BROWNE 1 ewe lamb. To the poor people of Great Totham 6s.8d. and of Tolleshunt Major and Little Totham 3s.4d. each, all at Christmas, with the consent of the 'chief of the parish'; the rest of my goods to my wife. I ordain her and John executors, and Edw. SAMMES supervisor, and for his pains 3s.4d. Witnesses: 'Sir' Lawrence AGOR [vicar of Great Totham], Stephen WITHERS, Henry STEPHEN, Henry BADCOCKE, John APRICE. Proved 8 Oct. 1577.

THOMAS NEWMAN of Elmdon labourer, 7 July 1577. (507)
To Henry my son my house and lands free and copy, in consideration that he shall pay Roger my son £5 at 21. To Wm. THORNE my son-in-law my house and yard for for 5 years after my decease, paying yearly to Henry 5s. and leaving it sufficiently repaired and discharge the yearly rent of 18d. to the lord [of the manor] of Lee Bury [in Elmdon]. To Mary my daughter my saffron grounds. To Mr Reynold MEAD my 2 kine, 3 ewes and 2 lambs, he to pay my three daughters Barbara, Dthy. and

Frances NEWMAN each 33s.4d. at marriage. To Frances my middle pot. The rest of my goods to Henry, whom I make executor. Witnesses Mr Reynold MEAD, John KETRIDGE the elder, James ENGLISHE. Proved 10 Oct. 1577.

JOAN DIGLETT of Colne Engaine widow, 27 Aug., 19 Eliz. [1577]. (508)
To Th. DIGLETT my son the cow which is in the keeping of Stephen BECHAM of Pebmarsh; if Th. do depart this world or [n]ever come again from the sea, to Cecily my daughter. To Joan CRABBE my daughter my 3 coats and 10s. To John CRABBE which I brought up 4d. To Joan CRABBE my goddaughter and Avice CRABBE 'my little mother' each 4d. All other my goods to Cecily, whom I ordain executrix. Witnesses: John POTTER, John CHAMBERLAINE, Stephen BECHAM. Proved 24 Sept. 1577.

THOMAS FREEMAN of Hadstock, 31 Mar. 1577. (Nuncupative.) (509)
He did give all his goods to Mary his wife, whom he did nominate executrix. Witnesses: John CLAYDEN, Geo. ONYON, Wm. BANCKES. Proved 30 July 1577.

HENRY CAVELL of Black Notley, 29 May 1577. (510)
To the poor at my burial 3s.4d. To my children, i.e. Wm., Sarah and Th., each 26s.8d. at 18, Th.'s money to remain in my brother LEONTON's hands. To my son John my red bullock. The residue of my goods to Eleanor my wife, whom I make executrix. I ordain my well-beloved friend John COLLETTE overseer. Witnesses: Cyprian GARRARD, Th. STEBBINGE, John FRANCKE, John DRAKE, Rt. EVERED, John BEDELL the writer. Proved 14 July 1577.

THOMAS SPENCER of Great Tey husbandman, 26 June 1577. (511)
To Joan my wife my houses, i.e. Bucklers and Pickes, for her life, to bring up my children; after her death, to my eldest son John, on condition that he pay Samuel £6 13s.4d. To John my youngest son £5. To Ellen my daughter a cow worth 40s. or 40s. [in money]. The rest of my movables to my wife, whom I make executrix. I make Th. UNDERWOOD supervisor, and for his pains 3s.4d. Witnesses: Wm. SPENCER, Rt. BESOUTH, Rd. RAMPTON, Wm. DAMPTON [*sic*]. Proved 3 Sept. 1577.

JOHN WILSON of the Old Hythe in Colchester tailor, 10 Sept. 1577. (512)
To the poor people of East Donyland 2s. To Mary my wife my house called Warmans, on condition that she shall see the bringing up of my three children, viz. Wm., John and Mercy, in the fear of God for 10 years; after it shall be sold and the money equally divided into four parts, viz. to my wife and my children. To my sons Wm. and John each 2 beasts and a bullock. To Mary 2 beasts, my wife to occupy them for bringing up my children for 10 years. To Wm. and John each a flockbed. To my three children 2 sheep apiece. The rest of my goods to my wife. I make Th. PILGRYME of Sudbury [co.Suffolk] and John HASYLL of East Donyland executors, and to John HASYLL for his painstaking my buck's leather doublet. To my brother[-in-law] DARBY my red saddle and my boots. Surrender to the lord by Th. ESTWOOD and John SMYTH, tenants of the manor, and John HASELL instead of the bailiff. Witnesses: John ALLEN the elder, Edw. DARBY, John LAMBE. Proved 19 Sept. 1577.

ELIZABETH HEARDE of Wivenhoe widow, [date not given]. (513)
To Joyce daughter of John BUSHE my son £10; Th. CLERKE shall receive it at Our Lady Day in Lent next coming of Wm. LUSON and pay it at her marriage day. To Joyce a featherbed, the cupboard in the hall, 12 pieces of pewter standing on it, a chest that my best linen is in, a lockram tablecloth, 4 kerchers, 2 fine kerchers, 1 neckercher laid with bone lace, a great kettle, a little brass pot, an a little latten kettle. To John BUSHE my son £21 to receive of Wm. MORLEY of Wivenhoe at Midsummer next £11 and of Chris. DENMARKE of Alresford the same day £10. To Thomasine daughter of John my son £10 that he shall pay her at her marriage. To her a great kettle, a latten kettle, 2 holland kerchers, 2 holland quarters, and 1 neckerchief. To Joyce a chest under the parlour window. To mother UPPERGRAVE [UPPERGRANE?] a russet petticoat, a smock, a neckerchief, and an apron; John BROWNE's wife a black saveguard, a red petticoat with a red cotton upperbody, 1

smock, a neckerchief, and an apron; LANGLE's wife a frize petticoat, 1 apron, 1 smock, and 1 neckerchief; Joan LUCAS a rug petticoat, 1 smock, 1 apron, and 1 neckerchief; Besse PUPLETT a selfgrown petticoat, and a waistcoat; and MUNDAYE's wife a puke cassock that I made the other day. LUSON of the 'Heath' [Hythe in Colchester] oweth me 15s.; Chris. DENMARKE oweth me 16s.8d. To DENMARKE's maid a frize gown; John DENMARKE's wife of 'Old Hythe' a frize cassock; Joyce BUSHE a round puke kirtle; and mother DENNYS a coverlet, a sheet, a pillow, and a pillowbere. The rest of my goods to John my son, whom I make executor. Witnesses: Wm. MORLY, John MILLER, Wm. LUSON. Proved 6 July 1577.

JOHN JAMES of Rivenhall, 15 Apr. 1577. (514)
To every one of my six children, i.e. Mary, Rd., Mgt., Clare, Agnes and Leonard, each a cow at marriage or 20. The rest of my goods to Dthy. my wife, whom I make executrix. Witnesses: John FAWNT parson of Rivenhall, Rd. WARRE gentleman. Proved 22 June 1577.

LAWRENCE POTTER of Layer-de-la-Haye husbandman, 28 May 1577. (515)
To Mary my daughter £10 at 18; if she decease before, to Anne my wife; if she decease before Mary is 18, to Wm. POTTER the younger, my brother, now dwelling in Bocking, until Mary is 18, he to enter into bond to Th. DUKE of Layer-de-la-Haye for payment of the £10; if Mary decease before 18, the £10 in Wm.'s hands to be equally divided to his children at 18. To Wm. my dun mare. To his children, i.e. Th., Wm., Rd., Rt. and John, 20s. to be equally divided at 18. To Joan THURGOE my servant 1 black weaned calf. To Wm. ROSHYE, the lad that dwelleth with me, 1 ewe lamb. The rest of my goods to my wife, whom I ordain governor to my daughter, and executrix; provided that, if she marry, he to whom she shall be married shall enter into bond to Th. DUKE for the £10. I ordain him supervisor. Witnesses: Wm. TEY [rector of Peldon], Nich. BREST, Rt. BRACKETT. Proved 6 July 1577.

ELIZABETH LARRETT of Messing widow, 4 Feb. 1576/7. (516)
To John LEVERITCHE my son my table which doth stand on the bench in the hall, my form, and my flockbed on the sollar called the trundle bed. To Rt. LEVERYTCH my son my featherbed, 3 pair of my best canvas sheets, 1 lockram sheet, my hutch with the spring lock, and my bedsteadle with the hangings. To him £6 which I have of his. To Lawrence LEVERETCH my son my counter table. To Al[ice?] daughter of Kath. LARRETT 13s.4d. at 18 or marriage. To my son John's wife my holland sheet and my wearing woollen to her and her children. To his wife and my son Th.'s wife my wearing linen. To Th.'s wife my worsted kirtle. To Geo. FILLEBROWNE son of Geo. my bell candlestick. The rest of my goods to be equally divided between Rt. and Th. I ordain my beloved in Christ Geo. FILLEBROWNE executor. Witnesses: Rt. LEVERITCHE, John LUFKIN. Proved 20 July 1577.

JOHN BARNARD of Fairstead tanner, 11 Apr. 1577. (517)
[Religious preamble.] To the poor of Fairstead 2s. All my goods to Mary my wife, whom I ordain executrix. I desire Rt. SORRELL of Great Leighs yeoman to be overseer, to whom for his pains 5s. Witnesses: Rt. SORRELL, Stephen SPILLMAN, Wm. CARTEWRYGHT. Proved 8 July 1577.

AGNES ROBERTES of Wivenhoe widow, 12 May 1577. (Nuncupative.) (518)
She gave to her son Wm. ANDERSONNE all her goods, he paying to Mark ROBERTES, her husband's son, 26s.8d. at 21. Witnesses: Edw. BURGES, Wm. MORLEY, Erkenwald TYLER, James SYDAYE. [No probate clause.]

ROBERT TURNER of Littlebury, [date not given]. (519)
To Agnes my wife my house and land which is copy[hold] for 5 years after my decease towards bringing up my children; after to Th. my son. I will that he pay to my four other children, Wm., Rt., Rd. and Geo., each £5 at 26; if any marry and have a child, yet the father die before 26, his child shall have the £5 at 21. I surrender the house and land before John COLE to Th. TURNER my brother until such

legacies be paid. The rest of my goods to my wife towards bringing up my children. I ordain Th. my brother and Frs. LINDSELL parson of Strethall executors. Witnesses: Nich. FELSTEAD, Rt. PARMENTER, Th. TURNER, John COLE, Frs. LINDSELL. Proved 30 July 1577.

THOMAS CAMPYON of Springwell in [Saffron] Walden, 1 June 1574. (520)
Towards the reparations of Little Chesterford church 12d. and of Walden church 2s. To the poor men's box in Walden 12d. and to the poor in Little Chesterford 4d. To my six [*recte* five?] daughters, Grace, Mary, Dthy., Anne and Alice CAMPYON, 40s. apiece at 21. The residue of my goods to Alice my wife, whom I make executrix. I request my dear friends John HARVEY and Wm. AYLEWARDE of Walden to be overseers. Witnesses: Th. TITTERINGTON, Rd. THAKE, Roger HUEN. Proved 30 July 1577.

AGNES REASON of Great Tey widow, 29 Apr. 1577. (521)
To Wm. BREWER my son 1 black garled cow and 1 bullock of a year at 18, 1 tick bed in the chamber, 2 pewter platters, my great kettle and the next to it, my little brass pot, my latten chafing dish, a brazen mortar, a hutch in the chamber, a great and a little spit, my plough chains and the rest of my old iron, my table and the form and the cupboard in the hall, my salt trough, and the hangings about the chamber, all at 18. To Mgy. ABBOT, my daughter's child, a cow worth 40s. or 40s. in money, a great pewter platter, my best flockbed, and 1 pair of sheets next the best; and to Eliz. ABBOT, my daughter's child, a bullock of 1 year, a flockbed next the best and the bedsteadle, a great pewter plater, a kettle that holdeth 2 gallons, and a pair of sheets next to the 2nd pair; all at 15. To Edw. ABBOTT, my son-in-law, 3 acres of wheat growing in Hedge Croft at Great Tey, except to Wm. 1 acre of wheat or 20s., at 18 and the half of 3 acres of bullimong which I have sown to halves with Rd. BREWER the elder under the wood in Great Tey, to which Rd.'s three children a black sheep and her lamb to be parted equally. To Edw. 5 sheep and their lambs, 2 calves of this year's weaning, and my hogs. To widow MARTEN of Great Tey 1 bushel of wheat. To the poor 2 bushel of wheat to be ground and baked and given in bread at my burial and 1 bushel of malt to be brewed. To Agnes REASON my sister-in-law 1 flockbed and 1 pair of hempen sheets. The rest of my goods to Edw. I will that Edw. shall have the government of Wm. for 3 years and find him meat, drink and apparel and keep him at school to write and read, and for such term to have my house and lands. I ordain Edw. and Rt. AMIES of Feering executors, and for their pains 40d., and my cousin Th. UNDERWOOD supervisor. Witnesses: John CUTLER of Earls Colne, Anthony GYMBLETT the writer, Th. UNDERWOOD. Proved 5 June 1577.

WILLIAM NORTHEN of St. Nicholas, Colchester, shearman, 12 July 1576. (522)
[For abstract of this Will, proved 12 Sept. 1576, see previous volume, no.846.]

THOMAS WILDE of Pattiswick, 24 Apr. 1577. (523)
To Rt. WYLDE my son, after the decease of Eliz. my wife, all my 'housen' and lands belonging in Pattiswick and Stisted; if he die before he enjoy this gift and without issue, to my daughters Joan and Francis; if all die before, to be divided equally among the [blank]; if he come to enjoy my gift, he shall pay Joan and Frances £10 apiece. I will that my wife shall pay my three children each £5 at 21. The rest of my goods to my wife, whom I make executrix. Witnesses: John COPLANDE parson of Bradwell[-juxta-Coggeshall], Nich. PAGE, John CHAMBERLAYNE. Proved 15 May 1577.

THOMAS RAYNER of Great Braxted, 4 May, 19 Eliz. [1577]. (524)
To Joan my daughter 40s. and all my silver 'games' [dice?, see no.813] being 5 or 6, a pair of silver hooks, and a tick bed in the chamber in the east end of the house, a pair of sheets on which I lie, a silver pin, a latten chafing dish, a scummer, a pewter dish, 1 old platter, and 1 saucer, all at 18 or marriage; if she die before, to remain to the residue of my children equally to be divided. If my brother SALTER or any other goodbody will take Joan until then, her part to be delivered to him or them to her use until then. To my brother RAYNER my best hat. To John my son the

table in the hall with 40s. at 18. To my daughters Anne and Dorothy 26s.8d. at 18 or marriage. The residue of my movables to Dthy. my wife, to bring up my children honestly. If she marry before their ages, I will that he who shall marry with her shall put in bond for performing my Will to my father-in-law BYETT and my brother-in-law SADLER, whom I make overseers. I make my wife executrix. Witnesses: Rd. BARNARD, Th. RAMSOLDE. Proved 5 June 1577.

ALICE WILSON of Wendon Lofts widow, 11 Feb. 1576/7. (525)
To Eliz. daughter of Th. STAGGE 1 cow now in the hands of John TRIGGE of 'Dudnham' [now Duddenhoe] End in Elmdon. The residue of my goods to Th., whom I make executor. Witnesses: Wm. ALEXANDER, John TRIGGE, Th. FREMAN. Proved 18 Apr. 1577.

JOHN son of John POLLY of Brightlingsea late deceased esquire, 16 Dec. 1576. (526)
To be buried in [Saffron] Walden church. My brother[-in-law] Th. ROBERTES shall take 26s.8d. that I left with John HARISON that was my father's man and my quarter's rent, to bear the charges about my burial. To Rd. ROBERTES my colt that I have with my brother[-in-law] MORDEN in Norfolk. The rest of my goods to my brother[-in-law] ROBERTES, whom I make executor. Witnesses: Rt. CORNELL, Wm. CORNELL. Proved 18 Apr. 1577.

WILLIAM BROWNE of Little Wenden, 28 Mar. 1577. (527)
To be buried in Little Wenden churchyard. To Wm. KINGE bailiff my best shirt of the 3, 1 pair of boots, and a pair of spurs. The rest of my goods to Agnes daughter of Henry SEARSON of Great Wenden. Witnesses: Nich. YORKE rector of Little Wenden, John ROMBOULDE, John FELSTED. [No probate clause.]

RICHARD LANE of Wix husbandman, 3 June 1576. (528)
To Mary my wife my house and lands called Busses for her life; after her death, to my son Theophilus, on condition that he pay his sister Joan LANE £10; if both depart without issue, to my sister Anne STONE; if Theophilus do not pay Joan, she shall have my land, paying Theophilus £20. To 'Austone' my sister 13s.4d. in consideration of such friendship as she have shown me. To my mother [not named] every year 1 load of wood, part cubit, part logs, which best may be made of my lands for her life, and 6s.8d. every year so that she make quittance for a bond for which I stand bound to her. The rest of my goods to my wife, whom I make executrix. I make John PAYNTER supervisor. I have delivered a surrender to Geo. TOOS bailiff [of the manor] and Th. STEPHEN and Edw. BATEMAN tenants this day. Witnesses: Th. STEPHEN, John WHYMPERS, Geo. ROOS writer hereof. Proved 12 Dec. 1576.

CHRISTOPHER WESTWOOD of Goldhanger husbandman, 13 Apr. 1577. (529)
I will that my tenement and lands called Skottes in which I dwell in Goldhanger be divided into two equal parts by my executor, the hallhouse and the buttery with 2 sollars or lofts over the same to be one part, and the residue of the house the other. To Ellen my wife the one half for 20 years after my decease if she do so long live in satisfaction of her third part or dowry and to the use and for bringing up Josias my son; if she decease before, my executor shall have it in his custody, yielding and allowing for the profits to Josias at 20. My executor shall hold the other half of my lands until my son John is 24, paying yearly 40s. towards payment of my debts and bringing up Mary, John, and Lettice WESTWOOD my children and to yield to them accounts thereof when John is 24. If John decease before, I will that my tenement be sold and the money distributed, half amongst my children part and part like at 20 or marriage and the other half to the poor people and to the church of Goldhanger. The residue of my goods to be divided equally, half to my wife, the other half equally amongst my four children at 20 or marriage. My wife shall be bound with sufficient sureties in £40 to perform my Will. I ordain Rt. OSBORNE of Little Totham executor, and for his pains 6s.8d. I assign John HENNINGHAM the younger of the same place overseer. Witnesses: Barnaby DICKMAN, Lawrence VALENCEBY. Proved 15 May 1577.

JOHN STREAT of Earls Colne, 17 Jan. 1576/7. **(530)**
To Joan my wife 40s. To Anne STREAT my daughter 20s. To Mgy. STREAT my daughter 20s. at 17. To Martin WATSON my wife's son my horse. The rest of my goods to my wife, whom I make executrix. Witnesses: Wm. ADHAMS vicar [of Earls Colne], Rt. JERVES, Henry PULLEN. Proved 6 Apr. [1577].

WILLIAM MYLLS [MILLS *in margin*] of West Bergholt ploughwright, 18 Jan. 1576/7. **(531)**
To my two sons Wm. and Edw. all my occupation with all my tools, my timber, 3 horses, and 1 mare between them, with 2 [blank], plough and cart, and all that belongs to them. To Wm. my great pot, the biggest that I have, and to each 2 pewter platters. To them the bed that they lie in. To Wm. a quern, a brass mortar and a hutch in the sollar. To Edw. my hutch in the hall and my black cow calf. To Wm. 13s.4d. To each of my three daughters, Joan, Mgt. and 'Prisca' MYLLS, 40s., which shall be due on an obligation of one John GOODWYNE of [blank]. To Joan 1 dun bullock of 2 years, Mgt. 1 'howed' [for meaning see p.xvii] cow, and Joan and 'Prisca' 1 flockbed; and 2 brass pots, 2 pewter platters and 1 candlestick, the best I have, to each. To Joan 1 little cushion. To Mgt. the other brass pot, 1 great cauldron, 2 pewter platters, and 1 great skillet. To Eliz. my wife my best mare. To John MONNEY 20s., on condition and at such time as the parishioners of West Bergholt will make it 30s. to be employed to the use of the said John MUNNEY by the discreet and ablest of the parish till he is 24, then he to have the 30s. with the profits; if he die before, to my wife. The rest of my goods to her. I make Wm. my son executor, and to him more my saddle and my new bridle. Witnesses: John MILLS, Wm. AUDLEY, Wm. MILLS of Acton [co. Suffolk]. Proved 4 June 1577.

JOHN SMYTH of Stansted Mountfitchet husbandman, 7 May 1577. **(532)**
I will that my five daughters, Blanche, Mgt., Joan, Agnes and Eliz., each have 40s. at 25. If it please God to take my wife before they be paid, my son and heir to have that I have given her — an acre and a half of free land at that age according to my surrender of my lands to my wife till my son is 30, and at 30 he shall have half and my wife the other half for her life. The rest of my goods to Mgt. my wife. [No executor named.] Witnesses: John NORTHAGE, Rt. WOOD, John GYRTON, John LACE. Proved 11 June 1577.

ROBERT GOODDAY of Little Totham, 26 March 1577. **(533)**
To Agnes my wife my house for her life; after her death, to Alice and Joan GOODDAY my daughters; for lack of heirs, to remain to the children of my brother John GOODDAY the elder. To Alice the hutch with the spring lock, 1 kettle, 1 platter, and 1 pair of silver hooks that were her own mother's. To Joan 1 hutch with a plain lock, 1 basin, 1 kettle of the middle sort, and 1 odd silver hook. The residue of my goods to my wife, whom I make executrix. I make my brother John supervisor. Witnesses: Lawrence AGAR of Great Totham vicar, John GOODDAY the elder, John UPPRICE. Proved 15 Apr. 1577.

JOHN BROOKE, son of late George BROOKE of Tolleshunt Major, seaman and apprentice to William KINGE of Tollesbury mariner, 26 Mar. 1577. **(534)**
I make my Will, being in the town of Orford (co. Suffolk). I ordain my well-beloved and trusty master Wm. KINGE executor and John HAUCKES of Tollesbury the elder overseer. To Geo. BROKE my eldest brother £13 6s.8d. and to Stephen BROOKE my youngest brother £10, each at 21. To Mgt. BROOKE my sister £5 at 20. To Geo. my featherbed, bedstead, half my pewter, a brass pot, and my cupboard. To Stephen a flockbed, half my pewter, 2 old kettles, and a spit. My debts to be paid: Mich. GRIFFIN of Tolleshunt 30s., Stephen his brother 20s., and Stephen OSKIN 3s.4d. Also for John HAWKES taking pain herein 13s.4d., praying him for God's sake to fulfil my Will. The rest [of my goods] to my master and his children [not named]. Witnesses: Leonard BRYANT writer hereof, SAUNDER's dame, my host, Rd. TATTELL of East Donyland, John NEWLAND of Old Hythe [Colchester], Wm. SAMPSON of Orford. Proved 14 Apr. 1577.

STEPHEN GRIFFIN of Tolleshunt Major, 27 Oct. 1578. (535)
To Nich. GRIFFEN my brother £6, 1 leather doublet, my best hat, and my lockram shirt. To Edw. his son 20s. at 20 and to Eliz. his daughter 20s. at marriage. To my sister Mgt. SPOONER £5. To Anne daughter of Michael [*sic*] GRIFFEN my brother 30s. at 21 or marriage. To Joan and Eliz. BOWEN my sisters, daughters of my father-in-law Th. BOWEN each 40s. at 21 or marriage. To John FANNE of Tolleshunt Major my fustian doublet. To the poor people of the parish 20s. The rest of my goods to my brother Michael, whom I make executor. I will that my father-in-law shall be my overseer. Witnesses: Th. BOWEN, John MATHER my vicar [of Tolleshunt Major]. Proved 27 Nov. 1578.

THOMAS SAFFOULDE [SAFFOLDE *in margin*] of East Mersea, 30 June 1577. (536)
To Francis [Frances?] FLOWER £3 6s.8d. and a pewter dish, which £3 6s.8d. was the bequest of Agnes POLLARD. To Josias SAFFOLDE my son half of my monger [boat] called the 'Anne' with half of her apparel and furniture belonging, he claiming no legacy from Agnes POLLARD his granddame. I will that Wm. LOWINGE shall go still in my monger this 12 months, he to have half the profits and my wife and my son the other half; at the 12 months' end the half to be sold and 20 marks of the money to Anne my wife and the rest to my son. To my wife 10 ewe sheep on condition that she give my five godchildren each a lamb before Midsummer. To her all the household stuff that she had when I married with her, also the third part of my household stuff (except my best bedstock and best cupboard and table which I do give to my son). To my son the yellow hutch and the little coffer. To my wife my tenement and land that I dwell in, for 15 years if she live so long; if she die before, to my son; the term of years being expired, I will it to my son. To her my 2 brass [pots omitted?] that were hers. I appoint John PORTER and Rd. SOMMER, both of 'Braxted', to be 'gardiners' [guardians] of my son's lands until he is 21 and to let them to the best advantage. To my sister Agnes 4 marks when my boat be sold. To John GYBB and Th. TAYLER my boat called the 'Rose' with all that belongeth to her, they paying £10 towards paying my debts and legacies. The rest of my goods to remain in the hands of my wife, she being bound to Josias to pay him the worth at 21; if he die before age and not married, to Agnes my sister and her child and Rd. SOMMERS my godson equally divided. To Grace WRIGHTE 20s. at 16. I appoint John GYBB and Th. TAYLER executors, and for their pains each 20s. I will that Wm. LONGE shall bear the half charges of all the 'wast' of [blank] during the year that he shall have the half profit of the monger called the 'Anne'. To Josias 2 silver spoons that were his granddame's [not named]. If any of my executors or guardians shall renounce the fulfilling of my Will, I institute Wm. SMYTHE and my wife executors or guardians. Winesses: Nich. MIDDLETON, Wm. SMYTHE writer, Edm. SMYTH, Nich. WOODWARDE, John ELLETT. Proved 7 Apr. 1578 by Wm. SMYTHE, the others renouncing.

WILLIAM LITTLEBURY of Great Bromley labourer, 30 Dec. 1580. (537)
To Wm. my son my house and land at 21, conditionally paying my daughter Mercy 20s. within 2 years and 40s. at 20. To him a brass pot, a saw, 7 iron wedges , and a hutch. To Mercy a posnet and a kettle. To my daughters Eliz. a cauldron and Faith a kettle, a skillet and a hutch. The rest of my goods to my children part and part like. I make my brother Geo. Littlebury executor, he to keep Faith and have the profit of my land until my son come of age. I make Geo. COLL supervisor. Witnesses: [blank. Surrendered to the lord of] the manor of Great Bromley, where the same lieth, to the use of my Will in the presence of Wm. TONGET in place of the lord's bailiff. [No probate clause.]

WILLIAM BRIDGE of Colne Engaine, 17 Dec., 23 Eliz. [1580]. (538)
To the poor of the parish 6s.8d. and of Earls Colne 6s.8d. To John my son my messuage called Trerdgall Fen. To my son Abraham my copyhold land called Banlyes belonging to the manor of Shrives in Colne Engaine. To my daughters Mgt. £6 13s.4d., Audrey, Agnes and Joan each £20, within 1, 2, 3 and 4 years after my decease. To my son Wm. my best joined bed in the parlour. The residue of my household stuff to the residue of my children, i.e. Roger, John, Abraham, Mgt., Audrey and Joan, to

be equally divided. To Roger and John my lease of my farm in which I dwell, with the rest of my goods; they shall take up £5 13s.4d. of Wm. PARKER the butcher of Earls Colne, whereof John shall receive 53s.4d. and the residue of this debt I give to my youngest son Wm. to be put to some good use for him by Roger until he is 21. I ordain Roger and John executors. Witnesses: Geoffrey POTTER, Th. SMYTH, Roger LAUESOLL. Proved 17 Jan. 1580/1.

ALICE FRANCKAM of St. Nicholas, Colchester, widow, 8 Jan.1580/1. (539)
To John TYLL my son-in-law my tenement in West Bergholt called Nicholls. To Mgy. GOSSE that was my maid a weaned bullock and the vantage, a furred gown, and a piece of stammel. To Anne FOKES my kinswoman my black gown with billiment lace, a stammel [red] petticoat and a worsted apron. To WELL's wife my old cassock at Bergholt. To ROADES' wife my russet petticoat. To Rt. SPARLINGE the bed he lieth on and all the old shafts when he come out of his years [of apprenticeship], on condition that he tarry and remain with John TILL the full term, and at the end 10s. The rest of my goods to John, whom I ordain executor. I make John LAMBE supervisor. Witnesses: Martin EDWIN, Eliz. HARWOOD, John LAMBE, Wm. LAMBE. Proved 10 Feb. 1580/1.

JOHN MARSHE of Great Bentley, 3 Dec. 1580. (540)
To 'Matha' my wife my house and lands in Great Bentley for her life; after her decease, to John my son, he paying Joan my daughter £8 and 'Rodeya' his sister 20s., after he come to the houses and lands that I have given him. The residue of my goods to 'Matha' my wife, to bring up my children withal, whom I make my executrix. Surrender into the hands of the lord [of the manor] in the presence of John COLL instead of the bailiff and John GREEN and John NEWMAN tenants. Witnesses: John COLL, John NEWMAN, Wm. NEVEARDE. Proved 12 Jan. 1580/1.

STEPHEN DUNTON of Dedham, 19 Nov. 1580. (541)
To every one of my children 40s. apiece, i.e. to Rt., Joan, Agnes, Mgt., Martha and Grace, all to be paid by Mgt. my wife out of such goods as I shall have at the hour of my death. Witnesses: Wm. DUNTON, Th. BUNE, Wm. COLLE, Ellen DUNTON. Proved 17 Dec. 1580.

MARGARET HEDGE of Ramsey widow, 3 Sept. 1580. (542)
To my son Anthony WICKES my house and lands in Great Oakley called Kings, on condition that he pay yearly for the lives of Rd. HEDGE my son and Reynold WICKES my late son's child 33s.4d. apiece at 19 and shall keep the two children or see them provided for and placed well to be brought up with meat, drink and clothes to 19; if Anthony should neglect payment, I will my son John to enter on Kings as his own for his life and pay the portions and Anthony to be void of my gift. If all my children die except Reynold and Eliz. HEDGE my daughter, Reynold shall have the house and lands, conditionally that he pay her for her life 40s. yearly and after her death 40s. yearly to her child or children if she have any. I will that my supervisors shall buy as much land or house and land with £20 to her use. To her 1 flockbed the worst, a transom, and a pair of boarded bedsteadles. To Reynold my best flockbed, a transom, and the bedsteadles. To John, Reynold and Eliz. 1 piece of pewter at 20 or marriage. To the poorest people of Needham Market [co. Suffolk], Great and Little Oakley, and Ramsey 6s.8d. each parish in Lent. To my godchildren 6s. apiece. To my three servants, viz. John HEDGE, Nich. HAYWARDE and Cecily HEDGE, each 1 ewe sheep. To Reynold £4 and a grey horse. I make Anthony WICKES executor if he live and recover [from] his sickness; if he die before he prove my Will I choose John my son and John HAYWARDE executors, and I choose Th. PAKEMAN of Wrabness and John HAYWARDE [*sic*] supervisors, and for their pains 10s. apiece. To Wm. HEDGE's wife 20s. If all my goods when they shall be inventoried do not amount to such sums sufficient enough to pay all legacies, my executors and supervisors shall abate of every of my children's portions as much to fulfil my Will. Witnesses: Simon CAWSON, John HEDGE, John HAYWARDE. Proved [no name given], 4 Feb. 1580/1.

MARGARET SMYTH of Wrabness single woman, 17 Nov. 1580. (Nuncupative.) (543)
She delivered into the hands of Th. PAKEMAN 50s., whereof she willed Susan SMYTHE, her sister's daughter, to be paid 20s. The rest of her money she gave to the poor in Wrabness at Th.'s discretion. All her other goods to the poor to be distributed by Th. and other of the parish at such time as they shall see need. Witnesses: Th. GODFREY, Wm. STELMAN, Edw. MAYER. Proved 9 Feb. 1580/1.

HENRY BREATT senior of Great Sampford husbandman, 8 Jan. 1577/8. (544)
To the poor 6s.8d. To Rt. my son my messuage and lands called Mariotts in Sampford aforesaid after the decease of Mary my wife; if he die before her, to Alice my daughter. To her £10 at 20. To my wife all my goods to bring up my children in learning, whom I make my executrix. I make Rt. SMYTH *alias* AGNES supervisor. Witnesses: Wm. SAUNDERS, John FITCHE, John ROLFE, Oliver CLARAUNCE. Proved 16 Feb. 1581/2.

JOAN FORDHAM of Great Chishall, 3 Nov. 1580. (545)
To John FORDHAM my father 8s. to be taken out of 18s.4d. which my brother-in-law ASPINALL doth owe me, to be bestowed on a coat for my father by my executor. To my father 1 bolster, 2 pillows, 1 pair of sheets and 1 mattress which I lie on, for his life; after his decease, to Joan wife of John FORDHAM my brother. To John my brother 20s. and to Joan my cupboard, my newest gown, my red petticoat, a pair of flaxen sheets, a pair of towen sheets, a flaxen tablecloth, 4 towen table napkins, my best covering, and 2 kettles. To my sister Julian my other gown, a russet petticoat, a pair of flaxen sheets, a pair of towen sheets, a kettle, and a pot posnet. To Rd. FORDHAM my brother 5s. and my best hutch; Mgt. FORDHAM daughter of Mich. FORDHAM 1 sheet, and Eliz. and Joan his daughters each a pewter dish. To Th. ASPINALL son of my brother ASPINALL 10s.4d., the residue of the 18s.4d. remaining in my brother's hands. To Eliz. and Kath. his daughters each a sheet. To Magdalen SEWETT a pewter dish and a napkin. To Eliz. LORKIN and Agnes MARCHALL each a petticoat. I will that Th. FORDHAM my brother shall be executor. Witnesses: Wm. BIRD clerk [vicar of Great Chishall], Rt. PLUCKROSE, Wm. FORDHAM. Proved 6 Dec. 1580.

ROBERT PLATFOOT of West Mersea, husbandman, 9 Jan. 1577/8. (546)
To Wm. son of Th. WAULD of West Mersea late deceased and to Parnell, Mary and Kath. WAULDE, sisters of Wm., each 20s. at marriage. To Mary and Kath. each 1 cow of a year, to be put forth to their most profit and to receive them at 21. To Anthony HARRISON of Colchester shearman and John GARDINER of Coggeshall tailor each 1 lamb at May Day after my death. To Wm. HAWLE of Colchester the younger 1 sheep of 2 years at marriage and to Joan, Eliz. and Alice HAWLE his sisters each a lamb. To Eliz. daughter of Anthony HARRISON 40s. at marriage. To the children of Th. HARVY of West Mersea late deceased, i.e. John, Th. and Eliz., each 2s.6d. at marriage. To John KINGE servant [blank]. To Wm. HAWLE the elder of Colchester 2s.6d. at marriage. The residue of my goods to Anne my wife, whom I ordain executrix. I make my father-in-law Wm. HAWLE the elder of Colchester supervisor, and for his pains 10s. Witnesses: Wm. SMYTH, John HARVY. Proved 12 Jan. 1580/1.

SAVEN AGLYNTINE of Ramsey single woman, 10 Dec., 23 Eliz. [1580]. (547)
To 'Kirchian' HEWETT widow my part of my house called Needs in Ramsey. To Th. BROWNE 10s. To Rt. BORFLETTE's three children, Mgt., Eliz. and Susan, each 5s. To Barbary JELLETT a sheep and a lamb which were given me by the Will of Joan MARVEN. To Frances HEWETT 5s. To Th. HEARD the elder 5s. which he laid out for me at the court. To John TACKN[ER] 2s., Eliz. CAPON 2s., Rt. BLOSSE 12d., Rd. HEARDE 3s.4d., and Geo. HERDE 3s.4d. I make John HEARD executor. The residue of my goods to him. Witnesses: Wm. WALTERS, Nich. MAYE. Proved 14 June 1580.

JOHN LITTLEBURY of Great Bromley, 14 Dec., 23 Eliz. [1580]. (548)
To my daughters Mgt. a flockbed, Frances a pewter platter, a candlestick, a pewter

sallet for salt, and a brass posnet, Besse a pewter platter, a pewter dish, and a little candlestick, and Kath. a pewter platter, a pewter dish, a 3-legged skillet, and a candlestick. To Th. my son a hutch with lock and key, a brass pot bought at UNDERWOOD's, 1 of the best [blank], and my best doublet. To Margaret a little table bought of father WELE, the best candlestick, a scummer, and a pewter platter. The rest of my goods to Jane my wife, whom I make executrix. I make Nich. FREND supervisor. Witnesses: Nich. FREND, Wm. [blank], Rd. GOLDIN. Proved 9 Jan. 1580/1.

ROBERT DICKSON of St. Leonard, Colchester, yeoman, 6 Dec. 1580. (549)
To the poor people of the parish 10s. at Christmas and 10s. at Easter. To my sons Rt. and John each £20 at 21. If my wife shall not be with child at my decease or the child shall not live to 21, each of my said sons shall have £6 13s.4d. at 21; if she be with child, she shall be bound to my supervisor to pay £13 6s.8d. to the child at 21. She shall have the use of the £40 till my children are 21 in consideration of the bringing up and education of my children. If my wife marry, she and he with a surety shall be bound to my supervisor in £60 for payment of the legacies to my sons. The residue of my goods to my wife, whom I name executrix. I ordain Benjamin ANDROWES of Colchester oatmealmaker supervisor, and for a remembrance towards his pains 20s. Witnesses: Edw. FULLER, Benjamin ANDREW, John FRANKLIN, Th. WELDE. Proved 12 Jan. 1580/1.

RICHARD WHELER the elder of Witham husbandman, 20 Dec. 1577. (550)
[Religious preamble.] To Kath. my daughter, now wife of John OSMONDE, 6s.8d. To Gilbert her son and Ellen, Agnes and Jane CRACKBONE her daughters 6s.8d. If Kath. and all her children die before receiving their legacies, all to Joan my daughter, now wife of Jerome WEBB, and her children, to be equally divided. To Joan 6s.8d. and to Rebecca and Agnes WEBB her daughters each 6s.8d.; if Joan and all her children die, to Kath. and her children. The residue of my goods to Eliz. my loving wife, whom I ordain executrix. Witnesses: John GLASCOCKE writer hereof, Th. SMEE, Th. HAVEN, Geo. HAVEN, Jerome WEBB. I ordain my very loving nephew Rd. BACON of Ulting overseer and 6s.8d. for his pains. Proved 18 Jan. 1581/2.

THOMAS BUCKE of Littlebury husbandman, 17 Feb. 1579/80. (551)
To Wm. my son, after the decease of Joan my wife, a tenement with two pightles in the bridgefoot in Newport in the tenancy of Rt. and another messuage and customary land in the town of Littlebury towards the Water End called Smythes with 8½ acres of arable land, whereof 3 half-acres lie at Stickling Croft, 3 half-acres at Perchers Hill, 2 half-acres both in one shot [furlong] at Langland, 1 half-acre abutting on Lilland Bank, 1 half-acre leading towards Audley End [in Saffron Walden] called Lewdmare, 1 acre in a field called Stockinge, 1 acre lying on Lilland Bank, 1 half-acre abutting on Lilland Bank and on the same shot, 2 half-acres in West Croft, with 1 acre of wood being customary land between Snakes Lane and Crispes Croft. To Wm. my 3rd horse as shall fortune to be in my stable at my death and 5 quarters of barley every year so often as Grove Field Piece shall be sown with wheat or barley. To Mgt. my daughter a messuage being free land in North End in Walden, on condition that, if she sell it, one of my sons shall have the offer thereof before any other person better cheap than any other by 20s., if willing to buy. To John son of John BUCKE my son deceased 1 acre of arable being customary lying on Perchers Hill in the tenure of Peter PYTYE. To Joan and Mgy. BUCKE, daughters of my son John deceased, each 50s., and to Eliz. BUCKE and Mgy. PARKER each 3s.4d., all to be paid by Erasmus my son. To Simon, Th., Edith and John PAYNE each 3s.4d. to be likewise paid within 8 years after my decease. To my sister Constance 5s. To Erasmus a messuage called Marions with my other lands free and customary in Littlebury and Elmdon. To Erasmus all my horse not before bequeathed, my carts and cartgear, ploughs and ploughgear. All my beasts shall be equally divided between my wife and him. The corn in my barn at my decease shall remain to my executors for the maintenance of my house and sowing my land. My wife shall have her dwelling and honest and comely boarding there for her life at the cost of Erasmus; he shall give her yearly 1 acre of barley, 1 acre of wheat and 1

acre of oats, with 4 loads of firewood if she shall spend so much, and shall reap, mow and dress the barley, wheat and oats and make them ready to the cart and cart and lay them where she think convenient, all at his cost. The rest of my goods to my wife and him, whom I make executors. Read in the presence of Th. CLOUGH, Th. FENNER, Rt. TURNER, James TURNER. Proved 16 Mar. 1580/1.

JOHN WATSON of Ardleigh, 12 Sept. 1580. (Nuncupative.) (552)
He did give his house and all his goods to Mgy. his wife, his house for her life, the goods to enjoy as her own; after her decease, the house to John his son, on condition that he pay his four daughters, i.e. Alice, Joan, 'Milcha' and Abigail his sisters [*sic*], each 6s.8d. after his mother's decease, every year. [No executors or witnesses.] Administration committed, 12 Feb. 1580/1.

THOMAS SEARLE of Elmdon husbandman, 28 Nov., 23 Eliz. [1580]. (553)
All my freehold lands [no details] to Wm. my son at 24; and 4 sheep which were his grandfather's gift at 24, being worth 4s. each at delivery. To Geo. my son £20 at 21; and 4 sheep likewise t 21. To Dthy. my daughter 20 marks at 21 or marriage; and 3 sheep likewise. To the child which my wife is now withal, if a manchild £20 or a daughter 20 marks at 21. My wife shall occupy my freehold lands and tenements for 7 years after my decease; after the 7 years all (my wife's third excepted) shall be let at the discretion of Rt. SEARLE and John PERRIN my brothers until Wm. is 24 towards payment of the legacies to my children. I will that Kath. my wife shall see them well brought up; in consideration thereof the residue of my goods to my well-beloved wife, whom I make executrix. [No witnesses.] Proved 16 Mar. 1580/1.

ROBERT FORDHAM of Great Chishall, 13 Feb. 1580/1. (554)
To Wm. my son a piece of meadow with the hedgerows about the same (2 acres) in Little Chishall, customary to the manor of Little Chishall; the hedgerow at the upper end lieth next a watercourse. To Th. my son £4. To Alice my daughter one upper chamber in the south end of my house behind the chimney for so long as she is single, chaste and unmarried; 1 hutch, 1 chest, and one half rood of saffron ground in Twifflye Field this year to be raised. To Mary my daughter 1 bullock of 2 years and my red hutch. To Isabel my daughter one half rood of saffron ground in Ashdon and my cupboard and table. To all my daughters except Joan 40s. apiece as soon as it can conveniently be raised by my son John. To Joan 6s.8d. and her two children other 6s.8d. as soon likewise. Witnesses: John COOKE, John HAGGER, John FORDHAM the elder. Proved 16 Mar. 1580/1.

RICHARD COLLETT of Dedham, 6 Oct. 1580. (555)
To Th. GULL my son-in-law and my daughter Mary his wife my house in North Street in Dedham called Snellinges and Sowters for 4 years after my decease; then to be sold by my executors, the money to be divided equally among my three daughters, i.e. Mary GULL, Christian FISHER and Alice KELLER, Th. to have the first preferment in buying the house and land if able to do so; if not, to Rd. and John in turn; if none able, to be sold to any other man. To Stephen DUNTON and Eliz. DUNTON 40s. each at 19. To Mary MASCALL 20s. at 19. To Rd. son of Th. GULL 40s., whom also I will shall be heir to Stephen, Eliz. and Mary, if all die. To John KELLER my son-in-law 20s. and his three children [not named] 20s. To the five children of Rd. FISHER £5. To him £4 which he oweth me. To Rd. GULL my son[-in-law] £10. To my daughter Mary GULL my household stuff, except 1 bed which I give to her son Rd. at 19. To Joan COCKE widow 40s., Th. PACKYNE 10s. and widow BANNES in the Row 5s. To my sister's daughter Eliz. CHETTELL 20s. I make Th. my son-in-law executor, to whom for his painstaking I give the residue of my goods. Rd. COLLETT surrendered his house and lands to Edm. ROBERTSONNE and Rt. LITTELBURYE tenants of the manor to the use of his Will in the presence of Timothy FITZALLEN standing for bailiff. Witnesses: Timothy FITZALLEN, Wm. WARNER, Edm. ROBINSON [*sic*], Rt. LITTELBURY. The testator requested that his house be appraised at £20 at the end of 4 years. Proved 10 Feb. 1580/1.

ABRAHAM CLERKE of Langham husbandman, 23 Sept. 1580. (556)
To Alice my wife for her life, if she keep herself a widow, her dwelling in the house wherein I dwell and the occupying of the three crofts and two groves belonging; if she marry, she shall lose my gift, and then to Abraham my son. To him my copyhold called Perries to take the use and profit at 22; in the meantime my wife shall have the use, on condition that she give Alice my daughter £10 at marriage so that she marry not before she be 21 without the consent of her mother and other her friends. To my wife 2 milch beasts, i.e. the 2 black. To Abraham the brown cow that I bought at Lawford. To Alice my daughter the youngest cow. My wife shall have liberty to hire the same beasts of them before any other. To my brothers Nich., Rt., and Rd. CLERKE, each 20s., and Methuselah CLERKE 13s.4d. To Abraham a bed and he shall have chamber room for the same and ingress and egress at all times so long as he keepeth himself unmarried. To the poor 10s. I ordain my wife executrix, to whom the rest of my goods. Witnesses: John REIGNOLDE, John WENLOCKE, Th. FARRER, John COPPINGE, Rt. POTTER. He gave surrender of his copyhold into the hands of John REIGNOLDE and Rt. STARLINGE tenants, Rt. POTTER being in stead of the bailiff, 12 Nov. 1580. Proved 9 Dec. 1580.

JOHN ASKEU *alias* CUNSTABLE of Lawford, 25 Nov. 1580. (557)
To John my son, Bridget my daughter and Ralph my son each £20 at 21. To Wm. LEACH 40s. To Nich. my brother £6 which he doth owe me. To John LEACHE [*sic*] that he owe me. The rest of my goods to Grace my wife, whom I make executrix. I make Roger VAUGHAM supervisor. Proved 3 Dec. 1580.

GILES PENSEPAWLE of Bradwell near Coggeshall, 3 Nov. 1580. (558)
To Joan my wife my 2 beasts, my mare and my colt. To Dthy. my daughter my cupboard and 1 bullock. To my wife the bed that I lie in and to Dthy. my other bed. My wife shall have the occupying of my brass pot for her life; after her decease to Dthy. My other brass and pewter shall be divided between them, Dthy.'s part at 21; if she die without issue, to my daughter Kath. All other my goods to my wife for her life; after her death, to Kath. and Dthy. and Dthy.'s child that she hath called Peter DINES, part and part like. My other cow shall be sold, and 4 nobles of the money paid to Peter and the rest to my wife. To her my cloth that is at JOBE's at Braintree containing 11 or 12 yards, and my cloth in my sollar to her, Dthy. and Kath. equally to be divided. To my wife my corn growing on my ground and my part of the rye and the dredge in my barn. To my brother John PENSEPAWLE my best cloak, black paned hose and best doublet. The rest of my goods to my wife. To John my brother all my white rods, paying my wife 6d. for every bunch bearing 3 foot about. I make her my executrix. Witnesses to the reading before the maker: Rt. RAVEN the elder, John BACON, John MILES, John INGRAM, John COPLAND parson of Bradwell. Administration committed, 17 Nov. 1580, to Joan PERSEPAWLE in the person of John PERSEPAWLE [*sic*], her proctor.

JOHN COLLMAN of Weeley husbandman, 19 Nov. 1580. (Nuncupative.) (559)
He willed his debts to be paid, namely, his rent to his landlord HARRIS and to Rt. COWYE of St. Osyth 38s.4d. for a cow. The rest of his lands and goods to be equally divided between Joan his wife and his five daughters, viz. Joan, Rose, Dthy., Mgy. and Agnes COLLMAN. Witnesses: Wm. ALLEXANDER, James RIDESDALE, Rt. COWYE, Peter RIDESDALE the younger. Administration committed, 22 Nov. 1580, to Rose NOBLE daughter of the deceased.

EDWARD TRIGGE of Elmdon tailor, 29 Nov. 1580. (560)
To Grace my wife, after my mother's decease, such lands as were given me by the Will of my father John TRIGGE until Grace my daughter is 16, then to her; if she die, not having issue, to my brother Wm. TRIGGE. To my wife to the better bringing up of my daughter the close which I bought of Henry TRIGGE until she is 16; if she die before, to Wm. in consideration that he pay my brother Henry and my sister Kath. TRIGGE each £6. To my wife my saffron grounds, my sheep, 1 cow, 4 quarters of barley, 4 quarters of oats, 1 comb of wheat, 1 comb of rye, with such stuff as shall be brought to me. If she refuse to bring up my daughter, some

reasonable portion as shall be thought meet by four honest men indifferently chosen shall be deducted out of her legacies. The rest of my goods to Mgt. TRIGGE my mother and Grace my daughter equally to be divided. I make my brother John TRIGGE executor. Witnesses: Th. CLOUGHE, Barbary MAYDE. Proved 6 Dec. 1580.

JOHN BOWIN of Great Bentley, 26 Oct. 1580. (561)
To Th. BOWIN my son 4 ewe lambs at May Day after my decease, also 20s. at 21; if he die before, to be parted amongst my children. To John and Wm. my sons each 20s. at 18. The residue of my goods to Mgy. my wife, whom I make executrix. Witnesses: Wm. THORNE vicar, Wm. HARRIS, John COLE, Rt. KINGE, John BOFFLEY. Proved 9 Nov. 1580.

WILLIAM SIDEY of Great Bromley tailor, 7 Nov. 1580. (562)
To Agnes my wife my house and land called Wrytes and my land I last bought called Stead Pickells [Pightles] for her life; after her decease, Writes to my son Stephen on condition that he pay my daughter 'Mathye' £5. To him my table in the hall with the board that is nailed to the wall, my shop board with all the boards that be nailed fast in the shop, my shears and my pressing iron, and my pewter basin. To Wm. my son Stead Pickells after my wife's decease. The rest of my goods to my wife, whom I make executrix. I have surrendered my lands into the hands of the lord [of the manor] by Miles CLARKE his bailiff in the presence of Rt. PARSONNE and John BELL tenants of the manor. Witnesses: Rd. GOLDINGE, Miles CLERKE, Rt. POOLE. Proved 18 Nov. 1580.

THOMAS HANES of East Mersea, 3 Feb., 23 Eliz. [1580/1]. (563)
To John HANES my brother £4. I will that my half quarter of the ship called the 'John' shall be appraised by four indifferent persons and the money coming from [the sale] thereof to John, provided that Rt. BURDE shall have the first offer to buy the half quarter, and on his refusal to sell the same to some other that will buy and the money to rest in my executor's hand in the meantime. To John SLYE my best cloak, if God send him home; if not, to my brother John. To Edw. OSBORNE, if he come home, my best jerkin; if not, to my brother. To John SALMON my best breeches, if he come home, if not, to my brother. To Habakkuk FINER my best doublet, if he come home; if not, to my brother. To my godchildren 2s.6d. apiece. To East Mersea church 10s. where is most need. To goodman POLLARDE my best shirt and best shirtband; Th. WALDEN and my godson the next shirtband; goodman POLLARDE a quarter of fine holland in my hutch and the blue Coventry thread to work it withal; Rowby WEALDE 2 of my best kerchers; John WALDEN the widow's son my 2nd best hat; Wm. LONGE my best sea cassock; and John WEBB 2 canvas shirts. To the children of Th. WEALDE sometime dwelling at the Strood [the causeway to Mersea Island] 2s. To Wm. WALDEN my best handkerchers in the hands of Robin BURDE. To my mother [not named] my part of the ship now going at the goodman RITCHMONDE's. The rest of my goods to John my brother. I make Roger PRENTICE executor, giving him for his pains 5s. Witnesses: Wm. SMYTHE writer hereof, Wm. BAWE, goodwife BAWE, goodwife E---. I make goodman POLLARD superviser, giving him for his pains 5s. to see my Will proved and my goods appraised by indifferent men. Roger PRENTICE hath still in his hands of my money £5 and in single pence 6s.8d. There is owing by goodman POLLARD to me and Roger PRENTICE for 6lb. wool. These parcels following are owing to me. Mine host POLLERD oweth me 44s.10d.; I owe him for fire and lodging and my two keepers' boards. Goodwife POLLERD oweth me for canvas and lockram 4s.4d. Wm. SMITH oweth me 6s.9d. The money that is owing me by poor folks and not here named I clearly forgive it them. I owe Wm. BEALD of Colchester Hithe about 10s. and that is the most. NELSUM hath of mine a firkin of butter price 13s.4d. and John NELSUM hath remaining in his hand of my candle 3 dozen lb. and 2lb. of candle; John NELSUM hath more a roundlet of vinegar containing 8 gallons and 2 quarts price about 3s.; and NELSUM hath more another roundlet of 6 gallons worth about 2s.4d. John NELSUM oweth for a pair of new shoes 14d. There is in the ship called the 'John' my part of stock that is in money 5s. and in other wares about 6s. Proved 6 Mar. 1580/1.

THOMAS TOMSON of Great Horkesley, 5 Mar. 1580/1. (564)
To my father [not named] £5. To my mother 2 sheep and 1 lamb, the sheep both white, the lamb 'bowked'. To my sister 'Edon' 5 marks at marriage and 6 sheep at Michaelmas. To my sister Eliz. 2 neat beasts at Hollomas, and her children each 1 lamb at May Day come 12 months. To my brother-in-law Wm. LONGE 5s. which is owing me by him. To the poor people of [Great] Horkesley, viz. Anne CUTTINGE, mother STERE, mother BAKER, mother PONDE and mother LAME, each 12d., and Dthy. KEYTER 4d. I appoint my brother John executor. All other things to him. These are my debts. Of Peter SMITHE 40s. wanting 4d. to be paid before Our Lady next; of Henry WAIGHT 18s.; of John CRADOCKE 8s.1d.; of Th. WARDE 13s.4d.; of John ROOSE 10s.; of John CARDYE £3 13s.4d.; of Amos COOKE 4s.; of Rd. SMYTH 11s.; of Wm. FOX 5s. Sum £9 2s.5d. Witnesses: Chris. SYDAY, Rd. BARKER, Th. WENIFFE junior. Proved 13 Mar. 1580/1.

JOHN HEDGE of Wrabness, 14 Jan. 1578/9. (565)
To John and Th. my sons my houses and lands in Ramsey free and copy by equal portions for 6 years after my decease, except that Rd. my son will presently become bound to them to pay each £10 when they are 20, the bonds to remain in the hands of Th. PAKEMAN of Wrabness the elder; then to Rd. To John and Th. each 4 kine, 1 bullock of a year, 10 ewes, and a brass pot of the best. To Th. a featherbed. To John a colt. To Joan my daughter 2 kine, 1 bullock, and 1 flockbed. My pewter shall be divided among my children by even portions. To my servant Mgt. SMYTHE 1 cow and a flockbed. The rest of my goods, saving corn, malt, cheeses, and butter for provision, to all my children part and part like at 20. I will that Rd. shall keep the rest of my children till they shall be able to go to service where he shall see meet. I ordain him executor; if he die before, I make Wm. HEDGE my brother executor. I make Th. PAKEMAN supervisor. Witnesses: Th. GODFREE, Th. HUR[RIER]. Surrender delivered into the hands of Wm. STILLEMAN in place of the bailiff in the presence of Th. HURRIER and Wm. HEDGE tenants. Debts owing to him, 17 Aug.: Wm. TURNER 44s.; LEACH of Stutton [co. Suffolk] 19s.4d.; widow LEWES 45s.11d. Proved 11 Mar. 1580/1.

THOMAS AYLETT of Great Oakley, 7 Jan. 1580/1. (566)
To Rebecca and Joan ROOTE my wife's daughters, my 4 milch kine to be equally divided at marriage or 21; if both decease before, to my son John AYLETT and his children if he be departed. My wife shall have the profit and letting of the beasts until received. To John 1 cow, 1 flockbed, 1 brick axe, and a hammer. The residue of my working tools to Nich. CHAUNDELER. To Rd. MARTIN my servant 5s. at 20. To Rebecca and Joan each a flockbed. To Alice BOWNE a hutch. To John a hutch bound with iron and 1 quarter of oats. To my neighbour Th. WARDE of Moze my brown bay colt, hoping that he will be executor with my wife. To John my other 2 colts. The rest of my goods to Sabine my wife, whom with Th. WARDE I nominate executors. Witnesses: John STOKES, James SPURLINGE, Th. ROCHESTER parson of Oakley, this writer. Proved 8 Jan. 1580/1.

JOHN CHURCHMAN of Bradfield, [no date given]. (567)
To Grace MARTIN a young cow and 4 ewes. To my daughter Alice a cow, she to choose it, also 10s. a year to be paid by my wife as long as she live. To Wm. GRENE, my sister's son, an ewe and a lamb. To Alice a great kettle and a brass pot. To my sister CRUE and her children each an ewe. To Joan my wife 4 horses and an axe to give and to sell at her pleasure; also 48 sheep to occupy so long as she live; after her death, my daughter to have one half of them. To my wife my goods unbequeathed. To Alice 4 milch beasts, a featherbed, a great kettle, and a brass pot after my wife's decease; also a cow at Easter next. To the poor 20d. I make my wife executrix and Barthw. JENNINGES supervisor, and for his expenses 10 groats. Witnesses: Nich. CONNEN [*recte* CONVEN], Th. ATTON, Th. WINGE. Proved 13 Feb. 1580/1.

ROSE WARDE of Earls Colne widow, 10 Mar. 1579/80. (568)
To the poor 12d. To Rt. WARDE my son a bullock of 2 years. To Mgt. PRENTIS

my daughter a cow, a cupboard, a flockbed, a brass pot, 2 pewter dishes, a chest, and a trundle bed where I lie. To my son a posted bed where I lie. To Christian my daughter a posnet and a pewter dish. To John WARDE my son 4 [blank], a posted bed, a featherbed, a brass pan, a salt, a latten chafing dish, and a platter. To Mgt. the rest of my goods to John my son [*sic*], whom I make executor. Witnesses: Rd. ENNOWE, Rd. PRENTIS, John CAUT. Proved 17 Jan. 158[0/1].

GEORGE TAYLER the elder of Coggeshall weaver, 6 Dec. 1580. (569)
To Rt. my son my house wherein I dwell in Stollon [Stoneham] Street, except that Rose my wife shall have half of my house for her life. To Geo. my son my broad loom and all things belonging. Witnesses: Edm. TILER, Peter SAUNDER, Alan HAYWARDE, Anthony GYMLET. Administration committed, [date not given], to Rose the widow and Rt. the son.

JOHN RICHE of 'Bromley', 13 Oct. 1580. (570)
To Agnes PATEN my daughter 5 marks and 24 cheeses. To Ellen POLLE my daughter 40s. To my son Stephen £5 and my house and lands in Ardleigh. To Ellen RICHE my [blank] 40s. To the four children [not named] of my son Stephen 6s.8d. apiece. I make executors Stephen and Nich. FREND. Proved 9 Dec. 1580.

WILLIAM BROMEFEILDE of Great Wigborough, 24 June 1578. (571)
To my daughter Edith 1 cow at the discretion of her mother. The residue of my goods to Eliz. my wife, whom I make executrix. Witnesses: Randall WYMSLEY clerk [rector of Great Wigborough], writer hereof, Anne MOTT, Mgt. ALLEN. Proved 27 June 1578.

WILLIAM the son of John FREMAN of Ashdon, 31 Mar. 1578. (572)
[Religious preamble.] To Rt. FREMAN my brother my grove called Onvers [Ouvers?] ($3\frac{1}{4}$ acres), he paying 40s., viz. 16s. to my father [not named] and the rest to the poor folks. To Rt. all my sheep and lambs with my barley and malt to sell and to take up all sums of money which I lent to any person and owing to me, also to pay my debts and pay John FREMAN my brother 20s. and my three sisters Alice MASON, Grace JAGGER and Joan FREMAN £5 apiece, John NEWMAN servant to John FREMAN my father 13s.4d., and my godchildren 12d. apiece, and the rest to my father and mother. I make Rt. executor and my father overseer. Witnesses: John FREMAN, John NEWMAN, Joan FREMAN. Proved 10 Apr. 1578.

JOHN BREWER of Great Tey husbandman, 26 Feb. 1577/8. (573)
To Rd. my son 40s. at 20. To Dorcas and Rebecca my daughters £3 6s.8d. each at 20 or marriage. To the poor people of Great Tey the bread of a bushel of wheat. The rest of my goods to Joan my wife, whom I make executrix. If she marry again, he whom she shall intend to take in marriage shall with sufficient surety be bound by their bill obligatory to Ralph NORTHEN and John ROOTE to perform my Will. Witnesses: John MOOTHAM, John HILLS. Proved 5 Apr. 1578.

WILLIAM BITTEREDGE of Great Bromley husbandman, 22 March 1577/8. (574)
To Wm. REIGNOLDE my cousin a red bullock of 3 years, 1 of my best ewes after sheartime, a flockbed that I lie on, a pair of bedsteads that goeth with pins, a stained cloth to hang over it, my best brass pot, a trammel, 2 pewter platters, an axe, a scythe, 2 beam hooks, a wood hook, a chair, a grindstone, a frize jerkin, a canvas doublet, a petticoat, a pair of shoes, a pair of high shoes, a pair of new low shoes, 2 shirts (1 of lockram, 1 of canvas), a bow and 4 shafts, a grained staff, a girdle, a knife, and a lockram napkin. To Henry REIGNOLDE 3 ewes after sheartime, a lockram napkin, and a pair of gloves. To John BALL my leather jerkin. To Chris. WANLY my brother-in-law my best sacking doublet [sackcloth]. More to Wm. REIGNOLDE my best cap and best hat. To Wm. LUNGETT [*recte* TUNGETT] £6 to discharge me of my bond to the parish for the keeping of Joan [blank] daughter to Sybil CAULTON and he to keep the child in like manner; to Joan a petticoat, 2 smocks, and 2 kerchers of new cloth. The rest of my goods to Agnes my wife. I appoint her and Nich. FREND executors and Wm. TUNGETT supervisor, and to Nich.

and Wm. 2s. apiece for their pains. I will that my executors pay Wm. TANGETT at Midsummer £3 of his £6 and at Shrovetide £3 in satisfaction of the £6. Witnesses: John SEAMAN, Chris. WANLYE, Wm. RAVENS, Rd. GOULDINGE. Proved 6 Apr. 1578.

MARGARET COOLE of Little Bentley widow, 13 Mar. 1577/8. (575)
To the poor folks 10s. To Joan my maid my best russet petticoat. To Agnes HECKFORDE my sister my best hat.. To Constance my daughter all my wearing woollen and linen apparel and my little coffer and all therein, also my new red cloth containing 3 broad yards. The residue of my goods to be d vided into four equal parts by the advice of Geo. MARTIN, John PAYNE and John RELESON and to be given to my four children Chris., Constance, Edm. and Geo., to have choice in turn. I make Chris. executor. I ordain Geo. MARTIN and John PAYNE supervisors. Witnesses: Roger HECKFORDE, Stephen ESTWOOD the elder. Proved 7 Apr. 1578.

JOHN PIGGET [PIGGETT *in margin*] of St. Peter, Colchester, smith, 26 Apr., 20 Eliz. [1578]. (576)
To Mgt. my wife my tenements in St. Peter's parish, on condition that she pay John my son £16 at 21 and each of my daughters, i.e. Eliz. and Mgy., £5 at 21. To Joan PIGGETT my mother 10s. a year for her life. The rest of my goods to my wife, whom I ordain executrix. I ordain my brother John STONNARDE supervisor, and for his pains 3s.4d. Witnesses: John STONARD, Roger SPARRINGE, Jerome GILBERT. Proved 28 May 1578.

JOHN RELESON the younger of Little Bentley labourer, 9 Feb. 1577/8. (577)
To John RELESON my father my best axe. To Wm. CORBALL of Great Bromley my best hat. The rest of my goods to Mgt. my wife to the bringing up of my child [not named]. I make her my executrix. Witnesses: John PAYNE, John RELESON. Proved 7 Apr. 1578.

WILLIAM CAMPYON of St. Runwald, Colchester, 3 June [year not given]. (578)
To Agnes my wife all my goods. Written with mine own hand. Administration committed, 13 June 1578, to Agnes the widow; John GOODWIN clerk, surrogate of Mr Fabian WITHER, Official of the Archdeacon of Colchester.

JOHN POTTER of Earls Colne yeoman, 27 Feb. 1577/8. (579)
To Geoffrey POTTER my brother and Clement KETTELL my kinsman all my goods, corn, implements and household stuff equally between them to be divided, whom I ordain executors and to bestow some part of the overplus, if any remain, amongst such of kinsfolks as they shall think good. Witnesses: John AYLEMOR, Rd. BRAGGE, Wm. TURNER, Rt. BOYES, Wm. VIGEROUS. Proved 26 May 1578.

THOMAS GAMMIGE [of Saffron Walden], 15 Feb. 1577/8. (580)
To John, Th. and Nich. my sons each £20 at 24 and to Mary my daughter £10 at marriage. This is my whole Will. I crave it to be written in form of law. I make my wife executrix and 'gardener' [guardian] to my children. I make my brother Nich. GAMIGE supervisor, and to him 10s. Witnesses: John LASON clerk, vicar of [Saffron] Walden, Rt. TURNER, Rd. TURNER, Nich. GAMEDGE. Proved 10 Apr. 1578.

ROBERT PEACOCKE of St. James, Colchester, carpenter, 4 Mar. 1577/8. (581)
To Th., John and Timothy my sons and Mary my daughter each 40s. at 21. To Th. all my working tools, if he go to the science of a carpenter when he hath served his apprenticeship thereunto. To John my little copper kettle; to Timothy the best flockbed in my house; and to Mary my great copper kettle and a featherbed at the discretion of Joan my wife. To Eliz. KEBALL my goddaughter 5s. and Rd. KEBALL her brother 12d. To Susan HYARDE 5s. to be delivered to Rd. COCKE in Wivenhoe to the use of the said Susan HYRDE and the profits at 15. To Anne SANDER my servant 3s.4d. The rest of my goods to my wife, whom I ordain executrix. I make Rt. HILLES supervisor, and for his pains 3s.4d. Witnesses: Rt. HILLES, Wm. REVILL, Rd. SANFORDE, Rt. STEVEN writer hereof. Proved 7 Apr. 1578.

WILLIAM KELLOGGE of the Rose *alias* Roose [now the Roos] in the parish of [Saffron] Walden, 20 Apr. 1578. (582)
To Th. son of John KELLOGGE my son £10 at 21. To Mary KELLOG daughter of John £10 at 21 or marriage. If both die before, to the children of John, if he shall have any then living. To Joan WARMAN that was my servant a cow at marriage. To Alice my wife my corn and cattle with all my movables and such money as is owing to me for her life; after her decease, to John son of John my son. She shall enter into bond to John son of John for such sum as shall be thought fit by Th. BRADBURYE gentleman, Phillip BIRD gentleman and Rd. HAMONDE the elder for payment thereof. I make my wife executrix. Witnesses: Th. BRADBURYE, Philip BIRDE, Rd. HAMONDE, James CROFTE the writer. Proved 15 May 1578, before Mr Rd. HODGESON, A.M., surrogate of Mr Fabian WITHER, the Official of Mr Geo. WITHER, Archdeacon of Colchester.

ROBERT HASELDON of Terling, 17 Dec. 1577. (583)
To Rd. HASELDON my son ½ quarter of wheat and ½ quarter of malt. To John my younger son a cupboard in my bedchamber and my best flockbed in my little chamber. To Rt. all other the hangings and painted cloths in my chamber where I lie. To John HASELDON my eldest son a platter, a pewter dish, a saucer, a brass pan with 2 ears, a bell candlestick, a little spit, the hutch in my little chamber, my great pitchfork, and a flockbed. To John my youngest son 2 platters, a pewter dish, a saucer, a canvas sheet, my best blanket, my unbound brass pan, a brass pot, a little posnet, a great hutch bound with iron, my bell candlestick with another little candlestick, a spit with holes, a little pitchfork, an iron peel, a pair of trammels, a pair of pothooks, a gridiron, and a saddle with stirrups. To Rd. £4, John my younger son £3, and John my eldest son 45s., all by 20s. a year. To the children [not named] of Rd. each an ewe. To Wm. HASELDON my godchild 2 ewe sheep; to every one of my [other] godchildren 4d. To John my younger son my short table in the hall and an axe. The residue of my goods to Rt. my son, whom I make executor. I appoint John my younger son supervisor. Witnesses: John ORVICE clerk [vicar of Terling], Nich. WARRENER, Henry RAYNER, Proved 26 June 1578.

PHILIP BATEMAN of [Saffron] Walden single man, 9 Apr. 1578. (584)
To be buried in Walden churchyard by [i.e. beside] my mother [not named]. To my sister Mary all my goods. To my aunt STRACHYE 40s. To Mary GOODDINGE, Anthony GOODDINGE and Mgt. BIRD each 6s.8d. I make Mary executrix and Andrew BIRDE supervisor, and for his pains 10s. To Anthony my coat laid with green lace and the hose suitable to it, 1 blue coat, and a green doublet. To Geo. DEVELL 6s.8d. Witnesses: Jonas CORBYE, Wm. YONGE, Geo. DEVELL, Wm. GOODWINE. Proved, 1 May 1578, before Mr Rd. HODGESON [as in no.582].

THOMAS STEVEN of Wix, 1 May, 20 Eliz. [1578]. (585)
To my son John STEVEN a bullock of 2 years. To Priscilla, my son's daughter, a yearling bullock at Michaelmas come twelvemonth. To Rt. my son half my sheep and lambs. The rest of my goods to Agnes my wife, whom I make executrix. I desire that John BATEMAN, my wife's son, shall be overseer. The debts which I owe: to the executors of Wm. PORTER 7s.; Wm. TOWNET 26s.4d.; James LUCAS 6s.8d.; Matthew CHALETS 2s.4d.; Wm. TAYLER 3s. Debts owing to me: Henry STEVEN 15s.4d.; Edw. MANNINGE of Harwich [blank]. Witnesses: Edw. WALKER, James LUCAS, Wm. BATEMAN, John CONVEN, Wm. LYNE. Proved 28 May 1578.

WILLIAM STEVEN of Witham single man, 18 July 1578. (586)
To the poor 20s. To Mary DYKES 50s. To Joan GUTRIGE half my apparel, the other half and 20s. to Hum. DALOM. I will that my house in Witham be sold by Wm. DIKES my father-in-law and Wm. SOMMER my brother, and the money to be equally divided betwixt Wm. SOMMER and Joan FAYREHED and Grace [blank] my sisters, on condition that, if one Mgy. HEVERS be with child and the child come into the world mine which as I have deserved it with Mgy. 5 weeks before Our Lady Day in Lent or thereabouts, I will Wm., Joan and Grace shall bring up the child. The rest of my goods to the said brother and 'sisterne' on the said condition. I

make Wm. SOMMER executor and Wm. DIKES supervisor, to whom I give £6 13s.4d. to do withal as he thinketh best. To Wm. NEWMAN 10s. if I die before Michaelmas next. Witnesses: Th. GELDER, Wm. NEWMAN, Th. BROWNE. Proved 22 July 1578.

EDWARD HAMONT servant with Adam WELLCOCKE of Boxted, — 1578. (Nuncupative.) (587)

He bequeathed to Rose REIGNOLDE and John REIGNOLDE his lease of his ground in Langham Park; to Wm. and Alice children to Adam WELLOCKE his master each a bullock of a year. The rest of his goods to Adam WELLOCKE, [he] paying Ralph HAMMONT his brother 13s.4d. Witnesses: Mr Th. MORS minister [vicar of Boxted], John REIGNOLDE of Langham, Th. DEBNAM writer hereof. [No probate clause.]

AGNES WEDE of Peldon maiden, [date not given]. (Nuncupative.) (588)

These are the words spoken before Jane HERDE, Kath. ARCHER widow, Ellen BISHOPPE widow and Rt. COPPIN. 'I give to Rt. COPPIN all that I have, he to take all and to pay all'. [No probate clause.]

WILLIAM LUFKIN of Elmstead husbandman, 29 Nov. 1578. (589)

To Elmstead church 5s. To the poor 12d. To my brother John LUFKIN 20s. To John and Stephen my brother Edw. LUFKIN's children my 2 wennels that are at Edw.'s. To the child that my wife is withal whether son or daughter £5 at 21, my wife to have the occupying of the £5 to keep the child so long as she keep herself a widow; if he with whom she marry will put Edw. in surety for payment and see my child honestly brought up or else Edw. to take so much of my goods in his hands; if my wife die before the child, the £5 to be distributed between Edw.'s and John's children. I will that my wife shall keep the child that I had of Ardleigh men [a poor parish child?], whose name is [blank] and discharge my executor against them. The residue of my goods to my wife. I make Edw. LUFKIN my brother executor. Witnesses: Rd. CAZER writer hereof, Th. BROWNINGE, John RICHE. Administration committed, 19 Dec. 1578.

RICHARD UNDERWOOD of Great Bromley, 15 May, 20 Eliz. [1578]. (590)

To Agnes LITTELBURYE widow 1 cow for her life; after her decease, to Eliz. my daughter. All other my goods to Kath. my wife, whom I appoint executrix, she to bring up my children [not named]. Witnesses: John SHEPPARDE, John WOODLANDE, John SEAMAN. Proved 27 June 1578.

THOMAS SEAMER of Debden yeoman, 2 June 1574 [*sic*]. (591)

To Eliz. my wife such goods as she brought to me at marriage; and 10 acres of my free land called Cage Morrelles, which she claims by marriage, for her life. To Th. my son my tenement wherein I dwell with the 'housen' thereunto built, 10 acres of customary land called Swetmilkes, a tenement and 5 acres of land called Wills; also 3 acres of free land called called Long Croft in Debden; if he decease without issue, all to Jeremy my son; for default of issue, the remainder to all my daughters Alice, Joan, Mgt., Mary and Frisewide equally amongst them to be divided. To Th. 1 chair, the best table, and the form with all the benchboards in the hall. To Jeremy my tenement with 2 'housen' thereon built and 5 acres of customary land, sometime Rt. PARKER's, in Debden; also, after my wife's decease, the 10 acres called Cage Morrelles; if he decease without issue, all to Th.; for default of issue, the remainder to all my said daughters likewise. To Jeremy 1 of the joined chairs and the least table. To Mary £4. To Frisewide £10 at 21 or marriage, also 1 cupboard and 1 bed in the entry chamber on the same day. The residue of my goods to all my said daughters equally to be divided. I ordain executors Th. and Jeremy. Witnesses: Rd. HODGESON, Henry HAMMON, John RISE, Philip BIRDE, Rd. HAMMOND, Rt. ANDREW. Proved 3 July 1578.

ROBERT AUNGER of Little Bentley single man, 15 June 1578. (592)

To the poor folks 10s. To Mgt. DARBY my sister 40s. To Thomasine HECKFORDE 10s. and the steer bullock which her husband hath in keeping for me. To Bridget WRIGHTE £6 13s.4d. To Rd. HORTON the hose he hath of mine. To John STEVEN my old hat and 1 of my working-day shirts. To Constance PAYNE 5s. To Edm. KINGE my worst breeches and a pair of short blue hose. To Geo. SMYTHE my pair of russet short hose. To my brother John's man my leather doublet. To Eliz. daughter to Rd. KINGE of Weeley 40s. at 21. To my uncle PAYNE the 40s. he oweth me. To John MUNTE a sheep and a lamb. To Th. POLLEY 5s. and a jerkin. To my brother John £25, the most part of which he oweth me, at Candlemas next. The rest of my goods to my brother Wm., whom I ordain my executor. Witnesses: Edw. JYLER [*recte* TYLER?], John PAYNE, John ESTWOOD. Proved 27 June 1578.

WILLIAM SPOONER of Coggeshall tailor, 15 June 1578. (593)
To Mgt. my wife for her life my house and garden being copyhold; after her decease, to John my youngest son, he to pay my sons Th. and Geoffrey and my daughters Anne, Susan and Jane each 13s.4d.; he shall have 8 years in paying these legacies. The residue of my goods to my wife, whom I ordain executrix. Witnesses: Th. DUNSELL, Wm. DERE, John JENNWE, Hugh WHITINGE. Proved 26 June 1578.

STEPHEN WITHERS of Great Totham husbandman, 7 Apr. 1578. (594)
To be buried in Great Totham churchyard near Joan my late wife. To the poor people of the parish 10s. at the discretion of the curate and churchwardens. To the poor people of Heybridge 3s.4d. Towards the reparations and building of Heybridge steeple [i.e. tower] whensoever they shall go about the same 10s. To Henry WITHERS, my brother's son, 6s.8d. and 2 lambs. To Rd. SCOTT my son-in-law 1 cow or 40s. for her at his own choice. To every of my covenant servants each a lamb. To John TOMPSON my godson 2 lambs. To Agnes and Bridget, two of the daughters of Rd. SCOTT, each 1 ewe sheep. To the wife of John TOMPSON 3s.4d. To Sarah EGAR 1 lamb. To Stephen NORRIS 1 lamb or 3s.4d. To Rt. NORRIS 6s.8d. To Martha WITHERS my daughter £13 6s.8d. at 18 or marriage, the legacy to remain in the hands of Edw. SAMMES; if she die before, to Joan my wife, her mother. Whereas I am seised of lands and tenements in Heybridge called Pages, Haywerdes, Long Croft and 1 acre of meadow holden of the Dean and Chapter of St. Paul's in London as of their manor of Heybridge by copy of court roll, I will the same to my wife until Martha is 15; until then the profits to the use and the education and bringing up of Martha; for want of issue, to the said Stephen and John [*sic*]; for want of issue, to the issue of Mgy. WITHERS my daughter, now wife of John ARGENT. Whereas I am to answer Mgt. daughter of Rt. WITHERS deceased 10s. as of the gift of John WITHERS her grandfather, she shall have as of my gift other 10s. at 18, and 1 little cupboard, a little joined form, a table, and 1 cow or 26s.8d. All other my goods, money, plate and jewels to my wife, whom I constitute executrix. I ordain my trusty and well-beloved friend Edw. SAMMES supervisor, and for his pains £3 6s.8d. or 1 mare, at his choice. [No witnesses.] Proved 22 July 1578.

THOMAS HALE, [abode not given], — 1577. (595)
To Mgt. my daughter a featherbed with a post bed, also a cow at marriage; and all my lands free and copy; if she die before, to Mary my wife to give and sell. To Joan BATES my servant 10s. at marriage. The rest of my goods to my wife, making her my executrix. I make overseer my brother Frs., and for his pains 3s.4d. Witnesses: Rt. SARTANE clerk [not identified], Henry STEVEN, Giles BRETT, Th. BOWEN. Proved — 1577.

JOAN BESOUTH [BESYTHE *in margin*] of Fordham widow, 1 Jan. 1577/8. (596)
To Rt. JOLLYE my son 2 pewter platters, the best. To Rd. JOLLY my son 1 brass pot. To Wm. JOLLYE and Joan WHITER my children 1 cow, to be sold by my executors and the money equally divided between them. To Alice JOLLY, my son Wm.'s daughter, 1 kettle and 1 chafing dish. To Joan my daughter 1 flockbed in the sollar, 1 hutch, all her wearing linen which she use to wear, and all her coats except her best gown. To Walter WHITER and Mich. WHITER, my son-in-law John WHITER's children, my best hog. To my son John JOLLYE 1 cow, the best kettle, the little posnet, and the best flockbed. To Walter my son my best featherbed, 1 brass pot, 1 kettle, 1 posnet, 1 chafing dish, the great candlestick, 1 flockbed, and the best gown. To Joan WHITER my daughter 1 sheet with an open seam. To John

my son 1 lockram shirt. To my daughter £10. To Agnes JOLLYE, John JOLLYE's daughter, 1 pewter dish. To Mgt. WHITER 1 pewter candlestick; when John my son die, she shall have my best kettle. To John and Walter my sons all my goods unbequeathed, whom I ordain executors. Witnesses: Wal. FESEY, Alice STOWE, John TWEDE writer. Proved 1 Sept. 1578.

ALICE CONY [abode not given], 9 June 1578. **(597)**
To be buried in Thorrington churchyard. To [blank] a flockbed, an ewe and a lamb, a little kettle, 2 pewter dishes, 2 platters, and a candlestick. To Mgt. BYNDER 6s.8d. The rest of my goods to 'John' [*sic*] CONY my daughter, my executors to sell them and to buy such cattle as may be most for the profit of my poor daughter, she to have towards her keeping yearly all that cometh of the said cattle and at the end of 10 years the stock wholly; if she die before, the stock shall go to the parish of Thorrington and the profits to the poor to be bestowed by the churchwardens and two or three of the chief parishioners and the stock to remain for ever to the parish. I make John CERLINGE and John HUBBERT executors. Witnesses: [blank] WYEALL, Wm. COLMAN, John HUBBERD, Wm. BUTLER. Proved 1 Sept. 1580.

ROBERT BRACKETT of Layer-de-la-Haye husbandman, 27 July 1578. **(598)**
To my son Anthony £5. To my son Rd. £5 at 21, but, if my wife decease before, then to him presently. To my son Edw. £10 at 21; if she die before, the £10 to remain in the hands of the worshipful Kath. AWDLEY widow of Berechurch, and if she die before then he to have the £10. To Edw. my best bed, the brass pot and the kettle that I bought of Nich. AWDEN, 2 great and 2 smaller pewter platters, 1 ewe and 1 lamb. To Mistress Bridget AWDLEY my red 'howed' [for meaning see p. xvii] cow calf. To Th. DUKE the younger my black garled cow calf. To Th. LITTELBURY my sister's son and Agnes LITTELBURY her daughter each 1 ewe sheep. To Edw. BRACKETT my brother's son 1 sheep. To Eliz. CRAMER 12d. To widow GEORGE of this parish, Rd. GYLDER and widow COCKLE of Langenhoe each ½ bushel of rye. To widow SQUIRE 12d. The rest of my goods to Helen my wife, whom I ordain executrix. Witnesses: Th. DUKE, Henry SALLMON, Rd. GYLDER, Wm. SALMON, Roger GOODWINE. Proved 1 Sept. 1580.

JOHN FLACKE the elder of Radwinter, 25 Aug. 1574 [*sic*]. **(599)**
To the poor men's box 12d. To the poor in the first week of Clean Lent 6s.8d. To Eleanor NEWBURNE 30s. at 24 or marriage and the cupboard in the hall. To my son John's wife 3 bushels of bread corn and drink corn this winter and to his three children [not named] 3s.4d. apiece at 16. To my godson John son of John GARDINER 6s.8d. To Joan wife of Rt. CORNELL to the use of Rose her daughter at Candlemas next a seam of barley. To Mgt. MEASANT 5s. To Amy BARKER 5s. To Rt. my son the 2 greatest chests, also that which is in the chest in the sollar. To Ralph HOYE my best russet coat. The rest of my goods to my sons Rt. and Giles to be divided, whom I make executors. I make my son Wm. and Rt. MASCALL supervisors. Witnesses: Th. MUMFORD, Rd. ROGERS, John JUDE, Rd. COOTE. Proved 3 July 1578.

THOMAS RADLE [RADLEY *in margin*] of Great Bentley, 25 June 1578. **(600)**
To Joan my wife all my houses and lands for her life; after her decease, to Grace my daughter the part that was her mother's and to Besse my daughter the part that I purchased. To Grace and Besse each 1 cow bullock and the vantage, 5 young ewe sheep, 1 flockbed, 1 pewter platter, 2 pewter dishes, and 1 candlestick at Michaelmas 1579. The residue of my goods to my wife, whom I make executrix. Witnesses: Wm. THORNE vicar [of Great Bentley], Wm. HAYS, John MONT the younger and John MONT the elder. Proved 13 July 1578.

JAMES LOCKE of Colchester, 11 July 1578. (Nuncupative.) **(601)**
To James his son 2 sheep. To his three daughters, i.e. Agnes, Lucy and Kath., 26 sheep to be equally divided [*sic*], also the rest of his goods, Agnes to have first choice. He ordained them executrices and James overseer. Witnesses: Wm. SURFLETT, Wm. CHILVER. Proved 2 Oct. 1578.

THOMAS MONY of Lexden, — 1577. (602)
To 'Stace' my wife my tenement in Lexden called the Forge for her life; after her decease, to Geo. my son; if he die without issue, to Joseph BARROWE my godson. To my wife my orchard in Lexden sometime Wm. RICHE's for her life; after her decease, to Geo. and to Joseph as aforesaid. To Geo. 2 pewter platters at 19. I appoint my wife executrix, to whom the rest of my goods. I constitute Th. PECHE of Fordham supervisor, and for his pains 2 wethers. Witness: Rt. SEARES [*recte* SEARLE] minister of Lexden. Proved 2 Oct. 1578.

JOHN COOKE of Coggeshall clothier, 30 Sept. 1578. (603)
To my sisters Ellen WISTO and Mgy. PERETRE, Kath. SAUNDER, Mary FINCHE my wife's daughter, Judith HAWKINS, Rd. FINCHE and Eliz. HAWKINS each 10s. To John COKE, Lawrence COKE and Rt. COKE each 2 yards of kersey. To my sister WYSTO's children and my sister PERETRE's children 5s. apiece at marriage or 21. The rest of my goods to Mgy. my wife, whom I appoint executrix. I desire my uncle Wm. SAUNDER to be supervisor, and for his pains 12d. Witnesses: John SAUNDER, Th. SYMON. Proved 21 Oct. 1578.

RICHARD PAYCE of Little Tey, 27 Sept. 1578. (604)
To the poor people 20s. To Henry LODGE 40s., he to be double arrayed, i.e. cleanly for the holy day and profitably for the workingday by Hallowmas next. To Jeremy DO 20s. To Eliz. and Ellen daughters of Th. AYLEWARDE deceased 40s. apiece at 18. I ordain John PAYCE my brother executor, to have the governance of my goods to bring up Th. my son virtuously with them, and for his pains 10s.; provided that the residue of my goods which shall surmount the charges of my Will shall remain to Th. at 20; if he die before, equally divided between my brother and all my 'sistern' [not named]. Witnesses: Nich. BUCKE, Joan FULLER widow, Henry DAMYON clerk [rector of Little Tey]. Proved 15 Oct. 1578.

JOHN PRENTIS of Great Chishall, 18 Mar. 1576/7. (605)
To the reparations of the church 6s.8d. To John my son the third part of the houses and lands that I bought of Th. COCKE and Joan his wife in Chishall next the land of Nich. FORDHAM on the north and a tenement of Edw. MODYE's called the Grange on the south, one head abutting on the highway from the church to Melbourn [co. Cambridge] on the east. To my son's son Wm. PRENTIS at 21, 1 acre of land in Ashdon which I bought of Mr CRAWLY next the land of Shingay [co. Cambridge] on the north and that of Chishall Hall on the south, the east head abutting on the highway from Chishall to Foulmere [co. Cambridge]. To John my son pasture in a close called Curtis next his land on both sides, the east head abutting on the highway from Chishall to Langley, which I bought of Henry HAGGAR, also all my copyhold lands (18 acres) belonging to the manor of Shingay lying in Great and Little Chishall and to the manor of Chishall Hall, 3 roods lying in Curtis. The residue of my goods to John, whom I ordain executor. Witnesses: Th. COOKE, Edw. MODEY, Th. WALLIS. Proved 13 Oct. 1578.

WILLIAM BARKER of Colchester tiler, 30 Jan. 1575/6. (606)
To my son Peter my tenement in Wire Street [in Colchester] and a garden plat in the tenure of Wm. MAKEN schoolmaster; for want of heirs, to my son John. To Peter 2 pewter dishes, 1 pewter porringer, 1 saucer, 1 salt, and my best doublet at 21. To my son John my land and tenement in Oakley [*sic*] called Masons; for want of heirs, to Peter. To John 4 pewter platters, 1 pewter basin, 1 salt, and 1 silver spoon at 21. To my daughter Joan BELL my tenement wherein widow SYMOND dwelleth for her life, conditionally that she and her husband keep it in good reparations; after her decease, to Peter. To Joan 1 silver spoon, 1 pewter platter, 2 pewter dishes, 1 porringer, 1 saucer, and a pewter salt. To my cousin Kath. MAKEN widow 20s. To my cousin Wm. MAKEN 20s., his wife 6s.8d., and her three children Mary, Abigail and Eliz. 6s.8d. between them. To Rd. PROFFETT of Cornard [co. Suffolk] the cow which he hath of mine. To Th. KINGE my kinsman 20s. I will that the rent of my lease called Fremans and my rent of Masons these 2 years at Michaelmas next and the stock which doth remain in Mr CLERE's hands, which is 2 milch beasts, 2 calves, 26 ewes and 7 lambs or £10 to be at their choice, to take

the stock or the £10. The rest of my household stuff to pay my debts and see my legacies discharged; of the overplus of the rents, stocks and household, to Joan 40s. and what remains to be equally divided between Peter and John. My cousin Wm. MAKEN shall remain in the house wherein he dwelleth for 6 years, paying yearly 6s.8d. and bestowing yearly other 6s.8d. on reparations; he shall have the garden plat for 6 years, paying the rent to the town. To Mary BLYAUNT 6s.8d. To Sabin my wife my cupboard in the hall and 6 of my best pewter platters, conditionally that she shall not claim any of the thirds of my 'housen'. She shall have all her goods to herself that she had when I married with her. I ordain Rt. BARINGTON and Adam REVE executors, and for their pains each 6s.8d. Witnesses: Wm. BARINGTON, John BARNARD, Jerome BURTON, Rd. BELL. Proved 28 Nov. 1578.

AGNES POTTER of White Colne widow, — 1577. **(607)**
To my son Henry the best wennel calf and a kettle, the biggest of 3, to his wife a petticoat, and his children 6s. apiece. To my daughter Agnes my best petticoat and her children 16s. between them. To my daughter Joan a petticoat, the best of 3; to my daughter Mgy. a petticoat, the best of 2. To my son Geoffrey's wife my worst petticoat. To John POTTER my godson 12d. and a lamb and his sisters 6d. between them. To my godchildren Mgt., Agnes and Hugh POTTER 12d. and Mgt.'s children 6d. To my three daughters 3 kerchers and Henry's wife a rail. To my sons John and Geoffrey 12d. apiece. To Mgy. POTTER a lamb. To John POTTER's children 8d. The rest of my goods to my son Hugh that my husband gave him in his Will. To Hugh's wife my best gown. Witness: Geoffrey POTTER. Administration committed, 25 Oct. 1578, to Hugh.

MARGARET THOMPES [abode not given], 10 Nov. 1578. **(608)**
To Mary my eldest daughter a great brass pot, 1 kettle of the middle sort, a skillet, half a dozen of pewter one with another, a featherbed tick, my greatest bolster, a holland pillowbere, a mattress, 4 pair of sheets, 2 fine rails, 2 table napkins, 1 silver spoon, a yard kercher of holland of the finest, 2 kirtles, 1 train, the other without, and my best petticoat. To Mgt. my daughter a brass pot, 2 kettles, a frying pan, a spit, a pair of andirons, a skummer, and a dripping pan, half a dozen of pewter, 4 pair of sheets, 2 tablecloths, 2 table napkins, 2 fine rails, a yard kercher of holland, my best covering, a mattress, a pillow, my best cassock, my 2nd petticoat, a round worsted kirtle, a safeguard of black cloth, half a dozen of tin spoons, my new chest, a chamber pot, my table, my cupboard, 3 little stools, a little chair, a pair of bellows, a pair of tongs, and a candlestick. To Mary and Mgt. £5 to be equally divided at 21, which remaineth in the hands of my cousin Geo. SAVILL. The rest of my goods to them, to be divided by Geo., whom I make executor. Witnesses: John LASON, Paul SEAMAN. Proved 25 Nov. 1578.

WILLIAM UNDERWOOD of Great Tey, 24 Dec. 1578. **(609)**
To the poor people 2s. To Joan my daughter my free lands, pastures, meadows and messuages in Tey Mandevyle *alias* Marks Tey called Bullheds and Smith Field, on condition that she pay Agnes her sister 6s.8d. yearly for the term of my wife's life. The residue of my goods to Rose my wife, on condition that she shall not meddle with the third of my free lands. I ordain her my executrix and John ABBOTT supervisor, to whom 2s. for his pains. Witnesses: Rd. MERRELL, Th. UNDERWOOD, Nich. BUCKE, Roger PUDNEY, John PUDNEY, Henry DAMYON clerk [rector of Little Tey]. Proved 30 Dec. 1578.

PETER CHAPMAN of Ardleigh blacksmith, 16 Nov. 1578. (Nuncupative.) **(610)**
To Grace my wife this my house called Whippetts with the yard or backside in Ardleigh for her life and all my goods. I ordain her my executrix. Witnesses: Wm. BALDEN, Th. PARKER, John BONDE. Proved 19 Dec. 1578.

ANNE HARLOWE of [Saffron] Walden widow, 26 Dec. 1578. **(611)**
To the poor men's box 2s. To Joan my daughter my messuage in Walden copy and free in which I dwell, with 1 acre of land in Hethe [Common] Field *alias* the Vineyard; my 3 acres of land at Meres Harp with a little pasture called the hoppet which I purchased of Th. GODFRE of London gentleman; and my grove which I

purchased of John TAYLOR my son sometime called Senneschells Grove and now Howlatts Grove. To Wm. my son £20. To Edw., Ezechiel TAYLOR's son, 20s. To Susan TAYLOR, my son John's daughter, and Mary and Eliz. TAYLOR, her sisters, each 3s.4d. The residue of my goods to Joan, whom I ordain executrix. Witnesses: Th. CLERKE, Henry WEBB, John SHELLFORD. Proved 23 Jan. 1578/9.

WILLIAM TURNOUR of [Saffron] Walden yeoman, 20 Feb. 1577/8. (612)
To be buried in Walden church. To Agnes my wife Stubbard Field and Tans Mead, two several parcels lying in Thaxted for her life so that she keep herself unmarried; also another parcel called Gulpes in Thaxted, until Wm. my son is 24. To Ursula my daughter the house in Thaxted where John LAMMAS dwelleth, after my wife's death; and £10 at 21 or marriage; if Ursula die before marriage, to be paid to Wm. at 21 towards his better maintenance and bringing up. To Ursula 1 featherbed, the best tablecloth, 2 platters, 2 dishes, 3 porringers, and 2 saucers. To Wm. and Ursula my dozen of silver spoons to be equally divided. To Wm. my best joined bed, with the best tester of vestment work and the curtains, my best brass pot with the long feet, the best carpet, 2 of my best cushions with a pillow of silk and vestment work, my best table and the form, the livery table in the hall, the new press or cupboard with the best cupboard cloth, the best basin and ewer, 2 platters, 2 dishes, 4 porringers, 2 saucers, the best chafing dish, the best latten candlestick, the best pewter candlestick, my best cobirons, a tablecloth next the best, half a dozen napkins to the same, the best chair, 2 of the best stools, and the chest where I put my writings. To 'Fabye' my daughter the best cupboard which was her grandmother's, the brass pot next the best, a latten basin, 1 pair of sheets, a mattress, 2 latten [*sic*], 2 saucers, a candlestick, and a kettle. To 'Fine' my daughter a pair of sheets, a brass posnet, a candlestick, a chafing dish, 2 platters, 2 saucers, 2 little pewter pots, and 2 flower pots. To Eliz. my daughter a featherbed, a candlestick, an old brass pot with the broken ear, a kettle unbound, and 3 cushions stuffed with feathers which was her grandmother's. To Clemence my daughter my greatest kettle, the greatest latten basin, and a painted cloth of half a dozen yards. All which goods my wife shall hold for her life. To Urias BARKER my son-in-law my joined square table and a cupboard in the house at Thaxted in the occupation of John THORNE, the fairest chest, and a joined bed next the best with the tester, after my wife's death. To Sarah my daughter-in-law, after my wife's death, a cupboard that was her own father's, the little brass pot, and a flockbed. To Th. my son-in-law my great cauldron, a moulding trough, and the great chest bound with iron, after my wife's death. To Agnes my own daughter a mattress, a pair of sheets, a cupboard in the house at Stebbing, 2 bedsteads, with all other my movables there in the tenure of Chris. HUNT. I will that £40 of the £50 which shall be paid by John GYVER of Walden locksmith at Candlemas 1578 shall on receipt thereof be paid to Geoffrey POOLE of Great Bardfield to discharge the land now to him being in mortgage. To Agnes, Clement, Eliz., 'Fine' and 'Fabye' my moiety of the copyhold land called M[er]eyes with the land belonging in Stebbing purchased of Rd. PURCAS, on condition that they and the husbands of them as shall be married shall on request make a sufficient release to my executors and to Wm. of all actions and demands which they might have against me, also surrender that part of copyhold land according to the custom of the manor of Stebbing to John PLAYLE of Stebbing lately purchased of me. The residue of my goods to my wife, whom I make with John THORNE executors, to whom for his pains 10s. I make supervisor Urias BARKER, to whom for his pains 20s. Witnesses: John JACKSON, Wm. KINGE, Rt. COWLEY, James CROFT. Proved 30 Sept. 1578.

MARGARET MARSHALL of Springwell in the parish of Little Chesterford widow, 6 Mar. 1578/9. (613)
To Agnes and Eliz. MARSHALL my daughters 3 roods of saffron ground as it lieth by equal seasons in the fields to be equally divided between them. To Agnes MARSHALL my daughter, Eliz., and John MARSHALL, my son each 2 pair of sheets at 21 or marriage, and to Thomas MARSHALL 1 pair. To John and Th. my two sons 2 acres of wheat and rye in the fields to be equally divided. The rest of my goods in the house to Agnes and Elizabeth equally divided. To the poor men's box 6d. and

towards repairing Little Chesterford church 6d. The residue of my goods to Th. and Agnes, whom I make executors. I desire my two brothers John CAPPE and Th. CAPPE to be supervisors. Witnesses: Rt. PEPPER, Philip KOCKE, John HAUGHTON. Proved 10 March 1578/9.

BEATRICE UPCHER of Great Fordham, widow of Richard UPCHER, 28 Dec. 1578 (614)

To 'Jocabeth' my daughter, wife of Th. MILBEY, my best featherbed, a garled cow, and a pair of mustard querns. To Joan my daughter, wife of Walter GENNOR, a brown bullock and 1 featherbed. To Rt. and Susan GENNOR, my daughter's children, my dun cow and to Rt. 1 flockbed. To Mercy GENNOR and Rebecca GENNOR my red cow. To Eliz. DEKES my servant 5s. To the children of 'Adrian' SPOONER deceased, the late wife of Henry SPOONER, each 5s. To the daughter of Alice SPOONER my daughter deceased, late wife of Rt. SPOONER, 6s.8d. To eight poor folks of Fordham each a peck of wheat. The rest of my goods to Walter GENOR my son-in-law, whom I ordain executor. Witnesses: Wm. LOVENEY, John POTTER, Roger BAKER. Proved 13 March 1578/9.

MARY DRYEWOOD of St. Peter, Colchester, single woman, 24 Jan. 1578/9. (Nuncupative.) (615)

She did give to her mother Beatrice £6 which was in her mistress's hands, to Anne EUSTACE her felt hat, her new smock and her old petticoat, to Mgt. SMYTHE her russet petticoat and her waistcoat, and to her mother the rest of her goods, whom she made executrix. Witnesses: Rd. SAYER, Th. PORYFOOTE. Proved 18 Feb. 1578/9 by Beatrice STAMEDGE executrix.

THOMAS DOCKER [abode not given], 4 Jan. 1574/5. (616)

I have owing to me £20 for my half year wages at Michaelmas last of my master, Mr Th. TAYE esquire. There was a bill between him and me, out of which there is £10 due, and 20s. that I lent my mistress at Layer[-de-la-Haye] Hall. My master gave me a white nag going at 'Wyvenhalle' [Wivenhoe, not Rivenhall]. Th. PURSE oweth me 10s. I lent him, due at Midsummer next. I have a hutch in my chamber at Wivenhoe, 2 pair of new shoes and a pair of boots and spurs and in the old chamber there is my sword and dagger. I have certain gear in my chamber at Layer, besides certain things in the storehouse there. All these goods I give to Wm. DOCKER my brother, whom I make executor. Witnesses: Wm. HARVYE the writer, Rt. COFILDE. Proved 17 Feb. 1578/9.

RICHARD DEKES of Lexden yeoman, 27 Jan. 1578/9. (617)

To my son Wm. 12 beasts or bullocks, 1 mare, my hogs, my corn in the house and on the ground, and all my household stuff; on condition that he shall honestly keep Anne my wife, his mother, with meat, drink and clothes for her life; if she refuse to be kept, Wm. out of my goods shall give her £4; and on condition that he deliver to my son Frs. the young bullock of 3 years or 33s.4d. and the like bullock or like sum to Geo. my son, both at 24. I charge Wm. upon my blessing to be friendly and helping with the rest of my children [not named]. I ordain him executor. Witnesses: Wm. LINNE, Chris. DEANE. Proved 17 Feb. 1578/9.

EDWARD KINGE of Little Bentley yeoman, 25 Dec. 1578. (618)

To Agnes my wife all my goods for her life; after her decease, to be equally divided amongst my daughters [not named]. To my wife my house and land called Cowey House in Little Bentley for her life; after, to John my son, conditionally that he pay his five sisters each 20s. I make her my executrix. Witnesses: John PAYNE, Geo. SMYTHE, John ESTWOOD. Proved 17 Feb. 1578/9.

WILLIAM HARVY of East Donyland mariner, 14 Dec. 1578. (619)

To Helen my wife my customary messuage called Butlers with the lands belonging for her life, on condition that she bring up my children; after her decease, to John my son; for want of issue, successively to Eliz. my daughter and to John son of Th. HARVY, on condition that, if it happen to come to John son of Th., he shall pay to

Emme WHINNOCKE £6 13s.4d. and to John, Alice and Frs. CUKOKE £3 each; provided that, if it come to John my son, he shall pay to Eliz. within 8 years after my wife's decease £3 13s.4d. To John my son a posted bedstead with my best featherbed. To Eliz. my best cupboard after my wife's decease. The residue of my goods to my wife, whom I make executrix. I ordain Th. HARVY overseer, praying him to be an aider to my wife and children. Witnesses: Wm. KIRCKBYE, Th. HARVY, John WHITACRES. Proved 17 Feb. 1578/9.

ROBERT PALMER of Lawford, 14 Dec. 1578. (620)
To the poor people of Lawford and of Melton 3s.4d. To my brother John SPYAR all my lands in Melton, Bradfield, Boulge, and Ufford (all co. Suffolk). To my brother Frs. SPYAR and my sisters Eliz. PARKER and Barbara SPYAR each £10, all to be paid by John within 4 years after the decease of Kath. my mother. I make Rt. HALIBRED my uncle and Th. LUFKIN of Dedham executors, and for their pains 10s. apiece. Witnesses: John MANNINGE, Rd. THOMPSON, John PYKE, Rd. CLERKE. Proved 17 Feb. 1578/9 by Th. LUFKIN, power reserved to Rt. HALIBRED.

ELEANOR BRACKETT of Layer-de-la-Haye widow, 2 Jan. 1578/9. (621)
To Edm. BRACKETT my son 20s. presently and 40s. at 21 which shall remain in the hands of the worshipful Kath. AWDELY of Berechurch till then. To him 1 black colt of 2 years. To Anthony my son 2 horse which are the forebald and the bay mare. To my brother Stephen 1 cow bullock of a year old. To Rd. GELDER 1 bushel of rye, SEBOROUGHE and mother JORGES each half a bushel of rye. To mother SQUER 12d. The rest of my goods to Anthony and Rd. my sons to be equally divided by Mr Th. AWDELY, Mr John AWDELY, goodman REDE and Th. DUKE. If Anthony to obtain goodwill occupy the farm till Rd. is 21, then Anthony shall have the occupying of Rd's legacy, except the household [stuff], till he is 21. I ordain Anthony executor. Witnesses: Henry READ, Henry SAMMON, John SEARLES, Th. DUKE. Proved 17 Feb. 1578/9.

JOHN BRETT of Tolleshunt D'Arcy yeoman, 29 Dec. 1578. (622)
To be buried in Tolleshunt Major churchyard. To the poor of five parishes, i.e. Tolleshunt Major 20s. and Tolleshunt D'Arcy, Tolleshunt Knights, Great Braxted and Goldhanger, each 10s. To Mary my well-beloved wife all my freehold and copyhold lands in Tolleshunt Major and D'Arcy and my copyhold lands and tenements in Great Braxted for her life; after her decease, those in Great Braxted to Anne MELLOWES; if she die without issue, to Abraham and Th. MELLOWES equally to be divided; if they die without issue, to Giles BRETT of Tiptree [in Tolleshunt D'Arcy] and Henry BRET his brother equally. To Mr Th. BECKINGHAM of Tolleshunt Major the elder a close being freehold called Gun Croft in Tolleshunt Major after my wife's decease. I will that my copyhold lands in Tolleshunt Major called Mytchelles or Shubbardes after her decease shall be sold by the churchwardens (they to have 10s. for their pains) and the money shall be equally divided among my three sisters' children, viz. the youngest children of Mgt. WARMAN, i.e. John and Daniel WARMAN, Marian WILCOCKE's four children, i.e. John the elder, John the younger, Hugh and James, and THOURLETHORPE's daughter Valentine. To John son of Giles BRETT of Tolleshunt Major a freehold close called Little Round Field in Tolleshunt D'Arcy. To Mr Th. BECKINGHAM the son of Mr Th. BECKINGHAM of Tolleshunt Major 10s. To Jane FENNER my servant 6s.8d.; to three of my servants, i.e. Th. the Northern man, Edw. GYLL and the Northern maid 3s.4d. apiece. To my sister Mgt. NEWMAN 1 bullock, the price 13s.4d. To my cousin John BRETT the elder of Tolleshunt Major (whom I make overseer) 20s. For certain sermons to be preached in Tolleshunt Major church 20s. To Mary my well-beloved wife all my goods unbequeathed, whom I make executrix. To Mr Th. son to Mr Th. DARCYE 20s. Witnesses: John MATHER, John LUFKIN, Rt. MELLOWES, Th. SOUTHMAN. Proved 29 Jan. 1578/9.

EDITH GOORE widow of Th. GOORE of Great Fordham, 25 Jan. 1577/8. (623)
To Alice wife of Wm. AYLEWARDE my daughter my tenement and lands called Fellpott Lands (16 acres) holden by copy of court roll of the manor of Bures-at-Mount lying in Great Fordham, to her and her husband and the longer liver accord-

ing to the custom of the manor; they to pay in consideration of this gift £4 equally to my other two daughters, i.e. Rose wife of John ROOTE and Christian wife of John MORCOCKE, each 40s. To Rose my black garled cow, 1 candlestick, 1 salt, and 4 pieces of pewter. To every one of my three daughters 1 lockram shirt. To Alice and Rose my greatest kettle. To Edw. GOORE my godson my greatest latten posnet and 2 pewter platters. To Anne WALES my little posnet, my best gown, and 6s.8d. To Rachel AYLEWARDE my great chest. To Christian my red kirtle, my black russet petticoat, 2 pillowberes, and 1 flockbed. To my three daughters the residue of my linen part and part like. To the poor of Great Fordham 20d. The residue of my goods, cattle and implements to Wm. my son-in-law, whom I ordain executor. I ordain Henry QUELTER supervisor. Witnesses: Th. SMYTHE, John GENOR, John SPARKE. Proved 13 Mar. 1578/9.

THOMAS STRACHYE of [Saffron] Walden yeoman, — Aug. 1578. (624)
To be buried in Walden church by [nearby] my father [not named] in the chapel if it may be or some other place in the church at my executor's appointment. To Mercy my wife for her life my house wherein I dwell, both free and copy, with the gardens, orchards, closes and land on the backside, she to repair it continually when need be. If she shall join herself in marriage with any man, he shall enter into bonds in £100 to my son-in-law John LASON, vicar of Walden, and my son Elias STRACHYE for repairing the house and not suffer to be sold or taken away any brick, tile, timber, joists, boards, planks, doors, locks, ceiling, plaster, joined work, portal, 'pentise' [penthouse], partition, glass, lattice, window or lead belonging to the house, barns, stables, dovehouse or outhouses. After my wife's decease, in performance of the legacies of Ralph BIKADICKE, sometime alderman of Cambridge, my father-in-law, in his Will, the house, [etc.] shall by my wife's executor or executors be sold, and the money I ordain to be divided equally amongst my children then being 21, within a week after the sale. It shall be lawful for my wife at any time to sell the house, [etc.] with the consent of the more part of my children being 21 so that before the sale be made she with two sufficient sureties approved by John LASON and Elias be bound in £400 for the distribution of the money to be paid to my children by equal portions. To my wife my land called the Grove, copy and free (10 acres of pasture) for her life; after her decease, to Elias; if he die without issue, successively to Ralph my son, to Edw. my son, and to my daughters and their children to be divided equally among the daughters. I will that my lease of the Parsonage of Pentlow shall within 2 years after my decease be sold by John LASON and Elias, and the money for the performance of the Will of Ralph BIKADICKE, to be distributed as followeth. To my wife £40, to Elias £20, to Eliz. LASON my daughter £20, to Rebecca and Susanna STRACHYE my daughters each £20, to Ralph my son £20 at 24, to Bridget STRACHYE my daughter £20 at 21, and to Edw. my son £20 at 24; the residue shall be reserved by my wife for her life, and after to be divided equally among my children living at her decease; and the portions for Ralph, Bridget and Edw. shall be in my wife's hands until their ages. My wife shall be bound in £200 to John and Elias for the payments and in a further £200 to John and Elias, if she shall contract herself in matrimony, for the payments. To Elias 1 great charger, 4 platters, 4 pewter dishes, 4 saucers, 1 great brass pot, 1 great spit, and my best joined chair, also the great [blank] table in the hall, and 2 long settles standing by the chimney. To Ralph my son 1 great charger, 4 platters, 4 pewter dishes, 4 saucers, 1 great brass pot, 1 great spit, and my joined chair with the broken panel at 24, also the great cupboard in the hall after my wife's decease. To Edw. my son 1 great charger, 4 platters, 4 pewter dishes, 4 saucers, 1 great brass pot, 1 great spit, my joined chair I do daily occupy, at 24, also the great press in the parlour after my wife's decease. To Eliz. my daughter 1 great silk pillow for a window, and 2 bell candlesticks. To Rebecca 1 great charger, 4 platters, 4 pewter dishes, 4 saucers, 1 great brass pot, 1 great spit, 1 great kettle, 1 little kettle with bails on them, 1 [blank] table in the ceiled chamber, 1 wicker chair, 1 great hutch next the fish chamber. To Susanna [as to Rebecca, to '1 little kettle with bails on them'], 1 table in the shop with the trestles, 1 wicker chair, and the great red hutch in the chamber where my study is. To Bridget [as to Susanna, to 'where my study is'], 1 plain hutch which lacketh a joint in the same chamber, and a panel

chair in the fish chamber at 21. To Mercy, Mary and Susanna LASON daughters to John my son-in-law each 6s.8d. I give toward 'Colletts Haven' [Colyton, co. Devon] 3s.4d. To the most needy of the poor and the most godly 10s. to be divided at my son-in-law's discretion. The rest of my goods to my wife, whom I make executrix. I make John and Elias supervisors. Witnesses: John STRACHYE, Wm. MALBYN, Th. COOPER. Proved 5 Sept. 1578.

WILLIAM CRABBE of Colne Engaine miller, 14 Aug. 1578. (625)
To Agnes my wife for her life my tenement with the garden and 1 croft of land adjoining (2 acres) in Colne Engaine which I bought of one John LYTILL of 'Melford' [Long Melford, co. Suffolk, or mill-ford in Colne Engaine?]; after her decease, to remain to Th. the elder and Th. CRABBE the younger, my brethren, for their lives and the longer liver equally between them; after their deceases, to their children, if either have any which be in poverty; after that, the yearly rents and profits shall be distributed amongst the poor people at the discretion of the churchwardens and chiefest inhabitants. To the poor of 'Gaynes Colne' [alternative form of Colne Engaine] 5s. and to the poor of Halstead 5s. To Th. the elder and the younger each 13s.4d. To Matthew and Jacques my brethren each 10s. The rest of my goods to my wife, whom I ordain executrix. Witnesses: Th. HUNWICKE the elder and the younger, Wm. VIGORUS of Halstead. Proved 3 Oct. 1578.

JOHN POTTER of Great Fordham yeoman, 26 Feb. 1578/9. (626)
To Kath. my wife my tenement called Hayes that I dwell in and my free lands in Fordham for her life; on condition that he whom she shall chance to marry shall put in bonds to Geoffrey POTTER that he make no waste, keep the house in sufficient reparations, taking timber only for the same and to have sufficient firebote, hedgebote, ploughbote, cartbote and harrowbote for her necessary use on the house and lands. If my sister do live unmarried and not of service, she shall come and have her dwelling with my wife in my house with firewood sufficient for her needs; if she marry before, she shall have a cow at marriage and a tenth part of the fruit. To John my son my tenement called Hayes, with a joined bed and a cupboard in the nether chamber, also a joined table in the hall standing on a frame, on my wife's decease, also my free land after her decease, except Gannocks and Heath Field, which I give to the child that my wife is withal, if she be with any, or else £30, at 21; if John and the child both decease within age without issue, the tenement and lands to Rt. son of Rt. POTTER my brother deceased. To my wife my lands holden by copy of court roll of the manor of Crepping Hall [in Wakes Colne] and to John at 21; if he decease without issue and before 21, to Rt. my brother's son, surrendered into the hands of Rd. BARRETT and Wm. BRETT in the presence of Geoffrey POTTER instead of the bailiff. To Christian POTTER my sister 26s.8d. To Joan POTTER my sister a coat to be delivered at May Day 1579, to Isabel POTTER a cow in 1580, and to Rose POTTER a cow in 1581. To Wm. BECQUITHE my brother-in-law 2 seams of wheat. To Rt. my brother's son my steer. To Mary LOVENEY my servant 6s.8d. To the poor of Fordham 6s.8d. All other my goods to my wife, whom I ordain executrix. I will that Geoffrey my brother's son shall be supervisor, and for his pains 6s.8d. Witnesses: Th. UPCHER, Joseph UPCHER, Geoffrey POTTER, Walter GENER. Proved 31 Mar. 1579.

MARK COUPER of Tolleshunt D'Arcy bachelor, 17 Apr. 1574. (627)
To my brother Frs. £3 and his two sons [not named] at 20 each 20s. To my brother Edm. £9 6s.8d. which he oweth me in ready money that I lent him, which I freely forgive him, on condition that he pay every child of his out of the £9 at 20, 20s. apiece. To my brother James' children £3 part and part like. To my sister Joan's two daughters, i.e. Joan and Agnes, at marriage or 20, 20s. apiece. To all my sister's sons [not named] at 20 £3, her eldest son excepted. To my brother Wm.'s children both sons and daughters at 20, 10s. apiece. The residue of my goods freely to my executor towards his pains, whom I ordain Wm. POTTES of Tolleshunt D'Arcy clerk [the vicar]. I will that my brothers Wm. and Th. be overseers, they to take a bond of Wm. POTTS to perform my Will. Witnesses: Rt. PANNELLE, Wm. JANSON. Proved 21 May 1574 [*sic*].

WILLIAM PROYER of Colne Engaine carpenter, 22 Jan. 1578/9. **(628)**
To every one of my daughter's children [not named] 12d. To my son Aubrey PROYER and his children 12d. apiece. To my son Mich. 3s.4d. The rest of my goods to Agnes my wife, whom I make executrix. Witnesses: John PERKINSON clerk [rector of Colne Engaine], Henry PRYOR. Proved 1 Apr. 1579.

MARGERY BOWEN of Great Bentley widow, 11 Nov. 1580. (Nuncupative.) **(629)**
She did give to Th. BOWEN her last husband's son 20s. at 21. To Wm. BOWEN her son £6 at 18, 1 fair cupboard, a joined table with a frame, a featherbed, 1 brass pot, 2 candlesticks, half a dozen pieces of pewter, a new little kettle, and a latten mortar with a pestle at 18; if he should die before, £4 thereof to the 'said' John son of Th. BOWEN and the rest to the use of her executor. To Matthew WILLSON her brother 1 bullock of a year and the vantage. The rest of her goods to Rt. WILLSON of Weeley, whom she did ordain executor. Witnesses: John MARSHE, Rt. POTTER. Proved 18 Nov. 1580.

ELIZABETH DAVE of Messing widow, 20 Oct. 1580. **(630)**
To Edw. DYNES my son £3. To Gilbert DYNES my son 20s., a bullock, a kettle, a candlestick, a platter, a spit, an andiron, a chest, and a chair. To Wm. DYNES my son a cow, a brass pot, my table in the hall with the form, and my cupboard. To Ralph DYNES my son 10s. To Prudence my daughter a cow, a candlestick, a pewter dish, 2 pillowberes, 1 pillow, my white covering, my red petticoat, my russet cassock, and half of my wearing linen not bequeathed. To Faith my daughter a cow, a bed, my best cassock, and the other half of my wearing linen. To Kath. DYNES my girl 40s., a flockbed with the bedsteadle, a frying pan, a kercher, a rail, a holyday apron, a neckercher, a quarter, and a piece of russet of 3½ yards. To Wm. PUR my brother 10s. and a bushel and half of such corn as I have, my pot of butter, and 6 cheeses. To his wife 12d. and my black russet petticoat. To Theophilus PUR 16d. and to three of my brother PUR's children 6s. apiece. To Ellen GOWERS 12d. The rest of my corn to Wm. POLLARD my son-in-law. I will that the 'gardner' [guardian] of my girl shall have her bequest to her use. The rest of my goods shall be divided equally amongst my said children by my executors, whom I ordain Wm. PUR and Wm. POLLARD. Witnesses: Mr MARCHE, John LUSKIN [*recte* LUFKIN]. Proved 18 Nov. 1580.

ELIZABETH SORRELL of Cressing widow, 22 Apr. 1580. **(631)**
To my daughter Eliz. CLARKE my featherbed, 1 kercher, 1 rail marked with a blue mark, 1 kercher more (a fine one with a little black mark), also 2 neckerchers (1 of the best and another of the worst), 2 lockram aprons and 2 more lockram kerchers, my best black apron, 2 canvas aprons, 2 fine quarters, the best and worst tablecloths, my best gown, my worst red petticoat, a candlestick, and a cow. To her two daughters, i.e. to Frances CLERKE my hutch by my bedside, a pewter dish and 1 pair of the best [salt] cellars , and to Agnes CLERKE a round table with a chest in the frame of it and a joined table. To Agnes, a pewter dish and 1 of the best cellars. To Eliz.'s sons, i.e. John her eldest a latten chafing dish and her youngest [not named] a pewter dish and a cellar. All the things to Eliz.'s four children to be delivered to their father and mother to their behoof at 20. To Daniel son of my son Rt. STOKES a joined bedsteadle, my cupboard in the chamber and 1 brass pot, to be delivered by the father to Daniel at 21; if he die before, to Thomasine my daughter-in-law, Daniel's mother. My son Rt. doth owe me 40s., which he shall deliver to my executor; whereof 5s. each to Eliz.'s four children at 18 or marriage, 13s.4d. to John son of John HAYWARDE, and 6s.8d. to Daniel son of Rt. STOKES at 21. To Thomasine STOKES my 2nd gown and my best petticoat. To the poor of Cressing at the day of my burial 2s. The rest of my goods to Rt. I ordain John HAYWARDE my son-in-law executor, and for his pains 3s.4d. Witnesses: Rd. DYNES, John HUBBERD curate. [No probate clause.]

HENRY THORNE, [abode and date not given]. (Nuncupative.) **(632)**
To Dthy. my wife £3. To Wm. my brother my 2 best doublets for they are good ones. To Agnes his wife 2 shirts. Witnesses: John COWELL, Wm. CLERKE, Frs. LINDSELL parson of Strethall. [No probate clause.]

THOMAS MYDSON of Little Walden [in Saffron Walden], 23 Feb. 1579/80. (633)
To Joan my wife a meadow called Wynhall (1 acre) lying beneath Crowally [Common] Field on one side and the highway from James FLEMMINGE's towards Water End; a parcel of arable, parcel of 6 acres of ware land in Crowally Field (2 acres); and my tenement called Godfreys; all for her life; on condition that she shall see my children brought up. After her decease, to Henry MYDSON my son. I will that my wife shall pay to my four daughters, i.e. Susan, Alice, Joan and Winifred, £5 apiece at marriage. The rest of my goods to my wife, whom I make executrix. Witnesses: Th. PETTIT, John FREMAN, Henry PETTIT. Surrender given according to the custom of the manor into the hands of Th. PETTIT, one of the tenants of the lord, in the presence of John FREMAN and Henry PETTIT. Proved 6 Oct. 1580.

MARGERY NEWBOLTE of Brook Walden in [Saffron] Walden widow, 13 Sept. 1580. (Nuncupative.) (634)
She did bequeath to Joan her daughter her customary tenement holden of the manor of Brook Walden and one half-acre of land holden of the manor of Littlebury. To Joyce NEWBOLTE her daughter another half-acre of land customary holden of the same manor. To Mary her daughter 3 roods of land customary holden of the same manor. She did will that all her goods and cattle and crop of saffron and saffron heads should be divided equally between John NEWBOLTE her son and Joan, Joyce and Mary. She did ordain John and Mary executors. Witnesses: Rt. FRITH the writer, Nich. LOSHE, Th. CURRE, Joan CLERKE. Proved 6 Oct. 1580.

JOHN BORRE of Tolleshunt Knights, 10 Apr. 1580. (635)
To Rt. BURE my eldest son, John and Matthew my son each £3 at 21. To the poor 12d. The residue of my goods to Joan my wife, whom I make executrix. Witnesses: Th. SYMOND minister of the church [the clergy list for Tolleshunt Knights is deficient at this period], John BURE his father, Rd. BRIDGEMAN his brother-in-law, Henry BREDGEMAN. Proved 30 May 1580.

THOMAS TAYLER of Great Chesterford the elder, yeoman, 25 June 1573 and 15 Eliz. (636)
To the poor people 10s. To Th. my son my messuage wherein I inhabit, with the buildings, yards and gardens belonging, in Great Chesterford, and my 4 acres of land in the [Common] Fields of Littlebury; and my land, wood and pasture enclosed in Burton in the parish and [Common Fields] of Great Chesterford, with my orchard in the 'town' [i.e. village] of Great Chesterford adjoining the messuage, all holden of the manor of Great Chesterford. To Th. my 2 acres of land in the Fields of Littlebury; and my 2 acres of land in Strethall holden of the manor of Strethall. Which premises I have surrendered by the hands of Th. SWALLOW in the presence of Philip SWALLOW and into the hands of Th. WESTON in the presence of John STALLEWORTHMAN and Wm. STALLEWORTHEMAN, tenants of the same manors. To Samuel son of John RUNHAM my son-in-law 4 bushels of barley. The residue of my goods to my son Th. , whom I make executor. Witnesses: John PAXSTON writer hereof, Th. SWALLOWE, Th. WESTON, John STALLWORTHMAN, Th. SWALLOW , [*sic*], Philip SWALLOWE, John SAYER, Wm. STALLWORTHMAN. Proved 3 Apr. 1580.

JOHN RELESON of Little Bentley chapman, 30 Jan. 1579/80. (637)
To the poor of Cattaway Street [Cattawade, co. Suffolk] the money which HARRIS's wife oweth me. I forgive the poor folk of Walton [co. Essex or Suffolk?], Th. CARTER the minister of 'Chilforde' [Chillesford, co. Suffolk?], COLLIN the summoner, THOMPSON of Magdalen Street [in Colchester], BLAKFORDE of Colchester Hythe, STONE of Elmstead, and Th. STRINGE of Little Bentley all the debts that they owe me. To my host BULVAN of 'Inverston' [Ingatestone?] 3½ yards of white sacking to make him a doublet. To Rt. STEEDE's son 3s. To Constance daughter and Wm., Rt. and Th. sons of Geo. SMYTHE each 50s. at 21, all the £10 to be delivered to Barnard SURFLYTTE of Colchester, he to put into bonds for the payment. To Constance my cupboard and table in the hall, 10 lb. of flat pewter, my best brass pot, and a brass chafer, after the death of Anne my wife. To Constance DENICE a cow or 4 nobles at 21, the cow to be delivered to Geo. SMYTHE my

son-in-law; he shall pay yearly on Midlent Sunday 2s. for the hire of her to the poor of Little Bentley and shall put in good assurance for the stock and increase of the same as the minister and churchwardens shall think good. To Mgt. my daughter 6s.8d to buy her a brass pot. To Wm. KEBALL my black doublet. To Bridget GRUBBE 3s.4d. to buy her a petticoat. To Rd. SHERMAN my house on the Green and the pightle adjoining it and the field against the Parsonage and the meadow belonging to the house lying by Paunkowe, for 17 years after my death; on condition that he shall pay for the house and lands 30s. a year and the lord's rent, whereof 10s. I will to be bestowed on the reparations of the house yearly and 20s. he shall pay to Barnard SURFLTT of Colchester; after the 17 years, the house and lands to remain to Anne daughter whilst he lived of John RELESON my son; if she die before the time, to the children of Geo. SMYTHE equally divided. To Anne my wife my tenement called Stourges for her life; after her death, to Geo. my son. To Geo. SMYTHE 40s., a cloak, and 2 bushels of barley. The residue of my goods to my wife, whom I make executrix, on condition that she shall neither suffer any of the children to dwell with her nor she shall dwell with them; if she do, my gift to be void. To Barnard SURFLITT her gift and he to be executor. I ordain Rd. SHERMAN supervisor. Witnesses: John PAYNE, Edw. GYLES, Barnard SURFLITT, Rd. SHERMAN. Proved by Anne, 6 Apr. 1580.

WILLIAM WILLOWES of Ashdon yeoman, 20 Feb. 1579/80. (638)
To Mich. my son my lands, meadows, pastures and woods called Muchfields which I bought of Wm. LESTRICHE *alias* BUTCHER late before Mr Rd. TERREL's, specified in the deeds of purchase. My executors shall have the herbage thereof till Mich. is 21 and shall find him sufficient meat, drink, apparel and schooling until he is 21. To him £10 at 21. To Eliz. my daughter £40 at 21 or marriage, my executors to find her meat, drink and apparel until then. To Anne FRENCH my daughter 6s.8d. To Anne daughter of Anne FRENCHE 20s. or a bullock worth 20s. To Th., Wm. and Th. sons of Anne my daughter 6s.8d. each at 10. To the poor of Ashdon 10s. I ordain my wife Anne and Wm. my son executors and my brother John WILLOWES supervisor, and to John 20s. for his labour. The residue of my goods to my wife and Wm. equally divided; but if she marry, she shall have no part of the movables but only £30 or else £6 13s.4d. by year or else the third part of my lands for her life. Witnesses: Rd. SLANYE, Rt. CLAYDON, Wm. HUMFREY. Proved 13 Apr. 1580.

ROBERT FRANKHAM of St. Nicholas, Colchester, 20 July 1577. (639)
To Alice my wife my messuage in West Bergholt called Nicolls for her life, conditionally that she give to the maintenance of an almshouse there, if any be erected within these 2 years, 3s.4d. yearly as long as she live; if no almshouse, she shall give the 3s.4d. to the collector of the parish for the poor yearly. After her decease, the tenement to Eliz. my daughter with the same condition; if she die without issue, the churchwardens with four other honest men yearly appointed by the parish shall appoint an honest tenant in the tenement, they keeping it sufficiently repaired, and shall distribute the rent yearly to the poor of the parish of St. Nicholas in Colchester 13s.4d. for ever. Also I will that the churchwardens and the four men shall distribute to the poor in Bergholt the 13s.4d. taken out of the rent to the poor of St. Nicholas, the overplus of the rent to the use of the poor in Bergholt. To Eliz. 2 milch beasts, 10 good sheep and my posted bedsteadle in Colchester, a joined table with a frame and turned posts, 4 joined stools, a trundle bedsteadle with a flockbed, a chest with iron bars, a fair flat chest standing on 2 feet, 4 platters, 2 saucers, 2 porringers, 2 good bell candlesticks, a brass pot, a kettle that will seethe, a pair of sheets, a posnet, a gridiron, a spit, a frying pan, a silver spoon of a ounce and a half, a needlework cushion, a canvas tablecloth 3 yards long, another featherbed, and £5, all at 18 or marriage. To Agnes FOKES 2 sheep at 18 or marriage. I will that my wife shall put in sufficient sureties to Adam REVE of Colchester (whom I ordain supervisor) in £10 that my wife shall not take away any glass, ceiling or anything that is joined to the house but let them remain for Eliz.'s use on pain of forfeiture of the bond. The rest of my goods to my wife, whom I ordain executrix. Witnesses: Adam REVE, Th. FIRFANNE, John LAMBE. Proved 14 July 1579.

JOHN SMYTHE of Great Birch, 16 March 1581/2. (640)
To Mary my wife my house in which I dwell in Great Birch with the lands belonging in Great Birch, Stanway and Copford, both free and copyhold, for 18 years, on condition that she pay my debts and bring up and nourish Anne the daughter of Anne GODARD and the base child and discharge the parish of Great Birch in respect that I have received £10 for the same, and also John son of Nich. SMYTHE until 18 years are expired. If he can be well placed by my wife with the advice of my supervisors for the said time, I will that she give his master 40s. and at the end of 18 years to pay John £4, if he be living. To my wife my wood and soil of ground containing 3 acres and half an acre of meadow in Layer-de-la-Haye, to be sold to the performance of my Will. To her my house called the Gatehouse as it is divided from my mansion [i.e. dwelling house]. To Hugh SMYTHE my son after the 18 years my house that I dwell in with the said lands, on condition that he pay my son John £3 when he enter on them. I will that my wife bestow 10s. yearly in reparations of my house. To my godchildren 12d. apiece. I will that Anne FORDE have her habitation for her life as she hath had. To my wife all my goods, whom I make executrix. I ordain Rt. WORDYSWORTH and John NOTHE supervisors, and for their pains 5s. apiece. Witnesses: Rt. WORDYSWORTH, John NOTHE, Rt. UBBERDE, Andrew KABELL. Proved 30 Apr. 1582.

THOMAS ROOFE [ROOFFE *in margin*] of Little Bromley, 5 Nov. 1582. (641)
To the poor folk 10s. To 'Grisell' KINGE my servant a wennel. To Hum., John and Chris. LOVELL, my wife's children, each a bullock. To Mgt. my daughter £40 at 21 or marriage. To Mgy. my wife my houses and lands in Thorpe in the tenure of Geoffrey BANBRICK for her life; after her decease, to Leonard my son. To him my houses and lands in Little Bromley called Drapers and Gyddye Pightle. I will that my cousin Rt. RUNTINGE be his 'gardiner' [guardian]. To Th. my son my houses and lands in Little Bromley called Lockes and Fur Lands. To John my son a tenement called Laymes (20 acres) in Little Bromley with Megg Pightle and another tenement and 7½ acres called Stevens in Little Bromley. The rest of my goods to Mgt. [*sic*] my wife, whom I make executrix. I request Mr Charles CARDINALL to be supervisor, and for his pains 10s. Witnesses: John STEVEN, Th. ADAMS, Nich. STRICKLANDE, Edw. GYLES. Proved 13 Dec. 1582 by Mgt. executrix.

THOMAS MURCOCKE of Hatfield Peverel, 30 Nov., 25 Eliz. [1582]. (642)
To Alice MURCOCKE my wife, whom I make executrix, all my goods. I make John GURLIVAUNCE overseer, and for his pains 20d. Witnesses: John SEA curate, Wm. BORNDE, John HORNSEY. Proved 14 Dec. 1582.

STEPHEN RICHE of Lexden husbandman, [no date given]. (643)
To Mary my wife my house wherein I dwell and my land free and copy until John my son is 21, then to him. To my daughters Susanna and Agnes each 2 milch beasts and 6 sheep at 21, also £3 2 years after my son is 21; if they decease before, to my wife for her life and after her decease to my brother John RICHE. To him 2 lambs. The rest of my goods to my wife, whom I make executrix. I make overseer Rd. GOSNOLL. Witnesses: Rd. STEWARD, Rd. GOSNOLL, Hugh WILLSON, Edm. ALLEYN, Edw. WHITTAM, Th. ALLIN. Proved 13 Dec. 1582.

AGNES CLERKE of Littlebury Green [in Littlebury] widow, 28 May 1582. (644)
To Wm. CLERKE my son an ewe and a lamb, my table with 2 trestles in the hall, and my timber in the yard. To Alice THORNE my daughter an ewe and a lamb, my cloak, and my best cassock. To John CLERKE my son my red cow called Cherry, an ewe and a lamb, 2 pair of sheets, 3 towen and 1 flaxen. To Rt. CLERKE my son a dun cow called Mouse, an ewe and a lamb, and 2 pair of sheets. To Th. CLERKE my son a yellow cow called Lillye and a calf weaned this year, an ewe and a lamb, and 2 pair of sheets. To Erasmus CLERKE my son a grimbled bullock of 2 years, 2 sheep and 1 lamb, and 2 pair of sheets. To Henry CLERKE my son my brown cow, an ewe and a lamb, and 2 pair of sheets. To Mgt. CLERKE my daughter my black grimbled cow, an ewe and a lamb, 2 pair of sheets, my cupboard in the hall, my best great hutch, my best dornix coverlet, all my wearing linen, my

sheep's russet cassock, my best petticoat, and a towel. To Agnes daughter of Wm. CLERKE my son a bullock and a lamb. The rest of my household stuff to be equally divided between six of my children, i.e. John, Rt., Th., Erasmus, Henry and Mgt. The rest of my movables to be sold and the money equally divided among my six children. I make executors John and Rt. CLERKE my sons and Rt. TURNER my brother supervisor, and for his pains 12d. Witnesses: James TURNER, Frs. LINDSELL, parson of Strethall. Debts — I owe to Erasmus CLERKE £3 and 1 coomb of barley, to Henry my son 40s., and Mgt. CLERKE 20s. Proved 17 Dec. 1582.

THOMAS PILGRAM, [abode and date not given]. (645)
To Ellen my wife all my goods. She shall pay Grace my daughter £15. If my wife marry again, she shall pay Grace £15 more. To Rt. PILGRAM's children 6s.8d. apiece at marriage. I will that my wife give to the poor 10s. I choose her my executrix and desire my brother SMYTHE to be supervisor. [No witnesses.] Proved 24 Nov. 1582.

THOMAS HARRIDAUNCE of [Saffron] Walden yeoman, 16 Jan. 1581/2. (646)
To Th. my son 3 acres of land in Heath [Common] Field in Walden, with the deeds. To Jeremy my son 1 tenement and 3 acres 'warland' [land originally held by villeins] in Little Walden [in Saffron Walden] called Watatholteryes and 1 acre of land called Wakesacre, 3 roods called Hayells, 1 acre parcel of the tenement, 10 acres 'warland' called Borouz in the occupation of John PETITT and holden of the lord of [the manor of] Walden by copy of court roll, as I have surrendered the same to the lord by John HEDGE in the presence of Rt. EARTHFEILDE and Stephen STEWARDE customary tenants of the manor, one ½-acre of land, parcel of the tenement lately Rt. STOCMER, lying at the Scavers Ashes in Little Walden, and one ½-acre of wood holden likewise. To Edw. my son 1 shop in Walden market place holden of the Treasurer and Chamberlains of Walden by copy of court roll and 3 half-acres of land in Willow Field in Walden. To Wm. my son 1 featherbed and bedstead, 1 charger, 1 basin, 1 brass pot, 1 posnet, 1 spit, 1 great dripping pan, 1 kettle, 1 table with the frame and 2 forms usually in the parlour, 6 table napkins, 1 short towel, 1 tablecloth, 3 silver spoons, 1 moulding trough, 1 pair of andirons, 1 chest, and 1 cupboard in the chamber. To Jeremy 1 featherbed, 6 table napkins, 1 table with the frame in the inner parlour, 1 form, 2 silver spoons, 1 brass pot, 1 skillet, 1 spit, 1 counter table, 2 chests in the chamber over the shop on each side of the bed, and 1 candlestick. To Edw. 1 featherbed and 1 bed in the same chamber, 2 silver spoons, 1 quilt, 1 joined cupboard in the kitchen, 2 brass pots, 1 footed table in the chamber over the hall with the longest form, 1 round table in the hall, 1 chest bound with iron, 6 table napkins, 1 chair in the hall, 1 little chair table having a cupboard in it in the parlour, with 1 spit and a dripping pan. To Samuel my son 1 goblet parcel gilt which I lent to Geo. NICHOLLES esquire and remaineth in his hands. The residue of my goods to Th. my son and Mark DOWLINGE my son-in-law, whom I make executors. Witnesses: John HEDGE, Simon WILLMOTT, Rt. EARTHFEILDE, Stephen STEWARDE. Proved 21 Nov. 1582.

JOHN HARRIS of Hatfield Peverel husbandman, 18 Sept. 1582. (647)
To Rd. CHILDE my son-in-law 2 bushels of wheat and 2 bushels of malt. To Jane CHILDE his daughter a brass pot. To Wm. son of John BRAYNEWOOD 10s. at 21. The residue of my goods to Mgt. my wife, whom I make executrix. I make Alex. WYMOTT overseer. Witnesses: Alex. WILLMOTT, John HAYLLES. Proved 2 Nov. 1582.

THOMAS MAYDWELL *alias* CHAPMAN of Langley husbandman, 26 Mar. 1582. (648)
To the reparations of Langley church 3s.4d. To the poor 6s.8d. To Joan my daughter £3 6s.8d. at 26 [*sic*] or marriage, also 1 cow, my benchboard, 1 hutch made of walnut tree boards, and 1 kettle. To Mary and Eliz. daughters and Rt. son of Rt. CHEPPERFEILDE each 6s.8d. at 21. To Philip son of and Agnes daughter of John MELLERD each 6s.8d. at 21. The residue of my goods to Eliz. my wife and Henry my son, whom I make executors. Witnesses: Wm. LETCHFEILDE, Wm. COLLYN, Rt. SMYTHE. Proved 30 Oct. 1582.

WILLIAM HECKFORDE of Beaumont single man, 13 Sept. 1582. (Nuncupative.) (649)
He did bequeath to Lawrence HECKFORDE his brother all his goods. [No witnesses or date of probate or administration.]

JOHN TOMSON the elder of Debden carpenter, 9 Sept. 1582. (650)
To Mgy. my wife all such household stuff as was hers before that I married her; also 1 joined bed, all my leases in my occupation [no details], all my corn in the field or in my house, my horses, carts, cart harness, ploughs and plough irons, all my beasts and bullocks, sheep, hogs and poultry, all for her life; after her decease, the goods to be appraised and equally divided amongst my children, i.e. John, Th., and James RABLE and Rd., Geo., Eleanor, Mary, Joan and Anne TOMSON. If my wife chance to marry again, she shall give them £10 between them. To Mary TOMSON my cupboard in my chamber and all that is in it to be equally divided between Mary and Joan. To Anne 1 joined bed above in the chamber where my 'Ladyes' [*recte* maids?] lie. To Rd. my son 1 long table, 4 joined stools belonging to it, and 1 chair at the table's end in the hall, 1 coffer at Joan OVERAL's at Horsehamper Gate, with 1 new chair. To Eleanor my daughter the lesser chest in my chamber. The residue of my goods to be equally divided between my four children, Rd. taking his first choice. I will that my wife shall deliver the goods as my children stand in need of them or at marriage. I make her my executrix and ordain my trusty and well-beloved John GATTES supervisor. To my wife 1 pair of cobirons, 2 great kettles, 1 brass pot, and 1 little brass pot. Witnesses: Rt. BUCKE, Nich. WOOD. Proved 8 Nov. 1582.

ROBERT SPENSER of Ramsey single man, 25 Dec. 1580. (651)
To Agnes MARVIN my dame all my goods except my apparel and that I give to Reynold MARVIN my master. I appoint him executor. Witnesses: Henry TUNMER, Rd. WRITE. Proved 12 Oct. 1582.

HENRY OZELL of Colchester alien, 7 Sept. 1582. (652)
To the poor people of the Dutch [i.e. Flemish] congregation in Colchester 10s. and to the poor people of the Dutch congregation in Halstead 10s. To every one of my children which I have in Colchester 10s. The rest of my goods to my three daughters, i.e. Jakemynken, Gaengen and Mayken, equally to be divided. I ordain Christian de FREND my son-in-law and the said Mayken executors. Witnesses: Wm. VIGERUS writer hereof, Edm. SMYTHE, Jan Van ROOKE, Joos MYNER. Proved 26 Oct. 1582.

JOHN PRENTISE the elder of Colne Engaine yeoman, 3 Aug., 24 Eliz. [1582]. (653)
To be buried in Colne Engaine church or churchyard. To the poor people thereof 20s. for 4 years at 5s. a year. To Alice my wife for life the messuage in Colne Engaine wherein I dwell, with the yards, orchards and gardens, the croft adjoining and a free croft called Redinge belonging, and Grey Croft which I bought of Geo. HASSATT and Alice his wife in Colne Engaine; after her decease, to Wm. my son, except Gray Croft to John the elder my son. To John the younger my son my customary lands of the manor of Wakes Colne called Frenches in Colne Engaine. To my wife for life my third part of a messuage and croft adjoining called Biglands in Halstead which I purchased of John PRENTICE of London. To John the elder my messuage called Goor[es?] and the lands belonging in Colne Engaine in his occupation; for lack of issue, to John the younger. To Mary my daughter my tenement and lands in Colne Engaine which I purchased of John LYNTON and Rt. LYNTON, with liberty to set a ladder when they shall tile any building thereof on any free croft belonging to the house wherein I dwell. To Agnes the younger my daughter my tenement and garden called Skottes in Colne Engaine. To my wife for life my moiety of the manor with the appurtenances called Bromptons and the lands belonging which I purchased of Roger MARTIN esquire in Colne Engaine; after her decease, to John the elder and Wm. equally to be divided, i.e. each half of the moiety. To Wm. my tenement called Warkemans with the gardens and orchards in Earls Colne in the occupation of Clement TURNER, on condition that Wm. pay to my three daughters, i.e. Joan, Agnes the elder and Agnes the younger, each £5 6s.8d. To Eliz. my daughter, wife of James RICHARDSON, £3 6s.8d. To Mary my daughter £10.

To Mary PRENTISE, daughter of the late Rt. PRENTISE my son, £3 6s.8d. at 20. To every one of my children's children 3s.4d. and to every one of my godchildren 12d. To John the elder, John the younger and Wm. each 2 of my horses or colts. To every one of my children a cow to be delivered to them at Michaelmas after my decease. To Wm. 1 featherbed next the best, after my wife's decease. The rest of my goods, corn, cattle, ready money and household stuff to my wife, whom I ordain executrix. I ordain my well-beloved friends James RICHARDSON my son-in-law and Wm. VIGORUS of Halstead supervisors, and for their pains 20s. Witnesses: Nich. BUNTINGE, John CHAMBERLAIN, John OFFIN, Wm. VIGORUS. Proved 11 Oct. 1582.

HENRY RUSSELL of St. Leonard in Colchester beerbrewer, 9 Mar. 1581/2. (654)
I will that all my goods shall be sold by my executrix. Of the money arising, I give to Mary DUNSTONE and her three children, viz. Daniel at 21, and Priscilla and Sarah at 21 or marriage, by equal portions. I nominate Mary executrix, and for her pains and the sustentation and bringing up of her children £5. I name my trusty friend Mr John HUNWICKE, one of the aldermen of the town of Colchester, supervisor, and for his painstaking 5s. If Mary shall contract with any man, he with whom she shall marry shall enter into bond to John HUNWICKE for the education of the children and payment of their portions; if he refuse, the portions to be paid to John HUNWICKE, who shall have the placing of the children withal. My executrix shall bestow on the poor of the parish at my burial 10 dozen of bread and a barrel of beer. Witnesses: Rd. LITLEWOOD, John COLE, John HUNWICKE, Th. LAMBERT. Proved 12 Oct. 1582.

RICHARD LESTRICHE *alias* BUTCHER of Ashdon, 26 Oct. 1580. (655)
To Blanche my wife all the stuff in the chamber wherein I lie. The rest of my goods to Alex. my son, he to pay to David BUTCHER my son 10s., Joan WATSON my daughter 20s., and to my sons Th. BUTCHER, Wm. BUTCHER the younger, John BUTCHER and Rd. BOCHARD [*sic*], each 20s., Edw. BOCHARD 20s., Rt. BOCHER and Rd. BOCHER each 20s., to be paid within 1, 2, 3, 4, 5, 6, 7, 8 and 9 years after my wife's decease. I ordain Alex. BOCHER executor. Witnesses: John FREMAN, Wm. FREMAN, Wm. FITCHE. Proved 8 Oct. 1582.

MARGARET WARNER of Coggeshall widow, 16 June 1582. (656)
To Mary and Priscilla WARNER, being the wives of Edw. and Henry WARNER my sons, all my linen and wearing apparel to be equally divided, my old frize gown excepted which I give to Joan HUAR of Kelvedon widow and a red petticoat which I have delivered to Mgt. SLAUGHTER. To Henry 1 'stawle' [stall?] of bees and Edw. and Cyprian WARNER each a swarm of bees. To Priscilla, my son Cyprian's wife, the painted cloths about the chamber where I lie and 1 turned chair. I will that Edw. and Henry shall be executors. Witnesses: Walter OWSOLDE, Mgt. SLAUGHTER. Proved 6 Sept. 1582.

JOHN BARRETT of Earls Colne yeoman, 23 Aug. 1582. (657)
To be buried in the church or churchyard of Earls Colne. To the poor people 20s. at the day of my burial. To Mgy. my wife my customary messuage wherein I dwell, with the buildings, yards, gardens, orchards, lands, meadows and pastures belonging, in my own occupation in Earls Colne, which I hold by copy of court roll of the Earl of Oxford as of his manors of the Earldom and of the Priory, until my son John is 21; then to him. If he die without issue, to my wife until my two daughters Agnes and Mary are 21; then to them. To my wife my two customary tenements with the yards, orchard and gardens belonging in Earls Colne in the several occupations of [blank] HARDINGE and Wm. TAYLER, for her life; after her decease, to John. To my wife my free croft of land in Earls Colne in the occupation of Barthw. CHURCHE. To her my lease and term of years in a tenement and lands in Earls Colne in the occupation of John SKOTT. To Agnes and Mary each £100 at 21 or marriage. The rest of my goods to my wife, whom I ordain executrix. I ordain my brother-in-law Mr Rt. CHURCHE executor with her, and for his pains 20s. If my wife happen to marry, he that shall marry with her shall be bound with two sufficient sureties to Rt. CHURCHE in £400 for the payment of my legacies. Witnesses: Barthw. CHURCHE, Th. LEFINGWELL, Wm. VIGORUS, John CHURCHE. Proved 6 Sept. 1582.

JOHN METCHILL of Brook Walden in parish of [Saffron] Walden, 14 Jan. 1573/4 and 16 Eliz. (658)
To Jane my daughter the interest of my house for the term of years that I have according to the custom of the manor of Brook Walden, the bench with the painted cloths in the hall, my quern and a coop, the brewing and baking vessels, two sideboards, and all the movables in the house, save that I mind to give with my hand. I make her my executrix. Witnesses: Rt. BURRE, Geo. FURLOWE, Th. CUR, Chris. PARKER. Proved 18 July 1582.

MARGARET LINNE of Wormingford widow, 10 Apr., 22 Eliz. [1580]. (659)
To Eliz. ALLEN my daughter 2 of my best kine. To John GOLDINGE, Erasmus GOLDINGE, Geo. GOLDINGE, Wm. LINNE, Anne BLITHE and Alice BECHUM, my six children, each a cow. To John, Geo. and Wm. all my sheep. To Eliz. my daughter 3 of my best hogs. To Eliz. Blithe a bed. To my three said daughters Anne, Alice BECHUM and Eliz. ALLIN all my beds unbequeathed. To Mary POTTER, Eleanor POTTER and Agnes GOLDINGE each 20s. To Mary BLITHE a pair of sheets. To John WENDE, Joan ALLIN, Mgt. GOLDINGE and Mary LINNE my four godchildren 20s. apiece. To Joan ALLIN 20s. To John GOLDINGE my son my mare. To Mary POTTER 2 or 3 of my best kerchers and a piece of plate or 'macier' [mazer] called an ox eye. To Anne BLYTHE, Alice BECHUM and Eliz. ALLIN all my woollen and linen and wearing clothes to be equally divided. To Wm. LINNE my son all my silver spoons and my best coverlet. To Erasmus 2 of my hogs and a cupboard. To Wm. my mare colt and £6 13s.4d. which I lent him before the death of my husband his father. To my three daughters my 3 best chests. To my five children all my corn in the barns or chambers equally and the rest of my goods and ready money equally among them. To Wm. the corn growing on my ground. I ordain him executor; if he refuse, I will my son John GOLDINGE to be executor. Witnesses: Rt. ANDREW vicar of Wormingford, Th. COO, Rt. POTTER, Th. BARKER. Proved 7 Nov. 1582.

THOMAS ROCHESTER of Ramsey sailor, 24 June, 23 Eliz. [1581]. (660)
To Cecily my wife my house with the lands belonging in Ramsey for her life; after her decease, to my son John; if he die without heirs, to one Davy Celty. To John the best bed in my house, the best cupboard and my best chest, after his mother's decease. I will that Edw. HAYWARD my son-in-law shall have my house which he holdeth of me for 4 years without paying any rent. I ordain my wife and one Hugh CAVELL executors. Witnesses: John HARVYE, Rt. WYRE, Rd. WOOD. Proved 7 Sept. 1582.

RICHARD HECKFORDE of Ardleigh husbandman, 17 May 1582. (661)
To my six children called Rd., Th., Daniel, Wm., I[s]rael and Sarah each £5 at 21. To my brother Th. HECKFORD 10s. The rest of my goods to Mgt. my wife. I ordain Th. my executor. My brother Wm. HECKFORD I desire to be supervisor. Witnesses: Lawrence LYDE minister [vicar of Ardleigh], Giles ALLEN, Wm. HECKFORD. Proved 21 July 1582.

THOMAS FAIRSTEAD of St. Botolph, Colchester, 21 June 1582. (662)
To be buried in the churchyard either of St. Giles or of St. Botolph. To Lucy my wife my houses and lands in the town of Colchester for her life, i.e. my house in which I last dwelt in St. Giles; 2 tenements in St. Botolph with the garden; 1 tenement that Rt. RASHEBROOKE dwelleth in with a garden in St. Giles; 2 orchards, 1 called the saffron pane in St. Botolph under the town wall, the other called the vicar's garden in St. Giles; which house and 2 orchards are in the hands of Rt. SMYTHE, she to enjoy them after his death; after her death to John FAIRSTEAD my son; if he die without heirs, to my two daughters, i.e. Eliz. DEXTER and Mgy. EVANCE, to be divided equally. To Susanna my youngest daughter, after my wife's decease, the house in St. Giles in which Mr SQUEAK dwelleth, also the orchard called the saffron pane, she paying Elizabeth DEXTER £10 and her children 20s. apiece at marriage or 21; if Susan die without heirs, to John my son, he paying his sisters Eliz. DEXTER £10 and Mgy. EVANCE £5 and their children 20s. apiece. To Mgy.

my daughter for her life and after her decease to her children my 2 tenements with 2 gardens in St. Botolph which I bought of Stephen MOUNFORTH the minstrel and Rt. BURGESS innholder; if she and her children die, to th. DEXTER; after him to John his son. To Susanna my new post bed wherein I lie. To Th. DEXTER 1 great brass pot or a mark of money, which he will. To John FAIRSTEAD all my apparel. The residue of my goods to my wife, whom I make executrix. Witnesses: John BARNARD, John LOVEDAY, Th. DEXTER, John FAIRSTEAD. Proved 21 July 1582.

WILLIAM MATHEW of Lexden husbandman, 12 June 1582. (Nuncupative.) (663)
Geoffrey his son should have the bed he did lie on with the furniture (except the coverlet which he said was his daughter Eliz.'s), his wearing apparel, with his wedges, hook, axe and other working tools. To Wm. DUNSTONN 4 of his best wether sheep or so much money as they should be worth at Michaelmas next, to be delivered to Geoffrey NEWTON of Stanway. He set over his corn to his son of London for 40s. which he was indebted to him but if worth more his son should pay over the overplus to his daughters. He willed that Eliz. should not go to London to dwell but remain at Geoffrey NEWTON's appointment till able to provide for herself. The rest of his goods to be parted between his two daughters Ellen and Eliz. by Geoffrey, whom he appointed overseer. Witnesses: Rt. SEARLE, Walter PECHYE, Anthony RAMPTON, Geoffrey NEWTON. Administration committed, 21 June 1582, to Geoffrey NEWTON.

JANE FRENCH of Terling widow, 20 Apr. 1582. (664)
To John FRENCH my eldest son 1 croft of land called Three Ashes, a cauldron, and a wicker chair. To Rebecca FRENCH his daughter 20s. To Rt. son of Geo. FRENCH a little brass pot and Geo.'s wife my best gown. To my sister Joan WATSON, if she be alive, a pair of canvas sheets. To my brother John CLANCHE a little flockbed and Rt. CLANCHE a pewter dish. I give a bushel of wheat if it be in the house and a bushel of malt among eight poor householders in Terling as my overseer think meet. To Julian CHAMBERLAYNE an old covering on my bed. I constitute Mr James ROBINSON clerk, vicar of Terling, overseer, and for his pains 2s.6d. The rest of my goods to Rt. my son, whom I make executor. Witnesses: James ROBINSON, John STEVEN, John WRITELL. Proved 21 July 1582.

CHRISTOPHER DAGNET of Terling husbandman, — Jan. 1581/2, (665)
To Wm. BOWSEY at the brook, my son-in-law, 7 beasts, 40 sheep, 4 seam of wheat, 20 bushels of malt, and the lease of the house and ground wherein he dwelleth, the rent whereof is paid for 2 years, he to find my wife Florence dwelling with him sufficient meat, drink, washing, wringing, and houseroom and to be bound for the performance thereof if she shall require it. To my son Wm. DAGNET the lease of Hogwell abutting on Hogwell Grove and Bromely Field on Brockmore. To him my lease of Phinex or Bishop's land in Fairstead and Terling, and 2 horse, 2 sheep, my ploughs and carts, plough and cart harness and chains; also my house [called] Chamberlaines after my wife's death, he paying John my son £6 13s.4d. at Lammas Day next. To Wm. 1 horse more in consideration of a cow he should have had. To John my apparel, with the rest of my sheep, 1 seam of wheat, and the 20 nobles which Wm. is to pay him. To the children of Wm. JACKSON, my son-in-law, 8 lambs equally divided. All other my goods to my wife, whom I appoint executrix. Witnesses: Henry ROBINSON clerk [vicar of Terling], Wm. DAGNET, John DAGNET, Th. FINCHE. Proved 22 May 1582.

AGNES LITTELBURY of East Mersea, [date not given]. (666)
To Rt. CROMMER and Wm. son of Wm. CROMMER each 20s. at 21 and to Rose CROMMER 10s. at 21 or marriage. To Anne WALDEN my best russet petticoat, Alice WALDEN a double kercher, 'Edey' WALDEN a single kercher, and Jane LONGE a russet petticoat. I ordain Wm. CROMMER executor. The rest of my goods to Wm. CROMMER the elder. Witnesses: Rd. BAINE, Rt. GODDINGE. Proved 22 June 1582.

WILLIAM PATTEN of Ardleigh shoemaker, 29 Mar. 1582. (667)
To Rose my daughter my little house with the backside in Boxford (co. Suffolk) let for 20s. a year to her; to Arthur and Henry my two sons the other part. To Agnes my wife the said houses for her life, but Rose to have hers at marriage. To Wm. and Rd. my sons my house wherein I dwell with the grove wherein it standeth in Ardleigh to be equally divided, my wife to have it till they are 22. To my four sons 30s. each at 21 out of the stock of my son Th. which he hath now in occupying. The rest of my goods to my wife, whom I ordain executrix. I make Wm. overseer. Witnesses: Lawrence LYDE clerk [vicar of Ardleigh], Wm. COOK, Rt. LYNES. Proved 21 May 1582.

ROBERT HALE of St. Nicholas, Colchester, gardener, 12 Jan. 1581/2. (668)
To Love HALLE my wife my house in which I dwell for her life; after her decease, to Rt. HALE my son; if he die without heirs, to Edw. son of Walter HALE my brother, Edw. paying 10s. to Joan SMYTHE my sister and 5s. each to Martin, Th. and Mgt. SMYTHE her children. To Rt. my house and ground in West Bergholt in the tenure of Edw. BROWNE. To my wife my house in which one John ROGERS dwelleth for her life; after her decease, to Grace HALE daughter of Walter. The residue of my goods to my wife, whom I make executrix. Witnesses: Rt. SMYTHE, Nich. TAYLER, John BANESTER. Proved 21 May 1582.

JOHN BAKER the elder of Fordham husbandman, 22 Mar. 1581/2. (669)
To my son John my house called Perrylandwith the lands belonging; if he decease without issue, to my son Simon. To Simon 6 kine, 10 sheep, and the bed whereon I lie. To Lucy and Frances his daughters each a bullock, Rt. BAKER a bullock, Joan BARNARD my servant a sheep and a lamb, Mary daughter of my son John 2 sheep, Joan BAKER dwelling with Rt. SURRAY a sheep, and Grace ALDEN my goddaughter a lamb. Towards the pulling down of the painted glass on the south window right against the steeple [i.e. tower] that I do use to sit in, 3s.4d., in token that I do utterly disallow all manner of idolatory as well in glass windows as in all other places, to be bestowed at the discretion of Mr Th. UPCHER our minister [the rector]. Towards the making of Porters Bridge 3s.4d. I surrender the house to Th. PECHYE and Th. BERIFF tenants of this manor in the presence of Wm. SWAN who supplied the room of the bailiff. The residue of my goods to John BAKER my son, whom I make executor. Witnesses: Th. UPCHER, Rt. SURRAY, Th. PETCHYE, Th. BERIFF, Wm. SWANNE, John GOODWYN clerk [rector of Stanway?]. Proved 21 May 1582.

JOHN BURRE of Marks Tey yeoman, [date not given]. (670)
To Matthew my son the tenement in Marks Tey called Longes. To Wm. my son my tenement called Christmas with the ground belonging and a parcel of land called Tyalls and Earls and to Rd. my son my tenement called Talbotes and Balls, both in Thorrington. To Susan my daughter £10. To Joan, Agnes and Mgt. my daughters a featherbed each. To Susan my son John's daughter 20s. at marriage or 20. To Wm. and Rd. each a brass pot. To my six children each a candlestick. To Wm. the greatest kettle and 1 of my round chests, Rd. the broad chest, and Susan the little white chest. To Susan the 3rd salt and a featherbed. To the poor of the parish 6s.8d. by goodman LAWRENCE and other of my neighbours. The rest of my goods to Emme my wife and Matthew my son equally, whom I constitute executors. Witnesses: Henry CORNEWALL minister [the clergy list for Marks Tey at this period is deficient] and writer hereof, Th. LAWRENCE.

Codicil 19 Mar. 1581. To Matthew my son my tenement called Augers with the ground belonging, on condition that he pay his brothers Wm., Rd. and Th. each £6 13s.4d., that for Th. to be in the hands of Matthew to the best comfort of Th. To Matthew my free cottage in the lordship of Frating Hall and my meadow in it ($1\frac{1}{4}$ acres copyhold) in consideration of keeping his brother. Witnesses: Henry CORNWALL, Th. LAWRENCE. Proved [date omitted in error].

WILLIAM STEVEN of Little Bromley husbandman, 15 Mar. 1581/2. (671)
To Edith my wife my lands and tenements called Bearlands and Stevens in Little Bromley for her life; after her decease, to be sold by my trusty friends and neigh-

bours Th. CAUNDLER, Th. ROLFE, John STEVEN and Rt. MAIND, tenants of the manor of Little Bromley, and the money equally divided between my three daughters 'Awdryan', Barbara and Edith STEVEN. To 'Awdryan' my greatest brass pot, a candlestick and 3 pieces of pewter, Barbara my greatest kettle, a candlestick and 3 pieces of pewter, and Edith a broad pan, a little brass pot, 3 pieces of pewter, and a candlestick, all at marriage. To Agnes STEVEN a black wennel. My wife shall lawfully take on the premises sufficient timber for reparations, firewood and fencing without making any strip or waste. The rest of my goods to my wife, whom I make executrix. Witnesses: Th. CAUNDLER, John STEVEN, Rt. MAIND, Ralph KINGE clerk [rector of Little Bromley], writer hereof. Proved 30 Apr. 1582.

JOHN SOMMER of Pontisbright *alias* Chapel, 1 Jan. 1581/2. (672)
To Joanmy wife all my household stuff. To my brother BARNARD's two sons Andrew and John each 20s. at 21; if both die before, equally among the children of my two sisters Kath. and Agnes. To the children of Rose now wife of Timothy PAYNE 20s. To Mary POWELL 2s. To my mother [not named] 1 bushel of wheat and 1 bushel of malt. The rest of my goods, cattle, corn in the field and barn, hay and other stover, with my implements of husbandry, to my wife, whom I make executrix, she to pay my debts to the sum of £18 10s. and discharge my legacies. I appoint my trusty and well-beloved neighbour and friend Rt. HAWKINS supervisor. Witnesses: Samuel LONDON, Th. BAKER, Rt. UPTCHER. Proved 30 Apr. 1582.

JAMES LARRANCE of Dovercourt husbandman, — '1581'. (Nuncupative.) (673)
He bequeathed to Wm. his son a cow and his cloak. He would not give any of his goods from his wife [at marriage?] but willed them to remain in her hands, she to be executrix. Witnesses: John COTINGHAM his master and others hereunder written [not given]. Proved 30 Apr. 1582.

WILLIAM PARKER servant with John COLE of Great Bentley, 23 Feb. 1581/2. (674)
To the poor's box of Great Bentley the money that John SMYTH of 'Horkesley' doth owe me after he hath paid my executor. To Susan AWSTEN of Great Bentley 3s.4d. To the poor's box of Thorrington 10s. that Wm. LOCKE of Great Bentley doth owe me. To John GALE, late servant with Wm. DANYELL of Tendring, my hutch with lock and key, my best hat, best shirt band, a pair of handruffs, best jerkin, best doublet, best pair of canvas breeches, and a pair of blue stockings. To Lawrence BYNDER of Great Bentley my best welted canvas doublet and russet breeches as they are tied together, frize jerkin with leather sleeves, a new pair of russet stockings, and a new pair of low shoes. To Anthony his son a sheep's leather jerkin new sleeved. To John my master COLE's son my wether sheep. To Anne DURRELL my dame COLE's daughter my white ewe sheep, but the lamb (if it stand to health until able to [be] put from the dam) to John WENT my fellow servant. To Emme MUNT my dame COLE's maid my russet ewe with her lamb by her side. The residue of my goods to John COLE my master, whom I ordain executor. Witnesses: John BACKLER, John DEARE, John BUSHE writer. Proved 23 Mar. 1581/2.

WILLIAM ROLPHE of Helions Bumpstead (co. Cambridge [*sic*]), 23 Nov. 1568 and 11 Eliz. (675)
To Rd. my son £40, half within 3 years after my decease, half within 3 years ensuing; if he die before, the £40 to Basil his son at marriage. To Joan my daughter £4 and 1 cow, or for default of a cow 20s.; if she die before, equally divided among her children at marriage. To Eliz. my daughter £5; if she decease before, to be divided among her children, Abraham her son shall have the greatest part, but if she have no more children then the £5 to Abraham at marriage. To Mary my daughter £5 and 1 cow, or for default of a cow 20s.; if she decease before, equally among her children, To Kath. my daughter £10 at marriage and my great brass kettle that I last bought. I will that Wm. my son pay Eliz. STUBBINGE £6 13s.4d. and 2 seam of barley at 21. To Wm. my indenture of lease and years to come and 2 kine that I have of the Master and Fellows of the Queens' College in Cambridge of a tenement and lands in [Helion] Bumpstead called Hempstead Hall; if he decease without issue, the lease to Rd. my son, permitting Eliz. now wife of Wm. to have her dwell-

ing therein for a whole year afterwards, the lord's rent due to the College only [to be paid], and paying her £40. The rest of my goods to Wm., whom I ordain executor. Witnesses: Peter LYNDSELL, John POOLE, NICHOLAS the writer. Proved 27 Mar. 1582.

WESTON WARNER of Langham single man, 5 Apr. 1581. (676)
To the poor of Langham 20s. To my sister CHILLON 40s. To Anthony BORODALE beside that I owe him 10s. To my brother John WARNER 40s. and Geoffrey WARNER 20s. and to my brother John my tenements at the church gate. The rest of my goods to the disposition of my executors, whom I ordain Th. SADLER and John. Witnesses: Th. WARNER, Anthony BORODALE, Geoffrey WARNER, John WARNER, Th. FARROR, Th. SADLER. Proved 9 May 1581.

WOLSTONE BARINGE of Thorrington, 26 Jan. 1581/2. (677)
To James and Daniel my two sons each 6 bushels of wheat and rye at harvest next, a store pig, 1 sow and half her pigs, 1 pewter dish of the best, half the brass, half the tubs, a cart, 1 pair of querns, 1 horse, and 1 colt; they shall pay Amy my daughter 40s. out of the same. To them each 1 cow, James to have the garled cow. To each of my sons a featherbed, 1 iron wedge of the best, 1 piece of cloth, 1 axe, and 1 hook, saving that Amy my wife shall have a gown cloth of the same. To Daniel my best scythe and James a shirt cloth. The rest of my goods to my wife, whom I make executrix. Witnesses: John HUBBERD, Philip KIDMUS, Matthew SAWKES. Proved 23 Mar. 1581/2.

GILLIAN widow of George BROWNINGE [abode not given], 31 Jan. 1580/1. (Nuncupative.) (678)
She gave to her eldest daughter Dorcas her best bed, the 2nd bed to Agnes her daughter, the 3rd to Anna, and the 4th being the worst to John her youngest son; more to Dorcas her father's hutch; and the hutch at the chamber door to Agnes; to John her cupboard; and her money equally divided amongst her youngest children, with the rest of her movables. This she affirmed again 2 days after, before the wife of Th. HOPPER and others, when she requested Th. PEIRSON and Rt. LITHERLAND to go into her sollars and take view of such things as there were, to which Rt. she reposed her trust for the placing of her child and the equal distributing of her movables. Administration committed, 7 Feb. 1581/2, to Rt. LETHERLAND.

RICHARD BOWSEY of Terling husbandman, 27 Oct., 22 Eliz. [1580]. (679)
To 'Levinge' and John BOWSEY my sons and Mgt. WADE my daughter 20s. apiece to be paid by Joan my wife out of my lands called Lingwoodes. To Ambrose BOWSEY 5s., his brother 'Just[yne]' 10s., and their sister Jane BOWSEY 5s., all at 20. If Joan my wife die before, James BOWSEY my son, whom I make executor, shall pay the rest of the money orderly. To Mgt. my daughter 1 featherbed which I lie on. To 'Leving' and John each 1 featherbed. The rest of my goods to be divided in even portions among 'Leving', and Mgt. after my wife's decease. I ordain John executor and Rt. CRACKBONE my neighbour overseer. Witnesses: Nich. WARRENER the writer hereof, Rt. CRACKBONE, Wm. BRETT, Fabyan FOKES. Proved 10 May 1581.

JOHN SOLE of Witham husbandman, 25 Apr., 22 Eliz. [1580]. (680)
To Peter son of John FAIREHEAD of Witham farmer my messuage in Witham called Gybes in the fee [manor] of 'Hulbredge' [now Howbridge] Hall in Witham, in the tenure of John CARTER tanner; on condition that John the father may hold a lease of the messuage from Michaelmas next ensuing, or after the end of the lease of John CARTER if he have any, to the end of 40 years, paying Peter the rent of 20s.; Gybbes to remain to Peter; if he decease before 21, to Elias FAYREHEAD his brother. The leases for 40 years shall be to the use of John FAYRHEAD. To my two brethren Rd. and Wm., if living, £10 by 20s. yearly out of the rent; if both be deceased, £5 to the poor people of Witham an £5 towards repairing Witham chuch. I ordain John executor. Witnesses: Th. GRENE of Witham husbandman, Edw. HALES clerk, vicar of Witham. Proved 10 May 1581.

ALEXANDER USBOUNDE [OSBOUND *in margin*] of Hatfield Peverel husbandman, 1 May 1581. (681)
To Mgy. my daughter my customary tenement called Woodhouse Crofts in Hatfield at 18; if she decease before, to Joan my daughter at 18; if both die before, to Geo. OSBOUND my brother. To Joan my freehold tenement called Lockes and 1 garden plat called Masons garden in Hatfield at 18; with remainders to Mgy. and to Joan my wife for her life, she to keep the house and barns in good reparations, and after her decease to Geo. She shall have the profit and occupation of my 2 tenements during my children's minority in consideration that she bring them up to 18. To her all my goods, whom I ordain executrix. Witnesses: James WILLMOTT, Th. NEWMAN, Matthew JENEE. Proved 7 June 1581.

JOHN ALLEN senior of Dovercourt, 31 May 1580. (682)
To the poor people 3s.4d. To Rd. my son my house in which I dwell called Allens. To Joan my wife my house and land called Vales in Dovercourt for her life, not to waste any of my woods and timber there except for firing and fencing and to disburse yearly to repairing the wall 20s. After her decease, Vales to my son Wm.; if he die without heirs, to his brother Godfrey ALLEN. To Godfrey my lands free and copy in Great Oakley; if he die without heirs, to Wm. To my wife a posted bedstead and a trundle bedstead in the sollar, which sometime was her own, 5 chests (2 of them Dansk chests, the rest small) in my bedchamber, 4 milch kine and 6 ewes. To Agnes ALLEN my daughter £10, a milch cow, a featherbed, and a bedsteadle. To Mgt. a milch cow. To Godfrey my joined bedsteadle and bed which I lie on, the greatest chest in my chamber, and 2 milch kine. To Wm. a posted bedsteadle, a featherbed, 1 great chest next the biggest in my chamber, and 2 milch kine. To my wife £4. To Wm. £10. To Godfrey my cart and 1 plough with a coulter and share, my bay horse called Dunne, my old mare, and my young horse called Byrd. To my wife my horse called Brown. To Rd. my mare called Hobb, a plough with a coulter and share, a pair of wheels with the tumbril, and a seam of wheat and a seam of barley at Michaelmas after my decease. To my wife 12 bushels of rye and a seam of barley to make her malt. To Godfrey 12 bushels of rye and a seam of barley. My wife and Godfrey shall occupy and dwell together in the 'said' farm of Mistress LAMBE's called East House from Michaelmas after my decease for a year, then she to depart and to have all her said goods except she can otherwise agree with him. To her a brass hanging in the backhouse and a salting trough which sometime were her own. To Godfrey my long salting trough. To Rd. the shortest salting trough and the lead in the backhouse. Godfrey and my wife shall have all my wood for firing and keep all the said beasts and cattle bequeathed in any wise with meat and fothering [fodder] until Easter after my decease; therefor they shall have all the hay and straw on the lands I hold. I will my wife to be the governor of Mgt. and have the use of her goods until she is 20 or married. To Mgt. the residue of my goods after my wife's decease. To every one of my servants and my godchildren 3s.4d. To the poor people of the parish a seam of barley, i.e. each ½ bushel so far as it will reach. To Eliz. FRENCH my kinswoman 20s. To my wife's daughters Agnes MUNSEN 2 ewes and Susan BREDGE an ewe. The residue of my goods to my wife, Godfrey, Wm., Agnes and Mgt. equally between them. I make my beloved wife and Godfrey executors. I ordain for supervisor Rd., and for his pains a seam of rye. Witnesses: John SACKE at 'marche' [marsh?], John BREDGE junior, Th. PANNET, John COTTINGHAM. Surrendered his copyhold lands in Great Oakley to the lord by John BREDGE, James BAYLYE, Rd. ROFFE, Gilbert WODE, tenants of the manor, 6 Apr. 1581. Memorandum that my heirs or executors which shall have the use of lands pertaining to the 'town' [parish] put in trust by the townsmen to me shall redeliver them at the request of the churchwardens and so for the use of the town. Surrendered, 7 Apr. 1581, his copyhold lands to the Queen's Majesty, lady of the manor of Dovercourt, by John SACKE junior bailiff, Th. PANNETT and John ALLEN junior, to the use of his Will. Proved 8 June 1581.

JOHN SMYTHE of Weeley yeoman, 3 Apr. 1581. (683)
[Religious preamble.] To John my son my 2 kine called Garle and Golde. To my godson [not named] a wennel calf and an ewe lamb and to Rd. my son John's son an ewe lamb, all to be delivered to John presently to their use, he entering into bond

for delivery with the increase thereof, at 21. To Henry GAWNSLEY my son-in-law my sorrel horse, my daughter Alice GAWNSLEY a cow, Anne GAWNSLEY my god-daughter a wennel calf, and Wm., Th. and [blank] the three children of Henry, each a lamb, all to be delivered to Henry likewise. To Geo. my son a cow, a cupboard, a trundle bed, a flockbed, a table, a joined stool, a candlestick, 2 pewter platters, a chair, a spit, and 20s. To Philip my son 40s. To 'Josian' my daughter 1 cow and 20s. at 21; I will that she shall remain with my wife at her appointment until then. To John CHRISTMAS my servant 20s. and an ewe sheep at 21. To Kath. DEATH 10s. To Rose COLLEN my servant a lamb. To Geo. and Th. POTTER my wife's sons each a cow at 21. To the poor people of Weeley 3s.4d. The rest of my goods to my wife, whom I ordain executrix. Witnesses: John HAMER, Samuel WILKINE, Matthew FISHE, John GOODAY, Wm. CHAPLIN. Proved 19 June 1581.

ANNE RELESON of Little Bentley, widow, 12 May 1581. (684)
To the poor's box 5s. To Geo. RELESON my son 3 milch kine, viz. the great Northern cow, 'Bruster', and a black 'shilde' [piebald] bullock. To Geo. my best featherbed, 1 holland tablecloth, 3 table napkins, 2 of the best hutches, 3 pewter platters, 3 pewter dishes, 3 pewter porringers, 3 saucers, a basin, 2 saltcellars, 6 pewter spoons, 2 candlesticks, my best cauldron, best great kettle, best little kettle, a little brass pot, a scummer, a dripping pan, a fire pan, a spit, a cobiron, a trammel, a chair, and 1 of the best cushions. To Anne RELESON my son John's daughter 3 milch kine, viz. the red 'shylde' cow, Black String, and a black bullock, and 4 ewes and 4 lambs by their sides. My executors shall take an indifferent man and my supervisors another to divide these sheep and their lambs. My executors to have the wool of the 4 sheep and their lambs and the commodity of the 3 kine towards the keeping of Anne until Michaelmas after my decease. To Wm. and Rt. sons of Geo. SMYTHE each 2 ewes and 2 lambs and 10 lb. of pewter, to Th. SMYTHE their brother 1 cow and 10 lb. of pewter, and to Constance SMYTHE their sister 2 ewes and 2 lambs; all at 18. To Geo. SMYTHE that married my daughter 20s., on condition that he keep WILBOYE until he is 21. To Wm. BRIGGES 2s. to buy a lamb with it. To Thomasine BROWNE and HORTON's wife each a petticoat. The rest of my goods to Geo. and my wife, whom I ordain my executors. I constitute overseers Geo. MARTIN and Rt. WADE dwelling both in Little Bentley. Witnesses: John P[ER?]YE the elder, Rt. WADE, John BUSHE writer. Proved 3 July 1581.

RICHARD TEWED of Stanway yeoman, 26 May 1581. (685)
To Mgt. my wife 3 pewter dishes, 1 featherbed next the best, and 1 brass pot next the best. To Th. my son 1 cow and 1 bedsteadle that is drawn with curtains in the sollar. To Wm. my son my sow hog. The rest of my goods to John my son, whom I ordain executor. Witnesses: Th. PAWFFELD, David LENNT. Proved 27 July 1581.

HENRY SWALLOW of Great Bentley, 11 June 1581. (686)
To Th. SWALLOW my brother my 2 beasts now in the occupying of John NEWMAN of Great Clacton, to be delivered before Michaelmas after my decease; if he die before, to Wm. my brother's son. To my three sisters, viz. Barbara, Ellen and 'Joyzan', each 6s.8d. The rest of my goods to John BACKLER my father-in-law, whom I ordain executor. Witnesses: Rt. KELER, John BUSHE. Proved 8 July 1581.

JOHN WEALE of Earls Colne yeoman, 27 Oct. 1578. (687)
To my daughters Susan, Grace, Mgt., Sarah and Anne WEALE, each £5 at marriage or 21. To my sons Wm., Henry and John my youngest each £5 at 26 [*sic*]. The rest of my goods to Joan my wife and John my eldest son, whom I make executors. Witnesses: Hum. TREEK, John TREGGE, Wm. ADHAMS clerk [vicar of Earls Colne]. Renounced by the executors; administration committed to John WELD, son of the deceased, 10 May 1581.

ALICE widow of Robert LAMBE of Greenstead-juxta-Colchester carpenter, 3 Mar. 1580/1. (688)
To the poor folk of Colchester 30s. and of Dedham 10s. To Rt. LAMBE, son of my daughter Alice widow of Th. LAMBE of Greenstead, £12 at 24 and to Wm. her son

£12 at 24; if both die before, the £24 equally among Anne LAMBE daughter of Alice and Eliz. NEWMAN, 'Wellshyan' NEWMAN and Anna NEWMAN, daughters of my daughter Eliz. wife of Edw. NEWMAN sailor of Alresford. To Alice LAMBE my daughter my posted bedsteadle with a featherbed in the lower chamber. To Eliz. NEWMAN my other featherbed. To Anne LAMBE, Elizabeth, 'Wellshyan' and Anna NEWMAN 25s. apiece and 7 milch beasts, with the residue of my goods, which shall be sold and the money divided and paid at marriage or 24. I ordain executors Henry USBORNE of Colchester glover and John VIGORUS of Stratford (co. Suffolk) fishmonger. Witness: Rt. LEWIS. Proved 27 July 1581.

THOMAS CULVERTON of Earls Colne, 10 July 1581. (689)
To the poor in Earls Colne 3s.4d. and to the reparations of the church 15d. which is already paid in cloth for the desk. To my two daughters Thomasine and Joan CULVERTON all my goods, except my apparel, to be equally divided at 20. To Thomasine my lands called Pery Croft, Coxe Croft and Sede Croft holden of the manor of the Priory in Colne; my lands there holden of the [manor of the] Earldom being 3 crofts called H[a?]shes; 2 acres in the Common Meadow; and Tyle Kiln Croft. To Joan the tenement in which I dwell with the garden and orchard holden of the manor of the Priory and a croft now divided into 2 called How Field holden of the Earldom. I ordain Rt. PERSON my father-in-law my executor, provided that he see my two daughters brought up, except that they in the meantime marry. Witnesses: Barthw. CHURCH, Th. BREDGE, Th. POLLYE, Th. ALLEN, Wm. BONNER, 'Benyt' WATSON, Henry ABBOTT, Rd. WILLIAMSON. Proved 5 Sept. 1581.

THOMAS PAYSE of Hatfield Peverel labourer, 24 Aug. 1581. (690)
To Rt. PEVERILL and John AUNGER my two sons-in-law all my goods part and part like, whom I make executors. Witnesses: Alex. WILLMOTT, John HATCHMAN. Proved 5 Sept. 1581.

ALICE ONYON of Little Sampford widow, 14 Feb. 1580/1. (691)
To the poor of Little Sampford 3s.4d., of Great Sampford 6s.8d., and of Steeple Bumpstead 6s.8d. To Th., John and Rt. sons of the late Wm. ALLEN my son each £3 6s.8d. at marriage or 21 and Agnes and Barbara his daughters each 40s. at 21. To Th. a flockbed in the sollar behind the chimney and to Agnes another flockbed being the maiden's bed. To Th. ALLEN my godson, son of Th. my son, 1 little silver spoon, a pair of sheets, and 5s., and Mary daughter of Th. my son 5s. and a pewter platter at marriage or 21. To Rt. ALLEN my son 1 horse now in his occupying. To Rt., Edw. and Henry his sons each 20s. at marriage or 21. To Th. ONYON my godson, son of Rd. ONYON my son, 40s. at 21, and Rt., John, Zachary and Matthew, and Mary, Frances and Thomasine, daughters of Rd., each 5s. at 21 or marriage. To Rt. ALLEN son of Mgt. my daughter 1 silver spoon; Mgt., Alice, Jane, Anne, Eliz. and Bridget daughters of Mgt. each 5s. at 21 or marriage; and Barbara daughter of Mgt. a flockbed, 2 joined stools, a yellow cushion, and a red hutch at marriage or 21. To the children of Edw. CHAPLIN and of Barbara his wife my daughter, i.e. Edw. a silver spoon with an acorn and my lesser brass pot and Th., Peter, Alice, Barbara and Mgt. their children each 5s. at marriage or 21. To Barbara my little press in my chamber, a pewter platter, and the hutch in the maids' chamber. To Edw. MUMFORD my godson, son of Edw. MUMFORD and of Alice his wife, my daughter, 1 silver spoon, and Agnes and Alice their daughters, each 5s. at 21 or marriage. To the children of Joan CRANE my late daughter, i.e. Wm. and Alice, each 20s. at 21 or marriage. To Mgt. SMYTHE my servant a pair of sheets and a bushel of wheat, Agnes GOSE that was my servant 3s.4d., and John HASTLER my servant a lamb. To Barbara CHAPLEN my daughter my great wicker chair. To Th. ALLEN my son 20s., and James son of Wm. ALLEN 10s. at 21. I will that £6 13s.4d. which remaineth in my hands to the use of Geo. ALLEN my son late deceased, which was given him by my late husband Th. ONYON, be paid thus, to the children of Joan my daughter, widow of Lionel CRANE, each 3s.4d. at 21, Th. my son 26s.8d., the two children of Rt. my son, i.e. Rt. and Edw., each 20s., and the children of Wm. my son 40s. amongst them all, according to a note dated 20 Feb. 1573/4. To Wm. ALLEN my servant, son of Wm. my son, my lease and

term of years in the tenement and lands called Parkers which I hold of Rd. ONYON my son, on condition that Wm. my son's son permit Thomas my son to occupy the lands and tenements called Hownesbrigges in Old and New [now Great and Little] Sampford so long as my lease continue, so that Th. perform the covenants in the lease of Hownebrigges and pay Wm. yearly 40s. towards the rent of Parkers. The rest of my goods to Wm. HALES my son's son, whom I ordain executor. I ordain my well-beloved son Rd. ONYON and Edw. CHAPLEN my son-in-law overseers, and for their pains 6s.8d. Witnesses: Rd. SMYTHE, Edw. CHAPLEN, Wm. VIGORUS. Proved 12 July 1581.

THOMAS RAWHEAD of Manningtree shearman, 2 May 1580. (692)
I ordain my uncle and cousin Wm. GONNE [GOUNE?] of 'Braxted' and Abraham GONNE of Manningtree to receive and recover such goods and debts to me due and with the same to repay debts I owe, and that which remaineth to be reserved towards the bringing up of my children [not named]. Witnesses: Chris. COCKE, John COLLENE. Proved 22 Aug. 1581.

THOMAS PARNELL the elder of [Saffron] Walden wheelwright, 26 Sept. 1581. (693)
[Religious preamble.] To Alice my loving wife my messuage in Walden called the 'Gree[n] Dragon' for her life; after her decease, to Josias, Th. and Samuel my sons, on condition that they pay Geo. my eldest son £10 at the porch on the south side of the church. To Alice COCKETT my daughter, Agnes PARNELL wife of Geoffrey GAMADGE, and Sarah PARNELL wife of Th. PUMFRETT, each £5. To Th. my son all my timber concerning my occupation and my tools, he not to trouble his mother by any ways. I ordain my wife executrix, to whom the rest of my goods. I constitute John COCKETT and Geoffrey GAMAGE supervisors, and for their pains 10s. apiece. Witnesses: Wm. BARRYE, Th. [blank], Geo. WOOD. Proved 19 Oct. 1581.

FRANCIS LISTER of Great Horkesley husbandman, 5 Nov. 1581. (Nuncupative.) (694)
He did will that Joan his wife should take all his goods in consideration that she should pay his debts. Witnesses: John BOUND parson of Great Horkesley, Geo. CHASE, John CLERKE of Great Horkesley. Proved 18 Nov. 1581.

JOHN WESTWOOD of Fingringhoe widow, 20 May 1581. (695)
To Joyce Westwood, my sister's daughter, 2 sheep of the best at her choice. To Anne SAYER and Th. KELLSYE each 20s. at 23; if both die before, to the poor people of Fingringhoe. To widow BURTON my old self-grow cassock, best russet petticoat, 2 kerchers, a quarter, and a neckerchief. To Anne SAYER 1 quarter and a neckercher. To John WESTWOOD my servant my best brass pot, my featherbed, 2 pair of sheets next the best, 2 diaper pillowberes, and a pitch pot. To Dthy. WESTWOOD my daughter my linen and woollen unbequeathed, the flockbeds, a little brass pot, an iron pot, and a posnet. The rest of my goods to John my son and Th. HARRIS my son-in-law, whom I ordain executors; if John doth not live to come home of this voyage, I give Joyce my sister's daughter my great black cow and Joyce LITLEBURY and Anne LITLEBURY my eldest and youngest brother's daughters my youngest red cow. Witnesses: Rd. WISEMAN, Rd. BRYAN. Proved 4 Sept. 1581.

EDWARD MALLSOMME of Lexden husbandman, 25 June 1581. (Nuncupative.) (696)
Being demanded by Rd. STOWERS of Lexden whom he would have to see his children brought up and his goods ordered, he appointed Rd. BRAGGE [and his?] brother both to see his children brought up and to dispose of his goods to their use. Witnesses: Rd. STOWERS, Rd. AYLEWARDE. [No probate clause.]

JOAN COOLE of Boxted single woman, 12 May 1570 [*sic*]. (697)
To the poor 13s.4d. To Jasper son of my brother John COOLE 13s.4d. To Mgy. HUNTAM, my brother John COLLE's daughter, my great kettle and 13s.4d., Agnes CHANDLER his daughter, 13s.4d., my red coffer and my basin, and Alice COOLE his daughter 13s.4d., my long chest and a platter. To Rachel MILLES my best blanket; John COOLE 13s.4d.; Jeremy COOLE 13s.4d.; Alice CHANDLER 5s.; Jeremy CHANDLER 5s.; Rd. CULPACKE 6s.8d.; Wm. CLERKE 6s.8d.; Joan COOLE 3s.4d.;

Rose COOLE daughter of Nich. COOLE 3s.4d.; and James MORRIS 3s.4d.; all to receive their legacies in 4 parts over 4 years. The rest of my goods to Stephen son of Jasper, whom I ordain executor. Witnesses: Th. NEVARD, John COOLE, John NEVARD, James MORRIS. Proved 2 Oct. 1581.

JOHN COCKSON of Tollesbury labourer, 11 Nov., 23 Eliz. [1581]. **(698)**
To the poor of Tollesbury 20s. Toward the making of a new pulpit 12d. To Edw. CLEMENT my house that I dwell in, my cupboard, best trundle bedstead with best bed, and quern. To Eliz. SMYTH a flockbed that lieth upon the sollar; Gilbert son of John SMYTH my biggest brass pot and 2 platters; middle John SMYTH my little brass pot and 2 platters; Eliz. CLEMENT my biggest kettle and 2 pewter platters; Th. SMYTH a kettle and 3 pewter dishes; and to John SMYTHE the younger 2 posnets and 3 pewter dishes. The table and the form shall remain at the house to the use of Edw. CLEMENT. To Joan CLEMENT my part of a lease now in the hands of my brother[-in-law] Wm. HUTT [HURT?] for the term of years. The rest of my goods to John BRASFOOT, whom I make executor. I appoint overseer John COURTMAN. Witnesses: Rt. GROVE, Wm. AKLYE, Th. RICHMOND, Henry GYLL. Proved 17 Nov. 1581.

MARGARET TRIGGE of Elmdon widow, 8 Nov. 1581. **(699)**
To TRIGGE my son my powdering trough; John son of John 1 calf; Henry TRIGGE my son 1 brass pot and 1 pair of sheets; Wm. TRIGGE 1 latten and 1 pewter basin; and my daughter Kath. TRIGGE my lead, best brass pot, saffron grounds, my cupboard furnished, 3 porringers, 1 pewter basin, and my best latten basin. To Mary TAYLER daughter of Henry TAYLER 1 pewter platter and 1 pewter dish, to be delivered to Mistress Mary MEAD for her behoof. To Mgt. THORTON 1 old petticoat, 1 pewter platter, 1 pewter dish, 1 porringer, and 1 stock of bees. To Mistress MEAD wife of Reynold MEAD 1 latten strainer. To Th. SEARLE and John SEARLE each 1 hive of bees. The rest of my goods to Wm. and Kath. to be equally divided. I ordain Wm. executor. Witnesses: Th. CLOUGHE, John TRIGGE, James ENGLISHE. Proved 13 Dec. 1581.

JOHN PYTTYE of Great Chishall carpenter, 21 Feb. 1580/1. **(700)**
To Wm. PYTTYE my son my term of years in a close (5 acres) in Chishall, being part of Barons. To Agnes my wife all my goods, whom I make executrix. To Rd. my son my interest and term of years in half a close (5 acres), i.e. 2 acres, in Chishall next Bilden land. To the poor of Chishall 6s.8d. Witnesses: Wm. COOKE, Wm. BIRD, Wm. FORDHAM, Wm. WALLIS the elder. Proved 13 Dec. 1581.

JOHN HARDINGE the elder of Witham yeoman, 20 March 1580/1. **(701)**
To John my son all my lands free and copy in Witham, on condition that he suffer Jane my wife, his mother, to have a convenient portion of the house where I dwell for her own habitation and half the fruit yearly growing in the orchard for her life and pay her for her sustentation £4 yearly and to Clement, Wm. and Henry my sons, and Prudence, 'Emelyn' and Eliz. my daughters £6 13s.4d. apiece at 18 or marriage; if John die, my lands to remain to Clement on like conditions. To Henry my chest at the bed's feet. To the poor of Witham 3s.4d. The residue of my goods to my wife, whom I make jointly with John executors. I make Adrian SMARTE of Braintree overseer. Witnesses: James STANFORTH, Wm. SAFFOLDE, John GRENE, Edm. SWANSON, Rt. CLERKE, Nich. DAY clerk [not the rector of Witham], Frs. SEA vicar of Ulting, writer hereof. Proved 15 Dec. 1581.

RICHARD WAKELIN of Hempstead, 19 June, 23 Eliz. [1581]. **(702)**
To Joan my wife 2 acres of copy ground for her life; after her decease, to Rd. the son of John my son. To my wife all my goods. To John my son 1 cow. Witnesses: John LUDDINGTON [vicar of Great Sampford], Rd. BAKER, Rd. WESTLY, John WESTLYE. Proved 12 July 1581.

JOHN WORTHE clerk, parson of Great Bromley, 8 Aug., 23 Eliz. [1581]. **(703)**
To be buried in the chancel of Bromley. To Joan my wife a good cow (to take her

choice), my grey mare with the foal, 10 bushels of rye, and all the household stuff that she brought to me when I did marry her, my sow and her 4 pigs, 2 silver spoons (she to take her choice of my 6 spoons), 1 pair of sheets that she made of late, the third part of my wood, and half of my poultry. To Prisca CLERKE my wife's daughter 1 cow. My hay shall be equally divided between my wife and her and my children. I appoint my wife executrix. Witnesses: John SEAMAN the writer, John STENE[R?], John HARRIS, Rt. STANTON. Proved 26 Aug. 1581.

THOMAS REIGNOLDES of Great Bromley, 2 June 1579. (704)
To Agnes my wife my best featherbed, my worst cupboard next the entry, 8 pieces of pewter (4 platters and 4 dishes), 2 saucers, 2 latten candlesticks, 1 latten chafing dish, 2 kettles (the greatest with a bail, the other of 3 gallons), best brass pot, my middle posnet with iron feet, a fillet pan, a frying pan and a spit next the best, a chair, a stool, my great hutch that hath ledges on the lid, a little hutch that her linen lieth in, my table in the parlour, a tablecloth, 2 towels, a tub, a firkin, a keeler, a drinking pot, 2 salts, a form, and the little new salting trough. To my wife 4 milch neat (2 of the best and 2 at my executor's discretion, so that she shall not have the worst cow of all), 6 ewes, 2 sheats, 4 hens, a cock, 2 geese and a gander, 2 ducks and a drake, 3 comb of rye, a comb of oats, 2 bushels of wheat, and my sorrel bald mare with a panel and bridle; if she embezzle or convey away any of my goods, she shall be void of all that I have given her. To Joan BIRKETT my sister 2 bushels of rye. To David STONE the younger 1 bullock. To the poor people of the parish 3s.4d. The rest of my goods shall be equally divided between my two sons John and Th. I make executors John and John THURGODE of Harkstead (co. Suffolk). Witnesses: Rt. MAYNARD, Wm. STEVEN, John BLOSSE the writer. Proved 13 Mar. 1581/2.

JOHN WILLOWES of Elmdon labourer, 7 June 1581. (705)
To Mgt. my wife for her life my house and lands free and copy; after her decease, to John my son; on condition that he put in bonds to Rt. SEARLE and Rd. HUMBERSTONE for performing my Will and for payment of £10 each to Henry my son and Joan my daughter. Joan shall have 1 bedchamber next the street door with free egress and regress until she be married. All my movables to my wife, whom I ordain executrix. Witnesses: Th. CLOUGHE, Rt. SEARLE, Rd. HUMBERSTONE. Proved 27 Mar. 1582.

MATTHEW WEST of Great Bromley single man, 21 Oct., 23 Eliz. [1582]. (706)
To John MONTE of Great Bromley all my copyhold lands and tenements, on condition that he pay Wm. and Joseph MONT his sons £10 each, also Constance MONT his daughter £30 at 21 or marriage. To John ABRAHAM my kinsman £3. To Stephen MUNT my godson 20s. To the poor people 20s. To my farmer [lessee] John JENYTOR 20s. To John, Mgt. and Joan MUNT each 20s. The residue of my goods to John MUNT, whom I make executor. Witnesses: Chris. MANLYE [MAULYE?], Wm. MAN, Stephen MUNTE. Proved 13 Jan. 1581/2.

MARGARET SMYTH of Dovercourt widow, 12 July 1581. (707)
To the poor people 6s.8d. and 1 seam of barley. To 'Leom' SMYTHE and Susan SMYTHE that late were the daughters of Nich. SMYHE my son 40s. apiece at 21 or marriage; after my decease, Rd. ALLEN their father-in-law to have the use of the money until then. To Eliz. PARNELL and Mgt. that late were the daughters of young John SMYTHE 40s. apiece at 21 or marriage. More to Mgt. 20s. likewise. To Christian the daughter of Th. SMYTHE 40s. at 21 or marriage. To Thomasine BARNABYE my servant a flockbed that she lieth on, a pewter platter, a candlestick, and a salt. To every godchild that I have 12d. To Roger PAKEMAN and John HARVYE each 2 bushels of wheat and 2 bushels of barley. To John HARVY all the 'leapers', fans and sieves that I made oatmeal withal except 1 fan. To my sister Joan FOWNDE and her two daughters Mgt. and Susan each 20s. To my brother BROWNE's children 6s.8d. apiece. To my daughter-in-law Rd. ALLEN's wife 2 bushels of wheat. To my daughter-in-law Eliz. FRENCH 3s.4d. To John son of young John SMYTHE deceased 40s. to be kept by Wm. SILVESTER until his apprenticeship be expired. To

John GRAYE 1 sheep. To John LAYNE a flockbed. To John CONVIAS' wife of Wix my kinsman 6s.8d. To John LAYNE £6 13s.4d., on condition that he abide and continue in my service for my life. At my burial my executor shall bestow a sheep, bread, cheese, drink or other such necessaries as they think meet to make the poor cheer withal. A sermon shall be made for the edifying of the people at the day of my burial. The rest of my goods shall remain amongst young John SMYTHE late my son's children, Nich. SMYTHE's children, and Christian SMYTHE, equally divided. I ordain executor Wm. SILVESTER of Dovercourt, and 30s. for his pains. I ordain supervisor Th. LECHE, and for his pains 5s. Witnesses: Rd. ALLEN, John HARVYE, Th. LEACHE, John COTTINGHAM. Proved 6 Mar. 1581/2.

JOHN HEWE *alias* STALLWORTHE of Great Chesterford yeoman, 4 Feb. 1580/1. (708)

To Th. REVE my son-in-law and Joan his wife my daughter and her heirs my messuage in Great Chesterford wherein I dwell, with the buildings, orchards, yards, closes and garden; and my arable lands and wood grounds there, except my other messuage there in the occupation of one Wm. REIGNOLDE the younger; all holden by copy of court roll of the manor of Great Chesterford; suffering Eliz. my wife to have the use of the parlour with lock and key for herself without paying any rent and finding her meat, drink, and apparel, washing and wringing, and the use of the hall, kitchen, well and such like necessaries at all times; also finding at their own costs meat, drink, harbouring, and clothing for my son Wm. HUGHE *alias* STALLEWORTHE for his life. To Henry HARVEY my other son-in-law and Mary his wife, my other daughter, my other said customary messuage. To my wife all my goods for her only use. I make her and Th. executors. Witnesses: John PAMFLIN, John SWAN, Wm. HANGETT. Surrendered to the Queen's Majesty [owner of the manor] by John SWAN gentleman in the presence of John PAXTON gentleman, customary tenants. Proved 12 Jan. 1581/2.

RICHARD CHASE of Ardleigh weaver, 22 Jan. 1581/2. (709)

To Sybil my wife 1 bed which is half-headed, 2 cow beasts with 1 cow bullock, a sheep with the profit, 2 hutches, 2 tables, 2 kettles, 2 pewter dishes, 1 pot, 1 pair of malt querns, 1 piece of old pewter, the brewing vessels, 2 small chairs, the churn with the cheesemotes, 1 flitch of bacon, my swine (saving 1 sheat which I give to Wm. my son), and my poultry. To Rt. and John my youngest sons each £5 at 20, my wife to have the use till then towards their bringing up. To Nich. my son my best cloak, the posted bed on the sollar with the featherbed, the stained cloth hanging by the bed, my best shirt, the great hutch in the chamber, the latten chafing dish, the biggest kettle, my 'moule' [see no.501] spade, the table with the frame and form in the hall, 1 little table in the kitchen which should serve for a cheese, 1 'lare', 1 cow calf, and 2 ewe sheep with the profit, 1 trammel, 1 pulling hook, and 1 chair. To Wm. my eldest son 1 cow bullock, 3 sheep with the profit, the biggest brass pot, 2 pieces of pewter, 1 saucer, 1 old piece of pewter, 1 candlestick, 1 great 'maunde' [wicker basket], 1 cleaver, 1 pitchfork, 1 bill, 1 leather doublet, 1 russet jerkin, 1 canvas doublet, 1 lockram shirt, and 1 pair of russet hose. To Rd. my son 1 bed, 1 latten pot, 2 pewter dishes, 1 saucer, 1 old piece of pewter, 1 candlestick, 1 pair of new quern stones, 1 cheese 'layre', 1 puke coat, and 3 sheep with the profits. The rest of my goods to Wm. and Rd., whom I ordain executors. Witnesses: Lawrence LYDE clerk [vicar of Ardleigh], John STEVEN the elder and the younger, Leonard PYKE. In the hearing of us, the witnesses, he did give to his wife the keeping and pasturing of 4 cow beasts until Michaelmas after his death, reserving to his executors 3 calves and 1 quarter of cheese; also to her 10 bushels of rye then in the sollar and 1 remnant of cloth to make the said two little children coats. He did appoint Lawrence LYDE supervisor. Proved 10 Feb. 1581/2.

NICHOLAS HILLIERD of 'Salcott Wigborough' [now Salcott] weaver, — 1581. (710)

To Mgy. my wife her wearing linen and her apparel and cloth already provided to make her more apparel so that she have need of it and wear the same. To Th. MYNKES my loving friend 1 new jerkin and a pair of upper gaskins, both violet colour, in consideration of the payment of 2s. to the tailor which made them. To Wm. son of Wm. BASTWICKE of Hatfield Peverel my 2 kine and all other my goods, on condition that he Wm. the elder do keep my wife with meat, drink and all other necessaries for her life, which Wm. I make executor. I make Geo. CHAPMAN surgeon of Boreham supervisor. Witnesses: Th. MYNKES, John SPARROW clerk [rector of Virley], writer. Proved 6 Mar. 1581/2 by Wm. BASTWICK, to whom administration committed.

RICHARD DYNES of Cressing, 9 Jan., 24 Eliz. [1581/2]. (711)
To Thomasine my wife my customary tenement and lands called Petfyrs for her life; after her decease, to my three sons, i.e. Th., John and Rd. To Rd. a featherbed. To my three daughters Agnes £4 and 'Gryzzell' £5, each at 21 or marriage. To my wife a casting sheet, a holland bearing sheet, and a diaper tablecloth. The rest of my goods to my wife towards the virtuous education and bringing up of 'Gryzzel'; after her decease, to my children equally parted. I ordain John KINGE my brother-in-law and my wife executors. Witnesses: Peter WITHAM, Frs. RAVEN, Henry BACON. Proved 6 Mar. 1581/2.

JOHN BEANE of Fordham husbandman, 1 Mar. 1581/2. (712)
I will that my goods be appraised by four or five honest neighbours. For the bringing up of my three children John, Dthy. and Mary. I ordain John BAKER and Wm. PETCHYE executors and also 'gardiners' [guardians]. To them all my goods, household stuff and cattle, viz. 7 beasts, 3 mares, 5 sheep, 2 yearling calves and 2 yearling colts, in consideration of the pains and charges for bringing up my children, paying themselves such as in conscience they shall think meet, reserving the overplus for the children's use at marriage or 20. If both children die before, the implements and profits which shall surmount the charges for bringing them up shall be delivered, half to my sister Mary BEANE and half to my three other sisters, Martha, Mgt. and Kath. Witnesses: John BAKER, Wm. PECHYE, Emery ROCHESTER gentleman, Rd. KIRBYE preacher, the writer. Proved 6 Mar. 1581/2.

RICHARD TITTERILL of Little Sampford yeoman, 27 Mar. 1581. (713)
To Collet my wife my lands called Shepecote Field (6 acres), a parcel of land called Carters (2 acres), and 3 closes called Potters Field (20 acres), all in Little Sampford, until Wm. my son is 23, when he shall enter on them. To my wife my tenement in Old [now Great] Sampford in the tenure of Gregory ROBERTES carpenter with the lands belonging (16 acres), for 5 years after my death; to Geoffrey my son. To Gregory my close in Little Sampford called Birdeswell (6 acres) at 22, until which time my wife shall have the use. To her my close in Little Sampford called Matthew or P[itt?] Croft with a pightle adjoining (5 acres) until my son John is 22, then to him. To Gregory and John each £40 at 21. To Alexander TITTERILL my servant and Joyce HELY my maid each 1 bullock. To Joan PAULE 10s. at 18; my wife shall reasonably apparel her. To the poor people of Little Sampford 6s.8d., 6s.8d., of Old Sampford 3s.4d., of Thaxted 3s.4d., and of Little Bardfield 2s.6d. To Wm., Geoffrey, Gregory and John each 1 joined bedsteadle, 1 flockbed, 1 milch cow and 2 sheep at 21. The residue of my goods to my wife. I appoint her my executrix. Witnesses: Peter PURCAS, Austen LINDSELL, Nich. HUMFREY, John MORE. Proved 12 July 1581.

JOHN WARNER of Langham yeoman, 30 July 1577. (714)
To the poor of Langham 40s. To Frances [blank] my sister 40s. To my executors 20s. and my supervisor 5s. The rest of my goods in the house and without, in the yards and the fields, to Mgt. my wife. She shall dwell in my house and occupy all my houses and lands towards bringing up my children for 5 years after my decease, laying 20s. yearly on the reparations of the houses and discharging the lord's rent. To her 8 loads of wood yearly during the term out of my grove at Boxted and 4 loads out of my other grounds, she paying for the making and carriage; and the same number of loads and no more shall remain to the house for fuel after the 5 years until my heir come to occupy the house and lands. After the 5 years, they shall be letten by my executors for 6 years, so that John my eldest son, Th. and Rd. each have £20 from the rent. My wife shall have the first offer in the hiring of the house and lands. After the 11 years John to have the house and lands, 1

acre of meadow called Hunters acre only excepted, on condition that he put in bonds with sureties to my executors for payment of £66 13s.4d. as followeth: to pay for 8 years after entering on the house and lands £5 a year to the use of Wm. and young John my son, £20 to John my youngest son at 24, and John my eldest son shall lay in bonds for the yearly payment to Th., Rd., Wm. and John the younger each £3 13s.4d. for 2 years. [Followed by several lengthy provisos of little significance.] I ordain John UPTCHER my brother-in-law and my brother Th. executors, and for their pains 20s. I constitute Th. DEPNAM supervisor, and for his pains 5s. Debts due to me: my brother Th. oweth me for malt 40s.; Th. DEPNAM of Boxford (co. Suffolk) oweth me 18s.8d. Debts I owe: to young John WARNER 10s.; to TOWLES 3s.4d. Witnesses: Th. SADLER, Wm. SEAMAN, Th. WARNER, Th. FARRUE writer hereof. Proved 13 Dec. 1577 [*sic*].

JOHN STORYE *alias* BEALLE of St. Leonard, Colchester, cooper, 26 Oct. 1579. (715)

[Religious preamble.] To the poor of the parish 30s. To Geo. STORYE *alias* BEALL my son my wearing apparel and my tools belonging to my occupation. To the child that my wife is now pregnant with £10 at 21, she to have the use of the £10 and to put in bonds with one surety of 40 marks for payment. To Helen my wife her wearing apparel linen and woollen. To Rt. DIXSON my godson, Wm. DAGLES my boy, and John BALLE and Rt. BRERLY my prentices, each 6s.8d. To Rt. DIXSON the elder and Geo. DIXE sailor, both of St. Leonard's, each 20s., whom I nominate supervisors. The residue of my goods to my wife, Geo. my son and Alice my daughter equally parted. I name Geo. executor. To Geo. my house wherein I dwell; my wife shall have the dowry of the third part of the same for her life as the law will permit. Witnesses: Wm. RAM writer hereof, Rt. DIXSON, Geo. DYX. Proved 12 Mar. 1579/80.

ROBERT BALLE of White Colne yeoman, 29 Nov. 1578. (716)

To Joan my wife for her life my tenement and lands I bought of Wm. HOYE deceased and my 2 crofts called Bridges Fields there bought of my brother John BALL of Little Horkesley yeoman, all in Wiston (co. Suffolk), on condition that she stand bound to my executor in £100 not to claim any dower or third part of my lands. After her decease, to John my brother and John his son. To them my tenements and lands called Church Field and Jenkins in Great Holland which I purchased of Th. CORBY and my lands called Smales (21 acres) and a piece of meadow purchased of Th. CARTER and Mary his wife and one John HOLLAND, all in Great Holland. To my wife half my household stuff, 4 kine and 20 sheep, and 5 seams or quarters of hard corn and 5 of soft corn on my farm. To my brother and his son my manor or capital messuage called Bart Hall with the lands belonging in White Colne, and my title to the manor or capital messuage called Loveney Hall and the lands belonging [in Wakes Colne] now demised, which late were of John SYDAYE of Great Horkesley, and my title to such money as the manor and lands are mortgaged for; also my title to such lands in Colne Engaine as I have in mortgage of Rt. BUNTINGE for £40. To Th. CLERKE a cottage and 3 acres of land in White Colne. I ordain that my brother shall be 'his' guardian during 'his' nonage. If Rd. SIDAYE my son-in-law shall be living at Michaelmas come 12 months after my decease and enter into bond with two sureties to my executor for payment to him of £6 13s.4d. for every year unexpired of my lease of my farm called Barwick [now Berwick] Hall [in White Colne], he shall have my lease; but if he refuse to be bound, my lease shall remain to my executor towards the performance of my Will. If I shall happen to have any issue begotten at the time of my decease, my lands and tenements devised to my brother and his son shall remain to such issue. To John TURNER of Crepping Hall [in Wakes Colne] esquire £3 6s.8d., Matthew CRACHRODE esquire £3 6s.8d. Rt. READ of Earls Colne 40s., Wm. RYCE of Bures St. Mary [co. Suffolk] 40s., Rd. FOOTE 10s., Mary daughter of my brother John BALLE 40s., John SMYTHE of Great Horkesley the elder £3 6s.8d., Anthony SMYTH of Great Horkesley the elder 6s.8d., Geoffrey, John and Rd. SYDAY and Christian SYDAY now wife of John BURTON of White Colne, each 20s., and Rt. SYDAYE my godson 40s. To my servants Rt. HASSETT, Rt. UNDERWOOD, Rd. BYNES, and Mgt. FOOTE each 40s.., and Geo.

FEYSYE 6s.8d. The residue of my goods to John BALLE my brother, whom I ordain executor. I ordain John SMYTHE of Horkesley and John FLUDD of Colchester notary public supervisors, and to John FLUDD for his pains 40s. To Wm. HALLE of Colchester the elder 10s., John GURLIVANT of White Colne 20s., Geoffrey his son 20s., Rd. FOOTE's wife 10s., and Edith wife of Wm. CLERKE 10s. To Mgt. KINGE my servant 6s.8d. Witnesses: John FLUDD, Edw. FULLER, Th COSYN. Proved 26 Nov. 1579.

NICHOLAS WILBORE of Colchester woollendraper, 26 June 1577. (717)
To Emme my wife my lands free and copy in West and East Mersea in the occupation of PLATFACT [*sic*], for life; to remain to Edw. my son; for want of issue to Nich. my son. To my wife my capital messuage wherein I dwell and my rentary with 2 gardens in St. Martin's parish for life, to remain to Nich.; for want of issue to Edw. All my ceilings, glass and glass windows, benches, portals, hangings, doors, locks, settles, wainscots and keys to remain to the capital messuage for ever and not to be removed by my wife. To Nich. £10 at 21. To Anne my daughter £30 at 18 or marriage; if she marry without the consent of her mother and friends before 18 she shall not have £30; to her my stone pot lipped and footed with silver and the 2 silver spoons which I had of John PULLEN clothier, at age or marriage in form aforesaid. To Joan my daughter £10 as is limited to Anne. My wife shall have my silver goblet parcel gilt and my dozen silver spoons for life, and after to Nich., and the goblet to Edw. or else my executor to pay him £4. To my daughters Mary, Grace and Mgt. each £5 at marriage. To my brother Rd. WILBORE my furred gown I bought of Geo. HARRISON. To my sisters GRENE and CATLES and my cousin SYMNELL's wife each an angel. To my cousin SYMNELL my own shutting bow. To Matthew BROWNE's wife the gold ring that Mr LATYMER gave me. To my cousin Th. BUXTON my dagger and 2 arrows. To Wm. HILL 2 prickshafts. To Mr MOTT my mool spade staff with the prynes and to Matthew BROWNE my other mool spade. To my brother Edw. COMBES my gold ring. To my cousin Th. BUCKSTON's wife an angel. Rt. PLATFOOTE shall not be put out of his farm as long as he liveth but to have it for £6 a year. The rest of my goods to my wife, whom I make executrix; if she be minded to marry, he with whom she marry together with two sureties to enter into bond in £200 to my cousins Th. BUCKSTONE and Rd. SYMNELL for the performance of my Will. Witnesses: Rd. COLLETT, Matthew BROWNE, Rd. SYMNELL, Th. BUXSTON, Th. POLLIFOOTE, [blank] GRENE. Proved 1 Sept. 1579. Memorandum, 27 Sept., 20 Eliz. [1578], Nich. WILBORE did surrender the 2 tenements to the right honourable [John 2nd] Lord DARCYE, lord of the manor of West Mersea, by Th. BUXSTON in place of the bailiff in the presence of [blank] FEILD and Wm. FROKES.

GEORGE HOYE of 'Salcott Wigborough' [now Salcott] butcher, 6 Apr. 1579. (718)
To Jane my mother, wife of Rd. BAYLY of Colchester brazier, my tenement and ground in Acton (co. Suffolk) called Heynes for her life. To Rose my wife the remainder after my mother's death towards bringing up my children. To John my son my greatest brass pot at 21. To Kezia HOYE my daughter my joined table in the hall with the frame at 20. The residue of my goods to my wife, whom I make executrix. I make Nich. GRYFFIN my brother-in-law supervisor, and for his pains 3s.4d. Witnesses: Toby EDEN, John GALE, John SPARROWE clerk [rector of Virley], writer. Proved 27 Apr. 1579.

AGNES PAKEMAN of Wrabness single woman, 27 May 1579. (Nuncupative.) (719)
She gave to her sister Joan PAKEMAN all her goods, whom she ordained executrix. Witnesses: Agnes WRIGHT, Joan WYET. Proved 19 May 1579.

WILLIAM TURNOR of Wakes Colne husbandman, 9 Mar. 1578/9. (720)
To Alice my wife the parlour where I lie with the chamber over it for her life; to remain to my son John. To my wife 3 beasts (the whiteback bullock, the youngest red cow, the red 'howed' [for meaning see p. xvii] cow with a white face) and 7 sheep with lambs by their side. To her and John my tenements called Frostes and Lyrdwothes with a garden and 6 acres, 2 parcels called Smythes garden and Cattes

Mere, and lands called Cobesland or Cobbesseez (60 acres), together or divided as they can agree equally between them; after her decease, wholly to John. The rest of my lands and tenements free and copy to my son Roger, saving the house where UNDERWOOD dwelleth in, he to take his crop without paying anything. To Roger 1 cow and a seam of wheat. To Agnes LAWRETT, Rose TOWNSEND, father BARRETT and father HARMEWOOD each ½ bushel of wheat. To each of Roger's and John's children a sheep. To my maid Mgy. BRUCE and Agnes LAWRETT each a sheep. To John my great hutch, the great brass pot, rack for the spit, greatest candlestick, and 6 sheep with lambs. My wife shall have my brewing vat equally with John for her life. To them my corn in my barn and house and on my ground. The rest of my goods to my wife, whom with John I make executors. Witnesses: Rt. MONKE, John KEBBLE, Rt. WARREN, Th. UNDERWOOD, Th. SEYSTON, Geoffrey KINGE. The copyhold lands were surrendered in the presence of Th. SEYSTON, Rt. WARREN, John ALLCOCKE, Th. UNDERWOOD, and Wm. LAWRETT [tenants of the manor]. Proved 18 Mar. 1578/9.

WILLIAM RYDING [RIDINGE *in margin*] of Thorrington husbandman, 3 May 1579. (721)

To Susan my daughter £5 at 21 or marriage. If she die before, 20s. each to my sister's children, viz. Joseph, Simeon, Judith, Mary and Hester HUTTEN. To my cousins Judith HUTTEN 10s., and Simeon HUTTEN and Mary HUTTEN each 10s. at 21 or marriage. I will Kath. my wife to pay Wm. BUTLER of Thorrington the 30s. and to keep it until then. The residue of my goods to my wife, whom I make executrix. Witnesses: Wm. COLLMAN, John SMYTHE, Wm. BUTLER, John WYERD. Proved 23 June 1579.

WILLIAM HUTT the elder of Great Braxted yeoman, 10 Apr. 1579. (722)

To Wm. my son all my freehold lands and tenements, i.e. a meadow lying at Allingford Hedge [*recte* Bridge?], my long orchard or croft lying before my door where I dwell in Great Braxted, and my other orchard being towards Allingford Bridge which I call Wren Park, which [I] rent yearly to the owner of May House and Faycelands in Great Braxted [for] 8d. The rest of my freehold lands are in Little Tolleshunt [now Tolleshunt Knights], Goldhanger, Little Totham and Great Totham. To Wm. my cottage in Great Braxted called Rawteys wherein I dwell with the lands belonging. To Tabitha my daughter 40s.; to Joan AYLETT my daughter 40s. yearly to be paid out of my lease of Pages and my cottage called Cuteys, until £15 be paid; to Th. and Joan her children £3 6s.8d. at 21. To my son John 40s. above his portion already paid. To [blank] WALLAKER my servant 1 of my best kine and 1 of my best sheep. To my cousin John HUTT the younger 40s. and my best gown. To Leonard SKINNER 1 bullock. To my servants Mgt. AYERS 2 good ewes, Anne WILSON 6s.8d. and Timothy CLEMENT 1 cow bullock at 20. The rest of my goods to Wm. HUTT my son, whom I appoint my executor. Witnesses: Arthur BREDE gentleman, Simon BREWER, John HOWE, Edw. HALES clerk [vicar of Witham]. My executor shall pay John BECQUITHE eldest son of Tabitha my daughter £10 at 23; if he decease before, £5 equally divided between Arthur and Elias her other children at 21 and £5 to my executor. To Arthur and Elias each 20s. at 23. To the poor people of Great Braxted 10s. Witnesses: Arthur BROCKES gentleman, Simon BRUAR weaver, John HOWE of Great Braxted, Edw. HALES clerk [vicar of White Notley]. Proved 8 Jan. 1579/80.

THOMAS UNDERWOOD of Fordham husbandman, 5 Nov. 1579. (723)

To Wm. my eldest son, Ellen and Kath. my daughters, and John my son, each 40s. at 21. The rest of my goods to Joan my wife, whom I make executrix. Witnesses: Th. UPTCHER, Th. REASON. Proved 9 Jan. 1579/80.

MARGERY SPINNYE of Black Notley widow, 11 March 1579/80. (724)

To the poor people 2s.4d. To my son-in-law John BRIDGE for the use of his three children [not named] 10s. To him and my daughter Eliz. such goods as they now have and my featherbed, he to pay 'Zachis' SPINNYE my son 10s. for the same. The rest of my goods to Zachis, whom I ordain executor. I appoint my good friend

John BEDLE of Notley overseer. Witnesses: Wm. CHAPMAN, Walter OWSOLDE, John LAMSON, John WEST, Davy ANDERSON. Proved 22 Mar. 1579/80.

MATTHEW STUTEVILE of Wormingford minister, 30 Dec. 1578. (725)
To be buried in the churchyard. To six poor folks 2s. and to those that shall bear my body to the funeral 16d. The residue of my goods to Mgy. CLARKE widow, whom I make executrix. Witnesses: John SEMER, Nich. CLERKE, Th. COE, Th. MANNOCKE. Proved 4 Feb. 1579/80.

JOAN CHASE of Elmstead widow, 19 Aug. 1579. (726)
To the reparations of Elmstead church steeple [i.e. tower] 20s. To every one of the children of John STEVEN of Elmstead 12d. To Kath. LIBBIS 12d. To John HECKFORD my nephew the 2 beasts that he hath already and 2 other beasts, half the dry bullocks saving the 2 oxen, and £5 in Mr Edm. PYRTON's hand, which he shall take up. He shall pay SPALDINGE that I owe him. To Joan GRIMMELL my maid 20s. To Kath. MERRILL 5s. To David HECKFORD and John HECKFORD my nephews all my household [stuff] part and part like, saving that David shall have the new kettle. To Hugh BANINGE 2s. To John HECKFORD my black horse. The residue to David HECKFORD, whom I ordain executor. Witnesses: Kath. MERRILL, Joan GRYMMELL, Rd. CAZER writer hereof. Proved 28 Aug. 1579.

THOMAS BEANE of Fordham carpenter, 18 Mar. 1577/8. (727)
To Agnes my wife my tenement called Akermans and the copy lands belonging holden of the manor of Mount [i.e. Mount Bures], both free and copy, for her life, on condition that she keep thge house in good reparations, such to be adjudged by the tenants of the manor, surrender thereof delivered to Rt. POTTER bailiff and John MORE tenant of the manor. After my wife's decease, to John my son, on condition that he pay Th. and Edm. the sons of John LEA 20s. by equal parts. My son shall pay Agnes and Mary my daughters each 20s. To Martha my daughter my best feather-bed after my wife's decease. To my daughters Martha, Kath. and Mgt. 20s. apiece at marriage. To Agnes and Mary each a sheep. If John die before my wife, not having any heir, the house and lands shall be sold by John CLAY of Bures and John MORE of Mount Bures and the money equally divided among all my children. To the poor of Fordham 2s. To John my carpenter's tools. My wife shall have the rest of the years of the lease of the house wherein I dwell. The rest of my goods to my wife, whom I make executrix with Geoffrey NEWTON of Stanway. I ordain John CLAYE supervisor, and for his pains 3s.4d. Witnesses: 'Barthamus' ANDREWES the writer hereof, John JOLLYE. Proved 30 Oct. 1579.

THOMAS MORRIS of Dedham shearman, 1 Feb. 1579/80. (728)
[Religious preamble.] To Mr [Edm.] CHAPMAN of Dedham preacher 20s., Mr RICE minister 10s., Simon HURLESTON [*recte* HARLESTONE] of Cavendish [co, Suffolk] preacher 10s., and James ANDERTON minister 6s.8d., to be paid shortly after my burial. To the poorest people of Dedham 10s. To my sister Elizabeth £5 at 10s. a year. To Nich. ROSE her son my 7 pair of shearman's shears in my shop (5 pairs whereof are French shears) and all other stuff belonging to my occupation at 21; if he die before, all to be sold by my executrix, half the money given to such as fear God and love the Gospel of Jesus Christ which are known to have most need, to the glory and praise of Almighty God, by my wife's good discretion, and the other half to Eliz. my sister if she live or else to the poor. To John BRAXTED my wife's kinsman 20s. and his sister [not named] 20s. To Th. SWANSON my wife's kinsman 10s. I will that she deliver to Simon HARLESTON 10s., he to bestow it as I have appointed. To the making of the long bridge to 'Barfolde warde' [towards East Bergholt, co. Suffolk], if there be any made that men may travel over, 6s.8d. To the repairing of Stratford [St. Mary] Bridge [over the Essex-Suffolk county boundary] 3s.4d. The rest of my goods to Eliz. my wife, whom I ordain executrix. I make supervisor my neighbour Henry SHERMAN of Dedham, and for his goodwill 10s. Witnesses: Henry SHERMAN junior, Wm. PETFEILD, Hugh MAYE. Proved 8 Mar. 1579/80.

JOHN STONARD of Wormingford yeoman, 20 Sept. 1579. **(729)**
To Anne STONARD my eldest daughter the house wherein I dwell with barns, stables, yards, orchards and gardens, for her life; after her decease, to John son of my late son John deceased. To Anne and Marion STONARDE my two daughters the rest of my copyhold lands to be equally divided, for their lives; after the decease of the longer liver, to John son of John. To Anne and Mary 20s. [each] at 21. To Anne JENNER my kinswoman 6s.8d. at 30 [*sic*]. The rest of my goods to Anne and Mary, whom I ordain executrices. I request my very faithful and well-beloved friends Wm. LYNN and Th. SADLER to be supervisors. Witnesses: Wm. LYNNE, John PRESNE, Th. SADLER, John LAYE. Proved 18 Mar. 1579/80.

JOHN SUMMER the elder of Pattiswick husbandman, 6 Feb. 1579/80. **(730)**
I will that Agnes my wife shall have my chamber wherein I lie and all things therein, also my 2 several butteries being parcels of my tenement in Pattiswick called Adam Bacons, with free ingress, egress and regress, for her life, without any let of John my son. She and John shall occupy jointly the residue of my tenement and lands belonging, portion and portion like for her life, on condition that he use her in all things as his natural mother, also that they pay Agnes and Mary SOMMER my two daughters each 5 marks in the 6th year after my decease. After my wife's decease, the tenement to remain to John for his life; after the decease of John's next heir, to remain to my children's children. To Wm. SUMMER my son my tenement called Godsave with the lands, pastures and meadows in Pattiswick for his life; after his decease, to John SUMMER my godson, Wm.'s son. To Joseph SOMMER my son 6s.8d. To Mary and Agnes each 1 bullock. The residue of my goods to my wife and John my son evenly parted. I make them executors and supervisor Edw. GRENE my son-in-law, and for his pains 6s.8d. Witnesses: Geo. PARE, Th. WADE, John SPARHAUKE. [No probate clause.]

EDWARD WELDINGE of Little Walden in parish of [Saffron] Walden yeoman, 26 Nov. 1579. **(731)**
To Edw. my son Tinne Croft ($1\frac{1}{2}$ acres). To Sarah WELDINGE my daughter my messuage with the land, meadow and pasture holden of the manor of Chipping Walden, if Edw. die before 21 or Sarah before 18, to the other. To Mgt. my wife the messuage till Sarah is 18 towards the bringing up of her small children. To Samuel my son 2 of my best beasts and 2 of my best horse after her decease. The rest of my goods to my wife, whom I make executrix. Witnesses: Henry WEBB, John FREMAN, Geo. WAKEFEILDE, Rt. NOTAGE. Proved 1 Dec. 1579.

THOMAS KETTELL [KETTLE *in margin*] of Pattiswick husbandman, 2 Aug. 1579. **(732)**
To John KETTELL my son the 16s.4d. in the hands of my cousin Anthony GYMBLETT of Coggeshall, which debt is due to me on 26 Aug. 1579; to Eliz. his daughter 16d. out of the 16s.4d.; my brother Rt. KETELL of Fingringhoe shall have the 15s. and keep it for John until he cometh out of his apprenticeship at Michaelmas 1582. To John my 12 sheep, Eliz. my wife's daughter my 3 lambs, and Mgt. my wife 4 sheep. Rt. shall use John's sheep as his own until John's coming out. To John my best flockbed and 1 pair of bedsteads in the chamber, $\frac{1}{2}$ dozen pewter, 2 platters, 4 pewter dishes, 2 saltcellars, 1 saucer, 2 small candlesticks, the biggest kettle without a band, 1 little kettle, 1 posnet, 1 spit, 1 tunnel, and 2 hutches (1 in the sollar, the other in the hall). The rest of my goods to Rt., to be executor. Witnesses: Th. ROWTEN, John CHAMBERLYN, John BUCKE, Wm. CHAMBERLYN, Anthony GYMLETT. Proved 1 Sept. 1579.

WILLIAM PEREN of Elmdon yeoman, 30 May 1579. **(733)**
To the poor 2s. to be bestowed by the collectors. To Mgt. my wife my lands in Stansted Mountfitchet for her life, she to make no claim to any other my lands; after her decease, to John PEREN my son. To her 1 cupboard, 6 sheep, 2 roods of saffron ground (1 being raising ground, 1 being 2 years set), my best featherbed, the bedstead wherein I lie, hangings in the parlour, great red chest, 4 buffet stools, with my linen, brass and pewter not given. To John and Wm. PEREN my sons jointly my lease of the Parsonage of Elmdon, with my houses and cattle not otherwise given,

and my carts and ploughs, for the better occupying of the lease or farm. To John my table in the hall and my form, 2 pair of sheets, 1 tablecloth, my lead, and best chest (my great red chest excepted). To Wm. my great brass pot, 2 pair of sheets, 1 tablecloth, and my table in the parlour. To my daughter Kath. SEARLE 40s. and 1 rood of saffron ground 12 month set. To Wm. SEARLE my godson, Geo. SEARLE and Dthy. SEARLE each 2 sheep. To Agnes PEREN my daughter 2 acres of land bought of John PARKER in the [Common] Fields of Elmdon; if she die before 21 without issue, to John and Wm. To her 1 bullock, 1 rood of saffron ground 12 month set, 1 featherbed, 1 tablecloth, and 2 acres of tilth to be sown with wheat, rye or barley at my executors' discretion who shall sow it at their costs only for 2 years after my decease. They shall find to their mother meat, drink and houseroom and my parlour such as shall be comely and necessary during the years of my lease; if she mislike of such, they shall pay her yearly £5. The rest of my goods to John and Wm. equally, whom I make executors. Witnesses: Th. CLOUGHE, John DRYVER, Frances YLGER. Proved 28 July 1579.

WILLIAM BURLE of Black Notley, 30 May 1577. (734)
In consideration that Mgt. my wife honestly keep and bring up all my children until 20 and my houses in sufficient reparations, without felling any of my timber. I give her all my houses and lands free and copy in Black Notley for her life; after her decease, to Wm. my son; if he die before 21, successively to John the younger my son and to Th. my son; provided that which of my sons shall have them shall be friendly in helping and gentle towards the bringing up of all the other of my children to the uttermost of his power. If my wife die before Wm. is 21, Rt. RANKE, my brother-in-law, shall occupy my houses and lands until then and bring up my children. To Geoffrey my son £3 within 2 years after my decease, Th. and John the younger each 40s. at 20, Barbara, 'Dennys' and Ellen my daughters each 20s. at marriage, Mary my daughter 10s. within 2 years, John the elder my son 20s. within 4 years, and Mgt. my daughter 20s. at marriage. If my wife marry again, she shall enter into bond in £100 with sureties to my overseer for performing my Will or else my gifts to be void. The rest of my goods to my wife, whom I ordain executrix. I will John FRANKE and Rt. RANKE to be overseers, and for their pains 3s.4d. apiece. Witnesses: Wm. BRETT *alias* SPOONER, John WREST, Th. TANNELL, Rt. EVERED, John FRANCKE. [No probate clause.]

RICHARD GENT of West Bergholt weaver, 14 June 1579. (735)
To Rd. my son a red cow, a black 'howed' [for meaning see p. xvii] bullock, a colt, a square framed table with a framed form, and a 2-eared pan, all to be appraised by four indifferent persons chosen by my executor and then delivered to Henry CREKE of Little Horkesley my brother-in-law so that he put in bond to Rt. RAYSBOOTE of Colchester my brother-in-law for the delivery of the stock or the value thereof to Rd. at 20. If he die before, 40s. of the stock to Geoffrey RAISBOOTE my sister's son and the residue to John RUDLAND my son-in-law. The rest of my goods to Alice my wife, whom I make executrix. Witnesses: Wm. DOBNEY, Rt. RAISBOOKE [*sic*], John HUBBERD. [No probate clause.]

JOHN LAVENDER of Little Bentley yeoman, 15 Jan., 22 Eliz. [1579/80]. (736)
To Edm. son of Edm. the elder my son my bed. To Olive daughter of my son John LAVENDER a coverlet. To John 2 beasts and 30s. which Henry BRUSTER oweth me, half of my linen in my hutch, 3s.4d. which Peter SMYTHE oweth me, and half my debts. The residue of my goods to Edm., whom I make executor. Witnesses: Wm. WOFFIN, Mgt. WOFFIN, Edm. LAVENDER. Proved 5 Feb. 1579/80.

ROBERT BUNTINGE of Colne Engaine husbandman, 5 Jan. 1577/8. (737)
To 'Em' my wife my messuage wherein I dwell, with the buildings, yards, orchards and gardens and my lands free and customary in Colne Engaine, for her life; on condition that she keep and bring up Agnes BUNTINGE daughter of Kath. my sister for her life. All to remain to John PRYOR my sister's son, he paying yearly to Agnes 20s. or else keeping her with meat, drink and apparel, also paying Rt. BALLE of White Colne £40 in 1581 for redeeming of certain lands there belonging to my

messuage which Rt. hath now in mortgage, and paying my sister's children 5s. apiece, the poor of Colne Engaine 10s., and towards the reparations of the church 5s. To Agnes wife of John THURSTON 1 sheep. To John PRYOR my long table and the form in the hall after my wife's decease. To my godchildren 12s. apiece. The rest of my goods to my wife, whom I make executrix. I ordain my well-beloved friends Wm. LESINGWELL and John PRYOR supervisors to be aiders to her, and to each for their pains 5s. Witnesses: John [LAW?]RENCE the elder, John LEFINGWELL, Th. LEFINGWELL, Wm. VIGERUS the writer. Proved 13 June 1579.

AGNES BAKER of Wakes Colne widow, — 1571 [*sic*]. **(738)**
To Wm. KINGE my son a table, a form, a kettle the best, and 1 hog. To the poor people 12d. To Joan ALLEN and Alice MYLLES my daughters a brown cow, 4 bushels of wheat, and 4 of barley, equally parted. To Alice MILLES a cupboard, a mustard quern, a basin, a strained cloth, and 3 chests. To Kath. TURNER and Christian WEBBE my daughters a red bullock, 4 bushels of wheat and 4 of barley, and 3 chests, equally divided. To John son of Wm. KINGE a lamb. To Joshua BAKER a [word illegible] and a bushel of wheat. To Geoffrey [MIL?]LES, Bridget ALLEN, Geoffrey WEBBE, John TURNOR, and Christian RUFFLE each a lamb. To Christian daughter of John WEB a bushel of wheat. The residue of my goods to Geoffrey my son, whom I ordain executor. Witnesses: Wm. TURNOR, Th. SEVER, John WEBB, Th. VINCENT. Proved 27 Apr. 1579.

EDWARD SAMWELL of Great Totham, 23 Oct. 1579. **(739)**
To the poor people of Geat Totham 20s., of Langford 20d., and of Heybridge 20d. To Rt. DOE my servant all my apparel except my 2 cloaks and my best hat, and a little brown bullock and the vantage. To my other three menservants each 20d., 1 hog and a lamb. To Mary and Olive DORRE my servants 20s. To my brother Wm. PECKE 2 angels to make him a ring and all my 'hopressor' [hop press?]. To my mother Mgt. SAMWELL 40s., 1 seam of wheat, and 1 seam of barley. To Joan HARVYE my mother-in-law ½ seam of wheat. To my aunt SAWKIN 2 ewe lambs. If my wife be with child and God give her a son, to him all my freehold lands, on condition that he pay his sisters each £30 when he is 21. My brother Th. SAMWELL shall have the occupying and letting of my lands during the nonage of my children and at their several ages to make an account of the profits and then pay them. The residue of my goods to my wife on condition that she bring up my children. I ordain her my executrix and Henry SAMS and Edw. SAMS supervisors, and for their pains each one bow of ewe. Witnesses: Lawrence AGAR [vicar of Great Totham, Rd. OWGHAM, Edw. SAMMES, Henry SAMMES. Proved 3 Dec. 1579.

CHRISTIAN ABELL of Colchester, 10 Mar., 21 Eliz. [1578/9]. **(740)**
To be buried in the churchyard of St. Giles in which parish I dwell. To Mistress Mary ROCHESTER my niece and goddaughter my bed. To my cousin Mgt. MALLOWES 2 cushions of my best, a candlestick, a basin, and my carpet for my table. To my cousin Eliz. ALLEN and Mary SAWEN each 2 platters; Kath. POORE, Emme POORE and Grace POORE each 2 pewter dishes and a saucer; Mary POORE 2 porringers and a saucer; Joan NICHOLLS a spit and a skillet; Wm. AYER's wife, my woman, a pair of sheets, a petticoat, a cassock of her choice, my white coffer, a pair of cobirons, a pair of blankets, a pillow, a pillowbere, and a kettle. To my cousin NICHOLLS a brass pot; Eliz. ALLEN a kettle; and Anne DEANE a cassock and a cupboard. To four poor women appointed by my executors to go to the church with my body each a kercher and to those four [men?] which bear me to church 4d. apiece. The residue of my goods to my executors, whom I make my cousin Wm. MALLOWES and Wm. BARRINGTON my neighbours, and to Wm. BARRINGTON for his pains a pair of my best canvas sheets. Witnesses: Th. TURNOR, Wm. AYERS, Rebecca AYERS. Memorandum, 7 Aug. 1579. She did nominate the women to go with her body to the church, viz. Eliz. BARRINGTON, mother SOME, AYER's wife and mother BERY. Her wood in her house and yard to be bestowed to the poor of St. Giles, AYER's wife to have 1 load of billet and 1 load of cubit. 2 Oct. 1579.

JOHN NORRIS of Great Totham, 3 Sept. 1579. **(741)**
To my daughter Joan NORRIS the biggest candlestick and a pewter dish. The residue

of my goods to Rt. NORRIS my son, whom I make executor. Witnesses: Lawrence AGAR vicar of Great Totham, Edm. WASTENER, Wm. FREER. Proved 30 Sept. 1579.

'TYTUS' DYNES of Bradwell-juxta-Coggeshall husbandman, 14 Jan. 1579/80. (742)
To be buried in Cressing churchyard. To Peter my son 1 cow, the price of 40s. and also 13s.4d. at 18; if he die, to Kath. my wife his mother. To Agnes CODWELL 1 black lamb. The residue of my goods to my wife. Giles PENSPAULE my father-in-law and John WOODWARD my brother-in-law to be executors. Witnesses: John HUBBERD, vicar of Cressing, Th. DYNES, John PENSPAULE, Proved 8 Feb. 1579/80.

ELIZABETH WHALE of Hatfield Peverel widow, 20 Sept. 1579. (743)
To my daughters Mgy. and Mgt. HARRIS the 4 years yet to come in the lease made to my husband and me by John STRAIGHT of Wethersfield (a parcel of ground called Gaulden excepted which I give to my daughter Anne AUGIER for the 4 years, not paying any rent). To Anne my best flockbed, cloth for a petticoat, and a piece of cloth ready to go making. To my daughter Margery my 2nd flockbed at 18 and Mgt. my 3rd flockbed at 18. To Agnes BERMAN which was my servant my best cassock. To Mgt. WATTSON my best russet petticoat. I appoint Rt. SWANSON to be overseer of my daughters Mgy. and Mgt.'s goods. The rest of my goods to my son John AUGIER, whom I make executor, he to bring up my son Nich. and my daughter Mgt. at his own charges until they come to their full ages, and John AUGIER to be 'gardiner' [guardian] to my son Rd. WHALE until he is 14. Witnesses: James ROBINSON curate, Rt. SWANSON, Th. PAGE, John HAYLE, Rd. POOLE. Proved 29 Oct. 1579.

WILLIAM GOODDINGE of [Saffron] Walden, 10 June 1579. (744)
To my father Rd. GOODDINGE and Annabel his wife my mother, £12 which Th. ADAM the younger son of Th. the elder, late of the 'Rose' [manor of Roose?] in the parish of Walden [oweth me omitted?]. To Mary BATEMAN £12. To Samuel GOODDING my brother all my apparel and 20s. To Annabel STRACHYE my grand-mother 40s. to be paid this side Cold Fair Day [the fair at Newport near Walden, 6 Nov. [1]]. To Mary GOODDING my sister 1 rood of saffron ground lying in the Long Lane turning to 'Jhurdlye' [Yardley in Thaxted] in the tenure of Th. MARTIN. To Dthy. GOODDING my sister ½ acre of saffron ground adjoining to the said rood. To Anthony GOODDING my brother 1 rood of saffron ground lying in a close leading towards Thaxted in the occupation of Alexander RAYE, which rood Mark HILLE must set of this present season at his own costs. The residue of my goods to my mother, whom I make executrix. Witnesses: John LARKE, Nich. REVE, Wm. BOYTON writer hereof. Proved 30 June 1579.

JOHN HARRE of Markshall husbandman, 23 Apr. 1579. (745)
To Alice my wife all my goods, implements and cattle, viz. 8 beasts, 3 bullocks, 1 horse, 1 mare, 7 sheep, 6 lambs, 1 hog, 6 sheats, my corn in the house, and half the corn on the ground. If she marry again, £9 6s.8d. to be equally distributed to my seven children, John, Anne, Wm., Mary, Mgt., Rt. and Th. HARRE before the day of her marriage. I ordain her my executrix. Witnesses: John RAND the elder and John RAND the younger. Proved 15 July 1579.

JOAN TOMPSON of Great Bromley, 10 Jan. 1579/80. (746)
To David STONE my brother-in-law 20s. To the poor 20s. To Th. STOW and Joan his wife 10s., and Eliz. STOWE 20s. To Mgy. SUMMERSON, my father-in-law's maid 3s. and a lamb. To John HARRIS my brother-in-law 3s., Kath. HARRIS 6d., Th. HARRIS 6d., and Wm. HARRIS 4s. To Mark BARKER 6d. The rest of my goods to Wm. CHURCHE and Mgy. CHURCHE my sister and brother[-in-law]. I ordain John HARRIS my father-in-law executor. Witnesses: John MUNT, John HARRIS. Proved Proved 19 May 1579.

[1] *The Description of England*, by William Harrison (ed. G.Edelen, U.S.A., 1968), p.396.

RICHARD FAWKENER *alias* STOCKMER of [Saffron] Walden, 9 June 1579. (747)
[Religious preamble.] To my daughter Eliz. my house wherein I dwell with the yards and buildings in Castle Street; if she die without heir, to my daughter Mgt. wife of Wm. MARSHALL. To my daughter Agnes 20s. to be paid by Eliz. within 3 years after my decease or at her marriage, 1 black coat which was her mother's, my best coat, 1 chafing dish, a posnet, 2 pewter dishes, and a saucer. To Mgt. 10s. To my daughter Dthy. 1 table that was her grandmother's and 5s. My brother-in-law Rd. PAGE shall have the oversight and governance of my house and Eliz.'s goods until she is 22 and the profits to redound to her benefit. To Agnes RABBETT my old covering called an 'hapharlott' [coarse coverlet]. The rest of my goods to Eliz., whom with Rd. PAGE I make executors, and for his pains 3s.4d. Witnesses: Nich. AYLEWARDE, Anthony THORNE, James CROFTE the writer. Proved 30 June 1579.

JOHN HAULLE of Lawford glover, 8 Apr. 1579. (748)
To my eldest son John £4 at 21. To my son Barthw. £4 at 21 and 1 double platter. To my sons Edw. and Rt. and my daughter Eliz. HAULLE each £4 at 21. To Rt. BROOKE the elder, gentleman, 3 does' skins already dressed. To my servant John POZKIN 2 horse hides of the best. The rest of my goods to Alice my wife, whom I make with Rt. COOKE executors. Witnesses: Matthew KETTS, Mich. CRAYNAME, Chris. HOWES, Rt. POOLE the writer. Proved 19 May 1579.

STEPHEN RULE of Great Sampford husbandman, 23 Feb. 1578/9. (749)
To Th. my brother 33s.4d. To my four sisters [not named] and my brother John's two children 2s.6d. apiece. To mother CLERKE my mother 5s. To Mary PEPPER 12d. The rest of my goods to Mgt. my wife, whom I make executrix. Witnesses: John BULLOCKE, John MOSSE, John STABBINGE. Proved 10 Mar. 1578/9.

JOAN THURGOOD widow, [abode not given], 13 May 1577. (750)
[Long religious preamble.] To Joan daughter of Geo. MEDE 1 little brass pan unbound. To every one of my son Rt. THURGOOD's daughters [not named] 20d. To John THURGOOD, son of my son John of Fairstead, my best chest where I now lie, great brass pot, 2 joined stools, and cupboard in the parlour, at 21 or marriage. To Agnes ORGAR my least chest, 1 brass pot broken on the side, 3 little pewter dishes, and a pair of towen sheets. The rest of my goods to my son John, whom I make executor. I freely forgive Rt. £20 that he oweth me. Witnesses: Wm. CARTWRIGHTE curate, John FREBORNE. Debts owing to me: of Edw. SAGAR 12s., of Geo. KINSEY 10s.8d. Proved 12 Dec. 1578.

JOHN MOYDE of Heydon, 5 Oct. 1579. (751)
To Eliz. my wife the house that I dwell in with the yards, orchards and buildings, for her life; after her decease, to Th. my son, on condition that he pay Eliz. my daughter £4; if he die without issue before my wife, the house to Simon my son and Joan, Anne and Eliz. my daughters equally divided. To Joan 1 acre of free land in Great Chishall [Common] Field called Alkesder Field next the land of Chishall Hall on the south and that of Rt. MOWLE on the north, the east head abutting on that of Th. HAGGAR. To Joan my cupboard, a pair of stools, a pewter dish, a platter, a kettle that was her mother's, and my 5 roods of copyhold land lying divided in the Fields of Great Chishall Hall belonging to the manor of Shingay [co. Cambridge]. To Anne and Eliz. each a pair of sheets, a pewter dish, a platter, a hutch, also my saffron ground, equally divided. The residue of my goods to my wife. I ordain her and Nich. WARYNE executors. Witnesses: Th. COOKE, Edw. MODYE. Anthony GODHAND. Proved 1 Dec. 1579.

ROBERT BARKER the elder of Debden yeoman, 30 June 1579. (752)
To the poor folks 3s.4d. To Agnes BARKER my daughter £20, my best coverlet, and 40s. to buy her a bed, but my wife to choose 5 of the best beasts, then Agnes to choose her 1. To John my son my lease and term of years of Wood Field which I hold of Mr WYSEMAN, he paying the rent, the corn growing there, Brendly Field (16 acres) during my term, 3 beasts or bullocks after the said choices, a bedstead, and a flockbed. To Joan ANDREW my daughter £10, Eliz. ANDREW her daughter a

cow, and Rt. ANDREW my godson 20s. at 18. To Blanche my wife all my lands and tenements [no details] for her life; the remainder to John. The residue of my goods to my wife, whom I make executrix. If any years remain of my lease in Tenderinges [Tendrings Farm, in Debden] after her death, to John. I appoint Wm. BOWTELL and John supervisors, and for their pains 3s.4d. apiece. Witnesses: Rd. HODSHON, Th. BOWTELL of Debden, Geo. BOWTELL, Lawrence NORCOATE. Proved 27 June 1579.

EDWARD CREFEILD [CREFFEILD *in margin*] of Messing yeoman, 18 July 1579. (753)
To the poor 10s. on the day of my burial and 10s. within a quarter of a year following. To Edw. son of Rt. CREFEILD my brother all my lands and tenements free and copy in the parishes and [common?] fields of Chapel *alias* Pontisbright and Great Tey, on condition that he pay Joan my wife yearly at the mansion [i.e. dwelling] house called Popes in Chapel in satisfaction of her dowry £3 6s.8d., also to Jane HUDSON my servant yearly 20s. If Edward die without heirs male, to remain successively to Rt., to Peter, and to Th. his brothers, and their heirs male, under like conditions. If my wife or Alice GARLINGE my sister-in-law or either of them die before Edw. is 21, the sums payable to them out of my lands shall remain to Agnes CREFEILDE, my brother Rt.'s daughter, yearly until Edw. is 21, except 40s. thereof to be paid to Agnes wife of Th. UNDERWOOD my brother's daughter. To Edw. 6 silver spoons; if he die before 21, to remain successively to Rt. and Peter. To Edw. my bed in the sollar wherein I lie, a flockbed and a featherbed, with the bedstead and ceiling, my great spit, my hutch at the chamber door, my almain corselet with the whole furniture, i.e. sword and dagger. To Th., Rt. and Peter each 20s. and Agnes 26s.8d. To John WEBB and Agnes WEBB each 10s. To my brother Rt. my best coat, best cloak, and best doublet. To Wm. FORD and Joan WRIGHTE each 3s.4d., Edw. FOOTE 1 lamb or 2s.6d. and all my arrows, Rd. BECQUITHE 1 lamb or 2s.6d., and Mary BARDWELL daughter to John FAKEN 10s. if living, if not to Eliz. his daughter. The rest of my goods, corn, money, and plate to my wife, whom I make executrix. I make John LUFKIN overseer, and 3s.4d. for his pains. Witnesses: John COCKERILL, John WARDEN, Clement COWELL, Wm. HYLLES. Proved 2 Sept. 1579.

HUGH WHITE of Coggeshall, [date not given]. (754)
To my daughters Agnes and Mgt. each £15. To Agnes the little counter table and little form in the parlour. To Mgt. the counter table and a frame above the chamber. To my wife [not named] £7 and my house for her life; after her decease, to my two children part and part alike. The rest of my goods to my wife. I will that she and Th. FICH her brother be executors. Witnesses: John LEE, Wm. CAVELL, Barnard BESLEY. [No probate clause.]

JOHN GROVE of Elmstead labourer, 25 Mar. 1579. (755)
To my daughters Joan, Eliz. and Dthy. GROVE each 3s.4d. at 21. The residue of my goods to Cecily my wife, whom I ordain executrix. Edw. LUFKIN, John SHEPERD, Rd. CAZER writer hereof, Joan PAYNE widow. Proved 27 Apr. 1579.

'PHILLIP' WYER of Great Oakley single woman, 12 Nov. 1580. (756)
To John NOBLE my nephew my little brass pot and 2 pewter dishes. To my father-in-law John MAWDLYE my tenement and lands in Kirby within the Soken and all my other goods. I ordain Mr Th. ROCHESTER, parson of [Great] Oakley, my executor, and for his pains 10s. Witnesses: Th. STOWE, Th. PALMER, Toby COOKE. The said day, she surrendered the premises in the presence of Toby COOKE, Th. STOWE and Th. PAGE tenants of the lord [of the manor] to the use of John MAWDLYE. Proved 18 Nov. 1580.

NICHOLAS PRATT of [Saffron] Walden, 26 Mar. 1579. (757)
[Religious preamble.] To Adam my son 1 featherbed, 2 pewter plates, 2 pewter dishes, 2 saucers, 1 candlestick, 1 great brass posnet, 1 spit, and 10s. To John my son and Eliz. CHAUNDLER my wife's daughter each 2 pewter dishes, 2 pewter platters, 2 saucers, 2 pair of sheets, 1 candlestick, 1 spit, 1 brass pot, and 10s. The rest of

my goods to Kath. my wife to use at her pleasure, whom I make executrix. Witnesses: James CROFTE, John BAKER, John DISEBEROW, John WEEKE. Proved 30 Apr. 1579.

PAUL SEAMAN of [Saffron] Walden yeoman, 19 Apr. 1579. (758)
To Paul my son my 7 acres of land bought of Mr Wm. SMYTHE gentleman lying in ground enclosed called Stone Close wherein Joan my wife shall have them for her life; after her decease, to Paul; if he decease without issue, to the rest of my children to be divided equally. To Mercy, Susan, Sarah and Annabel, my daughters, each 20 marks at 24 or marriage. Witnesses: John LASON, Rt. TARNTE [TARUTE?], John BANKES. Proved 30 Apr. 1579.

JOHN WOODWARD of St. Trinity, Colchester, 5 Oct. 1579. (759)
To my wife Ellen my dwelling house at 'Sheare' Gate, with all my goods, to give and to sell. I make her my executrix. Whereas she and I together purchased my house of old Rt. LADEN *alias* GLADEN and of his son Th., having a release of Th., the deeds were made and estate given to me and my wife, I give her my house. I make John BEWICKE of St. Giles overseer, and for his pains to be my wife's friend 20s. To my brother Rt. WOODWARD of St. Giles 20s. To Th. WOODWARDE of [blank] 40s. To my cousin Rt. LADEN all my apparel as a gown and 2 cloaks. All my debt in money, cloth and wool is to answer and pay my debts which I owe as followeth: to Mr BROWNE to pay 4 Aug. next £28; to John TURNER £7 6s.8d.; to Mr PERE 53s.4d.; to Mr BLOKE [blank] of wood [*recte* wool?]; I give Mr Bayly THURSTON £5; I owe Mr TEY of Ipswich [co. Suffolk] a bale of wood [*recte* wool?] £8 10s.; to John THORPE of [blank] £9. Witnesses: John BEWICKE, Rt. LADEN. Proved 27 [blank] 1578 [*recte* 1579].

JOHN OVERED of Hempstead, 22 Jan. 1578/9. (760)
To Agnes my daughter 20s. within a year after my decease; if she die before, 13s.4d. thereof to be divided amongst the rest of my children each at 21. To Eliz. my daughter and Rt. and Th. my sons each 10s. at 21. To John my son my cupboard in the hall after my wife's decease, and 2 of my best livery coats (1 of blue, the other of plunket [kind of woollen cloth]); the 2 white livery coats shall be sold, the price 10s., and the money to be employed to John's behoof until he is 20. To him my yew bow and my hand saw at 20. The rest of my goods to Agnes my wife, whom I ordain executrix. Witnesses: Wm. REIGNOLDE, Wm. AGNES, Henry LAGDEN, John ROLPHE, Rt. SHIPWRIGHTE, Wm. FARRANT. Proved 10 Mar. 1578/9.

JOAN WAKELIN of Great Oakley, 12 Dec. 1582. (761)
To John KEBELL my son my corn and hay in my houses and sheds, my table and form in the hall, 1 of my chests at his election, my hogs great and small, my bedstead in the chamber with the featherbed, a pewter dish, a platter, my great brass kettle, a black bullock, a salting trough, a pair of querns, a pair of sheets, a little kettle, a counter table, a spit the best, a cobiron, a chair in the hall, a cushion, and a candlestick. To Dthy. BETTS my daughter my other black cow, 3 porringers, my best hat, a fine sheet, a pair of fine pillowberes, a kettle of white brass of the least sort, a little chafer, a little chair, a basting ladle, 1 sheet, a pillow, a little table, and my silver whistle. To Mgt. KEBELL my daughter my bedstead that I lie on with the featherbed, my cupboard, a fine sheet, a fine pillowbere, a fine tablecloth of holland, my gown, a brass pot, my kettle of white brass of the biggest sort, 3 porringers, a great chest, a pewter dish, a platter, my best chafing dish, a joined chair, a cushion, a pillow, and a candlestick. To Edm. KEBELL my son my posted bedstead with the featherbed, a pewter basin, a kettle, and a roast iron [gridiron]. To Henry KEBELL my son a black bullock with the white face, a chest by the bedside, and a kettle. to Rd. KEBELL my son my brended cow called Shortbig, a table and trestles, a little brass pot, a pewter dish, a saucer, a little [blank], a coverlet, a pot with butter, a coffer, a salting trough in the milkhouse, and a pair of mustard querns. To Joan his wife a kercher, an apron, and 2 quarters. To Wm. KEBELL my son my great red cow, my brass chafing dish, a table in the chamber, a candlestick, a little pot with butter, and 4 cheeses. To Mary his wife my blue apron. To Rt.

KEBELL my son my mortar and pestle and 2 platters. The residue of my linen to Mgt. and Dthy. To Eliz. KEBELL a pewter dish and a platter. To my sister Mgt. BROUGHTON my frize cassock. To Joan CLERKE my servant my russet petticoat and a white apron. To Rd. a stained cloth in the chamber. The residue of my goods to John, whom I nominate executor. Witnesses: John UPGRAVE, Wm. AYLEWARD, Th. ROCHESTER clerk [rector of Great Oakley], the writer. Proved 21 Jan. 1582/3.

ROBERT SNODOUN [SNODONN?] of Berechurch, 12 Nov. 1582. (762)
To Ellen my wife 6 milch beasts. To Simon SARELLS, my wife's son, 2 draft oxen Black and Bell, my black horse and my sorrel mare. To Rt. SNODEN my son 2 bullocks Haste and Tawboote, and 2 horses. To Simon and Rt. my sons my cart, harness, yokes and chains, equally divided. They shall occupy these oxen, bullocks, horses and cart for the use of their mother and shall be at their mother's commandment at all times, so long as she keepeth herself a widow. To James BUTLER my son-in-law a calf and a pewter dish. To Anne my daughter his wife a flockbed after her mother's decease. To Mary my daughter a flockbed. To Joan MASON my sister a bushel of oats. My geld ox called Buck to be sold to buy lambs for the increase of Rt. To my wife, Simon SEARLES and Rt. all my household stuff and goods equally divided, to occupy together so long as she keep herself a widow. To Rt. and Simon my cart nag to go with the team for their mother's use, to be parted at 21. To Rt. my suckerel colt. To John BROWNE the elder and his son and daughter John and Mary an ewe sheep. To Rt. my 7 sheep with the increase to 21, then to have them all, also my 2 bullocks at 21 if they be spared or else to be sold to buy stover for the rest of the cattle. The rest of my goods to my wife and Simon, whom I make executors. To James BUTLER £5 and Simon £5 that are John HASSMYTHE's debt and the obligation that was NOBLE's to be divided part and part like. Witnesses: John BROWNE the elder, Wm. CHRISTMAS, James BUTLER, Mgt. CHRUSTMASSE, Simon SEARLES. Proved 1 Jan. 1582/3.

WILLIAM LANE of Little Oakley husbandman, 5 Nov. 1582. (763)
To Benet my wife all the goods which I had with her. To Wm. and Joan LANE my son and daughter the goods which were mine before I married, equally divided at 18, my wife to occupy them until then. I appoint her my executrix. Witnesses: John SALLOWES, Wm. HICKMAN, Andrew WEST. Proved 1 Jan. 1582/3.

EDMUND ROCHELL of Kelvedon, 19 Dec. 1583 [*recte* 1582] and 25 Eliz. [1582]. (764)
To the poor 6s.8d. to be delivered to the collectors. To all my children, i.e. Joan, Rd., John, Eliz., Agnes, Edm. and Wm. ROCHELL, 40s. apiece at 21 or marriage. The residue of my goods to my executors to bring them up in good order in the fear of God. I constitute Rd. NORTHIE my father-in-law and Eliz. my wife executors. Witnesses: John LAMBE, Rt. SLOWMAN, Henry PARSCELY, Anthony PICKNUTT, Walter RICHARDSON the writer. [No probate clause.]

HENRY ALLMAN of Bradfield, 20 Nov. 1582. (765)
To the poor 6s.8d. To my brother Th. ALLMAN 10s., my petticoat, and my russet jerkin. To goodwife CONVEN my mortar. To John COPER 12d. I give my household [stuff] and the rest of my goods to be sold by my executor with the counsel of my supervisor and this house to be let till Michaelmas next. My house and lands called Kents to be sold and the money to my three children part and part like, to my two sons Philip and Simon at 21 and to my daughter Mary at 18. I ordain my executor John MARTEN and for his pains 20s. and Nich. CONVEN supervisor and for his pains 3s.4d. Witnesses: Nich. CONVIN, Th. WAGE, Th. ALLMAN, Ralph SHEPHEARDE. [No probate clause.]

PRUDENCE SCRUTE of Fingringhoe maid, 14 Feb. 1582/3. (766)
To the poor 12d. To Agnes WOOD a lockram apron and a new holland quarter. To RICHMAN's wife an old red petticoat; Anne WALSTOME [WALFTOME?] the best black cassock; and Anne STRAUNGER's wife [*sic*] a frize cassock and an old russet petticoat. The residue of my goods to the discretion of my executor; Tobias MAKIN

my master to see my Will observed. Witnesses: Hugh RAYLAND, Th. SHARPE clerk [not the vicar of Fingringhoe.] [No probate clause.]

JOHN CUCKOE of Wix, 22 Jan. 1582/3. (767)
To my four daughters, i.e. Joan YONGE, Joan [*sic*], Mary and Mgt., each 1 pewter dish after the decease of Mgt. my wife. To Nich. my son my best jerkin, best breeches and best short hosen, brazen mortar, and best shirt after my wife's decease. The residue of my goods to my wife, whom I make executrix. Surrendered to Geo. TOOS bailiff and John CONVEN and Wm. BATEMAN tenants [of the manor], the same day. Witnesses: John CONVEN, Wm. BATEMAN, Geo. TOSE writer hereof. [No probate clause.]

THOMAS BRETT of Cressing bachelor, 8 Jan. 1570/1 [*sic*]. (768)
To the poor people of Chelmsford 6s.8d. and of Cressing 8s. To Joan SMITHE my sister £10 at Michaelmas 1573; if she die, to her sister Bridget. To my brother[-in-law] Wm. SMYTH £4 on the same day. To Joan SMYTHE my house in Chelmsford, being a smith's forge, in the occupation of goodman TYE the smith, for her life; after her decease, to Bridget. To Edm. SMITHE my brother[-in-law] my house and lands in Springfield. Edm. and Joan shall each pay 10s. a year to my mother to discharge my obligation to pay her 20s. a year for her life. The rest of my goods to the discretion of John WALFORD of Cressing, whom I make executor, and for his pains 3s.4d. If anything remain, I will it to the amending of the highways. Witnesses: John WALFORD, Rd. DYNES, [one name blank], John HUBBERD writer hereof. [No probate clause.]

ROSE KENT of Lexden widow, 26 Feb. 1582/3. (769)
To Rd. AYLEWARDE my son all my son all my lands and goods, whom I ordain executor. To Mary WADE my daughter 5 marks and a couple of beasts; Thomasine KENT my daughter 5 marks; [blank] PEPPER £5 at his marriage; and [blank] CULLPACKE 5 marks. To my daughter WADE half my wearing linen and my best coverlet. To Mary CROWE now dwelling with me [blank] marks at marriage. To the poor of Lexden 5 marks. To Mary BURE 5 marks at marriage. To Mary daughter of my daughter WADE 40s. at 21. Witnesses: Nich. BUER, Th. NEWMAN, Nich. PEPPER, [blank] NEVE. Proved 28 Feb. 1582/3.

RICHARD BERDEN of Black Notley, 19 Jan. 1582/3. (770)
To ten of the poorest householders in Black Notley 3s.4d. at the day of my burial. The 2 tenements and the lands belonging in Black Notley called Hosyers and Tilles house *alias* Tyles Hall shall remain after the decease of 'Dennys' my wife to Th. my eldest son. To Wm. my 2nd son my customary tenement with the lands belonging called Trippes in Black Notley, holden of the manor of Black Notley, on condition that he suffer my wife 'Benet' [*sic*] to hold my farm called Tanners wherein I dwell with the crop growing at the time of my decease and the profits for 16 years. To Rt. my son my frehold tenement called Rowes in Black Notley and my customary lands in Black and White Notley, holden of the [manor of the] late Priory or Nunnery of Little Leighs, on condition that he shall not trouble or expel 'Dennys' my wife from Tanners. To Th. 5 quarters or seams of good barley at 21. To my five daughters called Eliz., Mgt., Anne, Ellen and Mary £6 13s.4d. apiece at 18. To Rt. HUNT my servant 20s. To 'Dennys' my wife Tanners for 16 years, also all other my goods to her own maintenance and bringing up of all my children, on condition that, if she marry again, she enter into bond to Th. for the performance of my Will. I ordain her my executrix and John GOODDAY of Roxwell my brother-in-law overseer, and for his pains 6s.8d. Witnesses: John GLASCOCK, John BEDLE. Proved 14 Mar. 1582/3.

AGNES INKLE of Goldhanger widow, 22 Jan. 1582/3. (771)
To be buried in Goldhanger church or churchyard. To my daughter Mary, my legitimate child, all my goods, provided that she discharge the bond wherein her uncle Th. READER is bounden. I ordain him executor. Witnesses: Th. FINCHE, Th. SEARLES. Proved 8 Mar. 1582/3.

RICHARD WELL of Ashdon, 18 Nov. 1582. (772)
To Joyce my wife my house wherein I dwell with the close, on condition that she keep herself unmarried; if she marry, Rd. my son shall enter on them and she to be utterly void thereof. To her all my goods for her life; if she marry, to be equally divided at the discretion of Th. FREMAN, Th. COOK and Rt. SNOYE, my wife to have 1st choice, my son 2nd and my daughter 3rd. To Rd. after my wife's decease, my house and close, he to pay Eliz. my daughter £8 within 4 years after my wife's decease. I ordain her and him my executors. Witnesses: Th. FREMAN, Rt. SNOYE. [No probate clause.]

JOHN ROSSE the elder of [Saffron] Walden, 1 Apr. 1580. (773)
To Edm. the son of John ROSSE 1 of my beds of saffron ground in Clay Pit Close at the discretion of his father and the profits. To Adam son of Wm. PASFEILD of Walden and Mercy PASFEILD 5s. apiece. To Rd. PASFEILDE now servant with Wm. PASFEILDE 3s.4d., the said Wm. 10s., and Alice his wife 5s. The residue of my goods to my three sons, i.e. the said [*sic*] John, Stephen and Wm., by equal parts. I ordain John my executor and Wm. PASFEILD supervisor. To Mgt. wife of my son John my biggest brewing pan. Witnesses: Henry LOADER, Matthew RANDE, Wm. BOYTON. [No probate clause.]

AGNES MINICASE of Hatfield Peverel maiden, 12 Mar. 1582/3. (Nuncupative.) (774)
She gave Th. COLLINS her kinsman £8 which he 'ought' [owed] her by a bond. The residue of her goods she gave to John BROMLY of Hatfield in consideration of his charges and goodwill in taking her into his house and relieving her in her sickness and extremity. Witnesses: John SEA curate of Hatfield, Rd. BARRETT of the same. [No probate clause.]

ANNE ASHFEILDE of Earls Colne, 6 Mar. 1581/2. (775)
To the poor 3s.4d. To Dthy. BURNDISHE and Frances ERWIN my two daughters my free houses and lands, land called Brokhole excepted which I give to Avice ASHFEILD. To Mgt. daughter of Giles ASHFEILD 1 posted bedstead with a satin tester over it, 1 featherbed, and 1 holland casting sheet. To Avice 1 cupboard, 1 cupboard cloth, and 1 cushion with columbines. To Frances a trundle bed, a featherbed and a strawbed, a red petticoat, 1 black coffer, a brass pot, a counter table, 2 forms, a chair, a buffet stool, 1 cushion of dornacles, 2 wrought cushions, 2 silver spoons, a pair of curtains, all the old pewter, 5 pieces of stainings [stained cloths], 1 little churn, 2 firkins, a dripping pan, an andiron, a bolting tub, 2 other tubs, a cheese press, 1 spice mortar, and a little chafer. To Dthy. 1 velvet hat and 1 great kettle. To my two daughters my apparel equally divided. To Bridget BURNDISHE 1 trundle bed, 1 flockbed, and 1 holland casting sheet. To [illegible] 1 bullock, 1 great coffer with iron bars, 1 little chair with a great cushion, 1 middle kettle, 1 posnet, 1 little table, and 1 skillet. To Anne ERWIN 1 little skillet and 1 little Dutch wheel. To Nich. ASHFEILD 6s.8d. To Prudence ERWIN 1 little kettle and 1 spinning wheel, Frances ERWIN cooper 5s., and Mary ERWIN 1 buffet stool. To Henry son of Bridget HARTE 1 silver salt. To Joan COOKE 1 pewter dish and 1 pair of sheets. All my goods to be divided between Dthy. and Frances, being executrices. Witnesses: Rt. READ, John WOOD, Frs. WHISTON clerk [the clergy list for Earls Colne at this period is deficient]. Proved 16 Apr. 1583.

HECTOR OSKIN of Great Braxted husbandman, 1 May 1583. (776)
To the poor people of Great Totham 5s. and of Great Braxted 5s. To Mark and Giles my sons equally between them £20, which Reynold BIRCH of Stratford [Stratford St. Mary, co. Suffolk?] oweth me. To Mark my house wherein I dwell in Great Braxted with the lands belonging; for default of issue, successively to Giles and to Joan my daughter, according to a surrender to the lord [of the manor] to them. To Mark my bed in the sollar or chamber. To Roger HARROLDE of Braxted 2 sheep. The residue of my goods to Giles, whom I make executor. John HOLME clerk, parson of Wickham [Bishops], and John AYLETT of Great Braxted to be overseers, and for their pains 3s.4d. apiece. Witness: Th. WOODWORTH. Debts owing to me: of Reynold of Stretford [Stratford co. Suffolk?] £20; LITTELBURYE of Totham £4 for a

yoke of oxen. [More] witnesses: Roger HOOD [altered to WOOD?], John HOWE. [No probate clause.]

THOMAS WASHINGTON of [St.] Mary Magdalen, Colchester, mercer, and free[man] of the [Mercers'] Company of the City of London, 5 Nov. 1579. (777)
To Agnes my wife for her life my house wherein I dwell called 2 tenements or rentaries, which I had of the free gift of Rd. OSBORNE of Tillingham gentleman; on condition that she bring up my five children Mary, Sarah, Andrew, Rebecca and Peter WASHINGTON in the fear and service of God and with sufficient meat, drink and apparel during their minorities; after her decease, to be sold by Lawrence my son, Rd. OSBORNE, Geo. BROWNE my son-in-law, and Benjamin ANDREWS my neighbour, and the money equally divided amongst my children at 18 or marriage for my daughters and 21 for my sons. To James WASHINGTON my son my say jacket, my gown I made last lined with white bays and faced with fur, and a chest bound with iron bands and 2 locks. The rest of my goods shall be divided, half to my wife and half to my children, to remain in her hands to their education and bringing up. I make her my executrix. Witnesses: Ralph HARGRAVE, John BATTELL, Rd. MASON. [No probate clause.]

THOMAS SEAMAN of Heydon husbandman, 17 Oct., 24 Eliz. [1582]. (778)
To Mercy my wife 30s. which Rt. COLTE oweth me and all such furniture and household stuff as she brought to me [at marriage] and her own apparel. To Chris. my son £10, and to my daughters Joan £6 13s.4d., Kath. £4, and Ellen wife of Leonard FARDELL, Mgy. wife of John THORNE, Mary wife of Th. THORNE, and Eliz. wife of John ROMBOLDE each 20s. To the poor of Heydon 6s.8d. To John my son 40s. To Chris., Joan and John all my household stuff, bedding, brass, pewter utensils and necessaries equally divided by the oversight of Th. SEAMAN the younger, Wm. MOWLE and Rt. MOWLE. To the parson 12d. for my tithes forgotten. The residue of my goods to John, whom I constitute executor. Witnesses: Wm. BARLEE, Edw. BARLEE, Mgt. COLTE, John COSEN, John SEAMAN. Proved 18 Apr. 1583.

GEORGE WOLLWARD of Little Walden [in Saffron Walden], 23 Mar., 25 Eliz. [1582/3]. (779)
To my father [not named] 20s. in his hands. My mother shall have its use for her life; after her decease, to Wm. my brother; if he die before her without issue, to be equally divided between my brother KNOTTE's children. To Geo. my godson, son of John WOLLWARD of Hadstock, 5s. and his other two children, and Geo. FARRAUNT my godson, each 12d. The residue of my goods to Frances my wife, whom I make executrix. Witnesses: Th. PETTIT, Henry PETTIT. [No probate clause.]

JOHN WARMAN of Ashdon, 29 Jan. 1582/3. (780)
To Mgy. my wife my house and lands wherein I dwell; after her decease, all my 'housen' and lands in Ashdon and Bartlow [in Ashdon] to John my son. To my wife all my goods to occupy for her sustentation; after her decease, to John to pay my legacies. To my daughters Ellen £3 6s.8d. and Mgt. GYLLE 20s. To Ellen RAYNFORDE my daughter's daughter 1 bullock at 18. To John SEWELL my wife's son 1 cow. I ordain John executor. Witnesses: Th FREMAN, Rt. BACKER, Rt. SNOYE. [No probate clause.]

ANNABEL RAYMOND of Littlebury widow, 13 Mar. 1582/3. (781)
To Edmond my son 50s. within 30 weeks after my decease; if he die before, to his two children Anne and Rt. at 21. To Edm. my corn growing in the [Common] Fields of Littlebury and my tillage, and my standing bed with the featherbed. To John HUES my son-in-law. To 'Phillip' HUES my daughter my best coverlet and best gown. To Wm. one of the sons of Th. SELL 13s.4d. and Mgt. his daughter 10s. at 21. To her my hutch and a pair of sheets. To Anne RAYMOND my goddaughter my great skillet, best pewter platter, and 1 pair of sheets. To Rt. son of Edm. RAYMOND my cupboard. To 'Mathye' my son my grove which I hold of the manor of [Saffron] Walden (2¾ acres). The rest of my goods to him, whom I ordain executor. Witnesses: Rt. PERKIN, John HEDGE, Stephen STEWARDE, John HELYE. Proved 18 Apr. 1583.

RICHARD RAMPTON of Great Tey husbandman, 29 Mar. 1583. (782)
To the poor men's box 2s. To Alice my wife for her life my messuage wherein I dwell, with the barns, stables, yards, orchards, gardens and lands, and my lands called Gulles, Wymlottes, Brodgores, Aungevins and Shotbowtes in Great Tey in my own occupation; after her decease, to Samuel my son. To my wife Donylands Croft holden by copy of court roll in Great Tey for her life; after her decease, to Th. my son, on condition that he pay 20s. to Mary SPOONER, and if she die, to Judy SPOONER her sister. To Samuel my joined table with a form, my iron wedges, and best bedsteadle and featherbed. To my daughters Susan SPOONER and Clement and Dorcas RAMPTON each 40s. To Agnes BODE my kinswoman a bullock. The rest of my goods to my wife, whom I ordain executrix. I name my well-beloved friend Andrew LONDON of Great Tey supervisor, to whom 12d. Witnesses: Samuel MOOTHAM, Rd. UNDERWOOD, Andrew LONDON. [No probate clause.]

ANDREW WEST of Little Oakley, 26 Jan. 1582/3. (783)
To my three children [not named] my part of the house that I dwell in equally divided at 24; until then it and the rest of my goods to my debts and bringing up my children. I surrender it and my land to the lord [of the manor] by John WADE instead of the bailiff and John HEARD and Th. CARTWRIGHTE tenants. I ordain my cousin Th. WADE of Beaumont Hall executor. Witnesses: Th. CARTWRIGHTE, John HERDE, John WADE. [No probate clause.]

JOHN WOOD of Wix husbandman, 7 Mar. 1783. (784)
To my dearly-beloved mother [not named] the 40s. that my brother-in-law HAYWARDE oweth me, to be paid at the Lawrence Day [10 Aug.] next, 6s. that Edw. TWYLTE and 13s. that Reynold HAVELOCKE oweth me. To my sister HAYWARDE 1 cow that HAYWARDE hath already, and to her three daughters [not named] each 1 sheep, to be put into some honest man's hand where they may be forthcoming or else into their grandmother's hand. To my master RADLAN's daughter Joan 1 sheep. To six poor folks each 12d., i.e. mother DABNEY, mother HALLE, 'Saunder' [Alex.] BRANDEN, Christian GYDNEY, Frs. BREWER, and WRITE. The rest of my goods to my brother Rt., whom I make executor. Witnesses: James LUCAS, Wm. RADLAND, John GYLLAT, Frs. BREWER. [No probate clause.]

THOMAS ESTWOOD of East Donyland sailor, 17 Mar. 1582/3. (785)
To the poor 12d. To John my son my monger [fishing vessel] with the furniture belonging and £6 13s.4d. at 21, half to be paid by Mgy. my wife, half by my eldest son, both to occupy the monger, but the £6 13s.4d. to see my Will discharged. To Mary ESTWOOD my daughter and Th. my youngest son each £10 at 21. To Joyce LITTELBURYE my goddaughter 6s.8d. To my wife and Edw. my son my ketch [small trading vessel] with the furniture, each half; if it please God to send her [home] from the North Seas safe and sound the ketch to be equally divided, and so if they sell it. To them my house that I dwell in for her life according to the last surrender to Th. HARVYE, Wm. DEANE and John WOLLMAN bailiffs [of the manor]; if it please God to move my son to marry and his wife and mine cannot agree, to my wife my house for her life and a new chimney to be set up at both their charges for a better quietness of my wife, and she and Edw. each to have half the occupying of the fish houses. The residue of my goods to them, whom I make executors. Witnesses: John PARISHE, Wm. KYRBYE parson [rector of East Donyland]. [No probate clause.]

RICHARD GALLAWAYE of Ramsey, 1 Dec. 1582. (786)
To Eliz. my wife 2 of my best beasts, 1 seam of rye, 1 seam of wheat, 1 seam of barley, my household stuff ungiven hereafter, and all my swine and poultry, and 4 loads of cubit [wood] delivered to her house in Bridge Street at Michaelmas after my decease, and her dwelling and occupying of my house and lands that I occupy until then with the profits of cattle now feeding on the ground (except my corn) freely without paying any farm [rent] for it. The timber with the lord's [lord of the manor's?] that I have prepared necessary for reparations of my houses, with a long ladder and all other out stuff as cart, plough and harrows, to be sold to help pay

my debts, and my other goods, the rest of my lease and other cattle and corn likewise sold. The residue, if any be spared, to be equally divided among my children. To Eliz. my daughter 1 featherbed, a bedsteadle, a Dansk chest that was her mother's, a wainscot table at my son-in-law PAKEMAN's house, also £4 to be paid to her or to him that she shall dwell with, he or she to put in surety to my executors to pay the £4 again to her. My lands and houses free and copy in Ramsey called Frysells to my very friend Wm. SILVESTER of Dovercourt, conditionally that he pay my executors £80 within 2 years after he have assurance of the premises. After the sale of my houses, lands and my goods, my debts paid, and judgement in the law that I am given, that which may be spared shall be equally divided among my children. Whereas I owe Agnes BLOSSE my daughter-in-law £5, she shall have 20s. more. My executors shall buy as much cloth as will make my wife, Eliz. my daughter, and Agnes BLOSSE each a gown and a petticoat. I ordain Edw. DERIVALE and John HAYWARDE executors and Wm. SILVESTER supervisor, and for their pains 20s. apiece. Witnesses: Rt. WYER, John HARVYE, Rd. HOWARDE. [No probate clause.]

ROSE BEARD of Wivenhoe widow, — 1582. (787)
To Joan BROME my kinswoman a new canvas apron, 2 pair of sheets, and 2 pair of hosen. To 'Lydda' GYLSE a canvas apron. To Agnes COOKE a fair candlestick. To my son Th. the lease of my house. To my daughter Rose all my apparel and 1 mortar and her children each 1 pewter dish and a platter; also to Rose the bed which I lie in. The rest of my goods equally between Th. and Rose. I constitute Th. executor. Witnesses: Edw. BURGES, Jeremy BURGES. [No probate clause.]

THOMAS CAUNDLER of Little Bromley yeoman, 15 Oct. 1582. (788)
To Jane my well-beloved wife my messuage called Cowyes with 40 acres of land in Little Bromley for her life; after her decease, to Geo. my son; for default of issue, successively to John my son and to Geo. my son and Anne my daughter equally divided. To Geo. £20, John £26 13s.4d., and Anne £20, all at 21. To Roger £20 2 years after my decease and 4 ewe sheep conditionally that he make no further demands on my goods. To my cousin Wm. CANDLER a bullock and a seam of rye. To Rd. FULLER my servant 2 lambs. To the poor people of Little Bromley 5s. My wife shall enter into bond to my trusty friend and brother-in-law John STEVEN in 200 marks to perform my Will and pay my legacies. The rest of my goods to my wife, whom I ordain executrix. I cause John STEVEN to be supervisor, and to him 6s.8d. Witnesses: John STEVEN, Rt. SOUNDE, Rt. CAUNDLER, Ralph KINGE. Proved 15 Apr. 1583.

WILLIAM COSSEN of West Bergholt yeoman, 19 Mar. 1572/3 [*sic*]. (789)
To Alice my wife my house and land called Ardens with the profits for her life; after her decease, to Wm. my son. To the poor 3s.4d. a year for 10 years out of ELENGAME's house, to be paid by my wife if she live so long; if not, by my son. Wm. shall pay out of Ardenes to his sisters £5 apiece. To my daughter SPARLINGE's seven children [not all named] each 1 bullock, to Rt. the garled, to Eliz. the dun. To my daughter Mgy. the 2 beasts that she hath and a bed [short blank here] pleaseth her mother. To Agnes my daughter a cow. To PRESTEN's two children each 1 beast. To Wm.'s three children my 3 beasts at FEILDE's. To John STONARD an ewe and a lamb. To my daughter PRESNEY a brass pot and to Wm. another. To him the lease of Mothes which he hath already and £5 of the money that he oweth me. The rest of my goods, leases, corn, cattle, household [stuff], and money to my wife. I make Wm. executor and Geoffrey NEWTON overseer. Witnesses: Geoffrey MOTE, Henry SICKER. Proved 6 May 1582.

MARY STERNE [abode not given], 6 Aug. 1582. (790)
To be buried in Heydon church or churchyard. To my brother Geo. STERNE ½ acre of saffron ground in Heydon [Common] Field, 2 milch kine whereof 1 is at Melbourne Bury [in Melbourne, co. Cambridge], the other at Nether [Little] Chishall, 1 quarter of malt in the house of Rd. COTTES of Heydon, and 4 sheep at Melbourne. To my sister Bridget STERNE a rood of saffron ground in Heydon Field, 2 quarters of malt, a bullock, and 3 sheep. To Grace FELTON 1 ewe and a [blank]. To my

cousin Mistress BURLYE 20s. which she oweth me. To Rt STERNE my brother 20s. To my aunt ASPLEND 1 acre of lintels in Heydon Field. To Eliz. STERNE my best gown and Mary STERNE my best kettle. To the poor of Heydon 13s.4d., and of Chrishall 6s.8d., and of Great Chishall 6s.8d. The residue of my goods to my aunt ASPLEND to divide at her discretion among my brethren and sisters and their children. I appoint her my executrix. Witnesses: John STERNE, John FELLTON, Edw. BARLEE. [No probate clause.]

ROBERT WADE of Great Holland, late of Moze, 4 Nov. 1582. (791)
To Daniel my son my tenemnt called Cotymakes with 10 acres of ground in Moze paying my son Th. £3 and Rt. son of Rt. JARMEN and Ellen his wife £5 at 21. To Daniel son of Gilbert WADE 6s.8d. at 21. Rd. SKOTTELL my son-in-law shall pay £10 to Rt. and Ellen, and so doing he shall have 10 acres, parcel of Cottywades, to him and Martha his wife. To the poor of Moze 20d., whereof mother BERDELL to have 12d. To Daniel a cupboard and a table in the house at Moze, a great brass pot, and my bed that I lie in at Holland. To my daughter Ellen a bed in my house at Moze, a cauldron at Holland, and the trivet at Moze. To Martha a copper kettle, a little brass pot, and a bed on the sollar at Moze. The rest of my goods shall be divided by my neighbours indifferently between Daniel (to have 1st choice) and Ellen's husband. I ordain Rd. CARTER executor, and for his pains 20s. Surrendered my tenement in Moze to the lord [of the manor] by Th. MERYFEILDE instead of the bailiff in the presence of Wm. GARDNER and John CARTER tenants. [No probate clause.]

THOMAS HARRIS of Great Wigborough, 26 Apr. 1583. (792)
To Grace and Faith my daughters each a cow and £5 at 21. To Faith my wife my lands in Fingringhoe called Tye House for 7 years towards the bringing up and keeping of my children; then to Th. my son, paying his brother Edw. £20 within 6 years after he shall enjoy the lands. The residue of my goods to my wife to bring up my children. I constitute her my executrix. Witnesses: Edw. BULLOCKE, Th. FOSTER, Isaac ALLEN. Surrendered my land in Fingringhoe in the presence of two tenants Isaac ALLEN and Th. FOSTER and of Edw. BULLOCKE instead of the lord's bailiff. By me Randall WYMSEE parson of Great Wigborough. [No probate clause.]

AGNES PROWSE of [Saffron] Walden widow, 7 Apr. 1583. (793)
To Wm. MOYSE my kinsman a chest of walnut, a pair of new towen sheets, a towen tablecloth, my best joined bedstead, my middle kettle, and 4 of my best painted cloths. The rest of my goods to Rd. JOHNES. I ordain Joyce GYVER my executrix. Witnesses: Geo. AMIE, Anthony CLEMENT, Peter FYEFF writer. [No probate clause.]

RICHARD SANDFORD of Great Tey, 22 Apr. 1581. (794)
[Religious preamble.] To the poor 2s. To 'Aunstace' [Annastace] my dearly-beloved wife my lease and term of years of the manor or farm called Marks Tey Hall and Ditches wherein I inhabit and of my lands, meadows and pastures belonging, with such corn, cattle, household stuff, and husbandry implements on the premises; on condition that she, at the request of Th. my father, quitclaim to him her right to the messuage called Dukes in Willingale Doe and Shellow Bowells in the tenure of Th. KILLETT; if she refuse, she shall lose my legacy and have only 100 marks and such household stuff as I had with her [at marriage], and the residue of my goods to my father to perform my Will. To him my right to the said lands. To every one of my brethren and sisters, i.e. Rt., Th., Wm., Geo. and Edm. SANDFORD, and Eliz. FISHPOOLE, Susan SANDFORD and Judith SANDFORD, each 20s. I ordain my wife executrix. Witnesses: Wm. SAMMES, Th. HAVEROCKE. Proved 9 May 1581 [*sic*] in the person of Ralph NORTHYE proctor of Annastace.

ROBERT PARKER clerk, parson of Little Bardfield, 1 June 1581. (795)
To Alice my wife my house in Thaxted which is 2 tenements with the yards and gardens as I purchased it. To my four sons Th., Rt., John and Matthew PARKER each 40s. to be paid by my wife when she thinketh good; the rest of my goods to her, whom I make executrix. I ordain John my son overseer, and for his pains 2s.6d.

Witnesses: Wm. RUST clerk, vicar of Felsted, Stephen RICHE, Edw. RICH, Barthw. CHISSHULL. [No probate clause.]

JOHN FINTNER of Little Totham, 25 July, 25 Eliz. [1583]. (796)
To Collett my wife my house called Brookes for her life; after her decease, to John my son, on condition that he pay my daughter Joan £3. All my goods to my wife, whom I ordain executrix. I make Henry BADCOCKE overseer, and for his pains 12d. Witnesses: wm. RIPPINGALE, Henry BADCOCKE, John BUER, Stephen BRIDGES. Proved 1 Oct. [year not given].

WILLIAM NEVILL of Witham smith, 15 Mar. 1582/3. (797)
To John my son all my lands and tenements in Stow [Maries] and Danbury. To Agnes wife of John KNIGHTE butcher £10. To Joan CHAPMAN £10 at marriage or 22, 1 bedstead with the featherbed on which I usually lie, and 1 hutch at its foot. To Wm. PRENTICE my daughter's son 10s. and Agnes PRENTICE his sister 40s. at marriage or 22. To Mary MOTHOWSE and Prudence her sister each 40s. at marriage. To Bridget COUNSELY 5s. To the poor in Witham 20s. To Eliz. wife of Th. COWLINGE fletcher 5s. The rest of my goods to John, whom I ordain executor. I make Edm. TEELE of Witham mercer overseer, and for his pains 20s. Witnesses: Wm. BECKE, Edm. TEELE, Vincent CURTIS, Edm. HALES clerk [vicar of Witham]. [No probate clause.]

RICHARD NORKOTT of [Saffron] Walden tailor, 23 Oct. 1583. (798)
To be buried in Walden churchyard amongst my children there. To Joan my wife the messuage wherein I dwell in Walden for her life; after her decease, to John my son, on condition that he pay Susan NORKOTT my daughter £20; the remainder of the messuage to Samuel and Wm. my sons. To Samuel £5 within 2 years after my decease, Sarah £10 at marriage and Wm. £5 at the end of his apprenticeship, so that he honestly serve his master and they both be obedient to 'his' mother. To my daughter-in-law Susan NORKOTT an angel to make her a ring. To my brother Rt. NORKOTT my coat, best doublet and hose and oldest cloak. To Mgy. MORLY my sister-in-law 5s. To my maidservants Susan and Barbara each 3s.4d. at marriage. The residue of my goods to my wife, whom I make executrix. I make my cousin Nich. GAMEDGE supervisor. Witnesses: Roger BYBBYE, Th. MARTIN, Nich. GAMEDGE, Edm. POUNSONBIE, James CROFTE. [No probate clause.]

THOMAS SEVER of Wakes Colne, 17 Oct. 1583. (799)
To Mgy. my wife for her life my house and lands called Jordens holden by copy of the manor of Wakes Colne and free land (3 roods); if she have any issue by me, to my issue; after her death, to my cousin Ellen SEVER my brother John SEVER's daughter, she to pay her sister's children £10. To twelve of the poor of Wakes Colne 6s.8d. To six of my godchildren 20d. apiece. To my sister HARVEY 2s., my cousin SAWKINS 5s., Lettice BOVER 1 lamb, and John CREFFEILD dwelling in Hockley 5s. The rest of my goods to my wife, whom I make executrix. I ordain John HAWKINS supervisor. Witnesses: James DIGLETT, Wm. MEDOWE, John COCKERTON, Rt. MONKE, Rd. BOVER. Surrendered to Wm. MEDOWE and John COCKERTON, tenants of this manor. Proved 25 Nov. 1583.

JOHN FENNER of Wivenhoe husbandman, — 1583. (800)
To Joan my wife 8 silver spoons for her life; after her decease, to my son John. To her the best and fairest chest in the chamber and the cupboard in the hall for her life, all her household [stuff] which was hers before we married, a seam of rye, and 20 loads of wood of cubit logs and brush or billet; the rest of my wood to be sold to help pay my debts and legacies. I will that she be governess to John, but if she die before he is of sufficient age to govern himself, my son Rt. to have his government, and for his pains the commodity of his legacy house, so that he doth conveniently keep him to school. To Rt. my counter table with the form and carpet, all my apparel, saddle, bridle and boots. To my son Wm. £30 and the flockbed and the hutch in the chamber at 22. To my son Th. my house in Wivenhoe Street called Puplats, my featherbed in the little parlour, the hutch at the bed's feet, the

small round table, and a brass pot next to the best, all at 22. To John the house that I dwell in called Rogers after my wife's decease, my table in the hall with the form, 2 joined stools, the press in the little parlour, 5 cushions in the hall, with such light stuff as doth appertain to the house as the trammel and such old irons as are necessary to the same. I will that the copper in the kitchen be not removed and remain with the house and to John's use. To him the bed I lie in and my best brass pot. To Susan my daughter the cupboard in the great parlour and the trundle bed in the small parlour. To Bridget my daughter a worsted gown with half sleeves. All my pewter and candlesticks which were mine before I was betrothed, to my wife and children equally divided. To John SMYTH my son-in-law 20s. To the poor of Wivenhoe 6s.8d. To Wivenhoe church 6s.8d. The rest of my goods equally divided between my children. Rt. to have the government of Wm. to see him well placed and of Th. to keep him to school so long as he may conveniently until able to write some plain indifferent and legible hand. I ordain Rt. executor and Th. ROGERS supervisor. Surrender given to Henry FOOTE as the lord's bailiff and Th. SAMMON and John MILLER tenants [of the manor] in the presence of Rt. FENNER, Th. ROGERS, Jeremy BURGES and John BRAGGE. [No probate clause.]

JOHN SHELFORD the elder of Great Wenden husbandman, 8 Apr. 1579. (801)
To Kath. my wife the free messuage wherein I dwell and 5½ acres of free land belonging for her life; and my 3 half acres bought of Th. LYON; after her decease, to John my son, on condition that he pay Ellen my daughter 5 marks, the reversion to Ezechiel my son. To my wife a customary tenement and all other my customary lands holden of the manor of Wenden Hall for her life; on condition that she honestly bring up my young children; after her decease, he reversion of the customary lands, pastures, meadows and pightles which I bought of WRIGHT (together 10 acres) to Th. my son, on condition that he pay Roger my son £20. After my wife's decease my customary land which I bought of Rt. WATSON and John BYE (4¼ acres) to Ezechiel, and to Kath. my daughter a pightle called Jeynes (½ acre). All which customary lands I have surrendered by John BONKES [*recte* BANKES] the elder in the presence of Geo. DAYE to the use of my Will. To my wife all my goods to bring up my children well and honestly until they come to the age to help themselves; if she die before, my friend and brother-in-law John BURLINGE shall have my goods and lands until Th. is 21 and so to part my goods equally between them. I make my wife and John BYRLINGE executors. Witnesses: Nich. YORKE, Anne HARLOWE, Wm. BOYTON. [No probate clause.]

THOMAS BEFINE of Great Totham husbandman, 1 Apr. 1583. (802)
To Mary, Anne and Kath. BEFINE my three daughters each £6 13s.4d. at marriage; if all die, to Joan my wife for her life, then to Wm. BEFYNE my brother; the £20 to remain in the custody of [Wm. HUNT omitted in error] of Great Totham gentleman. The residue of my goods to my wife, whom I ordain executrix. I require Wm. HUNT my master to be overseer. [No witnesses.]

RICHARD GOODWYN of [Saffron] Walden yeoman, 2 Oct. 1583. (803)
To Annabel my wife all my lands and tenements free and customary for her life; after her decease, to Samuel my son my 2½ acres of customary land called Jermins lying together [in the Common Fields] between the land late of Th. ROPER and Annabel his wife on one part and that of me on the other, and to Mary GOODWYN my daughter 1 acre of customary lnd, parcel of a tenement called Swaynes in Willow Field in Walden, and my ½ acre of customary land called Pigges which I had by the surrender of Wm. STRACHYE. To Anthony my son my piece of free land with ditches enclosed in Farrenden [Common] Field and a piece (1 rood and 17¾ perches or poles) which I bought of John SPRUCE. To my wife all my goods, household [stuff], corn, saffron, plate, and ready money. I make her my executrix. Witnesses: James GOODWYN, John SHELLFORDE, James CROFTE scrivener. Proved in the chamber of the executrix in her own person before Anthony HARTFORDE, A.M., deputy of the Official of the Archdeacon of Colchester, 22 Nov. [1583].

JOHN ROOTE of Chapel *alias* Pontisbright husbandman, 31 Mar. 1583. (803A)
To John ROOTE my eldest son my tenement called Middells with my customary lands holden of the manor of Great Tey. To Anne my wife, in consideration that she shall not claim dower or thirds of my lands and shall bring up the children which I had by her, £13 6s.8d. To her the bed wherein I lie and 1 bed more, the 2 best kettles save 1 and the least kettle, 4 pewter dishes, 1 saucer, 1 salt, 2 candlesticks, the least trammel, 1 brass pot which she brought with her [at our marriage], the ladle with the pothooks, the little spit, 2 stand tubs, 2 keelers, 1 scummer, 1 frying pan, 1 hutch which she brought with her, 1 little cupboard at John ROOT's house, 1 buffet stool, and a chair. John shall provide for my wife within the parish of Chapel a convenient house for her to dwell in for a year after my decease at his charge; to whom I give the government and education of Daniel my second son to the age of 21. To Agnes my daughter a hutch that was her mother's [not named], a kettle, a pair of silver 'dies' [dice], a pair of silver hooks, a silver pin, a silver and gilt marrying ring, a silver aglet [metal lace tag], 2 rails, and a bed. To Th. my son my mattock and best spade, a latten pot, and a candlestick. To Rt. my son my best cart, the biggest brass pot, a posnet, a candlestick, a pewter dish, and a saucer. To Samuel my son a bullock. To Joseph my son 1 joined bedstead, a pewter dish, an axe, and a bill. To Rt. my son my greatest kettle, on condition that he pay Th. and Joseph 20d. apiece. To Simon my son a table in John ROOTE's house with a form in the milkhouse. To Th., Rt., Samuel, Joseph, John, Mgt., Emme and Agnes my children each 25s. [between 1 and 4 years in turn] after my decease. To Simon, Mary and Eliz. my three youngest children each £4 at 18 and Simon at 21. The rest of my goods to John my eldest son, whom I make executor. Witnesses: Samuel MOTHAM, John KEBELL, John BAKER. Proved [blank].

HENRY HOYE of White Colne husbandman, 18 Sept. 1583. (804)
To the poor 12d. at the day of my burial. To Henry CRABBE a bullock and a flock-bed at 20. The rest of my goods to Clement my wife, whom I make executrix. Witnesses: Wm. ADHAMS clerk [vicar of Earls Colne], Th. WELYE, Nich. BRETT. [No probate clause.]

JOHN BRAUNCH of Little Braxted husbandman, 27 Oct. 1583. (805)
All my goods to John LOWE of Witham my brother-in-law to the end he pay my debts. The rest of my goods shall be equally divided among my six children [not named] at his discretion, whom I ordain executor. Witnesses: James HURRELL rector there, John GRENE of Great Totham yeoman. Proved 26 Nov. 1583.

JOHN SOWTH of St. Giles, Colchester, 20 Aug. 1583. (806)
To Eliz. my wife my house called Hawkins with the fields that doth not only lie within my Lord of Oxford's manor [Edw. de VERE, 17th Earl of Oxford] but all my lands in the manor [of Berechurch] held of Mr Edw. JOBSON, for her life; after her death, to John SOWTH my son; if he die without heirs, to my father-in-law John GRENE. The residue of my goods and cattle to my wife, whom I make executrix. Witnesses: Adam HOLLAND, Th. HARVYE, Wm. KYRBYE parson of East Donyland, Rt. GOSNOLL. [No probate clause.]

THOMAS GOWARS of Little Totham, [date not given]. (807)
To the poor people of Little Totham 3s.4d. to be distributed by my executrix with the consent of Ralph CORTMAN and 'C.' MEDCALFE. To Anne ROTTE £3 6s.8d. at 22 or marriage. To Nich. GOWARS my son £10 at 22. My executrix to do her best endeavour to bring up Nich. in learning or some other good trade or occupation, whereby he may get his living. The residue of my goods to Audrey my wife, whom I make executrix. I make Ralph CORTMAN my brother-in-law supervisor. Witnesses: Chris. MEDCALFE, Henry SAMS. [No probate clause.]

THOMAS NICOLLS of [Saffron] Walden yeoman, 8 Dec. 1583. (808)
To Joan my wife my messuage in Newport with my lands belonging for her life; after her decease, to be sold by the Treasurer and Vicar of Walden and the money divided amongst my four children, i.e. John, James, Rt. and Henry, part and part

like. To John NICOLLS my son £10. For certain causes I freely forgive my son Geo. such sums as he doth owe me. To James, Rt. and Henry each £10 at 24. To Nich. ALDRICHE *alias* BEADLE my servant 20s. The residue of my goods, cattle, ready money and plate to my wife, whom I ordain executrix. I ordain my son Geo. supervisor. Witnesses: Mark DOWLINGE, Edw. BRAUNE, James CROFTE the writer. [No probate clause.]

THOMAS DAGNET of Hatfield Peverel, 10 Dec. 1583. (809)
To Florence my wife the best flockbed, a pair of bedsteadles, 2 painted cloths, a little square table, a short form, a pair of dormans, a chair, a joined stool, a brass pot next the best, a kettle, 2 pewter dishes, a saucer, a candlestick, a saltcellar, and 30s. To Joan DAGNET my eldest daughter 1 flockbed, a brass pot, 3 pewter dishes, a saucer, and a chest. To Anne DAGNET my youngest daughter a flockbed, 1 little brass pot, 3 pewter dishes, a saucer, and a little chest. To Joan and Anne 20s. apiece at 21. If my wife do refuse her gift, she shall at choice take 4 marks and so to depart quietly. I make John SEA clerk [vicar of Hatfield Peverel] executor to see my two children brought up and placed at his discretion, and 10s. for his pains. I will that all my goods are to bring them up. I appoint Th. SACHE to see that they have their legacies at 21 and not before, and for his pains 5s. Witnesses: Rd. BARRETT, Th. TYCHEW. [No probate clause.]

WILLIAM ABBOTT of Wakes Colne weaver, 29 Jan. 1583/4. (Nuncupative.) (810)
To Th. my son 58 at 21; if he die before, to be divided amongst my five younger brothers [not named] by even portions, the poorest to have twice so much as the other. The rest of my goods to Agnes my wife. I will that the £8 remain in the hands of John ABBOT my elder brother, he paying the profits yearly for the bringing up of my son Th. until 14; then the profit to him until he is 21. I ordain my wife and John my elder brother executors. Witnesses: Rt. HAWKINS, John ABBOT the elder, John CHAMBERLIN. [No probate clause.]

ALICE CRADACK [CRADOCKE *in margin*] of Great Horkesley widow, 21 Dec. 1583. (811)
To Alice CRODOCKE my daughter my best bed, great brass pot, and the cupboard. To Rd. CRADOCKE my son 1 cauldron, 1 latten chafing dish, 1 spit, and 1 trivet. To Henry CRADOCKE my son 1 old brass pot. The residue of my goods to Alice, Rd. and Mgt. TREDGOLD my daughter; they shall lay out 13s.4d. to be bestowed at my burial by the discretion of my executors, i.e. Wm. STREAT, my son-in-law, of Colchester shoemaker, and Rd. my son of Ballingdon shoemaker, and for their pains 6s.8d. Witnesses: Th. KEN, John NORMAN, John STANSTEAD. [No probate clause.]

EDMUND HUNWICKE of Wivenhoe yeoman, 24 Jan. 1583/4. (812)
To Mary my wife my lands and tenements in Halstead and a messuage called Degens in Messing for 20 years to the bringing up of my children; if she die before, my cousin Th. HAM shall have them likewise. Forasmuch as my wife is with child, if it be a son he shall have all my lands at 21; if no son, after the 20 years to Th. HUNWICKE, my brother's son, on condition that he pay to my daughters each £30 at 21; if he refuse such condition, my lands to my daughters at 21. To my wife for her life all my goods; after her decease, to my daughters to be equally divided. To Ge. HURRELL's children all my looms, whereof 2 are broad and are at Th. BENTALL's of Halstead, 1 narrow at John BRAUNCHE's of Halstead, 1 narrow at John BURIE's of Halstead, and my loom at Wivenhoe. To Th. HAM my cousin 14s. that JASPER of Shalford oweth me. To 'Eleazer' ARDLE $8\frac{1}{2}$ bushels of wheat that he oweth me. I ordain my wife executrix and 'Eleazer' ARDLE overseer. Witnesses: Th. SYMONDE, Nich. MACHYN, Wm. BROWNE. Proved [date not given].

MARGARET PETER *alias* PETERSON of Salcot Virley [i.e. Virley], widow of Henry PETER *alias* PETERSON of the same, mariner, 14 Nov. 1583. (813)
To Joan HOWNAYLE my daughter the lease and term of years which I hold of the right honourable Sir Henry PARKER, Lord MORLEY, with the consent of the Lady MORLEY his widow and assent of the right honourable Edward PARKER, according

to the gift and condition that Henry PETER *alias* PETERSON bequeathed it to Mercy GARED my daughter; 1 joined chest, 1 piece of new woollen cloth, a gown of my husband's, and all my wearing apparel except my wearing linen, which linen to be equally parted between my two daughters. To Mgt. GARED my niece 1 black-legged sheep, and a joined table with a frame and a form. To Mgt. HOWNELL my niece 1 joined cupboard and 1 cow with 1 eye. To Mercy my best bed with a bedsteadle. My other linen except sheets to be divided between my daughters. To Th. HOWNELL my son-in-law a coat and a pair of gaskins of my husband's. To Mgt. 1 little brass pot. To Mercy and Joan half of my pewter equally apportioned, also 1 flitch of bacon, half my corn, half my cheese, and 1 pot of butter on my sollar. The residue of my goods to Th. my son-in-law and Joan, on condition that he pay my legacies. I ordain him executor and John STONE supervisor, to whom for his pains 2s.6d. Witnesses: John STONE, John SPARROW clerk [rector of Virley]. [No probate clause.]

JOHN PUMFRET the younger of [Saffron] Walden butcher, 28 Dec. 1576. (814)
To Agnes my wife my house in which I dwell for her life; after her decease, to Edw. my son. To him my shops and slaughter 'housen' in the Market Place in Walden at 21; if he die before, to Geo. PUMFRET my servant [*sic*] at 21 and likewise my house after my wife's decease. To Edw. £10 at 21 and Geo. 5 marks at 21. If Edw. die before, the £10 to Th. PUMFRET the younger, my brother. To my brothers John the elder, Wm. and Th., and to my sister Mgy. BUSHE each 10s. The residue of my goods to my wife. I ordain her and Edw. executors and Miles PUMFRET overseer, and for his pains 5s. Witnesses: Edw. BROWNE, John EVERED, Rt. SEARLE, Miles PUMFRET, Adam PRATT. Proved 7 Mar. 1576/7 by Agnes, power reserved to Edw.

WILLIAM CARTER of East Donyland salter, [date not given]. (815)
To my cousin 'J.' CLERKE's wife of Bradfield 1 little coffer with a key and lock. To my sister Joan PARSON 1 flockbed in the chamber next to the window. The residue of my goods to James WARRINDER and John WARER, whom I make executors, equally divided between them. Witnesses: Rt. PARKER, Wm. KYRBYE parson [of East Donyland]. Proved 8 Mar. 1584/5.

THOMAS HARVEY of St. Giles, Colchester, yeoman, 5 Feb. 1583/4. (816)
To be buried in East Donyland churchyard. To the poor of St. Giles 3s.4d., to be bestowed by Wm. BARRINGTON, churchwarden. To Joan my wife my customary land called Reignoldes in East Donyland for her life; after her decease, equally divided between my six children Stephen, Anne, Mary, John, Th. and Rd. HARVEY; excepted from this my orchard belonging to Reignoldes which I give to my eldest son John. To my wife my reversion after the death of Jane WOD of Felsted of the tenement and lands called [blank] in the tenure of John NEWLAND and Wm. NEWLAND in East Donyland, for her life; after her decease, to my seven children, i.e. John, Stephen, Anne, Mary, Joan, Th. and Rd., by equal parts. If my goods shall not amount to the sum of my debts, my wife shall sell Reignoldes except the orchard. The rest of my goods to her to bring up my children in the fear of God during their minorities. I nominate her my executrix and Rt. GOSNOLL of St. Giles supervisor. Witnesses: Th. BAKER, John DUFFEILDE, Edw. ESTWOODE, Wm. PARRIS. Memorandum, 5 Feb., Th. HARVEY did surrender his copyhold land to the lord of the manor of East Donyland by Th. BROKEMAN instead of the bailiff in the presence of John DUFFEILDE and Edw. ESTWOOD tenants. Witnesses: Wm. PARRIS, John FOXE, Rd. MASON, Rt. PILGRAME. [No probate clause.]

JOHN COLLYN [COLLIN *in margin*] of Wivenhoe sailor, 20 Aug. 1583. (817)
To Th. my son my house called Barris in Wivenhoe Street at 21, paying my children £6 apiece from the eldest to the youngest within 6 years after Th. enjoy my house; if he die before without seed of his body, to my sons John and Wm. likewise, and after in the same order. To Wm. my son and Ruth COLLEN my daughter each 1 of my best kettles or 8s. apiece. To John my best brass pot or 6s. I make Emme my wife executrix and Wm. CANNON supervisor. Surrender to John MAYER as the

lord's bailiff and Wm. LEAY and Wm. CANON tenants, these being present, John MAYER, Jeremy BURGES, Wm. LEAY, Wm. CANON. [No probate clause.]

ROBERT LITTELBURYE of East Mersea, 8 July 1583. (818)
To Rt. and Wm. sons of Wm. CRAMMER and Rose LITTELBURYE his wife each 6s.8d. at 19 or marriage. To him more a Dansk chest which was his uncle Geo.'s and a brass pot at his father's. If both die, to be equally divided between the children of my brethren and sisters. If Wm. on behalf of his children disturb my executor for any legacy ensuing from my son Geo. deceased, my gifts to be void. To Agnes wife of Abraham WEB 5s. and my wife's russet petticoat. To Wm. LONGE my grey russet breeches, a pair of short russet hosen, my old canvas doublet, frize coat, and a canvas shirt. To Jane LONGE my servant 3s.4d. To my brother Geo. LITTELBURYE 3s.4d. All other my goods to my wife Joan, whom I make executrix. For my children's legacies, she shall pay my brother-in-law Frs. HUBBERD, he putting in bond for payment. If my wife be with child at the time of my decease, I will it to have £4 at 19. I make overseer Frs. HUBBERD, and for his pains 6s.8d. Witnesses: Frs. HARFORD writer, Rt. GOODMAN, Th. YOLLE, Geo. LITTELBURYE. [No probate clause.]

JOHN CULLPACKE of Great Tey husbandman, 13 Apr. 1584. (819)
To the poor men's box of St. Peter, Colchester, 6s.8d. To Mgt. my wife my free land in the parish of Mile End by Colchester in the tenure of Arthur WILLSON. My house in St. Peter shall be sold for payment of my legacies and debts. To Barthw. TILL my son-in-law £6 13s.4d., Joan TILL my daughter-in-law £20, John TILL 5 marks. To Grace BARKEWAYE £3. To John BREWER my godson a red lamb. The rest of my goods, plate, money and cattle to my wife, whom I ordain executrix. I name my friend John UPTCHER supervisor, and 10s. to him. Witnesses: Th. BREWER, Henry JACKSON, Rt. UPTCHER, John UPCHER. To John WADE, my son-in-law, £5 which he oweth me in recompense of Barthw. TILL's rent. Proved 2 May 1584.

3

ARCHDEACONRY OF MIDDLESEX

The proper name of this archdeaconry, the Archdeaconry of Middlesex (Essex and Hertfordshire Jurisdiction), distinguished it from the Archdeaconry of Middlesex (London Jurisdiction). It covered 39 parishes in west and north Essex (for north-west Essex Wills, see Section 2) and 25 parishes in east Hertfordshire. The present series of publications excludes the Wills of Hertfordshire[1]. The abstracts were prepared from the Wills Registers [Essex Record Office reference D/AMR 3 and 4], nos. 820-911 from D/AMR3 and nos. 912-997 from D/AMR 4. No original Wills of this archdeaconry are extant before 1602.

JOHN BENOLD of King's Hatfield [Hatfield Broad Oak] poulterer, 24 Apr. 1574. (820)
To my daughters Joan, Mary, Eliz. and Audrey BENOLD each a pair of towen sheets, 1 pillow, and 40s., at marriage. To John my son a featherbed and 40s. at marriage. The rest of my goods to my wife Joyce, whom I ordain executrix. I make supervisor John. Witnesses: Wm. GOODWIN, Th. PAVELYE, John BROWNE, John SMITH. To my mother PUMFRITT 4 bushels of wheat and 4 of malt the next harvest after my decease. Proved 16 May 1576.

AGNES FOSTER of Willingale Doe widow, 18 July 1571. (821)
To the poor 13s.4d. To repairing of Beach Lane 6s.8d. To John GEFFERY my son 5 marks and 1 hutch; Wm. FOSTER my son £3; Mgy. HAWKYN my daughter £3 and my russet covering; Agnes SALINGE my daughter £3 and my best covering; and Eliz. ODYN[N]E my daughter 40s.; Joan REVE daughter of John SOR[R]ELL my son-in-law 13s.4d.; and Agnes ASHEWELL daughter of John GEFFERY my son 3s.4d.; all within 2 years after my decease. To Mary, Marion and Edw. HAMOND children of Th. HAMMOND my son late deceased [each] 13s.4d. at 16. To Ellen and Agnes FOSTER daughters of Rd. FOSTER my son 10s. To Edw. NEELL 2s. All my other goods to Rd. FOSTER, whom I ordain executor. I make Rd. SAMPFORDE supervisor, and 5s. for his pains. Witnesses: Edw. NEEL, Edw. WALL, Wm. NEELL. Proved 12 Apr. 1576.

[1] They are listed in *Wills at Chelmsford, 1400-1620*, ed. F.G.Emmison (British Record Society, Vol. 78, 1958), which brings them together in the Index of Places.

SIMON LORKYN of Wimbish, 2 Mar. 1575/6. **(822)**
To the poor people of Wimbish a bushel of wheat among them. To Mgt. LORKYN my daughter a cupboard in the parlour, 2 bedsteadles, a flockbed, 6 painted cloths in the parlour, a bearing sheet, a yard kercher, a towel, a flaxen tablecloth, 1 black 'howed' [for meaning see p. xvii] bullock, the biggest kettle but 1 and the 2nd of the least sort, 2 little pewter dishes, the best salt, the whole candlestick, and my spit and andirons; both winter stover and pasture for her 3 beasts until the Feast of SS. Philip and Jacob [1 May] next; also 4 yards of the russet piece of cloth (and the rest to Jane daughter of Wm. WAKELENN). To 'Diones' my daughter the least kettle of 3 of the biggest sort, a 'mantill' [meaning?] and covering, 2 pewter dishes with a cross on the bottom, the worst salt, and the old cupboard in the hall; also 1 acre of wheat lying next her brother James's. To Th. BARNES her son a red 'howed' bullock of a year to be kept as aforesaid, 1 pewter dish, and a brass pot. To Wm. WAKELIN my quern as it stands and 1 acre of wheat next to the barley land, and to his wife 2 pewter platters with cracked brims and 2 saucers. Also to Wm. 1 bed, conditionally that he give Henry his son 3s. at 16 and 13s.4d. that I laid out for the colt that we bought together. To Jane WAKELYNE his daughter a yard kercher, my greatest kettle, and 1 pewter platter. To James LORKYN my son 1 acre of wheat next Wm. WAKELIN's, my best coat and best hose, a 'bendless' [bandless] kettle, and the bed in the parlour. To Simon son of James LORKIN 1 black cow to be kept as aforesaid. To Mary LORKIN daughter of James the candlestick with the broken brim and a bedsteadle. To Mgt. LORKIN daughter of James the longest tablecloth, a skillet, and a pewter pot. To Simon LORKYN my son my cloak, a flaxen sheet, 1 acre of wheat, 1 acre of bullimong [mixed corn], the best horse, and 20s. To Th. son of Simon my other hutch. To Joan LORKIN daughter of Simon the shortest tablecloth and a scummer. To John LORKYN my son an acre of wheat next to Diones' wheat, the biggest bedsteadle in the chamber, and the form in the hall. To Mary LORKYN daughter to John a dun bullock of a year to be kept as aforesaid. To John LORKYN, WAKELEN's wife and BOUTELL's wife, my children, each 1 pair of sheets. To Simon and Wm. sons of James LORKYN, Th. BARNES son of Diones, and Henry my godson son of Wm. WAKELIN each a sheep. To Ambrose WILSMER my servant the sow that I bought of his father [not named]. The rest of my goods divided equally among all my children by the advice of John BARKER the bailiff and Rt. SHEDDE, whom I have appointed supervisors. I make my son Simon executor. Witnesses: Rt. SHEDDE, Rd. HOLTON, Henry FRANKELYN. Proved 6 June 1576.

JOHN SAVELL of Thaxted, 18 Mar. 1575/6. **(823)**
To my sons Moses £6 13s.4d. and Josias £3 6s.8d. and my daughter Agnes £3 6s.8d., all at 21. The residue of my goods to Joan my wife, whom I make executrix. I make Wm. SAVELL my brother supervisor, and for his pains 6s.8d. Witnesses: Allen RAYMENT, John KNAPPINGE, Peter PURCAS. Proved 12 Apr. 1576.

HUGH SUTTLE of Ashen husbandman, 28 Apr., 19 Eliz. [1577]. **(824)**
To Joan my wife all my goods. To Eliz. FRANKE my daughter my bakehouse and bakehouse chamber for her life, with free egress and regress. To my wife the rest of my buildings and all my lands belonging for her life; after her decease, my house and lands shall be sold, reserving the bakehouse and chamber to Eliz., and the money indifferently divided amongst all my children [not named]. I make my wife executrix. [No witnesses.] Proved 7 June 1577.

JOHN OVERED of Stebbing shearman, 31 July 1577. **(825)**
To Julian my wife my messuage with a garden in Great Bardfield bought of Th. RUSTE of Clare (co. Suffolk) glover for her life; after her decease, to John my son; for default of issue, successively to Th. my 2nd son, Hester my youngest daughter, and Eliz. my eldest daughter. To John 20s. at 21, Th. £3 at 21, and Eliz. and Hester each 40s. at 21 or marriage. To the poor people of Stebbing 3s.4d at the day of my burial. The residue of my goods to my wife, to see my children honestly brought up, putting in bonds for payment of their legacies to my well-beloved friend Th. HALLE of Stebbing or else to let him apply the money to their commodity and

to stand bound likewise. I ordain my wife executrix. Witnesses: Th. HALLE junior, Rd. SMITHE the writer. [No probate clause.]

JOHN SALMON of Thaxted, 21 Feb. 1576/7. **(826)**
To Mgt. my wife my croft or close in Thaxted called Tewes purchased of Sir John CUTT knight for her life; after her decease, to Martin SPARROWE my son-in-law. To him my wheat growing on the farm land except 4 acres which she shall have and the wheat belonging to Davy COWELL; to him also my yellow dun colt and best cow except 1 which he shall not have until 1 year after the decease of Isabel RYCE widow. To Joan AYLMER 1 bullock. Martin shall pay to Ellen COWELL my wife's daughter £10 which I owe her as parcel of a legacy from her father and mother, to John SALMON 53s.4d. which I owe him, to the executors of John BOUGHTEL 40s., and to Jeremy KEY 46s.8d. which I owe him. To the poor people of Thaxted 3s.4d. To Agnes my daughter 1 pair of my best sheets, the 2nd bed, the latten pan, and great brass pot. The obligation which I have of John COLLEN for John PLEDGER's money shall remain in my executor's hands to his use. The residue of my goods to my wife. I nominate Martin executor. Witnesses: Wm. KEY, James COWELL, Peter PURCAS. Proved 22 May 1577.

EDWARD CLYFTON of Roydon yeoman, 18 Dec. 1556 [*sic*]. **(827)**
To be buried in Roydon churchyard near the sepulture of Alice my late wife. To Th. my eldest son the lease of Alice Down, 5 acres in Lady [Common] Mead and 1 acre in Lies. He shall have the keeping of 5 kine for 1½ years and enter on the lease of Alife [*sic*] Down at Michaelmas after my decease. Edw. my son and Eliz. my wife shall have my lease of the manor of Down Hall [in Roydon], on condition that they pay Rose my daughter £20 within 1 year, Martha my daughter £20 likewise or at marriage, Geo. my son £20 at 20, Eliz. and Jane my daughters each £20 at marriage, Rt. my son £20 at 21, and Mary my daughter £20 at 21. To John SHETTLETON's three children Edw., Kath. and Eliz. and the child that Rose is now great with each a bullock. To Eliz. CLYFTON, Th.'s daughter, 1 bullock. John SHETTLETON shall have the keeping of my lease of the manor of Down Hall, forbidding my executors to sell the lease, for performing my legacies, bringing up my children, and paying my debts. My executors shall keep Rt. in learning 4 years where some good school is. To my wife if she marry £20, 4 kine, 2 featherbeds, 6 pair of sheets, 2 pots, 6 platters, 6 pottingers, and 2 chests, and so to depart. I make her and Edw. executors, to have the lease jointly during the years I have, if she marry not. My earnest desire and humble request is that, if it will please my master to be overseer, [to] whom I give 10s. towards his pains. Witnesses: Gabriel GRENE curate of Roydon, Th. PEAKES, John WILLET, Miles RODGERS. Proved 16 Dec. 1577.

THOMAS [surname omitted] of Middleton, 5 Nov. 1577.
[No Middleton burials register extant before 1700.] **(828)**
John BRAGGE 'moning' [reminding] him to take order for his goods, he answered, I have before this time promised them all to my wife, and according to that promise I give them all to her, for I know she loveth my children all well, for they are hers as well as mine, and therefore if she spare anything I leave the distribution thereof to her discretion. Witnesses: John BRAGGE, Rd. HITCHCOCKE and Mgt. HITCHCOCKE his wife. Administration committed, 13 Dec. 1577, to Alice the widow.

JOAN WETHERSTREATE [*recte* NETHERSTREATE] of Thaxted widow,
1 Aug. 1577. **(829)**
To Wm. WETHERSTRETE my son 6s.8d. and Alex. and John WETHERSTRETE my two younger sons each 6s.8d. To Alice NETHERSTRETE my daughter my best bedstead and best flockbed, best cupboard with 2 little joined tables, 2 little joined stools, greatest kettle and next best kettle, biggest brass pot, 1 latten chafing dish, 1 great latten candlestick, 1 brazen mortar with an iron pestle, 1 pewter charger, and 1 great pewter saltcellar. Also to Alice NETHERSTRETE 1 linen tester with fringed valances and the white linen curtains belonging and 1 painted tester. I make her and Eliz. my daughters executrices and Th. HALLIDAY supervisor. Witnesses: Edw. ROBINSON, Th. HALLIDAY writer hereof. Proved 26 Sept. 1577.

HENRY JYES [*recte* JOYCE] of Great Dunmow clothier, 20 July 1577. **(830)**
Agnes my wife and Simon my son shall have and occupy my tenement and backside jointly so long as she keep herself unmarried; if she marry this gift shall be void to her and she only to have her thirds in my tenement. To the poor people of Great Dunmow 30s. To Ralph JYES my brother 10s. The residue of my goods to my wife and Simon, whom I make my executors. Witnesses: Henry BARKER, Wm. CLERKE the writer hereof. Proved 20 Sept. 1577.

JACOB BROWNING of Pleshey, 30 Apr. 1577. **(831)**
To Joan my wife my tenement in Pleshey for her life; after her decease, to Th. my son to give and to sell. To Th. my tenement in Chelmsford and £20. To my daughters Mgy. £20 and Joan £10. I make my wife and Th. executors. To the poor in Pleshey 40 'pieces' of wheat to be paid by and by. Witnesses: Geo. BAY, James PEKER, Rt. HORSNAILE, Hugh BARKER. Proved 21 May 1577.

JOHN CHOPPYN [CHOPPING *in margin*] of High Roothing, 3 Jan. 1576/7. **(832)**
To the poor 12s. [*sic*]. To Joan DAWSON and Alice DAWSON 5s. each. To Mgt. my wife my best bed in the chamber next the street door where I dwell, with 2 hutches, all other linen, also 20s. yearly from my land called Fyshes for her life, on condition that she keep the houses at Fysshes in sufficient reparations. To Wm. my son my houses and land in Barnston called Fysshes; notwithstanding that Geo. BARNARDE my son-in-law shall have Fyshes for 10 years after my decease, paying yearly 20s. to my wife if she live so long. To John my son my free land in High Roothing on condition that he give yearly to the poor of High Roothing 20d. To my daughters Mary £3 6s.8d. and Julian 40s. To Wm. my son 6s.8d. To Wm. CRABBE 5s. To my son Wm.'s three children [not named] each 2s.6d. To my wife my pewter and latten, little brass pot, and 1 kettle. To six of my last godchildren each a piece of pewter. To Joan daughter of my brother Th. CHOPPYN a lamb. To Geo. BARNARDE's children 20s. among them. The residue of my goods to my son John, whom I ordain executor. I make my brother Rd. CHOPPYN overseer, and for his pains 5s. Witnesses: Rd. CHOPPYN, John HALL, Geo. BARNARD, John LACYE, Henry DREWRIE. Proved 21 May 1577.

WILLIAM HAYWARDE of Sturmer, 29 Apr. 1577. (Nuncupative.) **(833)**
To be buried in Sturmer church or churchyard. He did give to 'Phillip' his daughter 1 lamb. To Eleanor his wife his goods not bequeathed towards the helping and bringing up of his children [not named]. He did appoint his wife executrix. Witnesses: Geoffrey PHILLIPS parson of Sturmer, Th. FRENCH, Geoffrey WHYFFINE. Proved 22 May 1577.

WILLIAM ASHEN of Gosfield yeoman, 13 Mar. 1576/7. **(834)**
To Wm. my son at 21 the best table in the hall, best joined bedsteadle, best featherbed, a coverlet of tapestry work lined with canvas in the parlour, 6 of the biggest pewter platters standing on the cupboard in the parlour, and my great cauldron with 2 ringles, at 21; if he die before, to Joan my wife. To the repairing of Gosfield church 3s.4d. The residue of my goods to my wife, whom I make executrix. Witnesses: Matthew STUTVILE vicar [of Gosfield], James CLERKE, Nich. OVERAL. Proved 22 Apr. 1577.

RICHARD BERLEY (or BERLE) *alias* SPONER of Felsted, 12 Apr. 1577. **(835)**
Agnes my wife and Francis my son shall occupy quietly together my lands in Felsted for her life; after her decease, to him; if he die without heirs, to my three daughters Joan, Agnes and Denis by equal portions. To Joan 26s.8d., Rt. PAFFLYN my godson 6s.8d., and Agnes 53s.4d., paid by Frs. within 5 years after my wife's decease; if not paid to Joan and Rt. PAFFLEN, my tenement and croft called Suddes or Sagges to remain to Joan and my godson; if not paid to Agnes, my croft called Bradfield to her; and if not paid to Denis, my croft called Cookes Croft to her. All my goods to my wife and Frs., whom I ordain executors. I ordain Th. TANNER supervisor. Witnesses: Th. TANNER, John FRENCHE, Rd. DRANE. I have surrendered my lands by Th. TANNER in the presence of John FRENCHE and Rd. DRAKE tenants [of the manor]. Proved 21 May 1577.

JOHN SAVAGE the elder of Roydon husbandman, 4 Nov. 1574. (836)
To Ellen my well-beloved wife my house, barns, cottages and lands and goods whatsoever for her life; after her decease, to Nathaniel my son a cottage over against the house I dwell in with the backside and the 2 closes adjoining (9 acres) and to John my eldest son the house I dwell in with the rest of my lands. They shall pay Alex. my youngest son each £4. I make my wife executrix and Edw. CLEFTON and James BOREHAM of Roydon [overseers]. Witnesses: Gabriel GRENE curate of Roydon, Simon RUNINGTON, Stephen LENARD, Nich. SMITHE. Proved 20 May 1577.

AGNES FOSTER of Matching widow, 15 Oct., 18 Eliz. [1576]. (837)
To my sister Agnes' children £3 6s.8d. equally divided. To Rd. YONGE my sister Agnes' daughter's son £5 at 21. To Anne KYNGE my brother John's daughter 26s.8d. and a pair of sheets. To my sister FYNCHE's children 20s. apiece and to the daughters a pair of sheets each, i.e. her children by Andrew FINCH. To Joan GYBBEN 20s., Rd. MORTON our servant, Agnes BYLL, Geo. BRIDGES and John GRAVE my godson, each 5s. To Agnes my brother Andrew's daughter a featherbed, the great cauldron, and the best spit. To the poor folk of Matching 30s. and of Hatfield [Broad Oak] 30s. To Andrew KINGE my brother's children £3 6s.8d. of the money that is in Reynold FOSTER's hands evenly divided. To Arthur YONGE 10s. To Agnes KINGE, Andrew's daughter, a cupboard in the parlour. To Agnes BYRLIE a pair of sheets and a kettle with a basin in the bottom. To Joan GYBBEN a pair of sheets and a little brass pot. To the poor folk of Matching £3 6s.8d. The residue of my goods to Reynold FOSTER, whom I ordain executor. I ordain Wm. KINGE and Andrew KINGE supervisors. To Wm.'s children £3 6s.8d. equally divided. Witnesses: Th. KINGE, Arthur YONGE. Proved 17 Apr. 1577.

RICHARD ABELL of Matching, 2 Jan., 21 Eliz. [1578/9]. (838)
To Avice my daughter my best flockbed. To Avice, Eliz. and Agnes my daughters all my brass and pewter with the tubs and other such implements equally divided, Avice to have the 1st choice. To Agnes a flockbed. To Eliz. my best cow for money that I owe her, Agnes my red cow bullock, Roger my son my black wennel bullock and my little anvil, John my son my little bulchin [bull calf], and Frs. my son my cow that is now for milch for money that I owe him. The rest of my goods to Th. my son, whom I make executor on consideration that he keep Avice until she be married. I make Wm. and Frs. supervisors, and for their pains 3s.4d. Witnesses: Th. PAGE vicar [of Matching], John PALMER. Proved 7 Mar. 1578/9.

JOAN STALLOM of Foxearth widow, — '1578'. (839)
To the wife of John HEDDE the bed that I lie on. To the wife of Rt. SWANNE the best flockbed, my best gown, and my red petticoat with the chamlet overbody. To Rt. SWANNE my quern and all that belongeth thereto. To every poor house in Foxearth [sum not given]. To Rt. SWANNE a seam of malt and 2 bushels of wheat. To John HEDDE's children 6 bushels of malt and 2 bushels of wheat. To Grace [surname not given] my goddaughter my cupboard. The rest of my goods to John HEDDE [*sic*] and Rt. SWANNE equally between them. To every of my goddaughters 12d. To my daughter Eliz. the widow [surname not given] 20s. Witnesses: Wm. LODER, Th. SOMERTON. Administration committed, 11 Mar. 1578/9, to Rt. SWANNE.

WILLIAM MONKE [abode not given], 18 Sept. 1576. (840)
To be buried in Sheering churchyard. To John MONKE of Sheering my son my cupboard in the hall and at harvest next 2 bushels of wheat and 4 bushels of barley. To Geoffrey MONKE a quern after the death of his mother. To Mgt. PORTER a sheep. To Geo., Anthony and Rd. my sons each 6s.8d. and my daughter Mgt. at marriage 20s. To Leonard son of Th. MONKE 2s. To Th. MONKE and Leonard his brother 2s. To John their brother my best coat. The residue of my goods to Joan my wife, whom I appoint executrix. I make John STANE overseer. [No witnesses.] Proved 7 Mar. 1578/9.

PHILIP STANTON of Birdbrook husbandman, 14 Feb. 1577/8. (841)
To Rose my daughter and Wm. CONSTABLE her husband my house and ground,

paying my other three daughters Alice, Mgt. the elder and Mgt. the younger each £4 in the 1st, 2nd and 3rd years after his entry to the house. To Wm. son of Th. TYLER 20s. and a pair of andirons. To Kath. SYMONTE daughter of John SIMONTE 20s. The rest of my goods shall be equally divided amongst my four daughters. I make John MORE clerk, Th. MORE clerk [neither was rector of Birdbrook], Henry WARDE. Proved 16 Feb. 1578/9.

RICHARD BARBER of Gestingthorpe, servant to the goodman KETTLE, — '1578'. (842)

To my father-in-law Cuthbert GASKYN 40s. and his wife [not named] 40s., Joan JOHNSON her daughter 20s., my brother[-in-law] Hugh POLLEY 30s., my sister his wife 30s., his three children 5s. apiece, and John and Rt. CARTCEN my brother's sons 6s.8d. apiece. To my godson at Th. HUMFREYS 20d. To my master KETTLE's children Agnes, John, Mgt., Rt. and Joseph 12d. apiece. To bringing me into the earth 40s. To Rt. KETTLE my master 3s.4d. and John TYFFEN 3s.4d., whom I ordain executors. All other my goods to Cuthbert and Hugh equally divided. Witnesses: Rd. BERE, Rt TOMPSON. Proved 17 Feb. 1578/9.

ALICE BAFFORDE [abode not given] widow, 29 Nov. 1578 (843)

To the poor of Barnston 20s. and of [Great] Dunmow 20s. To Agnes BARNARDE the best velvet partlet in my chest; goodwife Stephen WADE's wife 2s.6d. and his children 4s.; my sister BASSE 10s.; my brother-in-law Rt. BASSE 3s.4d. and Joan EMPSON his sister 20d.; and goodman Th. BARNARD 3s.4d. and his servants each 3s.4d. The residue of my goods I refer to the discretion of my executors Mr Chris. SCOTT, Th. BARNARD, Rt. BASSE and Stephen WADE, and supervisor shall be Rt. BARNARD, to whom for his pains 2s. Witnesses: Henry FLETCHER, Th. SMYTH, Gervase FISHER. Proved 10 Jan. 1578/9.

RICHARD CHOPPYN of High Roothing yeoman, 20 Nov. 1578. (844)

To the poor of High Roothing 20s. To Phyllis my wife my house in High Roothing Street called Hills for her life; after her decease, to Chris. my son. To my wife for her life 2 crofts of customary land called Ricardes and another croft of customary land called Ayres Field, all in the parish. To Agnes my daughter £10 and 1 cow. To my sons Th. £3 6s.8d. and Geo. £6 13s.4d. To my wife my best horse and the brass and pewter that was hers before I married with her. To Wm. my son a parcel of free ground called Ayres Acre in a Common Field. To Chris. a parcel of customary ground called Rowland Field. To Rd. son of my son Th. 20s. at 21. To Th. BELCHAM my servant 40s. at 21 or money's worth. My wife shall have a chamber in my house wherein I dwell until Michaelmas after my decease and wheat and malt to live withal until then. To her my best bed in the parlour. To Wm. my wife [*recte* son] £6 13s.4d. My executors shall have my house and lands quietly until Michaelmas. To Agnes a great brass pan with 2 ears, a great platter, a lesser of pewter, a pewter dish, a porringer, a saucer, a candlestick, a salt, a pair of sheets, a bed in the chamber between the doors, a tablecloth, 2 napkins a great chest, and 2 sheep. To Chris. a great brass pan unbound, 4 porringers, a brass pot, 2 platters, a pewter dish, a candlestick, a red bullock, a pair of sheets, a pillow, and £3 6s.8d. To Wm. a great kettle, a brass pot, as much pewter as I have given to Chris., a pair of sheets, a candlestick, and my crumple bullock. To my wife 2 silver spoons, a latten posnet, and 2 porringers. To my single godchildren 12d. apiece. To Joan LACYE my servant 6s.8d. To my godson Rd. SPITYE 2s. To my son Th.'s four children 2s.6d. apiece and the four children of my daughter Joan 12d. apiece. To my son Simon my house called Roses with the land free and copy for his life; then to James my son. To Chris. my cupboard in the hall and Agnes and Wm. each a frying pan. All my other goods to James and Rd. my sons, whom I ordain executors. I assign my cousin John CHOPPYN overseer, and for his labour 10s. Witnesses: John CHOPPYN, John HALLE, Th. ELLYS, Henry DREWRIE. Proved 16 Dec. 1578.

THOMAS CORBIE of Thaxted cutler, 24 Sept. 1578. (Nuncupative.) (845)

He gave to Rose his wife the tenement wherein he dwelt for her life; after her decease, to be sold and the money employed to the bringing up of four of his children,

Stephen, Frs., Anne and Mgt. To his wife 26s.8d. to be paid by Wm. his son yearly for her life out of a copy[hold] in Bardfield Saling. To Eliz. his daughter 26s.8d. To Stephen and Frs. and five of his daughters Alice, Eve, Mercy, Jane and Mgt. each 26s.8d. at 21. To Wm. his son and Eliz. his daughter each a hutch. All other things to his wife, ordaining her and Wm. executors and John THORNE supervisor. Witnesses: John THORNE, John WALER. Proved 13 Oct. 1578.

JOHN WAKELYN [WAKELINGE *in margin*] of Great Oakley yeoman, 31 May 1578. (846)
To Joan my wife such implements of household stuff as I had with her at marriage, 4 beasts, the corn on the ground, and 3 hogs. To Stephen my son my 2 obligations with the money specified, whereof 1 is due at Michaelmas come twelvemonth for £30. I appoint Rd. and Peter my sons to receive the £30 to the use of Stephen at 23 and Peter to keep the other obligation to the use of Stephen when due. To Grace WAKELYN my daughter 5 beasts in the hands of Roger SHEPPERDE my son-in-law, he to deliver them or else £8 on 7 Jan. next. To Jane, Eve, Mgt. and Eliz. my daughter Emme COOKE's children 20s. apiece at 23. To Eliz., Mary and Dthy. my daughter Rose SKOOLE's children each 3 bullocks in the keeping of John SKOLE my son-in-law. To Dthy. KEBLE my daughter-in-law 6s.8d. To Lucy COOE my sister 6s.8d. To the poor people in Shalford 6s.8d., in Panfield 6s.8d., and in Oakley 6s.8d. Rd. shall have some consideration of Peter for the cost of reparations of my house wherein he now dwelleth. The rest of my goods at the disposition of my executor, whom I ordain Rd. Witnesses: Barnaby GAYMER, Rt. STANTON, John BEALE. Proved 23 Oct. 1578.

JOHN GOOGE of Roydon husbandman, 15 June 1578. (847)
To the poor of Roydon 2s. and of Nazeing 2s. To Rt. my son my tenement with my land in Roydon wherein I dwell, my brass pot, my woollen cloth and wearing raiment, my timber and boards in or about my grindstone, my kneading trough and salt trough, and 2 milch kine. To Mary my daughter 2 milch kine, the rest of my household [stuff], and the corn due to me. To John BERDDE my son-in-law the money due to me with the price of 3 hogs, 5s. apiece, contained in a bill between us. To John son of Rd. GOOGE my son £5 at 21, 1 milch cow with the profits in the custody of Th. WOODE his father-in-law, a kettle, and a brass pot which his mother hath. John BERDE shall have his dwelling in my house and the occupying of the land until Michaelmas and 1 year more, paying yearly 26s.8d., and Rt. half the fruit. To John and Wm. sons of Simon GOOGE my son 20s. apiece at 21. The rest of my goods to Rt., whom I ordain executor. I desire Wm. CAMPE of Roydon to be overseer, and for his pains 20d. Witnesses: Wm. CAMPE, Edw. HOPKYNSON. Proved 1 Sept. 1578.

JOHN SPAROWE of Finchingfield, 3 Apr. 1578. (848)
To Mgt. my daughter my 3 hutches at Th. SMYTHE's and the linen and woollen and other things in them, a silver pin, 3 of my worst kettles, 6 of my worst pewter platters, 7 saucers, my spice mortar and the 'stampell'. The residue of my goods to Rt. my son to bring him up and set him in some good service. I ordain John COO my brother-in-law executor, and for his pains 12d. Witnesses: Alex. BAYLYE, Jerome BAYLYE, Wm. BENNYTT clerk [not the vicar]. Proved — Sept. 1578.

HENRY WOODLAND of Hatfield Broad Oak, [date not given]. (Nuncupative.) (849)
He appointed his wife [not named] to pay his debts which he confessed. The residue of his goods, corn, cattle, beasts and implements of household to his wife. Witnesses: Philip KENT the elder, Wm. SWORDER, Philip KENT the younger. [No probate or administration clause.]

JOHN STANES [STANE *in margin*] of Sheering yeoman, 8 Oct., 19 Eliz. [1577]. (850)
To Joan my wife the half part of my tenement called Clementes wherein I dwell in Sheering holden by copy of court roll of the manor of Sheering Hall and half of my lands, meadows and pastures in Sheering held likewise, for her life, or else to have at her choice a yearly rent of £6 13s.4d. from the premises. To her 1 chamber

therein with free ingress, egress and regress, also the pasturing and keeping for 1 cow winter and summer. To my son Wm. after her decease the other half part of my tenement and other lands, conditionally that he pay my children Edm., Joan, Rd., Roger, Ellen, Bridget and Mgt. each £5 and Frances [my daughter?] 40s. within 1, 2, 3, 4, 5, 6, 7 and 8 years respectively after my death. To my wife the corn or grass and other profits of the premises and the residue of my goods. I ordain her my executrix. To Wm. son of Edm. STANES 1 lamb. I ordain Frs. FRANCKE gentleman and Rd. ALWARDE yeoman overseers. To Wm. my sorrel horse. To Joan daughter of Roger STANES 1 quarter of barley. Witnesses: Th. HOCKLEY, John PORTER. Proved 28 July 1578.

THOMASINE DAVIE of Harlow widow, 23 Dec. 1577. (851)
To Mgy. BEDFORD widow my wearing apparel both linen and woollen, a blue blanket, a pair of towen sheets, a carpet coverlet, and a little kettle. To Joan BRIDGMAN daughter-in-law of John BREDGE my great kettle and a dornix coverlet. To Andrew PLANCKE the younger a towen sheet. To John BROWNE a mattress and a pair of flaxen sheets and Rd. HARRISON a little round table. To mother HAVER a towen sheet. To John BRIDGE 2 great bell candlesticks and 1 of my best pewter platters. I ordain the same John of Harlow my executor, and for his pains-taking 2s.6d. The residue of my goods shall be sold by him and my overseers [not named] to pay my debts and legacies. Witnesses: John GLADWYNE the younger, Rd. HARRISON. Proved 23 June 1578.

MICHAEL WILLIAMS of Hatfield Broad Oak yeoman, 18 May 1578. (852)
To the poor people of Hatfield 5s. and of Takeley 5s. To my son Rt. my house wherein I dwell with the orchard, pond, barns, garden and my land called Madge HARRIS's and Madge HARRIS's garden, paying £10 to my creditors towards my debts. To him my tenement and land in Takeley called Paykyns after 2 years for my land and after 10 years for my house unless he can redeem it sooner, also my field and land called Bunes Field on condition to pay £40 towards the discharge of my debts. To him after the custom of the manor Cockes Croft paying therefor to Th. my son £6 and so to be enrolled in the [manor] court. To my son Wm. likewise after the decease of me and my wife my tenement and land called Hills in Takeley. My messuage and garden wherein Nich. TRESURE dwelleth to be sold towards paying my debts. To my son John £21 so that he see my debts paid to the Warden and Scholars of New College in Oxford to be taken by my executors of my corn and movables. To my daughter Eliz. 5 marks besides the portion that was her husband's [not named]. To my daughter Thomasine £5 and as much timber as will make her a joined bedstead. To my daughter Joan MILLER 40s. To Eliz. ARCHER 20s. To Mich. MYLLER my godson 40s. To Mgt. MILLER 6s.8d. at 8. To Joan my wife £3. The residue of my goods to Rt. and Wm. on condition to see my debts and legacies paid, whom I ordain executors. I make John PAVETT of [Great?] Dunmow overseer, and for his pains 10s. Witnesses: Rt. LEWKYN, John CLERE. Proved 28 July [1578].

RALPH SELLE of [Little] Dunmow Priory [i.e. Little Dunmow] shoemaker, 20 June 1578. (Nuncupative.) (853)
He gave to John SELL his son a bullock and the vantage, to be kept by Agnes his wife until it be a cow and then let forth to John's use until he come to lawful age. To her all his goods, corn and cattle. Witnesses: Th. EMERSON, John LEWES. Proved 28 July 1578.

ROBERT TAYLER of Felsted blacksmith, 23 May 1578. (854)
To Mgy. my wife for her life the house that I dwell in with the buildings, yards, gardens and orchards if I do not sell it before I die; if she enjoy my house or else by exception by sale, she shall let the shop to my partner John PETCHE blacksmith before all other if he will have it, giving as another will or as he and she can agree reasonably. To John my son 20s., 1 anvil in the hands of John TAYLER of Stebbing blacksmith, 2 pairs of smith's tongs to nail tools, and a middle hammer. To Mgt. my daughter 40s., Wm. my son 40s. and my hutch, and Joan and Mgy. my daughters each 40s. To Joan WORTHAM 40s. to be paid to John COORTMAN the elder of Felsted Bury for her at 20 or marriage, a hutch bought of John PETTCHE the elder,

and a kettle, after my wife's decease; if she die before receiving the 40s., to be paid to the rest of Mgt.'s children that she had by her husband Rd. MARYS. To the maintenance of Felsted church 12d. My wife shall 'sett' [*recte* sell] all my shop implements to pay my debts withal. The rest of my goods to my wife, whom I make executrix. I constitute John COORTMAN the elder, John CRANE of Green Street [in Felsted?] and Wm. THEDAM overseers, and for their pains 3s.4d. apiece. Witnesses: Wm. RUSTE [vicar of Felsted], John PETCHE, James COPPINE, John COPPIN. Proved 22 June 1578.

AGNES GOWER of Matching widow, 19 May, 12 Eliz. [1570]. (855)
To James YONGE's children a pair of sheets and 6s.8d. apiece. To his wife [not named] my woollen raiment. All my linen to be equally divided between my three children [not named]. The residue of my goods to John GOWER my son-in-law, whom I make executor. I make Rd. PECOCKE my son supervisor, and for his pains 3s.4d. Witnesses: Th. LYNDSEL, Arthur YONGE. Proved — 1578.

JOAN INGER of Harlow, 31 Jan. 1577/8. (856)
To Eliz. wife of Nich. LENTRESSE [LEUTRESSE?] my russet petticoat with a pair of russet sleeves. To Agnes PRENTICE widow my black kirtle. To Agnes PRENTICE my master CRAMPHORNE's servant my best knit sleeves, best hosen, and waistcoat. To Wm. CRAMPHORNE my master's son my best brass pot, little chest, and the painted cloths at Sawbridgeworth [co. Hertford]. To Rose FAWCETT my featherbed, great hutch, boulting tun, kneading tub and sieve, a little kettle, a hatchel [for combing flax or hemp], and a frying pan. The rest of my goods to John CRAMPHORNE, whom I make executor. I ordain Rd. HARRISON vicar of Harlow overseer. Witnesses: Th. CLAYE the elder, Wm. WRIGHT of Potters [Potter Street, in Harlow], Rd. CLAYE. Proved 18 May 1578.

THOMAS LAMBERTE of Thaxted, 6 Apr. 1578. (857)
To Joan my wife my messuage with the yards and gardens belonging in Thaxted, which I dwell in. The residue of my goods to her. I nominate her my executrix and Th. PURCAS supervisor. Witnesses: Th. ARGEN, Henry HOLLANDE, Peter PURCAS. Proved 16 May 1578.

NICHOLAS SAPSFORDE of Harlow husbandman, 1 Dec. 1577. (858)
To the poor people 3s.4d. To John my son my tenement called Robertes with the land belonging in White Roothing; if he die without heirs, to Mgt. my daughter. To John my 2 cows to be kept by my wife a year after my decease, then sold to my son's use to 15. To him a great pewter dish, my great candlestick, a little pewter basin, and the greater hutch. To Mgt. 2 cow bullocks to be let out to her use when she is 15, £6 at 18 or marriage, 4 pewter dishes, 2 candlesticks, a tablecloth, my green coverlet, the lesser hutch of those 2 I brought to my wife, and a new salt. John FINCHE of Great Parndon my landlord and Th. WRIGHT of Sawells in Harlow shall be guardians to John until he come to 21 and to Mgt. to 18. To my wife 2 years' rent out of my tenement in White Roothing immediately after the new barn there [is built?], on condition that she shall indemnify my overseers. The residue of my goods and the lease of my farm to my wife, on condition that she pay my debts and legacies and bring up my said children. I make her my executrix and overseers John FYNCHE and Th. WRIGHT, and for their pains 3s.4d. Witnesses: Th. HOSKIN clerk [rector of Magdalen Laver], Th. WRIGHT, Rt. BENTON, Rt. ADAM. Proved 17 May 1578.

RICHARD SPILLMAN of Thaxted shearman, — 1577/8. (859)
To Lettice my wife my house that I dwell in and the house on the backside with my yard, sometime twain together, for her life; after her decease, the said houses to my two daughters [not named]; provided that, if she stand in any need to pay my debts or toward the bringing up of my children or her own sustentation, she have power to sell the yard and take the profits. To her all my tenters, shop tools, and all other my goods. I ordain her my executrix. Witnesses: Rd. SPILMAN the younger, John SCOTTE the elder, John CHAPMAN writer hereof. Proved 15 Apr. 1578.

'ALBERIE' [AUBREY] VEER of Hedingham Castle esquire, 18 Jan. 1579/80. (860)
To be buried in Castle Hedingham church. I make my well-beloved friends Th. ATKYNS gentleman and Wm. ADAMS of Castle Hedingham executors. To them my goods and household stuff to the intent that they pay my debts; after paying all charges as my executors, the remainder to John my son and Bridget my daughter equally betwixt them, provided that my executors be not charged in further paying my debts than my goods shall come to. Witnesses: Giles WHITINGE, Geo. WARDE, Rt. OSBORNE, Wm. VIGORUS. The executors refused executorship; administration committed to them.

JOHN BROMLEY of Wethersfield, 13 July 1579. (861)
To Kath. my wife all my brass and pewter little and great, my cupboard in the hall, all kind of bedding, with all my other goods within and without the house. I constitute her my executrix. Witnesses: John WALFER, John PARKER, Wm. NASHE, Th. CRANE, Paul INGRAM. Proved 1 Mar. 1579/80.

HENRY GRAYE *alias* POOLE of Halstead weaver, 11 Oct., 22 [*recte* 21?] Eliz. [1580, *recte* 1579?]. (862)
To the poor 6s.8d. To Alice COCKRILE and Blanche KINGE each 1 bullock to be taken out of 3 of 2 years old. The rest of my goods to Mgt. my wife, whom I make executrix. Witnesses: Wm. MALTE, Wm. WATSON, Th. SWETINGE. Administration committed, 24 Feb. 1579/80, to Mgt. widow of Henry GRENE [*sic*] *alias* POOLE.

JOHN HEMPSTED of Steeple Bumpstead labourer, 28 Dec. 1579. (863)
To Edw. and Rd. my sons at 21 and Eliz., Mgt. and Alice my daughters at 21 or marriage the profits and rents equally of my tenement and Frees Croft for 7 years after my decease, to be let according to the custom of the manor at the discretion of my trusty friend Edw. HAWKYNS, whom I ordain executor. To Wm. my son part of Frees Croft now being enclosed; he shall have free ingress, egress and regress through the nether part of Frees Croft with horse, cart or any other cattle, paying yearly for the drift 2d. to John his brother, if demanded, and half the lord's rent. My children being brought up, my executor shall take out of my goods as much as it cometh to for his discharge. The rest of my goods to my first-mentioned five children equally. Witnesses: Rd. ONYON, Edw. HAWKYNS. Proved 6 Feb. 1579/80.

AGNES BASHE of Matching widow, 14 Nov., 26 Eliz. [1584, *recte* 20 or 16 Eliz.?]. (864)
To Clemence GERVELL my daughter a russet coat. To Agnes KYNTO [LYNTO?] my daughter's children 2d. apiece. The residue of my goods to Dthy. my daughter, whom I ordain executrix. Witnesses: Wm. CLARKE, Arthur YOUNGE. Proved 8 Jan. 1579/80.

EDMUND REVE of High Easter husbandman, 3 Jan. 1579/80. (865)
To Mgy. my wife my tenement with the lands free and copy in High Easter for her life; after her death, my tenement called Harveys with the said land to Wm. my eldest son, also another croft called Blondes (2 acres). To my 2nd son Rd. my other tenement called Smithes with half a yard [about 15 acres] of land belonging, a parcel being half an acre, parcel of Sawkins half acre, 3 acres of land in Little Baveley [now Bavley, in High Easter] being customary land, and 1 acre of meadow being parcel of Bawlde Eves Quarter at West End. To my youngest son Th. a croft being free called Halles Bewley (10 acres) and Garters Mead (2 acres) being parcel of Gacers Quarter; if he die before 21, to be sold by four honest men and Rd. to have the proffer thereof. To Wm. my croft called Eves at Bishop Wood Green in Great Dunmow (2 acres), on condition that he pay out thereof to Fortune REVE my daughter £10 at 50s. yearly. To Eliz. my daughter £7 13s.4d. to be paid by my wife out of my goods. To Bridget REVE my daughter £10 to be paid by my wife at 20. The residue of my goods to her and Rd. my executors, and for his pains 3s.4d. Witnesses: John ROOF, John NOKE, Lawrence REVE. Proved 6 Feb. 1579/80.

JOHN ASSER of Mashbury husbandman, 10 Aug. 1579. (866)
To my eldest son Th. my mansion [i.e. dwelling] house in Good Easter, 4 crofts of pasture and arable adjoining (8 acres), Hamstole Field (8 acres), Clobbes (5 acres), and Sowterly (3 acres) in High Easter. To my 2nd son John my tenement called Woodes with Woodes Croft (1 acre), St. James Croft (1 acre), and Munnes Croft (1 acre) in High Easter, Clayes with a garden plat (10 acres) and Robbyns (8 acres), Robbyns Meadow (6 acres), with 5 acres of land, all in Good Easter. To my son Wm. Goldenwell Field with a meadow adjoining (2 acres) in Wares Leet and 1 acre of free ground in the same field (in all 12 acres) and land adjoining (2 acres) in Newarks Leet, abutting on a meadow of Mr GROVE's belonging to Bedfordes. To John my son Warebordes Croft in Mashbury (2 acres). To Joan my wife the years that I have of Mashbury Hall, with the stock, corn, cattle and all other things not before bequeathed, to her own sustentation and bringing up of my children. To my daughter Mary £20 when my lease of Mashbury Hall is expired and my daughter Joan £20 4 years after my decease to be paid by my sons Th. and John the elder equally. My wife shall pay my son Edw. £10 6 years after my decease and my son Th. £20 at 22, also Th. ASSER my kinsman 20 nobles at Michaelmas next and 20 nobles at Michaelmas after. Th. and John the elder shall pay my wife yearly £5 and Wm. pay her 40s. yearly. To my godchildren 12d. apiece. I make my wife executrix and my brother Edm. ASSER of High Easter overseer, to whom I bequeath 5s. Witnesses: Rd. COFFEN, Andrew NOOKE, John NEWLANDE. Proved 6 Feb. 1579/80.

JOHN WODE of Little Yeldham, 29 Apr. 1579. (867)
To the child which my wife is now withal a freehold tenement caled Gyncoockes. To Eliz. my wife my copyhold in Stebbing for her life. If my child die, to her all my houses and lands free and copy for her life. If she decease and my child also without heir, all to John WOODE my kinsman, paying £40 [*sic*] to the poverty of Felsted and Stebbing and £4 to the children of Wm. WOODE of Felsted, cousin to John WOOD late deceased, and £6 to the children of John WOOD of Felsted. All my other goods to my wife. I ordain John WOODE my kinsman executor, and for his pains 20s. [No witnesses.] Proved [date not given].

ELIZABETH DERINGTON of Harlow widow [of George], 10 Apr. 1576. (868)
To be buried in Harlow church near my husband. To the poor people at the church at my burial 20s. among them in penny dole and 20s. in bread, drink and cheese. To widow MOYNE, widow CORNEY, widow STEVENSON the elder, John WILSON, widow PRENTICE the elder, widow CLERKE, and widow HAVER 4d. apiece. To my godchildren 12d. apiece. To my cousins Wm., Abraham the elder and Rt. SELL 13s.4d. apiece at any of their next coming to Harlow. To Mgt. BUCKMASTER my brother's daughter my best gown with a velvet cap, best kirtle, best petticoat, and best rail; my mother-in-law [not named] my frize cassock and my hat and cap which I wear every holyday; my sister WHALE my black cassock furred; my sister SKINGLE my train gown with 8 pleats; Susan MARCALE my frock; Mgt. BUCKMASTER my gold ring hoop which I wear on my finger with the letters E S within it, 2 silver spoons, and 40s.; Abraham SELL the younger, my brother John's son, 2 silver spoons, 1 gold ring with a stone in it, and £6 13s.4d.; Mgt. COXE my red petticoat with an upperbody of red mockado, a holyday kercher, and my worsted apron; Grace COOKE my 3 gold 'gymmers' [gimmals, divisible rings] all knitted in one; and Alice HAYDON an holyday kerchief. The rest of my goods, with the legacy due to me of the Will of Geo. DIRRINGTON my husband, to Th. SELLE my brother John's son, whom I ordain executor. I make John DERRINGTON of Harlow yeoman overseer. Witnesses: John COCKE, Rd. HARRISON [vicar of Harlow]. Proved 8 Jan. 1579/80.

MARGARET WALLIS of Stebbing widow, 25 Nov. 1579. (869)
To the poor people 3s.4d. To John WALLYS my son 20s., John and Samuel the sons and Alice the daughter of Rt. WALLIS my son, Agnes BUTLANDE my daughter, Rd. and Ellen son and daughter of Rd. BUTLANDE, and Alice daughter of Edm. WALLYS, each 6s.8d. To Joan WALLYS the base child of Edm. WALLYS 10s. The residue of my goods to be appraised by two indifferent men and equally divided between my four children Edm., Rt., Wm. and Agnes. I ordain my well-beloved in

Christ Wm. AYLWARDE executor. Witnesses: John SAWELL, Ralph SMITHE. Administration committed, 15 Dec. 1579, to Edm., Rt., Wm. and Agnes WALLYS, because the executor refused.

JOHN STAFFORDE of High Easter husbandman, 13 Dec. 1579. (Nuncupative.) (870)
To my two sons James and Wm. each £4 and my daughters Jane and Agnes each 53s.4d. The rest of my goods to my wife Mary to bring up my said children. I make her my executrix. Witnesses: Rd. VAUSE vicar there, John SORRELL, Wm. NOKE. Proved 15 Dec. 1579.

WILLIAM BYNDE of Alphamstone, 2 Mar. 1578/9. (871)
To Dthy. my wife my house and yard where I dwell in Alphamstone for her life; after her decease, to be sold and the money equally divided betwixt my seven children [not named]; the youngest daughter shall have 20s. more than the rest if it may be spared. To my wife all my goods for her life, then to be divided amongst all my children. I ordain Rd. my son and Rt. THOMSON executors, and for their pains 20s. apiece. Witnesses: John TOMPSON, Wm. BAKER, John WEKES. Proved 17 Nov. 1579.

AGNES NICHOLSON of Sible Hedingham widow, 14 Nov. 1579. (872)
To James my son my cupboard, counter table, press and painted cloths hanging in my hall. To Th. my son my trundle bed and featherbed. To Benet my daughter my posted bed and 1 featherbed. The rest of my linen equally divided to Benet and my daughter Anne by two discreet women and in like manner 4 of my gowns and 2 of my best petticoats. The rest of my woollen apparel to the poor. To my goddaughters Susan NICHOLSON, Emme NICHOLSON and Rebecca NICHOLSON each 1 pewter charger. To Th. my best kettle. The rest of my brass and pewter equally divided between my two daughters. The residue of my goods to James, whom I ordain my executor. Witnesses: Rd. TYFFIN, Wm. BARDE, John HUNTE. Proved 17 Nov. 1579.

JOHN ALLAM of High Easter husbandman, 24 Oct. 1579. (873)
To my son Geo. my customary lands and tenements in High Easter, i.e. a tenement called Mariotes with 30 acres appertaining, land called Chymebelles (2 acres), another parcel (1½ acres), and a half parcel of Baldewys Quarter, all at 25 and not before. I will that the money growing in the meantime of the premises may be let to any persons and remain with Joan my wife to the use of my son John for his maintenance at school and proceeding still in learning until Geo. is 25, when the money shall be paid by her to John's use to my cousin Geo. ALLAM, Edm. ASSER and John AYLET, all of High Easter husbandmen, my especial friends, at one whole payment without any deduction of the increasing money for the board and books and other necessaries of John, which board, books and necessaries I will my wife to give him freely for his preferment and furtherance in learning; the money to remain in my friends' hands until John is 21. To Alice my daughter 6s.8d. and a good cow at 20. All other my goods to my wife, whom I make executrix. I appoint Geo. ALLAM my cousin and Edm. ASSER overseers, and for their pains 3s.4d. Witnesses: Geo. QUILTER, Geo. ALLAM, Edm. ASSER, Geo. AYLYTE, Th. PLAYLE, Wm. BARNARD, John PIGBON clerk, writer hereof. Proved 21 Nov. 1579.

JOHN CHESSE of Barnston, 11 Feb. 1574/5. (874)
To be buried in Barnston church porch. To Mgt. my wife half the occupying of these tenements that I dwell in for her life, half the corn on the ground and in the barn, 2 beasts (1 a brown 'howed' [for meaning see p. xvii], the other a black 'howed'), 5 sheep of the best, 2 store hogs, my 'pullen', my best featherbed, and my best table in the hall. To my brother Wm. CHESSE the occupying of the other half of my lands during my wife's life and of such other goods not bequeathed, on condition that he pay Henry JUDDE my kinsman and servant £4 a year for 5 years from Michaelmas next and pay all my debts, after which all my household stuff, corn and cattle that remaineth shall be equally divided betwixt four of my kinsfolk, Alice KNATT, Mary HARTE, John CHESSE and Henry CHESSE. To my brother Wm.,

after my wife's decease, my tenement and lands that I dwell in and occupy, on condition that he let them for 10 years and my rents be divided equally amongst my said kinsfolk, after which he shall sell them and they shall have £20 apiece. To Th. CHESSE my brother, Wm. and Mercy BARNARDE my kinsmen, and Jane BARNARDE their sister, 40s. each and the residue of the money remaining. I appoint my brother Wm. executor, and for his pains 20s., and Rt. SAUNDER overseer, and I give him 10s. To my godchildren 12d. apiece. To twelve of the poorest households in Barnston 12d. apiece. My executor to bestow 8s. on a coat for Joan THEDAM my daughter-in-law. Witnesses: Wm. CHOPPIN, John JUDDE, Rt. SAUNDER. Proved 28 Oct. 1579.

LEONARD CORTMAN of Felsted, 20 Sept. 1579. (875)
To the poor people of Felsted 20s. To Andrew and Wm. COURTMAN my brothers each £3. To the children of my brother John COURTMAN, John and Mary, each 6s.8d. at 16 and of my brother Th. COURTMAN, Th., James and Wm., each 6s.8d. to be paid to their father. To five of my brother John's servants 3s.4d. apiece. To my brothers Th. and Rt. each 10s. The residue of my goods to my brother John, whom I make executor. To Leonard CRANE and Joan BREWET my godchildren 12d. apiece. [No witnesses.] Proved 27 Oct. 1579.

AGNES WRIGHTE of Sible Hedingham widow, 24 June 1579. (876)
To my son John WRIGHTE's children, seven in number, to six of them 4d. apiece and to the other, Agnes WRIGHTE, 12d. To five of my daughter Mgy. MORE's children each 4d. To Agnes MASON my godchild 4d. To seven of my son Rd. WRIGHTE's children, six of them 4d. apiece and the seventh, Titus, 3s.4d., to be paid out of 13s.4d. which Rd. oweth me. To my daughter Mgy. a pewter platter, a gridiron, and a frying pan. To my son Geo. WIGHTE's children, six of them 6d. apiece and to the other, John WRIGHTE, 12d. The rest of my goods and lands to Geo., whom I ordain executor. Witnesses: John DIGBIE, John FAWKON, Henry ORBEY. Proved 10 Sept. 1579.

ROGER NORMAN *alias* RENOLDE,
servant to Mr John WYSEMAN of Great Canfield esquire, 23 June 1579. (877)
To Reynold NORMAN my father 40s. a year for certain years as in a writing indented between Mr WYSEMAN and me, but, if my father die before the years be expired, the 40s. shall be equally divided between my brothers John and Th. and my sister Joan NORMAN, also to each 10s. To my godchildren 12d. apiece. To my fellows, now servants with my master, 4d. apiece. To Mistress Mgt. WYSEMAN my mistress for good considerations moving me, my houses and grounds in Great Dunmow. The residue of my goods to Mr John WYSEMAN my master, whom I make executor. Witnesses: Rd. RANBARDE, Chris. DAWSON, Rt. TURNER, Wm. CAWELL. Proved [date not given].

JOHN LYLEFORDE of Shalford labourer, 22 Apr. 1579. (878)
To my son Henry my house with the buildings and orchard in Great Bardfield after the decease of Anne my wife; if he die without issue, to my three daughters Anne, Clemence and Eliz. equally divided. To Eliz. my little house in the yard with a little garden plot in Shalford for her life, on condition that she goeth not to sell it; after her death, to Henry. To her a mattress. To my wife my great [*sic*] house in the yard with the ground. To Anne my black cow called Old Cnap. To Clemence my black bullock. To my wife all my other goods. I ordain her and Henry executors. Witnesses: Th. PRATT, Chris. PURPLE. Proved 7 July 1579.

WILLIAM THURGOOD of Felsted husbandman, 14 Nov. 1577. (879)
To Alice my wife my house and lands and all my movables after her decease, my house in Rayne Street to Barthw. my eldest son. To Gabriel my son Browninges Croft in Felsted ($5\frac{1}{2}$ acres); if he die without issue, to my six daughters [not named] part and part like. After my wife's decease the rest of my goods equally divided among my six daughters. I make my wife executrix and John ENNEWE overseer, and for his pains 3s.4d. Witnesses: Rd. USHER, John ENNEWE. Proved 23 July 1579.

ROBERT OSBORNE of Halstead fuller, 10 Feb. 1578/9. (880)
To Eliz. my daughter my term of years in the tenement in which Th. SWETINGE dwelleth with the hopyard and hoppoles and all my household stuff except 1 chest, 1 chair and 1 flockbed. To Alex. VYNE my term of years in the house in which I dwell. To Wm. son of Alexander VINE my term of years in my hopgarden which I hold of the demise of Wm. MARTYNE late of Halstead with the hoppoles, on condition that 20s. each be paid out of the profits by my executors to my sons Valentine and Vincent. To Wm. VINE 1 chest bound with iron. To Vincent 1 flockbed when he shall demand it. To William VINE, Rt. BRADLEY and Sarah ROME each 1 hive of bees. To Th. SWETINGE my cap which I bought of GRAYE. To four fullers to carry me to church four of my best 'twyches' [tweezers?]. I will that 1 kilderkin of beer and 20 pennyworth of bread be carried to the church to be eaten and drunk amongst the ringers and those which go with me to church. The residue of my goods to Eliz. I ordain her and Alex. VINE executors, and for his pains 1 silken cushion. To Eliz. my term of years in the dovehouse and parcel of land in Tenter Croft. Witnesses: Rt. ENEWE, John ROME, Wm. COLLISON, Rd. BAKER. Proved 4 June 1579.

JOHN SPITTLE of High Roothing yeoman, 10 Nov. 1578. (881)
To James my son my tenement called Paffermanes with the yards, hoppet and croft in High Roothing at 24; a croft called Waites in Great Dunmow after the expiration of a lease of Waites with other lands specified made by John SPITTLE to Wm. SKELTON, during which lease the rent of Waytes which I rate at 20s. a year shall remain to my executor towards paying my debts and legacies, and the rent of Paffermans likewise remain until James is 24. To Eliz. my wife for her life a tenement called Allens in High Roothing with the house belonging, 1 acre of free land called Allens hoppet, 1 acre of free land between Parsonage Croft and Carters Croft, and 1 acre of free land in Manges [Mauges?]; after her decease, to Th. my son. To my wife Parsonage Croft, Perrishe Field and Manges for her life; after her decease, to Th. To my wife and Rd. my son my other houses and lands in High Roothing, in consideration that they pay my debts and legacies. To John son of John my son £20 at 24 and £20 at 26. To Mgy. my daughter £10 a year until £40 be paid. To Winifred my daughter £10 at the end of 10 years after my decease. If John die before 26, the £40 to be divided betwen Mary SPITTLE daughter of my son Rd., Joan JACKSON daughter of my daughter Jane, and the two sisters of John son of John. To Rd. SWORDER and Dennys MACHYNE sometime my servants a seam of barley. To the poor people of High Roothing 20s. All my other goods to my wife and Rd., whom I make executors. Th. shall be overseer. Witnesses: Rt. WASKETT, Wm. HOWE, Henry BURTON, Th. PLAYLE. Proved 4 June 1579.

JOHN THURGOOD of Matching yeoman, 25 Apr. 1579. (882)
To the poor of Matching 20s., of Hatfield Broad Oak 10s., of Magdalen Laver 6s.8d., of Sheering 6s.8d., and of Harlow 6s.8d. To 'Colleton Haven' [Colyton, co. Devon] 2s. To Rt. my son my messuage in Magdalen Laver called Humfreys with the land belonging. To Wm. my son my lands in North Weald Bassett or High Ongar, provided that he pay Andrew my son £100 at such time as shall be thought good by my supervisors and Nich. THURGOOD my brother. To Th. my son my messuage in Matching called Taylers with the lands belonging free and copy and my lease of Highte Field in Epping. To John my son my purchase or bargain of the lands and houses of Th. KINGE of Bushes in Magdalen Laver with all debts due to me by him, on condition that John pay Andrew at the end of Th. KINGE's years £200 and acknowledge a recognizance for payment thereof to Andrew. To my three sons Rt., Wm. and Th. my lease or term of years yet to come in the manor of Ovesham [now Housham Hall, in Matching] with my corn and cattle on the manor, except 1 pease stack on land called Woodland which I give to Wm. I will that my sons pay my three daughters Kath., Mary and Agnes 300 marks, on condition that each [pay] 100 marks whereof 200 be paid to Th. LYNDSELL of Matching and Th. GYNINGES of Magdalen Laver my supervisors and Th. RAMSEY my son-in-law when the lease of the manor be expired, to be repaid by them to Mary and Agnes at marriage or 24, provided that if either contract matrimony without the assent of Th. KINGE and my supervisors, she shall have only £10 and the residue equally amongst my other children;

Kath. to have her 100 marks with convenient speed. To her 1 great brazen posnet, Agnes my best bed and 1 great chafer, Mary another bed of the best, and each ½ dozen of pewter, a saucer, a salt, a pottinger, a candlestick, 3 pair of sheets of the best, 2 tablecloths of the best, and ½ dozen napkins. To Andrew 1 bed of the best, ½ dozen of pewter, 1 candlestick, 1 saucer, 1 salt, 1 pottinger, the best chest, the long barred chest, ½ doz. napkins, and 2 tablecloths. To Mary and Agnes each 1 chest of the best. To Rt. and Wm. my timber lying at Humfreys. To Rt. the tile that I bought of Th. SOREHAM. To Wm. 1 great copper pan that I brew withal called the lead. To Rt., Wm., John and Th. the residue of my household stuff equally divided. To Rt., Wm. and Th. my carts, ploughs, plough irons, with collars and other things. To my two servants John BOREHAM and Ellen PARMENTER each 1 sheep and 1 lamb. Rt. shall pay my executor £20 and Th. pay £10 after my lease be expired. The residue of my goods to Wm., whom I make executor. I make Th. LYNSELL and Th. GENNINGES supervisors, and for their pains 20s. Witnesses: Th. PAGE vicar [of Matching], Th. KINGE. Proved 21 May 1579.

HENRY BREDGE of Felsted husbandman, 1 May 1577. (883)
To Rt. BREDGE my brother the dwelling in my house called Levels with the ground belonging as he doth now occupy it for 10 years after my death, paying the same 6s.8d. yearly and the lord's rent. To Henry son of Rt. my godson £3 6s.8d. at 21; if he die before, to my daughter Anne. To twenty of the poor householders of Felsted each 12d. The rest of my lands, goods, leases, corn and cattle to John CAVYLE my son-in-law, whom I make executor. Witnesses: Wm. RUST vicar of Felsted, Wm. SCOTTE, Rt. EVANS, John CAVYLE the elder. Proved 21 May 1577 [*recte* 1579].

JOAN GRYGMAN of Stebbing widow, 6 June 1577. (884)
To Joan PARRATE my daughter land in Stebbing called Perrie (2 acres). To Th. PARRATE my son my house with two crofts called Pylletes and Shortland, binding himself to John POLIE of Stebbing at the next [manor] court holden at Porters Hall in Stebbing after my decease to pay Henry and Mgy. GRIGMAN my children each 33s.4d. at 20. I make John POLEY executor. Witnesses: John DUDYN minister [John DURDEN vicar of Stebbing], John POLEY, Anthony POLEY, Wm. TURNER. Proved 2 Apr. 1579.

Joan STEWARDE widow, [abode not given], 11 Oct. 1578. (885)
To Kath. my daughter a casting sheet and all my wearing gear as linen and woollen. To Joan my daughter a fine sheet. To Wm. BARKER my son a painted cloth. The residue of my goods to Rd. BARKER my son, whom I make executor. Witnesses: Rt. HEYWARDE, Henry BARKER. Proved 28 Apr. 1579.

THOMAS BAKER [abode not given], 9 Apr., 21 Eliz. [1579]. (886)
To my sister's son Wm. RAWLINSON 20 nobles. To my sister's son Rt. HILLES, Edw. HILLES his other brother, and Mgt. RAWLINSON, each £6 13s.4d. I make my sister HILLES my executrix. The rest of my goods to be disposed at her discretion. Witnesses: Anthony WADDINGTON, Henry DOWDALE, Th. WICKLINGE. Proved 29 Apr. 1579.

THOMAS BROWNE of Great Parndon labourer,
22 Feb., 23 Eliz. [1580/1]. (Nuncupative.) (887)
To nine poor folk of the parish 4d. apiece. To John his youngest son 2 kine, 1 in the hands of Rt. SKYNNER of Netteswell, the other in those of John RAMSEY of Parndon aforesaid. To Rd. his son 2 kine, 1 with Rd. HALLE of Nazeing gentleman, the other with Wm. SHARPE of Harlow. To John 46s.8d. in the hands of John CLAYE and Rt. CLEYE his brother in Harlow. To Rd. 33s.4d. with Rt. SKYNNER. To John 1 featherbed, his great brass kettle which is bound, 1 spit, 1 pair of cob-irons, 1 trivet, 1 pair of pothangers, 1 powdering trough, 1 kneading trough, and all his painted cloths. To Rd. 1 flockbed and 1 brass pot. The residue of his goods to be divided between John and Rd. by his executors [not named], and for their pains 20s. apiece. Witnesses: James BUTLER, Wm. WALKER. Proved 9 Mar. 158-[1].
[[1] See fn. p.200].

THOMAS NICHOLSON of Halstead, 24 Oct. 158-[1]. **(888)**
I will that my house and lands called Partriches in Halstead and Gosfield be sold by Geo. NICOLSON my brother and that he pay Susan my wife £100 at Michaelmas next, on condition that she deliver up such dowry as she hath therein and bring up Anne my daughter to 21. To Anne £20 to be paid by Geo. out of my house and lands at 21. To Geo. £65 which I owe him. To my wife her dwelling in my house, the pasturing of 2 kine winter and summer until Michaelmas next, 1 bed with the casting sheet, the knit curtains and 3 holland pillowberes, with the household stuff, until then. The rest of my goods to Geo. towards the bringing up of my sons Th. and Rt. at 21; if all my children die before 21, their portions to be equally divided among all my brother's and sister's [brothers' and sisters'?] children. I ordain Geo. executor. Witnesses: Nich. WILLBOORE, Geo. NICOLSON, James NICOLLSON, Wm. JOHNSON, Rd. BAKER. Proved 14 Feb. 158-[1].

RICHARD GREENOUGHE of Great Parndon tailor, 22 Dec. 1580. (Nuncupative.) (889)
To the poor people 10s. To his sons Rt. his bald mare, Geo. £5 at 21, and Th. £5 at 21 and his black mare colt. The residue of his goods to Agnes his wife, whom he made his executrix. Witnesses: Wm. ADAM, Albone FLETCHER, Wm. GRAYGOOSE. Proved 13 Feb. 158-[1].

EDWARD NEALE the elder of Willingale Doe husbandman, 9 Nov. 158-[1]. **(890)**
To Eliz. my wife my mansion [i.e. dwelling] house called Wyndels with my lands in Willingale Doe and Willingale Spain for her life; if she marry again, she shall depart within half a year and yield up the premises to my two sons Edw. and Rd. To Edw. my eldest son the said house and land in Willingale Doe and to Rd. my younger son my lands in Willingale Spain. They shall pay my wife for her third or dower in my lands 40s. a year. To Edw. my table and form in the hall, greatest spit, 1 dripping pan, and malt quern. To Rd. my lands called Potmans and Parnell land in Willingale Spain; if both die without heirs, to Th. son of Ralph NEALE my brother deceased, also Wyndels after my wife's decease. To the poor householders in Willingale Spain 3s.4d. To Temperance LYCKERYS sometime my servant 1 bushel of wheat. The residue of my goods to my wife, whom I ordain executrix. I appoint supervisor Rd. DOWNHAM, and for his pains 12d. Witnesses: Gilbert SOMNER, Wm. GLASCOCKE. Proved 10 Jan. 158-[1].

THOMAS GARDINER of Pentlow, 8 Aug. 158-[1] and 22 Eliz. [1580]. **(891)**
To the poor people of Pentlow 5s., of Cavendish [co. Suffolk] 6s.8d., Belchamp St. Paul 3s.4d., of Clare [co. Suffolk] 6s.8d., and of Foxearth 3s.4d. To Christian my wife my 2 tenements and lands in Pentlow freehold and leased lands for her life. To Th. my son my customary lands and tenements holden of the manor of Bendish Hall in Radwinter, reserved therefrom a yearly rent of £3 during my wife's life, to be paid by Th., i.e. 30s. each to Geo. and John my sons. To Geo. after my wife's decease my tenement and lands called Clacksens and a close adjoining and a pightle called Lepingwell in Pentlow. To John after my wife's decease my tenement called Clerkes, a close called Close Laye, and Hook Meadow in Pentlow. To my daughters Joan HARDIE, Saphira and Agnes each £20. To Geo., John, Saphira and Agnes each 1 cow and 1 bedstead at marriage. The rest of my goods to my wife, whom I ordain executrix. I make Th., Geo. and John supervisors. I have surrendered my copyhold lands in Radwinter to the use of my Will by James COOKE and Henry BUTCHER copyholders in the presence of John LEECHE and Th. FURMAN. Witnesses: Th. DREWRIE, John SEXTON, Edw. RAYNISFORDE. Proved 10 Jan. 158-[1].

JOHN HOWE of Netteswell, 6 Dec. 1580. **(892)**
To the poor people 10s. To Anne my daughter my free tenement with an acre of land in Gilston [co. Hertford]. To Joan my sister 20s. which she oweth me for rent. To Rt. my servant 10s., my old leather doublet, an old pair of hose, and a pair of sky-coloured coats. To my cousin Th. HOWE 1 bushel of wheat. To Th. my servant

[1] On several folios of the Register the last digit of the year is missing (nos. 887-92, 901, 903); the year is 1580 or 1581.

20s. To Geo. YONGE 1 bushel of wheat. To Alice FULLER my servant 15s. I forgive my brother Herbert £3 of £10 which he oweth me. To Mary my daughter 20 marks at 21 or marriage. The rest of my goods to Mary my wife, whom I make my executrix. I make Th. HARRYS my father-in-law, Th. HARRYS and my brother Th. HOWE overseers. Witnesses: Th. GRAYGOOSE, Th. CARRE, Th. WOOD, Rd. HARRISON [vicar of Harlow]. Proved 9 Jan. 1580/1.

ELIZABETH TITRELL of Toppesfield widow, 4 Nov. 1580. **(893)**
To the poor men's box 3s.4d. To Rose and Mgt. my late husband's daughters besides his legacies each 20s. To Mgy. my daughter besides the legacy of her father, £4 and my wearing apparel linen and woollen, not before marriage and on condition that she marry with my executors' consent. To Mgy. GEORGE a pair of sheets and Joan GEORGE 2 pillows and a red petticoat. To Stephen my man a calf. To Wm. BIDGE and Henry SMITHE of Toppesfield each 15s. for their pains, whom I make executors. The rest of my goods to be sold by my executors, and what shall remain to my son Rd. at 21. Witnesses: Wm. WHITINGE the writer, Th. HAMONDE, Wm. BOCHER. Proved 17 Dec. 158-[1].

HENRY HARRINGTON of Toppesfield yeoman, 13 Nov. 1579. **(894)**
To the poor people of Wickham St. Paul 20s. To Simon my son my messuage called Walshes with the lands in Wickham and Gestingthorpe purchased of Rt. COTTEN gentleman and Lettice his wife, on condition that he pay Henry and Rd. my sons each £40. To Henry my messuage and lands in Steeple Bumpstead; my messuage and lands in Robin Hood's End in Stambourne in the occupation of widow HAUKYN bought of Th. NEWMAN gentleman; and my customary lands in Birdbrook in that of Edw. WADE. To Rd. my lands free and customary in Wickham St. Paul purchased of Peter GRENE and Wm. LAWSELL in the occupation of Wm. MILLER and my customary tenement and lands in Toppesfield severally holden of the manor of Skotneis and Cuntis [now Scotneys Farm and Cust Hall in Toppesfield] in the occupation of Rd. HALLE. To John my son my messuage and land adjoining and land called Maiden land in Toppesfield in that of Rd. POLLARD and my indenture of lease of the farm called Brownes tenement and the lands in Toppesfield. To Frances my wife 2 of my best kine and half my household stuff. To Collett my daughter £40. To Rd. my customary land called the Brook purchased of Rd. POOLEY gentleman in Wickham holden of the manor of Wickham St. Paul. To Henry Twist Meadow purchased of Rt. COMPTON in Stambourne. The rest of my goods, corn and cattle to John, whom I ordain executor. Witnesses: Wm. VYGORUS the writer, Hugh POLLIE. Proved 7 Dec. 158-[1].

WILLIAM FANNE of Thaxted yeoman, 1 May 158-[1], 22 Eliz. [1580]. **(895)**
To be buried in Thaxted church. To the poor people 20s. at the day of my burial. To the reparations of the church 12d. To John my son my messuage in which I dwell in a hamlet called Haggery or Standbrook in Thaxted with the lands belonging. To the poor of Thaxted yearly out of my lands 3s.4d. To Ellen BUCKE my daughter, if she keep herself unmarried, £6 13s.4d. by 13s.4d. a year, the bed in which I lie, and 1 cupboard and 1 hutch in my chamber. To my children's children [not named] £3 6s.8d. between them at 21. The residue of my goods to John. I nominate John and Ellen executors and Th. PURCAS supervisor. Witnesses: Th. PURCAS, James PURCAS, Mgt. PERRIE. Proved 4 Nov. 1580.

WILLIAM HUMFREY of Foxearth husbandman, 20 Oct. 1580. **(896)**
To Henry, Th. and Wm. my sons each 20 marks within 3 years after my decease. To 'Phillipe', Emme and Marion HUMFREY my daughters each £10 within 1, 2 and 3 years. To Wm. my eldest son 20s. To Alice my wife half of my goods. To Edw. HUMFREY's daughters [not named] each 10s. The residue of my goods and ready money to my executors, whom I ordain Edw. and Harry my sons, and to each for their labour 10s. To the poor people in Foxearth 10s. Witnesses: Wm. FYRMYN, Rt. DURANT. Proved 4 Nov. 1580.

[1]See fn. p. 200.

JOHN ANNYS *alias* SMYTHE of Halstead innholder, 23 Jan. 1579/80. (897)
To Rt. ANNYS my son £10 at 21 and my new bed in the middle guest chamber. To John ANNYS £10 at 21. If both die before, their portions to my wife's other children, Sarah, Ellen, Agnes, Alice and Joan SADLINGTON. To Chris. ANNYS *alias* SMYTHE 10s. The rest of my goods to Joan my wife, whom I make executrix, to see my children well bought up. Witnesses: Henry TOMSONNE, Rt. SMYTHE the elder and Rt. SMYTHE the younger, Chris. ANNYS, Th. NORMAN. Proved 29 Apr. 1580.

WILLIAM DENTE of High Easter yeoman, 17 Mar. 1579/80. (Nuncupative.) (898)
He did give all his goods to Mgt. wife of Th. RANDALL of High Easter. Witnesses: John RYCHARDSON and Allen LAMBERT, both of High Easter. Administration committed, 16 Apr. 1580, to Th. RANDALL.

MATTHEW KNOPPE of Alphamstone husbandman, 1 May 1580. (899)
To Agnes my wife my lease and term of years of the house and lands that I dwell in which I hold of Th. HAVERINGE; if she die before the end, to Th. PERYMAN and John KNOPPE my nephew, now my household servants, equally parted. To her all my household stuff, money, goods, and corn in the chambers, barn or growing, for her life. To Th. and John to be equally parted by the oversight of Mr Nich. le GRIS parson of Alphamstone [legacy not stated] after my wife's death; out of whose goods to Mgt. KNOPPE my maid and household servant £20 [*sic*], two parts which I have given to Th. and John, they dwelling and continuing with my wife. To the poor people of the parish 4s. To four men which shall bear me to church 4s. To Alice PERYE a dry sheep. To Wm. PERYMAN my wife's son 1 bullock. I ordain Th. and John executors. I make Mr Nich. le GRIS overseer, and for his pains 3s.4d. Witnesses: Nich. le GRYS the writer, John SIDAYE, James LORKIN. Proved 15 May 1580.

ROBERT GRENE the elder of Sible Hedingham husbandman, 30 Aug. 1579. (900)
To Eliz. my wife all my goods and my tenement in Alderford Street [in Sible Hedingham] in the occupying of Simon HULT for her life; after her decease, to Anne my daughter, wife of John CHAPMAN; after her decease, to be sold and equally parted among their children. To Hum. CHAPMAN's children (the two he hath now alive) 6s.8d. each. To John OCKLY and Anne BOUCHER my daughter's children a little tenement in Thaxted over against Wm. C[U?]RLES equally divided between them. To Th. BYFFORD my daughter's child 6s.8d., Eliz. BYFFORD 6s.8d., and the children of Wm. BYFFORDE my daughter's son 6s.8d. To Rt. OCKLEY my daughter's child 6s.8d., John OCKLEY 6s.8d., and Mgt. OCKLEY 6s.8d. To Rt. GRENE my son's child 20s. To three children of Anne BOWCHER my daughter's child 6s.8d. apiece. To the poor of this parish 20s. The rest of my goods to my wife, whom I make executrix. I make Rt. my son supervisor, and for his pains 6s.8d. [No witnesses.] Proved 16 May 1580.

RICHARD GENTRIE [GENTREY *in margin*] of Great Dunmow shoemaker, 16 Nov. 1580. (901)
To my sister Agnes WOOD's four children [not named] 13s.4d. apiece at 18 or marriage. To John and Mary children of my sister Joan CONNEY 13s.4d. apiece at 18 or marriage and Helen CONNEY her daughter 20s. To Simon GENTRIE my brother 20s. which he oweth me, my brother Th. GENTRY 25s., and my brother Gilbert GENTRIE 20s. To Peter and John sons of my sister Kath. CURTEIS 20s. apiece at 18 or marriage. To Kath. my featherbed. To the poor people of Great Dunmow 6s.8d. To Geo. AYLETT of the 'Swan' in Great Dunmow 10s. To the child which my sister-in-law, Simon GENTRY's wife, goeth withal 13s.4d. at 18 or marriage; if it die before, to Alice GENTRIE the mother. To her my great joined chest. To Joan CONNEY 6s.8d., also 18s.4d. which her husband Roger oweth me. To Simon GENTRIE my round green hose. To Th. GENTRIE my red gascon hose. To my sister Agnes WOOD 6s.8d. To Barbara WOOD daughter of my sister Agnes my lesser chest. To Simon, Agnes' son, my worst blue coat, my old canvas doublet, and my old russet hose. To Gilbert GENTRIE my best canvas doublet and best frize jerkin.

To Geo. AYLET's children 12d. apiece, and to Joan TOPLIE, Beatrice RAWLINSON and Helen AYLET his servants 12d. apiece. The residue of my goods to Kath. CURTEIS. I ordain Geo. AYLET executor. Witnesses: Henry BARNERD glover, Nich. AYLET, Wm. THWAITES. Proved 16 Apr. 158-[1].

GEOFFREY FYSHER of Great Henny yeoman, 16 Dec. 1572. (902)
To Geo. FISHER my son my ½ acre in Shalford [Common] Meadow in Little Cornard (co. Suffolk) and my messuage called Sparrowes with the buildings thereon and the lands free and copy belonging in Henny, Alphamstone and Twinstead for 1 year after my burial towards fulfilling my Will; then to Wm. my son on condition that he pay my executors £13 6s.8d. To Geo £6 13s.4d., 2 beasts, 1 flockbed with the bedstead and a tester and a side hanging, and a cupboard, all in my upper chamber, a shut table in the hall, my best brass pot, a cauldron, and a trivet. To Mgt SP[AR]-LINGE my daughter 5 marks and 1 calf of the last year's weaning. To Thomasine PARKER my daughter 26s.8d., 1 cow, 1 flockbed, and a brass pot. To Rose FYSH-ER my daughter 5 marks, 1 cupboard in the hall, 1 latten candlestick, 1 new hutch and a trundle bed with a tester in the upper chamber, a side cloth, my 2nd flock-bed, a feather transom, 1 pewter pot, a brazen posnet, a little kettle, and a skillet pan. To PARKER's wife a great chest. To Geo. a spruce hutch and a quern. To John and Marion SPARLINGE my daughter's children each a sheep to be delivered to Th. their father. To Geo., Thomasine and Rose all my pewter equally divided, viz. 13 platters, 1 basin, 4 salts and 3 saucers. To Alice DYER my servant 5s. The residue of my goods to Geo., Thomasine and Rose equally. I ordain Geo. and my cousin Wm. FISHER my executors. Witnesses: John FITZ the elder, Rt. FRIOTE [FRWTE?], Philip KENT. Proved 16 Apr. 1580.

THOMAS PUNVETT of Aythorpe Roothing, 1 Mar. 1579/80. (903)
To John PUNVETT my son 1 messuage parcel thereof called Gybbes in which Rt. CLERKE dwelleth, with the yards, gardens and orchards, a croft of copy land hold-en of the manor of Friers [in Aythorpe Roothing] called Five Acres, and a little copy croft of arable purchased of Th. STOKES holden of the manor of Aythorpe Hall. To John also the residue of my messuages and lands [no details] for the life of Eliz. my well-beloved wife, and for 4 years after her death the remainder there-of to Th. my son; in consideration whereof John shall permit her to enjoy the chamb-er wherein I lie and free ingress, egress and regress, and the hallhouse of the mess-uage wherein I dwell, and liberty to warm herself at the fire in the hallhouse and in every other place for all things necessary, and shall pay her yearly 4 marks. Th., after he enter on his inheritance, shall pay my daughters Frances and Mary 20s. apiece. To my wife and John all my goods (except 1 cow or else 5 nobles which I give to the little girl, my daughter's daughter, now remaining with me) equally divided, she to have the choice. John shall pay her yearly 1 seam of wheat and 1 seam of barley malt towards her bread corn and drink corn. I make John executor. Witnesses: Th. STOKES, Rd. COWLANDE, John CASSE, John STOKES, John GOWER, Rt. CLERKE, Th. EVE writer hereof. Proved 17 May 158-[1].

RICHARD HACHENET of Roydon weaver, 4 June 1581. (904)
To Mary my loving wife all my lands and goods for her life, on condition that she bring up my children as a mother ought to do; after her decease, to John my young-er son of that name my copyhold lands, whereof I have delivered a surrender the above date to Stephen GAUDGE and John SHIPPIE to my wife's use, and after her decease to John; if he die before, to John my eldest son of that name. To Rd. my eldest son the rent of my house and lands for 2 years after my wife's decease, then successively to Eliz. my daughter, then to John the eldest, then to Joan my daugh-ter, and to Th. my son, each for 2 years. I ordain my wife executrix. Witnesses: Gabriel GRENE, Stephen GOUDGE, John SHIPPE, Harry SLIPPER, Barthw. LIMMAN.

[1] See fn. p.200

I request Frs. SHARPE of Netteswell to be overseer to see my children brought up, to whom I give a bushel of wheat at harvest. Proved 5 July 1581.

JOHN FINCHE of Great Parndon yeoman, 2 May, 23 Eliz. [1581]. (905)
To the poor folk 20s. To Great Parndon church 20s. To Andrew son of Th. FINCHE my brother, after the decease of Mgt. my wife, my tenement called Shonkes in Harlow, with the lands belonging in Harlow, High Laver, Magdalen Laver and North Weald Bassett; for want of issue, to Wm. brother of Andrew. To John son of Th. my brother, after the decease of my wife and Th., my tenement and lands in Stondon [Massey]; for want of issue, to Wm. son of Th. To Wm., after her decease, my tenement called Tun[n]els in Harlow with the lands belonging; for want of issue, to Th. To John BEVYS of Great Parndon my sister's son £5. To Rt. son of Rd. SPENCER £5. To Rd. KINGE my sister's son £6 13s.4d. The rest of my goods to my wife, whom I make executrix. I make Th. SHIPTON parson of High Laver and John HELLHAM of Little Parndon overseers. Witnesses: Cuthbert CHAMBERS, John BEVYS, Wm. BREDSTRETE. Proved 30 May 1581.

JOHN BROWNE the elder of Toppesfield yeoman, 17 May 1579. (906)
To five of the poorest householders in Toppesfield 6s.8d. among them. To Alice my wife £10, according to a bond given by John my son to Rt. EDWARD for the same; 1 black horse or 33s.4d. for the same at her choice, 1 cow or 33s.4d., a little featherbed, a plain bedstead, 2 hutches in my bedchamber, an old hutch at the bedhead in the chamber under the window, and her apparel and linen. To John my tables, forms, cupboards, chairs, and stools, the painted hangings and my great chair, all in my hall, my posted bedstead, and the featherbed which came from my father [not named] in Laver, the great brass pot, the 'yeting' [for soaking barley] vat, the malt quern, a ship chest, my shod cart, and my counter table in my bedchamber. To my four children Th., and Eliz. EDWARD, Joan FITCH and Joan MAYE my daughters my corn growing and within my house equally among them, paying to my wife 1 seam of wheat and 1 seam of malt and to John 1 seam of wheat, 1 seam of barley and 1 seam of bullimong [mixed corn]. The rest of my goods shall be equally parted (except 1 brown horse which I give to John WES, and a sheep and a lamb each to Eliz. KENT and Rose EDWARDE) by four indifferent persons, i.e. John CHRACHROOD gentleman, Wm. BIGGE, Wm. BOTCHER and James EDWARDE, among my four children. To my children's children except those of late Wm. my son 6s.8d., sons at 21 and daughters at marriage or 21. To Rt. YLGATE, Eliz. STREAT and Rose EDWARDE my servants each 3s.4d. Alice THURKILLE shall have her dwelling in the house wherein she dwelleth 1 year after my decease. To John my customary lands and tenement which I hold of the right honourable [Edward de VERE 17th] Earl of Oxford as of his several manors of Berwicks, 'Scotnes' [now Scotneys Farm, both in Toppesfield], and Prayors [now Prayors Farm, in Sible Hedingham] (except Pipers Croft and Chere Meadow which I have already surrendered to the use of Th. my son), on condition that he execute my Will and discharge Th. and Wm. EDWARDE my son-in-law of their bonds to Geo. DEANE of Great Dunmow. If John refuse, the lands to Th. under like condition; if he refuse, to Wm. EDWARDE my son-in-law likewise. Witnesses: John CHAPMAN, Rd. POLLARDE, John HAMONDE, Wm. VIGORUS. Proved 1 Sept. 1581.

HENRY ROGERS of Liston yeoman, 10 May 1581. (907)
To Edw. my son 40s. To Parnell my daughter 40s. at 21. To Edw. my tenement called Knottes and Penny Maies and 4 acres of land belonging after my wife's decease; for default of heirs, successively to Parnell and to Mgt. PYNCHEBACKE. To Agnes my wife the lease of [my] farm [no details] for her life; after her decease, to Edw. To my wife all my horse, cattle, neat cattle, swine, cart gear and plough gear, brass, pewter, bedding, linen, woollen, and household stuff. I ordain her my executrix. Witnesses: Rd. CARTER, Rt. DORONTE. Proved 30 Sept. 1581.

THOMAS TURNER of Harlow, 7 Mar. 1580/1. (908)
To the poor people 5s. To John my son £6 at 21 and Geo. my son £6 13s.4d. at 21.

To Geo. my ½ acre in Well [Common] Mead in Latton. If any honest man will take any of them into their service, he shall have his or their portions, putting in sureties for payment at the end of their years. To my three daughters Eliz., Sarah and Mary £5 apiece at 18 or marriage. To my brother Henry TURNER my pellet bow. The rest of my goods to Joyce my wife, whom I make executrix to bring up my children honestly. I ordain Henry, Nich. SIBLEY and Giles HARDIE overseers, and to Nich. and Giles for their pains 6s.8d. apiece. Witnesses: John BREDGE, Henry DOWDALE, Giles SPICER, Rt. READE, Rd. HARRISON clerk [vicar of Harlow]. Proved 3 Apr. 1581.

WILLIAM SKANTE of Roydon yeoman, 7 Mar. 1576/7. (909)
To James SCANTE my nephew £5. To the poor 7s. The residue of my goods to Jane my wife, whom I make executrix. I ordain my well-beloved in Christ James BORHAM supervisor. Witnesses: Wm. CURTEIS, Stephen LEONARD, Th. FEASTE. Proved 28 Apr. 1581.

JOHN ALLEN *alias* BOTCHER, [abode not given], 15 Mar. 1580/1. (910)
To be buried in 'Sanbourne' [Stambourne] churchyard. To the poor 2s. To Jane my wife all my goods for her life; after her decease, equally divided amongst all my children, i.e. John, Th. and Anne, saving the lease of my farm, if there remain any years unexpired, to Th. I ordain my wife executrix. Witnesses: John EDWARDES, John STEBBINGE, Th. PAYNELLE. Proved 29 Apr. 1581.

JOHN BONNOM of Hatfield Broad Oak, 21 Dec. 1581. (911)
To Anne my wife my house in Hatfield for her life; after her decease, to John my eldest son, paying Joan and Agnes my daughters and Th. my son each 40s. within 6 years after he enter on the same. If my wife marry again, John shall enter into the house, she to go her way, and he to pay her 20s. a year. To my three children each a pair of sheets and a pewter platter. The residue of my goods to my wife, whom I make executrix. I make John JAWDYN supervisor. Witnesses: Geo. DIRRINGTON, Clement BENNET. Proved 15 Jan. 1581/2.

JOHN LYDDE of Castle Hedingham, 14 Feb. 1580/1. (912)
[Repeated, with witnesses and probate clause, no. 930.]

HENRY SAVEN of Felsted, 18 Apr. 1580. (913)
To Mgy. my wife all my household stuff, 2 beasts, 4 sheep, corn and hay in the barn, house, or on the ground, and £20, the money to remain in the hands of Anthony AVERELLE my son-in-law as appeareth by his writing obligatory [i.e. bond] to me made. To him 40s. To Reynold my son-in-law 1 bullock and 13s.4d. To my sons-in-law Wm. WATSON 13s.4d., Th. WATSON 20s., and John MARTYNE 20s. To John my son 1 milch cow, a bullock, and £3. To Ursula SAVEN 10s. I give £10 to be equally divided among such persons as my sons John and Henry SAVEN are indebted to, ratelike to the quantity of debt, the creditors to deliver to my executors the specialties that they had of my sons. The residue of my goods to Mgt. [*sic*] my wife, which Mgt. I ordain executrix. I make my well-beloved Henry RAYMOND [overseer]. Witnesses: Frs. RAYMONDE gentleman, Ralph SMITHE. Proved 8 Feb. 1581/2.

ROBERT GEALE of Felsted blacksmith, 27 Nov. 1581. (914)
To Wm. FRENCHE my son-in-law the 3rd bed in goodness which he hath already, a pewter platter, a saucer, a pottinger, my best russet hose, and the halling that hangeth at his brother Peter's. To Wm. GEALE my son 4 milch kine, 3 ewes and their lambs that they had last year, 2 score hogs, and all my shopward tools, iron and coal and other implements there, the duties that are owing to me on the scores [tallies], and a long table with a frame and the form I bought of Rt. STRAYTE. The rest of my goods to Agnes my wife. I ordain my trusty friend Simon BREDGE of Felsted executor, he to have the governance of my son Wm. and all that I have given him, to repay him at 21; if Wm. die before, his portion shall be parted equally between my brother Lancelot GEALE's children and Wm. FRENCH. To Simon

BREDGE for his pains 10s. I make Rt. BREDGE overseer, and for his pains 20d. Witnesses: Wm. RUSTE vicar of Felsted, Hugh BENEFEILDE, Rt. BREDGE. Administration committed [date not given] to Agnes widow of Rt. GEALE, Simon refusing executorship.

EDMUND BROUNE of Great Yeldham yeoman, 17 July, 23 Eliz. [1581]. (915)
To Edmund my eldest son and Th. my next son my farm [no details] and term of years which I hold of the right honourable [Edward de VERE, 17th] Earl of Oxford, with my stock and movables which I have in the occupying of the same; on condition that they pay my debts. To Joan my wife my croft in Kedington and Hundon [co. Suffolk] called Darishe (6 acres) in the occupation of Th. REDE of Kedington. I will that Edm. and Th. shall set up a house on the said land within 3 years after this day, containing in length 30 foot and in breadth 16 foot, finished to occupy; my wife shall have it for her life, also to have for 11 years 30s. to be paid out of the said farm. To her 2 beasts and yearly 1 seam of wheat and 12 bushels of malt to be delivered at the said house in Kedington, and 2 of the best beds. Edm. and Th. shall find her a sufficient house for 3 years at their cost and keep for her 2 beasts [with] winter and summer meat. After her decease, Rd. my youngest son shall have Darishe and they shall give him 20s. a year while my wife liveth. To my two daughters Cecily and Alice £15 apiece. To Rt., Wm. and John my sons each £20 within 5 years after my decease. I ordain Edm. and Th. executors and my brother Th. BROWNE supervisor, and for his pains 6s.8d. Witnesses: John BROWNE, Wm. BROWNE. Proved 11 Jan. 1581/2.

GEORGE RAMSEY of Sheering, 24 Oct. 1581. (916)
To Ellen my wife £20, yearly £4 until it be paid, and during her widowhood her dwelling, board and bedchamber with my daughter Frances; if she refuse, Frances shall pay her weekly 1 peck of wheat and 1 peck of malt and yearly 1 lead of cheese. To my wife the best cow to be kept where she shall dwell and half my inner household [stuff] to be divided by Wm. BEDWELL of Sheering, Wm. CLERCKE of Matching, my brother Nich. RAMSEY and John GLASKOCKE, reserved by them out of the same 1 pair of sheets, 1 pillowbere, and 2 table napkins to Joan, Mary and Jane RAMSEY my daughters. To my wife's children Rt., Th., Mary and Mgt. CLERKE 40s. yearly between them until £8 be paid. To Joan £6 and Jane £3 6s.8d. at marriage or 20. To Geo. my son £13 6s.8d. at Michaelmas 1589 and 10 lambs of that year, to be delivered to my brother Nich. and Wm. CLERKE to his use at 21; in the meantime they shall bring him up at school with sufficient meat, drink and clothing at the cost of my executrix. If he die before, to his sisters, whereof Joan to have £6 and the residue equally between Mary and Jane. To George EDIE 1 bushel of wheat and 1½ bushels of barley this year and 3 bushels of wheat then each year for 3 years; my executrix shall deliver the same to his house and make carriage of his wood and timber for his necessary use for 3 years without payment. The residue of my goods to Frances, whom I make executrix. Overseers I appoint Wm. CLERKE and Nich. RAMSEY, and for their pains 3s.4d. apiece. Witnesses: Roger CLERCKE of Harlow, John GLASKOCKE, Nich. RAMSEY, Wm. CLERKE. Proved 9 Jan. 1581/2.

JOHN JERMAYNE of Sible Hedingham single man, 4 Oct., 23 Eliz. [1581]. (917)
To my mother Jane [Joan?] wife of Th. TAYLOR of Broxted 40s., Mary CLAYDEN her daughter 40s., Mgt. CLAYDEN 40s., Th. son of Th. TAYLOR 10s., Josias TAYLOR 10s., and Ellen TAYLOR 10s. To my sister Eliz. wife of Wm. BRAGGE £10, Wm. £10 to the use of his son Marcellus my godchild at 20; if he die before, equally divided amongst the rest of his children. To Rt. CLAYDON 5s. To Agnes PARRET servant to Wm. BRAGGE 5s. To my brother Wm. JERMAYNE the corn and tillage which I have in a barn and other houses in Broxted with the use of the barn until Michaelmas next, which I had of the grant of Th. TAYLOR, also the use and commodity of Great Much Field, Little Much Field and Annys-at-Down to manure [work] and enjoy until then; 10 acres of wheat etch [stubble] for sowing bullimong [mixed corn] or suchlike corn in Middle Field; 1 acre of wheat land to be tilled and sown at Th.'s cost (seed only excepted); 12 sheep going on the same ground, a bullock

going among Th.'s cattle; and all other goods not bequeathed. I ordain Wm. executor and Wm. BRAGGE my brother-in-law supervisor. Witnesses: Wm. PARMETER, John PARKER, Rt. HARRINGTON. Proved 20 Oct. 1581.

WILLIAM COSSYN [COSSEN *in margin*] of Toppesfield yeoman, 6 Dec. 1575. (918)
To the poor at the day of my burial 20s. To Eliz. my wife my field called Swillande (12 acres), holden by copy of court roll of the right honourable [Edward de VERE, 17th] Earl of Oxford as of his manors of Barwick and Scotneys or one of them in Toppesfield, for her life; after her decease, to John COSSEN the younger, my son begotten of Eliz. my wife. To Wm. COSEN my son my free tenement called Turners and 2 crofts belonging in Toppesfield; my freehold tenement and barn with an orchard in Heydon (co. Essex [now co. Cambridge]) sometimes called Georges; and my customary lands in Heydon holden of the manor of Earls there. To my wife my messuage called Webbes at the Cross with the yards, orchards, gardens, lands, meadows and pastures in Heydon, Great Chishall (co. Essex [now co. Cambridge]) and Chrishall until Edw. COSSEN my son is 21, then to him. To my daughters Anne and Eliz. each £13 6s.8d. at marriage. The residue of my goods to my wife, whom I ordain executrix; if she marry again, equally parted among all the children which I have by her and only £10 to her. I ordain John the elder, my son, supervisor, and for his pains 20s. Witnesses: Wm. VIGORUS the writer, Rt. EDWARDE. Proved 20 Oct. 1581.

WILLIAM JACKMAN,[abode not given], 25 Sept. 1581. (919)
To be buried in Felsted churchyard. To Wm. my son 1 kettle without a band, 1 platter, 1 blue coat, 1 jerkin, 2 pair of hose, 2 doublets, and 1 pair of boots. To John FARRAR and Agnes FARRAR each 3s.4d. The rest of my goods to Alice my daughter, whom I make executrix. I make overseer John DRANE, and for his pains 6d. Witnesses: John DRANE, Rd. BREDGE, Th. BREDGE. Proved 20 Oct. 1581.

THOMAS BURREGE of Harlow, 14 Sept. 1581. (920)
To my children Wm., Edw., Ellen, Emme and Eliz. 10s. apiece at 21 or marriage. The rest of my goods to Mgt. my wife, whom I make executrix. I ordain my landlord John HARDIE overseer. Witnesses: Th. PERSE, Rd. HARRISON [vicar of Harlow]. Proved 12 Dec. 1581.

JOAN SKOTTE of Halstead widow, 15 Oct. 1581. (Nuncupative.) (921)
To Dorothy daughter of Henry SKOTTE 1 cupboard, 1 hutch, and a plank. To Wm. SPENCER 1 hutch. To Th. NORMAN 1 spit, 'Ewen' NORMAN a pottinger, Phyllis NORMAN a pewter basin, Rt NORMAN 1 pottinger, Agnes NORMAN a chair, Christian REWLE a chair, and Alice SERODE a pillow and a candlestick. To Agnes daughter of John SKOTTE a kettle and Agnes daughter of Wm. SKOTTE a pewter platter. To Joan SMITHE her daughter all her wearing apparel, 1 sheet, and a blanket. The rest of her goods to John SPENCER and Wm. SKOTTE. She did appoint John SPENCER to see her legacies performed. Witnesses: John SKOTTE, Wm. SKOTTE. Administration committed, 16 Nov. 1581,to John SPENCER.

JOHN SMEE of Wethersfield husbandman, 6 Nov. 1582. [See no. 955.] (922)
To my mother [not named] £6 13s.4d. To my sister Lucy 40s. To my brother Rt. 20s., a coat, 2 doublets, 2 pair of hosen, and 2 shirts. To my sisters Eliz. and Parnell each 20s. and Agnes and Mary each 10s. To Lucy's three youngest children 3s.4d. apiece. To Agnes GEORGE my best hutch. To my sister Mary's boy 10 groats. I appoint my master PARKER and my brother Rt. executors. Witnesses: Th. LEVERMORE, Wm. LIVERMORE, Geo. STRAYT. Proved 15 Dec. 1582.

WILLIAM RAYNER of Great Henny, 7 Apr., 19 Eliz. [1577]. [See no. 955.] (923)
To be buried in the churchyard of Great Henny amongst my other kindred. To Agnes my wife for her life my house wherein I dwell with my lands; after her decease, to Wm. my son. If he sell or mortgage it, Alexander my son shall enter on it; if he sell or mortgage it, likewise to Rt. my son. Wm. shall pay Alex. and Rt., also Martha, Eliz., Clemence, Joan, Kath. and Agnes my daughters, each 40s. at 20

after he hath the house and lands. If Wm. or Alex. die before 21 without issue, to Rt. To my wife all my goods in consideration that she bring up my children and discharge Wm. of £4 of the legacies; after her decease, the goods to Wm. I make her my executrix. Witnesses: Rd. MASON, Samuel NORCOT, Wm. RAYNER. Proved 10 Dec. 1582.

WILLIAM WOOD of Leaden Roothing husbandman, 6 Jan. 1581/2. [See no. 955.] (924)
To my sons Isaac and Nathan each 40s. at 20 and my daughters Susan and Rebecca WOOD each 30s. at 18. The rest of my goods to Mgt. my wife, to bring them up in the fear of God. I make her my executrix. I request John COLLYN husbandman and John PIGBON clerk to be overseers. Witnesses: John COLLYN, John CROSSYNGHAM the elder and John CROSSYNGHAM the younger, John PIGBON clerk, writer hereof. Proved 16 Feb. 1581/2.

RICHARD TIBOLTE of 'Maplestead' [probably Great Maplestead] husbandman, 6 Oct., 18 Eliz. [1576]. [See no. 955.] (925)
To Lettice my wife my best house with 2 crofts, Fourth Jorney Croft and Fyllepytte, in Great Maplestead, for her life; after her decease, to Henry my son; for want of issue, successively to Clemence my daughter and to the next of my kin. To my wife my house in Great Maplestead in which John MELTON dwelleth, for her life; after, to Clemence; for want of issue, successively to Henry and to the next of my kin. To my wife my house in 'Berstybe' [see no. 955] for her life, likewise. If she have need, she shall sell one croft. To Th. my brother my best coat. To Kath. my sister 5s. To the poor 12d. All my other goods to my wife, whom I make executrix. I ordain Wm. CRAB my supervisor, and for his pains 3s.4d. Witnesses: Wm. CRABBE, Lewis MILTON, Henry LUMRICKE [LAMRICKE?]. Proved 31 Mar. 1582.

ELIZABETH WILLOWES of Wimbish widow, 12 Nov. 1579. [See no. 955.] (926)
To Urias WILLSON my son my best joined bed with my featherbed that I lie on, my press, 1 little coffer, my 'sheet' table and the form, my cupboard in the hall, 1 cushion, 2 fustian pillows, 1 saltcellar, 1 candlestick, 6 pewter platters, my brass pot, my chafing dish; also 1 cow, 1 bullock, and my corn and stover to keep them withal. To Alice DREWE my kinswoman 1 cow, 1 post bed with the featherbed, my round table, 1 brass posnet, 2 pewter platters, 1 cushion, and my best gown. To Mgy. WILLSON my kinswoman 1 wennel so that she shall discharge the keeping of it, 1 sheet, 1 pewter platter, and my silver hooks. To Rd. WILSON my godson 1 of my greatest pewter platters. The residue of my goods to my four children, i.e. Th., John, Urias and Joan, equally to be divided. I make Urias executor and Th. supervisor, and for his painstaking 3s.4d. Witnesses: Th. CORNELL, Th. PAMFLYE, Th. DREWE. Proved 23 Jan. 1582/3.

THOMAS PANNELL of Belchamp Otton husbandman, 15 Apr. 1582. (927)
To Mgt. my wife all my goods, whom I make executrix, for her life. To Mgt. wife of Giles PANNELL, my son, after my wife's decease, 20s. If any of my goods be by my wife spared or unspent, to be equally divided among all my children, i.e. Giles, Th., Edm. and John PANNELL; if he [John] pay my executrix the 20s. which he oweth me, then he to be one of the partners, and Clemence my daughter, wife of Edm. GARVYS, to be another to have her part, so that Edm. do not trouble my executrix by any means. Witnesses: Wm. WOMOCKE parson there, John BROWNE, Rt. ALINGTON writer hereof. Proved 23 Jan. 1582/3.

JOAN DEANE, widow of Geoffrey DEANE, of Sheering, 15 Dec. 1582. (928)
To Wm. son of Andrew DEANE my red cow or 30s. and 1 lamb, and Frances his daughter 1 lamb. To Andrew DEANE my son the cupboard in my parlour and 1 of my flockbeds. To my daughter Frances a sheep, a mattress, 1 pair of sheets of tow, a bolster, and a coverlet. To Wm. my son my featherbed and my wafer irons. To James DEANE my greatest pewter platter and the mantle I had of him. The rest of my goods to my daughter Agnes DEANE, whom I make executrix. Witnesses: Rd. DEANE, Rd. AYSON of Sheering. Proved 25 Jan. 1582/3.

MARGARET URE *alias* WRIGHT of Wethersfield, 13 Jan., 24 Eliz. [1581/2]. (929)
To John my eldest son the whole joined bed in the parlour, the cupboard in the hall and the table, 3 beasts (black, red garled, and grimble), also my horse. To Edw. my youngest son the flockbed in the parlour, the 'stead' [bedstead], and the biggest kettle with the little one on it. To John the 2 lesser kettles, the cauldron, and the frying pan. To Edw. the brass pot and the dripping pan. To Joan SMITH my servant the unbound kettle with other kettles which used commonly to be occupied, ½ dozen of pewter, 1 salt, 1 candlestick, 1 saucer, the flockbed, also my white cow, and all my wearing apparel woollen and linen, except 3 of the best kerchers and a red petticoat, which petticoat I give to WEBE's wife. To John the biggest chest and brass basin, Edw. the 2nd chest with a pewter basin, and Joan the least chest. To John all my wheat on the ground, he giving Edw. 10 bushels of wheat and Joan ½ seam of wheat and ½ seam of malt at marriage. To my two sons all the barley and bullimong [mixed corn] on the ground. All my other goods to my two sons to be equally divided by Rd. GREENE and Th. CLARKE. I ordain John and Edw. executors. Witnesses: Rd. GREENE, Th. CLARKE, Jeremy WHIFFEN. Proved 3 Oct. 1582.

JOHN LYDDYE of Castle Hedingham, 14 Feb. 1580/1. [Cf. no. 912.] (930)
To Joseph my son £13 6s.8d., my bullock which I bought of Th. HARVEY, a featherbed, a round table, a chest in the sollar, 4 pewter platters, and 2 candlesticks. To Eleazer my son £13 6s.8d., my cow which I bought of Edm. WILLIAMSON, a featherbed, 4 platters, 2 candlesticks, the table in the parlour, and the little hutch there. If it shall please God of his goodness to send good increase of hops on my ground next year, then my wife shall pay my sons £5 apiece more. To the poor at my burial 10s. and part of my apparel to those as my wife shall think convenient. The residue of my goods to my wife, whom I ordain executrix. I make John JHEGONE and Edm. WILLIAMSON supervisors. Witnesses: Edm. WILLIAMSON, Mich. TILAR. Proved 31 March 1582.

ROBERT BLADWINE of Castle Hedingham, 18 Mar. 1574/5 and 17 Eliz. (931)
To the poor 20s. To 'Cisell' my wife £24, 3 of my best beasts at her choosing, my best featherbed, the transom, the curtains hanging about the bed, and a side saddle, my little table made of 2 boards, and all such household stuff as she did bring to me when I did marry her. To Geo. BLADWYNE my son £10, my bedsteadle in the great chamber, with the bed. To Ursula my daughter my bedsteadle and my bed and my chest in the chapel chamber and my cupboard in the milkhouse. To Mgt. my daughter the featherbed that I lie on, the bedsteadle, and my treadle bedsteadle and the bed thereupon and my cupboard, all in the chamber where I lie, and my chest with the spring lock. To my brother Rd. BLADEWYNE's wife 6s.8d. and to each of her two daughters 6s.8d. To Elizabeth BARNES, my daughter's child, 20s., and to each of her children that she hath by her husband Ralph BARNES 6s.8d. To my daughter Mgt.'s children 6s.8d. each. To Geo. GARDENER's children 6s.8d. each at 14. To Joan PORTWAYE late my servant 20s. at marriage. I will that my brass, pewter, spits, andirons, and kitchen implements be equally parted by my neighbours between Geo. BLADWYNE, Ursula and Mgt. The residue of my goods to John my son, whom I ordain executor. I ordain my brother Rd. BLADWYNE supervisor, and for his pains 20s. Witnesses: Wm. ETEY writer hereof, Th. PORTEWAYE, John BREWAR. Proved 2 May 1582.

WILLIAM STRONGE of Sible Hedingham clothier, 2 June 1580. (932)
To the poor people of Sible Hedingham 40s. at 10s. each year at the Feast of All Saints. To Phyllis my wife all such household stuff as brass, pewter and bedding as I had with her at marriage now in my possession. To her £6 13s.4d. in recompense of such money as I had with her. She shall have the occupying of my great bed with the bedstead and cupboard in the great parlour and my best hutch at her choice for her life if she live so long and dwell in Sible Hedingham and remain unmarried. After her decease or marriage, to Th. my son. She shall have yearly 1 cow's milk in summer and pasturing in my lease grounds in Sible Hedingham and Great Maplestead during the time of my lease under like conditions. To my daughters Agnes and Kath. each £5, the children of 'Arbrough' my daughter £5 among

them at 21 or marriage, and my daughters Joan and Eliz. each £5 within 1, 2, 3, 4 and 5 years [respectively]. To Wm. PRESSON my daughter's son 20s. at 21. To Th. my free houses and gardens and leases in Sible Hedingham and Great Maplestead and the reversion of the same, he paying every of my daughters' children 6s.8d. apiece until £5 be paid, at 21 or marriage. I forgive Geo. WEBB my son-in-law his debts to me. The rest of my goods to Th., whom I ordain executor. If any of my children carry away anything without his consent, their legacy shall be void. I appoint Mr Rt. HARRINGTON of the said parish and Geo. FYNCHE supervisors, and for their pains 10s. Witnesses: Geo. FYNCH, John HARRYS, Wm GREENE, Rt. HARRINGTON. Proved 23 May 1582.

Codicil, 24 Apr. 1582. To my sons-in-law Wm. PRESTON, James NICHOLSON and Geo. WEBB each £5, to be bound to my supervisors to pay the same to their children at 21.

FRANCES HARRINGTON of Birdbrook widow, 13 May, 24 Eliz. [1582]. (933)
To John CHATTERD's wife of Steeple Bumpstead my frize gown. The rest of my goods to Joan wife of Edw. WADE of Birdbrook my daughter, whom I make executrix. Witnesses: John STORIE schoolmaster, Rt. DONNELL clerk [rector of Birdbrook]. A note of the goods which I Frances give to my daughter — my featherbed, bedstead, cupboard and board or plank, 2 kettles, a posnet, 2 chairs, a trammel, a gridiron, a candlestick, 2 platters, a salt, a bedstead now at my son Simon's house at Wickham [St. Paul's], a hutch, a stool, a barrel, 4 bowls, and my apparel except 1 frize gown bequeathed to CHATTARD's wife — all these appraised at 53s.4d. Simon oweth me for a cow which he bought of me 26s.8d., John my son oweth me 5s., Henry my son oweth me which he borrowed 9s. and for my thirds 10s., Rd. my son oweth me for my thirds 10s. By Th. MORTLOCKE and Rd. CHOOTE, 22 May. Proved 20 June 1582.

WILLIAM RIDENHALL of Halstead fuller, 10 June 1582. (934)
To Rt. SMITHE of Halstead fuller my best coat, best doublet, best hosen, best shirt and best pair of shoes. To old father BALTAZER my russet frize coat, and a pair of shoes. To Henry Johnson my violet coat. To Rt. BARON 2s. and to every one of the poor aged people dwelling in the almshouses of Halstead 4d. apiece. To Rt. RIDNALL my kinsman, son of John RIDENHALL, 20s.; I forgive him 8s. which he doth owe me. The rest of my goods to my wife, whom I ordain executrix. Witnesses: Wm. VIGORUS, Th. JUMVICK, Th. TOTTENHAM. Proved 20 June 1582.

JOHN BARNARDE of Willingale Doe yeoman, 30 May 1582. (935)
To the reparations of the church 6s.8d. and the poor of the parish 3s.4d. To Joan my wife 2 kine, to choose them among my kine, 6 sheep, my white sow hog, 2 other hogs, my best featherbed and bedstock whereon I lie, half my tablecloths, 6 table napkins, 2 hand towels, all her apparel woollen and linen, 6 pieces of pewter great and small of the same that she brought with her and the same brass pot at our marriage, 1 iron pot, 1 chafing dish, 1 frying pan, 2 of the middle kettles next the best, 1 posnet, 1 spit, 3 bowls, 6 treen dishes, 1 dozen trenchers, 1 dozen pewter spoons, 1 chest, 1 little chair, 1 stool, 2 tubs, 2 milk pails, 1 boulting tub, 1 swine trough, 1 gridiron, my grindstone, half of my poultry, 1 quarter of wheat, 1 quarter of barley malt, 1 quarter of oats, and 1 mustard quern. To Ellen SAMPFORD my servant 1 pair of sheets, 1 tablecloth, 1 pewter platter next the best, and 20s., to be delivered to Edw. HAMMON of Willingale Doe until she is 20. To Agnes OSBORNE my daughter 40s., 1 cow, and my silver spoon that hath the print of a seal graven in the end of it. To Wm. son of Hugh BARNERDE my son deceased 40s. at 20. To Th. BARNARD my kinsman my corn and grass growing on my ground called Hatchmans in Beauchamp Roothing, my old cauldron, and 1 brass pot; to John his son 1 silver spoon. To the children of Th. OSBORNE my son-in-law 40s. equally. To Rd. BARNARD my kinsman 4 silver spoons, my cupboard in the hall, the table and form there, 1 featherbed, 1 joined bedstock, and my brewing vessel as it hangeth and commonly occupied. To Kath. COLE my servant 6s.8d. To John BARNARD my kinsman 1 brass pot in the hands of his mother Agnes wife of John POOLE.

The residue of my goods to Rd. and Th. BARNARDE, whom I ordain executors; if they refuse the execution of my Will, Edw. HAMMON and John HUTLY to be executors, otherwise they be supervisors, and for their pains 6s.8d. apiece. Witnesses: Edw. HAMMON, Wm. GLASCOCKE. Proved 15 June 1582.

JOHN HARVYE the elder of Finchingfield, 17 May, 24 Eliz. [1582]. **(936)**
To my son Walter HARVEY 3 beasts, the best of those 5 I have. My son Rt. HARVEY of 'Hawton' [not identified] hath in 'ferm' [i.e. lease] the rent thereof which is 18s. for the year next after my decease and then Walter to have the three beasts. To Walter 6s.8d. To my son Th. 3 beasts which are with John PASEFEILD of Wethersfield tailor, Giles HAWKESBE of Little Bardfield ploughwright and Eliz. AWGER of Shalford widow. To my daughter Barbara my 3 beasts. To Walter a seam of wheat and a seam of barley. To Th. and Barbara each ½ seam of wheat and ½ seam of barley. To Walter, Th. and Barbara each 2 sheep. To Joan HAMMANT my daughter 1 sheep and 4 lambs. To Rt. 20s. on condition that he pay out of it to Edw. [my son] 6s.8d. To 'Mathye' HAMMANT my son-in-law 20s., 2 bushels of wheat and 2 bushels of barley at harvest. My colt shall be sold by my execuitrix, out of which 20s. each to Th., Barbara and Mgt. my wife. To my wife 3 milch beasts and the residue of my corn and of my goods. I make her my executrix and my friend and neighbour Rt. EDWARDES overseer. Witnesses: Th. PRAT, Rt. EDWARDES, Wm. BENIT. Proved 20 June 1582.

JOHN BREDGE of Harlow joiner, 6 July, 24 Eliz. [1582]. **(937)**
To the poor men's box 13s.4d. To Edw. my son my house in Hatfield [Broad Oak] wherein my brother dwelleth with the lease of the woodyard and of the croft after the decease of Anne my wife, a joined bedstead with a featherbed, a cupboard, and a joined chest. To Anne and Mary my two daughters each a joined bedstead with a featherbed, a cupboard and a chest at marriage. If there chance any suit of law to my brother John for the house I sold him in Hatfield during my wife's lifetime, I give him 20s. to be paid by her. To my wife my tenement in Churchgate Street in Harlow with the lands belonging which I bought of Reynold FOSTER for her life; the remainder to my two daughters. To my wife the indenture of lease of Thremnall Fair or Hatfield Fair with the years to come, which I bought of Mr Rd. FRANCKE, also the lease of the same fair which I have of John WRIGHT. To Anne and Mary each £13 6s.8d. at marriage. The residue of my goods to my wife, on condition that she pay my legacies and recompense her two children according to conscience of the rents that I have taken of theirs, also bring up Edw., Anne and Mary without requiring any allowance. I ordain her my executrix. I desire Wm. SUMPNER the elder, John PERRYE and Edw. BENTON to be overseers, and for their pains 6s.8d. apiece. I desire my wife to be ruled by them in fulfilling my Will and paying my debts. I have written this with my own hand. If my wife marry again, she and he shall enter into bond of £30 to my overseers to pay to Anne and Mary at marriage 20 marks apiece. Witnesses: John READE, Th. WODD, John BREDGMAN, Th. RAYNER. Proved 29 Oct. 1582.

JOHN KINGE of Steeple Bumpstead tailor, — 1582. **(938)**
To Ellen my wife my messuage called May Pole Hall [Hill?] for her life; after her decease, to Rd. my son; if he decease without heir, to Wm. my son. I will that my shop with the yard be let by my executrix for 10 years after my decease, and the profits to remain to Mgt. and Eliz. my daughters; afterwards, to Wm. my eldest son; if he die without heir, to Rd. The rest of my goods to my wife, whom I ordain executrix. Witnesses: Reynold BAYNBRIGGE clerk [vicar of Steeple Bumpstead], John GOLDINGE, Wm. KINGE. Proved 22 Nov. 1582.

JOHN FRANCES of Toppesfield, — Oct. 1582. (Nuncupative.) **(939)**
He did give to Kath. his wife and 'Edye' his daughter all his goods, except 2 jerkins to Henry SPILTIMBER and John BROCKE. Witnesses: Wm. WHITINGE, Rt. EDWARDES, John BASTIAN. Administration committed, 22 Nov. 1582, to Kath. and Edith.

PETER ISAKE of Alphamstone husbandman, 30 Mar. 1582. (940)
To Peter my son my messuage that I dwell in called Linges with the lands, free and copy, on condition that he pay his brothers Hugh ISAKE £20 and John out of the said lands 26s.8d. yearly for his life. To 'Philip' PAKE my daughter £15, my featherbed that I lie in, the little cupboard, the hutch by it, the green hutch that was her grandmother's [not named], 1 hutch in the chamber, and all her mother's apparel linen and woollen and her jewels if she had any, also half the pewter, the greatest kettle, the best brass pot save 1, the best chafing dish, 2 of the best candlesticks, 1 chair, 1 buffet stool, 1 cow (whom she will), 6 sheep, 2 lambs, and 1 hog. To John my son £5, 1 flockbed, and 1 hutch. To Agnes ELLES my daughter 20s., a sheep and a lamb, and to her children Nan and Henry 10s. each. To the children of Hugh, i.e. Peter, Hugh and the girl, each 5s. and Wm. 10s. and a sheep and a lamb. To Agnes 4 bushels of white wheat and John 4 bushels. To Peter the lease of Mr WARREN. To four poor men to bear my corpse to the grave 16d. To Mary SKYNNER 5s. and John SALMAN 5s. The rest of my goods to my executor, whom I appoint my son Peter. [No witnesses or probate clause.]

THOMAS PANNELL of Belchamp Otton husbandman, 15 Apr. 1582. (941)
[Identical with no. 927, except that 'John CROWE' is substituted for 'John BROWNE' and there is no probate clause. See also no. 955.]

BENEDICT CLERKE *alias* COOKE of Matching, 14 Aug. 1582. (942)
To Lawrence CLERKE *alias* COOKE my father for his life my tenement at Matching called John Whites; after his death, to Joan CLERKE my goddaughter, daughter of Andrew my brother. To Clemence CLARKE my mother for her life my house and land in Sawbridgeworth [co. Hertford]; after her death, to Benedict FOSTER my godson, son of Agnes FOSTER my sister. I will that my father give Joan 6s.8d. a year and my mother give Benedict 3s.4d. a year, that Joan after she possess my tenement give her sisters Agnes and Eliz. each 40s. and her brethren Lawrence and Peter each 20s., and that Benedict give Eliz. 40s. and his brothers John, Reginald and Wm. FOSTER each 20s. To Agnes 6 sheep and lambs. To Eliz. MORRELL a sheep. I forgive my brother-in-law the money that he oweth me except 20s. that I will he give his wife's children Agnes, Mgt. and Rd. at marriage. To my brother Hugh's son John 2 sheep, my brother Andrew 2 cows and my colt with the bald face, my father the other colt and my horse, and my mother a cow. To Joan a sheep and a lamb. To Agnes FOSTER my sister all my barley except 2 quarters with the stover. To Andrew the lease of Park Mead. To my father the lease of Peacockes Acre. To Rd. CARTLE a sheep, John SPEDE the elder, John MARSHALL and Th. INGOLD of Matching Green each 2s., John STEVEN, Joan WISONE daughter of John STEVEN, Th. YOUNGE, and John DALE the Sexton each 12d., MARTIN and widow GRAVE each 6d., Th. DALE 4d., and Geo. MEAGER and Th. SPEADE my godsons each 2s. To my brother Andrew's child a lamb. The rest of my goods to my father, whom I make executor. I make Andrew supervisor, and for his pains 2s. Witnesses: Th. PAGE vicar [of Matching], Andrew CLERKE *alias* COOKE. Proved 20 Nov. 1582.

JOHN STONOM of Lamarsh husbandman, 23 Dec. 1582. (943)
Concerning my goods I am mindful to give them to my wife and children. To my four children John, Th., James and Mary STONOM each £8 at 24 and Mary then or at marriage. To John 1 postern bedstead, 1 flockbed which his grandmother [not named] did deliver me for him. To Mary a latten chafing dish, a latten candlestick, a casting sheet, and 40s. which her grandmother did deliver likewise. To the poor of Lamarsh, viz. Th. BOYTON, John REWE, Wm. LOVE, widow RYSBYE, Nich. SPENCER and John GOYMOR, each 1 peck of wheat. The residue of my goods to Alice my wife, whom I ordain executrix. I ordain supervisor Rt. LEVECHE of Bures St. Mary (co. Suffolk) yeoman, and for his pains 20s. Witnesses: Mr NICHOLAS le GRIS parson of Alphamstone, the writer, Rt. BEOLDE of Lamarsh, Rt LEVECHE my supervisor. Proved 13 Mar. 1582/3.

JOHN HARWOD of Belchamp Walter, 26 Aug. 1582. **(944)**
To Mgt. my wife my house in Belchamp Walter for her life and all my goods to her own use. To young John my son the said tenement, on condition that he pay these my gifts, i.e. to Wm. my son 13s.4d., his four children [not named] 20d. apiece, Rd. my son 13s.4d., his two children 20d. apiece, Anne my daughter 13s.4d., her four children 20d. apiece, Ellen my daughter 13s.4d., her child 20d., John my son 13s.4d., his three children 20d. apiece, and Geo. my son 20s. If young John refuse to pay them, Geo. my son shall have the house and pay them and give young John 13s.4d. and his two children 20d. apiece. My wife shall give Geo. 1 bed at marriage. I make her my executrix. Surrendered to Th. P[A?]TM[ER?] and Wm. PALTY in the presence of Edw. RIGGES and Th. STEELE. Proved 13 Mar. 1582/3.

AGNES GREENE of Sible Hedingham widow, 26 Oct. 1582. **(945)**
To Edw. GREENE my son £3 at 21, which remains in the hands of my brother Wm. FRAUNCES, and a pair of sheets. To Susanna my daughter 20s. at 18, which remains in the hands of Wm. MOTTE sometime dwelling in Sible Hedingham but now in Norfolk, and all my other goods, linen and woollen, 1 pewter dish, a brass pot, a pair of sheets, 1 bearing sheet, 2 saucers and 1 salt. I ordain Wm. FRAUNCES and Wm. GREENE my brother-in-law executors. Witnesses: 'Josephete' ALISTON, John SEGGES. Proved 13 Mar. 1582/3.

GREGORY BRETTEN of Finchingfield, 27 Nov. 1582. **(946)**
To the poor people 3s.4d. To Jerome BAYLY my son-in-law and Eliz. my eldest daughter, his wife, my messuage in Great Bardfield called Stewes with the gardens belonging for their lives; after their deceases, to Jerome their son; if he die without heir, equally divided among all their children. To Anne BRETTEN, Cecily BRETTEN and Ursula BRETTEN [my daughters?] my tenement called Wellstone with the lands belonging. To Mary my daughter my house and land in the occupation of widow ALCROFTE in Great Bardfield, also my stall in Braintree [market?] which I hold by copy of court roll. To my four youngest daughters my great brass pot to be equally divided between them [*sic*]. To Agnes my wife all my other goods, conditionally that she shall not claim any dower or third in my lands. I ordain executors my wife and Jerome BAYLY. Witnesses: Rt. WAYTE, John TAYLER, Rd. BRETTEN, Th. CRANFORDE senior. Proved 13 Mar. 1582/3 on the oath of Mr James THWAITES, proctor of Agnes; power reserved to Jerome.

GEORGE HARDY of Gosfield clothier, 6 Apr., 25 Eliz. [1583]. **(947)**
My executors shall call in my debts and pay all debts I owe. First John SEWELL hath £3 2s.6d. which I laid out in buying a piece of copyhold land before he married his wife a great while being the daughter of Sebastian JOHNSON; he and his wife hath of my goods 6 silver spoons which I lent them when their [land-?]lord Mr CHAMBERLYNE did dine and sup with them, also 1 great brass pot appraised at 26s. and another brass pot of a lesser sort which were sometimes Nich. HARDY's my father, 1 frying pan, 1 pewter basin, 1 carpet for a table, 3 curtains for a bed; John SEWELL and his wife owe me for schooling and boarding John their eldest son 10 weeks. Debts which I owe. To John SEWELL of Great Henny in right of his wife £10, the gift of her father Sebastian JOHNSON; to Mr Geo. GOLDINGE of Poslingford [co. Suffolk] my godfather, dwelling in the new house, 40s. which I borrowed of him when I had need; if Mr GOLDING will be so good as to remit any part of the 40s., my godson Geo., son of James INNOLDES, shall have it. I will that my executors take out my bond to John SEWELL for payment of the £10 and burn it in the fire and likewise a bond which my godfather Mr Geo. GOLDING hath of mine for the payment of the 40s., that no trouble be made when I am gone out of this wretched and miserable world to my heavenly Father everlasting God, Amen. I owe Wm. WASPE of Wethersfield 18d. To Rt. son of James INNOLDES of Sudbury [co. Suffolk] my posted bed with the ceiling and 1 featherbed. I owe Mr Henry HUNT of old debt 33s.4d., for tilth of late done 9s., and for ploughing 1 piece of land 3½ acres at 3s.4d. an acre 8s.2d. I owe Eliz. GROOME, my late servant, 9s. wages. To Rt. INNOLDES my black coat, black cloak, black gown, black doublet, russet hat, and 1 great chest for his books. To Geo. INNOLDES my godson a little

trundle bed with a little featherbed, 2 pewter platters, 1 saucer, and 1 kettle. To Joan daughter of the said James another trundle bed with a flockbed, 2 pewter dishes, 1 saucer, 2 kerchers, 1 rail, and 1 little chest which I lay my writings in. To Grace INNOLDES daughter of James 2 pewter dishes, 1 saucer, 1 kercher, 1 rail, and 1 neckercher or partlet. To Alice INNOLDE daughter of James 1 saucer, 2 pewter platters, 1 little kettle, 1 rail and 1 partlet. To Nich. son of Th. HARDY of Halstead my brother that was 1 bed in the chamber next the garden in which I lie, being a good flockbed, with the bedsteadle and the ceiling, 1 chest to lay linen in standing by my bedside, my best coat, best hat, best hoses with 2 pair of nether stocks the best, 1 leather doublet, and another doublet. To John son of Th. HARDY 1 bedsteadle, 1 flockbed, my old livery coat, a pair of hosen next my best, 1 pair of stockings, and 1 hat. To Eliz. daughter of Th. 2 pewter platters, 1 saucer, 1 kettle, 1 kercher, 1 partlet, and 1 rail. To John the younger, son of Nich. HARDYE of Halstead, my broad and narrow looms with the sleys and furniture, and they may be let out to his advantage and profit, and 2 young sheep to be let out to make him a little stock of money against he be able to shift for himself. To Abigail daughter of Nich. HARDYE 1 flockbed with a bedsteadle, 2 young sheep, 1 little brass pot, 2 pewter dishes, 1 saucer, to be kept safe, saving the sheep to be put forth likewise. To Alice daughter of Nich. HARDYE 2 young sheep likewise, 2 pewter platters, 1 saucer, 1 little kettle, and 1 little frying pan. The rest of my goods to James WARDE *alias* INNOLDE my brother-in-law and Eliz. [HARDY] my niece part and part like, whom I nominate executors. Witnesses: Henry HUNT, Th. LEAPER, Wm. HAYMAN minister [the clergy list for Gosfield is deficient at this period]. Proved 19 Apr. 1582 [*sic*].

JOHN BAKER of Alphamstone husbandman, 8 Nov., Eliz. [1582]. (948)
To the poor of this parish 3s.4d. and of [Mount] Bures 3s.4d. I will that Matthew and John my two sons shall have the occupying of my house in which I dwell called Awnselles with the lands belonging for 1 year after my death. To my eldest son Wm. and his heirs male my house and lands; on condition that he do not alien the lands; if he die without issue male, successively to Matthew and to John. To Matthew and John my house in Mount Bures called Normandise with the lands belonging part and part like and the longer liver and their heirs male. I will that Wm. pay my executors £5 to be paid to Mgy. my daughter. To Wm. 1 trundle bed in the lower chamber. To Matthew the bed therein that he lieth on and the tester over it. To John the bed in the sollar that I lie on myself. To Mgt. the other bed therein that she lieth on. To Agnes BRYANT my daughter the bed in the buttery chamber and 1 bullock. To Matthew my speckled cow, John my black cow, and Mgt. my brown 'howed' [for meaning see p. xvii] cow and my white linen tester for her bed. To John my black 'howed' bullock, Matthew the hutch which he doth occupy, John the great hutch in my chamber, Matthew the table in the hall and the form, John the table that standeth on the bench, and Mgt. the table in the buttery. To every one of my children 1 great charger and a porringer of the best. To Matthew and John my best cupboard and the other cupboard to Mgt. To my godchildren Edw. CROFTE, Agnes POLLING, John ISAAKE and Geo. BRYANT each 12d. To Wm. BAKER the younger, my nephew, 1 sheep. All my other goods to my executors, whom I ordain Matthew and John, they to bestow 10s. at my burial. I owe Mgt. 46s.8d. I ordain Wm. ISAAKE of Alphamstone and John BENNET of Chattisham [co. Suffolk] supervisors, and for their pains 3s.4d. apiece. Witnesses: Wm. ISAAKE, James LORKEN of Alphamstone, Peter ISAAKE. Proved 13 Mar. 1582/3.

THOMAS MORFEILD of Roydon, 10 May 1582. (949)
To the poor of Roydon hamlet 12d. To my daughters Mgt. RAYNER, Joan FOSTER, Agnes GUDGE and Kath. WEB each 20s. To Joan's children £4 to be paid to their mother to their use, and Joan GUDGE daughter of Agnes 20s. and Wm. GUDGE her brother 10s. I ordain my son-in-law Th. GUDGE executor. I ordain overseer my good friend Wm. CAMPE, and for his pains 2s. Witnesses: Stephen GUDGE, John HOPKYNS minister [vicar] of Nazeing. Proved 17 June 1582.

JOHN HAUKEN, [abode not given], 31 May 1582. (950)
To be buried in Finchingfield churchyard. To Ellen my wife my occupying of my farm which I dwell in as long as she keepeth herself unmarried, wherefor I desire and crave of you, master and mistress, your good wills to be so good as to let her have it before another; but if she marry I will my son Th. to have the farm, desiring your good wills for the same as I trust God and you he shall have before any other, and then I will that she take her crop that then is on the ground and all other movables unbequeathed and so to depart, and Th. to enter on the farm. To him 4 years after my decease £6 13s.4d. and my daughter Anne 40s. 5 years after. To Cecily my daughter a seam of wheat and a seam of barley between Michaelmas and Christmas after my decease, and a coverlet. To Cecily and Agnes my daughters each 1 bullock of 2 years at 20. To Mgt. my daughter 20s. at marriage. To Kath. my daughter 1 cow and 1 bed, the cow to be brought forth in a stock until she is 20 and then to her with the profits. The rest of my goods to my wife. I ordain her my executrix. Witnesses: Th. CHOOTE, Rt. MASCOLL, Chris. BENTING, John PEMBERTON. Proved 5 Sept. 1582.

CHARLES GODSCALK, late of 'Neuve Eglise par de la mer' [Newchurch-by-the-Sea] in Flanders and now of Halstead, [date not given]. [In French.] (951)
To Mary my wife all my goods and beasts in England, all debts that it is possible to receive, and £147 which my brother Wm. GODSCALKE sometime of Newchurch oweth me, and the residue. I make her my executrix. Witnesses: Rt. SMYTH, Henry THOMSON, Ed[mun?]d SMYTH, Th. VARMAN, Rd. COOKE writer hereof. Proved 5 Sept. 1582.

THOMAS CARTER of Foxearth gentleman, 13 May 1582. (Nuncupative.) (952)
To Anne his wife all his goods and his children honestly and in the fear of God to be brought up. He named her his executrix. Witnesses: Th. SCOTTE, Wm. FIRMYN, Chris. HARDY. Proved 19 July 1582.

JOHN STEELE of Belchamp Walter single man, 4 Sept. 1582. (Nuncupative.) (953)
To his sisters Eliz. STEELE, Mary STEELE and Joan STEELE each 1 quarter of barley, and Rose TITTERELL 2 quarters of barley. The residue of his goods to Th. STEELE his father, whom he desired to be executor. Witnesses: John COO, Cath. COO, Eliz. STEELE, Frances STEELE. Proved 29 Sept. 1582. Inventory exhibited at 76s.8d.

ROBERT BEALDE of Lamarsh husbandman, 2 Jan. 1581/2. (954)
To Rt. BEALDE my eldest son and his heirs male my house in which I dwell in Lamarsh called Wiggebowrise with the lands belonging, 2½ acres out of my land called Ibotts land on the side next to Wiggesbowrise between 2 ways leading to Bures and 1 acre out of meadow that belongeth to my house called Heardes next to the 'wasterside' [west] bank in the meadow, with the usual way through Heardes ground to fetch his hay with his cart, and my copy land called Axetedse and Axetedse Marsh and two crofts called Ash Croft and Plotts Hill. To Th. my son and his heirs male my tenement in Lamarsh called Heardes with the lands belonging, except 1½ acres out of Ibbotts land and the acre of meadow, and my copy land belonging to Heardes and Mittsons garden and Punttes and Salters. If Rt. die without heirs male, to go successively to Henry and to Wm. my sons and their heirs male; and if Th. die without heirs male, to Toby and to Edw. and their heirs male. I will that Rt. and Th. pay to Mgt. my daughter £7 apiece and in like sort to Henry, Wm., Toby and Edw. To Mgt., Henry, Wm., Toby and Edw. each a cow of the price of 30s., or 30s. in money, at their choice. To Henry, Toby and Edw. each a sheep and a pewter platter. All my other goods to Rt. and Th., but Th. to have the third part. I ordain them my executors. I appoint my cousins Rt. LINCHE of Bures St. Mary [co. Suffolk] and Wm. WHITE of Lamarsh supervisors, and for their pains 3s.4d. apiece. To Agnes RISBYE my sister 4 bushels of rye. Witnesses: Rt. LINCHE, Wm. WHITE, Peter ISAAKE minor. Proved 5 Sept. 1582.

[NOTE. Wills numbered herein 922-927 were entered again, by a different scribe, at the end of the Register on folios 343-346, that of Th. PANNELL appearing again on folio 333. The versions have been collated and the differences are recorded below and numbered 955 for convenience of indexing. The second versions of nos. 912 and 927 were both abstracted again, as nos. 930 and 941.]

Reference (955)

(922) [No probate clause.]

(923) Will of WILLIAM RAINER. Witness: Samuel NORCOCKE.

(925) Fourth Yornie Croft and Fill Pot Croft. In place of the parish of 'Berstybe' [the original Will doubtless illegible to the first scribe] the parish of Bocking. Witnesses: Wm. CRABB, James MILLER, Henry LEV[ER]ACKE.

(926) To sons and daughters WILSMER; which is the correct form: see Will of Eliz. WILSMER widow, proved 1593 (*Wills at Chelmsford, 1400-1620*, ed. F.G. Emmison, British Record Society, vol. 78, 1958, p.463). Witness: Th. PAMFLINE.

[End of Register D/AMR 3]

ROBERT HEARD of Wimbish bachelor, 27 Apr. 1583. (956)

To Th. HEARD my godson 5 marks, my sisters Eliz. and Joan each 10s., my brother Wm. HEARD and his wife [not named] 6s.8d., and my cousin[s?] Mary BARKER, Joan and Anne 20s. among them. To the poor folk of Finchingfield a quarter of wheat and of Wimbish 1 coomb [4 bushels] of wheat. To my brothers old John and young John each 3s.4d. I will that my uncle BARKER be executor and that my goods be divided. Witnesses: John BARKER, Rd. WILSMER, John EVES. Proved 8 Oct. 1583.

WILLIAM LOVE of Thaxted labourer, 31 May 1583. (957)

To Th. my son my messuage in which I dwell with the buildings, yards, orchards and gardens in Mill End in Thaxted now enclosed and not otherwise. To John ROBERDES my son-in-law my other tenement as he doth occupy it until Michaelmas come twelvemonth; then to Wm. my son. To Wm. my cupboard in the hall. To Anne LOVE my daughter the best chest in the parlour and my 2 milch kine which WADE doth farm [hire] of me, with the rent of the kine. To John ROBERDE's children 10s. out of the 14s. he doth owe me and Th. LOVE's daughter 13s.4d. which her father oweth me. The residue of my goods being debts owing me and in a note of the handwriting of Wm. SWALLOWE mayor [of Thaxted], after my debts be paid, equally divided among all my children by the good discretion of Mr Mayor, John SAME and Peter PURCAS. I nominate Th. my son and John ROBERTES my executors. Witnesses: Wm. SWALLOWE, Peter PURCAS. Proved 3 July 1583.

JOHN CRACKNELL of Hasted Green in Birdbrook [now Herksted Green, in Steeple Bumpstead] yeoman, 25 Mar., 20 Eliz. [1578]. (958)

To Mgt. my wife the occupying of my farm which I hold by lease with the profits belonging in Hasted Green for 7 years after Michaelmas next; all my corn, horses, beasts, bullocks, oxen, calves and other cattle. After the 7 years, she shall have her dwelling in my house called Whitlesse. To my son Robert, after his mother's decease, Whitlesse; if he die without heirs, to Barbary CRACKNELL my daughter. To her £13 6s.8d. at marriage or 21, and 1 featherbed with the standing bedstead in the sollar, which bed and the things belonging to it be worth 40s. The rest of my goods to my wife, whom I make executrix. [No witnesses.] Memorandum that this Will was exhibited in Anno 1583 but not to be proved for it was proved before [but no other record in the Registers].

THOMAS SERICHE of Wimbish yeoman, 14 Oct. 1583. (959)

To Alice my daughter £10 at marriage, £5 1 year and £5 7 years after the decease of Joan my mother. To Eliz. my daughter £5 6 years and £5 8 years after my mother's decease, also £5 to be paid by Cecily my wife. My wife and Wm. my son shall have jointly for my mother's life, if my wife keep herself a widow, the messuage wherein I dwell and the lands in my occupying and my horses, geldings, kine, sheep, hogs, and household goods, they to pay my mother equally for her life £4 and allowing her the chamber which she hath and sufficient meat, drink and other necessaries. After her decease, to Wm., my wife not to meddle any further with occupying the same; in consideration whereof he shall pay my wife yearly £4 and allowing her likewise, also firing and half such corn, cattle and other goods which they jointly have. To Alice 1 cow and 1 joined bed with a featherbed at marriage. To the child with which Eliz. is now, 1 bullock of 1 year when the child is three. To my godsons Th. HOLLAND and John WILSMER each 3s.4d. at marriage and to my other godchildren unmarried 8d. apiece. The residue of my goods to Wm. whom I make executor. Witnesses: Th. BARKER, John CLAY, John BARKER. Proved 6 Feb. 1583/4.

JOHN WAITE of Wethersfield, 9 May 1582. (960)
To Rachel my wife my messuage and lands in Wethersfield and Shalford for 16 years after my decease; then to Mgt. my daughter; if she die before 20 or after without heirs, to Henry my godchild, son of Henry WAITE of Sible Hedingham; after entering on the messuage and lands, he to pay the children of Mary WAITE and Joan WAYTE my two sisters equally the money that the half of my messuage and lands be esteemed to be worth at that time by four indifferent men chosen by both parties. To Mgt. my greater kettle, a brass posnet, 1 cobiron, and a spit. My wife shall not fell on my ground any oak, ash or other wood saving alder but only for necessary reparations of my messuage. She shall bring up Mgt. until of sufficient age in learning her to read English and pay Agnes WAITE my mother 18s. The rest of my goods to my wife. I ordain her and George WHIFFINE executors. Witnesses: John OVERED, Jerome WHIFFINE, Josias SAMPSONN. Proved 5 June 1583. Inventory exhibited at £9 18s. 8d.

WILLIAM MAYE of Little Yeldham, 9 Apr. 1583. (961)
To my children Wm., Henry, Edw., Eliz., Agnes and Th. each £5 at 21. The residue of my goods to Anne my wife, whom I make executrix. I ordain Geo. PERMITER and Henry FREMAN supervisors, and for their pains 3s.4d. apiece. Witnesses: Wm. PARMITER, Henry COOKE. Proved 9 May 1583.

HUMPHREY THOMAS *alias* WEAVER of Matching, 5 Feb. 1580/1. (962)
To John my son 2 pewter platters and my lamb that is pulled up [*sic*] in my shop. To Rd. my son 2 pewter platters. To Helen my daughter half of the rest of my pewter, 4 pair of sheets, my best bearing sheet, best pillowbere, my casket, the linen of both my wives, my best brass pot; and £20 paid out of my house and £10 at 30; Th. HOSKINS clerk [rector] of Magdalen Laver shall take the £20 and immediately deliver it to her. To Rd. the yearly annuity of 10s. out of my said tenement for his life, to begin at Michaelmas 1587, also 30s. beside the 30s. that I owe him, paid by my son Harry when Rd. is 30. If John be minded to dwell in my tenement, he shall have it for the yearly rent of £6 13s.4d. until Harry is 21. To Harry my tenement and land and my other land in Matching and High Laver; for want of heirs to John. The residue of my goods to Harry, whom with Th. HOSKINS I make executors, and for Th.'s pains 5s. I make supervisors Rt. KINGE the elder of High Laver and John INGOLD of Matching, and for their pains 3s.4d. apiece. Witnesses: Th. HOSKINS clerk, writer hereof, Th. PAGE vicar [of Matching], John COLLIN. To John my son 40s. Debts that I owe: to goodman COLLIN of Otes [in High Laver] about 30s.; Wm. THURGOOD of Magdalen Laver 5s.10d.; SIBLYE of Harlow 12s.; Edw. JENEN 3s.; Reynold FOSTER 14d.; Nich. SPEEDE 12s.; John INGOLD 4s.; CHAPMAN of Epping 3s.4d.; John my son £8; Rd. my son 30s.; the parson of Magdalen [Laver] for 2 bushels of wheat 5s. Debts owing to me: Nich. MARDEN of Stortford [co. Hertford] promised to pay for 5½ quarters of malt which Nich. his son had of me (witness John HORWOOD of Hockerill [co. Hertford] and Wm. JUST of Stortford bellow maker), of which money there is paid 15s.8d.; PLUMMER and his wife in gold oweth me 10s., Hugh AYLIES's wife beerbrewer oweth me to be paid next Midsummer 12s.; WRENNE of Nazeing for ½ seam of pease 5s. which I should have

had at the day of my marriage but we made a new condition. The £8 that I did owe my son is paid. Mr Th. HOSKIN refused executorship; afterwards proved 11 May 1583.

JOHN INGOLD of Harlow, 16 Apr. 1582. (963)
To the poor people 2s.6d. To Edw. my son my table, trestles and form in the hall, my shopboard and shelves in the shop, and the 'jestes' [joists] and boards over the shop and chamber as they lie. The rest of my goods to my three children Edw., Th. and Emme equally divided by my overseers. I ordain Edw. executor and my very friends Wm. SUMPNER of Harlow Bury and John WRIGHTE sexton overseers. Witnesses: [not given]. Proved 8 Jan. 1583/4.

ELIZABETH ROBINSON *alias* LUTHER of Stebbing, -- 1583. (964)
To Miles ROBINSONNE my youngest son both my looms, i.e. a bastard loom and a woollen loom, 2 pewter dishes (1 carved, the other broadbrimmed), and my little brass pot. To Wm. ROBINSONNE my son a pewter platter and a pewter dish, if he come again, else not. To my son Wyman ROBINSONNE's two sons Jehu and Jonas a pewter platter, a pewter dish, a chair, a black felt, and a testament. To Edw. ROBINSONNE's daughter Sarah my best pillowbere saving 1, a wrought neckercher, and a 'quoler' [collar?]. The residue of my goods to Joan wife of Wm. CLARKE my daughter. I make him executor. Witnesses: Wm. CHOPPINN, John BOOKER. Proved 23 Nov. 1583.

AUDREY REPINGALE of Belchamp Otton single woman, 17 Sept. 1582. (965)
To John REPINGALE my eldest brother £10 and Joan REPINGALE my sister £10. To the poor of Belchamp Otton £3 by 6s.8d. yearly on Good Friday at morning service by my executors and to the poor of Belchamp William [now Walter] 26s.8d. by 3s.4d. yearly likewise. To Mgy. CLARKE widow, Joan BEKERTONN and Agnes JACSONN each 3s.4d. To Amy PARMYTUR, Th. WHIFFINE and John HARDYE each 3s.4d. at 21 or marriage. All other my goods to Rt. REPINGALE my youngest brother and Joan my sister, whom I ordain executors. Witnesses: Rt. ALINGTON, Th. SADLINGTONN. Proved 7 Oct. 1583.

KATHERINE BROWNE of Felsted widow, 12 Dec. 1583. (966)
To my two sons Rt. ALBERT and Th. ALBERT each 20s. and the children of Stephen ALBERT my son 20s. amongst them. Towards the reparations of Felsted church 12d. To Mr William RUST vicar of Felsted 6s.8d. and to Rt. EVANS the church clerk 3s.4d. The rest of my goods to Mgt. ALBERT my daughter, whom I make executrix. I ordain Mr Wm. RUST overseer. Witnesses: John PORTER, Rt. BREDGE. Proved 5 Feb. 1583/4.

JOHN UNDERWOOD of Belchamp Walter joiner, 30 May 1580. (967)
To Eliz. my wife all my implements of household as brass, pewter, bedding, and apparel, praying her to be good to my brother Rt. UNDERWOOD in giving him houseroom and ministering to his necessity as occasion and her ability shall give. I ordain her my executrix, desiring Rt. TIFFINE to be supervisor. Witnesses: Edw. RIGGES, Th. COO, Rt. MATHEWE, John HOWE of 'Ausford' [Alresford?]. Proved 6 Feb. 1583/4.

THOMAS TAGELL of Harlow poulter[er], 22 Nov. 1582. (968)
To Rt. my son 40s. and my dun mare colt that I now have on Harlow Common. To Wm. my son 40s., my dun mare, and my bald colt. To Emme TAGELL my daughter 40s. and a black starred cow. To the children of Felix my son 3s.4d., the two daughters of Th. my son 3s.4d. apiece, and the two children of Rt. PRENTICE 3s.4d. apiece. To all my godchildren 4d. apiece at 10. The rest of my goods to Ellen my wife, whom I make executrix. I constitute Rt. PRENTICE my son-in-law overseer, and for his pains 3s.4d. Witnesses: John FUNTAYNE, John FOSTER, Giles KNIGHT. Proved 10 Dec. 1583.

MARGERY HUMFREY of Halstead widow, 8 Feb. 1583/4. (969)
To John my son a featherbed and bedstead. To Th. my son my flockbed. To Chris.

my son my cupboard. To the wife [not named] of John my son my great kettle and the wife of Rd. my son my best brass pot. To VIGOROUS' wife my best lockram tablecloth. To John my great hutch and Rt. his son my new hutch. To Wm. son of Rd. ESTERFORD my son the hutch that was his grandfather's [not named]. To Alice daughter of Rd. my casting sheet and Anne his daughter my lockram rail. To Joan my daughter my footed pan and the bed cloth that I bought of Wm. HUTSON. The rest of my linen to my son John's wife. To Th. and Chris. equally parted the money remaining in my executor's hands, i.e. £3 or what shall remain after my funerals. The rest of my goods evenly parted between Th., Chris. and Jane [*sic*] my daughter. I ordain my well-beloved cousin Wm. VIGORUS the elder of Halstead executor. Witnesses: John ESTERFORD, Rd. ESTERFORD. Proved 26 Oct. 1583.

REYNOLD INGOLD of Netteswell ploughwright, 26 Apr. 1583. (970)
To the poor 8d. To Reynold my son the bed wherein he lieth, the cupboard in the same chamber, and £3. To my son Henry £3. To John my son my red cow, and my right and interest in a house which I have in mortgage of one Th. PETCHYE of Hertford [co. Hertford] called the 'Lion'. To Mgy. my wife my dwelling house for her life, the furniture of the same, with the rest of my goods, whom I constitute executrix. Witnesses: 'Mathe' THOMAS, Th. GRAYGOSSE. Proved 11 May 1583.

REYNOLD JACKSON of High Easter, — 1583. (Nuncupative.) (971)
He gave to John NEWTON his landlord all his goods and household stuff, on condition that he John NEWTON should pay his debts. Witnesses: Wm. REYNOLD, John REYNOLD, Rd. CHURCHE. Proved 12 Dec. 1583.

RICHARD TIFFINN of Gestingthorpe single man, 6 May, 25 Eliz. [1583]. (972)
To Wm. WITTAM my sister's son £5, Th. WITTAM £5, Henry WITTAM £5, John WITTAM £4, five of my sister WALFORDE's eldest children £5 apiece at 21, six of my sister BUTLER's eldest children 30s. apiece at 21, and Mgt. GREENE my sister's daughter 20s. at 21. To Wm. TIFFINN of Gestingthorpe my copyhold in Belchamp Walter towards the performance of my Will, whom I make executor. To my cousin Rd. LAWSELL my best cloak and best black coat. To Alice LAWSELL my cousin my fire pan, tongs and cobirons in my chamber and roast iron. To Rd. ASTLEY my best doublet and best hoses. The rest of my goods to Wm. TIFFINN. Witnesses: Rd. LAWSELL, Rt. PARKE, Rd. ASTLEY. Proved 7 Oct. 1583.

[The next ten Wills in Register D/AMR 4, all proved in 1584/5, will be abstracted in the next volume.]

GILES WRIGHTE of Harlow, 24 Aug. 1584. (973)
To the poor 3s.4d. To Giles my son at 21 my free land in Harlow on condition that he make a good assurance of Yerd Mead in High Laver to Th. HOSKINN clerk, parson of Magdalen Laver, according to our bargain in writing; if Giles die without heirs, to Alice and Mary my daughters equally. I surrender to the use of Joan my wife for 20 years after my decease my customary land in Harlow, so that she honestly bring up my two children; if she die before, successively to Giles and to Alice and Mary, Giles to pay them if he possess it 40s. apiece. To both daughters 40s. apiece. The residue of my goods to my wife. I make overseer Wm. LINGWOOD, and for his pains 2s. Witnesses: Th. HOSKINN clerk [rector of Magdalen Laver], John SOMNER, Frs. FULSHIER, Wm. GLADWINN. The rent of FULSHIER's house to my daughters. Witnesses: Wm. LINGWOOD, Wm. GLADWINN. Surrender delivered by Th. HOSKINN and Felix WAILETT customary tenants of the manor of Harlow Bury. Proved 13 Nov. 1584.

LAWRENCE BARKER of Halstead labourer, 14 May 1583. (974)
To Marion my wife all my goods, also my house for her life; after her decease, the house to John my son, he to pay my children Th. 10s., Wm. 6s.8d., Thomasine BARKER 6s.8d., and Agnes BARKER my youngest daughter 10s. and a jointed hutch or coffer and my bedsteads. To John a chest after my wife's decease. To him all my

working tools. If any of my 'said' children, viz. Th., Wm., Anthony, Mgy., Thomasine and Agnes, die, his or her part shall be given to [another of the children, including Anthony]. I make my wife executrix. Witnesses: John GREENE the elder, John SCOTT the tailor, tenants of the manor of Abells [in Halstead] who have received surrender of my house. Witness: Rd. COOKE writer hereof. Proved 6 Feb. 1584/5.

THOMAS DOBIDEWE of Thaxted shoemaker, 10 July, 1577, 19 Eliz. (975)
To Joan my wife my messuage that I dwell in, except the shop, for her life; Th. my son shall occupy the shop during her life; after her decease, the messuage with the shop to Th. DOBYDEWE, on condition that he pay Wm. my son 20s., Sarah DOBIDEWE my daughter (or her children if she have any) 4 marks, and Simon my son 40s.; if Th. die before my wife, to Simon. The residue of my goods to my wife, whom I nominate with Th. executors. Witnesses: John MOREAKE [MORCOKE?] tailor, Th. PURCAS, Frs. RAM, Peter PURCAS. Proved 24 Sept. 1584.

JOHN HOCKLIE of Castle Hedingham husbandman, 13 Sept. 1584. (976)
To Dorothy my wife all my household stuff and goods, beasts, cattle, and money. I ordain her my executrix to see my children brought up in the fear of the Lord. Witnesses: Wm. BUCHER, 'Watte' WADE, John TILLE, John SEGGES. Proved 24 Sept. 1584.

HENRY CLARKE of Belchamp Walter single man, 10 June 1584. (Nuncupative.) (977)
He did give to Mary PETER his sister's daughter 53s.4d. and to Sarah PEWTER his sister's daughter 26s.8d., each at 21 or marriage. To Frs. PLUMLEY his brother a part in a colt to the sum of 6s.8d. and to Edm. PLUMLEY his brother a part out of the same colt 6s.8d. Towards the reparations of the bells 6s.8d. The residue of his goods to be disposed by Wm. PLUMLEY his father-in-law, whom he desired to be executor. Witness. Rt. TEBOLD. Proved 24 Sept. 1584.

RICHARD THORPE of Henny, 23 June 1584. (978)
To the poor 6s.8d. To Joan my wife all my goods, corn, cattle, debts, money, and household stuff. To Rd. my son, after her decease, 1 posted bedstead with a ceiling and tester, 1 featherbed, 1 flockbed, my best cupboard, ½ dozen of pewter, 1 brass pot, 1 kettle, 1 chair, and 1 hutch. My wife shall pay Rd. at full age £20, which shall be in discharge of 20 nobles which his aunt COCKE gave him. To Joan RAYNER my maid 5s. I ordain my wife executrix and Th. BORAM supervisor, and for his pains 6s.8d. Witnesses: Wm. BORAM, Wm. DIER, Matthew UNDERWOOD, Rt. TOMPSONN. Proved 24 Sept. 1584.

THOMAS FIRMEN of Middleton, — 1584. (979)
Towards the reparation of Middleton church 12d. My house wherein I dwell with the land and all my other goods shall be sold by John SEWELL my executor and the money be divided among my three children John, Th. and Rd. equally; he shall have their portions until they are 21; if all die before 21, their portions divided among the children of my brother Henry FIRMIN; in consideration of having their stocks, he shall see my children brought up in the fear of God. I ordain Rd. [my son?] and Rd. THORPE overseers. Witnesses: John OXBORROWE, Wm. BORAM, Rd. THORPE, Rd. BENTLIE. Debts owing: to goodman SEWELL 33s.4d., to Rt. TOMPSONN 5s., to the executors of John GATE 5s., to Wm. BORAM 4s.2d. Debts owing to him: by Henry CAUNT 8s. Proved 24 Sept. 1584.

EDMUND COOKE of Belchamp Otton, 18 May 1582. (980)
To Chris. my son my copyhold land with the houses belonging, paying the residue to my children thus: Henry £25 by £2 6s.8d. a year, and to my daughters Joan, Eliz., Marion and Agnes each 53s.4d. To Henry 1 bed and bedstead with a transom and the stained cloths about it, my quern and hutch, of everything one of the best apparel that I have, a mattock, a salting trough, and a pewter dish. To Henry, Eliz., Agnes, Joan and Marion each 1 sheep, and 2 kettles, 1 trivet, 1 frying pan and 2 skillet pans equally divided. The residue of my goods to Chris., whom I ordain executor. I make Rt. LAIE my son-in-law supervisor. Witnesses: Chris. COOKE, Henry FREMAN, Henry COOKE. Proved 24 Sept. 1584.

GEORGE WARD of Castle Hedingham 'chirugion' [surgeon], 25 Aug. 1584. (981)
To Mgt. my wife my tenement that I dwell in and my hopyard in Nunnery Street with the profits for her life. My tenement and hopyard shall be sold after her decease by my executor if he shall live so long or else by the constables and churchwardens and the money equally divided among my children. To Eliz. WARD my daughter, after my wife's decease or at 21, my best featherbed with the joined bedsteadle, table, frames and cupboard in the new parlour. To Mgt. WARD my daughter likewise 1 featherbed, the post bedsteadle in the new chamber, the long table there, form and cupboard. To Mary WARD my daughter likewise 1 featherbed, a post bedsteadle in the little new chamber, a great chest in the great new chamber, a press in my chamber over the hall, and the little table in the hall. To Th. BANNESTER 40s. To my wife all my leases for her life; after her decease, to be sold likewise. I ordain her and Edm. BASSAM executors, and for his pains 20s. To the poor of Castle Hedingham 20s. The rest of my goods to my wife. Witnesses: Dunstan BALDWINN, Wm. CATLEN. Proved 24 Sept. 1584.

HENRY YOUNGMAN *alias* CLERKE of Wethersfield, 17 July 1584. (982)
To Alice my wife my house wherein I dwell and my free land which I occupy until Michaelmas 1587, my copy land to remain to Henry my son, also my house and land after the 3 years, at which my wife shall have one-third part of them. To my son Lancelot and Samuel each £6 at 21. To my daughters Mary, Dorothy and Alice 3 years after my decease, and to Eliz. and 'Phillippe' at 18, each £3. To Henry the timber work of 1 bed standing in the outward chamber and 1 table, 1 benchboard and the backboard joined together in the hall with the hanging belonging. All other my goods to my wife for the better education and bringing up of my children. I make her my executrix. Witnesses: Lancelot WARD, Alex. DOD, Th. SPRINGE. Proved 24 Sept. 1584.

JOHN PEARSON of 'Eastaines at Mount' [Great Easton] blacksmith, 2 Aug. 1584. (983)
To Geo. PEARSONN my brother my debts due to me upon tally, score or otherwise, my iron tools and implements in my shop, and all other movables in the shop; conditionally that he pay my debts, viz. to Giles FLEMMINGE my debts due to him, Th. PEARSON my brother 20s., John FANNE 20s., and Mgt. BROWNING 12s., also satisfy my wife 53s.4d. and discharge the shop rent due at Michaelmas. The rest of my goods to Cecily my wife. I appoint Geo. PEARSONN executor. To John BAILIE and Roger POULTON each 3s.4d. Witnesses: Nich. NICHOLLS, Clement WRIGHT, Rd. BROWNING. Proved 24 Sept. 1584.

WILLIAM ALLEN of Gosfield husbandman, 20 July 1584. (984)
To Anne my wife my customary lands and tenements in Gosfield holden by copy of court roll of the right worshipful John WENTWORTHE esquire as of his manors of Shardlowes Belhouse and Holdinges [in Gosfield] until Wm. my son is 21; then all to him. If he die before, to my wife until Geo. my son is 21; if he die before, to my wife until Joan and Sarah my daughters are 21; all according to the custom of the manor. To Geo. £20 and Joan and Sarah £10 each at 21. To my wife towards the keeping and bringing up of my children the rest of my goods. I ordain her my executrix and my well-beloved brother Roger ALLEN supervisor. If my wife marry, he that shall marry her shall be bound in £100 to my supervisor to discharge my legacies. Witnesses: John SPENSER, Wm. GURDEN, Rt. SMITHE, Rd. SAWKINN, Wm. VIGORUS. Proved 4 Sept. 1584.

JOHN BUTCHER *alias* GARROLDE of Gestingthorpe blacksmith, 6 July 1584. (985)
To my sons John BUTCHER the younger and Rd. BUTCHER my gear in my shop with the iron, coals in the coalhouse, horse shoes and horse nails, and all other implements equally divided, my tallies and marks there only excepted. To John the younger and Rd. each 40s. at 21; if they do not discharge my executor of 40s. to them bequeathed by the Will of Rd. TENANT their grandfather, their legacies to be void. To Kath. my wife all my household stuff, my 5 milch kine, my 3 dry bullocks, and my sheep with their lambs. To Th. BUTCHER my son £12 at 21. To

Anne my daughter £8 13s.4d. [*sic*] at 21 or marriage. To Thomasine WHITEHEAD my daughter 40s. and 1 seam of white wheat, Edw. WHITEHEAD her son 40s. at 21, and John WHITEHEAD my son-in-law my best hosen, best doublet and best jerkin. The rest of my goods to my wife and John BUTCHER the elder, my son, whom I make executors. If John the elder do greatly trouble his mother by his disobedience and stubbornness, being well-seen and approved by their neighbours, he shall be void of executorship and my wife shall be executrix. Witnesses: John COO, Rd. ASTEY. Proved 30 July 1584.

THOMAS BIND of Pebmarsh husbandman, 26 June 1584. (986)
To Edith my wife my messuages and lands free and customary in Pebmarsh, Little Maplestead and Gestingthorpe for her life; then within 3 years after her decease to Rt. my son, paying out of the same to my three daughters Joan £5, Eliz. £7, and Dthy. £6 13s.4d. To John my son, after her decease, my said lands in Gestingthorpe in the occupation of Hugh POWELL. To her all my household stuff as bedding, brass, pewter, and such like. The rest of my goods to my executor towards paying my debts, whom I ordain Rt. I ordain Wm. VIGORUS of Halstead supervisor, and for his pains 10s. Witnesses: Wm. VIGORUS senior, the writer, Wm. HADDOCKE, Wm. FAWSCETT. Proved 30 July 1584.

GILES SPISER of Harlow smith, 10 Mar., 26 Eliz. [1583/4]. (987)
To my son Wm. the shop and the tools with the occupying thereof during his mother's life. To Joan my wife the rest of my tenement with the lands belonging, to bring up the rest of my children and pay my debts. To her the rest of my movables in consideration that she keep my mother. To Wm. the tenement after his mother's decease, on condition that he give his brother John 40s., his sister Thomasine 40s., Stephen his brother £4, and his sister Lettice £4, and see my mother honestly kept. To my wife the rest of my goods, whom I make executrix. I make goodman SUMNER overseer. Wm. shall pay his sister Mary 10s. To her three children [not named] 3s.4d. apiece. Witnesses: Wm. SOMNER, John GLADWIN, Th. RENOLD, John BREDGMAN. Proved 17 Apr. 1584.

GEORGE OSBORNE of Gosfied, 11 June 1584. (988)
To my two daughters Joan and Mary 40s. apiece. To my wife Eliz. all other my goods. I make my brother[-in-law] Matthew NEWMAN executor. To my wife £4 of the £10 which I must have of my brother Th. and the other £6 to my children £3 apiece. Witnesses: Th. OSBORNE his father, Th. his brother, Wm. HAGMAN minister of Gosfield [the clergy list for Gosfield is deficient at this period]. 9 July 1584, Matthew NEWMAN appeared and renounced executorship, and administration committed to Eliz. the widow.

JOHN BRANCHE of Halstead weaver, 8 Aug. 1583. (989)
To Henry my son 2 looms with sleys, reeds and all things belonging, a flockbed with the bedstead, tester and ceilure, my lesser brass pot, 1 hutch in my chamber at his choice, 2 pewter platters, a saucer, a salt, a candlestick, a kettle, 1 of my best tablecloths, and 2 table napkins. To Joan my daughter 1 flockbed in which she lies, a hutch in the sollar, my wife's best gown, a worsted apron, 2 platters, a salt, a candlestick, 2 table napkins, a kerchief, a holland quarter, an apron, 2 neckerchiefs, and my tinker's kettle. To Grace my daughter a flockbed in which she lies. The rest of my goods to John the elder my son in consideration that he bring up John the younger my son until he be of age to shift and provide for himself. I ordain John the elder executor. Witness: Wm. VIGORUS the writer. Proved 16 Apr. 1584.

ANTHONY RIDER of Liston yeoman, 13 Apr. 1584. (990)
To my well-beloved brother Wm. REEDER all my goods, whom I make executor. Witnesses: Wm. GREENE, John LEETCHE. Proved 6 May 1584.

HENRY TEBOLD [abode and date not given]. (991)
Being very weak. To be buried in Maplestead churchyard [probably Great Maplestead]. To Jane my wife my house and land which I hold until my daughter [not named] is

21; if she die before, to my wife for her life, then to my sister's daughter. To my wife half the corn and to my mother the other half, they to sow the barley land together and so to part the corn by the bushel and the straw by even portions, my wife to pay 30s. to TURNER of Halstead at Michaelmas next, 26s.8d. to my godfather BECKEWITHE at Braintree at Hallowmas next, and 12 bushels of barley to John TURNER at Hallowmas. To my sister's daughter 1 white pig. The rest of my goods to my wife, whom I make executrix. Witnesses: Martin BASTIAM clerk, Wm. PENNOCKE vicar [of Great Maplestead]. Proved 6 May 1584.

JOHN WATSONN of Steeple Bumpstead tailor, 3 Mar. 1583/4. (992)
To the poor people 2s.6d. To my sister LAMBERT 3s.4d. To Francis and Joan children of Th. WATSONN my son each 40s. at marriage or 21. To Eve my daughter £4. My messuages and lands in Bumpstead and Hempstead shall be sold by Rd. ONION of Bumpstead yeoman and John WATSONN my son and the money equally divided amongst all my children and Kath. my wife. The residue of my goods shall be divided likewise by the discretion of John RUNNELL and John COOTE of Hempstead yeoman, Eve my daughter excepted. If my wife refuse to release her right of dower in my lands, the legacies to her shall be void. I make Rd. ONION and John executors, and for their pains 3s.4d. Witnesses: Peter HASTELER, Rd. FITCHE the writer hereof. Proved 28 Mar. 1584.

ELIZABETH SMARTE of Thaxted widow, 10 Mar. 1583/4. (993)
To Rd. SMARTE my son all my goods. I nominate him executor. Witnesses: Peter PURCAS, Dthy. LAMAS. Proved 17 June 1584.

RICHARD LAWSELL of Sible Hedingham husbandman, 13 Jan. 1583/4. (994)
To Kath. my wife the use, profits and commodities of my house called Whelers wherein I dwell and another little house or cottage on Broad Marsh with the meadows and pastures in my occupation, for 6 years if she live so long; if not, to my two sons in manner following. She to maintain the houses in reparations, hedging, ditching and fencing; also my corn, cattle and other movables, except she leave the cupboard, long table in the hall with bench and backbench, bedsteadle, a great vat, 3 trammels, and the quern, the hop garden as now planted and the poles, all which to remain with my house to my son John; also 2 closes called Haukins Garden and Home Croft, a pightle called Davenaunt Marsh, 2 parcels of meadow called Mack Meadow and Holland Marsh, a pightle called Tilers Pightle or Coles Marsh, 2 fields called Gatward Mount and [illegible], and parcels called Much Sothecome. To Joseph my son the cottage and the pightle wherein it stands, 2 pightles called Conny Marsh and Geymor Marsh, and 2 parcels called Ofled Hill and Alcott Pond. To my daughters Mgt., Abigail and Dina each £4 at 21. All other my goods to my wife, whom I ordain executrix. I appoint supervisor John my son and Wm. COBBOULD. Witnesses: Rt. LOURELL [*recte* HOURELL], Wm. COBBOULD, John SEGGES. Proved 18 June 1584.

JOHN SKOOT of Thaxted cutler, 12 Dec. 1583. (995)
To Eve my wife my messuage which I purchased of Th. SAVIDGE my father-in-law in the Fish Row, late in the tenure of Th. COOKE *alias* FLETCHER, to be sold by her in fee simple and the money to pay my debts and legacies. To her all other my messuages and lands free and copy in Thaxted, provided that she permit my two sons John and Matthew SKOTT to use my 2 shops where I dwell and 1 chamber and room in the same house, so long as they shall dutifully as good children and servants behave themselves towards their mother, aiding her towards her living, which I hope she will perform towards them upon their good behaviour. To John and Nathan SKOOT my sons all my tools and things belonging to my occupation and all armour, swords, daggers, knives and such like equally divided, so long as they dwell and continue together; also 1 mattress, a bedsteadle, a bolster, a coverlet, a pair of sheets, and a blanket. The residue of my goods to my wife, whom I nominate executrix. Witnesses: John INNYVER, Peter PURCAS. Proved 18 June 1584.

JOHN ROGERS of Steeple Bumpstead smith, 13 Apr. 1584. (996)
To Eliz. my wife my tenement which I purchased of Th. GENT esquire with the croft for her life toward the bringing up of my children, reserved out of it the barn with a sufficient yard to be laid to the barn by the discretion of Rd. ONION, Edw. HAWKINS and Rd. FITCH; which barn and yard I bequeath to John my son. To him, after my wife's death, the tenement and croft, on condition that she [*recte* he] pay 'Phillippe', Agnes, Alice and Mary ROGERS my daughters 40s. apiece at 21 and Wm. and Rd. ROGERS my sons £3 apiece at 21. To John all my 'sceeches' [anvils?], hammers, bellows and other working tools, with my scales and weights belonging to the occupation. John shall have the use of my shop with the room for his coals during all the time that I have in the same [i.e. by lease], yielding yearly 10s. towards the payment of my rent, and shall have as much iron, coal and money of the tallies and marks as shall pay Mr LAMBERT so much money as I owe him, putting in surety to my wife for discharging her for the debt. The residue of my goods to her for paying Eliz. my daughter £4 and the residue of my debts. I ordain my wife executrix. Witnesses: Reynold BAMBRIGGE, Rd. ONION, Edw. HAWKINS, Wm. CONESTABLE, Wm. CLARKE, John MEVELIS, Rd. FITCHE writer hereof. Proved 29 May 1584.

CHRISTOPHER HARDIE of Foxearth tailor, 21 May 1584. (997)
To Joan my wife for her life my house and land called Sawyeeres copy and free, she bringing up Titus my son to school until he be able to shift for himself. After her death, to be sold to him especially above the rest if he be able, if not then from the eldest to the youngest [child] to buy it which is best able and equally divided amongst my children Titus, 'Frauncesse' [Francis or Frances?], 'Mathye', Mgt. and Hester, excepted that, if my wife die before Titus have sufficient learning he to have the profit of the house and land for 3 years, then to be sold and equally divided as before said, excepted that I give Mgt. and 'Mathye' 20s. more than the rest, to be paid by my wife if she be able at 20 or marriage, if not, to be paid out of the house and land. To all my children after her decease all my movables part and part like, excepted I give my great chest to Hester more than the rest, and that my daughters Joan and Bridget shall have their part with the rest equally. I except these two to have but 40s. apiece. I ordain my wife and Titus executors. Witnesses: John REINOLDE, Th. SCOOT, Geo. HARDIE, John FIRMYN. Administration committed, 22 July 1584, to John STALLON, uncle [on the mother's side, *avunculus*] of Titus, during his minority.

APPENDIX

Wills not registered

The following original Wills do not occur in the Register for the Archdeaconry of Essex; Will no. 1001 adds details not given in the registered Will no. 378.

WILLIAM DANWOOD *alias* BEANE
of Brentwood in South Weald blacksmith, 19 Nov. 1582. (998)
To be buried in South Weald churchyard. To John DANWOOD *alias* BEANE my eldest son my messuage that Rt. HATTER dwelleth in in Brentwood, a featherbed, and £5. To Elias DANWOOD *alias* BEANE my 2nd son my messuage in Brentwood that John SALMON dwelleth in, and another messuage in Brentwood that Hum. AME sometime dwelt in. To Susan DANWOOD *alias* BEANE my daughter my ground in Shenfield called the 'Sentorie' ground now in the tenure of Rt. HATTOR of Brentwood, and 1d. to be paid to the lord of the fee or fees if it be asked for; my new featherbed, my new cupboard, with a desk in the hall, a little square joined table in the hall that hath a cupboard in it, a long table with a frame in my chamber, and a long joined form in my parlour, my joined bedsteadle in my chamber, 3 curtains that hang on my bed, 6 pewter saucers, 6 of the best porringers, 4 pewter dishes, 1 of the best saltcellars, a qu[ern], a latten basin, 1 brass pot wrought with roman letters, 1 great kettle, 1 little kettle, another great brass pot being new, 1 old posnet, 1 chafing dish, the 2 best chairs in the hall, a great wicker chair in the parlour, 2 joined stools, 1 cushion wrought on the frame, and a little coffer that was her mother's. The rest of my goods to Elias. I make Susan executrix and John CRAMP of Shenfield and Rt. STAYNES of Tillingham Hall in Childerditch overseers, and for their pains 12d. Witnesses: Roger HALL, Lawrence MATHEW, [blank] ESSON of Bishops Hall [in South Weald]. Proved 28 Nov. 1583.

JOHN KNIGHT of Stanford-le-Hope, 13 Apr. 1583. (Nuncupative.) (999)
He spake to his wife and said she should have her dwelling in his house for her life; after her decease, to John their son; if he die without issue, successively to Wm. KNIGHT and Rd. KNIGHT each paying the rest of their brethren and sisters 40s. as appeareth in their father's [not named] Will. Witnesses: John STELLYMAN, John RATTELL, Arthur HARWOOD.

Inventory of the goods of John KNIGHT appraised by John Rattell and John OKLEY. A bed, 2 bedsteads, 2 mattresses, 2 coverlets, a bolster, and a pillow appraised at 13s.4d.; a cupboard, a table, a form, a benchboard, a great chair, 2 little chairs, 13s.4d.; 2 old chests 2s.4d.; brass and pewter 10s.; all implements of tubs and the painted cloths 6s.; a gridiron, a pair of trammels with the implements 5s.; the linen 4s. Total 54s.

MARGERY TENCH of BARKING, 21 Sept. 1584. (1000)
To my brother John 48s.6d. which my cousin BAKER of 'Elltam' [Eltham, co. Kent?] doth owe me for that I lent it him out of my purse. To him (BAKER) £10 which my brother Th. TENCH doth owe me likewise. To my mother 1 green gown, 1

petticoat, 2 holland smocks, 2 holland kerchiefs, and 1 neckercher. To my sister Mgt. 1 black gown, 1 petticoat, 2 holland smocks, 1 neckercher and 2 kerchiefs. To my cousin Eliz. BAKER of 'Elltam' 1 taffeta hat the best of the twain, 1 neckercher, and 1 purple girdle. To Mistress SIMPSON 1 neckercher, 1 kerchief, 1 purse and girdle of silk jersey. To widow BROOKE 1 neckercher, 1 kerchief, 1 petticoat, 1 waistcoat, and 1 gown. To Rd., Mr SIMPSON's son, 2s.6d., and Eliz. his daughter 2s.6d. I make my brother John TENCH executor. To goodwife SAMON the midwife 2s.6d. Witnesses: John TENCH, John SAMON, Paul TAFFTE. [No probate clause.]

WILLIAM NORRIS of Fyfield husbandman, 13 Aug. 1583. [See no. 378.] (1001)
To Mgy. my wife, whom I make executrix, all my goods. I make overseer Mr MAN our minister, and for his pains 2s. Witnesses: Mr MAN, Wm. KEYE the writer. Debts which I owe — to Hum. DANYELL 40s., Th. DANYELL 50s., Edw. DANYELL 40s., John CHAMPNEIS £3. Proved 3 Oct. 1583.

WILLIAM ECFORD of Eastwood labourer, 26 May —. (1002)
To be buried in Great Stambridge churchyard. To Bridget GODBOUT 1 russet petticoat, a red petticoat, a straw hat, and a pair of shoes. To mother ELDER 12d., John HUTSON 12d., Wm. HASELLWOD 12d., Denis wife of John ECFORD of Great Stambridge a new russet petticoat, and Mgt. daughter of John ECFORD a white apron, 2 neckerchers, and my black hat. To Denis a bushel of wheat at harvest next to be paid to her by John BROWN of Hockley. To my cousin Th. ECFORD of Great Stambridge 20s. to be paid by John ECFORD, parcel of £9 which he oweth me; the residue of the £9 I forgive him. To Denis £5, parcel of £9 debt by John BROWN which he standeth bound to me for payment at St Thomas' day 3 days before 'Christid' 1588, and to Mgt. daughter of John ECFORD the residue of the debt. I make John ECFORD executor; to him the benefit of the forfeiture of the bond of John BROWNE; if he pay not, the money to John ECFORD. I make Rt. KING of Great Stambridge carpenter overseer, and for his labour 2s. I will that my executor take up the debts owing to me to pay the legacies withal, i.e. of the wife of Rd. CANANDON 3s.3d. and of Geo. ENGELSBE servant to Th. WRITT 5s. Witnesses: Rt. KING, Geo. ALLEN. Proved 23 June 1587.

JOAN GYLMAN of Dunton widow, 26 Nov. 1584. (1003)
To Eliz. GYLMAN my eldest daughter my 2 biggest kettles, 1 pot brass posnet, 1 pair of andirons, 1 spit, 6 pieces of pewter, a great new tub, a brass spice mortar, my best candlestick, my salt, a pair of wafer irons, her father's [not named] hutch, a kneading trough, a pair of the newest sheets, a great bowl, a boulting tub, my cheese press, table, form, dun cow, black gown, russet petticoat, and best sow. To Joan GYLMAN my youngest daughter 1 cauldron, 1 kettle, 1 posnet of kettle brass, 1 firing pan, my best tablecloth, 3 pewter dishes, a saucer, my chair, my greatest tub, my new gown, my young sow, and 2 sheep. To John SAWELL my godson my old cow, my best hutch, a black sheep, and 12d. To Alice BRETTEN of Dunton and Mgy. WILLET of Bulphan my two goddaughters each 12d. To Alan BREWER 6d., Agnes JOAS 6d. and a pound of wool, John DAYNES 12d. and his wife a crosscloth, Frances GYFFORD a crosscloth, Alice FYFILD a new lockram kercher, and Joan SAWELL a deep pewter dish, a candlestick, a hutch, 1 sheep, and 12d. The residue of my goods to Eliz. and Joan my daughters to be equally divided, whom I make executrices; if they disagree on the division, I will that Rd. SAWELL and John NORRINGTON of Dunton husbandmen, whom I make supervisors, shall divide them. Witness: Th. ASPULL the writer hereof. Proved 29 Mar. 1585.

CHARLES WAD, [abode not given], 5 Mar. 1587/8. (Nuncupative.) (1004)
To be buried in Downham churchyard on the south side of the chancel. To my sister Eliz. 20 nobles that Edwin WALKER oweth me; if God take her away before the money be paid, the same to her brother Eustace, and to him the best featherbed. To my sister the other featherbed, the flockbed and the trundlebed. To my brother Edw. the little cauldron, the little brass pot, Eustace the great cauldron and the middle brass pot, Edw. the best posnet, my sister the least posnet, the little kettle, the scummer, the wafer irons, 6 pewter spoons, my brothers Eustace, John and Edw.

and my sister each 8 pieces of pewter, John a great kettle, my sister the pestle and mortar, a red bearing 'coll', and the little spit, Edw. the great cauldron and 1 spit, Eustace the 2nd cauldron and 1 spit, John the least candlestick and 1 spit, Eustace 1 fine sheet, 2 towen sheets, and my bow and quiver of arrows, my sister 2 blankets, Edw. 1 pair of towen sheets, 1 tablecloth, 3 table napkins, and 1 towel, Eustace the best chest, Edw. the 2nd chest, John the 3rd chest, my sister 2 chests, Edw. a round table, Eustace the long table, my sister the long settle, Eustace the chair, and John the leather bottle. [To] Henry BECKE the writer for 'falt' [default] of a better, 6s.8d. [I] make Rd. TARLING executor and Hum. GAROWLE overseer, and for their pains each 6s.8d. Witness: Rd. PETET. Proved 18 June 1588; administration to John her brother by reason of renunciation by the executor.

INDEX

Index of Persons

Some minor variants of spelling, e.g. Couper(e), Fysher, are not given or cross-referenced. A final 's' was a frequent alternative to many names, e.g. Adam(s), Grig(s).

The index references are to Will numbers. **Bold** type indicates a testator or testatrix.

ABBREVIATIONS: Ag Agnes; Al Alice; Alex Alexander; And Andrew; Ant Ant(h)ony; Art Arthur; Barb Barbara; Bart Bartholomew; Benj Benjamin; Brid Bridget; Cath Catherine; Chas Charles; Chris Christopher; Dan Daniel; Dthy Dorothy; Edm Edmund; Edw Edward; Eliz Elizabeth; Elr Eleanor; Frs Francis; Geo George; Geof Geoffrey; Greg Gregory; Hum Humphrey; Hy Henry; Jas James; Jer Jeremy; Jn John; Jos Joseph; Kath Katherine; Lawr Lawrence; Leon Leonard; Mat Matthew; Mgt Margaret; Mgy Margery; Mich Michael; Nich Nicholas; Nat Nathaniel; Phil Philip; Rd Richard; Reb Rebecca; Rh Ralph; Rog Roger; Rt Robert; Sam Samuel; Sar Sarah; Sim Simon; Ste Stephen; Sus Susan; Th Thomas; Wal Walter; Wm William.

Index of Places

This is an index primarily of parishes. Names of hamlets, manors (excluding references only to copyholds), manor-houses/halls, parks, streets, bridges, parsonages, almshouses, fairs, mills, inns, commons, marshes, and greens are indexed separately under the parishes in which they lie. (All, except hamlets and streets, also appear in the Index of Subjects.) Parishes *not in Essex* are brought together under their respective counties, e.g. SUFFOLK. See also *Editorial Method*.

Index of Subjects

All occupations are brought together under 'trades and occupations'; that entry is followed by 'social ranks' (gentlemen, etc.); for clergy, see separate entry.

Most of the unusual words are under 'words: rare, archaic, obsolete, local, or with earlier meaning' (see *Editorial Method*).

Bold type indicates reference to the subject in the Introduction.